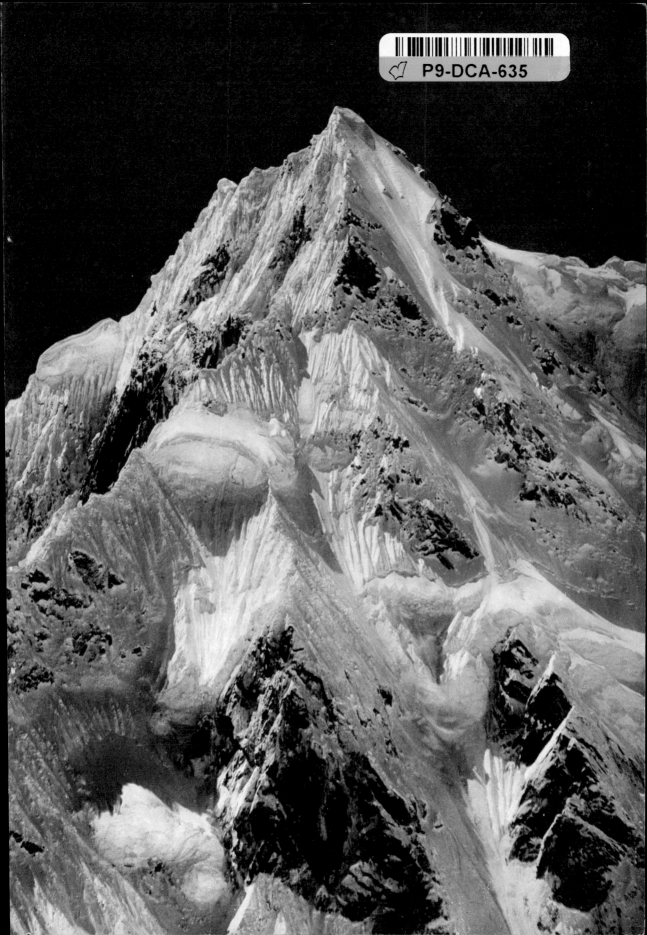

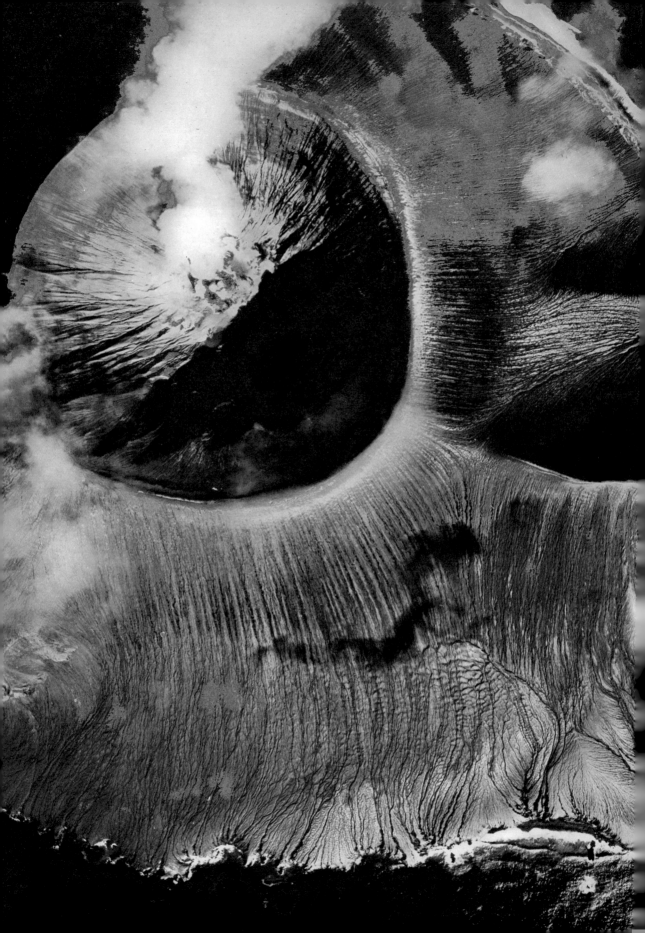

BEING A COLLECTION OF WRITINGS

ABOUT THE MOUNTAINS IN ALL

THEIR ASPECTS; WITH 64 PAGES OF

ILLUSTRATIONS IN HALFTONE AND

GRAVURE, AND MANY LINE DRAWINGS.

EDITED BY A. C. SPECTORSKY

APPLETON-CENTURY-CROFTS, INC.

NEW YORK

THE BOOK OF THE
MOUNTAINS

ACKNOWLEDGMENTS

The selections from the following books are reprinted by the kind permission of the publishers and copyright owners:

EARLY MOUNTAINEERS by Francis Gribble. Published in 1899 by T. Fisher Unwin Ltd. By permission of Ernest Benn Limited.

THE LAST SECRETS by John Buchan. Published 1923 by Thomas Nelson and Sons Ltd, and reprinted by their permission.

THE LETTERS OF JOHN KEATS, edited by Maurice B. Forman, 1935, Oxford University Press. By permission of the publishers.

THE WHITE TOWER, by James Ramsey Ullman. Copyright, 1945, by James Ramsey Ullman, published by J. B. Lippincott Company.

EXOTICS AND RETROSPECTIVES by Lafcadio Hearn. By permission of Little, Brown & Company.

JOHN OF THE MOUNTAINS: THE UNPUBLISHED JOURNALS OF JOHN MUIR. Copyright, 1938, by Wanda Muir Hanna. By permission of Houghton Mifflin Company.

COLLECTED STORIES OF H. G. WELLS, published by Ernest Benn, 1927. Used with the kind permission of the executors of the Estate of H. G. Wells.

THE MOUNTAINS OF YOUTH by Arnold Lunn. By permission of Eyre & Spottiswoode Ltd.

RELIQUIAE by Alfred Dennis Godley. By permission of The Clarendon Press.

HONEY IN THE HORN by H. L. Davis, copyright 1935 by H. L. Davis, by permission of William Morrow and Company, Inc.

TYROLEAN JOURNAL by C. Henry Warren. By permission of C. Henry Warren and Messrs. Robert Hale, Ltd.

"Deep in the Coca-Cola Belt" by Henry L. Mencken, the Baltimore Evening Sun, July 13, 1925. Reprinted with the permission of The Evening Sun, Baltimore, owner of the copyright, and the author.

GREEN HELL by Julian Duguid, copyright, 1931, The Century Company. Reprinted by permission of the publishers, Appleton-Century-Crofts, Inc., and Jonathan Cape Limited.

LISTEN FOR A LONESOME DRUM, by Carl Carmer, copyright 1936, 1950, by Carl Carmer, by permission of William Sloane Associates, Inc.

LOVE AMONG THE HAYSTACKS AND OTHER PIECES by D. H. Lawrence. Copyright 1933 by Frieda Lawrence. Reprinted by permission of The Viking Press, Inc., New York.

OUR LIFE IN THE SWISS HIGHLANDS by John Addington Symonds and Margaret Symonds, published 1892 by A. & C. Black, Edinburgh.

PIONEERS OF THE OZARKS by Lennis L. Broadfoot. Published by The Caxton Printers, Ltd., Caldwell, Idaho, and used by permission. Copyright 1944 by The Caxton Printers, Ltd.

CASUAL WANDERINGS IN ECUADOR by Blair Niles, copyright, 1923, The Century Company. Reprinted by permission of the publishers, Appleton-Century-Crofts, Inc.

OUR SOUTHERN HIGHLANDERS by Horace Kephart. Copyright 1913 and 1932 by The Macmillan Company and used with their permission.

THE MAGIC MOUNTAIN by Thomas Mann, translated by H. T. Lowe-Porter. By permission of Alfred A. Knopf, Inc. Copyright 1927 by Alfred A. Knopf, Inc.

THE MOTHERS by Vardis Fisher. Reprinted by permission of the Author. Copyright © 1943 by Vardis Fisher.

EXPLORING WITH BYRD by Richard Byrd, copyright, 1937, Richard Byrd. By permission of G. P. Putnam's Sons.

OTHER GODS by Pearl S. Buck. Copyright, 1938, 1939, 1940 by Pearl S. Buck. Published by The John Day Company, Inc. Reprinted by permission of the author's agent David Lloyd, New York, N. Y.

Extracts taken by permission of the Filson Club from William Calk's JOURNAL published in THE WILDERNESS ROAD (Filson Club Publications #2), by Thomas Speed.

CONQUEST OF MOUNT MCKINLEY by Belmore Browne, copyright, 1913, Belmore Browne. By permission of G. P. Putnam's Sons.

THE ASCENT OF F 6 by W. H. Auden and Christopher Isherwood, copyright 1936 by Wyston Hugh Auden and Christopher Isherwood. Reprinted by permission of Random House, Inc., and Messrs. Faber and Faber Ltd.

THE PATH TO ROME by Hilaire Belloc, copyright, 1902, 1936, Hilaire Belloc. By permission of G. P. Putnam's Sons.

THE TRACK OF THE CAT by Walter Van Tilburg Clark. Reprinted by permission of Random House, Inc. Copyright 1949 by Walter Van Tilburg Clark.

VISIBLE AND INVISIBLE, by E. F. Benson. Copyright 1924 by George H. Doran & Co. and, in Canada, by Messrs. Hutchinson & Co., Ltd. Reprinted by permission of the Executor of the Estate of E. F. Benson, by A. P. Watt & Son, and Hutchinson & Co. (Publishers) Ltd., London.

CONVERSATION WITH THE EARTH by Hans Cloos, translated by E. B. Garside, by permission of Alfred A. Knopf, Inc. Copyright 1953 by Alfred A. Knopf, Inc. Also with the permission of Routledge & Kegan Paul Ltd.

THE MOUNTAINS OF CALIFORNIA by John Muir, copyright, 1911, The Century Company. Reprinted by permission of the publishers, Appleton-Century-Crofts, Inc.

SWISS ESSAYS by Llewelyn Powys. Published by John Lane The Bodley Head Limited, 1947. Reprinted by permission of Alyse Gregory.

THE LAND OF LITTLE RAIN by Mary Austin, copyright, 1903, by Mary Austin. Reprinted by permission of the publisher, Houghton Mifflin Company.

"On the Behaviour of a Chamois" by Julian Huxley, from OXFORD MOUNTAINEERING ESSAYS, edited by A. J. Lunn, published by Edward Arnold, London, 1912. Reprinted by the permission of the author.

BIOGRAPHY OF THE EARTH by George Gamow. Copyright 1951 by George Gamow. Reprinted by permission of The Viking Press, Inc., New York.

SONG OF THE SKY by Guy Murchie, copyright, 1954, by Guy Murchie. Reprinted by permission of the publisher, Houghton Mifflin Company.

AMONG THE HILLS by Reginald Farrer, Headley Brothers Ltd., London, 1910. Reprinted by permission of George Allen & Unwin Ltd.

LIVY, VOLUME V, Loeb Classical Library, translated by B. O. Foster. By permission of the publishers, Harvard University Press.

THE GUN by C. S. Forester, copyright 1933, Little, Brown & Co., by permission of Little, Brown & Co. and A. D. Peters.

THE HORNED PIGEON, by George Millar. Copyright 1946 by George Reid Millar, reprinted by permission of Doubleday & Company, Inc.

WAR BELOW ZERO by Bernt Balchen, Corey Ford, and Oliver La Farge. Copyright 1944 by the Army Air Forces Aid Society.

NAPOLEON'S MEMOIRS, edited by Somerset de Chair, Harper & Brothers. Copyright, 1948, Somerset de Chair. By the kind permission of the editor.

COMSTOCK BONANZA edited by Duncan Emrich. Copyright, 1950, Duncan Emrich. By permission of the publishers, The Vanguard Press, Inc.

COMMANDO EXTRAORDINARY by Charles Foley. By permission of Longmans, Green & Company, Toronto.

Preface

CURRENTLY, THERE HAS BEEN AN EFFUSION OF WRITING ABOUT THE CONQUEST of heretofore impregnable peaks. Conquest is an odd word used thus: Months and years of planning, weeks and months of desperate and perilous toil are invested in a brief moment when perhaps two men, swaddled, numb, gasping like stranded fish, triumphantly stand with their heads some six feet higher than the hoary peak of a mountain which has—massive and impersonal—forced upon them adaptations almost beyond the limits of human flexibility and endurance. And then, of course, they must start the descent, at least as lethal as the trip up, and rendered more so by the fatigue and exposure of the ascent.

But what of the mountains themselves? There they stand, in great ranges all across the globe; the newer, wilder, craggier ones; the inaccessibles; the snow-capped with their feet in the tropics; the hot volcanic tops with their bases in ageless ice; the old and undulant ones standing as they have for millennia, made smooth by time, full of ancient secrets. All over the earth they march in motionless phalanx, and all over the earth, in all of man's brief history, he has informed them with mystical significance as they have inspired in him awe and fear and wonder. He has worshiped them, fought them, climbed them. His climate is affected by them wherever on this globe he may live, and the history of his battles and explorations, his language, his culture, his politics have all been shaped and influenced by the world's mountain masses.

It is the purpose of this collection to reveal the total sense of the mountain world and man's relationship to it, of which mountain climbing is only a part, as it is recorded in our literature.

To achieve that aim, it was deemed desirable to divide the book into sections each of which would deal with one aspect of the over-all subject. Before discussing and describing them, it may be of interest to set forth the three basic criteria by which the selections within all sections were chosen. Foremost was the aim to include only material of literary excellence, even though this meant the elimination of much writing whose subject matter was engrossing, or intriguing. Second, it was decided to exclude all but non-narrative selections from fiction; this was because so much fine fiction with a mountain locale is primarily concerned with interpersonal relationships uninfluenced by the mountains and having little direct bearing on them. Third was the desire to maintain a balance among the sections and within them, which may account for the absence of much that would otherwise have been included.

As to the sections, let's consider, first, *Men Climb the Mountains*. It might seem that here an editor would be confronted with an embarrassment of riches. But applying the principles set forth above, it became apparent that such was far from the case. Perhaps it is expecting too much to ask climbers to be writers, too; the fact is that, in the case of most of them, their skill as adventurous mountaineers is seldom approached by their literary efforts. Reading their accounts can be vicarious adventure of a high order, but it is infrequently a literary treat. Yet there is fine writing about that unique breed of men, and the best of it, by virtue of its literary superiority, achieves communication of the spirit of the act as well as of the act itself. It is believed the evidence will be found here. It was far to seek.

There is another group of mountaineers, perhaps less romantic than the "pure" climbers, to whom a section of this book is devoted, men whose courage and daring frequently match those of the adventurers, but whose feats largely have not found their way into popular literature. These are the mountaineering scientists: physicists, geologists, zoologists, chemists, botanists, meteorologists, mineralogists, biologists, doctors, geographers—the small and specialized army of explorers who must be doubly equipped, as mountaineers and men of science, to carry on their hazardous vocation. They infrequently reach the summits of the highest mountains, but their contribution is perhaps greater than that of the pure mountaineers. Possibly, it is modesty which keeps them from recording their exploits for the lay reader; more likely, their dedication to their chosen work disposes them to record it in the exact but cold language of science. Some of them, however, and some writers who have delved into the scientific world, have written superb accounts of man's continuing quest for knowledge of the mountain world. From this literature has been culled the material to be found in *Men Study the Mountains*.

The mountaineers and the mountaineering scientists go forth to challenge the mountain, to win it, to know it. The mountain may be their adversary or their prey, but it is not, in the true sense, their enemy. It was not so for those who came before: Mountains as enemies, as barriers, obstacles, impediments to movement, as upthrusting menaces of ice, rock, wind, avalanche, which must be circumvented or somehow crossed, have challenged man and been fought by him since the first *Pithecanthropus erectus* struggled up a high hill and looked over the edge toward a greener valley. The literature of man's conflict with the world's peaks and ranges is one of the richest in all writing about mountains; here some of the finest will be found under *Men Against the Mountains.*

Mountains have been not only barriers to men, they have also been boundaries and, often as a consequence, battlegrounds, too. In the history of war, few battles can compare in drama with those fought over and on the mountains. To the soldier, depending on his situation, the mountain can be an ally or an enemy deadlier than his human foe. In either case, the mountain is a major element in the fray, constantly to be dealt with, calling for daring, skill, and courage from each individual engaged. Perhaps the personal quality of mountain warfare is what has inspired so many writers and historians to surpass their customary literary level when writing about it. It is believed that the material in *Men Fight on the Mountains* is not only exciting, but demonstrates a high order of literary excellence.

So far, we have talked of men who seek the mountain realm for particular purposes. But wherever there are mountains, there are those who inhabit their flanks and plateaus. These, too, are a separate breed; whether they be Highlanders of Scotland or Andean Indians, Kentucky mountain folk or Tibetans, they have in common a way of life shaped by the exacting environment in which they live. This is not, of course, to imply that there is a similarity in their modes of living. On the contrary, the very fact of being mountain dwellers has insured to the people of the high altitudes a physical insularity which has permitted and even enforced the development—and then the stasis—of unique cultural patterns. Dwelling within these isolated cultural frameworks, knowing no other, the people of the mountains have rarely turned to literary expression, an artistic form which seems to thrive best in a cultural climate of movement, change, interaction of peoples and ideas. So the material in *Men Live and Work on the Mountains* is largely by lowlanders, observers from without—and this fact gives their writing a freshness of vision and a vigor which are richly rewarding to the reader.

Mention was made earlier of the awe and wonder with which mountains inspire man. Perhaps this is because there is nothing on earth or in the heavens which arouses man's awareness of his universe as do mountains. And this, in turn, may be attributable to the fact that there is no other natural phenomenon whose sheer, silent, forceful mass is so totally and impressively comprehensible. Sun, moon, planets, stars; deserts, oceans, the earth itself, these may be intellectually known to be vaster than a single peak, or even a mountain range, but the senses can, as it were, "grasp" a mountain—and reel back, and then the human spirit can wonder and the mind seek. This may illuminate to some degree the genesis of the passionate quality which imbues so much of the writing to be found under *Men Wonder at the Mystery of the Mountains.*

And so this volume is completed, containing something of the gamut of man's conflicts and compromises, reactions, adaptations, discoveries, ideas—in short, his life—as lived among the upthrustings of the earth's crust which we call mountains.

It would be gratifying to be able to say that all is in this book which one might wish. Various nonliterary considerations have made this impossible. Some material that was worthy of inclusion was omitted because its very excellence was responsible for its being overly familiar. Such work gave place, in some cases, to what it is hoped will be happy discoveries for many readers. There were other potential entries which, by virtue of the length of excerpt required to convey satisfactorily a complete facet of the mountain world, had to be excluded because of the physical limitations of a single volume such as this one.

Most readers who have delved at all into the literature of the mountains will, in all likelihood, find old favorites absent. It is hoped that they will reserve judgment until they consider the editor's hard choices in hewing to the basic aim, comprehensiveness, and the third criterion, balance. If they feel that these have been achieved on the whole, the time and work invested in preparing this volume will have been well spent. If others find the reading of this book as rewarding and aesthetically satisfying as the editor did its assembling, he will be content.

As in the companion volume to this book, *The Book of the Sea,* the pictures here were selected not to illustrate the text, but to supplement it with drawings and photographs which would convey visually the various aspects of the mountain world with which the text deals.

A final word, of deep thanks, to those who gave their invaluable assistance in this project: Louis Lerman, Patricia Schartle, Paul Jensen. Without them, it would not have seen completion.

A. C. SPECTORSKY

Contents

(Titles in center column are sources of selections)

2 MEN LIVE AND WORK ON THE MOUNTAINS

3 MEN AGAINST THE MOUNTAINS

4 MEN STUDY THE MOUNTAINS

5 MEN FIGHT ON THE MOUNTAINS

6 MEN WONDER AT THE MYSTERY OF THE MOUNTAINS

Illustrations

MOUNTAIN VILLAGE IN DAGHESTAN, IN THE CAUCASUS. CAUCASIAN PASSES WERE AGE-OLD INVASION ROUTES BETWEEN RUSSIA AND TURKEY AND PERSIA. NOTE THAT THE WATCH TOWERS IN THE VILLAGE ARE SUPPLEMENTED BY OTHERS SPACED UP THE VALLEY

HERDSMAN IN THE CAUCASUS WEARING SHEEPSKIN CAPE TYPICAL OF THIS MOUNTAINOUS REGION

A FIERCE PATRIARCH OF THE CAUCASUS

AN ETCHING OF CONSTANTINE, THE PLATEAU CITY IN ALGERIA, NOTED AS AN ANCIENT FORTRESS

PLATEAU AREA IN PERU SURROUNDED BY TERRACED MOUNTAINSIDES

LLAMAS CROSSING A HANGING BRIDGE ON THE TRAIL BELOW LIMBANI, PERU

NATIVES THRESHING GRAIN BY ANCIENT METHODS IN THE ANDES

A PEASANT COUPLE OF THE VAUDOIS, SWITZERLAND

following page 236

SHEPHERDING IN THE SCOTTISH HIGHLANDS

HIGHLAND DANCERS

GRAPE HARVEST NEAR BOLZANO, ITALY

GOLD MINE AT RED MOUNTAIN PASS, COLORADO

CANADIAN LUMBERJACKS AT WORK

EMIGRANTS CLIMBING THE PERILOUS CORDUROY ROAD OVER THE ROCKY MOUNTAINS, 13,000 FEET ABOVE SEA LEVEL, INTO LEADVILLE, COLORADO, 1879

PEASANTS OF MÜNSTER, A MOUNTAIN VILLAGE IN THE VALAIS REGION OF SWITZERLAND, TRANSPORT LOGS BY SLED

A THICK FROSTING OF SNOW COVERS THE HUTS ON ALP OBER-LAREIN, ALONG THE PARSENN DOWNHILL RUN TO JENAZ, SWITZERLAND

PINSEC IS A TYPICAL WANDERING SETTLEMENT IN VALAIS, SWITZERLAND. HERE THE HOUSES ARE INHABITED ACCORDING TO THE SEASONS. THE OWNERS MOVE TO SIMILAR SETTLEMENTS HIGHER UP THE MOUNTAINS AND IN THE VALLEYS BELOW WHEN WORK MUST BE DONE IN THE FIELDS ON THOSE LEVELS

SWISS SHEPHERDS CARRYING COWBELLS

CHAMOIS HUNTER

POSITANO, AN ITALIAN TOWN, CLINGS TO THE STEEP SLOPES OF THE MOUNTAINS RISING FROM THE MEDITERRANEAN

following page 268

JIM WHITTAKER, BELAYED FROM BEHIND BY HIS ROPE PARTNER, WHO IS OUT OF SIGHT, EXPLORES A BOTTOMLESS CREVASSE. THE LINES ON THE WALLS SHOW THE DEPTH OF SNOWFALL EACH YEAR

AN ETCHING OF THE CRATER OF MOUNT VESUVIUS

VESUVIUS ERUPTED VIOLENTLY IN 1944. THE VOLCANO IS ACTUALLY A SMALLER CONE WITHIN AN ENORMOUS CALDERA, THE RIM OF WHICH APPEARS AS A LOWER RING OF SURROUNDING MOUNTAINS

WHEN MT. PELÉE, A 4,000-FOOT VOLCANO ON THE ISLAND OF MARTINIQUE, ERUPTED IN A FLASH OF FIRE ON MAY 8, 1902, IT BLOTTED OUT ST. PIERRE, A SEAPORT SEVERAL MILES AWAY, AND KILLED 30,000 PEOPLE INSTANTLY. THIS PHOTOGRAPH, TAKEN A SHORT TIME AFTER THE ERUPTION, SHOWS A TOWER OF BLACK, GLASSLIKE ROCK, THEN CALLED PELÉE'S SPINE, WHICH WAS PUSHED UPWARD OUT OF THE CRATER TO A HEIGHT OF NEARLY 1,000 FEET. IT IS NOW BELIEVED TO HAVE BEEN THE PLUG THAT BLOCKED THE CRATER'S THROAT FOR HUNDREDS OF YEARS. IT DISAPPEARED FROM SIGHT AFTER A YEAR

AN AERIAL VIEW OF THE MOUTH OF BOQUERON VOLCANO, OFF THE WEST COAST OF MEXICO

IN 1883, KRAKATOA, A VOLCANIC ISLAND NEAR JAVA, EXPLODED IN ONE ENORMOUS BLAST, AND COLLAPSED INTO THE SEA. THIS IS ALL THAT IS LEFT: A RING OF LOW ISLANDS, AND AN OCCASIONAL PUFF OF STEAM. 35,000 PEOPLE WERE KILLED BY THE TIDAL WAVES

AN ETCHING OF THE DONNER PARTY, A GROUP OF EMIGRANTS WHO WERE TRAPPED IN THE HEAVY SNOWS OF THE SIERRA NEVADAS IN 1846–1847 AND SURVIVED ONLY THROUGH RECOURSE TO CANNIBALISM

IRONICALLY, THIS BEAUTY SPOT IN THE UINTA MOUNTAINS OF NORTHEASTERN UTAH BECAME A DEATH TRAP FOR A LUXURY AIR LINER THAT FAILED TO CLEAR THE TOP OF THE PEAK AND CARRIED 19 PERSONS TO THEIR DEATHS IN 1937. THIS PICTURE WAS MADE AS A RESCUE PARTY APPROACHED THE WRECKAGE OF THE FALLEN SHIP

TOURISTS OF 1885, REPLETE WITH WALKING STICKS AND PARASOLS, PICK THEIR WAY NEATLY OVER THE MER DE GLACE IN CHAMONIX, SWITZERLAND

CLIMBING THE CREST OF KLEINGLOCKNER IN THE DOLOMITES, AUSTRIAN ALPS

AVALANCHE ON BROAD PEAK IN THE KARAKORAM HIMALAYAS. THIS AVALANCHE WAS WELL OVER A MILE WIDE AND FELL MORE THAN 3,000 FEET

A JEFFREY PINE, NORMALLY A SYMMETRICAL TREE, ON THE SUMMIT OF SENTINEL DOME IN YOSEMITE PARK. THE GRIMNESS OF ITS STRUGGLE FOR SURVIVAL IS READILY APPARENT

A MOUNTAIN CARNATION IN BLOOM IN THE SWISS ALPS

GOLDEN EAGLES DEVOURING THE CARCASS OF A DEER

MOUNTAIN GOATS BECAUSE OF THEIR AGILITY AND INCREDIBLE SURE-FOOTEDNESS ARE ABLE TO MAKE THEIR HOME AMONG THE HIGH ROCKS AND CRAGS OF MOUNTAINS

A VIEW OF THE GREAT WALL OF CHINA, SNAKING ITS WAY OVER THE MOUNTAINS

AMERICAN INFANTRYMEN ON A RIDGE IN KOREA

A SWISS MOUNTAINEER PATROL DURING A DOWNHILL SKI RUN IN THE BERNE HIGHLANDS

SWISS ARMY RESERVISTS TRAINING IN WINTER WARFARE IN THE BERNE HIGHLANDS

SWISS SKI TROOPERS KNEE-DEEP IN NEW SNOW

following page 460

A SHRINE IN THE BAVARIAN ALPS

NOAH'S ARK LANDING ON THE TOP OF THE MOUNTAIN

CLOUD REFLECTIONS IN MONO LAKE, IN THE MOUNTAINS OF CALIFORNIA

A MOUNTAIN CABIN HIGH ABOVE THE ST. MORITZSEE, SWITZERLAND

YOSEMITE FALLS, 2,600 FEET, YOSEMITE NATIONAL PARK, CALIFORNIA

MASSIVE ICE BLOCKS AT AN ALTITUDE OF 10,000 FEET ON THE APPROACHES TO SILVERTHRONE PASS. NOTE ANNUAL ICE LAYERS

STORM, ON THE EAST SIDE OF THE SIERRA, TAKEN FROM NEAR BIGPINE, CALIFORNIA

MUSTAGH TOWER, ONE OF THE WORLD'S MIGHTIEST PEAKS, STILL UNCONQUERED IN THE KARA-KORAM HIMALAYAS

A PATH CUT INTO THE SIDE OF A CLIFF IN THE BLUE MOUNTAINS, AUSTRALIA

Men Climb the Mountains

It is no accident that men did not really venture to climb the mountains until the fifteenth century. To climb to the unknown needed the same boldness of spirit and resolution of soul that infused the early venturers upon unknown seas. The early climbers did not, like Columbus, find an America. But they found a new and challenging dimension. Later on, exploring climbers gave it a name: They called it the top of the world.

A literature and a people grew up out of the mountains. The literature rivals in movement and power the best of the writings on deep water; the people are a new and different breed, mountaineers—men who climb the mountains for pleasure.

These are people who have learned a balance between their strength and the strength of the mountain. They are not men who challenge blindly. It is an impermanent truce they have with nature. No one of them suffers more than once the illusion that man can conquer the mountain. He can at best understand it, with wisdom and skill and courage he can beguile it into his service.

The literature of mountaineering is a literature of personal authenticity, of rare triumphs and high moments, of frequent pain and frustration, and sometimes of accidents and sudden death.

A CERTIFIED CLIMB

FROM *The Ascent of Eguille-Fort, 1492*

DOMPJULIAN DE BEAUPRÉ

1492 is a memorable date in the history of mountaineering. It marks the first detailed account of a mountain climb; not alone that, but one attested to by a body of affidavits. Dompjulian de Beaupré, Captain of Montélimar and Sou, Chamberlain to his majesty Charles VIII of France, led the ascent of Mount Aiguille near Grenoble to satisfy a royal whim. When he reached the summit, he immediately sent his *procès-verbal* to the Parliament of Grenoble by special messenger. The Parliament debated the communication solemnly and then appointed a delegate to verify the facts therein. The delegate went to the *foot* of the mountain, looked up, took affidavits and reported back. The formidable documents were deposited in the Grenoble archives for posterity's edification. The mixture of legal phraseology, religious sentiment, and medieval naïveté makes delightful reading.

Monsieur the President,
I SEND YOU MY HEARTY GREETINGS. WHEN I LEFT THE KING HE CHARGED ME TO cause an attempt to be made to see whether it was possible to climb the mountain which was said to be inaccessible; which mountain I, by subtle means and engines, have found the means of climbing, thanks be to God; and now I have been here three days; and more than ten companions are with me—both Church men and other respectable people, and also one of the King's ladder-men; and I do not mean to leave here until I have received your answer, in order that, if you wish to send a few people to see us here, you may be able to do so; though I warn you that you will find few men who, when they see us up above, and see all the passage that I have caused to be made, will dare to come here; for it is the most horrible and frightful passage that I or any of my company have ever seen. I inform you of this in order that, having made sure of it at your pleasure, you may be so good as to write to the King by my lackey, the bearer of this; and I assure you that you will be causing him great pleasure, and me also, and you may be sure that if I

can do anything for you, I will do so according to the pleasure of our master, so that he may give you that which you most desire.

Written the 28th day of June, on Eguille-Fort, called Mount Inaccessible; for the people of the country call it Lèguille; and in order that I might not forget it, I have had the mountain named in the name of the Father, the Son, and the Holy Ghost, of Saint Charlemagne, for love of the name of the King; and I have had mass said upon it, and have caused three crosses to be set up. To describe the mountain to you—it is about a French league in circumference, a quarter of a league in length, and a cross-bow shot in width, and is covered with a beautiful meadow; and we have found a beautiful herd of chamois, which will never be able to get away, and some little ones of this year with them, one of which was killed, in spite of our intentions when we entered, for, until the King gives other orders I do not wish to have any of them taken. You have to ascend half a league by ladder, and a league by other ways, and it is the most beautiful place that I have ever visited.

Wholly yours,

Dompjulien

In 1492, and on the last day but one of June, the Parliament of Dauphiné, having received the above-mentioned letters, decided to send to the Mount Eguille, which is in Dauphiné, the noble Yve Lévy, Usher of the said Parliament, in order to ascertain whether the contents of the said letters were true: who returned therefrom on the 5th of July of the same year, and reported to the said Parliament that he had been to the place where the said mountain is situated, and that at the foot of that part of it where the cliff begins, he found that ladders had been placed against the rock, whereby one commences to ascend it. And he further reported that he, the said Usher, saw on the said Mount Eguille Dompjulian, Captain of Montélimar, above mentioned, and several other persons who were with him. He was unwilling to expose himself, however, by reason of the danger that there was of perishing there, and by reason of the impossibility of getting there, for fear less he should seem to tempt the Lord, since at the mere sight of this mountain everyone was terrified. He saw there, nevertheless, the said Dompjulian and the others, who begged him to draw near to them, which the Usher did not deign to do. He saw on the said mountain three crosses which had been recently erected, and there were with him several persons, some of whom went upon the said mountain, among others the Noble Guigue de la Tour, Châtelain of Cleles. As for the rest, they were so frightened when they saw this mountain that they would not draw near to it; but he did not fail to see several persons on it, who certified to him as follows:—

We, the undersigned, certify to the Usher of the Parliament, that to-day, the first day of July, we climbed the mountain which was formerly called Inaccessible, and is now called Eguille-Fort: on which mountain we report that we found Monseigneur Dompjulian, Captain of Montélimar, with his retainers, to the number of seven; and we heard mass on the said mountain and also (saw) three crosses, which the said Captain has caused to be set up.

GUIGUE DE LA TOUR, Châtelain de Cleles

F. DE COLAUS

SILVE

I, Pierre Liotard, Captain of the place of the Gates, certify that I went on the Mont Eguille, and that I found upon it Dompjulien, Captain of Montélimar, with five or six of his retainers, among whom were two priests, one of the order of the Lesser Friars, and the other a secular priest, who was celebrating mass on the same mountain. Several persons climbed with me, to wit:—the noble George Juvenis, the noble Pierre Blosset, the noble Gaspard Robert, the noble Gonnet-Bencot, Reymond du Collet, chaplain, J. Tobert, Pierre Espeil, of the place of Roisar, Claude Chevalier, of the place of the Gates.

Thus do I certify,

Pierre Liotard

BUT THE ROPE BROKE

FROM *Scrambles Amongst the Alps*

EDWARD WHYMPER

There is no sadder or more delusive victory in the history of mountaineering than Edward Whymper's successful climb of the Matterhorn. Whymper was an artist who received a commission from a London publisher to sketch the great Alpine peaks. He was possessed by the Matterhorn. In today's language of psychology one might almost talk of compulsions. Between 1861 and 1865 he made seven tries at the precipitous and icy peak—all defeated. His eighth try won the summit. The party remained on the summit for one hour, "one crowded hour of glorious life," Whymper quotes in his account. On the climb down, the rope parted. Four of the men were killed.

The accident evoked a great furor and controversy in the press and pulpit. Whymper, the organization of the climb, the guides, mountain climbing as a sport, were all attacked and defended by bitter partisans. In mountaineering circles one can still, with a word or two, provoke a heated discussion on how and why the rope parted—and this almost a hundred years after the climb.

Whymper is not a great stylist. His writing is factual, with few attempts at dramatization or embellishment, but its very bareness and lack of shading gives the account almost the fatal design of a Greek tragedy.

WE STARTED FROM ZERMATT ON THE 13TH OF JULY, AT HALF-PAST 5, ON A brilliant and perfectly cloudless morning. We were eight in number—Croz, old Peter and his two sons, Lord F. Douglas, Hadow, Hudson, and I. To ensure steady motion, one tourist and one native walked together. The youngest Taugwalder fell to my share, and the lad marched well, proud to be on the expedition, and happy to show his powers. The wine-bags also fell to my lot to carry, and throughout the day, after each drink, I replenished them secretly with water, so that at the next halt they were found fuller than before! This was considered a good omen, and little short of miraculous.

On the first day we did not intend to ascend to any great height, and we mounted, accordingly, very leisurely; picked up the things which were left in the chapel at the Schwarzsee at 8.20, and proceeded thence along the ridge connecting the Hörnli with the Matterhorn. At half-past 11 we arrived at the base of the actual peak; then quitted the ridge, and clambered round some ledges, on to the eastern face. We were now fairly upon the mountain, and were astonished to find that places which from the Riffel, or even from the Furggengletscher, looked entirely impracticable, were so easy that we could *run about*.

Before twelve o'clock we had found a good position for the tent, at a height of 11,000 feet. Croz and young Peter went on to see what was above, in order to save time on the following morning. They cut across the heads of the snow-slopes which descended towards the Furggengletscher, and disappeared round a corner; but shortly afterwards we saw them high up on the face, moving quickly. We others made a solid platform for the tent in a well-protected spot, and then watched eagerly for the return of the men. The stones which they upset told that they were very high, and we supposed that the way must be easy. At length, just before 3 P.M. we saw them coming down, evidently much excited. "What are they saying, Peter?" "Gentlemen, they say it is no good." But when they came near we heard a different story. "Nothing but what was good; not a difficulty, not a single difficulty! We could have gone to the summit and returned to-day easily!"

We passed the remaining hours of daylight—some basking in the sunshine, some sketching or collecting; and when the sun went down, giving, as it departed, a glorious promise for the morrow, we returned to the tent to arrange for the night. Hudson made tea, I coffee, and we then retired each one to his blanket-bag; the Taugwalders, Lord Francis Douglas, and myself, occupying the tent, the others remaining, by preference, outside. Long after dusk the cliffs above echoed with our laughter and with the songs of the guides, for we were happy that night in camp, and feared no evil.

We assembled together outside the tent before dawn on the morning of the 14th, and started directly it was light enough to move. Young Peter came on with us as a guide, and his brother returned to Zermatt. We followed the route which had been taken on the previous day, and in a few minutes turned the rib which had intercepted the view of the eastern face from our tent platform. The whole of this great slope was now revealed, rising for 3000 feet like a huge natural staircase. Some parts were more, and others were less, easy; but we were not once brought to a halt by any serious impediment, for when an obstruction was met in front it could always be turned to the right or to the left. For the greater part of the way there was, indeed, no occasion for the rope, and sometimes Hudson led, sometimes myself. At 6.20 we had attained a height of 12,800 feet, and halted for half-an-hour; we then continued the ascent without a break until 9.55, when we stopped for 50 minutes, at a height of 14,000 feet. Twice we struck the N.E. ridge, and followed it for some little distance—to no advantage, for it was usually more rotten and steep, and always more difficult than the face. Still, we kept near to it, lest stones perchance might fall.

We had now arrived at the foot of that part which, from the Riffelberg or from Zermatt, seems perpendicular or overhanging, and could no longer continue upon the eastern side. For a little distance we ascended by snow upon the arête—that is, the ridge—descending towards Zermatt, and then, by common consent, turned over to the right, or to the northern side. Before doing so, we made a change in the order of ascent. Croz went first, I followed, Hudson came third; Hadow and old Peter were last. "Now," said Croz, as he led off, "now for something altogether different." The work became difficult, and required caution. In some places there was little to hold, and it was desirable that those should be in front who were least likely to slip. The general slope of the mountain at this part was *less* than 40°, and snow had accumulated in, and had filled up, the interstices of the rock-face, leaving only occasional fragments projecting here and there. These were at times covered with a thin film of ice, produced from the melting and refreezing of the snow. It was the counterpart, on a small scale, of the upper 700 feet of the Pointe des Ecrins—only there was this material difference; the face of the Ecrins was about, or exceeded, an angle of 50°, and the Matterhorn face was less than 40°. It was a place over which any fair mountaineer might pass in safety, and Mr. Hudson ascended this part, and, as far as I know, the entire mountain, without having the slightest assistance rendered to him upon any occasion. Sometimes, after I had taken a hand from Croz, or received a pull, I turned to offer the same to Hudson; but he invariably declined, saying it was not necessary. Mr. Hadow, however, was not accustomed to this kind of work, and required continual assistance. It is only fair to say that the difficulty which he found at this part arose simply and entirely from want of experience.

This solitary difficult part was of no great extent. We bore away over it at first, nearly horizontally, for a distance of about 400 feet; then ascended directly towards the summit for about 60 feet; and then doubled back to the ridge which descends towards Zermatt. A long stride round a rather awkward corner brought us to snow once more. The last doubt vanished! The Matterhorn was ours! Nothing but 200 feet of easy snow remained to be surmounted!

You must now carry your thoughts back to the seven Italians who started from Breil on the 11th of July. Four days had passed since their departure, and we were tormented with anxiety lest they should arrive on the top before us. All the way up we had talked of them, and many false alarms of "men on the summit" had been raised. The higher we rose, the more intense became the excitement. What if we should be beaten at the last moment? The slope eased off, at length we could be detached, and Croz and I, dashing away, ran a neck-and-neck race, which ended in a dead heat. At 1.40 P.M. the world was at our feet, and the Matterhorn was conquered. Hurrah! Not a footstep could be seen.

It was not yet certain that we had not been beaten. The summit of the Matterhorn was formed of a rudely level ridge, about 350 feet long, and the Italians might have been at its farther extremity. I hastened to the southern end, scanning the snow right and left eagerly. Hurrah! again; it was untrodden. "Where were the men?" I peered over the cliff, half doubting, half expectant. I saw them immediately—mere dots on the ridge, at an immense distance below. Up went my arms and my hat. "Croz! Croz!! come here!" "Where are they, Monsieur?" "There, don't you see them, down there?" "Ah! the *coquins,* they are low down." "Croz, we must make those fellows hear us." We yelled until we were hoarse. The Italians seemed to regard us —we could not be certain. "Croz, we *must* make them hear us; they *shall* hear us!" I seized a block of rock and hurled it down, and called upon my companion, in the name of friendship, to do the same. We drove our sticks in, and prized away the crags, and soon a torrent of stones poured down the cliffs. There was no mistake about it this time. The Italians turned and fled.

Still, I would that the leader of that party could have stood with us at that moment, for our victorious shouts conveyed to him the disappointment of the ambition of a lifetime. He was *the* man, of all those who attempted the ascent of the Matterhorn, who most deserved to be the first upon its summit. He was the first to doubt its inaccessibility, and he was the only man who persisted in believing that its ascent would be accomplished. It was the aim of his life to make the ascent from the side of Italy, for the honour of his native valley. For a time he had the game in his hands: he played it as he thought best; but he made a false move, and he lost it. Times have changed with Carrel. His supremacy is questioned in the Val Tournanche; new men have arisen; and he is no longer recognised as *the* chasseur above all others: but so long as he remains the man that he is to-day, it will not be easy to find his superior.

The others had arrived, so we went back to the northern end of the ridge. Croz now took the tent-pole, and planted it in the highest snow. "Yes," we said, "there is the flag-staff, but where is the flag?" "Here it is," he answered, pulling off his blouse and fixing it to the stick. It made a poor flag, and there was no wind to float it out, yet it was seen all around. They saw it at Zermatt—at the Riffel—in the Val Tournanche. At Breil, the watchers cried, "Victory is ours!" They raised "bravos" for Carrel, and "vivas" for Italy, and hastened to put themselves *en fête.* On the morrow they were undeceived. "All was changed; the explorers returned sad—cast down—disheart-

ened—confounded—gloomy." "It is true," said the men. "We saw them ourselves—they hurled stones at us! The old traditions *are* true—there are spirits
on the top of the Matterhorn!"

We returned to the southern end of the ridge to build a cairn, and then
paid homage to the view. The day was one of those superlatively calm and
clear ones which usually precede bad weather. The atmosphere was perfectly
still, and free from all clouds or vapours. Mountains fifty—nay a hundred—
miles off, looked sharp and near. All their details—ridge and crag, snow and
glacier—stood out with faultless definition. Pleasant thoughts of happy days
in bygone years came up unbidden, as we recognised the old, familiar forms.
All were revealed—not one of the principal peaks of the Alps was hidden.
I see them clearly now—the great inner circles of giants, backed by the
ranges, chains, and *massifs*. First came the Dent Blanche, hoary and grand;
the Gabelhorn and pointed Rothhorn; and then the peerless Weisshorn:
the towering Mischabelhörner, flanked by the Allaleinhorn, Strahlhorn, and
Rimpfischhorn; then Monte Rosa—with its many Spitzes—the Lyskamm and
the Breithorn. Behind were the Bernese Oberland, governed by the Fin-
steraarhorn; the Simplon and St. Gothard groups; the Disgrazia and the
Orteler. Towards the south we looked down to Chivasso on the plain of
Piedmont, and far beyond. The Viso—one hundred miles away—seemed
close upon us; the Maritime Alps—one hundred and thirty miles distant—
were free from haze. Then came my first love—the Pelvoux; the Ecrins and
the Meije; the clusters of the Graians; and lastly, in the west, gorgeous in the
full sunlight, rose the monarch of all—Mont Blanc. Ten thousand feet
beneath us were the green fields of Zermatt, dotted with chalets, from which
blue smoke rose lazily. Eight thousand feet below, on the other side, were the
pastures of Breil. There were forests black and gloomy, and meadows
bright and lively; bounding waterfalls and tranquil lakes; fertile lands and
savage wastes; sunny plains and frigid *plateaux*. There were the most rugged
forms, and the most graceful outlines—bold, perpendicular cliffs, and gentle,
undulating slopes; rocky mountains and snowy mountains, sombre and
solemn, or glittering and white, with walls—turrets—pinnacles—pyramids
—domes—cones—and spires! There was every combination that the world
can give, and every contrast that the heart could desire.

We remained on the summit for one hour—

"One crowded hour of glorious life."

It passed away too quickly, and we began to prepare for the descent.

Hudson and I again consulted as to the best and safest arrangement of
the party. We agreed that it would be best for Croz to go first, and Hadow

second; Hudson, who was almost equal to a guide in sureness of foot, wished to be third; Lord F. Douglas was placed next, and old Peter, the strongest of the remainder, after him. I suggested to Hudson that we should attach a rope to the rocks on our arrival at the difficult bit, and hold it as we descended, as an additional protection. He approved the idea, but it was not definitely settled that it should be done. The party was being arranged in the above order whilst I was sketching the summit, and they had finished, and were waiting for me to be tied in line, when some one remembered that our names had not been left in a bottle. They requested me to write them down, and moved off while it was being done.

A few minutes afterwards I tied myself to young Peter, ran down after the others, and caught them just as they were commencing the descent of the difficult part. Great care was being taken. Only one man was moving at a time; when he was firmly planted the next advanced, and so on. They had not, however, attached the additional rope to rocks, and nothing was said about it. The suggestion was not made for my own sake, and I am not sure that it even occurred to me again. For some little distance we two followed the others, detached from them, and should have continued so had not Lord F. Douglas asked me, about 3 P.M., to tie on to old Peter, as he feared, he said, that Taugwalder would not be able to hold his ground if a slip occurred.

A few minutes later, a sharp-eyed lad ran into the Monte Rosa hotel, to Seiler, saying that he had seen an avalanche fall from the summit of the Matterhorn on to the Matterhorngletscher. The boy was reproved for telling idle stories; he was right, nevertheless, and this was what he saw.

Michel Croz had laid aside his axe, and in order to give Mr. Hadow greater security, was absolutely taking hold of his legs, and putting his feet, one by one, into their proper positions. As far as I know, no one was actually descending. I cannot speak with certainty, because the two leading men were partially hidden from my sight by an intervening mass of rock, but it is my belief, from the movements of their shoulders, that Croz, having done as I have said, was in the act of turning round to go down a step or two himself; at this moment Mr. Hadow slipped, fell against him, and knocked him over. I heard one startled exclamation from Croz, then saw him and Mr. Hadow flying downwards; in another moment Hudson was dragged from his steps, and Lord F. Douglas immediately after him. All this was the work of a moment. Immediately we heard Croz's exclamation, old Peter and I planted ourselves as firmly as the rocks would permit: the rope was taut between us, and the jerk came on us both as on one man. We held; but the rope broke midway between Taugwalder and Lord Francis Douglas. For a few seconds we saw our unfortunate companions sliding downwards on their backs, and spreading out their hands, endeavouring to save themselves. They passed from our sight uninjured, disappeared one by one, and fell from precipice to precipice on to the Matterhorngletscher below, a distance of nearly 4000 feet in height. From the moment the rope broke it was impossible to help them.

So perished our comrades! For the space of half-an-hour we remained on the spot without moving a single step. The two men, paralysed by terror, cried like infants, and trembled in such a manner as to threaten us with the fate of the others. Old Peter rent the air with exclamations of "Chamounix! Oh, what will Chamounix say?" He meant, Who would believe that Croz could fall? The young man did nothing but scream or sob, "We are lost! we are lost!" Fixed between the two, I could neither move up nor down. I begged young Peter to descend, but he dared not. Unless he did, we could not advance. Old Peter became alive to the danger, and swelled the cry, "We are lost! we are lost!" The father's fear was natural—he trembled for his son; the young man's fear was cowardly—he thought of self alone. At last old Peter summoned up courage, and changed his position to a rock to which he could fix the rope; the young man then descended, and we all stood together. Immediately we did so, I asked for the rope which had given way, and found, to my surprise—indeed, to my horror—that it was the weakest of the three ropes. It was not brought, and should not have been employed, for the purpose for which it was used. It was old rope, and, compared with the others, was feeble. It was intended as a reserve, in case we had to leave much rope behind, attached to rocks. I saw at once that a serious question was involved, and made him give me the end. It had broken in mid-air, and it did not appear to have sustained previous injury.

For more than two hours afterwards I thought almost every moment that the next would be my last; for the Taugwalders, utterly unnerved, were not only incapable of giving assistance, but were in such a state that a slip might have been expected from them at any moment. After a time, we were able to do that which should have been done at first, and fixed rope to firm rocks, in addition to being tied together. These ropes were cut from time to time, and were left behind. Even with their assurance the men were afraid to proceed, and several times old Peter turned with ashy face and faltering limbs, and said, with terrible emphasis, *"I cannot!"*

About 6 P.M. we arrived at the snow upon the ridge descending towards Zermatt, and all peril was over. We frequently looked, but in vain, for traces of our unfortunate companions; we bent over the ridge and cried to them, but no sound returned. Convinced at last that they were neither within sight nor hearing, we ceased from our useless efforts; and, too cast down for speech, silently gathered up our things, and the little effects of those who were lost, preparatory to continuing the descent. When, lo! a mighty arch appeared,

A CAMP ON MULDROW GLACIER ON MT. MC KINLEY, ALTITUDE 8,500 FEET, IN THE MIDDLE OF THE GREAT ICEFALL. THE CLIFFS OF MT. CARPÉ TOWER 4,000 FEET ABOVE THE BOTTOM OF THE VALLEY

A BALTI PORTER FOR THE AMERICAN ALPINE CLUB EXPEDITION TO K2, THE WORLD'S SECOND HIGHEST PEAK, IN THE KARAKORAM HIMALAYAS, CARRIES HIS 60-POUND LOAD ACROSS A BRIDGE MADE OF TWISTED WILLOW OVER THE RAGING BRALDU RIVER

ROCK CLIMBING AT JACKSON HOLE, WYOMING, IN THE TETON MOUNTAINS

Ewing Galloway

right: CLIMBERS, HIGH IN THE ALPS, WORKING THEIR WAY UP SHEER SLOPES OF SNOW AND ICE

FPG

CLIMBING SHOES ARE STUDDED WITH TRICOUNIS, TRICOUNI-EDGE NAILS, HOBS AND CALKS

EARLY 19TH-CENTURY MOUNTAIN CLIMBER WITH KNAPSACK MADE OF FUR

THE TOOLS OF THE MOUNTAIN CLIMBER: ICE AXE, ROPE, AND CRAMPONS

SITTING IN THE ROPE, WITH FEET BRACED AGAINST THE CLIFF, A CLIMBER LEANS WELL AWAY FROM THE ROCK AND SLIDES DOWN THE ROPE. SHOULD HE LEAN IN, HIS FEET WOULD PROBABLY SLIP AND HE WOULD SPIN IN MID-AIR

INCIDENT BEFORE REACHING THE GRANDS MULETS

TWO PARTIES OF CLIMBERS ON THE FIRST LEG OF THEIR ASCENTS

rising above the Lyskamm, high into the sky. Pale, colourless, and noiseless, but perfectly sharp and defined, except where it was lost in the clouds, this unearthly apparition seemed like a vision from another world; and, almost appalled, we watched with amazement the gradual development of two vast crosses, one on either side. If the Taugwalders had not been the first to perceive it, I should have doubted my senses. They thought it had some connection with the accident, and I, after a while, that it might bear some relation to ourselves. But our movements had no effect upon it. The spectral forms remained motionless. It was a fearful and wonderful sight; unique in my experience, and impressive beyond description, coming at such a moment.

I was ready to leave, and waiting for the others. They had recovered their appetites and the use of their tongues. They spoke in patois, which I did not understand. At length the son said in French, "Monsieur." "Yes." "We are poor men; we have lost our Herr; we shall not get paid; we can ill afford this." "Stop!" I said, interrupting him, "that is nonsense; I shall pay you, of course, just as if your Herr were here." They talked together in their patois for a short time, and then the son spoke again. "We don't wish you to pay us. We wish you to write in the hotel-book at Zermatt, and to your journals, that we have not been paid." "What nonsense are you talking? I don't understand you. What do you mean?" He proceeded—"Why, next year there will be many travellers at Zermatt, and we shall get more *voyageurs*."

Who would answer such a proposition? I made them no reply in words, but they knew very well the indignation that I felt. They filled the cup of bitterness to overflowing, and I tore down the cliff, madly and recklessly, in a way that caused them, more than once, to inquire if I wished to kill them. Night fell; and for an hour the descent was continued in the darkness. At half-past 9 a resting-place was found, and upon a wretched slab, barely large enough to hold the three, we passed six miserable hours. At daybreak the descent was resumed, and from the Hörnli ridge we ran down to the chalets of Buhl, and on to Zermatt. Seiler met me at his door, and followed in silence to my room. "What is the matter?" "The Taugwalders and I have returned." He did not need more, and burst into tears; but lost no time in useless lamentations, and set to work to arouse the village. Ere long a score of men had started to ascend the Hohlicht heights, above Kalbermatt and Z'Mutt, which commanded the plateau of the Matterhorngletscher. They returned after six hours, and reported that they had seen the bodies lying motionless on the snow. This was on Saturday; and they proposed that we should leave on Sunday evening, so as to arrive upon the plateau at day-break on Monday. Unwilling to lose the slightest chance, the Rev. J. M'Cormick and I resolved to start on Sunday morning. The Zermatt men, threatened with excommunication by their priests if they failed to attend the early mass, were unable to accompany us. To several of them, at least, this was a severe trial, and Peter Perrn declared with tears that nothing else would have prevented him from joining in the search for his old comrades. Englishmen came to our aid. The Rev. J. Robertson and Mr. J. Phillpotts offered themselves, and their guide Franz Andermatten; another Englishman lent us Joseph Marie and Alexandre Lochmatter. Frédéric Payot, and Jean Tairraz, of Chamounix, also volunteered.

We started at 2 A.M. on Sunday the 16th, and followed the route that we had taken on the previous Thursday as far as the Hörnli. From thence we went down to the right of the ridge, and mounted through the *séracs* of the Matterhorngletscher. By 8.30 we had got to the plateau at the top of the glacier, and within sight of the corner in which we knew my companions must be. As we saw one weather-beaten man after another raise the telescope, turn deadly pale, and pass it on without a word to the next, we knew that all hope was gone. We approached. They had fallen below as they had fallen above—Croz a little in advance, Hadow near him, and Hudson some distance behind; but of Lord F. Douglas we could see nothing. We left them where they fell; buried in snow at the base of the grandest cliff of the most majestic mountain of the Alps.

All those who had fallen had been tied with the Manilla, or with the second and equally strong rope, and, consequently, there had been only one link—that between old Peter and Lord F. Douglas—where the weaker rope had been used. This had a very ugly look for Taugwalder, for it was not possible to suppose that the others would have sanctioned the employment of a rope so greatly inferior in strength when there were more than 250 feet of the better qualities still remaining out of use. For the sake of the old guide (who bore a good reputation), and upon all other accounts, it was desirable that this matter should be cleared up; and after my examination before the court of inquiry which was instituted by the Government was over, I handed in a number of questions which were framed so as to afford old Peter an opportunity of exculpating himself from the grave suspicions which at once fell upon him. The questions, I was told, were put and answered; but the answers, although promised, have never reached me.

Meanwhile, the administration sent strict injunctions to recover the bodies, and upon the 19th of July, twenty-one men of Zermatt accomplished that sad and dangerous task. Of the body of Lord Francis Douglas they, too, saw nothing; it is probably still arrested on the rocks above. The remains of Hudson and Hadow were interred upon the north side of the Zermatt Church, in the presence of a reverent crowd of sympathising friends. The body of Michel Croz lies upon the other side, under a simpler tomb; whose inscription bears honourable testimony to his rectitude, to his courage, and to his devotion.

So the traditional inaccessibility of the Matterhorn was vanquished, and was replaced by legends of a more real character. Others will essay to scale its proud cliffs, but to none will it be the mountain that it was to its early explorers. Others may tread its summit-snows, but none will ever know the feelings of those who first gazed upon its marvellous panorama; and none, I trust, will ever be compelled to tell of joy turned into grief, and of laughter into mourning.

DE SAUSSURE ASCENDING MONT BLANC, AUGUST, 1787

''POPOCATEPEC, A HILL OF SMOAKE''

FROM *Purchas His Pilgrimes*

FRIAR LOPEZ DE GOMARA

Hakluytes Posthumous or Purchas His Pilgrimes appeared in 1625. Samuel Purchas worked with Richard Hakluyt in collecting materials for the monumental *Navigations*. When Hakluyt died in 1616, he left his papers to Purchas for posthumous publication.

This selection is an extract from *Antiquities Gathered out of the History of Friar Lopez de Gomara,* and describes Hernando Cortes' climb up Popocatepetl for his first sight of Mexico.

Bernal Diaz del Castillo, who was a member of the Cortes expedition, has the following comment to make in his *True History of the Conquest of Mexico:* "The historian Gomara says, that Cortes ascended a rock, in order to get a view of Zumpacingo. I say it was close to our station, and the man must have been blind indeed who could not have seen it from thence."

THERE IS A HILL EIGHT LEAGUES FROM CHOLOLLA, CALLED POPOCATEPEC, which is to say, a hill of smoake, for many times it casteth out smoake and fire. Cortes sent thither ten Spaniards, with many Indians, to carry their victuall, and to guide them in the way. The ascending up was very troublesome, and full of craggie rocks. They approached so nigh the top, that they heard such a terrible noise which proceeded from thence, that they durst not goe unto it, for the ground did tremble and shake, and great quantity of ashes which disturbed the way: but yet two of them who seemed to be most hardie, and desirous to see strange things, went up to the top, because they would not returne with a sleevelesse answer, and that they might not be accounted cowards, leaving their fellowes behinde them, proceeding forwards. The Indians said, what meane these men? for as yet never mortall man tooke such a journey in hand.

These two valiant fellowes passed through the Desart of Ashes, and at length came under a great smoake very thicke, and standing there a while, the darkenesse vanished partly away, and then appeared the vulcan and concavity, which was about halfe a league in compasse, out of which the ayre came abounding, with a great noise, very shrill, and whistling, in such sort that the whole hill did tremble. It was to be compared unto an Oven where Glasse is made. The smoake and heate was so great, that they could not abide it, and of force were constrained to returne by the way that they had ascended: but they were not gone farre, when the vulcan began to lash out flames of fire, ashes, and imbers, yea and at the last, stones of burning fire: and if they had not chansed to finde a Rocke, where under they shadowed themselves, undoubtedly they had there beene burned. When with good tokens they were returned where they left their fellowes, the other Indians kissed their garments as an honour due unto gods. They presented unto them such things as they had, and wondred much at their fact.

The simple Indians thought, that that place was an infernall place, where all such as governed not well, or used tyrannie in their offices, were punished when they died, and also beleeved, that after their purgation, they passed into glory. This Vulcan is like unto the Vulcan of Sicilia, it is high and round, and never wanteth snow about it, and is seene afarre off in the night, it lasheth out flames of fire. There is neere about this Hill many Cities, and Huexoxinco is one of the nighest. In tenne yeeres space this strange hill of working did expell no vapour or smoke: but in the yeere 1540. it began againe to burne, and with the horrible noyse thereof, the Neighbours that dwelt foure leagues from thence were terrified, for the especiall strange smoakes that then were seene, the like to their Predecessors had not beene seene. The ashes that proceeded from thence came to Huexo- zinco, Quelaxcopan, Tepiacac, Quauhquecholla, Chololla, and Tlaxcallan, which standeth ten leagues from thence, yea some say, it extended fifteene leagues distant, and burned their hearbes in their Gardens, their Fieldes of Corne, Trees, and cloathes that lay a drying.

He left the way that the Mexicans had perswaded him to come, for it was both evill and dangerous, as the Spaniard which went to the Vulcan had seene, he went another plainer way, and neerer. He ascended up a Hill covered with snow, which was six miles of height, where if the 30000. Souldiers had waited for them, they might easily have taken them, by reason of the great cold: and from the top of that Hill, they discovered the Land of Mexico, and the great Lake, with his Villages round about, which is an exceeding goodly sight. But when Cortes saw that beautifull thing, his joy was without comparison.

THE MOUNTAINS OF THE MOON

FROM *The Last Secrets*

JOHN BUCHAN

If we are to judge by such writers as Disraeli, prime minister of England under Queen Victoria, and John Buchan, governor general of Canada, it cannot be too far a cry from novel writing to statesmanship.

American readers will know John Buchan better as the author of *The 39 Steps,* from which the famous Hitchcock movie was made, than as the first Baron Tweedsmuir, representative of the king in Canada.

It would be vast understatement to say that Buchan led a full life. He was writer, soldier, publisher, lawyer, diplomat. His books, which give the reader an extraordinary feeling of reality, reflect his lifetime interest in mountaineering. This selection on the Mountains of the Moon was a product of a period early in his life when he worked in Africa.

TWENTY-FOUR CENTURIES AGO A LINE OF ÆSCHYLUS—"EGYPT NURTURED BY THE snow"—embodied a geographical theory which descended from Heaven knows what early folk-wandering. Aristotle with his ἀργυροῦν ὅρος, the Mountain of Silver from which the Nile flowed, continued the tradition in literature. Meantime Sabæan Arabs, trading along the east coast of Africa, and making expeditions to the interior, came back with stories of great inland seas and snow mountains near them. What they saw may have been only Kilimanjaro and Kenia, but the popular acceptance of their reports points to the earlier tale linking the snows with the Nile valley. Greek and Roman travellers spread the rumour, and presently it found its way, probably through Marinus of Tyre, into the pages of the geographer Ptolemy.

Ptolemy had no doubt about these snows. He called them the Mountains of the Moon, and definitely fixed them as the source of the river of Egypt. For centuries after him the question slumbered, and men were too busied with creeds and conquests to think much of that fount of the Nile which Alexander the Great saw in his dreams. When the exploration of Equatoria began in last century the story revived, and the discovery of Kenia and

Kilimanjaro seemed to have settled the matter. It was true that these mountains were a long way from the Nile watershed, but then Ptolemy had never
enjoyed much of a reputation for accuracy.

Still doubt remained in some minds, and explorers kept their eyes open
for snow mountains which should actually feed the Nile, since, after all, so
ancient a tradition had probably some ground of fact. Speke in 1861 thought
he had discovered them in the chain of volcanoes between Lake Kivu and
Lake Albert Edward, but these mountains held no snow. He received a hint,
however, which might have led to success, for he heard from the Arabs of
Unyamwezi of a strange mountain west of Lake Victoria, seldom visible,
covered with white stuff, and so high and steep that no man could ascend
it. In 1864 Sir Samuel Baker was within sight of Ruwenzori, and actually
saw dim shapes looming through the haze, to which he gave the name of
"Blue Mountains."

In 1875 Stanley encamped for several days upon the eastern slopes, but
he did not realize the greatness of the heights above him. He thought they
were something like Elgon, and he christened them Mount Edwin Arnold
(a name happily not continued); but he had no thought of snow or glacier,
and he disbelieved the native stories of white stuff on the top. In 1876 Gor-
don's emissary, Gessi, recorded a strange apparition, "like snow mountains
in the sky," which his men saw, but he seems to have considered it a hallucination. Stranger still, Emin Pasha lived for ten years on Lake Albert and
never once saw the range—a fact which may be partly explained by his bad
eyesight. Ruwenzori keeps its secret well. The mists from the Semliki valley
shroud its base, and only on the clearest days, and for a very little time, can
the traveller get such a prospect as Mr. Grogan got on his famous walk from
the Cape to Cairo—"a purple mass, peak piled upon peak, black-streaked
with forest, scored with ravine, and ever mounting till her castellated crags
shoot their gleaming tops far into the violet heavens."

The true discoverer was Stanley, who, in 1888, suddenly had a vision of
the range from the south-west shore of Lake Albert. Every one remembers
the famous passage:—

> While looking to the south-east and meditating upon the events of the
> last month, my eyes were directed by a boy to a mountain said to be covered
> with salt, and I saw a peculiar-shaped cloud of a most beautiful silver colour,
> which assumed the proportions and appearance of a vast mountain covered
> with snow. Following its form downward, I became struck with the deep
> blue-black colour of its base, and wondered if it portended another tornado;
> then as the sight descended to the gap between the eastern and western
> plateaus I became for the first time conscious that what I gazed upon was
> not the image or semblance of a vast mountain, but the solid substance of a
> real one, with its summit covered with snow. . . . It now dawned upon me

that this must be Ruwenzori, which was said to be covered with a white metal or substance believed to be rock, as reported by Kavali's two slaves.

In April, 1906, the Duke of the Abruzzi and his party left Italy to solve once and for all the riddle of the mountains. The Duke was perhaps the greatest of living mountaineers. As a rock-climber his fame has filled the Alps, and no name is more honoured at Courmayeur or the Montanvert. He had led Polar expeditions, and had made the first ascent of the Alaskan Mount St. Elias. His experience, therefore, had made him not only a climber but an organizer of mountain travel. It was to this latter accomplishment that he owed his success, for Ruwenzori was not so much a climber's as a traveller's problem. The actual mountaineering is not hard, but to travel the long miles from Entebbe to the range, to cut a path through the dense jungles of the valleys, and to carry supplies and scientific apparatus to the high glacier camps, required an organizing talent of the first order.

The Duke left no contingency unforeseen. He took with him four celebrated Courmayeur guides, and a staff of distinguished scientists, as well as Cav. Vittorio Sella, the greatest of living mountain photographers. So large was the expedition that two hundred and fifty native porters were required to carry stores from Entebbe to Fort Portal. It was not a bold personal adventure, like Mr. Wollaston's, but a carefully planned, scientific assault upon the mystery of Ruwenzori. The Duke did not only seek to ascend the highest peak, but to climb every summit, and map accurately every mountain, valley, and glacier. The story of the work has been officially written, not indeed by the leader himself, who had no time to spare, but by his friend and former companion, Sir Filippo de Filippi. It is an admirable account, clear and yet picturesque, and it is illustrated by photographs and panoramas which have not often been equalled in mountaineering narratives.

The charm of the book is its strangeness. It tells of a kind of mountaineering to which the world can show no parallel. When Lhasa had been visited, Ruwenzori remained, with the gorges of the Brahmaputra, one of the few great geographical mysteries unveiled. Happily the unveiling has not killed the romance, for the truth is stranger than any forecast. If the Mountains of the Moon are lower than we had believed, they are far more wonderful. Here you have a range almost on the Equator, rising not from an upland, like Kilimanjaro, but from the "Albertine Depression," which is 600 or 700 feet below the average level of Uganda; a range of which the highest peaks are 1,000 feet higher than Mont Blanc, which is draped most days of the year in mist, and accessible from the plains only by deep-cut glens choked with strange trees and flowers. The altitude would in any case give every stage of climate from torrid to arctic, but the position on the Line adds something exotic even to familiar mountain sights, draping a glacier moraine with a tangle of monstrous growths, and swelling the homely Alpine flora into portents. The freakish spirit in Nature has been let loose, and she has set snowfields and rock *arêtes* in the heart of a giant hothouse.

The Duke of the Abruzzi was faced at the start with a deplorable absence of information. Even the season when the weather was most favourable was disputed. Mr. Freshfield, following Sir Harry Johnston's advice, tried November, and found a perpetual shower-bath. Warned by this experience, the Duke selected June and July for the attempt, and was fortunate enough to get sufficient clear days to complete his task, though he was repeatedly driven into camp by violent rain. Another matter in doubt was the best means of approach to the highest snows. The obvious route was the Mobuku valley, but by this time it was pretty clear that Kiyanja, the peak at its head, was not the highest, and it was possible that there might be no way out of the valley to the higher western summits. Still, it had been the old way of travellers, and since the alternative was the Butagu valley right on the other side of the range, the Duke chose to follow the steps of his predecessors.

Just before Butiti he got his first sight of the snow, and made out that a double peak, which was certainly not Johnston's Duwoni, was clearly the loftiest. Duwoni came into view again in the lower Mobuku valley, and the sight, combined with the known locality of Kiyanja, enabled the expedition to take its bearings. Duwoni was seen through the opening of a large tributary valley, the Bujuku, which entered the Mobuku on the north side between the Portal Peaks. Now it had been clear from the lowlands that the highest snows were to the south of Duwoni, and must consequently lie between that peak and the Mobuku valley. The conclusion was that the Bujuku must lead to the foot of the highest summits, while the Mobuku could not. The discovery was the key of the whole geography of the range. But the Duke did not at once act upon it. He wisely decided to explore Kiyanja first; so, thinning out his caravan and leaving his heavier stores at the last native village, he with his party pushed up the Mobuku torrent.

The Mobuku valley falls in stages from the glacier, and at the foot of each stage is a cliff face and a waterfall. The soil everywhere oozes moisture, and where an outcrop of rock or a mat of dead boughs does not give firmer going, it is knee-deep in black mud. The first stage is forest land—great conifers with masses of ferns and tree-ferns below, and above a tangle of creepers and flaming orchids. At the second terrace you come to the fringe of Alpine life. Here is the heath forest, of which let the narrative tell:—

> Trunks and boughs are entirely smothered in a thick layer of mosses which hang like waving beards from every spray, cushion and englobe every knot, curl and swell around each twig, deform every outline and obliterate every feature, till the trees are a mere mass of grotesque contortions, monstrous tumefactions of the discoloured leprous growth. No leaf is to be seen

save on the very topmost twigs, yet the forest is dark owing to the dense network of trunks and branches. The soil disappears altogether under innumerable dead trunks, heaped one upon another in intricate piles, covered with mosses, viscous and slippery when exposed to the air; black, naked, and yet neither mildewed nor rotten where they have lain for years and years in deep holes. No forest can be grimmer and stranger than this. The vegetation seems primeval, of some period when forms were uncertain and provisory.

But the third terrace is stranger still. There one is out of the forest and in an Alpine meadow between sheer cliffs, with far at the head the gorge of Bujongolo and the tongue of the glacier above it. But what an Alpine meadow!—

The ground was carpeted with a deep layer of lycopodium and springy moss, and thickly dotted with big clumps of the papery flowers, pink, yellow, and silver white, of the helichrysum or everlasting, above which rose the tall columnar stalks of the lobelia, like funeral torches, beside huge branching groups of the monster senecio. The impression produced was beyond words to describe; the spectacle was too weird, too improbable, too unlike all familiar images, and upon the whole brooded the same grave deathly silence.

It is a commonplace to say that in savage Africa man is surrounded by a fauna still primeval; but in these mountains the flora, too, is of an earlier world—that strange world which is embalmed in our coal seams. Under the veil of mist, among cliffs which lose themselves in the clouds, the traveller walks in an unearthly landscape, which the gaunt candelabra of the senecios, the flambeaus of the lobelias, and the uncanny blooms of the helichryse like decorations at some ghostly feast. The word "helichryse" calls up ridiculous Theocritean associations, as if the sunburnt little "creeping-gold" of Sicily were any kin to these African marvels! Our elders were wise when they named the range the Mountains of the Moon, for such things might well belong to some lunar gorge of Mr. Wells's imagination. Beyond Kiyanja the Duke found a little lake where a fire had raged and the senecios were charred and withered. It was a veritable Valley of Dry Bones.

Bujongolo offered the expedition a stone-heap overhung by a cliff, and there the permanent camp was fixed. Among mildews and lichens and pallid mist and an everlasting drip of rain five weeks were passed with this unpromising spot as their base. The first business was to ascend Kiyanja. This gave little trouble, for the ridge was soon gained, and an easy *arête* to the south led to the chief point. The height proved to be 15,988 feet, and the view from the summit settled the geography of the range and confirmed the

Duke's theories. For it was now clear that the ridge at the head of the Mobuku was no part of the watershed of the chain, and that the Duwoni of Johnston was to the north, not of the Mobuku, but of the Bujuku. The highest
summits stood over to the west, rising from the col at the head of the Bujuku
valley. The Duke saw that they might also be reached by making a detour
to the south of Kiyanja, and ascending a glen which is one of the high afflu-
ents of the Butagu, the great valley on the west side of the system.

It may be convenient here to explain the main features of the range,
giving them the new names which the expedition invented, and which are
now adopted by geographers. Kiyanja became Mount Baker, and its highest
point is called Edward Peak after the then King of England. Due south,
across the Freshfield Pass, stands Mount Luigi di Savoia, a name given by
the Royal Geographical Society and not by the Duke, who wished to christen
it after Joseph Thomson the traveller. Due north from Mount Baker, and
separated from it by the upper Bujuku valley, is Mount Speke (the Duwoni
of Johnston), with its main summit called Vittorio Emanuele. West of the
gap between Baker and Speke stands the highest summit of all, Mount Stanley, with its twin peaks Margherita and Alexandra. North of Mount Speke
is Mount Emin, and east of the latter is Mount Gessi. Five of the great
massifs cluster around the Bujuku valley, while the sixth, Mount Luigi di
Savoia, stands by itself at the south end of the chain.

The assault on Mount Stanley was delayed for some days by abominable
weather. At last came a clear season, and the Duke with his guides crossed
Freshfield Pass and ascended the valley at the back of Mount Baker. There
they spent an evening, which showed what Ruwenzori could be like when
clouds are absent. They found a little lake, embosomed in flowers, under
the cliffs, and looking to the west they saw the sun set in crimson and gold
over the great spaces of the Congo Forest. Next day they reached the col
which bears the name of Scott Elliot, and encamped on one of the Mount
Stanley glaciers at the height of 14,817 feet. At 7.30 on the following morning they reached the top of the first peak, Alexandra, 16,749 feet high. A
short descent and a difficult piece of step-cutting through snow cornices took
them to the summit of Margherita (16,815 feet), the highest point of the
range:—

> They emerged from the mist into splendid clear sunlight. At their feet
> lay a sea of fog. An impenetrable layer of light ashy-white cloud-drift, stretch-
> ing as far as the eye could reach, was drifting rapidly north-westward. From
> the immense moving surface emerged two fixed points, two pure white peaks
> sparkling in the sun with their myriad snow crystals. These were the two
> extreme summits of the highest peaks. The Duke of the Abruzzi named
> these summits Margherita and Alexandra, "in order that, under the auspices
> of these two royal ladies, the memory of the two nations may be handed

down to posterity—of Italy, whose name was the first to resound on these snows in a shout of victory, and of England, which in its marvellous colonial expansion carries civilization to the slopes of these remote mountains." It was a thrilling moment when the little tricolor flag, given by H.M. Queen Margherita of Savoy, unfurled to the wind and sun the embroidered letters of its inspiring motto, "Ardisci e Spera."

BICYCLE FOR MOUNTAINOUS ROAD. AN AIR BALLOON HAS BEEN ATTACHED TO THE BICYCLE BY THE IN-VENTOR TO ASSIST THE RIDER TO HIS DESTINATION

A SONNET TO BEN NEVIS

FROM *Letters*

J O H N   K E A T S

In the Protestant cemetery in Rome there is a tombstone which bears no name. On it is cut the epitaph *Here lies one whose name was writ on water*. John Keats, great poet and poor prophet, lies buried there.

His letters give us a closer view of Keats than the convention of poetic form sometimes allows. There is the brilliant imagery and phrasing but in addition there is freedom and high humor and lack of restraint in these unstudied messages to friends and kinfolk—and also something perhaps of the bitter foreknowledge of his early death.

In 1817 he made a walking tour of the Lake District and Scotland. This letter was written to his invalid brother, Tom. It is a most unusual picture we get of John Keats sitting on top of Ben Nevis and writing nonsense verse.

To THOMAS KEATS. *Monday 3 August 1818.*
Address: Mr Thos Keats | Well Walk | Hampstead | Middx—
Postmarks: INVERNESS 6 AUG 1818; TOO LATE; AUG 9 1818 and 10 o'CLOCK AU 12 1818.

Letter Findlay, August 3rd

Ah mio Ben

My dear Tom,

We have made but poor progress Lately, chiefly from bad weather, for my throat is in a fair way of getting quite well, so I have had nothing of consequence to tell you till yesterday when we went up Ben Nevis, the highest Mountain in Great Britain—On that account I will never ascend another in this empire—Skiddaw is nothing to it either in height or in difficulty. It is above 4300 feet from the Sea level and Fortwilliam stands at the head of a Salt water Lake, consequently we took it completely from that level. I am heartily glad it is done—it is almost like a fly crawling up a wainscoat—Imagine the task of mounting 10 Saint Pauls without the convenience of Stair cases. We set out about five in the morning with a Guide in the Tar-

tan and Cap and soon arrived at the foot of the first ascent which we immediately began upon—after much fag and tug and a rest and a glass of whiskey
apiece we gained the top of the first rise and saw then a tremendous chap
above us which the guide said was still far from the top—After the first Rise
our way lay along a heath valley in which there was a Loch—after about a
Mile in this Valley we began upon the next ascent—more formidable by far
than the last and kept mounting with short intervals of rest untill we got
above all vegetation, among nothing but loose Stones which lasted us to the
very top—the Guide said we had three Miles of a stony ascent—we gained the
first tolerable level after the valley to the height of what in the Valley we
had thought the top and saw still above us another huge crag which still the
Guide said was not the top—to that we made with an obstinate fag, and having gained it there came on a Mist, so that from that part to the very top we
walked in a Mist. The whole immense head of the Mountain is composed
of large loose stones—thousands of acres—Before we had got half way up we
passed large patches of snow and near the top there is a chasm some hundred
feet deep completely glutted with it—Talking of chasms they are the finest
wonder of the whole—the[y] appear great rents in the very heart of the mountain though they are not, being at the side of it, but other huge crags arising
round it give the appearance to Nevis of a shattered heart or Core in itself—
These Chasms are 1500 feet in depth and are the most tremendous places I
have ever seen—they turn one giddy if you choose to give way to it—We tumbled in large stones and set the echoes at work in fine style. Sometimes these
chasms are tolerably clear, sometimes there is a misty cloud which seems to
steam up and sometimes they are entirely smothered with clouds.

After a little time the Mist cleared away but still there were large Clouds
about attracted by old Ben to a certain distance so as to form as it appear'd
large dome curtains which kept sailing about, opening and shutting at intervals here and there and everywhere; so that although we did not see one
vast wide extent of prospect all round we saw something perhaps finer—these
cloud-veils opening with a dissolving motion and showing us the mountainous region beneath as through a loop hole—these cloudy loop holes ever
varying and discovering fresh prospect east, west north and South. Then it
was misty again and again it was fair—then puff came a cold breeze of wind
and bared a craggy chap we had not yet seen though in close neighbourhood
—Every now and then we had over head blue Sky clear and the sun pretty
warm. I do not know whether I can give you an Idea of the prospect from a
large Mountain top—You are on a stony plain which of course makes you
forget you are on any but low ground—the horison or rather edges of this
plain being above 4000 feet above the Sea hide all the Country immediately beneath you, so that the next objects you see all round next to the
edges of the flat top are the Summits of Mountains of some distance off—as

you move about on all side[s] you see more or less of the near neighbour
country according as the Mountain you stand upon is in different parts steep
or rounded—but the most new thing of all is the sudden leap of the eye from
the extremity of what appears a plain into so vast a distance. On one part of
the top there is a handsome pile of stones done pointedly by some soldiers
of artillery, I clim[b]ed onto them and so got a little higher than old Ben
himself. It was not so cold as I expected—yet cold enough for a glass of
Wiskey now and then—There is not a more fickle thing than the top of a
Mountain—what would a Lady give to change her headdress as often and
with as little trouble!—There are a good many red deer upon Ben Nevis we
did not see one—the dog we had with us keep [*for* kept] a very sharp look
out and really languished for a bit of a worry—I have said nothing yet of
out [*for* our] getting on among the loose stones large and small sometimes
on two sometimes on three, sometimes four legs—sometimes two and stick,
sometimes three and stick, then four again, then two, then a jump, so that
we kept on ringing changes on foot, hand, stick, jump, boggle, s[t]umble,
foot, hand, foot, (very gingerly) stick again, and then again a game at all
fours. After all there was one Mrs Cameron of 50 years of age and the fattest
woman in all inverness shire who got up this Mountain some few years ago—
true she had her servants—but then she had her self—She ought to have hired
Sysiphus—"Up the high hill he heaves a huge round—Mrs Cameron" 'Tis said
a little conversation took place between the mountain and the Lady—After
taking a glass of Wiskey as she was tolerably seated at ease she thus began—

> M^{rs}. C.
> Upon my Life Sir Nevis I am pique'd
> That I have so far panted tugg'd and reek'd
> To do an honour to your old bald pate
> And now am sitting on you just to bate,
> Without your paying me one compliment.
> Alas 'tis so with all, when our intent
> Is plain, and in the eye of all Mankind
> We fair ones show a preference, too blind!
> You Gentleman immediat[e]ly turn tail—
> O let me then my hapless fate bewail!
> Ungrateful Baldpate have I not disdaind
> The pleasant Valleys—have I not madbraind
> Deserted all my Pickles and preserves
> My China closet too—with wretched Nerves
> To boot—say wretched ingrate have I not
> Le[f]t my soft cushion chair and caudle pot.
> 'Tis true I had no corns—no! thank the fates
> My Shoemaker was always M^r. Bates.

And if not M^r. Bates why I'm not old!
Still dumb ungrateful Nevis—still so cold!

Here the Lady took some more wiskey and was putting even more to her
lips when she dashed [it] to the Ground for the Mountain began to grumble
—which continued for a few Minutes before he thus began,

BEN NEVIS
What whining bit of tongue and Mouth thus dares
Distur[b]'d my Slumber of a thousand years!
Even so long my sleep has been secure—
And to be so awaked I'll not endure.
Oh pain—for since the Eagle's earliest scream
I've had a dam'd confounded ugly dream
                                              you?
A Nightmare sure. What Madam was it ~~true~~
It cannot be! My old eyes are not true!
Red-Crag,* My Spectacles! Now let me see!
Good Heavens Lady how the gemini
Did you get here? O I shall split my sides!
I shall earthquake——
M^rs. C
Sweet Nevis do not quake, for though I love
You[r] honest Countenance all things above
Truly I should not like to be convey'd
So far into your Bosom—gentle Maid
Loves not too rough a treatment gentle sir—
Pray thee be calm and do not quake nor stir
No not a Stone or I shall go in fits—
BEN NEVIS
I must—I shall—I meet not such tit bits—
I meet not such sweet creatures every day—
By my old night cap night cap night and day
I must have one sweet Buss—I must and shall!
Red Crag!—What Madam can you then repent
Of all the toil and vigour you have spent
To see Ben Nevis and to touch his nose?
Red Crag I say! O I must have you close!
Red Crag, there lies beneath my farthest toe
A vein of Sulphur—go dear Red Crag go—
And rub your flinty back against it—budge!
Dear Madam I must kiss you, faith I must!
I must Embrace you with my dearest gust!

---

* A domestic of Ben's.

Block-head,* d'ye hear—Block-head I'll make her feel
There lies beneath my east leg's northern heel
A cave of young earth dragons—well my boy
Go thither quick and so complete my joy
Take you a bundle of the largest pines
And where the sun on fiercest Phosphor shines
Fire them and ram them in the Dragons' nest
Then will the dragons fry and fizz their best
Until ten thousand now no bigger than
Poor Aligators poor things of one span
Will each one swell to twice ten times the size
Of northern whale—then for the tender prize—
The moment then—for then will red Crag rub
His flinty back and I shall kiss and snub
And press my dainty morsel to my breast
Blockhead make haste!
                               O Muses weep the rest—
The Lady fainted and he thought her dead
So pulled the clouds again about his head
And went to sleep again—soon she was rous'd
By her affrigh[t]ed servants—next day hous'd
Safe on the lowly ground she bless'd her fate
That fainting fit was not delayed too late

But what surprises me above all is how this Lady got down again. I felt it horribly. 'Twas the most vile descent—shook me all to pieces—Over leaf you will find a Sonnet I wrote on the top of Ben Nevis. We have just entered Inverness. I have three letters from you and one [from] Fanny—and one from Dilke. I would set about crossing this all over for you but I will first write to Fanny and Mrs Wilie. Then I will begin another to you and not before because I think it better you should have this as soon as possible —My Sore throat is not quite well and I intend stopping here a few days.

Read me a Lesson, muse, and speak it loud
    Upon the top of Nevis blind in Mist!
I look into the Chasms and a Shroud
    Vaprous doth hide them; just so much I wist
Mankind do know of Hell: I look o'erhead
    And there is sullen mist; even so much
Mankind can tell of Heaven: Mist is spread
    Before the Earth beneath me—even such
Even so vague is Man's sight of himself.
    Here are the craggy Stones beneath my feet;

---

* Another domestic of Ben's.

Thus much I know, that a poor witless elf
I tread on them; that all my eye doth meet
Is mist and Crag—not only on this height,
But in the world of thought and mental might—

Good bye till tomorrow

Your most affectionate Brother

John

ASCENDING THE LOWER DOME OF THE
YOSEMITE

E N E M I E S

FROM *The White Tower*

J A M E S   R A M S E Y   U L L M A N

James Ramsey Ullman is one of few writers who are able to communicate the intensity of a dangerous climb. In this selection from his novel *The White Tower,* the ascent is so vividly described, the suspense so sharply maintained that the reader feels as though he himself were one of the climbers.

This novel and the many mountain books which followed it grew out of Ullman's long-time avocation of mountaineering. He has climbed Mount Olympus in 110 degrees of heat and a Mexican volcano through six-foot snow drifts. He has climbed the Jungfrau, the Andes, the Tetons, the Rockies. But his most difficult climb, he says, was up Breakneck, opposite West Point on the Hudson.

THERE WAS THE SNOW AND THE FOOTPRINTS IN THE SNOW. THERE WAS THE SLOPE and the crest, and the next slope and the next crest, the slope and the crest beyond. There was the smooth, ice-veined wall of the Citadel rising sheer into the sky beyond the last crest. There was a ramp of snow curving around the wall to the right, and a sharp bend in the ramp, and the ramp narrowing and steepening, and beyond the ramp the summits of the Alps and the blue valleys that were Switzerland and the blue horizon that was France. There was Siegfried Hein standing beyond the next bend in the ramp and turning and looking at him, his eyes very gray and steady in his sun-blackened face.

Ordway stopped.

You must think clearly now, he thought. His eyes moved over the muffled figure, over the torn boots and the great jagged rents at the knees and elbows, and back to the burned, stubbled face and the gray eyes. You must think and talk very clearly now.

"You have changed your mind, I see," Hein said.

He nodded.

"A long, hard climb, is it not?"

"Yes."

"But you found the footprints and the piton helpful, perhaps?"

"Yes, I found them very helpful."

He could not feel his tongue or lips moving, and the words stuck like thick lumps in his throat. Suddenly he leaned against the rock-wall beside him, choking and coughing.

Hein watched him in silence. "You will excuse me if I go on now?" he said presently.

Ordway started to speak, choked again and stood crouched with his head against the rock. Then the paroxysm passed and he turned slowly back to the German.

"On?" he repeated thickly.

"To the top."

"I'm going to the top too."

Hein shrugged. "That is up to you, of course." His eyes were still fixed on Ordway's face. "Permit me to make a suggestion, however, *Herr Kapitän.* Do not waste your time trying to climb the rock."

Ordway's gaze moved slowly upward over the vertical ice-sheathed wall of the Citadel.

"It's the same all around?" he asked.

"Yes, it is the same all around. I have reconnoitred it for more than an hour and made a start in two or three places; but it is unclimbable. You will forgive me, perhaps, that I was not even able to hammer in a piton for our mutual convenience."

Ordway looked at him for a long moment in silence. Very steady now, he thought. Very clear and sure and steady . . .

"And this ledge?" he asked.

"Is the one possibility."

Ordway moved forward to a point a few feet beyond the German and peered around a protruding buttress in the rock-wall along the curving flange of the ramp. Only a short pitch of precipice remained above them— twenty vertical feet, perhaps, twenty-five at the most—with the ramp cutting diagonally upward across its face. It was far narrower and steeper than the section on which they stood—a mere ribbon of snow clinging to the mountainside. But it was there. It extended in an unbroken path to the top of the Citadel and ended in a broad, jutting platform of rock above.

Ordway turned back to Hein.

"It looks all right," he said.

"Yes, it does, doesn't it?"

"Let's go, then."

He took another step forward, but stopped suddenly when he saw that the other had not moved. For a moment the two men looked at each other in silence.

"I would not be quite so impatient if I were you, *Herr Kapitän*," said Hein quietly. "If, for example, you would take the trouble, as I did, to study the ledge ahead from various angles, you would perhaps notice something that will change your mind."

Ordway's eyes moved from Hein back to the ramp. He pressed himself in against the precipice wall and stared upward. Then he crouched and leaned outward. Digging his fingers and toes into the snow, he inched the upper part of his body out over the rim of the ledge until at last he could see what lay beyond and beneath it. And in that same instant he saw what Hein had meant. The section of the ramp on which they stood was, in effect, the sloping top of a bulge in the cliffs below, and the snow that covered it rested on a firm, if narrow, base of solid rock. But directly ahead, where the ramp steepened across the final pitch, the bulge no longer existed. The ribbon of snow that formed its surface was not a covering over rock beneath, but merely a cornice or unsupported platform, clinging of its own adhesiveness to the face of the precipice. Below it was no firm outthrust of the mountainside, but eight thousand feet of air.

Ordway stood up slowly.

"It wouldn't hold a man," he said.

Hein shook his head. "No, it would not hold a man."

"Then—"

He felt the gray eyes on his face again—the gray eyes, steady and mocking.

"Then if you will let me by, *Herr Kapitän*—" Hein moved past him for a step or two, stopped again and stood staring up along the ramp. "—I shall be starting now."

"But how can you? Which way?"

"You have heard of a hand traverse, perhaps?"

"Yes, but—" He broke off abruptly, his eyes following Hein's along the sheer face beyond. And now for the first time he saw that there was a crack in the smooth surface of the rock. Beginning not more than two yards ahead of where they stood, it slanted upward across the precipice, roughly parallel to the snow-ramp and about five feet above it, and ended where the ramp ended, at the base of the jutting platform above. It was a thin, hairline crack, far too narrow and shallow to hold a booted foot; but its lower lip seemed to curl upward and outward just enough to support the grasp of a man's tightly curved fingers.

Ordway's eyes went back to Hein.

"It's at least forty feet," he said.

"Yes."

"And a thirty-degree angle."

"Yes."

"But you think you can make it?"

"Yes, I think I can make it."

There was another silence between them. Ordway looked once again at the thin, slanting crack and the ribbon of snow beneath it and the gulf of space beyond. Then he quietly unslung his rope from his shoulder.

"All right," he said.

Hein looked at him without speaking.

"Shall we go?" asked Ordway.

The German shook his head slowly. "I'm going alone," he said.

"We're going together."

"No. Whether you try to follow me or not is your own affair, although having seen your attempts at climbing I would advise most strongly against it. But I am afraid I have finished with dragging you and your companions to the top of the Weissturm."

Ordway stood straight and still, his palms flattened against the rock behind him. For a moment the only sound was the deep rasping of his breath in his throat.

"I am not asking you to help me," he said quietly.

"No? What then?"

"I'm suggesting that we help each other."

"You are under the impression then that I need your help?"

"As much as I need yours." Ordway held out the rope. "Here. Tie it on."

Hein did not move.

"Tie it on, I say!"

He heard his own voice, tiny and hoarse and straining in the silence of snow and sky. He saw the gray walls of the Citadel and the white glint of a slope above the eaves. He felt the tautness of his body, the straining of his lungs, the wild pounding of his heart.

"We've come this far together, Hein," he said. "Let's finish it together. . . ."

The German stared at him silently for a moment. The eyes in the blackened, bearded, ice-crusted face were now no longer mocking, but as cold and hard and bleak as stone. "No," he said, his voice low and even, "we will not finish it together. I will finish it alone, and you will not finish it at all. And shall I tell you why that is the way it will be, Captain Ordway? It is because I am strong and you are weak. It is because I have the courage and the skill and the will to do it, and you have not. It is because I am a German climbing for Germany, and you are not climbing for anything, but only running away."

Ordway did not speak. He did not move. He stood there, as immobile and frozen as the mountain wall behind him, the coil of rope in his extended hand.

What happened then remained in his memory afterward not as remembered reality but as the blurred images and sensations of a half-apprehended dream. There was the sudden great surge of anger rising within him; an anger such as he had never felt in his life before; an engulfing and consuming tide that was more than anger, deeper and colder and more bitter than anger. There was Hein standing in front of him, Hein turning away again and moving slowly up the ramp. There was the wild, shaken, despairing instant in which he was about to hurl himself forward upon him. . . . But he did not hurl himself forward. He still neither spoke nor moved. . . . And now, as he stood watching, Siegfried Hein approached the lower end of the unsupported snow-ramp, studied the slanting crack in the rock above, and, grasping its lower lip with the fingers of both hands, swung himself out onto the face of the precipice.

With slow, measured movements the German pulled himself across and upward, his head and shoulders held close in against the line of the crack, his feet dragging without pressure along the surface of the snow below. His right hand slid forward, gripped and pulled. Then his body moved after it as the left hand slipped forward too. He reached, gripped, pulled, reached again. After each five or six swings he rested a moment, with his hands close together in the crack and his chin resting on its outcurving lip. Then he moved on again. Presently he was halfway to the rock platform above. Perhaps a minute later he was two-thirds of the way. And still he moved on, steadily and silently. The only movement in that enormous stillness of snow and air was the slow, rhythmic motion of his hands and body. The only sound was the faint scraping of his clothing against the wall of rock.

And then suddenly, startlingly, there was another sound. . . .

With a sharp, dry crack the lip of the crevice to which Hein was clinging broke away from under his hands. For a terrible, timeless instant Ordway heard the scratch of his bootnails against the rock and saw his fingers clawing at the wall. Then he was no longer clinging to the wall at all but standing on the unsupported snow-ramp below. The snow trembled, seemed for a moment to be slowly buckling under his weight . . . and held.

Then there was silence again. Hein did not move. Nothing moved.

"Can you get back on the wall?" Ordway called.

The German did not answer. For a few moments he remained frozen where he stood; then very slowly and cautiously, without moving his feet, he raised his arms and groped upward to the right along the rock-wall. Apparently, however, he could find no hold. Lowering his arms, he stood staring down at the snow, and Ordway could see that he was carefully shifting his weight and advancing one foot, inch by inch, in front of the other. He took one step, then a second. But he never took the third. For in the next instant the snow directly in front of him disappeared. It did not seem to break away or to fall. It was just soundlessly and magically no longer there. In the spot where Hein had been about to set his foot there was now revealed the blue sea of air that washed the eight-thousand-foot north face of the Weissturm.

Ordway shut his eyes, but only for a second, and when he opened them Hein was still miraculously there.

"Don't move!" he heard his voice calling. "Don't move an inch!"

And at the same moment he realized that, without having thought it or willed it, he himself had begun to move; that he had unslung his pack and dropped his ax and rope; that he was edging toward the snow-ramp, grasping the crack above it with bare hands, swinging himself out onto the precipice beyond. . . .

He kept his face to the mountainside and his eyes on the gray rock creeping past them. He reached, gripped, pulled, reached again. He clung motionless to the lip of the crack, counted ten and swung on again. When at last he turned and looked ahead he was no more than ten or twelve feet from the point where Hein stood. When he turned for the second time he was almost within arm's reach of him.

Directly ahead of him now was the section of the crack from which the lip had broken away in Hein's grasp. Slanting diagonally upward above the German's head, it was now no more than the merest fold in the vertical rock, shorn clean of all protuberances or roughnesses on which a hand or finger could secure a grip. It was not a long section—a yard across perhaps, four feet at the most—and beyond it the crack was deep and flanged again, cutting upward in its final stretch to the summit of the rock-wall and the jutting platform above. But the point at which the lip began was still a foot or more beyond Hein's grasp, and between him and its granite safety was the jagged hole in the snow-ramp and blue depths of space. Ordway's eyes moved back to Hein and from Hein to the point in the lower section of the crack to which he himself was clinging. Here, too, there was a distance of perhaps a foot between the German's farthest possible grasp and the nearest projection of the lip. But there was one difference. On the far side there was only one man's reach to bridge the gap, and on this side there were two.

"The crack's strong enough here to hold the two of us," Ordway said quietly. "I'm going to reach out my hand. Don't move until you're sure you have a grip on it. When I pull, jump."

He shifted his left hand to the securest grip he could find and jammed his elbow deep into the crack. Then he swivelled slowly around and extended his right hand until it was within two feet of Hein's shoulders.

"Take it," he said.

Hein did not move.

"Take it!"

But even as he spoke he knew now, with sudden and absolute certainty, that Siegfried Hein was not going to take his hand. The German stood, motionless and silent, looking at him, and Ordway looked back at him across the intervening yard of space and the arc of his extended arm. He saw the square-lined, blackened face and the tight, rigid flesh of the cheeks and jaw-line. He saw the snowflecked stubble of the beard and the greased, frozen crack of the thin lips and the minute glistening beads of sweat that coursed slowly down through the grease and stubble and flecks of snow. He saw the bleak-gray unmoving eyes and the bleakness behind the eyes. And in the same instant it seemed to him that he was seeing everything that was behind the eyes. For one flashing, timeless instant on that forlorn and timeless mountainside he looked into a man's eyes, and everything that the man was was there. He saw it all now, naked and manifest before him: the frustration and bitterness and contumacy; the fear and the pride and the bottomless sterility of pride; the despairing lonely hunger of the unloving and unloved; the will to conquer and the will to die. . . .

He saw it all. And then he saw the face turning from him, Hein turning away from him, advancing one foot slowly in front of the other, reaching out with both arms toward the upper section of the crack that slanted upward toward the platform at the summit of the cliff. He saw him stop and crouch, motionless. He saw him leap toward the rock-wall, hit it, grasp it, cling to it, claw at it, slip from it, fall slowly backward from it onto the snow-ramp. Hein did not seem to hit the snow. He simply disappeared through it, soundlessly. In the same instant the ramp itself was gone. Then there was only silence and stillness again, and the mountain wall curving downward, and a few puffs and shreds of spindrift wreathing gently in the windless air.

Martin Ordway hung from the crack and stared dully at the wall of rock from which the snow had broken away. The ramp was gone, and in its place was space—but not only space. For along the line where the concealing snow had joined the mountainside there was now revealed a narrow but solid flange of granite, banding the smooth face of the Citadel. He lowered himself to it, edged along it, grasped the lip of the crack on the far side, pulled himself forward and upward. . . .

F U J I - N O - Y A M A

FROM *Exotics and Retrospectives*

L A F C A D I O   H E A R N

Lafcadio Hearn has been called a decadent and there is some measure of truth in the evaluation. He created a world of half-lights, of soft, melancholy harmonies—but a beautiful world nevertheless, because it blurred the edges of reality.

His own life has the exotic character of his prose. He was born on a Greek island, the child of an Irishman and a Greek, with an added strain of Gypsy blood. He worshiped "the Odd, the Queer, the Strange," as he phrased it. He conceived a passionate interest in Japan and married into a Japanese family.

This essay from his *Exotics and Retrospectives* which describes his climb up sacred Fuji gives the singular quality of Hearn's writing—delicate and with a strange fragrance.

> *Kité miréba,*
> *Sahodo madé nashi,*
> *Fuji no Yama!*

> Seen on close approach, the mountain of
> Fuji does not come up to expectation.
>
> *Japanese proverbial philosophy*

THE MOST BEAUTIFUL SIGHT IN JAPAN, AND CERTAINLY ONE OF THE MOST beautiful in the world, is the distant apparition of Fuji on cloudless days— more especially days of spring and autumn, when the greater part of the peak is covered with late or with early snows. You can seldom distinguish the snowless base, which remains the same color as the sky: you perceive only the white cone seeming to hang in heaven; and the Japanese comparison of its shape to an inverted half-open fan is made wonderfully exact by the fine streaks that spread downward from the notched top, like shadows of fan-ribs. Even lighter than a fan the vision appears—rather the ghost or dream of a fan;—yet the material reality a hundred miles away is grandiose among the mountains of the globe. Rising to a height of nearly 12,500 feet, Fuji is visible from thirteen provinces of the Empire. Nevertheless it is one of the easiest of lofty mountains to climb; and for a thousand years it has been scaled every summer by multitudes of pilgrims. For it is not only a sacred mountain, but the most sacred mountain of Japan—the holiest eminence of the land that is called Divine—the Supreme Altar of the Sun;—and to ascend it at least once in a lifetime is the duty of all who reverence the ancient gods. So from every district of the Empire pilgrims annually wend their way to Fuji; and in nearly all the provinces there are pilgrim-societies —Fuji-Kō—organized for the purpose of aiding those desiring to visit the sacred peak. If this act of faith cannot be performed by everybody in person, it can at least be performed by proxy. Any hamlet, however remote, can occasionally send one representative to pray before the shrine of the divinity of Fuji, and to salute the rising sun from that sublime eminence. Thus a single company of Fuji-pilgrims may be composed of men from a hundred different settlements.

By both of the national religions Fuji is held in reverence. The Shintō deity of Fuji is the beautiful goddess Ko-no-hana-saku-ya-himé—she who brought forth her children in fire without pain, and whose name signifies "Radiant-blooming-as-the-flowers-of-the-trees," or, according to some commentators, "Causing-the-flowers-to-blossom-brightly." On the summit is her temple; and in ancient books it is recorded that mortal eyes have beheld her hovering, like a luminous cloud, above the verge of the crater. Her viewless servants watch and wait by the precipices to hurl down whosoever presumes to approach her shrine with unpurified heart. . . . Buddhism loves the grand peak because its form is like the white bud of the Sacred Flower—and because the eight cusps of its top, like the eight petals of the Lotus, symbolize the Eight Intelligences of Perception, Purpose, Speech, Conduct, Living, Effort, Mindfulness, and Contemplation.

But the legends and traditions about Fuji, the stories of its rising out of the earth in a single night—of the shower of pierced jewels once flung down from it—of the first temple built upon its summit eleven hundred years ago —of the Luminous Maiden that lured to the crater an Emperor who was never seen afterward, but is still worshiped at a little shrine erected on the place of his vanishing—of the sand that daily rolled down by pilgrim feet nightly reascends to its former position—have not all these things been written in books? There is really very little left for me to tell about Fuji except my own experience of climbing it. . . .

I arrived too late to attempt the ascent on the same day; but I made my preparations at once for the day following, and engaged a couple of gōriki ("strong-pull men"), or experienced guides. I felt quite secure on seeing

their broad honest faces and sturdy bearing. They supplied me with a pil-
grim-staff, heavy blue tabi (that is to say, cleft-stockings, to be used with sandals), a straw hat shaped like Fuji, and the rest of a pilgrim's outfit;—telling
me to be ready to start with them at four o'clock in the morning.

What is hereafter set down consists of notes taken on the journey, but
afterwards amended and expanded—for notes made while climbing are necessarily hurried and imperfect.

August 24, 1897
From strings stretched above the balcony upon which my inn-room opens,
hundreds of towels are hung like flags—blue towels and white, having printed
upon them in Chinese characters the names of pilgrim-companies and of
the divinity of Fuji. These are gifts to the house, and serve as advertise-
ments. . . . Raining from a uniformly gray sky. Fuji always invisible.

August 25th
3.30 A.M.—No sleep;—tumult all night of parties returning late from the
mountain, or arriving for the pilgrimage;—constant clapping of hands to
summon servants;—banqueting and singing in the adjoining chambers,
with alarming bursts of laughter every few minutes. . . . Breakfast of soup,
fish, and rice. Gōriki arrive in professional costume, and find me ready.
Nevertheless they insist that I shall undress again and put on heavy under-
clothing;—warning me that even when it is Doyō (the period of greatest
summer heat) at the foot of the mountain, it is Daikan (the period of
greatest winter cold) at the top. Then they start in advance, carrying provisions and bundles of heavy clothing. . . . A kuruma waits for me, with
three runners—two to pull, and one to push, as the work will be hard uphill.
By kuruma I can go to the height of five thousand feet.

Morning black and slightly chill, with fine rain; but I shall soon be above
the rain-clouds. . . . The lights of the town vanish behind us;—the kuruma
is rolling along a country-road. Outside of the swinging penumbra made by
the paper-lantern of the foremost runner, nothing is clearly visible; but I
can vaguely distinguish silhouettes of trees and, from time to time, of
houses—peasants' houses with steep roofs. . . .

What I have been taking for the horizon, in front of us, suddenly breaks
open, and begins to roll smokily away to left and right. In the great rift part
of a dark-blue mass appears—a portion of Fuji. Almost at the same moment
the sun pierces the clouds behind us; but the road now enters a copse covering the base of a low ridge, and the view is cut off. . . . Halt at a little
house among the trees—a pilgrims' resting-place—and there find the gōriki,

who have advanced much more rapidly than my runners, waiting for us.
Buy eggs, which a gōriki rolls up in a narrow strip of straw matting;—tying
the matting tightly with straw cord between the eggs—so that the string of
eggs has somewhat the appearance of a string of sausages. . . . Hire a
horse.

Sky clears as we proceed;—white sunlight floods everything. Road reascends; and we emerge again on the moorland. And, right in front, Fuji
appears—naked to the summit—stupendous—startling as if newly risen from
the earth. Nothing could be more beautiful. A vast blue cone—warm-blue,
almost violet through the vapors not yet lifted by the sun—with two white
streaklets near the top which are great gullies full of snow, though they look
from here scarcely an inch long. But the charm of the apparition is much less
the charm of color than of symmetry—a symmetry of beautiful bending
lines with a curve like the curve of a cable stretched over a space too wide
to allow of pulling taut. (This comparison did not at once suggest itself:
the first impression given me by the grace of those lines was an impression
of femininity;—I found myself thinking of some exquisite sloping of
shoulders toward the neck.) . . .

I see the gōriki hurrying forward far away—one of them carrying the eggs
round his neck! . . . Now there are no more trees worthy of the name—only
scattered stunted growths resembling shrubs. The black road curves across
a vast grassy down; and here and there I see large black patches in the green
surface—bare spaces of ashes and scoriæ; showing that this thin green skin
covers some enormous volcanic deposit of recent date. . . . As a matter of
history, all this district was buried two yards deep in 1707 by an eruption
from the side of Fuji. Even in the far-off Tōkyō the rain of ashes covered
roofs to a depth of sixteen centimetres. There are no farms in this region,
because there is little true soil; and there is no water. But volcanic destruction is not eternal destruction; eruptions at last prove fertilizing; and the
divine "Princess-who-causes-the-flowers-to-blossom-brightly" will make this
waste to smile again in future hundreds of years.

. . . The black openings in the green surface become more numerous
and larger. A few dwarf-shrubs still mingle with the coarse grass. . . . The
vapors are lifting; and Fuji is changing color. It is no longer a glowing blue,
but a dead sombre blue. Irregularities previously hidden by rising ground
appear in the lower part of the grand curves. One of these to the left—
shaped like a camel's hump—represents the focus of the last great eruption.

The land is not now green with black patches, but black with green patches; and the green patches dwindle visibly in the direction of the peak. The shrubby growths have disappeared. The wheels of the kuruma, and the feet of the runners sink deeper into the volcanic sand. . . . The horse is now attached to the kuruma with ropes, and I am able to advance more rapidly. Still the mountain seems far away; but we are really running up its flank at a height of more than five thousand feet.

Fuji has ceased to be blue of any shade. It is black—charcoal-black—a frightful extinct heap of visible ashes and cinders and slaggy lava. . . . Most of the green has disappeared. Likewise all of the illusion. The tremendous naked black reality—always becoming more sharply, more grimly, more atrociously defined—is a stupefaction, a nightmare. . . . Above—miles above —the snow patches glare and gleam against that blackness—hideously. I think of a gleam of white teeth I once saw in a skull—a woman's skull— otherwise burnt to a sooty crisp.

So one of the fairest, if not the fairest of earthly visions, resolves itself into a spectacle of horror and death. . . . But have not all human ideals of beauty, like the beauty of Fuji seen from afar, been created by forces of death and pain?—are not all, in their kind, but composites of death, beheld in retrospective through the magical haze of inherited memory?

The green has utterly vanished;—all is black. There is no road—only the broad waste of black sand sloping and narrowing up to those dazzling, grinning patches of snow. But there is a track—a yellowish track made by thousands and thousands of cast-off sandals of straw (waraji), flung aside by pilgrims. Straw sandals quickly wear out upon this black grit; and every pilgrim carries several pairs for the journey. Had I to make the ascent alone, I could find the path by following that wake of broken sandals—a yellow streak zigzagging up out of sight across the blackness.

6.40 A.M.—We reach Tarōbō, first of the ten stations on the ascent: height, six thousand feet. The station is a large wooden house, of which two rooms have been fitted up as a shop for the sale of staves, hats, raincoats, sandals— everything pilgrims need. I find there a peripatetic photographer offering for sale photographs of the mountain which are really very good as well as very cheap. . . . Here the gōriki take their first meal; and I rest. The kuruma can go no farther; and I dismiss my three runners, but keep the horse —a docile and surefooted creature; for I can venture to ride him up to Ni-gō-goséki, or Station No. 2½.

Start for No. 2½ up the slant of black sand, keeping the horse at a walk. No. 2½ is shut up for the season. . . . Slope now becomes steep as a stairway, and further riding would be dangerous. Alight and make ready for the climb. Cold wind blowing so strongly that I have to tie on my hat tightly. One of the gōriki unwinds from about his waist a long stout cotton girdle, and giving me one end to hold, passes the other over his shoulder for the pull. Then he proceeds over the sand at an angle, with a steady short step, and I follow; the other guide keeping closely behind me to provide against any slip.

There is nothing very difficult about this climbing, except the weariness of walking through sand and cinders: it is like walking over dunes. . . . We mount by zigzags. The sand moves with the wind; and I have a slightly nervous sense—the feeling only, not the perception; for I keep my eyes on the sand—of height growing above depth. . . . Have to watch my steps carefully, and to use my staff constantly, as the slant is now very steep. . . . We are in a white fog—passing through clouds! Even if I wished to look back, I could see nothing through this vapor; but I have not the least wish to look back. The wind has suddenly ceased—cut off, perhaps, by a ridge; and there is a silence that I remember from West Indian days: the Peace of High Places. It is broken only by the crunching of the ashes beneath our feet. I can distinctly hear my heart beat. . . . The guide tells me that I stoop too much—orders me to walk upright, and always in stepping to put down the heel first. I do this, and find it relieving. But climbing through this tiresome mixture of ashes and sand begins to be trying. I am perspiring and panting. The guide bids me keep my honorable mouth closed, and breathe only through my honorable nose.

We are out of the fog again. . . . All at once I perceive above us, at a little distance, something like a square hole in the face of the mountain— a door! It is the door of the third station—a wooden hut half-buried in black drift. . . . How delightful to squat again—even in a blue cloud of wood-smoke and under smoke-blackened rafters! Time, 8.30 A.M. Height, 7085 feet.

In spite of the wood-smoke the station is comfortable enough inside; there are clean mattings and even kneeling-cushions. No windows, of course, nor any other opening than the door; for the building is half-buried in the flank of the mountain. We lunch. . . . The station-keeper tells us that recently a student walked from Gotemba to the top of the mountain and back again—in geta! Geta are heavy wooden sandals, or clogs, held to the foot only by a thong passing between the great and the second toe. The feet of that student must have been made of steel! . . .

Though drenched with perspiration by the exertion of the first climb, I am already dry, and cold. . . . Up again. . . . The ascent is at first through ashes and sand as before; but presently large stones begin to mingle with the sand; and the way is always growing steeper. . . . I constantly slip. There is nothing firm, nothing resisting to stand upon: loose stones and cinders roll down at every step. . . . If a big lava-block were to detach itself from above! . . . In spite of my helpers and of the staff, I continually slip, and am all in perspiration again. Almost every stone that I tread upon turns under me. How is it that no stone ever turns under the feet of the gōriki? *They* never slip—never make a false step—never seem less at ease than they would be in walking over a matted floor. Their small brown broad feet always poise upon the shingle at exactly the right angle. They are heavier men than I; but they move lightly as birds. . . . Now I have to stop for rest every half-a-dozen steps. . . . The line of broken straw sandals follows the zigzags we take. . . . At last—at last another door in the face of the mountain. Enter the fourth station, and fling myself down upon the mats. Time, 10.30 A.M. Height, only 7937 feet;—yet it seemed such a distance!

Off again. . . . Way worse and worse. . . . Feel a new distress due to the rarefaction of the air. Heart beating as in a high fever. . . . Slope has become very rough. It is no longer soft ashes and sand mixed with stones, but stones only—fragments of lava, lumps of pumice, scoriæ of every sort, all angled as if freshly broken with a hammer. All would likewise seem to have been expressly shaped so as to turn upside-down when trodden upon. Yet I must confess that they never turn under the feet of the gōriki. . . . The cast-off sandals strew the slope in ever-increasing numbers. . . . But for the gōriki I should have had ever so many bad tumbles: they cannot prevent me from slipping; but they never allow me to fall. Evidently I am not fitted to climb mountains. . . . Height, 8659 feet—but the fifth station is shut up! Must keep zigzagging on to the next. Wonder how I shall ever be able to reach it! . . . And there are people still alive who have climbed Fuji three and four times, *for pleasure!* . . . Dare not look back. See nothing but the black stone always turning under me, and the bronzed feet of those marvelous gōriki who never slip, never pant, and never perspire. . . . Staff begins to hurt my hand. . . . Gōriki push and pull: it is shameful of me, I know, to give them so much trouble. . . . Ah! sixth station!—may all the myriads of the gods bless my gōriki! Time, 2.07 P.M. Height, 9317 feet.

Resting, I gaze through the doorway at the abyss below. The land is now dimly visible only through rents in a prodigious wilderness of white clouds; and within these rents everything looks almost black. . . . The horizon has risen frightfully—has expanded monstrously. . . . My gōriki warn me that the summit is still miles away. I have been too slow. We must hasten upward.

Certainly the zigzag is steeper than before. . . . With the stones now mingle angular rocks; and we sometimes have to flank queer black bulks that look like basalt. . . . On the right rises, out of sight, a jagged black hideous ridge—an ancient lava-stream. The line of the left slope still shoots up, straight as a bow-string. . . . Wonder if the way will become any steeper; —doubt whether it can possibly become any rougher. Rocks dislodged by my feet roll down soundlessly;—I am afraid to look after them. Their noiseless vanishing gives me a sensation like the sensation of falling in dreams. . . .

There is a white gleam overhead—the lowermost verge of an immense stretch of snow. . . . Now we are skirting a snow-filled gully—the lowermost of those white patches which, at first sight of the summit this morning, seemed scarcely an inch long. It will take an hour to pass it. . . . A guide runs forward, while I rest upon my staff, and returns with a large ball of snow. What curious snow! Not flaky, soft, white snow, but a mass of transparent globules—exactly like glass beads. I eat some, and find it deliciously refreshing. . . . The seventh station is closed. How shall I get to the eighth? . . . Happily, breathing has become less difficult. . . . The wind is upon us again, and black dust with it. The gōriki keep close to me, and advance with caution. . . . I have to stop for rest at every turn on the path;—cannot talk for weariness. . . . I do not feel;—I am much too tired to feel. . . . How I managed it, I do not know;—but I have actually got to the eighth station! Not for a thousand millions of dollars will I go one step farther to-day. Time, 4.40 P.M. Height, 10,693 feet.

It is much too cold here for rest without winter clothing; and now I learn the worth of the heavy robes provided by the guides. The robes are blue, with big white Chinese characters on the back, and are padded thickly as bed-quilts; but they feel light; for the air is really like the frosty breath of February. . . . A meal is preparing;—I notice that charcoal at this elevation acts in a refractory manner, and that a fire can be maintained only by constant attention. . . . Cold and fatigue sharpen appetite: we consume a surprising quantity of Zō-sui—rice boiled with eggs and a little meat. By reason of my fatigue and of the hour, it has been decided to remain here for the night. . . .

Squatting by the wood fire, I listen to the gōriki and the station-keeper telling of strange happenings on the mountain. One incident discussed I remember reading something about in a Tōkyō paper: I now hear it retold by the lips of a man who figured in it as a hero.

A Japanese meteorologist named Nonaka attempted last year the rash undertaking of passing the winter on the summit of Fuji for purposes of scientific study. It might not be difficult to winter upon the peak in a solid observatory furnished with a good stove, and all necessary comforts; but Nonaka could afford only a small wooden hut, in which he would be obliged to spend the cold season *without* *fire*! His young wife insisted on sharing his labors and dangers. The couple began their sojourn on the summit toward the close of September. In mid-winter news was brought to Gotemba that both were dying.

Relatives and friends tried to organize a rescue-party. But the weather was frightful; the peak was covered with snow and ice; the chances of death were innumerable; and the gōriki would not risk their lives. Hundreds of dollars could not tempt them. At last a desperate appeal was made to them as representatives of Japanese courage and hardihood: they were assured that to suffer a man of science to perish, without making even one plucky effort to save him, would disgrace the country;—they were told that the national honor was in their hands. This appeal brought forward two volunteers. One was a man of great strength and daring, nicknamed by his fellow-guides Oni-guma, "the Demon-Bear," the other was the elder of my gōriki. Both believed that they were going to certain destruction. They took leave of their friends and kindred, and drank with their families the farewell cup of water—midzu-no-sakazuki—in which those about to be separated by death pledge each other. Then, after having thickly wrapped themselves in cotton-wool, and made all possible preparation for ice-climbing, they started—taking with them a brave army-surgeon who had offered his services, without fee, for the rescue. After surmounting extraordinary difficulties, the party reached the hut; but the inmates refused to open! Nonaka protested that he would rather die than face the shame of failure in his undertaking; and his wife said that she had resolved to die with her husband. Partly by forcible, and partly by gentle means, the pair were restored to a better state of mind. The surgeon administered medicines and cordials; the patients, carefully wrapped up, were strapped to the backs of the guides; and the descent was begun. My gōriki, who carried the lady, believes that the gods helped him on the ice-slopes. More than once, all thought themselves lost; but they reached the foot of the mountain without one serious mishap.

After weeks of careful nursing, the rash young couple were pronounced out of danger. The wife suffered less, and recovered more quickly, than the husband.

The gōriki have cautioned me not to venture outside during the night without calling them. They will not tell me why; and their warning is peculiarly uncanny. From previous experiences during Japanese travel, I surmise that the danger implied is supernatural; but I feel that it would be useless to ask questions.

The door is closed and barred. I lie down between the guides, who are asleep in a moment, as I can tell by their heavy breathing. I cannot sleep immediately;—perhaps the fatigues and the surprises of the day have made me somewhat nervous. I look up at the rafters of the black roof—at packages of sandals, bundles of wood, bundles of many indistinguishable kinds there stowed away or suspended, and making queer shadows in the lamplight. . . . It is terribly cold, even under my three quilts; and the sound of the wind outside is wonderfully like the sound of great surf—a constant succession of bursting roars, each followed by a prolonged hiss. The hut, half buried under tons of rock and drift, does not move; but the sand does, and trickles down between the rafters; and small stones also move after each fierce gust, with a rattling just like the clatter of shingle in the pull of a retreating wave.

4 A.M.—Go out alone, despite last evening's warning, but keep close to the door. There is a great and icy blowing. The Sea of Milk is unchanged: it lies far below this wind. Over it the moon is dying. . . . The guides, perceiving my absence, spring up and join me. I am reproved for not having awakened them. They will not let me stay outside alone: so I turn in with them. . . .

6.40 A.M.—Start for the top. . . . Hardest and roughest stage of the journey, through a wilderness of lava-blocks. The path zigzags between ugly masses that project from the slope like black teeth. The trail of castaway sandals is wider than ever. . . . Have to rest every few minutes. . . . Reach another long patch of the snow that looks like glass beads, and eat some. The next station—a half-station—is closed; and the ninth has ceased to exist. . . . A sudden fear comes to me, not of the ascent, but of the prospective descent by a route which is too steep even to permit of comfortably sitting down. But the guides assure me that there will be no difficulty, and that most of the return journey will be by another way—over the interminable level which I wondered at yesterday—nearly all soft sand, with very few stones. It is called the hashiri ("glissade") and we are to descend at a run! . . .

All at once a family of field-mice scatter out from under my feet in panic; and the gōriki behind me catches one, and gives it to me. I hold the tiny shivering life for a moment to examine it, and set it free again. These little creatures have very long pale noses. How do they live in this waterless desolation—and at such an altitude—especially in the season of snow? For we are now at a height of more than eleven thousand feet! The gōriki say that the mice find roots growing under the stones. . . .

Wilder and steeper;—for me, at least, the climbing is sometimes on all fours. There are barriers which we surmount with the help of ladders. There are fearful places with Buddhist names, such as the Sai-no-Kawara, or Dry Bed of the River of Souls—a black waste strewn with heaps of rock, like those stone-piles which, in Buddhist pictures of the underworld, the ghosts of children build. . . .

Twelve thousand feet, and something—the top! Time, 8.20 A.M. . . . Stone huts; Shintō shrine with tōrii; icy well, called the Spring of Gold; stone tablet bearing a Chinese poem and the design of a tiger; rough walls of lava-blocks round these things—possibly for protection against the wind. Then the huge dead crater—probably between a quarter of a mile and half-a-mile wide, but shallowed up to within three or four hundred feet of the verge by volcanic detritus—a cavity horrible even in the tones of its yellow crumbling walls, streaked and stained with every hue of scorching. I perceive that the trail of straw sandals ends *in* the crater. Some hideous overhanging cusps of black lava—like the broken edges of a monstrous cicatrix—project on two sides several hundred feet above the opening; but I certainly shall not take the trouble to climb them. Yet these—seen through the haze of a hundred miles—through the soft illusion of blue spring weather—appear as the opening snowy petals of the bud of the Sacred Lotus! . . . No spot in this world can be more horrible, more atrociously dismal, than the cindered tip of the Lotus as you stand upon it.

But the view—the view for a hundred leagues—and the light of the far faint dreamy world—and the fairy vapors of morning—and the marvelous wreathings of cloud: all this, and only this, consoles me for the labor and the pain. . . . Other pilgrims, earlier climbers—poised upon the highest crag, with faces turned to the tremendous East—are clapping their hands in Shintō prayer, saluting the mighty Day. . . . The immense poetry of the moment enters into me with a thrill. I know that the colossal vision before me has already become a memory ineffaceable—a memory of which no luminous detail can fade till the hour when thought itself must fade, and the dust of these eyes be mingled with the dust of the myriad million eyes that also have looked in ages forgotten before my birth, from the summit supreme of Fuji to the Rising of the Sun.

"I HAD VOWED THAT I WOULD HURL MYSELF FROM THE FIRST CONVENIENT PRECIPICE"

FROM *Letter to an Unknown Lady*

RENÉ LE PAYS

In the courtly and full-blown language of gallantry, René le Pays, Sieur du Plessis-Villeneuve, has few superiors. From what scanty records are available, we can gather that he fancied himself a considerable lover and *littérateur,* in whatever order of precedence the reader may choose to place these two absorbing accomplishments. The "business" which brought him to the Alps of Savoy was tax collecting. He was *directeur-général des gabelles du Dauphiné et de Provence.* When he was asked to account for certain interesting discrepancies in his accounts, he replied simply that he was "too brilliant a man—*trop bel esprit*—to busy himself with bookkeeping," a disarming enough answer. But not sufficiently so, since it would appear that after this incident he found himself with a great deal of leisure to follow both his amorous and literary pursuits.

From Chamony en Fossigny,
The 16 May, 1669

Madame:

I CONFESS, MADAME, THAT I HAVE NOT DONE WHAT I PROMISED YOU THAT I would do, although I have found excellent opportunities of keeping my word. In the state of despair in which you had thrown me, when I parted from you, I had vowed that I would hurl myself from the first convenient precipice. Nevertheless, for the space of a fortnight, I have been ascending and descending the most dangerous mountains of Savoy, and have passed along the edges of a thousand precipices, and yet up to the present I have not thrown myself over them. I could easily tell you that my business occupations prevented me from thinking of it; but I must not deceive you. The

pleasure of seeing your likeness in this frightful country has always restrained me whenever I have had the thought of fulfilling my promise. I
could not make up my mind to die in places where, whenever I choose, I
can see this pleasing portrait of you. . . .

You will doubtless have some difficulty in guessing what is the portrait
of which I speak; you will go straight to some casket, and search to see
whether I have stolen that miniature which you so often refused to give me.
But you must know that I do not owe this pleasure to the art of painting;
Nature herself is the craftswoman. In fine, Madame, I see here five mountains which resemble you as though each of them were your very self.

Nay, do not laugh so. They are pictures which represent you far more
faithfully than do the Judith and the Pallas in your cabinet. Five mountains, Madame, made of pure ice from head to foot; but of an ice that may
be styled perpetual. One knows here, by tradition, that the ice has been ice
since the creation of the world. Neither the fires of five or six thousand dog-
stars, nor the waters of the universal Deluge, have had the power to melt it,
save in certain few places where one finds crystals and precious stones. But
to speak truly, it is dangerous to seek them there. The inquisitive and the
avaricious are often overwhelmed in summer beneath the ruin wrought by
the snows falling from their place, and their parents say, for their consolation, that art could not make them a tomb so stately and so brilliant as that
which they have received from Nature. For the rest, Madame, there is nothing in the world so magnificent as these mountains; when the rays of the
sun fall upon them, the different surfaces which a quaint Nature has given
to their ice flash back the light of this beautiful luminary in so many fashions
that you seem to see a thousand suns of different colours.

After that, can one find more faithful portraits of you? This perpetual
ice which surrounds you, those jewels which would be found in you by any
one who could melt the ice, this peril to which the rash adventurers who
undertake the quest expose themselves, the death of so many who have
ventured to undertake it, and finally those suns which shine in your eyes—do
not these things establish relations with the icy mountains, so exact that I
am entitled to regard them as finished portraits of you? Nature has done
five times for you what a famous sculptor wished to do once for Alexander.
You are here depicted on five mountains, and that is glory for you incomparably greater than if Appelles or Praxiteles were to return to the world
to engrave your image on copper, or to carve it in marble.

To conclude, Madame, we have here such lifelike portraits of you that,
in order to take vengeance on your cruelty in so often refusing me your
miniature, I should like to have one of these mountains hung like a medal
on my stock, or, if that cannot be, I should like to hang myself on to the
mountain, so as to die attached to your portrait. None the less, however, if

I must die of cold, I would rather that my death were caused by the ice of your heart than by the ice of the mountains. Wherefore, Madame, I am resolved to leave this frightful country as speedily as possible, in order to go and die at your feet. That is how I mean to keep my word with you. My death would not give full satisfaction to your cruelty if your eyes missed the joy of witnessing it.

MOUNTAIN LAUREL

EXPLORATIONS IN THE GREAT TUOLUMNE CANYON

FROM *John of the Mountains: The Unpublished Journals of John Muir*

JOHN MUIR

John Muir was the *genus loci* of the high Sierras. He explored its canyons and climbed its peaks with a bundle of bread and a notebook tied to his belt. What he loved best, because he knew it best, was the Yosemite region at the headquarters of the Tuolumne and Merced rivers.

Although he was a convinced evolutionist, he saw the hand of God behind all manifestations of nature and this mystical view of life, tempered with science, colors his carefully fashioned prose.

EARLY ONE AFTERNOON, AFTER EXPLORING THE PICTURESQUE DOMES AND ridges of the west rim of Yosemite Creek Basin, I reached the northmost tributary of the creek, a beautiful cascading stream with flowery banks which I followed to its head, wading across spongy patches of meadow, and climbing over fallen logs and heaps of boulders, to the top of the divide. This portion of the Merced and Tuolumne Divide is a smooth, sedgy tableland, holding a shallow lake. I made my camp in a grove of Williamson spruce [an old name for the mountain hemlock, *Tsuga mertensiana*] near the margin of the lake, and then proceeded to explore the plateau in a northeasterly direction. I had not gone far before I came in sight of a stately group of headlands, arching gracefully on the south, with here and there a feathery pine tree on their sides, but vertical and bare on the north, drawn up side by side in exact order, rigidly curved, like high-mettled cavalry horses ready for a charge. From the base of their precipitous fronts there extends a large, shallow mountain-bowl, in the bottom of which ten smaller bowls have been scooped, each forming the basin of a bright lakelet, abundantly fringed with spruce trees, and bordered close to the water with yellow sedge. Looking northward from the edge of this nest of lakes, I observed several gaps that seemed to sink suddenly, suggesting the existence of a deep gorge running at right angles to their courses, and I began to guess that I was near the rim of the Great Tuolumne Canyon. Then, looking back at the wild headlands, and down at the ten lakes, and northward through the suggestive gaps on the rim of the plateau, scarce able to decide where to go first, veering for some minutes like a confused compass-needle, I at length settled on a steady course, along the top of a ridge, from near the edge of the lake-bowl in a direction a little east of north, until suddenly halted by a sheer precipice over four thousand feet in depth.

This stupendous cliff forms a portion of the south wall of the Great Tuolumne Canyon, about halfway between the head and foot. Until I had reached this brink, I could see only narrow strips and wedges of landscape through gaps in the trees; but now the view was bounded only by the sky. Never had I beheld a nobler congregation of mountains. A thousand pictures composed that one mountain countenance, glowing with the life of the sun. I crept along the rugged edge of the wall until I found a place where I could sit down to look and think at rest. The Tuolumne River shimmered and spangled below, showing two or three miles of its length, curving past sheer precipices, and meandering through groves and small oval meadows. Its voice I distinctly heard, and it gave no tidings of heavy falls; but cascade tones and those of foaming rapids were in it, fused into harmony as smooth as the wind-music of the pines.

The opposite wall of the canyon, mainly made up of the ends of ridges shorn off by the great Tuolumne Glacier that once flowed over and past them, presents a series of elaborately sculptured precipices, like those of Yosemite Valley. Yet awful as is the scenery of this magnificent canyon, it offers no violent contrasts in general views; for the mountains beyond rise gradually higher in corresponding grandeur, and tributary canyons come in from the ice-fountains of the summits that are every way worthy of the main trunk. Many a spiry peak rises in sharp relief against the sky; in front are domes innumerable, and broad, whale-backed ridges, darkly fringed about their bases with pines, through openings in which I could here and there discern the green of meadows and the flashes of bright eye-lakes. There was no stretching away of any part of this landscape into dimness, nor possible division of it into back, and middle, and foreground. All its mountains appeared equally near, like the features of one face—on which the sun was gazing kindly, ripening and mellowing it like autumn fruit.

The forces that shaped the mountains—grinding out canyons and lake-basins, sharpening peaks and crests, bringing domes into relief, from the enclosing rocks, carving their plain flanks into their present forms—may still be seen at work at many points in the High Sierra. From where I was seated, on the brink of the mighty wall, I had extensive views of the channels of five large tributary glaciers that came in from the summits towards the northeast, every one of which had eroded its channel down to the bottom of the main canyon. I could also trace portions of the courses of smaller tributaries, whose canyons terminated a thousand feet above the bottom of the trunk canyon. So fully are the works of these vanished glaciers recorded upon the clean, unblurred pages of the mountains that it is difficult to assure ourselves that centuries have elapsed since they vanished. As I gazed, notwithstanding the kindly sunshine, the waving of grass, and the humming of flies, the stupendous canyon, with its far-reaching branches, seemed to fill again with creeping ice, winding in sublime curves around massive mountain brows, its white surface sprinkled with gray boulders, and traversed with many a yawning crevasse, the wide basins of the summits heaped with fountain-snow, glowing white in the thin sunshine, or blue in the shadows cast from the peaks.

The last days of this glacial winter are not yet past; we live in "creation's dawn." The morning stars still sing together, and the world, though made, is still being made and becoming more beautiful every day.

When the sun was nearing the horizon, I, looking once more at the shining river, determined to reach it if possible. To right and left, as far as I could see, the descent seemed impossible; but from another jutting headland about a mile to the westward I had a commanding view of a small side canyon on my left, running down at a steep angle, which I judged might possibly be practicable all the way. Then I hastened back among the latest of the evening shadows to my camp in the spruce trees, resolved to make an attempt to penetrate the heart of the Great Canyon next day. I awoke early, breakfasted, and waited for the dawn. The thin air was frosty, but, knowing that I should be warm in climbing, I tightened my belt, and set out in my shirt-sleeves, limb-loose and ready. By the time I reached the mouth of the narrow way I had chosen, the sun had touched the peaks with beamless light. Exhilarated by the divine wildness that imbued mountain and sky, I could not help shouting as I bounded down the topmost curves of the canyon, there covered with a dense plush of Carex, easy and pleasant to the tread.

After accomplishing a descent of four or five hundred feet, I came to a small mirror lake set here on the face of the canyon upon a kind of shelf. This side canyon was formed by a small glacier, tributary to the main Tuolumne Glacier, which, in its descent, met here a very hard seamless bar of granite that extended across its course, while the less resisting granite in front and back was eroded, of course, faster, thus forming a basin for the waters of the canyon stream. The bar, or dam, is beautifully moulded and polished, giving evidence of the great pressure exerted by even a very small glacier whose channel is steeply inclined. Below the lake, both the sides and bottom of the canyon became rougher, and I was compelled to scramble down and around a number of small precipices, fifty or a hundred feet high, that crossed the canyon like steps of a gigantic stairway.

At the foot of the stairs I found extensive willow-tangles, growing upon rough slopes of sharp-angled rocks, through which the stream mumbles and gropes its way, most of the time out of sight. These tangles would be too dense to walk among, even if they grew upon smooth ground, and too tall and flexible to walk on top of. Crinkled and loosely felted as they are by the pressure of deep snow for half the year, they form as impenetrable jungles as I ever encountered in the swamps of Florida. In descending, one may tumble and slide and crash over them in some way, but to ascend some of them with their longer branches, dry and sharp, presented against you like bayonets, is very nearly impossible. In the midst of these tangles, and along their margins, small garden-like meadows occur where the stream has made a level deposit of soil. They are planted with luxuriant Carices, whose arching leaves cover the ground. Out of these rise splendid larkspurs six to eight feet high, columbines, lilies, and a few Polygonums and Eriger-ons. In these moist garden-patches, so thoroughly hidden, the bears like to wallow like hogs. I found many places that morning where the bent and squeezed sedges showed that I had disturbed them, and knew I was likely at any moment to come upon a cross mother with her cubs, unless I made a good deal of warning noise. Below the region of bear-gardens and willow-tangles, the canyon becomes narrow and smooth, the smoothness being due to the action of snow-avalanches that sweep down from the mountains above and pour through this steep and narrow portion like torrents of water.

I had now accomplished a descent of nearly twenty-five hundred feet, and there remained about two thousand feet more before I reached the river. As I descended this smooth portion, I found that its bottom became more and more steeply inclined, and I halted to scan it closely, hoping to discover some way of avoiding it altogether, by passing around on either of the sides. But this I quickly decided to be impossible, the sides being ap-parently as bare and seamless as the bottom. I then began to creep down the smooth incline, depending mostly upon my hands, wetting them with my tongue, and striking them flatly upon the rock to make them stick by atmos-pheric pressure. In this way I very nearly reached a point where a seam comes down from the side to the bottom in an easy slope, which would enable me to climb out to a portion of the main wall that I knew must be available from the live-oak bushes growing on it. But after cautiously meas-uring the steepness—scrutinizing it again and again, and trying my wet hands upon it—I was compelled to retrace my devious slides and leaps, mak-ing a vertical rise of about five hundred feet, in order that I might reach a point where I could climb out to the main canyon wall, my only hope of reaching the bottom that day being by picking my way down its face, cling-ing to the bushes in the seams. I knew from my observations of the previous day that this portion of the canyon was crossed by well-developed planes of cleavage that prevented the formation of smooth vertical precipices of more

than a few hundred feet in height and the same in width. These may usually be passed without much difficulty.

After two or three hours more of hard scrambling, I at length stood
among cool shadows on the river-bank, in the heart of the great unexplored
canyon, having made a descent of about forty-five hundred feet, the bottom
of this portion of the canyon above the level of the sea being forty-six hundred feet. The river is here fully two hundred yards wide (about twice the
size of the Merced at Yosemite), and well timbered with Libocedrus and
pine. A beautiful reach stretches away from where I sat resting, its border
trees leaning towards each other, making a long arched lane, down which
the joyous waters sang in foaming rapids. Stepping out of the river grove to
a small sandy flat, I obtained a general view of the canyon walls, rising to a
height of from four thousand to five thousand feet, composed of rocks of
every form of which yosemites are made. About a mile up the canyon, on
the south side, there is a most imposing rock, nearly related in form to the
Yosemite Half Dome. This side canyon, by which I descended, looked like
an insignificant notch or groove in the main wall, though not less than
seven hundred to eight hundred feet deep in most places. It is one of the
many small glacier canyons that are always found upon the south sides of
trunk canyons that trend east and west.

The continuity of the north walls of such trunk canyons is also broken
by side canyons, but those on the north side are usually much larger, and
have a more steady and determined direction, being related to canyons that
reach back to high glacier-fountains, while many of those of the south side
are strictly local. The history of their formation is easily read: they were
eroded by the action of small glaciers that lingered in the shade of the wall,
long years after the exposed sun-beaten north wall was dry and bare. These
little south-side canyons are apt to be cut off high above the bottom of the
trunk canyon, because the glaciers that made them were swept round and
carried away by the main trunk glacier, at heights determined by the respec-
tive forces of their currents. This should always be taken into consideration
when we are weighing the probabilities of being able to reach the bottom
of a trunk canyon by these tributaries.

Immediately opposite the point I descended there are "royal arches"
like those of Yosemite, formed by the breaking-up and removal of a portion
of the concentric layers of a dome. All of the so-called "royal arches" of this
region are produced in the same way.

About a mile farther down the canyon, I came to the mouth of a tributary that comes in from the north. The glacier to which it belongs must have
been of great size, for it eroded its channel down to a level with the bottom
of the main canyon. The rocks both of this tributary and of the main canyon present traces of all kinds of ice-action—moraines, polished and striated

surfaces, and rocks of special forms. Just at the point where this large tributary enters the trunk canyon, there is a corresponding increase in size and
change in direction of the latter. Indeed, after making a few corrections
that are obviously required, for planes of cleavage, differences of hardness,
etc., in the rocks concerned, the direction, size, and form of any main canyon below a tributary are always resultants of the forces of the glaciers that
once occupied them, and this signifies that *glaciers make their own channels*. In front of this great tributary the canyon is about half a mile wide,
and nobly gardened with groves and meadows. The level and luxuriant
groves almost always found at the mouths of large tributaries are very distinct in appearance and history from the strips and patches of forest that
adorn the walls of canyons. The soil upon which the former grow is reformed moraine matter, collected, mixed, and spread out in the lake-basins
that are formed by the pressure of the incoming tributary. The trees are
closely grouped, social and trim; while those of the walls are roughish, and
scattered like storm-beaten mountaineers. Some of the lake-basin groves are
breezy from the way the winds are compelled to tumble and flow, but most
enjoy perpetual calm at the bottom of pits of air.

I pushed on down the canyon a couple of miles farther, passing over
level floors buried in shady greenwood and over hot sandy flats covered with
the common Pteris, the sturdiest of ferns, that bears with equal patience the
hot sun of Florida and the heavy snows of the Sierra. Along the river-bank
is an abundance of azaleas and brier roses growing in thickets, and in open
spots a profusion of golden Compositæ. Tall grasses brushed my shoulders,
and yet taller lilies and columbines rang their bells above my head. Nor
was there any lack of familiar birds, bees, and butterflies. Myriads of sunny
wings stirred the air. The Steller jay, garrulous and important, flitted from
pine to pine; squirrels were gathering nuts; woodpeckers hammering dead
limbs; water-ouzels sang divinely on foam-fringed boulders among the rapids;
and the robin redbreast of the orchards was in the open groves. Here was
no field, nor camp, nor ruinous cabin, nor hacked trees, nor downtrodden
flowers, to disenchant the Godful solitude, nor any trace of lawless forces,
no word of chaos or desolation among these mighty cliffs and domes; every
rock is as elaborately and thoughtfully carved and finished as a crystal or
shell.

I followed the river three miles. In this distance it makes a vertical descent of about three hundred feet in moderate deliberate rapids. I would
fain have lingered here for months, living with the bears on wild cherries
and berries. I thought of trying their board for a few days; but as I was in
my shirt-sleeves and without bread, I began my retreat. Let those who become breathless in ascending a flight of stairs think of climbing to a bedroom
four thousand or five thousand feet above the basement. Exhilarated and

buoyant by what I had reveled in, I pushed up the first three thousand feet almost without stopping to take breath, making only momentary halts to look at striated surfaces, or to watch the varying appearances of peaks and domes as they presented themselves at different points; but towards the summit I became tired, and the last thousand feet seemed long indeed, although I took many short rests, turning again and again to see the setting sun blessing the mountains.

DESCENDING THE YOSEMITE VALLEY

IN THE REGIONS OF
ETERNAL SNOW

FROM *Mont Blanc*

ALBERT SMITH

Had there been a Mont Blanc Booster's Club in the 1850's, Albert Smith would surely have been its president. He was self-appointed press agent for the mountain. At Chamonix he spent his honeymoon and every vacation thereafter and his annual return was celebrated with fireworks, speeches, and cannonades. His Mont Blanc "extravaganza" for the theatre, a lively variety of lantern-slide lecture in which he starred, and which had a fabulous run at the Egyptian Hall in London, had a most invigorating effect on the Swiss tourist trade. It would be carping on our part to ascribe the fireworks to that pecuniary fact. In this selection from his book which describes his momentous climb of Mont Blanc, the reader becomes aware that Mr. Smith did things in a large and public way.

THE SUN WENT DOWN MAGNIFICENTLY, AND EVERYTHING PROMISED A GLORIOUS day on the morrow. I collected all my requisites. Our host lent me a pair of high gaiters, and Madame Tairraz gave me a fine pair of scarlet garters to tie them up with. I also bought a green veil, and Jean brought me a pair of blue spectacles. In my knapsack I put other shoes, socks, and trousers, and an extra shirt; and I got a new spike driven into my baton, for the glacier. I was still far from well, but the excitement pulled me through all discomfort. I did not sleep at all that night, from anxiety as to the success of the undertaking: I knew all the danger; and when I made a little parcel of my money, and the few things I had in my "kit," and told my friend, Mr. William Beverley, who had come with me from London, to take them home if I did not return, I am afraid my attempt to be careless about the matter was a failure. I had set a small infernal machine, that made a hideous noise at appointed hours, to go off at six; but I believe I heard every click it gave, all through the night; and I forestalled its office in the morning by getting out of bed myself at sunrise and stopping it.

We met at seven o'clock on the morning of Tuesday the 12th, to breakfast. All our guides and porters had a feast in the garden, and were in high spirits—for the glass had gone up half an inch, and not a cloud was to be seen in the sky. Nothing could exceed the bustle of the inn-yard; everybody had collected to see the start: the men were dividing and portioning the fowls, and bottles of wine, and rugs, and wrappers; something was constantly being forgotten, and nobody could find whatever was of most importance to them; and the good-tempered cook—another Tairraz—kept coming forth from the kitchen with so many additional viands, that I began to wonder when our stores would be completed. The list of articles of food which we took up was as follows:—

NOTE NO. 1

Provisions for the Ascent of Mont Blanc

Hôtel de Londres, Chamouni,

August 12, 1851

			Francs
60 bottles of Vin	Ordinaire		60
6 do.	Bordeaux		36
10 do.	St. George		30
15 do.	St. Jean		30
3 do.	Cognac		15
1 do.	syrup of raspberries ..		3
6 do.	lemonade		6
2 do.	champagne		14
20 loaves			30
10 small cheeses			8
6 packets of chocolate			9
6 do.	sugar		6
4 do.	prunes		6
4 do.	raisins		6
2 do.	salt		1
4 wax candles			4
6 lemons			1
4 legs of mutton			24
4 shoulders, do.			12
6 pieces of veal			30
1 piece of beef			5
11 large fowls			30
35 small do.			87
		Total	456

About half-past seven we started; and as we left the inn, and traversed the narrow ill-paved streets of Chamouni towards the bridge, I believe we formed the largest caravan that had ever gone off together. Each of us had four guides, making twenty in all; and the porters and volunteers I may reckon at another score; besides which, there was a rabble rout of friends and relations, and sweethearts and boys, some of whom came a considerable distance with us. I had a mule waiting for me at the bridle-road that runs through the fields towards the dirty little village of Les Pélerins—for I wished to keep myself as fresh as I could for the real work. I do not think I gained anything by this, for the brute was exceedingly troublesome to manage up the rude steep path and amongst the trees. . . .

The ascent of this rock was the hardest work we had yet experienced: it was like climbing up an immense number of flag-stones, of different heights, set on their edges. Before we got half-way, we heard them firing guns at Chamouni, which showed us that we were being watched from the village; and this gave us fresh energy. At last we reached something like a platform, ten or twelve feet long, and three or four broad; and below this was another tolerably level space, with a low parapet of loose stones built round it, whilst here and there were several nooks and corners which might shelter people on emergency. We acknowledged the salute at Chamouni, by sticking one of our batons into a crevice, and tying a handkerchief to the top of it; and then set to work to clear away the snow from our resting-place. Contrary to all my expectation, the heat we here experienced was almost sultry, and even distressing. Those who have noted how long the granite posts and walls of the Italian cities retain the heat after the sun has gone down, will understand that this rock upon which we were was quite warm wherever the rays fell upon it, although in every nook of shade the snow still remained unthawed.

As soon as we had arranged our packs and bundles, we began to change our clothes, which were tolerably well wet through with trudging and tumbling about among the snow; and cutting a number of pegs, we strewed our garments about the crannies of the rocks to dry. I put on two shirts, two pairs of lamb's-wool socks, a thick pair of Scotch plaid trousers, a "Templar" worsted headpiece, and a common blouse; and my companions were attired in a similar manner. There was now great activity in the camp. Some of the guides ranged the wine bottles side by side in the snow; others unpacked the refreshment knapsacks; others, again, made a rude fireplace, and filled a stewpan with snow to melt. All this time it was so hot, and the sun was so bright, that I began to think the guide who told De Saussure he should take a parasol up with him, did not deserve to have been laughed at.

As soon as our wild bivouac assumed a little appearance of order, two of the guides were sent up the glacier to go a great way ahead, and then return and report upon the state of the snow on the *plateaux*. When they had started, we perched ourselves about on the comparatively level spaces of the rock, and with knife and fingers began our dinner.

We had scarcely commenced when our party was joined by a young Irishman and a guide, who had taken advantage of the beaten track left behind us, and marched up on our traces with tolerable ease, leaving to us the honour (and the expense) of cutting out the path. My younger friends, with a little ebullition of university feeling, proposed, under such circumstances, that we should give him a reception in keeping with the glacier; but I thought it would be so hyper-punctilious to show temper here, on the Grands Mulets rocks, up and away in the regions of eternal snow, some thousand feet from the level world, that I ventured on a very mild hint to this effect, which was received with all the acquiescence and good temper imaginable. So we asked him to contribute his stores to our table, and, I dare say, should have got on very well together; but the guides began to squabble about what they considered a breach of etiquette, and presently, with his attendant, he moved away to the next rock. Afterwards, another "follower" arrived with his guide, and he subsequently reached the summit.

We kept high festival that afternoon on the Grands Mulets. One stage of our journey—and that one by no means the easiest—had been achieved without the slightest hurt or harm. The consciousness of success thus far, the pure transparent air, the excitement attached to the very position in which we found ourselves, and the strange bewildering novelty of the surrounding scenery, produced a flowing exhilaration of spirits that I had never before experienced. The feeling was shared in by all, and we laughed and sang, and made the guides contribute whatever they could to the general amusement, and told them such stories as would translate well in return; until, I believe, that dinner will never be forgotten by them. A fine diversion was afforded by racing the empty bottles down the glacier. We flung them off from the rock as far as we were able, and then watched their course. Whenever they chanced to point neck first down the slope, they started off with considerable velocity, leaping the crevices by their own impetus, until they were lost in the distance. The excitement of the guides during this amusement was very remarkable: a stand of betting men could not have betrayed more at the Derby. Their anxiety when one of the bottles approached a crevice was intense; and if the gulf was cleared, they perfectly screamed with delight, *"Voici un bon coureur!"* or, *"Tiens! comme il saute bien!"* burst from them; and *"Le grand s'arrête!"* *"Il est perdu—quel dommage!"* *"Non—il marche encore!"* could not have been uttered with more earnestness had they been watching a herd of chamois.

FROM AN ENGLISH GENTLEMAN TO MR. ARLAUD, A CELEBRATED PAINTER AT GENEVA, GIVING AN ACCOUNT OF A JOURNEY TO THE GLACIERES, OR ICE ALPS IN SAVOY

FROM *a Letter, 1741*

WILLIAM WYNDHAM

The "English Gentleman" here referred to with the transparent anonymity of 18th-century writing was Mr. William Wyndham of Norfolk. His son became a parliamentary colleague of the great William Pitt. Mr. Wyndham must have been a man of parts. In London he was known as "Wyndham the Boxer" and in Geneva he was the leading spirit of a group of English hellrakes. Records show him cited for assault and battery, damage to farm property while hunting, and other such high-spirited pranks.

Like other young well-born Englishmen of the period, he made the Grand Tour with his tutor, the grandson of Edward Stillingfleet, Bishop of Worcester. Inevitably that would include a trip to the Alpine glaciers with instruments and other "scientific" paraphernalia. His biographer intimates that tutor Stillingfleet must have had a major hand in composing this narrative since Wyndham was very young at the time and the narrative is a product of mature judgment and composition. A later diary of Wyndham's travels in France and Italy, we are told, "is by no means so elegantly composed."

Sir,

ACCORDING TO YOUR DESIRE I SEND YOU AN ACCOUNT OF OUR JOURNEY to the *Glacieres*. I shall give it you in the plainest Manner, without endeavouring to embellish it by any florid Descriptions, although the Beauty and Variety of the Situations and Prospects that we observed in this unfrequented Part of the World, would well deserve to be described by one, who, like you, join to so great a Skill in Painting so lively and poetical an Imagination; but these not being my Talents, I will, as I said before, confine myself to the giving you a faithful Relation of the Incidents of our Journey, and acquainting you with the Observations we made. I shall add a few Hints, which may be useful to such as shall hereafter have the same Curiosity that we had, and who may perhaps have Advantages and Conveniences which we had not to make more accurate Observations. It is really Pity that so great a Curiosity, and which lies so near you, should be so little known; for though *Scheuchzer,* in his *Iter Alpinum,* describes the *Glacieres* that are in the Canton of *Berne,* yet they seem to me by his Description to be very different from those in *Savoy.*

I had long had a great Desire to make this Excursion, but the Difficulty of getting Company had made me defer it: Luckily in the Month of *June* last Dr. *Pococke* arrived at *Geneva* from his Voyages into the *Levant* and *Egypt,* which Countries he had visited with great Exactness. I mentioned to him this Curiosity, and my Desire to see it, and he who was far from fearing Hardships, expressing a like Inclination, we immediately agreed to go there; when some others of our Friends found a Party was made, they likewise came into it, and I was commissioned to provide what was necessary for our setting out.

As we were assured on all hands, that we should scarcely find any of the Necessaries of Life in those Parts, we took with us Sumpter Horses, loaded with Provisions, and a Tent, which was of some use to us, though the terrible Description People had given us of the Country was much exaggerated. I had provided several Mathematical Instruments to take Heights, and make Observations with, hoping that Mr. *Williamson,* an able Mathematician, Governor to Lord *Hadinton,* would have been of the Party; but he declining it, on account of the Fatigue which he fear'd he should not be able to support, I chose not to take the Trouble of carrying them, there being no Person in the Company so capable as he of making a proper use of them.

We set out from *Geneva* the 19th of *June,* N. S. we were Eight in Company, besides five Servants, all of us well arm'd, and our Baggage-Horses attending us, so that we had very much the Air of a Caravan. The first Day we went no farther than *Bonneville,* a Town about four Leagues distant from *Geneva,* according to the way of reckoning there; these four Leagues took us more than six Hours riding. This Place is situated at the Foot of the *Maule,* and close by the River *Arve;* 'tis surrounded with beautiful Meadows and high Mountains, covered with Trees, which form all together a very delightful Situation. There is a very good Stone-Bridge near the Town, but it had suffered in the late Innundation of the *Arve,* which had carried away part of it. Our Inn was a tolerable one for *Savoy* as to every thing but Beds.

The next Day being the 20th, we set out very early in the Morning, and passed the *Arve;* our Road lay between that River and the Mountains, all along which we were entertained with an agreeable Variety of fine Land-skips. They reckon two Leagues from *Bonneville* to *Cluse,* but we were three Hours and an half in going it.

Cluse is situated in a narrow Pass between the Mountains, which almost meet in this Place [leaving only room for the *Arve,* which is thus hemm'd in for above a League together]. Before you come to *Cluse* there is a kind of Hermitage, upon a Rock on the Right Hand, where we climb'd up in order to enjoy the Prospect, which is *delicious;* after that we passed the *Arve* over a fine Stone Bridge, of one very large Arch, and continued our Journey for about an Hour and an half through a narrow Road, along the *Arve,* between Rocks of a prodigious Height, which look'd as if they had been split on pur-pose to give the River a Passage. Not to mention the Beauty of the Views all along, we were extremely entertained by continual Echoes, and the pro-digious rattling, caused by cracking a Whip, or firing a Pistol, which we repeated several Times. We saw Cascades on every Side, which fell from the Top of high Rocks into the *Arve.* There is one among the rest of sin-gular Beauty, it is called the *Nan d'Arpena,* 'tis a great Torrent, which falls from a very high Rock; all the Company agreed it must be higher than *Saleve.* As for my Part, I will not pretend to decide about it, I however may venture to say, that the Cascade of *Terni* does not fall from near so great a Height; but then the Quantity of Water, when we saw it, was much less than at this last mentioned Place; tho' the People of the Country assured us, that at certain times the Water is much more abundant than it was then.

After about three Hours riding from *Cluse,* we came to Saint *Martin*'s Bridge, right against *Salanches,* which is on the other Side of the *Arve.* We did not care to go out of our Way into the Town; but chose rather to en-camp in a fine Meadow near the Bridge, in order to refresh ourselves. From thence we set out again on our Journey, and after four Hours riding through very bad Ways, being obliged to cross some dangerous Torrents, we arrived at a little Village called *Servoz.* Our Horses suffered here very much, being tied to Pickets all Night in the open Air for want of Stabling; besides, there was neither Oats, nor any other Forrage, but Grass fresh cut; as for our-selves, as we had brought all Necessaries along with us, we were well enough off, except as to Beds, and that want was supplied by clean Straw in a Barn.

From thence we set forward at break of Day, and passed the *Arve* once more over a very bad wooden Bridge, and after having clim'd over a steep Mountain, where we had no small Difficulty with our Horses, their Shoes coming off continually, and they often running the risque of tumbling into the *Arve,* which run at the Bottom of the Rock, we came into a pleasant Valley, where we pass'd the *Arve* a fourth time over a Stone Bridge, and then first had a View of the *Glacieres.* We continued our Journey on to *Chamouny,* which is a Village upon the North-side of the *Arve,* in a Valley, where there is a Priory belonging to the Chapter of *Salanches;* here we encamp'd, and while our Dinner was preparing, we inquired of the People of the Place about the *Glacieres.* They shewed us at first the Ends of them which reach into the Valley, and were to be seen from the Village; these appear'd only like white Rocks, or rather like immense Icicles, made by Water running down the Mountain. This did not satisfy our Curiosity, and we thought we were come too far to be contented with so small a Matter; we therefore strictly inquired of the Peasants whether we could not by going up the Mountain discover something more worth our Notice. They told us we might, but the greatest Part of them represented the Thing as very difficult and laborious; they told us no-body ever went there but those whose Business it was to search for Crystal, or to shoot *Bouquetins* and *Chamois,* and that all the Travellers, who had been to the *Glacieres* hitherto, had been satisfied with what we had already seen.

The Prior of the Place was a good old Man, who shewed us many Civilities, and endeavoured also to dissuade us; there were others who represented the Thing as mighty easy; but we perceived plainly, that they expected, that after we had bargain'd with them to be our Guides, we should soon tire, and that they should earn their Money with little Trouble. However our Curiosity got the better of these Discouragements, and relying on our Strength and Resolution, we determined to attempt climbing the Mountain. We took with us several Peasants, some to be our Guides, and others to carry Wine and Provisions. These People were so much persuaded that we should never be able to go through with our Task, that they took with them Candles and Instruments to strike Fire, in case we should be overcome with Fatigue, and be obliged to spend the Night on the Mountain. In order to prevent those among us who were the most in wind, from fatiguing the rest, by pushing on too fast, we made the following Rules: That no one should go out of his Rank; That he who led the way should go a slow and even Pace; That who ever found himself fatigued, or out of Breath, might call for a Halt; And lastly, that when ever we found a Spring we should drink some of our Wine, mixed with Water, and fill up the Bottles, we had emptied, with Water, to serve us at other Halts where we should find none.

These Precautions were so useful to us, that, perhaps, had we not observed them, the Peasants would not have been deceived in their Conjectures.

We set out about Noon, the 22ᵈ of *June,* and crossed the *Arve* over a wooden Bridge. Most Maps place the *Glacieres* on the same Side with *Chamoigny,* but this is a Mistake. We were quickly at the Foot of the Mountain, and began to ascend by a very steep Path through a Wood of Firs and Larche Trees. We made many Halts to refresh ourselves, and take breath, but we kept on at a good Rate. After we had passed the Wood, we came to a kind of Meadow, full of large Stones, and Pieces of Rocks, that were broke off, and fallen down from the Mountain; the Ascent was so steep that we were obliged sometimes to cling to them with our Hands, and make use of Sticks, with sharp Irons at the End, to support ourselves. Our Road lay slant Ways, and we had several Places to cross where the *Avalanches* of Snow were fallen, and had made terrible Havock; there was nothing to be seen but Trees torn up by the Roots, and large Stones, which seemed to lie without any Support; every step we set, the Ground gave way, the Snow which was mixed with it made us slip, and had it not been for our Staffs, and our Hands, we must many times have gone down the Precipice. We had an uninterrupted View quite to the Bottom of the Mountain, and the Steepness of the Descent, join'd to the Height where we were, made a View terrible enough to make most People's Heads turn. In short, after climbing with great Labour for four Hours and three Quarters, we got to the Top of the Mountain; from whence we had the Pleasure of beholding Objects of an extraordinary Nature. We were on the Top of a Mountain, which, as well as we could judge, was at least twice as high as Mount *Saleve,* from thence we had a full View of the *Glacieres.* I own to you that I am extremely at a Loss how to give a right Idea of it; as I know no one thing which I have ever seen that has the least Resemblance to it.

The Description which Travellers give of the Seas of *Greenland* seems to come the nearest to it. You must imagine your Lake put in Agitation by a strong Wind, and frozen all at once, perhaps even that would not produce the same Appearance.

The *Glacieres* consist of three large Valleys, that form a kind of Y, the Tail reaches into the *Val d'Aoste,* and the two Horns into the Valley of *Chamoigny,* the Place where we ascended was between them, from whence we saw plainly the Valley, which forms one of these Horns.

I had unluckily left at *Chamoigny* a pocket Compass, which I had carried with me, so that I could not well tell the Bearings as to its Situation; but I believe it to be pretty nearly from North to South. These Valleys, although at the Top of a high Mountain, are surrounded with other Mountains; the Tops of which being naked and craggy Rocks, shoot up immensely high; something resembling old *Gothic* Buildings or Ruines, nothing grows upon them, they are all the Year round covered with Snow; and our Guides assured us, that neither the Chamois, nor any Birds, ever went so high as the Top of them.

Those who search after Crystal, go in the Month of *August* to the Foot of these Rocks, and strike against them with Pick-axes; if they hear them resound as if they were hollow, they work there, and opening the Rock, they find Caverns full of Crystalisations. We should have been very glad to have gone there, but the Season was not enough advanced, the Snow not being yet sufficiently melted. As far as our Eye-sight could reach, we saw nothing but this Valley; the Height of the Rocks, which surrounded it, made it impossible for the Eye to judge exactly how wide it was; but I imagine it must be near three Quarters of a League. Our Curiosity did not stop here, we were resolved to go down upon the Ice; we had about four hundred Yards to go down, the Descent was excessively steep, and all of a dry crumbling Earth, mixt with Gravel, and little loose Stones, which afforded us no firm footing; so that we went down partly falling, and partly sliding on our Hands and Knees. At length we got upon the Ice, where our Difficulty ceased, for that was extremely rough, and afforded us good footing; we found in it an infinite Number of Cracks, some we could step over, others were several Feet wide. These Cracks were so deep, that we could not even see to the Bottom; those who go in search of Crystal are often lost in them, but their Bodies are generally found again after some Days, perfectly well preserved. All our Guides assured us, that these Cracks change continually, and that the whole *Glaciere* has a kind of Motion. In going up the Mountain we often heard something like a Clap of Thunder, which, as we were informed by our Guides, was caused by fresh Cracks then making; but as there were none made while we were upon the Ice, we could not determine whether it was that, or *Avalanches* of Snows, or perhaps Rocks falling; though since Travellers observe, that in *Greenland* the Ice cracks with a Noise that resembles Thunder, it might very well be what our Guides told us. As in all Countries of Ignorance People are extremely superstitious, they told us many strange Stories of Witches, &c. who came to play their Pranks upon the *Glacieres,* and dance to the Sound of Instruments. We should have been surprised if we had not been entertained in these Parts, with some such idle Legends. The *Bouquetins* go in Herds often to the Number of fifteen or sixteen upon the Ice, we saw none of them; there were some *Chamois* which we shot at, but at too great a Distance to do any Execution.

There is Water continually issuing out of the *Glacieres,* which the People look on as so very wholesome, that they say it may be drank of in any Quantities without Danger, even when one is hot with Exercise.

The Sun shone very hot, and the Reverberation of the Ice, and circumjacent Rocks, caused a great deal of thaw'd Water to lie in all the Cavities of the Ice; but I fancy it freezes there constantly as soon as Night comes on.

Our Guides assured us, that, in the time of their Fathers, the *Glaciere* was but small, and that there was even a Passage thro' these Valleys, by which they could go into the *Val d'Aoste* in six Hours: But that the *Glaciere* was so much increased, that the Passage was then quite stopped up, and that it went on increasing every Year.

We found on the Edge of the *Glaciere* several Pieces of Ice, which we took at first for Rocks, being as big as a House; these were pieces quite separate from the *Glaciere.* It is difficult to conceive how they came to be formed there.

Having remained about half an Hour upon the *Glaciere,* and having drank there in Ceremony Admiral *Vernon*'s Health, and Success to the *British* Arms, we climb'd to the Summit, from whence we came, with incredible Difficulty, the Earth giving way at every step we set. From thence, after having rested ourselves a few Minutes, we began to descend, and arrived at *Chamouny* just about Sun-set, to the great Astonishment of all the People of the Place, and even of our Guides, who owned to us they thought we should not have gone through with our Undertaking. . . .

Those who are desirous to undertake this Journey, ought not to set out till towards the Middle of *August;* they would at that time find not so much Snow on the Mountain. They might go to the Crystal Mines, and divert themselves with shooting of *Bouquetins;* the Oats would then be cut, and their Horses would not suffer so much. Although we met with nothing which had the Appearance of Danger, nevertheless I would recommend going well armed; 'tis an easy Precaution, and on certain Occasions very useful, one is never the worse for it, and oftentimes it helps a Man out of a Scrape. Barometers to measure the Height of the Mountains, portable Thermometers, and a Quadrant to take Heights with, would be useful, if there were a Mathematician in Company. A Tent would not be necessary, unless for those who had a Mind to examine every thing with the greatest Exactness, and make Observations; in this Case one might pitch it upon the Mountain, and pass the Night in it, if it were necessary, for it did not seem very cold there.

With these Precautions one might go through the other Parts of these Valleys, which form the Y, and one might find out whether the Cracks change daily as we were told; one might also Measure those excessive high Rocks which are on the Side of the *Glaciere,* and make many other curious Observations, according to the Taste and Genius of the Travellers; who, if they were inclined to Botany, might find an ample Field of Amusement.

One who understood Drawing might find wherewithal to imploy himself, either on the Road, or in the Place itself; in short, a Man of Genius might do many things which we have not done. All the Merit we can pretend to is having opened the way to others who may have Curiosity of the same Kind.

It would be right to take Victuals ready dress'd, and Salt Meat, Bread and Wine, for there are some Places where one can get no Provisions, and the little there is to be had in other Places, is very bad. We bought a Sheep, which we killed, and dressed upon the Spot.

It is necessary to carry Halters to tie the Horses, cut Shoes, Nails, Hammer, &c. for they lose their Shoes continually in those stoney Roads.

With such Precautions all kinds of Journeys become easy and agreeable, even in the most desart Countries, and one is then more in a Condition to observe with Care and Accuracy, whatever occurs worth Notice.

This is the Substance, Sir, of what I can recollect of our Journey. My having so long defer'd giving you this Account is owing to the Incapacity I found in myself to say any thing worth being presented to a Person of so good a Taste as yourself. However, upon the whole, 'tis your good Taste which ought to encourage me: Your lively and penetrating Imagination, which unites in one, both the Poet and Painter, will at once lay hold and perfect what I have but slightly sketched. I am, with the greatest Esteem,

S I R ,

Your most Obedient Humble Servant.

''SAFE AS TRAFALGAR SQUARE''

FROM *Little Mother Up the Mörderberg*

H . G . WELLS

One of the most curious pieces of literature which H. G. Wells wrote was his mock obituary. It was written in 1936, supposedly after he had died at the age of ninety-seven, a forgotten old man: "He was one of the most prolific of the literary hacks of his time. . . . It was his vanity to compare himself with Roger Bacon. . . . He was a copious and repetitive essayist upon public affairs and a still more copious writer of fiction. . . . Essentially an intellectual with an instinctive dislike for the intensities and emotional floods of life. . . . He was much more the scientific man than artist, though he dealt in literary forms."

Readers of Wells, whether of his prophetic science fiction, his erudite *Outline of History,* the sensibility and understanding of his modern novels of ideas, will evaluate Wells more kindly and certainly more accurately. His skill as storyteller is demonstrated in this delightful selection, one of the rare humorous stories in the fiction of mountaineering.

I MADE A KIND OF RECORD AT AROSA BY FALLING DOWN THREE SEPARATE crevasses on three successive days. That was before little mother followed me out there. When she came, I could see at a glance she was tired and jaded and worried, and so, instead of letting her fret about in the hotel and get into a wearing tangle of gossip, I packed her and two knapsacks up, and started off on a long, refreshing, easy-going walk northward, until a blister on her foot stranded us at the Magenruhe Hotel on the Sneejoch. She was for going on, blister or no blister—I never met pluck like mother's in all my life—but I said "No. This is a mountaineering inn, and it suits me down to the ground—or if you prefer it, up to the sky. You shall sit in the veranda by the telescope, and I'll prance about among the peaks for a bit."

"Don't have accidents," she said.

"Can't promise that, little mother," I said; "but I'll always remember I'm your only son."

So I pranced. . . .

I need hardly say that in a couple of days I was at loggerheads with all the mountaineers in that inn. They couldn't stand me. They didn't like my neck with its strong, fine Adam's apple—being mostly men with their heads *jammed* on—and they didn't like the way I bore myself and lifted my aviator's nose to the peaks. They didn't like my being a vegetarian and the way I evidently enjoyed it, and they didn't like the touch of colour, orange and green, in my rough serge suit. They were all of the dingy school—the sort of men I call gentlemanly owls—shy, correct-minded creatures, mostly from Oxford, and as solemn over their climbing as a cat frying eggs. Sage they were, great headnodders, and "I wouldn't-venture-to-do-a-thing-like-that"-ers. They always did what the books and guides advised, and they classed themselves by their seasons; one was in his ninth season, and another in his tenth, and so on. I was a novice and had to sit with my mouth open for bits of humble-pie.

My style that! Rather!

I would sit in the smoking-room sucking away at a pipeful of hygienic herb tobacco—they said it smelt like burning garden rubbish—and waiting to put my spoke in and let a little light into their minds. They set aside their natural reticence altogether in their efforts to show how much they didn't like me.

"You chaps take these blessed mountains too seriously," I said. "They're larks, and you've got to lark with them."

They just slued their eyes round at me.

"I don't find the solemn joy in fussing you do. The old-style mountaineers went up with alpenstocks and ladders and light hearts. That's my idea of mountaineering."

"It isn't ours," said one red-boiled hero of the peaks, all blisters and peeling skin, and he said it with an air of crushing me.

"It's the right idea," I said serenely, and puffed at my herb tobacco.

"When you've had a bit of experience you'll know better," said another, an oldish young man with a small grey beard.

"Experience never taught *me* anything," I said.

"Apparently not," said someone, and left me one down and me to play. I kept perfectly tranquil.

"I mean to do the Mörderberg before I go down," I said quietly, and produced a sensation.

"When are you going down?"

"Week or so," I answered, unperturbed.

"It's not the climb a man ought to attempt in his first year," said the peeling gentleman.

"*You* particularly ought not to try it," said another.

"No guide will go with you."

"Foolhardy idea."

"Mere brag."

"Like to see him do it."

I just let them boil for a bit, and when they were back to the simmer I dropped in, pensively, with, "Very likely I'll take that little mother of mine. She's small, bless her, but she's as hard as nails."

But they saw they were being drawn by my ill-concealed smile; and this time they contented themselves with a few grunts and grunt-like remarks, and then broke up into little conversations in undertones that pointedly excluded me. It had the effect of hardening my purpose. I'm a stiff man when I'm put on my mettle, and I determined that the little mother *should* go up the Mörderberg, where half these solemn experts hadn't been, even if I had to be killed or orphaned in the attempt. So I spoke to her about it the next day. She was in a deck-chair on the veranda, wrapped up in rugs and looking at the peaks.

"Comfy?" I said.

"Very," she said.

"Getting rested?"

"It's so nice."

I strolled to the rail of the veranda. "See that peak there, mummy?"

She nodded happily, with eyes half shut.

"That's the Mörderberg. You and me have got to be up there the day after to-morrow."

Her eyes opened a bit. "Wouldn't it be rather a climb, dearest?" she said.

"I'll manage that all right," I said, and she smiled consentingly and closed her eyes.

"So long as you manage it," she said.

I went down the valley that afternoon to Daxdam to get gear and guides and porters, and I spent the next day in glacier and rock practice above the hotel. That didn't add to my popularity. I made two little slips. One took me down a crevasse—I've an extraordinary knack of going down crevasses—and a party of three which was starting for the Kinderspitz spent an hour and a half fishing me out; and the other led to my dropping my ice-axe on a little string of people going for the Humpi glacier. It didn't go within thirty inches of anyone, but you might have thought from the row they made that I had knocked out the collective brains of the party. Quite frightful language they used, and three ladies with them, too!

The next day there was something very like an organised attempt to prevent our start. They brought out the landlord, they remonstrated with mother, they did their best to blacken the character of my two guides. The landlord's brother had a first-class row with them.

"Two years ago," he said, "they lost their Herr!"

"No particular reason," I said, "why you shouldn't keep yours on, is it?"

That settled him. He wasn't up to a polyglot pun, and it stuck in his mind like a fishbone in the throat.

Then the peeling gentleman came along and tried to overhaul our equipment. "Have you got this?" it was, and "Have you got that?"

"Two things," I said, looking at his nose pretty hard, "we haven't forgotten. One's blue veils and the other vaseline."

I've still a bright little memory of the start. There was the pass a couple of hundred feet or so below the hotel, and the hotel—all name and windows —standing out in a great, desolate, rocky place against lumpy masses of streaky green rock, flecked here and there with patches of snow and dark shelves of rhododendron, and rising perhaps a thousand feet towards the western spur of the massif. Our path ran before us, meandering among the boulders down to stepping-stones over a rivulet, and then upward on the other side of the stream towards the Magenruhe glacier, where we had to go up the rocks to the left and then across the icefall to shelves on the precipitous face on the west side. It was dawn, the sun had still to rise, and everything looked very cold and blue and vast about us. Everyone in the hotel had turned out to bear a hand in the row—some of the *deshabilles* were disgraceful—and now they stood in a silent group watching us recede. The last word I caught was, "They'll have to come back."

"We'll come back all right," I answered. "Never fear."

And so we went our way, cool and deliberate, over the stream and up and up towards the steep snowfields and icy shoulder of the Mörderberg. I remember that we went in absolute silence for a time, and then how suddenly the landscape gladdened with sunrise, and in an instant, as if speech had thawed, all our tongues were babbling.

I had one or two things in the baggage that I hadn't cared for the people at the inn to see, and I had made no effort to explain why I had five porters with the load of two and a half. But when we came to the icefall I showed my hand a little, and unslung a stout twine hammock for the mater. We put her in this with a rug round her, and sewed her in with a few stitches; then we roped up in line, with me last but one and a guide front and rear, and mummy in the middle carried by two of the porters. I stuck my alpenstock through two holes I had made in the shoulders of my jacket under my rucksac, T-shape to my body, so that when I went down a crevasse, as I did ever and again, I just stuck in its jaws and came up easy as the rope grew taut. And so, except for one or two bumps that made the mater chuckle, we got over without misadventure.

Then came the rock climb on the other side, requiring much judgment. We had to get from ledge to ledge as opportunity offered, and here the little mother was a perfect godsend. We unpacked her after we had slung her over the big fissure—I forget what you call it—that always comes between glacier and rock—and whenever we came to a bit of ledge within eight feet of the one we were working along, the two guides took her and slung her up, she being so light, and then she was able to give a foot for the next man to hold by and hoist himself. She said we were all pulling her leg, and that made her and me laugh so much that the whole party had to wait for us.

It was pretty tiring altogether doing that bit of the climb—two hours we had of it before we got to the loose masses of rock on the top of the arete. "It's worse going down," said the elder guide.

I looked back for the first time, and I confess it did make me feel a bit giddy. There was the glacier looking quite petty, and with a black gash between itself and the rocks.

For a time it was pretty fair going up the rocky edge of the arete, and nothing happened of any importance, except that one of the porters took to grousing because he was hit on the shin by a stone I dislodged. "Fortunes of war," I said, but he didn't seem to see it, and when I just missed him with a second he broke out into a long, whining discourse in what I suppose he thought was German—I couldn't make head or tail of it.

"He says you might have killed him," said the little mother.

"They say," I quoted, "What say they? *Let* them say."

I was for stopping and filling him up with a feed, but the elder guide wouldn't have it. We had already lost time, he said, and the traverse round the other face of the mountain would be more and more subject to avalanches as the sun got up. So we went on. As we went round the corner to the other face I turned towards the hotel—it was the meanest little oblong spot by now —and made a derisive gesture or so for the benefit of anyone at the telescope.

We did get one rock avalanche that reduced the hindmost guide to audible prayer, but nothing hit us except a few bits of snow. The rest of the fall was a couple of yards and more out from us. We were on rock just then and overhung; before and afterwards we were edging along steps in an ice-slope cut by the foremost guide, and touched up by the porters. The avalanche was much more impressive before it came in sight, banging and thundering overhead, and it made a tremendous uproar in the blue deeps beneath, but in actual transit it seemed a mean show—mostly of stones smaller than I am.

"All right?" said the guide.

"Toned up," I answered.

"I suppose it *is* safe, dear?" asked the little mother.

"Safe as Trafalgar Square," I said. "Hop along, mummykins."

Which she did with remarkable agility.

The traverse took us on to old snow at last, and here we could rest for lunch—and pretty glad we were both of lunch and rest. But here the trouble with the guides and porters thickened. They were already a little ruffled about my animating way with loose rocks, and now they kicked up a tremendous shindy because instead of the customary brandy we had brought non-alcoholic ginger cordial. Would they even try it? Not a bit of it! It was a queer little dispute, high up in that rarefied air, about food values and the advantages of making sandwiches with nuttar. They were an odd lot of men, invincibly set upon a vitiated and vitiating dietary. They wanted meat, they wanted alcohol, they wanted narcotics to smoke. You might have thought that men like these, living in almost direct contact with Nature, would have liked "Nature" foods, such as plasmon, protose, plobose, digestine, and so forth. Not them! They just craved for corruption. When I spoke of drinking pure water one of the porters spat in a marked, symbolic manner over the precipice. From that point onward discontent prevailed.

We started again about half-past eleven, after a vain attempt on the part of the head guide to induce us to turn back. We had now come to what is generally the most difficult part of the Mörderberg ascent, the edge that leads up to the snowfield below the crest. But here we came suddenly into a draught of warm air blowing from the south-west, and everything, the guide said, was unusual. Usually the edge is a sheet of ice over rock. To-day it was wet and soft, and one could kick steps in it and get one's toes into rock with the utmost ease.

"This is where Herr Tomlinson's party fell," said one of the porters, after we'd committed ourselves to the edge for ten minutes or so.

"Some people could fall out of a four-post bed," I said.

"It'll freeze hard again before we come back," said the second guide, "and us with nothing but verdammt ginger inside of us."

"You keep your rope taut," said I.

A friendly ledge came to the help of mother in the nick of time, just as she was beginning to tire, and we sewed her up all but the feet in her hammock again, and roped her carefully. She bumped a bit, and at times she was just hanging over immensity and rotating slowly, with everybody else holding like grim death.

"My dear," she said, the first time this happened, "is it *right* for me to be doing this?"

"Quite right," I said, "but if you can get a foothold presently again—it's rather better style."

"You're sure there's no danger, dear?"

"Not a scrap."

"And I don't fatigue you?"

"You're a stimulant."

"The view," she said, "is certainly becoming very beautiful."

But presently the view blotted itself out, and we were in clouds and a thin drift of almost thawing snowflakes.

We reached the upper snowfield about half-past one, and the snow was extraordinarily soft. The elder guide went in up to his armpits.

"Frog it," I said, and spread myself out flat, in a sort of swimming attitude. So we bored our way up to the crest and along it. We went in little spurts and then stopped for breath, and we dragged the little mother after us in her hammock-bag. Sometimes the snow was so good we fairly skimmed the surface; sometimes it was so rotten we plunged right into it and splashed about. I went too near the snow cornice once and it broke under me, but the rope saved me, and we reached the summit about three o'clock without further misadventure. The summit was just bare rock with the usual cairn and pole. Nothing to make a fuss about. The drift of snow and cloudwisp had passed, the sun was blazing hot overhead, and we seemed to be surveying all Switzerland. The Magenruhe Hotel was at our toes, hidden, so to speak, by our chins. We squatted about the cairn, and the guides and porters were reduced to ginger and vegetarian ham-sandwiches. I cut and scratched an inscription, saying I had climbed on simple food, and claiming a record.

Seen from the summit the snowfields on the north-east side of the mountain looked extremely attractive, and I asked the head guide why that way up wasn't used. He said something in his peculiar German about precipices.

So far our ascent had been a fairly correct ascent in rather slow time. It was in the descent that that strain in me of almost unpremeditated originality had play. I wouldn't have the rope returning across the upper snowfield, because mother's feet and hands were cold, and I wanted her to jump about a bit. And before I could do anything to prevent it she had slipped, tried to get up by rolling over *down* the slope instead of up, as she ought to have done, and was leading the way, rolling over and over and over, down towards the guide's blessed precipices above the lower snowfield.

I didn't lose an instant in flinging myself after her, axe up, in glissading attitude. I'm not clear what I meant to do, but I fancy the idea was to get in front of her and put on the brake. I did not succeed, anyhow. In twenty seconds I had slipped, and was sitting down and going down out of my own control altogether.

Now, most great discoveries are the result of accident, and I maintain that in that instant mother and I discovered two distinct and novel ways of coming down a mountain.

It is necessary that there should be first a snow slope above with a layer of softish, rotten snow on the top of ice, then a precipice, with a snow-covered talus sloping steeply at first and then less steeply, then more snow slopes and precipices according to taste, ending in a snowfield or a not-too-greatly-fissured glacier, or a reasonable, not-too-rocky slope. Then it all becomes as easy as chuting the chutes.

Mother hit on the sideways method. She rolled. With the snow in the adhesive state it had got into she had made the jolliest little snowball of herself in half a minute, and the nucleus of as clean and abundant a snow avalanche as anyone could wish. There was plenty of snow going in front of her, and that's the very essence of both our methods. You must fall on your snow, not your snow on you, or it smashes you. And you mustn't mix yourself up with loose stones.

I, on the other hand, went down feet first, and rather like a snow-plough; slower than she did, and if, perhaps, with less charm, with more dignity. Also I saw more. But it was certainly a tremendous rush. And I gave a sort of gulp when mummy bumped over the edge into the empty air and vanished.

It was like a toboggan ride gone mad down the slope until I took off from the edge of the precipice, and then it was like a dream.

I'd always thought falling must be horrible. It wasn't in the slightest degree. I might have hung with my clouds and lumps of snow about me for weeks, so great was my serenity. I had an impression then that I was as good as killed—and that it didn't matter. I wasn't afraid—that's nothing!—but I wasn't a bit uncomfortable. Whack! We'd hit something, and I expected to be flying to bits right and left. But we'd only got on to the snow-slope below, at so steep an angle that it was merely breaking the fall. Down we went again. I didn't see much of the view after that because the snow was all round and over my head, but I kept feet foremost and in a kind of sitting posture, and then I slowed and then I quickened again and bumped rather, and then harder, and bumped and then bumped again and came to rest. This time I was altogether buried in snow, and twisted sideways with a lot of heavy snow on my right shoulder.

I sat for a bit enjoying the stillness—and then I wondered what had become of mother, and set myself to get out of the snow about me. It wasn't so easy as you might think; the stuff was all in lumps and spaces like a gigantic sponge, and I lost my temper and struggled and swore a good deal, but at last I managed it. I crawled out and found myself on the edge of heaped masses of snow quite close to the upper part of the Magenruhe glacier. And far away, right up the glacier and near the other side, was a little thing like a black-beetle struggling in the heart of an immense split ball of snow.

I put my hands to my mouth and let out with my version of the yodel, and presently I saw her waving her hand.

It took me nearly twenty minutes to get to her. I knew my weakness, and I was very careful of every crevasse I came near. When I got up to her her face was anxious.

"What have you done with the guides?" she asked.

"They've got too much to carry," I said. "They're coming down another way. Did you like it?"

"Not very much, dear," she said; "but I dare say I shall get used to these things. Which way do we go now?"

I decided we'd find a snow-bridge across the bergschrund—that's the word I forgot just now—and so get on to the rocks on the east side of the glacier, and after that we had uneventful going right down to the hotel. . . .

Our return evoked such a strain of hostility and envy as I have never met before or since. First they tried to make out we'd never been to the top at all, but mother's little proud voice settled that sort of insult. And, besides, there was the evidence of the guides and porters following us down. When they asked about the guides, "They're following *your* methods," I said, "and I suppose they'll get back here to-morrow morning some-when."

That didn't please them.

I claimed a record. They said my methods were illegitimate.

"If I see fit," I said, "to use an avalanche to get back by, what's that to you? You tell me me and mother can't do the confounded mountain anyhow, and when we do you want to invent a lot of rules to disqualify us. You'll say next one mustn't glissade. I've made a record, and you know I've made a record, and you're about as sour as you can be. The fact of it is, you chaps don't know your own silly business. Here's a good, quick way of coming down a mountain, and you ought to know about it——"

"The chance that both of you are not killed was one in a thousand."

"Nonsense! It's the proper way to come down for anyone who hasn't a hide-bound mind. You chaps ought to practise falling great heights in snow. It's perfectly easy and perfectly safe, if only you know how to set about it."

"Look here, young man," said the oldish young man with the little grey beard, "you don't seem to understand that you and that lady have been saved by a kind of miracle——"

"Theory!" I interrupted. "I'm surprised you fellows ever come to Switzerland. If I were your kind I'd just invent theoretical mountains and play for points. However, you're tired, little mummy. It's time you had some nice warm soup and tucked yourself up in bed. I shan't let you get up for six-and-thirty hours."

But it's queer how people detest a little originality.

STONE AVALANCHE
IN WALES

FROM *The Mountains of Youth*

ARNOLD LUNN

In this personal account of a rock-climbing accident, Arnold Lunn omits the epilogue. As he lay on a narrow ledge after his fall with a leg not only broken but crushed, he vowed that he would never again climb alone, "for the horror of finding oneself alone with a broken leg must be experienced to be understood." But it was no more than two years after the accident, with a permanently crippled right leg, that he resumed his climbing—and alone. The stay-at-home will call it foolhardy, the mountaineer will call it guts. Thereby demonstrating once again, that what is one man's folly is another man's challenge.

Arnold Lunn became a mountaineer at the age of eight. He made the first ski ascent of many of the Alpine peaks and his books on ski-running are classics for *aficionados* of the craft.

IN WALES, MORE THAN ELSEWHERE, YOU ARE HAUNTED BY THE GHOSTS OF KINGLY ranges which have ceased to be. You realize the geological processes, not as academic facts, but as the *motif* of these senescent hills. The Alps, one feels, are still in their first heady youth, with all youth's love for bright colours and violent effects. But Cader and his peers are the Nestors of the mountains. They have suffered the incredible march of time. They move you with the beauty of old age, calm, resigned, and aloof. And their mature wisdom appeals no less surely to the imagination than the energy of the turbulent Alps. . . .

Two days after I first arrived at Tallylyn in 1909, I wandered up to Llyn Cae, surely the loveliest of all the Welsh tarns. A magnificent gully seamed the face of the dark cliffs beyond the lake. I did not then know that this was the Great Gully of Craig y Cae, Owen Glynne Jones's favourite Welsh climb. Had I known this I should not have started the ascent at 5 P.M.

Since then a miniature landslide has converted the famous cave pitch into an easy scramble, which is a pity. But when I first climbed the gully I could have dispensed with unnecessary difficulties, for I began the climb far too late in the day. Like most men who have learned to climb in the Alps, I tended to under-estimate the necessary allowance of time for a great Welsh gully, and before long I realized that if the last pitches should prove severe, I should not reach the top that night. Luckily, the last stages were interesting but straightforward, and as the light failed I scrambled out of the narrow exit of the final crack. I enjoyed that climb, and I have seen few more impressive sights than the black waters of the tarn far below, framed between the dark smooth cliffs which confine the recesses of the gully.

On the following day I met two friends, a little distance above Tallylyn. One of them was carrying a fisherman's rod, but the other was wearing well-nailed boots. This looked more hopeful, so I asked whether they would like to join me some day on a climb. Mr. Syme, the owner of the boots, had climbed before. His friend, Mr. Warren, was quite prepared to sample a Welsh gully, and they both agreed to meet me next day.

That night C. Scott Lindsay arrived, and next morning the four of us— Lindsay, my new friends and I—set out to climb the Great Gully. A casual remark of Mr. Syme's revealed the fact that Mr. Warren was a rising surgeon on the staff of the London Hospital. Another casual remark disclosed the name of the small village where Warren and Syme were staying. I should at this moment be wearing an artificial leg but for this lucky series of accidents, beginning with the nailed boots which Syme was wearing and which had effected our introduction.

On the following day Lindsay felt like a rest, so I set off alone and climbed the east ridge of Cyfrwy, off which I fell two days later. It is an interesting climb, not very difficult judged by modern standards, but quite amusing. A steep face . . . looks sensational but is really quite easy. The best thing on the ridge is a miniature Mummery crack which calls for skill if one wishes to climb it without disproportionate effort.

On August 28th I started for my last climb. Lindsay was not feeling fit, and he left me near the top of Cader Idris. I decided to descend the east and to climb the north ridge of Cyfrwy. I was carrying a short rope which I had brought along on the chance that Lindsay might join me.

The day was perfect. The burnished silver of the sea melted into a golden haze. Light shadows cast by scudding clouds drifted across the blue and distant hills. The sun flooded down on the rocks. I slid down the crack and reached the top of the steep face of rock above "The Table." The usual route dodges the top fifteen feet of this face, and by an easy traverse reaches a lower ledge. But on that glorious afternoon I longed to spin out the joys of Cyfrwy, and I found a direct route from the top to the bottom of this wall, a steep but not very severe variation.

It was one of those days when to be alive is "very heaven." The feel of the warm, dry rocks and the easy rhythm of the descending motion gave me an almost sensuous pleasure. One toyed with the thought of danger, so complete was the confidence inspired by the firm touch of the wrinkled rocks.

> In this short span
> Between my finger tips and the smooth edge,
> And these tense feet cramped to a crystal ledge,
> I hold the life of man.
>
> Consciously I embrace,
> Arched from the mountain rock on which I stand
> To the firm limit of my lifted hand,
> The front of time and space;
>
> For what is there in all the world for me
> But what I know and see?
> And what remains of all I see and know
> If I let go?

I was glad to be alone. I revelled in the freedom from the restraints of the rope, and from the need to synchronize my movements with the movements of companions.

I have never enjoyed rock-climbing more. I have never enjoyed rock-climbing since. But, at least, the hills gave me of their best, full measure and overflowing, in those last few golden moments before I fell.

A few minutes later Lindsay, who was admiring the view from Cader, was startled by the thunder of a stone avalanche. He turned to a stray tourist, urging him to follow, and dashed off in the direction of Cyfrwy. . . .

And this is what had happened. I had just lowered myself off the edge of "The Table." There was no suggestion of danger. Suddenly the mountain seemed to sway, and a quiver ran through the rocks. I clung for one brief moment of agony to the face of the cliff. And then suddenly a vast block, which must have been about ten feet high and several feet thick, separated itself from the face, heeled over on top of me and carried me with it into space. I turned a somersault, struck the cliff some distance below, bounded off once again and, after crashing against the ridge two or three times, landed on a sloping ledge about seven feet broad. The thunder of the rocks falling through the hundred and fifty feet below my resting-point showed how narrow had been my escape.

I had fallen a distance which Lindsay estimated at a hundred feet. It was not a sliding fall, for except when I struck and rebounded I was not in contact with the ridge. The fall was long enough for me to retain a very vivid memory of the thoughts which chased each other through my brain during those few crowded seconds. I can still feel the clammy horror of the moment when the solid mountain face trembled below me, but the fall, once I was fairly off, blunted the edge of fear. My emotions were subdued, as if I had been partially anæsthetized. I remember vividly seeing the mountains up-side down after my first somersault. I remember the disappointment as I realized that I had not stopped and that I was still falling. I remember making despairing movements with my hands in a futile attempt to check my downward progress.

The chief impression was a queer feeling that the stable order of nature had been overturned. The tranquil and immobile hills had been startled into a mood of furious and malignant activity, like a dangerous dog roused from a peaceful nap by some inattentive passer-by who has trodden on him unawares. And every time I struck the cliff only to be hurled downwards once again, I felt like a small boy who is being knocked about by a persistent bully—"Will he never stop? . . . surely he can't hit me again . . . surely he's hurt me enough."

When at last I landed, I tried to sit up, but fell back hurriedly on see-ing my leg. The lower part was bent almost at right angles. It was not merely broken, it was shattered and crushed.

I shouted and shouted and heard no reply. Had Lindsay returned home? Would I have to wait for hours before help came?

Solitude had lost its charm. I no longer rejoiced in my freedom from in-trusion. On the contrary, I raised my voice and called upon society to come to my assistance. I set immense store on my membership of the Human Club, and very urgently did I summon my fellow-members to my assistance.

And then suddenly I heard an answering cry, and my shouts died away in a sob of heartfelt relief.

And while I waited for help, I looked up at the scar on the cliff where the crag had broken away, and I realized all that I was in danger of losing. Had I climbed my last mountain?

During the war the cheery dogmatism of some second lieutenant home from the front was extremely consoling, for the human mind is illogical and the will to believe very potent. And so when Lindsay arrived and replied with a hearty affirmative when I asked him whether I should ever climb again, I was greatly comforted, even though Lindsay knew less of broken legs than the average subaltern of the chances of peace.

Lindsay was preceded by an ancient man who keeps the hut on Cader. He examined my leg with a critical eye and informed me that it was broken. He then remarked that I had been very ill-advised to stray off the path on to "rough places" where even the natives did not venture. He grasped my leg, and moved it a little higher on to the ledge. This hurt. He then uncoiled my rope and secured me to a buttress which overhung my narrow perch.

Then Lindsay staggered on to the ledge, gave one glance at my leg, turned a curious colour, and sat down hurriedly. He suggested breaking off a gate and carrying me down on it. The ancient man of Cader hazarded a tentative suggestion in favour of sacks. I demurred, for a sack may be appropriate to a corpse but is not conducive to the comfort of a wounded man.

Lindsay, by a lucky accident, remembered Warren's address, and so I sent him off to find him. He left me in charge of the tourist who had followed him, and departed with the man of Cader.

Lindsay's chance companion was useful while he stayed, for I was lying on a sloping ledge, and was glad of his shoulder as a pillow. Ten minutes passed, and my companion remarked that he thought he ought to be going. I protested, but could not move him. His wife, he said, would be getting anxious. I hinted that his wife's anxiety might be ignored. "Ah, but you don't know my wife," he replied, and, so saying, left me.

He consented to leave his cap behind as a pillow. A month later he wrote and asked me why I had not returned it. This struck me as unreasonable, but—as he justly observed—I did not know his wife.

I fell at 4 P.M. About 7.30 P.M. it became colder, and shivering made the pain worse. About 7.45 P.M. the old man of Cader returned with some warm tea which he had brewed for me, and for which I was more than grateful. Half-an-hour later the local policeman arrived with a search party and a stretcher.

Luckily the ledge ran across on to easy ground, but it was not until midnight—eight hours after my fall—that I reached the Angel Hotel.

My leg was broken, crushed and comminuted. Twice the preparations were made for amputation. Twice my temperature fell in the nick of time. At the end of a week I was taken home, and lay on my back for four months, much consoled by a Christian Scientist who assured me that my leg was intact. But it was not to Mrs. Eddy, but to the faint hope of the hills that I turned for comfort in the long nights when pain had banished sleep.

MERELY FOR PLEASURE

FROM *Reliquiae*

L FRED   DENNIS   GODLEY

The papers that Alfred Dennis Godley read to the Alpine Club, of which this selection is representative, are the best of his prose writings—gentle, witty, and urbane. Godley taught at Oxford for most of his life. He was a classics scholar and humorist, a seemingly unnatural combination of talents which, in his case, were admirably and mutually fused. He had a long and devoted attachment to mountain climbing and made some nineteen visits to the Swiss Alps. His colleagues describe him as having been an equally mighty walker in the English hill country.

I SUPPOSE THE FIRST AND OBVIOUS THOUGHT OF EVERYONE WHEN HE IS ASKED to read a paper before this Club (whether as a *lever de rideau* or otherwise) must be, that it is the proudest day of his life. The next and perhaps equally obvious reflection for myself personally was, that somehow or other the paper must be constructed; that after a number of years chequered by a great variety of hill-climbing expeditions there must be ample material; and the final conclusion of the whole matter seemed to be, that, however enthralling the subjective interest of one's own personal experiences, their objective value to an audience was absolutely nil; and that, in short, I had nothing to say. I communicated this fact to the Secretary. He, with a promptitude obviously born of experience, replied by return of post that the less I said the better. He did not put it precisely in that form. He spoke of mountains regarded from some other point of view than that of the mere (I am pretty sure he said "mere") climber or the commonplace explorer. This troubled me a little. From what other point of view can you regard a mountain? I cannot geologise; to photograph I am—incompetent. At one time I did think of reading a paper entitled "Mountains which I Have Not Climbed or Explored," and of hiring a set of slides illustrative of the Himalayas, the Caucasus, and the Breithorn. But eventually I thought I grasped the true inwardness of what the Secretary had said.

I appear, then, as a member of that class of perhaps not altogether respectable persons who ascend hills merely for pleasure. They have no particular principles, except the general maxim that it is better to be at the top of a hill than the bottom. They are not centrists nor excentrists; if they cannot have a peak, they will take a pass; if they cannot have a pass, they will be content with a glacier. Their object is to acquire such skill as will enable them to walk on steep places without danger to themselves and others. They are smatterers and general readers in an age of specialism; they are wedded to no dogmatic *formulae*, but are simple, undenominational (may one say?) Cowper-Temple Alpinists.

These are then mere Hedonists; and yet there is something to be said even for them. Their pursuit of pleasure is perhaps the less disreputable because they are in a sense martyrs. There are few to praise them. Within the circle of this Club they are regarded as lacking in seriousness and fixity of purpose, and that higher altruism which prompts to the increasing of knowledge by the ascent of untrodden peaks; mere voluptuaries, votaries of selfish pleasure. Outside, they are exposed to obloquy and detraction. To the public in general, which does not love mountains—except as a background to some scene of rational amusement—hill-climbing is either too difficult or too easy. Once it was too difficult, and Alpinists were condemned as bad citizens for their suicidal tendencies. Now, in general, the pendulum has swung the other way: it is too easy. With a vague consciousness of mountain railways—a distant recollection of *Tartarin sur les Alpes*—a hazy reminiscence of expressions perhaps used in the heat of the moment by members of this Club—with all this mass of imperfectly assimilated suggestion simmering in his mind, the uninterested outside critic is apt to conclude that mountaineering is a pastime where the facilities are too many and too obvious, and the need for personal exertion reduced to a minimum; and that on the whole a man who respects the dignity of human nature ought to be playing golf. Perhaps that is true. We are quite conscious of these variously unsympathetic attitudes; yet we persist in our vicious courses—being, as I said, mere voluptuaries, given over to self-indulgence and the gratification of appetite. And here the philosopher is confronted by what he must acknowledge to be a strange paradox. If we, being otherwise for the most part persons of moderate respectability, and not more obviously mad than other people, continue in these unremunerative pursuits merely for the sake of pleasure, and proclaim that our climbing days have been among the best days of our lives, we ought to be able at least to define that pleasure in an intelligible way.

It is every man's duty to attempt to arrive at truth. That is not easy in matters connected with mountains. Speaking (if one may say so) as an augur to augurs, one may confess that inaccurate statements have from time to time been made, and even printed. I have even heard mendacity and self-glorification described as part of the necessary equipment of a true Alpinist. Nevertheless, truth must be investigated. Now, if we are to take the aggregate of outside public opinion—if not *quod semper, quod ubique, quod ab omnibus,* yet what is held by most men at most times and in most places—we shall find that it speaks with no uncertain voice. I remember to have heard Mr. Edmund Gosse make an excellent speech when responding for the guests at the winter dinner of the Club. I shall always recollect his opening sentence, which claimed to interpret the real if unconfessed sentiments of the Alpine Club itself: "I dislike," he said, "a mountain as much as any of you." Mountains have only to be known to be disliked; and the Club, knowing them best, must dislike them most! A friend of my own, very highly placed in the University of Oxford, told me once that for him mountaineering held but two pleasurable moments—when you arrive at the top, and when you arrive (of course, voluntarily) at the bottom: nor did it appear that the sensual delights of the vanquished peak or the regained hotel were in themselves, for my friend, sufficient to balance the extreme agony incidental to the phases of existence preceding these two crises of achievement. Here, then, you have Literature and the Universities (for once) in agreement.

Any person of a candid and philosophic mind, not a mountaineer, must arrive at a like conclusion. The philosopher would say: Your expedition is made up of a series of acts which are either painful or unnatural or unnecessary or unremunerative, or (more commonly) all these at once. You get up at two in the morning—a thing horrible to imagine. Dragged or impelled by peasants of great strength and ferocious aspect, you ascend steep and slippery heights which no one will praise you for surmounting, while no sensible person would pity you if you fell. You eat and drink for the most part things from which at other times you would rightly recoil. Chicago supplies your viands, and the very name * of your so-called wine proves it (if proof were needed) the legitimate successor of that vinegar with which Hannibal, the first Alpinist, is fabled to have split the rocks. You are exposed to excessive cold and excessive heat; to the botanist who delays your advance by searching for probably non-existent vegetables, and the photographer who nails you like Prometheus to the rock. Can a succession of incidents, in themselves painful, compose an aggregate of pleasure? Apparently, it can.

If I may be autobiographical for a moment, I should like to describe to the Club my initiation into its pastimes a good many years ago. Hills, at that time, held no special attractions for me. I had no friends at that time who knew or cared anything about the Alps. From reading the usual kind of conventional descriptions of mountain ascents I supposed that the climber's choice lay invariably between the side of an overhanging precipice and

* Probably "fendant"—a pun on *fendre,* "to split."

the bottom of a fathomless crevasse. I recollected the perilous rock-and-glacier work which (according to Sir Walter Scott) menaces the incautious traveller on the route from Bâle to Lucerne. Altogether I do not suppose that a more crassly ignorant amateur than I was ever walked in a pair of improperly nailed boots. However, having been somehow imported into Switzerland, as I heard people talking about the so-called pastime of climbing, I thought I would demonstrate the futility of the thing *ambulando*. I therefore took to myself professionals and an alpenstock like "the mast of some tall ammiral"—the possession of an axe then implied some pretensions to being what is called an "expert"—and thus equipped I set out to walk over the Adler pass from Zermatt to Mattmark. This seemed to be a good test, as Baedeker said it was "wild and hazardous." We scaled those dizzy precipices; or rather, we walked and waded over leagues of very bad snow, which was naturally much more embarrassing to me than to the rest of the party. It was a misty day, and we saw no view. When we got to Mattmark my face felt a little hot after some eight hours of exposure to fresh snow, and I cooled it with very cold water (lanoline was not invented then). Over the agonies which my complexion endured some hours afterwards I can only draw a veil—and I remember wishing that I had drawn that veil before I started. Looking back on the cold details of that expedition, I can find nothing in it that a properly constituted mind could call enjoyable; yet I know very well that I seemed to myself to have discovered an entirely new and unmixed pleasure, and to have merely wasted all the years which I had spent outside Switzerland. I am almost ashamed to say how little I have changed my mind since then.

One cannot say what the pleasure is. It defies analysis into its agreeable or disagreeable parts. It appears to be independent of external accidents (the word is used in the logical sense); it exists on the Diablerets, which is as nearly flat as a mountain can be; it exists on the west face of the Pillar rock, which is not flat at all. Novelty is all very well. But however delightful to vanquish some rock pinnacle (*noch nicht gemacht*)—and possibly to find that your new peak is crowned by an old bottle, which you try to persuade yourself has been dropped by a passing balloon:—however fascinating to climb a gully, "equal to new," where the stones, accumulated by ages of justifiable neglect, only to fall on your devoted head, make you occasionally feel that you could be content with that gully in a slightly more used condition; whatever the charms of new ascents, it is not on these that the grovelling Hedonists for whom I speak primarily rely. As Aristotle might say, they do not need novelty, like an amulet. They recognise that if newness has its delights, so has familiarity; and, as I am professionally bound to think first of instruction, I ought to say that nothing is more educative from a climbing point of view than to make the same ascent under different conditions.

It may be urged that persons who approach the Alps in this casual and amateurish, and what I may call Bank Holiday, spirit are liable to be accused of forming an undesirable link between this Club and the ordinary tourist—in fact, of being ordinary tourists themselves. Now, no one can have studied the recent literature of Alpine adventure without realising that it is a very serious thing to be called a tourist. While the writer of an article in the *Journal* is almost invariably a hero—or at least *the* hero of the piece—the tourist, should he unfortunately appear, almost always takes the *rôle* of the villain.

And the worst of it is that it is so fatally easy to become one. The affliction may come upon a man quite suddenly; it is in a sense an accident of time and place. You may be successful in your profession and respected by your friends—so long as you keep below the snow-line; cross it and you may be at once described as *hostis humani generis;* in a moment you may find that you are one of a class of persons who are generally obese: who belong by preference to some alien nationality: in front of whom the rope is unduly taut as they ascend, and unduly slack as they descend; who regard the practised mountaineer with peculiar animosity, and take every opportunity of dislodging portions of the hillside on to his head: for whose sake mountains are draped with ropes and honeycombed by railways—while the true climber is driven far afield, before their locust-like advance, into distant and hotel-less solitudes.

Yet the harmfulness even of a tourist may be exaggerated.

After all, the crowds of persons only qualified for climbing by the possession of an ice-axe, who have certainly made some parts of the Alps less delightful in the past twelve or fifteen years, are not necessarily so baneful as we are sometimes given to understand—even granting the impossibility of their moral redemption. Natural gregariousness, which is perhaps the real *differentia* of the tourist, herds him into a few centres where he can dine off many courses and all the expeditions have sign-posts. But these are after all only a small part of the Alps. Fourteen years ago it was the singular good fortune of myself and a friend to find ourselves on five fine August days the sole visitors of five so-called first-class peaks. Allowing that now that would be a very unusual experience indeed—allowing the number of "hardest climbs in the Alps" which are now "an easy day for a lady"—granting that on fine mornings a *queue* has, I am told, to be formed from the door of the Matterhorn hut, and that every peak at Arolla, from the Petite Dent de Veisivi to the Aiguilles Rouges, is crowned by its own particular picnic—surely those are desperate counsellors who would have us retire (as does a recent and very eloquent writer in the *Journal*) to Parnassus or Olympus or Ida. We are not really crowded out of the Alps. Not to go far afield, it cannot be said the district between the Grimsel and the Gothard is over-populated. There is quite good climbing there, nor is the climber's initiative hampered or atrophied by the excessive skill of local guides. And any one who goes even to the Aiguilles of Mont Blanc with the *Climber's Guide* (a work which I mention for the sake of honour) will see at once that topography has not said its last word.

Why not accept the facts in an optimistic spirit, and acknowledge the potential perfectibility even of tourists? Many a man begins as a member of that class, yet afterwards lives quite respectably. Perhaps, among those who in later years have acquired quite enough knowledge to lead up (let us say) the Galenstock, more than would care to confess it have begun by going up the Matterhorn because it was the right thing to do. Even such are men and brothers. This Club is based after all on the desires that are shared by ourselves with the humblest tripper who crawls on all fours across the slab of the easy route up the Pillar—the desire for the high air and the sun shining on the peaks and the sense of something accomplished. In the "concentration camps" above described, much is being done for the moral, as well as the physical, elevation of the sojourner. When he ascends mountains, even those very boulders which he dislodges on to the head of the innocent mountaineer may be the "stepping-stones" of his tourist nature whereby he climbs "to higher things." Even when he only makes what I have heard a guide describe—in reference to the chief seats at feasts gradually attained by length of stay in hotels—as *la grande ascension de la table d'hôte*—even then he may be imbibing that enthusiasm for mountains, that *animus ascendendi* which is the sign of the true mountaineer; which will, one hopes, still send some Englishmen to the Alps when climbing as a fashion has passed into the limbo of forgotten pastimes. And here I seem to be getting near the subject which the secretary may have had in mind when he spoke of the Alps regarded from an unprofessional point of view; but as I have also got to the end of this unnecessary paper, I apologise for the length of the expedition.

2

Men Live and Work
on the Mountains

Of the vast overland migrations of prehistoric peoples we know little. That they had to overcome the dividing barrier of mountains we know from the artefacts and myths they left behind, scattered through widely separated areas of the world. Some, like the Incas, closed themselves in behind the mountain barriers and evolved their proud but insulated culture. For others, such as the Tibetans of the Himalayas, and our Southern Highlanders, time may seem to have stopped with their ancestors.

These are a distinctive people who live in the high altitudes of the Pyrenees, the Caucasus, the Andes, the Himalayas. Their lives and work have been shaped to the rocks, tempered by inordinate heat and cold; their houses, food, theology, tradition, stories have been fitted to the mountain slopes.

For the most part it has not been the mountain dweller who has written about himself. He is at once too isolated from the world outside and too close to his unchanging background to stand back and look on and write of what he sees. It has been the lowlander who has climbed upward from the valley to see what people dwell behind the mountain barriers, and how they lead their lives. Here we have collected the best of these records of the mountain life, from both lowlander and highlander, among them the writings of many of the world's great craftsmen in prose.

WOODCUT OF THE FIRST CONTINUOUS ORE SIFTER. AT A
COPPER MINE IN THE CARPATHIAN MOUNTAINS, 1530

THAT LAND AMONG THE CLOUDS, TIBET, HAS RIGHTLY BEEN CALLED THE ROOF OF THE WORLD,
AND HERE IS ONE OF THE ROOF-DWELLERS, WHO, WITH HIS PONY, LIVES AND TRAVELS WITH
COMFORT AT ALTITUDES THREE MILES ABOVE THE SEA

MOUNTAIN VILLAGE IN DAGHESTAN, IN THE CAUCASUS. CAUCASIAN PASSES WERE AGE-OLD INVASION ROUTES BETWEEN RUSSIA AND TURKEY AND PERSIA. NOTE THAT THE WATCH TOWERS IN THE VILLAGE ARE SUPPLEMENTED BY OTHERS SPACED UP THE VALLEY

HERDSMAN IN THE CAUCASUS WEARING SHEEPSKIN CAPE TYPICAL OF THIS MOUNTAINOUS REGION

Soxfoto

A FIERCE PATRIARCH OF THE CAUCASUS

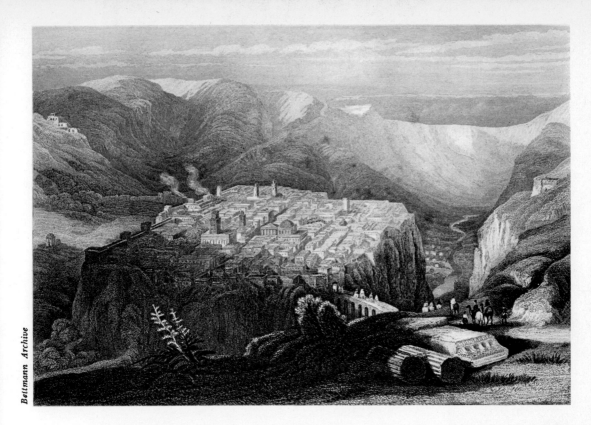

AN ETCHING OF CONSTANTINE, THE PLATEAU CITY IN ALGERIA, NOTED AS AN ANCIENT FORTRESS

PLATEAU AREA IN PERU SURROUNDED BY TERRACED MOUNTAINSIDES

LLAMAS CROSSING A HANGING BRIDGE ON THE TRAIL BELOW LIMBANI, PERU

NATIVES THRESHING GRAIN BY ANCIENT METHODS IN THE ANDES

American Geographical Society

A PEASANT COUPLE OF THE VAUDOIS, SWITZERLAND

CROSSING THE ALLEGHANIES

FROM *Excerpts from a Traveller's Note Book*

WALT WHITMAN

The old preachers used to say, "A man should have a glory." It's hard to think of six words that would better give the spirit of Walt Whitman's writing. Wherever human life was "magnificently moving in vast masses" Whitman was there to glory in it and to note it down. His *Leaves of Grass* on publication was attacked violently for its unorthodox poetic form, its frankness about sex, and its radical sentiments. Only Emerson, together with a few others, recognized that Whitman had given expression to the enormous diversity and potential of America and its people.

It was some little time before he published *Leaves of Grass* that Whitman got a job as reporter for the New Orleans *Daily Crescent*. He took the fourteen-day trip from Brooklyn to New Orleans by stagecoach with his brother Jeff. This selection from his notebook on the Alleghany crossing gives us an unusually intimate picture of the Whitman who found the raw materials for his poetry in the daily catalogue of man's life and work.

WE LEFT BALTIMORE ON SATURDAY MORNING AT SEVEN O'CLOCK, ON THE RAILroad for Cumberland, which is about a hundred and seventy miles distant, at the eastern edge of the Alleghanies. Of course, at this season of the year the country is not remarkably fascinating anywhere; and here a very large portion of the road is bounded on one side or the other by cliffs and steeps of an Alp-like loftiness. We seemed, for at least a hundred miles, to follow the course of an interminable brook, winding with its windings, and twisting with its twists, in a, to me, singular fashion. But even with so many circuits, the road had to be cut through very many bad places; and was probably one of the most expensive railroads ever built. It pays enormous profits, however; and they seriously "talk" about having it continued to some place on the Ohio, perhaps Wheeling. After "talking about it" awhile, it will very likely be done; it only wants money enough—and an enormous lot of that it *will* want, too!

At Harper's Ferry, where they gave us twenty minutes to dine, the scenery is strikingly abrupt and varied. Houses were perched up over our heads —backs in the ground—and others perched up over *their* heads, and so on. The finest scenery, though, even here (if it be not a bull to say so), is about half a mile off. As soon as the cars stopped, a frightful sound of bells and discordant screams surrounded us, and we were all but torn in pieces by the assault, as it were! Recovering from the first shock of such an unexpected salute, we found that there were several "hotels," each moved by a bitter rivalry for getting the passengers to eat their dinner. One "opposition house," in particular, seemed bent upon proceeding to extremities—and most of the passengers were fain to go quietly in. For a good dinner here, the price was only twenty-five cents.

Cumberland, at which we arrived about sunset, is a thriving town, with several public edifices, a newspaper or two, and those [institutions] invariably to be found in every western and southern community, some big "hotels." The town has a peculiar character, from its being the great rendezvous and landing place of the immense Pennsylvania wagons, and the drovers from hundreds of miles west. You may see Tartar-looking groups of these wagons, and their drivers, in the open grounds about—the horses being loosed—and the whole having not a little the appearance of a caravan of the Steppes. Hundreds and hundreds of these enormous vehicles, with their arched roofs of white canvas, wend their way into Cumberland from all quarters, during a busy season, with goods to send on eastward, and to take goods brought by the railroad. They are in shape not a little like the "Chinese junk," whilom exhibited at New York—being built high at each end, and scooping down in the waist. With their teams of four and six horses, they carry an almost incalculable quantity of "freight"; and if one should accidentally get in the road-ruts before their formidable wheels, they would perform the work of a Juggernaut upon him in most effectual order. The drivers of these vehicles and the drovers of cattle, hogs, horses, &c., in this section of the land, form a large slice of "society."

Night now falling down around us like a very large cloak of black broadcloth (I fancy *that* figure, at least, hasn't been used up by the poets) and the Alleghanies rearing themselves up "some pumpkins" (as they say here), right before our nasal members, we got in to one of the several four-horse stage coaches of the "National Road and Good Intent Stage Company," whereby we were to be transported over those big hills. They did the thing systematically, whatever may be said elsewise. All the passengers' names were inscribed on a roll (we purchased tickets in Philadelphia, at $13 a head, to go to Wheeling), and a clerk stands by and two or three negroes with a patent weighing machine. The clerk calls your name—your baggage is whipped on the machine, and if it weighs over fifty pounds, you have to pay extra. You are then put in the stage (literally put in, like a package, unless you move quickly), your baggage packed on behind—and the next name called off—baggage weighed—and so on to the end of the chapter. If six passengers desire it, or any smaller number who will pay for six, they can wait and have a coach sent with them the next morning, or at any hour they choose. One cunning trick of the company is, that they give you no check or receipt for your baggage, for which they pretend not to be responsible. It is best, therefore, if possible, for each passenger to have some witness to his baggage and its amount, in which case, if it be lost, the company will have to pay up—whatever they publish to the contrary.

So they boxed us up in our coach, nine precious souls, and we dashed through the town and up the mountains, with an apparent prospect of as comfortable a night as could be expected, considering all things. One or two of the passengers tried to get up a conversational entertainment; one old gentleman, in particular, *did* talk. He resided on a farm in the interior of Ohio. He had been on to Washington (I heard the fact at least twenty-five times in the course of that night and the next day), to claim a certain $5,000 from the Government for capturing a British merchant brig off the coast of Maine, in the last war. She got becalmed, or something of that sort, and he being thereabout, in command of a fishing smack, sailed or rowed up, captured her and brought her into port, where the Government functionaries took possession of her and sold her cargo for some $30,000. Our old gentleman, however (not *then* old, of course), had no privateering papers, and [was] consequently not a dollar the gainer. He had now been on to Washington to see about it, and was in hopes of getting at least his share of the sale. (Poor old man! if he lives till he gets Congress to pay him, he will be immortal.) This famous old gentleman moreover informed us that his wife had had thirteen children, one in every month of the year, and one over besides—all being alive and kicking! He did not know exactly what to think about the Mexican war; but he thought that Congress might at least grant decent pensions to those who were severely maimed in it, and to the widows of both officers and privates who were killed. Sage and sound conclusions, thought the rest of us too. And here I may say, once for all, that, though expecting to find a shrewd population as I journeyed to the interior, and down through the great rivers, I was by no means prepared for the sterling vein of common sense that seemed to pervade them—even the roughest shod and roughest clad of all. A satirical person could no doubt find an ample field for his powers in many of the manners and the ways of the West; and so can he, indeed, in the highest circles of fashion. But I fully believe that in a comparison of actual manliness and what the Yankees call "gumption," the well-to-do *citizens* (for I am not speaking so much of the country), particularly the young men, of New York, Philadelphia, Boston, Brooklyn and so on, with all the advantages of compact neighborhood, schools, etc., are not up to the men of the West. Among the latter, probably, attention is more turned to the *realities* of life, and a habit formed of thinking for one's self; in the cities, frippery and artificial fashion are too much the ruling powers.

Up we toiled, and down we clattered (for the first fifty miles it was nearly *all* up) over these mighty warts on the great breast of nature. It was excessively cold; the moon shone at intervals; and whenever we stopped, I found the ground thickly covered with snow. The places at which we changed horses (which was done every ten miles) were generally long, old, one-story houses, with stupendous fires of soft coal that is so plentiful and cheap here. In the night, with the mountains on all sides, the precipitous and turning road, the large, bare-armed trees looming up around us, the room half filled with men curiously enwrapped in garments of a fashion till then never seen —and the flickering light from the mighty fire putting a red glow upon most objects, and casting others into a strong shadow—I can tell you these stoppages were not without interest. They might, it seems to me, afford first rate scenes for an *American* painter—one who, not continually straining to be merely second or third best, in *imitation,* seizes original and really picturesque occasions of this sort for his pieces. There was one of the Alleghany inns, in particular, that we stopped at about an hour after midnight. (All the staging across these mountains, both to and fro, is done in the night, which engrafts a somewhat weird character upon the public houses—their busy time being from sunset to sunrise.) There were some ten or twelve great strapping drovers, reclining about the room on benches, and as many more before the huge fire. The beams overhead were low and smoke-dried. I stepped to the farther end of the long porch; the view from the door was grand, though vague, even in the moonlight. We had just descended a large and very steep hill, and just off on one side of us was a precipice of apparently hundreds of feet. The silence of the grave spread over this solemn scene; the mountains were covered in their white shrouds of snow—and the towering trees looked black and threatening; only the largest stars were visible, and they glittered with a tenfold brightness. One's heart, at such times, is irresistibly lifted to Him of whom these august appearances are but the least emanation. Faith! if I had an infidel to convert, I would take him on the mountains, of a clear and beautiful night, when the stars are shining.

Journeying in this manner, the time and the distance slipped away, until we welcomed the gray dawn of morning. Half an hour more brought us to Uniontown, at the western side of the Alleghanies—and glad enough were "all hands" to arrive there.

SHEEPHERDING IN
THE MOUNTAINS

FROM *Honey in the Horn*

H . L . D A V I S

H. L. Davis has been called a literary pioneer on the Oregon Trail. His *Honey in the Horn,* from which this selection has been taken, is happy reading—fresh, fluent, and without any of the heroics or whimsy which beset so many regional novelists. It won him the Harper and Pulitzer prizes.

He says of himself that he "lumbered" through school, worked as a cowboy, sheepherder, deputy sheriff, surveyor, and radio folk singer, and that he "favors a law imposing hanging as a punishment for fanaticism in any form, but has little hope of getting it passed." That is as good a clue to the special quality of both H. L. Davis and his books as anyone can write.

ON THE MORNING THAT THE STORM HIT THE SHEEP-CAMP IN THE MOUNTAINS, A shortage of bedclothes waked Clay Calvert at the exact time when a big coyote paid a before-daylight visit to the sheep to purvey himself a feed of fresh mutton. It was a lucky circumstance, though at the time it didn't seem one, because the purveying process had such an outlandish half-dreamy solemnity about it that he stood and watched it from start to finish without interfering until the sheep was killed and the coyote settled down to load up on her carcass. But merely watching it that far made the mountain sheep-camp seem new and a little disagreeable, so that he didn't feel homesick about leaving; and he learned a couple or three things about the power of intelligence over instinct that stood him in hand a good many times afterward, not merely in handling animals, but in looking out for himself.

The sheep were bedded in a high mountain meadow that was half a swale of red wild snapdragons and half blue-flowering wild pea vine. There were a couple of square miles of open ground in it, walled on three sides by a stand of black fir timber that looked solid until you got within two yards of it and on the fourth by a grove of mountain-ash saplings, fencing a chain of springs that were the headwaters of Little River. The sheep-camp was pitched close to the grove because it was handy to water; but the sheep insisted, principally because nobody wanted them to, upon picking open bed-ground in the middle of the meadow. There was no risk in it during the summer, but in the fall bears sometimes moseyed in to feed on the bitter scarlet berries of the mountain ash, and the herders took turns sleeping out with the sheep to see that they didn't get raided.

Guard duty was not burdensome in clear weather. A man didn't have to make any rounds or do any solitary vigils with his eyes propped open and a gun across his knees. He had only to keep his upper ear cocked for any unusual flurry or scuffling among the sheep, and to remember, whenever he turned over in his blankets, to reach out and lay a chunk or two of wood on the fire so it wouldn't go out. With a little practice one could do that without even waking up.

The herders kept a kind of off-and-on surveillance themselves when it was Clay's turn at it, because he was new to the responsibility; but they didn't watch one another because they were both veterans and touchy about it. Payette Simmons had herded sheep over thirty years, and Serphin Moss, the second herder, for considerably more than twenty. Between the pair of them, Clay got reminded of his inexperience and immaturity about every other time he turned round. It wasn't as if there had been any complicated mysteries about the business. The trouble was that they had both spent a good many more years learning it than their jobs were worth, and it hurt them to let on that anybody could acquire any understanding of it in less time than it had taken them. Their fussing and nosing and volunteering childish orders and supervising childish jobs made them hard to put up with. Clay got up with a chill when there was barely light enough in the tent to see by, and stole himself an extra blanket from old Moss. Before spreading it, he looked out the tent door and saw that the guard-fire was down to a couple of coals and that Payette Simmons had gone sound asleep with the bed-canvas pulled over his bald spot. The sheep were jammed together on account of the chill, and the close-packed yellowish fleeces pitched and heaved restlessly like the top of a forest catching the wind. Outside the pack, a few strays trotted uneasily, looking for an opening to crowd into. Not a sound came from them. They weren't wide awake enough to bawl, and their hoofs were cushioned on a couple of hundred years' accumulation of meadow-grass. The strays bored their way into the herd, which settled into drowsiness, with only one old ewe left moving around them at a worried sort of amble.

She raised her gait to a jog, glanced down at her side, and then put on still more speed, like an old lady being pursued by a cheap pitchman in the street. As she circled the herd she drew farther away from it, and, when her orbit brought her past the tent, Clay saw what ailed her. An old he-coyote was trotting beside her, his shoulder pressed against hers, holding a little back so she would keep trying to get ahead and rubbing her close so her shrinking from him would carry her out of range of the herd that she was working her best lick to get back to. He made no effort to hurry or hurt her; she was still so close to Simmons' guard-fire that he didn't dare to. If she had blatted or turned on him and started a rumpus, she would have been saved. But she was too scared to do anything but avoid him and try to outrun him. She trotted faster, and he let out another hitch of speed and rubbed her as if to remind her that he was still there. When they rounded the herd a second time, he had worked her a quarter of a mile away from it.

The promenade lasted a long time. Clay's legs hurt with cold. The light strengthened, and the sky bloomed full of light rose places where the dawn hit the bellies of black clouds. The sheep and the coyote trotted their round solemnly, pressed close like a pair of small-town lovers on Sunday afternoon, without noticing the daylight or each other. They went behind a stand of tall blue-joint grass, and Clay leaned a pack-saddle against the tent-pole and climbed on it to keep sight of them. When he picked them out, they had stopped. The sheep stood with her legs spraddled and her head dropped so it almost touched the ground, and the coyote stood watching her and waiting for her to look up. There was still time for Clay to have scared him off. A yell would have done it. But he held in because he didn't want to face a lifetime of wondering what the coyote had intended to do next, and because if he stopped the killing Simmons and Moss would claim it was all a yarn he had made up himself. He leaned against the tent-pole and waited, knowing perfectly what was going to happen, but willing to freeze his very liver to see how.

It was scarcely worth waiting for. As ceremonious as the preparation had been, the slaughter happened with no ceremony at all. The sheep lifted her head and the coyote trotted close and cut her throat with one swift open-fanged swipe. She knelt, folding her knees under her a good deal like the Lamb in pictures of the Holy Family, and died. It was so simple and she was so quiet about it that it scarcely seemed a finish to anything. But it was one, as the coyote proceeded to demonstrate sickeningly and unquestionably. He took a good long look around, and then dropped his muzzle and lapped the fresh blood under the sheep's chin.

The motion, as far as the coyote was concerned, was merely one of cashing in on a good morning's work. But it knocked the pictorial stateliness of the preliminaries plumb in the head. Clay didn't want to watch it, but he couldn't keep his eyes off it. To put a stop to it so he could go back to bed and get warm, he reached down Moss's rifle from the tent-pole and threw down and shot.

He didn't look at the sights, because he scarcely cared whether he hit the coyote or not. All he wanted was to make the brute leave. But the gun was a specially stocked one that Moss had bought for winter fur-gathering, and it handled so beautifully that it didn't need aiming. The bullet drove center with a smack. The coyote bounced a couple of feet in the air and hit the ground with his legs jerking slowly like a piece of machinery running down. The ordinary marksman's impulse would have been to gallop across and see where the bullet had connected and what damage it had done. Clay hung the rifle back on the tent-pole and climbed down from the pack-saddle. He wished he hadn't shot at all, because, in the moment that he pulled trigger, the coyote reminded him of Wade Shiveley, whom he had imagined he was shut of for good.

Both herders woke up at the shot. Serphin Moss reared up against the tent roof and grabbed his boots, yelling at old Simmons, who he supposed had done the shooting, to inquire what the dod-damn it was and whether he had dot it. Moss was long-faced and candid-looking with an expression which long years of herding had subdued almost to what he worked with. He looked so much like a sheep himself that when he opened his mouth you half expected him to blat, and he generally half did it. Payette Simmons was an older man with a considerably better flow of language, though he didn't use it for much except to tell lies with. On ordinary occasions he talked faster than Moss, but in emergencies he didn't talk at all. He bounced up from beside the dead guard-fire, his bald head shining in the cold light, his shirt-tail flapping on his bare stern, and his gray whiskers hackled up behind the sights of his rifle, which he pointed at the tent under the foggy-minded impression that somebody in it had taken a shot at him. Clay gave him no chance to get his head back in working order. When Simmons' thoughts were all hitting the collar together, he could lie himself out of a three-ton safe.

"You can go back under the blankets if you want to, Santa Claus," Clay told him. "It ain't Christmas yet. A coyote just got a sheep, and I got him. Lucky you had your head covered, or he'd have eat your nose off."

He would have had Simmons cured of ordering him around for life if Moss hadn't stuck himself in the tent door to take a hand in gouging it into him. "Yes, pile on back into bed, for Dod's sake," he chipped in, all hearty and sarcastic. "Dit through dreamin' about them doddam women, or you'll lose us every tockwallopin' sheep we doddam well dot."

According to Simmons' own representations, which he spun off by the mile when he felt good, he was a considerable hand as a stud. His gray whiskers didn't match up with his claims, but he explained that they had been caused by the strain of watching women try to kill themselves over him. He also had one lop-lidded eye which, by his account, had been disabled by a female lodge-organizer to keep other women from falling in love with

him. He could invent windies about his stand-in with the girls faster than
a turkey could gobble grasshoppers. None of them had much truth to them,
probably, for he passed among the stump-country roustabouts as a man who
spent his leisure in Mother Settle's straddling-house talking about sheep-
herding, and his work-season in the sheep-camp talking about the women
who had hung onto his shirt-tail to keep him from abandoning them.
Seniority made him the boss herder, and Moss had managed, by chesting
his own authority down on Clay Calvert, to get himself resigned to it;
but he still didn't believe that it was right. Moss himself was too bashful to
patronize Mother Settle's riding-academy, and played the more expensive
game of getting himself a wife through the Heart and Hand matrimonial
bureau as often as he could afford it for as long as she could stand him.
It came to about the same thing when you fractioned it down; but the fact
that Moss spent his money on marriage brokers and preachers and divorce
lawyers meant, to his notion, that he was moral and deserving of responsibility. Simmons squandered his on Mother Settle in smaller installments,
which meant that he was impure and shameless. Could anything be better
proof of it than his having lost a sheep on a worn-out old coyote-trick?
Moss thought not. "That's a hell of a fine fire you been teepin' up out there,
ain't it?" he inquired, sarcastic and glad of the chance. "Dit back into bed
or else put your pants on. You ain't on Front Street in town."

That was piling it on too thick. Instead of making Simmons meek and
humble, it made him mad, and it started the day off in a row with Moss
and Simmons digging on each other, and Clay, who had started the whole
thing, shoved back into the position of referee; not that his opinion
amounted to anything, but because it was the only one they had handy to
work on. Simmons climbed into his pants, ordered the dead sheep skinned
before the meat got to tasting of wool, and added that the next man he heard
any back-talk from had better get ready to draw his time and walk home.
Then he winked at Clay to indicate that the threat didn't apply to him
and made a vulgar gesture with his fingers toward Moss which was Indian
sign-talk to denote a simpleton who ran off at the mouth. Moss didn't get
that, but he muttered confidential opinions about Simmons' debauched
character and crumbling intellect all the way out to the dead sheep and all
the time they were working the hide loose.

They were skinning out the forelegs when a few flakes of snow fell on the
warm stripped meat between them, and Simmons yelled to them to give it
up and run in the horses. They were going to pull camp and move before
the storm hit, and there was no time to fool around about it. The air was
as dark as twilight, and tree outlines a mile away had gone out in a black
smudge like something scrubbed off a slate. But even in that Moss found an
excuse to bellyache, because they had been hectored off to pelt out a dad-

blasted forty cents' worth of second-rate mutton when any dod-damned fool might have known that there was a snowstorm working down on them.

The horses were forehobbled and easy to catch, and Simmons had the beds rolled and the canvas *alforjas* packed by the time they came crow-hopping in. The sheep needed only to be lined out and started moving, because the coyote had bunched them as competently as any herd-dog could have done. Each man singed a mammock of mutton on a stick and ate it in the empty tent, and then they struck and rolled it. It seemed almost like stripping something naked to expose the square of brown earth where they had come for meals and sleep and rest and shelter until, because it was used for a different purpose, it had got to seem a different species of ground from anything around it. Turning it back out-of-doors showed how little difference their living on it had made, after all. None, except that they had worn the grass down so the whirl of snowflakes turned it white while the deeper-grown meadow was still only a brindlish gray.

There was a good deal of cussing and yelling and chasing around about leaving, but there was no regretfulness. The herders had done it too many times, and they knew too well what they were getting out of. A storm so near the summit of the mountains could pile up snow from six to ten feet deep. As for Clay Calvert, the place was spoiled for him. The sheep-killing and the dead coyote had turned him against it. He felt every minute as if he was breathing a wind off Wade Shiveley. Clay hadn't felt any overmastering surge of affection for either of the Shiveley brothers, but he had liked the one who got killed the best, and he felt scared and sickened of Wade for having killed him.

They got the sheep moving with an hour's spanking and kicking and screeching and throwing rocks while the snow thickened. Then they lined the pack-horses in front and plodded across the clearing into the dark wall of timber, leading their saddle-ponies behind. When they looked back at the meadow, it had turned all white, and nobody could have told that they had ever been there. Even the dead ewe and the dead coyote were white humps that might have been snowed-in bushes. There was an easy and reassuring feeling about knowing that they were being put out of sight so peacefully. Wildness had destroyed them; now it was getting to work to cover up the mess and all the messes it had made during all that year in the mountains. Deer crippled by cougars, wild cattle hurt fighting among themselves, hawk-struck grouse, stiff-jointed old dog-wolves waiting in some deep thicket for death to hit them and get it over with. The snow would cover them, more snow would fall and cover them deeper, and when spring came it would melt and the freshets would carry what was left of them away. Even the bones wouldn't last, because the little wood-mice would gnaw them down to the last nub.

They trailed down through heavy timber all that day, and made camp, when it was too dark to see, by spreading the tent over some huckleberry bushes and crawling under it. The sheep lay down in their tracks, too tired to browse, because deep pasture had put more tallow on their ribs than they were built to pack. The trail hadn't been particularly hard, because the snow hadn't yet started sliding from the trees into it. There was not room under the tent for more than one bed, so all three men slept in it, Clay in the middle and Moss and Simmons on the outside, squabbling and arguing back and forth across him. Whenever he tried to sleep, they would wake him up to prove something by; and when he stayed awake and ordered them to shut up they would ignore him completely. Moss maintained that the sheep were going to be lost and that it would be Simmons' fault for not having started them out sooner. Simmons insisted that he had started in plenty of time and that if he lost them it would be Moss's fault for throwing off on him.

The second day's trail was harder. Trees dripping turned the ground into red greasy mud, and horses kept going down in it and having to be unpacked before they could get up. There were also clearings where the snow had drifted in a couple of feet deep, and the sheep, whenever they struck one, would either break back for the timber or give up and lie down. The two herders had to kick them up and keep them moving while Clay broke a trail across for them. He chopped down a small fir tree, looped his rope into the top branches, and rode through, dragging it behind him. Where the snow was wet and heavy, he had to drag back and forth three or four times to wear off a track that the sheep would tackle, and the herders would be almost worn out with work before he was ready for them. They would come wallowing across with the sheep, slipping and falling and crawling and cussing one another in a kind of windbroken cackle as if they were getting ready to cry.

Nothing but personal ill-feeling could have made those two herders put in the work they did to keep the sheep moving. They cared nothing about the sheep or about old Shiveley, and they were legally assured of getting paid off, whether they came in with all the sheep or ten or none. But they wanted to work each other down, and they fought brush and climbed logs and fell into stump-holes and carried broken-down strays into line on their backs, and, at a couple of clearings where the herd got halfway out and balked, they simply got down and boosted, like a couple of logging-engines horsing a string of flats up a grade. By the second night they had got to the small-timber belt well down the mountain. They camped in a deserted post-camp on Plum Creek. The sheep lay in wet snow and went for another night without anything to eat. The next day they dropped below the snow-storm into hazel-brush country where it was raining, and the sheep began to take spells of balking and lying down on the open trail.

It was about time. For two days they had traveled without food, their wind and strength were shot and their fleeces water-soaked and loaded with mud till their bellies dragged their tracks. Half a mile of shoving through dripping brush and soapy mountain mud fetched them to the ground as if they had been clubbed, and no amount of heaving and hauling could get them up again until they had blown and rested. The two herders tried plenty of it, and Clay helped until he saw that they were working merely because neither wanted to be the first to quit. After that he sat under a bush with the horses when the herd stalled, and let the two bull-headed old reprobates have both the work and the argument to themselves. It was hard to tell which wasted the most time, but the argument gave them the most satisfaction. Simmons brought up the string-halted old story about one of Moss's Heart and Hand wives, who, after comparing him with the photograph he had sent her, chased him down the road with a grubbing-hoe, explaining to everybody she passed that she was going to fix his face to match his picture; and Moss recalled the time when Simmons had made one of Mother Settle's veteran boarders a birthday present of a pink silk corset, and that she had raised considerable hell around town about it because it was of a design intended to disguise impending maternity.

That was the worst day of all, and the worst night followed it. The fir timber got small and then changed into alder and willow. About dark they dragged clear of that and struck open country, with a last streak of watery light breaking circles in the flooded stubble before them. Beyond was a rise, with the black rails of a stack-yard corral making a rib-bone pattern on the sky. The stage-station itself was maybe eight miles off, but it was all open going. They could see the yellow dot of a lamp in one of the windows, and Clay had to grab ropes and mill the pack-horses to keep them from stampeding for it. Even the sheep brisked up, broke line, and jounced into the water, ignoring the herders who tried to hold them and hunt up a shallow place to cross. Both men jumped in after them. Moss grabbed his chaps from his saddle and whacked heads, trying to drive them back before they got in too deep. Simmons yanked a limb off a tree and spanked tails with it to get them across with a rush before they got time to think how deep it was. Clay fought the horses to a standstill and jumped down to help, but he was too late. An old ewe let out a resigned blat and knelt, and, with the trustfulness of wild geese settling to a pond behind their leader in the night, the whole herd caved down around her. They lay still, with the muddy water swishing as it roiled round them and worked into their wool.

This time they meant it for keeps. Moss and Simmons flogged and kicked and whacked the water to scare them, and Clay tried throwing them out bodily. But the ones who were in stayed in, and the ones who got helped out simply came back in and lay down again. It was jesusly hard work, waist-deep in mud with the rain and dark and weariness. Nobody would have minded if it had shown signs of getting them anywhere, because it would have been something to brag about afterward; but it was all useless. The sheep had decided to die, and there was no way of scaring them out of the notion, because there was nothing worse that they could be scared with.

HAYMAKING IN THE ALPS

FROM *Tyrolean Journal*

C . HENRY WARREN

Most travelers see no more than the surface aspects of the life of the people they visit. Occasionally they are witness to the more apparent troubles and joys. But few travelers have any awareness of the smaller tragedies and more intimate pleasures which make up the daily round of life and work. In this selection from his *Tyrolean Journal,* a record of a happy Alpine year, C. Henry Warren writes with sympathy and understanding of the mountain peasant at haymaking.

Warren is a countryman both by work and avocation. He lives in the country, writes of the countryside and gardens for recreation.

June 23. THROUGHOUT THE SULTRY MORNING THE HAYMAKERS WERE AT WORK. Every hour of dry weather has to be snatched now, for the grass gets tougher in the stalk every day. It was a rather frantic haymaking: everybody knew that this morning's scowling sunshine boded no good: we should be lucky if we got through the day without a storm. However, by noon many hundred more "hay men" had been added to the already considerable ranks deployed across the valley. But after dinner, I noticed, only those farmers returned who had not yet been able to cock all their cut hay. They seemed to know what was coming. And then, very early in the afternoon, the clouds began to pile up. One could see the rain already in the mountains, and sudden flicks of wind foretold the storm. The haymakers hurried to fork the last hay on to the crosses before fleeing for shelter, with scythes and forks shining in the glowering light. They were away only just in time.

The storm broke with a ferocity the like of which I have never known. The valley was soon completely obscured. There were no raindrops, only a grey, blinding sheet of water. Even the lightning could not pierce it to reveal the hidden haycocks. The storm seemed to rush towards the Wetterstein, which drew it like a magnet; and the thunder that cracked overhead suggested that the rocks were splitting wide open. It was no longer a storm, it was a cloudburst. And in half an hour it was all over. But in that time we had been not so much rained on as buried under seas of rain.

Even so, it was not until the skies had cleared a little and I had gone outside, that I realized just how much water had fallen in that little while. Behind the house there was a roar in the forest like an express train approaching. For the moment I was dumbfounded: it was a sound I shall never forget, elemental, terrifying. And then, looking up, I saw the face of the Wetterstein streaming and shining with water as if it were one gigantic waterfall. And all this water was collecting and pouring down through the forest to the valley with a speed and a menace thrilling to hear. Good reason then had Ehrwald to thank those engineers who had built the great stone and concrete channels through which the flood poured—built them for just such an emergency as this. Strangers invariably comment with surprise when they see those strongly constructed channels leading down from the Wetterstein to the valley. Mostly only a trickle of water flows through them, lost among the scattered rocks and stones; and even when the snows melt in spring, the amount of water is quite out of proportion to their size and strength. But to-day's cloudburst explains all. Without their safeguard there would now be disaster in the village. Mixed with earth and rock and stone, the flood was more like lava than water; and the noise of it was heard all over the village, bringing men, women and children, some on bicycles, some hurrying on foot, to see the wonder.

Standing by the brown cataract, one had to shout to make oneself heard. An old peasant farmer was beside me, his hay-fork still hoisted over his shoulder, his features tense with excitement. Five years ago, he said, there had been a similar cloudburst on the Wetterstein, and the damage up there (he was referring to the repair work necessitated in the channels from time to time) had cost thousands of schillings. "You wouldn't think so much water could fall out of the skies in that little time," he said. He turned his back on the flood and looked over the drenched meadows. "As for our hay," he began; but he got no further, as if no words would touch even the fringe of what he was feeling. The grass lay flat. The ground beneath it was a bog. The old man pointed with his fork to the strip where he had been working when the storm came up. Never did hay look more dreary; however, he had managed to get it cocked, and that was something. "But," he said, "I have five other strips, and not one of them is cut yet. It's a catastrophe." We left the crowd by the roaring flood and walked some of the way home together. "I've known some bad seasons in my day," the old man continued, "but this looks like being worse than any. Nothing has gone right from the start. A freeze-up in May; snow in June; and now this!" Farmers are traditionally a pessimistic lot, and sometimes I think the Tyrolean peasant farmer tops them all. This year, however, there really is something to be pessimistic about. . . .

July 3–5. When I was in the Stubai valley last October, I promised myself, and Herr Falbesonner, that I would come again before I left the Tyrol. Time was getting short, and so I arranged to go right away. I could not have chosen a worse time: the rain fell ceaselessly, from beginning to end of my brief stay. In that steep, narrow valley, I had hoped, I would see the hay-making as it really is in the mountains, where the fields fall at so sharp an angle that the grass has to be carried on the back in panniers and the scythesmen must wear crampons as they mow.

In fact, the thing I recall most vividly about those three blind, rainy days is a pair of bare feet in the wet grass. For they were no ordinary feet, and they seemed, somehow, to epitomize both the disastrous weather and the hard lot of those mountain peasants who had to battle with it. The feet belonged to one of the three young men who were scything an almost perpendicular slope of grassland. There was, of course, for them, nothing exceptional about this: most of the haymaking in the Stubaital has to be done on slopes that would seem to the stranger to render such a job all but impossible. Two of these young men wore the usual crampons, to give their feet a grip on the incline; but this one apparently preferred to trust in his own feet. They were about level with my eyes as I stood in the rain watching the trio work down the steep slope in echelon, their scythes swishing through grass that was so wet it sounded more like rushes than grass. Maybe they were not the feet to delight a sculptor of classical form; they were big and crusty, they were hard and well-arched; and if there was anything beautiful about them it was the beauty of sheer adaptability. They gripped the earth like great hands. Years of going up and down these mountain-sides had given them a knotty strength; and just now the bright wet grass and flowers, brushing against the dark, red-brown skin, emphasized their strength by juxtaposition. They seemed to me, far more than the crampons on the other men's feet, to sum up the harsh life's work of the mountain peasant, whom no machine can help. Every blade of grass, for the cattle by which they live, must be cut and carried the hard way—scythed, as these young men were scything it, on slopes that were nearly perpendicular, and then carried in stout panniers strapped on the back. Yet they seemed to think nothing of it. When they came down to the narrow, muddy path where I stood, they laughed at my interest. Relaxing for a moment they stood there, hats pushed back from weather-tanned faces, eyes bright as raindrops, answering my questions about their work and, in return, asking me how the grass was harvested in England. Then they shouldered their scythes and clambered easily up the slope again. For a while they stood clear against the sky, honing their blades, until, with a smile and a farewell, they bent to the job, scything in slow, steady strokes.

It was on the way back, where the path entered the forest, that I came upon one of those naïve, ex-voto paintings—*Marterl* is the local name for them—which have been put up by the peasants on the scene of some accident in which a friend or relative was killed. These paintings, done on wood and as graphically representative as a child's, are both memorials and warnings. They are a feature here, as they also are in Bavaria, over the border; and this was one of the best I have seen. It was in memory of a local villager, who, in 1884, had been bringing a load of wood down the mountain when he had been killed. There he was, stretched full-length on the ground beside the ox-drawn load of timber. Close behind came his wife, her hands raised in horror, while their little son, as children do, stood looking on, seemingly quite detached and unmoved. For nearly seventy years this painting had hung here, fastened to a tree, but the weather had not much harmed it: the stolid ox and the horrified woman, in particular, were as clear and fresh as if they had been painted yesterday. Underneath was a crucifix, as usual, into which pious hands had tucked a bunch of *Almrauschen:* perhaps some relative had put them there, or some climber, coming down from the mountains, had pulled them from his rucksack and made an offering of them.

I confess I always find these wayside peasant-paintings rather moving, not only for the childlike *naïveté* with which the incident is depicted but also for the simple faith they express: who pauses to read the bare record and gaze on the painted scene may perhaps be prompted to add a prayer for all who, in the course of their daily work, may fall into danger, as this woodman had done. Simple they are—the act and gesture of a child—and that is their virtue. They are no more irrelevant today than they were a hundred years ago, for at heart every genuine peasant is still a child. (The young scythesman's feet were the feet of a giant, but his eyes, bright and unequivocal, were the eyes of a child.)

Were a similar fashion to prevail today, the scene recorded would almost certainly involve a motor-car, with, as likely as not, an implied recklessness on somebody's part. But the *Marterl* is, almost without exception, concerned with somebody who lost his life in the ordinary course of his daily work, bringing down wood from the forest, as this man was doing, or felling trees, or sledging hay over icy tracks in midwinter, or scything grass on the steep slopes, as I had watched them doing half an hour ago. As I walked away from the crucifix, while the rain dripped from the trees, I could not but reflect again how little, in the course of the years, the life and work of these mountain peasants has changed its essential character: danger is still inherent in all their routine jobs and is accepted as being in the inevitable course of things. A machine-age has brought them very little amelioration indeed, in so far as their work is concerned. Their trust is still and only in their hands—and God.

November 29. One of the routine jobs for these mountain farmers in winter (it is also one of the most exciting jobs) is that of bringing down the hay from the log-huts on the high slopes where it has been stored since one or other of last season's two hay harvests. The huts are often sited in the most difficult places, wherever, in fact, the farmer's strips happen to be—and that may well be three or more miles from home and perched on almost vertical slopes. While the weather is still open enough, ox or horse will be used to bring down the loads of hay; but once the snow has arrived, the only possible way to get it in is by sledge, stoutly built to stand the strain and far too big, you would suppose, for the farmer to pull. Yet pull it he does, harnessed to it like an ox. The harness consists of broad straps of leather, riveted together, which he fastens over his shoulders and round his waist. Slowly he makes his way up the steep mountain-side, through the deep snow, dragging his heavy (though as yet empty) sledge behind him, and using a strong, sloping stride, his body swinging from the hips with every pull. His eyes are fixed on the track at his feet, his whole self is centred on the physical effort of pulling the sledge up the steep slopes. But at last he arrives at the hut, and, with scarcely a pause (so well has he conserved his strength all the way), he begins to load the sledge, using a fine knack in doing so, lest it should topple over on the way home, with disastrous results.

A full load, lodged securely between the two uprights attached to the sledge, back and front, will be as much as seven feet high and four to five feet broad. The last thing to be done is to rope the load together, and then the fun begins. The farmer slips the harness over his shoulders, gives the sledge a sharp pull or two to get it on the move downhill, and then, squatting almost on his haunches and digging his heels into the snow, he slithers down the track with the whole weight of the load pressing hard on to his back. All his lifelong prowess in travelling over deep snow, whether by ski, sleigh, sledge, or nothing but his iron-shod boots, now comes to his aid as he steers his heavy cargo so unerringly round the bends and curves of the track, often at an incredible speed, till at last he reaches the more or less level road home through the village. It is strenuous and exciting work, but the Tyrolean farmer enjoys it: here is one more opportunity for the exercise of that sporting instinct which he shares with all his fellow-countrymen. It can also be dangerous work—but not so dangerous as it is when wood, and not hay, makes up the sledge-load. Then the great logs, piled with even finer skill and care, require the trickiest handling: the united strength of two men will be required to get the sledge on the move. But the danger comes when

the sledge gathers momentum. The tragic instance is still fresh in memory
here of a young farmer who, last year, was coming down a steep slope from
the forest with a load of wood when it got out of control, and a broken neck
was the immediate result.

It is always a pleasant thing to come on these loads of hay as they slither
through the village street on their way to the farmers' stalls. Six months have
gone by since the first hay harvest; and yet, when the hay is brought into the
village today, it is still astonishingly green and quite unlike our stacked hay
at home. In that hot sunshine it is much more quickly made, which is one
reason: another may be the fact that it is stored loose in the airy log huts.
However it may be, the result, as the loads of green hay ride the white snow,
is strangely incongruous. The piercingly fragrant scent of the sapless stalks
and burnt flower-heads brings to the cold white scene a whiff of summer.

MOUNTAIN GLOBE FLOWER

HOLY ROLLERS

FROM *Deep in the Coca-Cola Belt*

HENRY L. MENCKEN

The generation of the 1920's was a short-lived but merry one—articulate, contentious, and heretic. Iconoclasm was its religion and Henry L. Mencken its prophet. Perhaps the high point in this noisy period was the Monkey Trial. The state of Tennessee had passed a law making it a crime for any teacher in the state "to teach the theory that denied the story of the divine creation of man as taught in the Bible." Here was a fantastic legal battle in this sleepy southern town of Dayton, Tennessee: William Jennings Bryan, three times almost president of the United States, attorney for the Bible; Clarence Darrow, pleader for unpopular causes, counsel for the theory of evolution. It was a circus for the world. And Mencken, the gadfly, came to report it for the Baltimore *Sun*. Mencken could have invented no happier subject for his stinging rhetoric. While the trial was in progress, he visited a Holy Roller revival in the mountains behind Dayton. Here is his comment on the proceedings.

The Sun, Baltimore, July 13, 1925

Dayton, Tennessee, July 13—THERE IS A UNITARIAN CLERGYMAN HERE FROM New York, trying desperately to horn into the trial and execution of the infidel Scopes. He will fail. If Darrow ventured to put him on the stand the whole audience, led by the jury, would leap out of the courthouse windows and take to the hills. Darrow himself, indeed, is as much as they can bear. The whisper that he is an atheist has been stilled by the bucolic make-up and by the public report that he has the gift of prophecy and can reconcile Genesis and evolution. Even so, there is ample space about him when he navigates the streets. The other day a newspaperwoman was warned by her landlady to keep out of the courtroom when he was on his legs. All the local sorcerers predict that a bolt from heaven will fetch him in the end. The night he arrived there was a violent storm, the town water turned brown, and horned cattle in the lowlands were afloat for hours. A woman back in the mountains gave birth to a child with hair four inches long, curiously bobbed in scallops.

The Book of Revelation has all the authority, in these theological uplands, of military orders in time of war. The people turn to it for light upon all their problems, spiritual and secular. If a text were found in it denouncing the antievolution law, then the antievolution law would become infamous overnight. But so far the exegetes who roar and snuffle in the town have found no such text. Instead they have found only blazing ratifications and reinforcements of Genesis. Darwin is the devil with seven tails and nine horns. Scopes, though he is disguised by flannel pantaloons and a Beta Theta Pi haircut, is the harlot of Babylon. Darrow is Beelzebub in person, and Malone is the Crown Prince Friedrich Wilhelm.

I have hitherto hinted an Episcopalian down here in the Coca-Cola belt is regarded as an atheist. It sounds like one of the lies that journalists tell, but it is really an understatement of the facts. Even a Methodist, by Rhea County standards, is one a bit debauched by pride of intellect. It is the four Methodists on the jury who are expected to hold out for giving Scopes Christian burial after he is hanged. They all made it plain, when they were examined, that they were freethinking and independent men, and not to be run amuck by the superstitions of the lowly. One actually confessed that he seldom read the Bible, though he hastened to add that he was familiar with its principles. The fellow had on a boiled shirt and a polka-dot necktie. He sits somewhat apart. When Darrow withers to a cinder under the celestial blowpipe, this dubious Wesleyan, too, will lose a few hairs.

Even the Baptists no longer brew a medicine that is strong enough for the mountaineers. The sacrament of baptism by total immersion is over too quickly for them, and what follows offers nothing that they can get their teeth into. What they have is a continuous experience of the divine power, an endless series of evidence that the true believer is a marked man, ever under the eye of God. It is not enough to go to a revival once a year or twice a year; there must be a revival every night. And it is not enough to accept the truth as a mere statement of indisputable and awful fact; it must be embraced ecstatically and orgiastically, to the accompaniment of loud shouts, dreadful heavings and gurglings, and dancing with arms and legs.

This craving is satisfied brilliantly by the gaudy practices of the Holy Rollers, and so the mountaineers are gradually gravitating toward the Holy Roller communion, or, as they prefer to call it, the Church of God. Gradually, perhaps, is not the word. They are actually going in by whole villages and townships. At the last count of noses there were 20,000 Holy Rollers in these hills. The next census, I have no doubt, will show many more. The cities of the lowlands, of course, still resist, and so do most of the county towns, including even Dayton, but once one steps off the state roads the howl of holiness is heard in the woods, and the yokels carry on an almost continuous orgy.

A foreigner in store clothes going out from Dayton must approach the sacred grove somewhat discreetly. It is not that the Holy Rollers, discovering him, would harm him; it is simply that they would shut down their boiling of the devil and flee into the forests. We left Dayton an hour after nightfall and parked our car in a wood a mile or so beyond the little hill village of Morgantown. Far off in a glade a flickering light was visible and out of the silence came a faint rumble of exhortation. We could scarcely distinguish the figure of the preacher; it was like looking down the tube of a dark field microscope. We got out of the car and sneaked along the edge of a mountain cornfield.

Presently we were near enough to see what was going on. From the great limb of a mighty oak hung a couple of crude torches of the sort that car inspectors thrust under Pullman cars when a train pulls in at night. In their light was a preacher, and for a while we could see no one else. He was an immensely tall and thin mountaineer in blue jeans, his collarless shirt open at the neck and his hair a tousled mop. As he preached he paced up and down under the smoking flambeaux and at each turn he thrust his arms into the air and yelled, "Glory to God!" We crept nearer in the shadow of the cornfield and began to hear more of his discourse. He was preaching on the day of judgment. The high kings of the earth, he roared, would all fall down and die; only the sanctified would stand up to receive the Lord God of Hosts. One of these kings he mentioned by name—the king of what he called Greece-y. The King of Greece-y, he said, was doomed to hell.

We went forward a few more yards and began to see the audience. It was seated on benches ranged round the preacher in a circle. Behind him sat a row of elders, men and women. In front were the younger folk. We kept on cautiously, and individuals rose out of the ghostly gloom. A young mother sat suckling her baby, rocking as the preacher paced up and down. Two scared little girls hugged each other, their pigtails down their backs. An immensely huge mountain woman, in a gingham dress cut in one piece, rolled on her heels at every "Glory to God." On one side, but half visible, was what appeared to be a bed. We found out afterward that two babies were asleep upon it.

The preacher stopped at last and there arose out of the darkness a woman with her hair pulled back into a little tight knot. She began so quietly that we couldn't hear what she said, but soon her voice rose resonantly and we could follow her. She was denouncing the reading of books. Some wandering book agent, it appeared, had come to her cabin and tried to sell her a specimen of his wares. She refused to touch it. Why, indeed, read a book? If what was in it was true, then everything in it was already in the Bible. If it was false, then reading it would imperil the soul. Her syllogism complete, she sat down.

There followed a hymn, led by a somewhat fat brother wearing silver-rimmed country spectacles. It droned on for a half a dozen stanzas, and then the first speaker resumed the floor. He argued that the gift of tongues was real and that education was a snare. Once his children could read the Bible, he said, they had enough. Beyond lay only infidelity and damnation. Sin stalked the cities. Dayton itself was a Sodom. Even Morgantown had begun to forget God. He sat down, and the female aurochs in gingham got up.

She began quietly, but was soon leaping and roaring, and it was hard to follow her. Under cover of the turmoil we sneaked a bit closer. A couple of other discourses followed, and there were two or three hymns. Suddenly a change of mood began to make itself felt. The last hymn ran longer than the others and dropped gradually into a monotonous, unintelligible chant. The leader beat time with his book. The faithful broke out with exultations. When the singing ended there was a brief palaver that we could not hear and two of the men moved a bench into the circle of light directly under the flambeaux. Then a half-grown girl emerged from the darkness and threw herself upon it. We noticed with astonishment that she had bobbed hair. "This sister," said the leader, "has asked for prayers." We moved a bit closer. We could now see faces plainly and hear every word.

What followed quickly reached such heights of barbaric grotesquerie that it was hard to believe it real. At a signal all the faithful crowded up to the bench and began to pray—not in unison, but each for himself. At another they all fell on their knees, their arms over the penitent. The leader kneeled, facing us, his head alternately thrown back dramatically or buried in his hands. Words spouted from his lips like bullets from a machine gun—appeals to God to pull the penitent back out of hell, defiances of the powers and principalities of the air, a vast impassioned jargon of apocalyptic texts. Suddenly he rose to his feet, threw back his head, and began to speak in tongues—blub-blub-blub, gurgle-gurgle-gurgle. His voice rose to a higher register. The climax was a shrill, inarticulate squawk, like that of a man throttled. He fell headlong across the pyramid of supplicants.

A comic scene? Somehow, no. The poor half-wits were too horribly in earnest. It was like peeping through a knothole at the writhings of a people in pain. From the squirming and jabbering mass a young woman gradually detached herself—a woman not uncomely, with a pathetic homemade cap on her head. Her head jerked back, the veins of her neck swelled, and her fists went to her throat as if she were fighting for breath. She bent backward until she was like a half of a hoop. Then she suddenly snapped forward. We caught a flash of the whites of her eyes. Presently her whole body began to be convulsed—great convulsions that began at the shoulders and ended at the hips. She would leap to her feet, thrust her arms in air, and then hurl herself upon the heap. Her praying flattened out into a mere delirious caterwauling, like that of a tomcat on a petting party.

I describe the thing as a strict behaviorist. The lady's subjective sensations I leave to infidel pathologists. Whatever they were they were obviously contagious, for soon another damsel joined her, and then another and then a fourth. The last one had an extraordinarily bad attack. She began with mild enough jerks of the head, but in a moment she was bounding all over the place, exactly like a chicken with its head cut off. Every time her head came up a stream of yells and barking would issue out of it. Once she collided with a dark, undersized brother, hitherto silent and stolid. Contact with her set him off as if he had been kicked by a mule. He leaped into the air, threw back his head, and began to gargle as if with a mouthful of BB shot. Then he loosened one tremendous stentorian sentence in the tongues and collapsed.

By this time the performers were quite oblivious to the profane universe. We left our hiding and came up to the little circle of light. We slipped into the vacant seats on one of the rickety benches. The heap of mourners was directly before us. They bounced into us as they cavorted. The smell that they radiated, sweating there in that obscene heap, half suffocated us. Not all of them, of course, did the thing in the grand manner. Some merely moaned and rolled their eyes. The female ox in gingham flung her great hulk on the ground and jabbered an unintelligible prayer. One of the men, in the intervals between fits, put on his spectacles and read his Bible.

Beside me on the bench sat the young mother and her baby. She suckled it through the whole orgy, obviously fascinated by what was going on, but never venturing to take any hand in it. On the bed just outside the light two other babies slept peacefully. In the shadows, suddenly appearing and as suddenly going away, were vague figures, whether of believers or of scoffers I do not know. They seemed to come and go in couples. Now and then a couple at the ringside would step back and then vanish into the black night. After a while some came back. There was whispering outside the circle of vision. A couple of Fords lurched up in the wood road, cutting holes in the darkness with their lights. Once someone out of sight loosed a bray of laughter.

All this went on for an hour or so. The original penitent, by this time, was buried three deep beneath the heap. One caught a glimpse, now and then, of her yellow bobbed hair, but then she would vanish again. How she breathed down there I don't know; it was hard enough ten feet away, with a strong five-cent cigar to help. When the praying brothers would rise up for a bout with the tongues their faces were streaming with perspiration. The fat harridan in gingham sweated like a longshoreman. Her hair got loose and fell down over her face. She fanned herself with her skirt. A powerful mortal she was, equal in her day to obstetrics and a week's washing on the same morning, but this was worse than a week's washing. Finally, she fell in a heap, breathing in great, convulsive gasps.

We tired of it after a while and groped our way back to our automobile. When we got to Dayton, after eleven o'clock—an immensely late hour for these parts—the whole town was still gathered on the courthouse lawn, hanging upon the disputes of theologians. The Bible champion of the world had a crowd. The Seventh Day Adventist missionaries had a crowd. A volunteer from faraway Portland, Oregon, made up exactly like Andy Gump, had another and larger crowd. Dayton was enjoying itself. All the usual rules were suspended and the curfew bell was locked up. The prophet Bryan, exhausted by his day's work for Revelations, was snoring in his bed up the road, but enough volunteers were still on watch to keep the battlements manned.

Such is human existence among the fundamentalists, where children are brought up on Genesis and sin is unknown. If I have made the tale too long, then blame the spirit of garrulity that is in the local air. Even newspaper reporters, down here, get some echo of the call. Divine inspiration is as common as the hookworm. I have done my best to show you what the great heritage of mankind comes to in regions where the Bible is the beginning and end of wisdom, and the mountebank Bryan, parading the streets in his seersucker coat, is pointed out to sucklings as the greatest man since Abraham.

RIP VAN WINKLE AWAKENING

OIL IN THE ANDES

FROM *Green Hell*

JULIAN DUGUID

Julian Duguid is that fortunate traveler who can re-create for the reader not alone places and people but the mood and excitement of an exploratory voyage to a little-known part of the world. His writing is quick and active and he spares the so frequently ill-used reader those tedious scenic descriptions which are always hurried over guiltily.

The expedition to the jungle country of Bolivia was to survey and film the forest areas, but, admits the author, these were weighty and official reasons to justify a *wanderlust* and venture into this fantastic country, the Switzerland of South America, nine-tenths of whose people live on the tops and sides of the high Andes.

UP TO A FEW YEARS AGO A RAGING WILDERNESS LAY TO THE SOUTH AND WEST OF the Waters of Death. It lay to the east as well, of course, and so it does to this day, but it was in the slanting forests of the Andean foothills that the Chiriguano Indians, keening like ghosts, harried the Spaniards with flame and arrow to the memory of Atahualpa. A narrow, tree-girt road twisted along the valley as far as the Argentine border, but it was a bold man who faced it when every yard was a potential ambush. To a nervous muleteer the silence must have been appalling.

In their rough and eager way the Chiriguanos were men of humor. Since the days when a mad, white race had dropped from the sky on to the Cordilleras, a black gown and a shaven pate had spelt danger. Captured tribesmen, dying in agony at the stake, had glowered bitterly at the unctuous, mumbled spells, and the clicking waistbands of dark beads with which they passed the remaining moments of their lives. Wherefore, although the natives loathed all foreigners with every muscle of their yellow bodies, they reserved a peculiar and sardonic hatred of the priests; and with the pure joy of Robin Hood castigating prelates, they indulged in a little fun before spitting them to a tree. They jumped out from the shadows like so many prancing fiends, and chased the reverend fathers for miles, until the comic aspect began to pall, and they made an end—eventually. And so the missionaries for the most part ceased to roam and kept behind the stone walls of the monasteries of Tarija and Macheriti.

Religion having retired from the fray, it was left to commerce to open up the district. Somewhere about 1912 a rumor blazed throughout America that deep under the ridged *sierras* of Bolivia there was oil. Instantly the inferno of uncharted forest was invaded by a band of men who held their lives so lightly as to scorn the Chiriguanos. They were spare and slight, northerners for the most part, narrow of feature, tough and resilient as whalebone. Drawn from every nation of the world they gathered under the joint banners of the United States and the Standard Oil Company of New Jersey, and wandered out alone among the hills. For six months at a stretch they clambered and slipped and wrestled with Green Hell, breaking off bits of mountains and entering the facts in a notebook. They peered about for seepages—which are never directly above the oil field, but are diagonal backwashes from a layer some miles away—and grew daily leaner. They called themselves with characteristic modesty, geologists. I met one of them, a grave, pinched man, a little white about the temples, but when he tried to tell me of his job the loneliness had dried the words out of him. I expressed wonder that he could enjoy so grim a vigil in a country where trees grow like bristles on the faces of sheer cliffs. Drily he smiled:

"It's a good life on the whole," he said. "Better than a pot belly, anyway." . . .

Early next day we began the ascent. A pleasant freshness lingered in the trees, and as we wound in and out along the broad mule path, the sound of splashing water disturbed the great silence. Thirty or forty times a cascade dropped on to the track and fell bubbling into the rocky depths hundreds of feet below. A green, majestic emptiness, heightened by the cool shadows, set off our own insignificance, and made us realize the gigantic labor that had gone to the building of the road. Slowly we mounted.

At four thousand feet we emerged from the tree-line, and, like swimmers breaking surface after a dive, we gasped at our freedom from Green Hell. For six strenuous months we had plowed our way through the hills and thickets of the forests; our lungs had grown accustomed to the strange, dead atmosphere of decay; and our eyes had almost forgotten the existence of space. Now we stood and wondered, and our feelings might have been compared to those of prisoners long buried in the Bastille on climbing Notre Dame after their release.

In an angle of the path with the noise of water in our ears we looked out across the rolling leagues of the Gran Chaco. It was a brilliant day, and we could see for a hundred miles beyond the wooded folds of mountains that twined about our feet. Mile upon mile of silent, motionless green tapestry, it stretched away to the horizon that was slightly blurred by heat. To the southward the silver snake of the Rio Pilcomayo uncurled itself in the sunlight, only to be lost in the marshes beyond before it pitched over the edge of our vision. Suddenly, a stone rattled at my side, and Tiger-Man ran his mule against mine.

"There are five such horizons," he said, "between us and the Rio Paraguay."

Thus simply, as was his wont, the bearded philosopher-hunter showed me the dangers we had been spared. We had traversed the whole of that vast plain, in which streams were few and water holes fewer; we had starved and thirsted and gone without our sleep, and had gloried in the greatness of companionship; and yet it was only at this moment when we saw with the eyes of vultures, that awe, overwhelming and unshakeable, took possession of us. We felt like flies on the surface of the sea.

We sat without moving for twenty minutes in this unaccustomed temper of humility, and then Tiger-Man pointed to the foothills. A little puff of cloud, soft and round and opaque shot out of a concealed valley and started to climb towards us. Another followed, and yet another, until the entire plain was mottled by these curious white billows.

"Wind-dogs," said Tiger-Man. "We must hurry."

Sure enough, within a quarter of an hour, the main army of mist had caught up with the wind-dog vedettes, and the sun went quietly to sleep. In an instant we were isolated, pushing through a moving veil. It was cold and wet as a sea-fog, swirling and tossed, chilling us to the bone. It shut out the perspective of Green Hell, and made us wonder what precipice we should fall down next. The mules, born and bred in the plains, took fright, and whinnied their distress into the unresponsive gloom of the ascent. Soon we were groping in grim earnest, feeling our way along the rock wall, and guided only by the roar of the cascades. A few inches ahead I could see Tiger-Man, a bronze figure in the saddle, trying to induce his animal to walk in a straight line. Then it took to its heels, my mount bolted in sympathy, and for a mile we swept round corners at terrifying speed, until the gradient proved too steep and our beasts breathed themselves to a halt.

Half an hour later, guided by the snorting of a steam-engine, we bumped into the steel triangle of the oil derrick, and demanded lunch.

That afternoon revealed to us a Standard Oil Company in time of stress. As we toiled up the bare mountain from the living huts to the mine, a green and yellow torrent rushed past us down the hill. We followed it to its source, to where it splashed over the steps of the engine shed, and then, high above the racket of machinery, came a burst of nasal oaths. Tempestuous and florid, obviously from the heart, they poured through the cracks in the high, wooden walls, and halted us in our stride, for, deeply as we desired to explore the mysteries of petroleum, we did not wish to prejudice our chances by intrusion at such a moment. Suddenly, while we gazed at each other in disappointment, a glistening, oily head was poked round a corner, and a weary smile welcomed us.

"Guess you're intelligent beings," said a voice which was harsh from thirst. "Just bum around, keep clear of the wheels, and don't ask questions till your wits have done their damnedest. We're busy."

At first, everything seemed pointless in that smelly, din-filled shack. In consequence details piled themselves up in our brains and refused to fall into any ordered scheme. A filthy teapot, broken at the spout, lay on a shelf in the corner. A more than filthy man in overalls swayed on a step-ladder and grasped a handle that was clamped to a thick steel rope, one end of which disappeared into the ground, while the other curled over a pulley at the apex of the triangle, dizzily distant in the sky. With each beat of the engine the rope, taut as a bar, was lifted six inches into the air, and as it bumped down into place the man gave it a deft half turn. Over and over again this happened, and each time it dropped he listened for the sound of the fall with an anxious expression on his face. From time to time a lively, serious-looking native leaped from the floor into a pit that was lined with slimy balks of timber. It was all rather puzzling.

Then, without warning, the American held up his hand, and the engine groaned to a halt. Almost at once another one started, and the rope began to wind itself round a gigantic drum. Our friend came down from his ladder.

"Everything's gone wrong this afternoon," he said cheerfully, "we're in a seam of black shale, and the bit keeps sliding out of the true. The oil has been spurting up the shaft—possibly you met the surplus as you came up the hill. It will happen again before dark, sure as I'm a naturalized American."

By this time our minds had become attuned to the easy problems, and we were ready for technicalities.

"I'm called a tool-pusher," he explained, his lips glued to the spout of the teapot. "Yeah, water gets greasy if it ain't covered. I'm responsible for running a chain of steel pipes plumb vertical into the ground till they connect up with the petroleum, and God help me if I don't keep straight. How do I do it? That's simple. I just stand on that ladder and hold that rotten little handle and make a guess as to what my drill is doing half a mile away, somewhere round where you started to climb this morning."

The light of the true craftsman came into his eyes, and he grinned. "Say, you need imagination in my job."

"How do you know what you're hitting?" asked Tiger-Man.

The American glanced at his wrist watch and walked over to a lever.

"I'll show you in a minute," he said.

Suddenly, out of the depths of the pit, a long, narrow yellow-green cylinder, dripping with oil, shot towards the summit of the triangle, in another second it would have crashed into the peak, but directly the gleam of it emerged, the lever was pulled down and the engine ceased. With intense curiosity we craned our necks and marveled at the majesty of the drill that hung, swaying slightly, half way up the tower.

"Now," said the tool-pusher, "watch me."

He lowered it into the pit and made a sign to the agile Indian. In an incredibly short time the little fellow had unhooked it from the rope and had replaced it with a similar instrument that shone like silver. A turn on the engine and it swung easily at the level of our heads.

"This," remarked the American, "is a valve."

He detached a fish-tailed appendage at the bottom of the cylinder and pressed it home.

"When it reaches the floor, nearly four thousand feet below, this head is driven into the barrel, and the mud squirts into the hollow interior. As you can see, it's twenty-five feet long and pretty wide. Directly I release the pressure the head falls back and the mess is trapped inside. Neat, eh?"

It was—very neat—and we watched the rope uncoil off the drum as it journeyed once more down the shaft. This time we looked at our watches when it started to come up, and it took eight solid minutes to ascend. That little fact more than any other convinced us of the imagination requisite to tool-pushers.

Towards evening, as we stood chatting to our new friend, there came a noise that sent him racing to the shaft. It was a curious sound, midway between a bubble and a hiss, almost as though some one was sucking at an enormous and unclean pipe while waves broke on the shingle. Quickly the disturbance grew, and before we could reach the pit the floor was covered with a seething tide of raw petroleum. We drew back in alarm, for it had the appearance of intense heat, frothing its energy in angry petulance, but when we stooped to dip our fingers it was harsh and cold with a peculiar gritty feeling all of its own. Higher it mounted and still higher, until it was several yards up the triangle in a feathery column of green and yellow foam. We watched entranced, hoping it would prove a real gusher, but the American did something technical and the flood fell away.

On the walk back to the living huts he pointed to a number of ten-foot tanks that made an ugly blot on the mountain.

"Funny birds, Indians," he said. "They know petroleum quite well, both by feel and smell, yet one of 'em tried to swim across that refinery. Naturally, he sank like a rock, and we had to send to the Pilcomayo for a boathook."

TOURISTS AT
SAINT BERNARD

FROM *Little Dorrit*

CHARLES DICKENS

🦅 It seems almost gratuitous to acquaint the reader with Charles Dickens.
The world of characters he created—Oliver Twist, Mr. Micawber, Sarah
Gamp, Martin Chuzzlewit, and a host of others—is one familiar in every
language which has readers. Even his minor characters are memorable,
as evidenced by this selection from *Little Dorrit* which describes an
overnight stay at the Saint Bernard hospice by a Dickensian group of
English tourists.

SEEN FROM THOSE SOLITUDES, AND FROM THE PASS OF THE GREAT SAINT BER-
nard, which was one of them, the ascending Night came up the mountain
like a rising water. When it at last rose to the walls of the convent of the
Great Saint Bernard, it was as if that weather-beaten structure were another
Ark, and floated away upon the shadowy waves.

Darkness, outstripping some visitors on mules, had risen thus to the
rough convent walls, when those travelers were yet climbing the mountain.
As the heat of the glowing day, when they had stopped to drink at the
streams of melted ice and snow, was changed to the searching cold of the
frosty rarefied night air at a great height, so the fresh beauty of the lower
journey had yielded to barrenness and desolation. A craggy track, up which
the mules, in single file, scrambled and turned from block to block, as
though they were ascending the broken staircase of a gigantic ruin, was their
way now. No trees were to be seen, nor any vegetable growth, save a poor
brown scrubby moss, freezing in the chinks of rock. Blackened skeleton
arms of wood by the wayside pointed upward to the convent, as if the ghosts
of former travelers, overwhelmed by the snow, haunted the scene of their
distress. Icicle-hung caves and cellars built for refuges from sudden storms,
were like so many whispers of the perils of the place; never-resting wreaths
and mazes of mist wandered about, hunted by a moaning wind; and snow,
the besetting danger of the mountain, against which all its defenses were
taken, drifted sharply down.

The file of mules, jaded by their day's work, turned and wound slowly up the steep ascent; the foremost led by a guide on foot, in his broad-brimmed hat and round jacket, carrying a mountain staff or two upon his shoulder, with whom another guide conversed. There was no speaking among the string of riders. The sharp cold, the fatigue of the journey, and a new sensation of a catching in the breath, partly as if they had just emerged from very clear crisp water, and partly as if they had been sobbing, kept them silent.

At length, a light on the summit of the rocky staircase gleamed through the snow and mist. The guides called to the mules, the mules pricked up their drooping heads, the travelers' tongues were loosened, and in a sudden burst of slipping, climbing, jingling, clinking, and talking, they arrived at the convent door.

Other mules had arrived not long before, some with peasant-riders and some with goods, and had trodden the snow about the door into a pool of mud. Riding saddles and bridles, packsaddles and strings of bells, mules and men, lanterns, torches, sacks, provender, barrels, cheeses, kegs of honey and butter, straw bundles and packages of many shapes, were crowded confusedly together in this thawed quagmire, and about the steps. Up here in the clouds, every thing was seen through cloud, and seemed dissolving into cloud. The breath of the men was cloud, the breath of the mules was cloud, the lights were encircled by cloud, speakers close at hand were not seen for cloud, though their voices and all other sounds were surprisingly clear. Of the cloudy line of mules hastily tied to rings in the wall, one would bite another, or kick another, and then the whole mist would be disturbed: with men diving into it, and cries of men and beasts coming out of it, and no bystander discerning what was wrong. In the midst of this, the great stable of the convent, occupying the basement story, and entered by the basement door, outside which all the disorder was, poured forth its contribution of cloud, as if the whole rugged edifice were filled with nothing else, and would collapse as soon as it had emptied itself, leaving the snow to fall upon the bare mountain summit.

While all this noise and hurry were rife among the living travelers, there, too, silently assembled in a grated house, half a dozen paces removed, with the same cloud enfolding them, and the same snow flakes drifting in upon them, were the dead travelers found upon the mountain. The mother, storm-belated many winters ago, still standing in the corner with her baby at her breast; the man who had frozen with his arm raised to his mouth in fear of hunger, still pressing it with his dry lips after years and years. An awful company, mysteriously come together! A wild destiny for that mother to have foreseen. "Surrounded by so many, and such companions, upon whom I never looked, and never shall look, I and my child will dwell together inseparable, on the Great Saint Bernard, outlasting generations who will come to see us, and will never know our name, or one word of our story but the end."

The living travelers thought little or nothing of the dead just then. They thought much more of alighting at the convent door, and warming themselves at the convent fire. Disengaged from the turmoil, which was already calming down as the crowd of mules began to be bestowed in the stable, they hurried shivering up the steps and into the building. There was a smell within, coming up from the floor of tethered beasts, like the smell of a menagerie of wild animals. There were strong arched galleries within, huge stone piers, great staircases, and thick walls pierced with small sunken windows—fortifications against the mountain storms, as if they had been human enemies. There were gloomy vaulted sleeping rooms within, intensely cold, but clean and hospitably prepared for guests. Finally, there was a parlor for guests to sit in and to sup in, where a table was already laid, and where a blazing fire shone red and high.

In this room, after having had their quarters for the night allotted to them by two young Fathers, the travelers presently drew round the hearth. They were in three parties; of whom the first, as the most numerous and important, was the slowest, and had been overtaken by one of the others on the way up. It consisted of an elderly lady, two gray-haired gentlemen, two young ladies, and their brother. These were attended (not to mention four guides) by a courier, two footmen, and two waiting-maids: which strong body of inconvenience was accommodated elsewhere under the same roof. The party that had overtaken them, and followed in their train, consisted of only three members: one lady and two gentlemen. The third party, which had ascended from the valley on the Italian side of the Pass, and had arrived first, were four in number: a plethoric, hungry, and silent German tutor in spectacles, on a tour with three young men, his pupils, all plethoric, hungry, and silent, and all in spectacles.

These three groups sat round the fire eyeing each other dryly, and waiting for supper. Only one among them, one of the gentlemen belonging to the party of three, made advances toward conversation. Throwing out his lines for the Chief of the important tribe, while addressing himself to his own companions, he remarked, in a tone of voice which included all the company, if they chose to be included, that it had been a long day, and that he felt for the ladies. That he feared one of the young ladies was not a strong or accustomed traveler, and had been over fatigued two or three hours ago. That he had observed, from his station in the rear, that she sat her mule as if she were exhausted. That he had, twice or thrice afterward, done himself the honor of inquiring of one of the guides, when he fell behind, how the young lady did. That he had been enchanted to learn that she had recovered her spirits, and that it had been but a passing discomfort. That he trusted (by this time he had secured the eyes of the Chief, and addressed him) he might be permitted to express his hope that she was now none the worse, and that she would not regret having made the journey.

"My daughter, I am obliged to you, sir," returned the Chief, "is quite restored, and has been greatly interested."

"New to mountains, perhaps?" said the insinuating traveler.

"New to—ha—to mountains," said the Chief.

"But you are familiar with them, sir?" the insinuating traveler assumed.

"I am—hum—tolerably familiar. Not of late years. Not of late years," replied the Chief, with a flourish of his hand.

The insinuating traveler, acknowledging the flourish with an inclination of his head, passed from the Chief to the second young lady, who had not yet been referred to, otherwise than as one of the ladies in whose behalf he felt so sensitive an interest.

He hoped she was not incommoded by the fatigues of the day.

"Incommoded certainly," returned the young lady, "but not tired."

The insinuating traveler complimented her on the justice of the distinction. It was what he had meant to say. Every lady must doubtless be incommoded, by having to do with that proverbially unaccommodating animal, the mule.

"We have had, of course," said the young lady, who was rather reserved and haughty, "to leave the carriages and fourgon at Martigny. And the impossibility of bringing any thing that one wants to this inaccessible place, and the necessity of leaving every comfort behind, is not convenient."

"A savage place, indeed," said the insinuating traveler.

The elderly lady, who was a model of accurate dressing, and whose manner was perfect, considered as a piece of machinery, here interposed a remark in a low soft voice.

"But, like other inconvenient places," she observed, "it must be seen. As a place much spoken of, it is necessary to see it."

"Oh! I have not the least objection to seeing it, I assure you, Mrs. General," returned the other, carelessly.

"You, madam," said the insinuating traveler, "have visited this spot before?"

"Yes," returned Mrs. General. "I have been here before. Let me recommend you, my dear," to the former young lady, "to shade your face from the hot wood, after exposure to the mountain air and snow. You too, my dear," to the other and younger lady, who immediately did so; while the former merely said, "Thank you, Mrs. General, I am perfectly comfortable, and prefer remaining as I am."

The brother, who had left his chair to open a piano that stood in the room, and who had whistled into it and shut it up again, now came strolling back to the fire with his glass in his eye. He was dressed in the very fullest and completest traveling trim. The world seemed hardly large enough to yield him an amount of travel proportionate to his equipment.

"These fellows are an immense time with supper," he drawled. . . .

With the supper came one of the young Fathers (there seemed to be no old Fathers) to take the head of the table. It was like the supper of an ordinary Swiss hotel, and good red wine grown by the convent in more genial air was not wanting. The artist traveler calmly came and took his place at the table when the rest sat down. . . .

"Pray," he inquired of the host, over his soup, "has your convent many of its famous dogs now?"

"Monsieur, it has three."

"I saw three in the gallery below. Doubtless the three in question."

The host, a slender, bright-eyed, dark young man of polite manners, whose garment was a black gown with strips of white crossed over it like braces, and who no more resembled the conventional breed of Saint Bernard monks than he resembled the conventional breed of Saint Bernard dogs, replied, doubtless those were the three in question.

"And I think," said the artist traveler, "I have seen one of them before."

It was possible. He was a dog sufficiently well known. Monsieur might have easily seen him in the valley or somewhere on the lake, when he (the dog) had gone down with one of the Order to solicit aid for the convent.

"Which is done in its regular season of the year, I think?"

Monsieur was right.

"And never without the dog. The dog is very important."

Again Monsieur was right. The dog was very important. People were justly interested in the dog. As one of the dogs celebrated everywhere, Ma'amsclle would observe. . . .

"Ask him if he has saved many lives," said, in his native English, the young man who had been put out of countenance.

The host needed no translation of the question. He promptly replied in French, "No; not this one."

"Why not?" the same gentleman asked.

"Pardon," returned the host, composedly, "give him the opportunity and he will do it without doubt. For example, I am well convinced," smiling sedately, as he cut up the dish of veal to be handed round, "that if you, Monsieur, would give him the opportunity, he would hasten with great ardor to fulfill his duty."

The artist traveler laughed. The insinuating traveler (who evinced a provident anxiety to get his full share of the supper), wiping some drops of wine from his moustache with a piece of bread, joined the conversation.

"It is becoming late in the year, my Father," said he, "for tourist-travelers, is it not?"

"Yes, it is late. Yet two or three weeks, at most, and we shall be left to the winter snows."

"And then," said the insinuating traveler, "for the scratching dogs and the buried children, according to the pictures!"

"Pardon," said the host, not quite understanding the allusion. "How, then the scratching dogs and the buried children according to the pictures?"

The artist traveler struck in again, before an answer could be given.

"Don't you know," he coldly inquired across the table of his companion, "that none but smugglers come this way in the winter, or can have any possible business this way?"

"Holy blue! No; never heard of it."

"So it is, I believe. And as they know the signs of the weather tolerably well, they don't give much employment to the dogs—who have consequently died out rather—though this house of entertainment is conveniently situated for themselves. Their young families, I am told, they usually leave at home. But it's a grand idea!" cried the artist traveler, unexpectedly rising into a tone of enthusiasm. "It's a sublime idea. It's the finest idea in the world, and brings tears into a man's eyes, by Jupiter!" He then went on eating his veal with great composure.

There was enough of mocking inconsistency at the bottom of this speech to make it rather discordant, though the manner was refined and the person well-favored, and though the depreciatory part of it was so skillfully thrown off, as to be very difficult for one not perfectly acquainted with the English language to understand, or, even understanding, to take offense at: so simple and dispassionate was its tone. After finishing his veal in the midst of silence, the speaker again addressed his friend.

"Look," said he, in his former tone, "at this gentleman our host, not yet in the prime of life, who in so graceful a way and with such courtly urbanity and modesty presides over us! Manners fit for a crown! Dine with the Lord Mayor of London (if you can get an invitation) and observe the contrast. This dear fellow, with the finest cut face I ever saw, a face in perfect drawing, leaves some laborious life and comes up here I don't know how many feet above the level of the sea, for no other purpose on earth (except enjoying himself, I hope, in a capital refectory) than to keep an hotel for idle poor devils like you and me, and leave the bill to our consciences! Why, isn't it a beautiful sacrifice? What do we want more to touch us? Because rescued people of interesting appearance are not, for eight or nine months out of every twelve, holding on here round the necks of the most sagacious of dogs carrying wooden bottles, shall we disparage the place? No! Bless the place. It's a great place, a glorious place!"

The chest of the gray-haired gentleman who was the Chief of the important party, had swelled as if with a protest against his being numbered among poor devils. No sooner had the artist traveler ceased speaking than he himself spoke with great dignity, as having it incumbent on him to take the lead in most places, and having deserted that duty for a little while.

He weightily communicated his opinion to their host, that his life must be a very dreary life here in the winter.

The host allowed to Monsieur that it was a little monotonous. The air was difficult to breathe for a length of time consecutively. The cold was very severe. One needed youth and strength to bear it. However, having them and the blessing of Heaven—

Yes, that was very good. "But the confinement," said the gray-haired gentleman.

There were many days, even in bad weather, when it was possible to walk about outside. It was the custom to beat a little track, and take exercise there.

"But the space," urged the gray-haired gentleman. "So small. So—ha—very limited."

Monsieur would recall to himself that there were the refuges to visit, and that tracks had to be made to them also.

Monsieur still urged, on the other hand, that the space was so—ha—hum —so very contracted. More than that. It was always the same, always the same.

With a deprecating smile, the host gently raised and gently lowered his shoulders. That was true, he remarked, but permit him to say that almost all objects had their various points of view. Monsieur and he did not see this poor life of his from the same point of view. Monsieur was not used to confinement.

"I—ha—yes, very true," said the gray-haired gentleman. He seemed to receive quite a shock from the force of the argument.

Monsieur, as an English traveler surrounded by all means of traveling pleasantly; doubtless possessing fortune, carriages, servants—

"Perfectly, perfectly. Without doubt," said the gentleman.

Monsieur could not easily place himself in the position of a person who had not the power to choose, I will go here to-morrow, or there next day; I will pass these barriers, I will enlarge those bounds. Monsieur could not realize, perhaps, how the mind accommodated itself in such things. . . .

"It is true," said Monsieur. "We will—ha—not pursue the subject. You are—hum—quite accurate, I have no doubt. We will say no more."

RATTLESNAKE HUNTER

FROM *Listen for a Lonesome Drum*

CARL CARMER

Carl Carmer has taken title to the upstate New York country. He has written about it engagingly in his many books and has told its folk tales over the radio. He knows its people, the Indians who are the older up-staters and the newer ones. Carmer was born in the York State hills, the Onondaga country on top of whose mountains the old Indian gods used to walk. In this selection from *Listen for a Lonesome Drum* we meet one of his Adirondack neighbors with a strange trade.

THE DARK, WINDING ROAD THROUGH THE ADIRONDACKS, SPLASHED HERE AND there by spring sunlight, guided me past lake after lake, high summit after high summit. I saw Saranac, then Placid, and I turned south at Elizabeth-town, preferring the tree shadows of the Schroon Lake road to the more open highway that rims the waters of Champlain and Lake George. A few minutes after I had left Schroon, I took a dirt road that seemed to lead southeast toward my destination. It was steep and it branched often. Soon I realized that I had in all probability taken a wrong turn and I looked eagerly ahead for human aid.

It seemed to have materialized in a lank, middle-aged fellow in overalls and black shirt who was hoeing dispiritedly at a rocky patch of earth near the road. His jaws were moving rhythmically, and occasionally he spat a yellow stream toward the blade of his hoe.

"Can you tell me how to get to Bolton's Landing?" I said.

He stopped work, leaned on his hoe-handle and regarded me solemnly.

"Well," he said, "if I was goin' to Bolton's Landing, I wouldn't *start* from here."

I laughed, but his weather-seamed face did not change expression.

"There must be a way," I said.

"Take the next turn left. That'll bring you into Padan-Aram. Ought to help some."

"I suppose you're glad of a warm day," I said. "Your farming season can't be long in this northern part of the state."

"Only lasts about fifteen minutes," he said very seriously, "and *they* seem to come around lunchtime."

When I first saw Bill Clark he was down in one of his back lots mending fence. I had parked my car close to the edge of the narrow winding road that leads over the mountains back of the lake and I had reached his porch, littered with pails, baskets, milk pans, bits of old machinery and ears of seed corn before he saw me. He waved then and came slowly up the rise toward his little house.

"Yesterday was my sabbath," he said, "so that's why you catch me workin' on your Sunday."

"I don't mind," I assured him hastily. "I just wondered if you wouldn't take me out to hunt rattlesnakes with you."

He smiled and his mouth spread to each side of his face—paralleling the lines about his blue eyes. His squat figure was firmly planted on the stony soil.

"Don't get many requests like that," he said. "Folks don't care much about catchin' snakes. But I guess I could oblige you. When c'n ye go?"

"I'm ready any time," I said.

"Ain't no time like the present," said Bill. "We may be a little late startin' since it's near nine o'clock but maybe we can pick one up before very long, certainly before dark."

"One'll be enough," I said. "I just want to see how you do it."

Bill stepped to the wall of the porch and picked up a long stick with some sort of metal contraption on the end.

"You see this," he said impressively; "this is what's known as the Bill Clark rattlesnake tongs. I do practically all my snake catchin' with it. Fifty years ago I used to use a forked stick—or my hands—but by and by I invented this an' it's the best thing for takin' a rattler that I know."

"How does it work?" I said.

"Well, it's really a broomstick with a wire run through eyelets along the side. They's a handle at your end and at the business end it's got a pair of steel jaws like pincers an' they work the same way. When I see a rattler I get up on him and get his neck between them jaws. Then I pull on the handle an' the jaws close on his neck, an' I've got him. I usually carry a basket to put him in because he might be a her and have five or six little ones down her gullet. I git jest as much bounty for little rattles as I do fer big ones. But if I'm in a hurry I jest put my foot on his neck and jerk his head off with the tongs. Then I bury the head under a stone and go ahead. Well, I reckon I'm ready. Here's a pair o' tongs fer you."

We put the tongs in the back of the car and started driving south along the west shore of the lake.

"How much can you make out of one average-size rattlesnake?" I said.

"Well, now, that depends," said Bill. "We used to get three dollars a rattle regardless o' size. Then they reduced it to a dollar 'n' a half, but now it's back up to two-fifty. Then there's all the oil you can try out of him. May amount to three-four dollars' worth."

"Oil?" I said.

"Sure. Rattlesnake oil. Good for what ails ye, whatever it is. Drugstores buy it an' these doctors that goes out with a tent and an Indian through the country sells lots of it. Mighty good for rheumatism—makes ye soople. Feller I know says he knew a man wunst used too much of it—got so soople he couldn't stand up."

His blue eyes sought mine in kindly seriousness.

"I take it the female rattler carries her young in her gullet," I said sternly.

"Yep. But they ain't no way o' tellin' unless ye take her home an' put her in a box an' wait fer 'em to crawl out. Then ye can get bounty fer all the little rattles. That's a damn sight better than doin' like a rattlesnake feller on the other side of the lake did a couple years ago. He broke the big rattles in two an' tried to collect bounties fer both ends. He's still in the penitentiary."

We were crossing the southern end of the lake now. The great cliffs on the east side were looming above us and the water at their feet was very blue. Far to the north green islands seemed to be floating on the still surface.

"I like livin' back from the water," said Bill suddenly. "A lake always looks better when you come up on it. Here's where we stop an' hit a trail."

Through an upward slanting field we strode, tongs dragging behind us, then climbed along a creek bed until we reached a wooded ridge.

"There ought to be some in the rocks at the end of this ridge," said Bill.

"Isn't this business a little dangerous?" I said.

"Ain't been struck in fifty years."

"Yes, but suppose there's more than one at a time."

"More than one!" He struck his thigh with his open palm. "Guess I ain't told ye 'bout the time round ten years ago when Dal Pratt an' I was huntin' on this very ridge. We was separated. Pratt had gone on up the mountain an' I come into a little rocky ravine not much bigger'n a minute and there, by God, was all the rattlesnakes in this whole Adirondack country a-sunnin' 'emselves. They'd jest come out o' their winter dens an' was gettin' ready to move to their summer ones. Five hundred to a thousand rattlers, by God, a-turnin' and twistin' there in the sun an' all of 'em singin' so's you could hear 'em a half-a-mile."

Bill's eyes gleamed, his face seemed contorted with joy. I imagined that he was counting up the grand total of rattles and rattlesnake oil in terms of dollars.

"I called to Pratt an' he heard me and come along the mountain to the edge of the ravine. He jumped down on a boulder just beside my shoulder an' then not payin' any attention landed right beside me an' there we both was with all them rattlers raisin' hell around us. I seen Pratt's eyes sort o' flicker so I says to him, I says:

" 'If you be scared you better git back up thar on that rock.'

" 'Waal,' he says, sort o' slow an' careful, 'I be.' "

Bill waited for this monosyllabic expression of emotion to sink in, his eyes twinkling. Then he said, "I sure was a fool to use my shotgun that day. I got seventeen on the first shot and I got about seventy-five that morning—but I could of got the whole lot if I'd took my time and used these here tongs."

We had come to a pile of dark rocks and Bill began poking around under them with the tongs. Once he turned one over, looking expectantly at the spot beneath while I stepped back and felt frightened. At last he said:

"We'll rest here a bit," and sat down on a rock. Fearfully I sat beside him.

"Why can't you breed rattlesnakes?" I said. "Then you wouldn't have to go to all this trouble and you'd get your bounty and oil just the same."

"I thought o' that," said Bill reflectively. "Fact is I tried it once. I got a lot o' rattlers an' put 'em all in box all winter and all spring an' nothin' happened. Didn't get no little rattlers at all. Then Henry Hall, friend o' mine lives down in the town o' Lake George, come by and he says, 'Ye won't git no little ones unless you put a blacksnake in there.' So I put a blacksnake in there and by God it wan't no time 'fore there was six little fellers crawlin' around. So I'd say it would be my conclusion after fifty years o' huntin' rattlers that the blacksnake is the papa rattler."

"I didn't know they ever mated," I said.

"Oh, sure. One mornin' I seen a big blacksnake come out from under a rock and a rattler followed him out and they mated right there—you know how they do—twistin' and turnin' sort of like they was dancin'. Well then, I'm damned if he didn't get back under that rock and bring out another rattler and mate with her, and then he went back again and when a third rattler come out I jest went on about my business."

"You haven't told me why you aren't breeding blacksnakes with rattlers to get more rattlers," I said.

"Well, that was Henry's fault, too, really. He seen I had some luck, so he tried it. He put some blacksnakes and rattlers in a big wire cage and kept 'em there a long time. But nothin' happened. So he kept 'em a couple o' months more and still he didn't get none and somehow he got to blamin' it on the female rattlers. Henry's house is right plumb on the street in Lake George an' one mornin' his wife woke up and there sits Henry in the doorway with his shotgun on his knees.

" 'You goin' huntin'?' she says.

" 'Nope,' says Henry.

" 'What you plannin' on?' she says.

" 'I'm figgerin' on shootin' the first female that comes down the street.'

" 'You can't do that,' she says.

" 'I'm goin' to,' says Henry.

"Well, then she screamed an' some men come in an' satcheled onto Henry an' by God they had to take him to the crazy house. He's sane enough 'bout everything else except females but he's bound to take a shot at the first one o' *them* he sees. So they have to keep him locked up. He's up there now."

Bill pulled some sandwiches and two bottles of milk from his basket and we ate and talked a while. Then we dozed off and midafternoon had come before we felt like continuing our quest. Neither of us expected it to have so sudden an ending.

For as Bill rose, the rock on which his feet rested tilted slightly. From under it came a prolonged buzz not unlike the note of a cicada but lower and harder. The shambling ease of the old man vanished. With one quick movement he kicked the rock over and there beneath it in a writhing coil lay a snake. His head was already moving back making ready to strike. His mouth was open very wide and his eyes were darkly gleaming beads above it.

"See if you can catch him by the neck," said Bill and I pushed my tongs awkwardly forward. As I pulled the wire handle the rattler struck and his head lunged up the pole, the jaws at the bottom catching him toward the middle of his body. Again he struck, coiling about the steel teeth that held him, his dripping fangs reaching halfway up to my rigid hands while I stood paralyzed, gazing at him.

"Hold tight," said Bill sharply, and I heard the sharp click of his tongs as they bit into the snake just behind the head.

I must have had sense enough to loosen my hold then, for I remember Bill's raising the twisting burden and turning away from me. Then he had the snake firmly held, his right hand close up to the head, and he was stuffing it into a wicker fish-basket lined with felt and hung by a strap over his shoulder.

"Well, that's one," he said.

"I was too scared to do a good job," I said miserably.

"It takes practice," said Bill, "but you weren't in much danger. I was ready to hit him if he got too close to ye. A rattler ain't much of a fighter.

One lick and he gives up and runs. Looks like we might find some today. Blamed if I didn't think that C.C.C. camp had driven most of 'em back into the mountains."

"No," I said, "I've had enough."

Bill followed me down the trail in reproachful silence. Finally he said:

"I reckon you'll want this one killed so's you can show it to your friends. We better stop and kill it now, for it takes a rattler a long time to die."

"How long?" I said.

"Depends—but my son and me cut the heart out of a big one once and laid it on a rock in the hot sun. It was beatin' forty-seven times a minute then and when we come back three hours later it was still beatin'—twenty-three times a minute."

"You'd better keep it," I said as we reached the car and climbed in. "Perhaps it's a female carrying a lot of little ones."

"Perhaps," said Bill pessimistically, and then we both lapsed into a long silence as we rolled along the side of the lake. The sun was out of sight somewhere beyond Bill's house and its rays were almost level as they struck against the rock cliffs on the eastern shore. The water below them seemed covered with a golden sheet.

We were approaching Bolton's Landing when Bill spoke again.

"Sometimes," he said, "the rattlers cross the lake."

"Ever see 'em?" I said.

"Sure," he said. "Lots o' times. They take the little ones down their gullets and set out. You can see the mother snake's head above the water and she keeps her tail out, too. You can hear it rattlin' away—sort o' like an outboard motor. In the spring o' the year, in the moonlight, it makes a mighty pretty sight."

COUGAR

A METHODISTICAL BOOK

FROM *Wild Wales*

G E O R G E   B O R R O W

"A Norwich young man is construing with me Schiller's *Wilhelm Tell*, with a view to translating it for the Press. His name is George Henry Borrow and he has learned German with extraordinary rapidity; indeed, he has the gift of tongues, and though not yet eighteen, understands twelve languages." A most extraordinary young man was George Borrow. Employed by the British and Foreign Bible Society to translate the New Testament into Manchu, he borrowed a few books and three weeks later wrote to the secretary of the society that if he only could get hold of a Manchu grammar, "I should in a month's time be able to send a Manchu translation of *Jonah*."

Borrow traveled on foot through Spain, Portugal and Wales selling the Bible and writing his curious travel, adventure and Gypsy books in which one finds it hard to know where autobiography leaves off and fiction begins. This selection is from his peregrinations in 1854 through the mountains of "Wild Wales."

HAVING LEARNT FROM A NEWSPAPER THAT A WELSH BOOK ON WELSH METHODism had been just published at Wrexham I determined to walk to that place and purchase it. I could easily have procured the work through a bookseller at Llangollen, but I wished to explore the hill-road which led to Wrexham, what the farmer under the Eglwysig rocks had said of its wildness having excited my curiosity, which the procuring of the book afforded me a plausible excuse for gratifying. If one wants to take any particular walk it is always well to have some business, however trifling, to transact at the end of it; so having determined to go to Wrexham by the mountain road, I set out on the Saturday next after the one on which I had met the farmer who had told me of it.

The day was gloomy, with some tendency to rain. I passed under the hill of Dinas Bran. About a furlong from its western base I turned round and surveyed it—and perhaps the best view of the noble mountain is to be obtained from the place where I turned round. How grand though sad from there it looked, that grey morning, with its fine ruin on its brow above which a little cloud hovered! It put me in mind of some old king, unfortunate and melancholy but a king still, with the look of a king, and the ancestral crown still on his furrowed forehead. I proceeded on my way, all was wild and solitary, and the yellow leaves were falling from the trees of the groves. I passed by the farmyard, where I had held discourse with the farmer on the preceding Saturday, and soon entered the glen, the appearance of which had so much attracted my curiosity. A torrent, rushing down from the north, was on my right. It soon began to drizzle, and mist so filled the glen that I could only distinguish objects a short way before me, and on either side. I wandered on a considerable way, crossing the torrent several times by rustic bridges. I passed two lone farm-houses and at last saw another on my left hand—the mist had now cleared up, but it still slightly rained—the scenery was wild to a degree—a little way before me was a tremendous pass, near it an enormous crag of a strange form rising to the very heavens, the upper part of it of a dull white colour. Seeing a respectable-looking man near the house I went up to him. "Am I in the right way to Wrexham?" said I, addressing him in English.

"You can get to Wrexham this way, sir," he replied.

"Can you tell me the name of that crag?" said I, pointing to the large one.

"That crag, sir, is called Craig y Forwyn."

"The maiden's crag," said I; "why is it called so?"

"I do not know sir; some people say that it is called so because its head is like that of a woman, others because a young girl in love leaped from the top of it and was killed."

"And what is the name of this house?" said I.

"This house, sir, is called Plas Uchaf."

"Is it called Plas Uchaf," said I, "because it is the highest house in the valley?"

"It is sir; it is the highest of three homesteads; the next below it is Plas Canol—and the one below that Plas Isaf."

"Middle place and lower place," said I. "It is very odd that I know in England three people who derive their names from places so situated. One is Houghton, another Middleton, and the third Lowdon; in modern English Hightown, Middletown, and Lowtown."

"You appear to be a person of great intelligence, sir."

"No, I am not—but I am rather fond of analyzing words, particularly the names of persons and places. Is the road to Wrexham hard to find?"

"Not very, sir; that is, in the daytime. Do you live at Wrexham?"

"No," I replied, "I am stopping at Llangollen."

"But you won't return there tonight?"

"O yes, I shall!"

"By this road?"

"No, by the common road. This is not a road to travel by night."

"Nor is the common road, sir, for a respectable person on foot; that is, on a Saturday night. You will perhaps meet drunken colliers who may knock you down."

"I will take my chance for that," said I and bade him farewell. I entered the pass, passing under the strange-looking crag. After I had walked about half a mile the pass widened considerably and a little way farther on debouched on some wild moory ground. Here the road became very indistinct. At length I stopped in a state of uncertainty. A well-defined path presented itself, leading to the east, whilst northward before me there seemed scarcely any path at all. After some hesitation I turned to the east by the well-defined path and by so doing went wrong as I soon found.

I mounted the side of a brown hill covered with moss-like grass, and here and there heather. By the time I arrived at the top of the hill the sun shone out, and I saw Rhiwabon and Cefn Mawr before me in the distance. "I am going wrong," said I; "I should have kept on due north. However, I will not go back, but will steeple-chase it across the country to Wrexham, which must be towards the north-east." So turning aside from the path, I dashed across the hills in that direction; sometimes the heather was up to my knees, and sometimes I was up to the knees in quags. At length I came to a deep ravine which I descended; at the bottom was a quagmire, which, however, I contrived to cross by means of certain stepping-stones, and came to a cart path up a heathery hill which I followed. I soon reached the top of the hill, and the path still continuing I followed it till I saw some small grimy-looking huts, which I supposed were those of colliers. At the door of the first I saw a girl. I spoke to her in Welsh, and found she had little or none. I passed on, and seeing the door of a cabin open I looked in—and saw no adult person, but several grimy but chubby children. I spoke to them in English and found they could only speak Welsh. Presently I observed a robust woman advancing towards me; she was barefooted and bore on her head an immense lump of coal. I spoke to her in Welsh and found she could only speak English. "Truly," said I, to myself, "I am on the borders. What a mixture of races and languages!" The next person I met was a man in a collier's dress: he was a stout-built fellow of the middle age; with a coal-dusty surly countenance. I asked him in Welsh if I was in the right direction for Wrexham, he answered in a surly manner in English, that I was. I again spoke to him in Welsh, making some indifferent observation on the weather, and he answered in English yet more gruffly than before. For the third time I spoke to him in Welsh, whereupon looking at me with a grin of savage contempt, and showing a set of teeth like those of a mastiff, he said, "How's this? why you haven't a word of English? A pretty fellow you with a long coat on your back and no English on your tongue, an't you ashamed of yourself? Why, here am I in a short coat, yet I'd have you to know that I can speak English as well as Welsh, aye and a good deal better." "All people are not equally clebber," said I, still speaking Welsh. "Clebber," said he, "clebber! what is clebber! why can't you say clever! Why, I never saw such a low, illiterate fellow in my life"; and with these words he turned away with every mark of disdain, and entered a cottage near at hand.

"Here I have had," said I to myself, as I proceeded on my way, "to pay for the over-praise which I lately received. The farmer on the other side of the mountain called me a person of great intelligence, which I never pretended to be, and now this collier calls me a low, illiterate fellow, which I really don't think I am. There is certainly a Nemesis mixed up with the affairs of this world; every good thing which you get, beyond what is strictly your due, is sure to be required from you with a vengeance. A little over-praise by a great deal of under-rating—a gleam of good fortune by a night of misery."

I now saw Wrexham Church at about the distance of three miles and presently entered a lane which led gently down from the hills, which were the same heights I had seen on my right hand, some months previously, on my way from Wrexham to Rhiwabon. The scenery now became very pretty —hedge-rows were on either side, a luxuriance of trees and plenty of green fields. I reached the bottom of the lane, beyond which I saw a strange-looking house upon a slope on the right hand. It was very large, ruinous and seemingly deserted. A little beyond it was a farmhouse, connected with which was a long row of farming buildings along the road-side. Seeing a woman seated knitting at the door of a little cottage I asked her in English the name of the old ruinous house?

"Cadogan Hall, sir," she replied.

"And whom does it belong to?" said I.

"I don't know exactly," replied the woman, "but Mr. Morris at the farm holds it, and stows his things in it."

"Can you tell me anything about it?" said I.

"Nothing farther," said the woman, "than that it is said to be haunted and to have been a barrack many years ago."

"Can you speak Welsh?" said I.

"No," said the woman, "I are Welsh but have no Welsh language."

Leaving the woman I put on my best speed and in about half an hour reached Wrexham.

The first thing I did on my arrival was to go to the bookshop and purchase the Welsh methodistic book. It cost me seven shillings, and was a thick bulky octavo with a cut-and-come-again expression about it, which was anything but disagreeable to me, for I hate your flimsy publications.

A CHAPEL AMONG

THE MOUNTAINS

FROM *Love Among the Haystacks*

D . H . LAWRENCE

🐉 Much like Ibsen, if with a somewhat narrower scalpel, D. H. Lawrence anatomized middle-class morality of the early twentieth century. The intent of his books, widely read and significant in changing attitudes, was to restore the balance of living which he thought had been lost by prudishness about sex and by the dehumanizing pressures of industrial society.

He himself, in spite of his freedom with the much-censored theme of sex relations, was described by many who knew him as a man who lived simply, almost abstemiously. From our modern point of view his own marriage was not overly complicated. He fell in love with a married woman, Frieda von Richthofen, and lived with her until he died. When the two found they loved each other, Frieda left her husband and with Lawrence went to Austria and from there on foot over the Brenner Pass to Italy. This selection describes an incident in their trip. They lose their path and find a mountain chapel.

IT IS ALL VERY WELL TRYING TO WANDER ROMANTICALLY IN THE TIROL. SADLY I sit on the bed, my head and shoulders emerging from the enormous over-bolster like a cherub from a cloud, writing out of sheer exasperation, whilst Anita lies on the other bed and is amused.

Two days ago it began to rain. When I think of it I wonder. The gutter of the heavens hangs over the Tirolese Alps.

We set off with the iridescent cloud of romance ahead, leading us southwards from the Isar towards Italy. We haven't got far. And the iridescent cloud, turned into a column of endless water, still endures around the house.

I omit the pathos of our setting forth, in the dimmery-glimmery light of the Isar Valley, before breakfast-time, with blue chicory flowers open like wonder on either side the road. Neither will I describe our crawling at dinner-time along the foot of the mountains, the rain running down our necks from the flabby straw hats, and dripping cruelly into one's boots from the penthouse of our rucksacks. We entered ashamed into a wayside inn, where seven ruddy, joyous peasants, three of them handsome, made a bon-fire of their hearts in honor of Anita, whilst I sat in a corner and dripped. . . .

Yesterday I admit it was fine in the afternoon and evening. We made tea by a waterfall among yellow-dangling noli-me-tangere flowers, whilst an inquisitive lot of mountains poked their heads up to look, and a great green grasshopper, armoured like Ivanhoe, took a flying leap into eternity over a lovely, black-blue gentian. At least, I saw him no more.

They had told us there was a footpath over the mountain, three and a half hours to Glashütte. There *was* a faint track, and a myriad of strawber-ries like ruddy stars below, and a few dark bilberries. We climbed one great steep slope, and scrambled down beyond, into a pine wood. There it was damp and dark and depressing. But one makes the best of things, when one sets out on foot. So we toiled on for an hour, traversing the side of a slope, black, wet, gloomy, looking through the fir trees across the gulf at another slope, black and gloomy and forbidding, shutting us back. For two hours we slipped and struggled, and still there we were, clamped between these two black slopes, listening to the water that ran uncannily, noisily along the bottom of the trap.

We grew silent and hot with exertion and the dark monotony of the struggle. A rucksack also has its moments of treachery, close friend though it seems. You are quite certain of a delicate and beautiful balance on a slippery tree-root; you take the leap; then the ironic rucksack gives you a pull from behind, and you are grovelling.

And the path *had* been a path. The side of the dark slope, steep as a roof, had innumerable little bogs where waters tried to ooze out and call themselves streams, and could not. Across these bogs went an old bed of fir-boughs, dancy and treacherous. So, there was a path! Suddenly there were no more fir-boughs, and one stood lost before the squalor of the slope. I wiped my brow.

"You so soon lose your temper," said Anita. So I stood aside, and yielded her the lead.

She blundered into another little track lower down.

"You *see!*" she said, turning round.

I did not answer. She began to hum a little tune, because her path de-scended. We slipped and struggled. Then her path vanished into the loudly snorting, chuckling stream, and did not emerge.

"Well?" I said.

"But where is it?" she said with vehemence and pathos.

"You see even *your* road ends in nowhere," I said.

"I *hate* you when you preach," she flashed. "Besides it *doesn't* end in nowhere."

"At any rate," I said, "we can't sleep on the end of it."

I found another track, but I entered on it delicately, without triumph. We went in silence. And it vanished into the same loudly snorting stream.

"Oh, don't look like that!" cried Anita. So I followed the bedraggled tail of her skirts once more up the wet, dark opposition of the slope. We found another path, and once more we lost the scent in the overjoyed stream.

"Perhaps we're supposed to go across," I said meekly, as we stood beside the waters.

"I—*why* did I take a damp match of a man like you!" she cried. "One could scratch you for ever and you wouldn't strike."

I looked at her, wondering, and turned to the stream, which was cunningly bethinking itself. There were chunks of rock, and spouts and combs and rattles of sly water. So I put my raincoat over my rucksack and ventured over.

The opposite bank was very steep and high. We were swallowed in this black gorge, swallowed to the bottom, and gazing upwards I set off on all fours, climbing with my raincoat over my rucksack, cloakwise, to leave me free. I scrambled and hauled and struggled.

And from below came shriek upon shriek of laughter. I reached the top, and looked down. I could see nothing, only the whirring of laughter came up.

"What is it?" I called, but the sound was lost amid the cackle of the waters. So I crawled over the edge and sat in the gloomy solitude, extinguished.

Directly I heard a shrill, frightened call:

"Where are you?"

My heart exulted and melted at the same moment.

"Come along," I cried, satisfied that there was one spot in this gloomy solitude to call to.

She arrived, scared with the steep climb, and the fear of loneliness in this place.

"I might never have found you again," she said.

"I don't intend you should lose me," I said. So she sat down, and presently her head began to nod with laughter, and her bosom shook with laughter, and she was laughing wildly without me.

"Well, what?" I said.

"You—you looked like a camel—with your hump—climbing up," she shrieked.

"We'd better be moving," I said. She slipped and laughed and struggled.

At last we came to a beautiful savage road. It was the bed of some stream that came no more this way, a mass of clear boulders leading up the slope through the gloom.

"We are coming out now," said Anita, looking ahead. I also was quite sure of it. But after an hour of climbing, we were still in the bed of clear boulders, between dark trees, among the toes of the mountains.

Anita spied a hunter's hut, made of bark, and she went to investigate. Night was coming on.

"I can't get in," she called to me, obscurely.

"Then come," I said.

It was too wet and cold to sleep out of doors in the woods. But instead of coming, she stooped in the dark twilight for strawberries. I waited like the shadow of wrath. But she, unconcerned, careless and happy in her contrariety, gathered strawberries among the shadows.

"We *must* find a place to sleep in," I said. And my utter insistence took effect.

She realized that I was lost among the mountains, as well as she, that the night and the cold and the great dark slopes were close upon us, and we were of no avail, even being two, against the coldness and desolation of the mountains.

So in silence we scrambled upwards, hand in hand. Anita was sure a dozen times that we were coming out. At last even she got disheartened.

Then, in the darkness, we spied a hut beside a path among the thinning fir trees.

"It will be a woodman's hut," she said.

"A shrine," I answered.

I was right for once. It was a wooden hut just like a model, with a black old wreath hanging on the door. There was a click of the latch in the cold, watchful silence of the upper mountains, and we entered.

By the grey darkness coming in from outside we made out the tiny chapel, candles on the altar and a whole covering of ex-voto pictures on the walls, and four little praying-benches. It was all close and snug as a box.

Feeling quite safe, and exalted in this rare, upper shadow, I lit the candles, all. Point after point of flame flowed out on the night. There were six. Then I took off my hat and my rucksack, and rejoiced, my heart at home.

The walls of the chapel were covered close with naked little pictures, all coloured, painted by the peasants on wood, and framed with little frames. I glanced round, saw the cows and the horses on the green meadows, the men on their knees in their houses, and I was happy as if I had found myself among the angels.

"What wonderful luck!" I said to Anita.

"But what are we going to do?" she asked.

"Sleep on the floor—between the praying-desks. There's just room."

"But we can't sleep on a wooden floor," she said.

"What better can you find?"

"A hay hut. There must be a hay hut somewhere near. We *can't* sleep here."

"Oh yes," I said.

But I was bound to look at the little pictures. I climbed on to a bench. Anita stood in the open doorway like a disconsolate eternal angel. The light of the six dusky tapers glimmered on her discontented mouth. Behind her, I could see tips of fir-branches just illuminated, and then the night.

She turned and was gone like darkness into the darkness. I heard her boots upon the stones. Then I turned to the little pictures I loved. Perched upon the praying-desks, I looked at one, and then another. They were picture-writings that seemed like my own soul talking to me. They were really little pictures for God, because horses and cows and men and women and mountains, they are His own language. How should He read German and English and Russian, like a schoolmaster? The peasants could trust Him to understand their pictures: they were not so sure that He would concern himself with their written script.

I was looking at a pale blue picture. That was a bedroom, where a woman lay in bed, and a baby lay in a cradle not far away. The bed was blue, and it seemed to be falling out of the picture, so it gave me a feeling of fear and insecurity. Also, as the distance receded, the bedstead got wider, uneasily. The woman lay looking straight at me, from under the huge, blue-striped overbolster. Her pink face was round like a penny doll's, with the same round stare. And the baby, like a pink-faced farthing doll, also stared roundly.

Maria hat geholfen E. G.—1777.

I looked at them. And I knew that I was the husband looking and wondering. G., the husband, did not appear himself. It was from the little picture on his retina that this picture was reproduced. He could not sum it up, and explain it, this vision of his wife suffering in childbirth, and then lying still and at peace with the baby in the cradle. He could not make head or tail of it. But at least he could represent it, and hang it up like a mirror before the eyes of God, giving the statement even if he could get no explanation. And he was satisfied. And so, perforce, was I, though my heart began to knock for knowledge.

The men never actually saw themselves unless in precarious conditions. When their lives were threatened, then they had a fearful flash of self-consciousness, which haunted them till they had represented it. They represented themselves in all kinds of ridiculous postures, at the moment when the accident occurred.

Joseph Rieck, for example, was in a toppling-backward attitude rather like a footballer giving a very high kick and losing his balance. But on his left ankle had fallen a great grey stone, that might have killed him, squashing out much blood, orange-coloured—or so it looked by the candle-light—whilst the Holy Mary stood above in a bolster-frame of clouds, holding up her hands in mild surprise.

Joseph Rieck
Gott sey Danck gesagt 1834.

It was curious that he thanked God because a stone had fallen on his ankle. But perhaps the thanks were because it had not fallen on his head. Or perhaps because the ankle had got better, though it looked a nasty smash, according to the picture. It didn't occur to him to thank God that all the mountains of the Tirol had not tumbled on him the first day he was born. It doesn't occur to any of us. We wait till a big stone falls on our ankle. Then we paint a vivid picture and say: "In the midst of life we are in death," and we thank God that we've escaped. All kinds of men were saying: "Gott sey Danck"; either because big stones had squashed them, or because trees had come down on them whilst they were felling, or else because they'd tumbled over cliffs, or got carried away in streams: all little events which caused them to ejaculate: "God be thanked, I'm still alive."

Then some of the women had picture prayers that were touching, because they were prayers for other people, for their children and not for themselves. In a sort of cell kneeled a woman, wearing a Catherine of Russia kind of dress, opposite a kneeling man in Vicar of Wakefield attire. Between them, on the stone wall, hung two long iron chains with iron rings dangling at the end. Above these, framed in an oval of bolster-clouds, Christ on the Cross, and above Him, a little Maria, short in stature, something like Queen Victoria, with a very blue cloth over her head, falling down her dumpy figure. She, the Holy Mother of heaven, looked distressed. The woman kneeling in the cell put up her hands, saying:

O Mutter Gottes von Rerelmos, Ich bitte mach mir mein Kind von Gefangenschaft los mach im von Eissen und Bandten frey wansz des Gottliche Willen sey.

Susanna Grillen 1783.

I suppose Herr Grillen knew that it was not the affair of the Mutter Gottes. Poor Susanna Grillen! It was natural and womanly in her to identify the powers that be with the eternal powers. What I can't see, is whether the boy had really done anything wrong, or whether he had merely transgressed some law of some duke or king or community. I suppose the poor thing did not know herself how to make the distinction. But evidently the father, knowing he was in temporal difficulty, was not very active in asking help of the eternal.

One must look up the history of the Tirol for the 1783 period.

A few pictures were family utterances, but the voice which spoke was always the voice of the mother. Marie Schneeberger thanked God for healing her son. She kneeled on one side of the bedroom, with her three daughters behind her; Schneeberger kneeled facing her, with a space between them, and his one son behind him. The Holy Mary floated above the space of their thanks. The whole family united this time to bless the heavenly powers that the bad had not been worse. And, in the face of the divine power, the man was separate from the woman, the daughter from the son, the sister from the brother—one set on one side, one set on the other, separate before the eternal grace, or the eternal fear.

The last set of pictures thanked God for the salvation of property. One lady had six cows—all red ones—painted feeding on a meadow with rocks behind. All the cows I have seen in these parts have been dun or buff coloured. But these are red. And the goodwife thanks God very sincerely for restoring to her that which was lost for five days, viz. her six cows and the little cow-girl Kate. The little girl did not appear in the picture nor in the thanks: she was only mentioned as having been lost along with the cows. I do not know what became of her. Cows can always eat grass. I suppose she milked her beast, and perhaps cranberries were ripe. But five days was a long time for poor Kathel.

There were hundreds of cattle painted standing on meadows like a child's Noah's Ark toys arranged in groups: a group of red cows, a group of brown horses, a group of brown goats, a few grey sheep; as if they had all been summoned into their classes. Then Maria in her cloud-frame blessed them. But standing there so hieroglyphic, the animals had a symbolic power. They did not merely represent property. They were the wonderful animal life which man must take for food. Arrayed there in their numbers, they were almost frightening, as if they might overthrow us, like an army.

Only one woman had had an accident. She was seen falling downstairs, just landing at the bottom into her peaceful kitchen where the kitten lay asleep by the stove. The kitten slept on, but Mary in a blue mantle appeared through the ceiling, mildly shocked and deprecating.

Alone among all the women, the women who had suffered childbirth or had suffered through some child of their own, was this housewife who

had fallen downstairs into the kitchen where the cat slept peacefully. Perhaps she had not any children. However that may be, her position was
ignoble, as she bumped on the bottom stair.

There they all were, in their ex-voto pictures that I think the women
had ordered and paid for, these peasants of the valley below, pictured in
their fear. They lived under the mountains where always was fear. Sometimes they knew it to close on a man or a woman. Then there was no peace
in the heart of this man till the fear had been pictured, till he was represented
in the grip of terror, and till the picture had been offered to the Deity, the
dread, unnamed Deity; whose might must be acknowledged, whilst in the
same picture the milder divine succour was represented and named and
thanked. Deepest of all things, among the mountain darknesses, was the ever-
felt fear. First of all gods was the unknown god who crushed life at any
moment, and threatened it always. His shadow was over the valleys. And a
tacit acknowledgment and propitiation of Him were the ex-voto pictures,
painted out of fear and offered to Him unnamed. Whilst upon the face of
them all was Mary the divine Succour, She, who had suffered, and knew.
And that which had suffered and known had prevailed, and was openly
thanked. But that which had neither known nor suffered, the dread unnamed, which had aimed and missed by a little, this must be acknowledged
covertly. For his own soul's sake, man must acknowledge his own fear,
acknowledge the power beyond him.

Whilst I was reading the inscriptions high up on the wall, Anita came
back. She stood below me in her weather-beaten panama hat, looking up
dissatisfied. The light fell warm on her face. She was discontented and
excited.

"There's a gorgeous hay hut a little farther on," she said.

"Hold me a candle a minute, will you?" I said.

"A great hay hut full of hay, in an open space. I climbed in——"

"Do you mind giving me a candle for a moment?"

"But no—come along——"

"I just want to read this—give me a candle." In a silence of impatience,
she handed me one of the tapers. I was reading a little inscription.

"Won't you come?" she said.

"We could sleep well here," I said. "It is so dry and secure."

"Why!" she cried irritably. "Come to the hay hut and see."

"In one moment," I said.

She turned away.

"Isn't this altar adorable!" she cried. "Lovely little paper roses, and
ornaments."

She was fingering some artificial flowers, thinking to put them in her hair.
I jumped down, saying I must finish reading my pictures in the morning.

So I gathered the rucksack and examined the cash-box by the door. It was open and contained six kreutzers. I put in forty pfennigs, out of my poor pocket, to pay for the candles. Then I called Anita away from the altar trinkets, and we closed the door, and were out in the darkness of the mountains.

ANXIOUS TOURISTS PROCEED ALONG AN ALPINE PATH, 1861

THE HORRID MOUNTAINS

FROM *Diary, 1646*

J O H N   E V E L Y N

John Evelyn led a busy and varied life in the rapidly shifting political life of 17th-century England. He must have had a pleasing and adaptable personality for he had friends in Cromwell's court at the same time that he was corresponding with his father-in-law, Sir Richard Browne, ambassador of Charles II to France. He held public office, wrote with that curious encyclopedic diversity so characteristic of the time—on navigation, forestry, science, even "Mundis Muliebris: or the Ladies Dressing Room Unlocked—an enumeration of the immense variety of the modes and ornaments belonging to the sex." He traveled widely and not merely to count steeples, as he phrased it in one of his letters, but to inquire into manners and customs and to talk with eminent men of learning.

That Evelyn should have found the Alps "horrid" was to express the convention of the period which required nature to be wigged and beruffled if she were to be received at court.

THE NEXT WE SAW WAS ISOLA, AND WE LEFT ON OUR RIGHT HAND THE ISLE OF St. Giovanni; and so sailing by another small town built also on an island, we arrived at night at Margazzo, an obscure village at the end of the lake, and at the very foot of the Alps, which now rise as it were suddenly after some hundreds of miles of the most even country in the world, and where there is hardly a stone to be found, as if Nature had here swept up the rubbish of the earth in the Alps, to form and clear the plains of Lombardy, which we had hitherto passed since our coming from Venice. In this wretched place, I lay on a bed stuffed with leaves, which made such a crackling, and did so prick my skin through the tick, that I could not sleep. The next morning, I was furnished with an ass, for we could not get horses; instead of stirrups, we had ropes tied with a loop to put our feet in, which supplied the place of other trappings. Thus, with my gallant steed, bridled with my Turkish present, we passed through a reasonably pleasant but very narrow valley, till we came to Duomo, where we rested, and, having showed the Spanish pass, the Governor would press another on us, that his Secretary might get a crown. Here we exchanged our asses for mules, sure-footed on the hills and precipices, being accustomed to pass them. Hiring a guide, we were brought that night through very steep, craggy, and dangerous passages to a village called Vedra, being the last of the King of Spain's dominions in the Duchy of Milan. We had a very infamous wretched lodging.

The next morning, we mounted again through strange, horrid, and fearful crags and tracts, abounding in pine-trees, and only inhabited by bears, wolves, and wild goats; nor could we anywhere see above a pistol-shot before us, the horizon being terminated with rocks and mountains, whose tops, covered with snow, seemed to touch the skies, and in many places pierced the clouds. Some of these vast mountains were but one entire stone, betwixt whose clefts now and then precipitated great cataracts of melted snow, and other waters, which made a terrible roaring, echoing from the rocks and cavities; and these waters in some places breaking in the fall, wet us as if we had passed through a mist, so as we could neither see nor hear one another, but, trusting to our honest mules, we jogged on our way. The narrow bridges, in some places made only by felling huge fir-trees, and laying them athwart from mountain to mountain, over cataracts of stupendous depth, are very dangerous, and so are the passages and edges made by cutting away the main rock; others in steps; and in some places we pass between mountains that have been broken and fallen on one another; which is very terrible, and one had need of a sure foot and steady head to climb some of these precipices, besides that they are harbours for bears and wolves, who have sometimes assaulted travellers. In these straits, we frequently alighted, now freezing in the snow, and anon frying by the reverberation of the sun against the cliffs as we descend lower, when we meet now and then a few miserable cottages so built upon the declining of the rocks, as one would expect their sliding down. Amongst these, inhabit a goodly sort of people, having monstrous gullets, or wens of flesh, growing to their throats, some of which I have seen as big as an hundred pound bag of silver hanging under their chins; among the women especially, and that so ponderous, as that to ease them, many wear linen cloth bound about their head, and coming under the chin to support it; but *quis tumidum guttur miratur in Alpibus?* Their drinking so much snow-water, is thought to be the cause of it; the men, using more wine, are not so strumous as the women. The truth is, they are a peculiar race of people, and many great water-drinkers here have not these prodigious tumours; it runs, as we say, in the blood, and is a vice in the race, and renders them so ugly, shrivelled and deformed, by its drawing the skin of the face down, that nothing can be more frightful;

to this add a strange puffing dress, furs, and that barbarous language, being a mixture of corrupt High German, French, and Italian. The people are of great stature, extremely fierce and rude, yet very honest and trusty.

This night, through almost inaccessible heights, we came in prospect of Mons Sempronius, now Mount Sampion, which has on its summit a few huts and a chapel. Approaching this, Captain Wray's water-spaniel (a huge filthy cur that had followed him out of England) hunted a herd of goats down the rocks into a river made by the melting of the snow. Arrived at our cold harbour (though the house had a stove in every room) and supping on cheese and milk with wretched wine, we went to bed in cupboards so high from the floor, that we climbed them by a ladder; we were covered with feathers, that is, we lay between two ticks stuffed with them, and all little enough to keep one warm. The ceilings of the rooms are strangely low for those tall people. The house was now (in September) half covered with snow, nor is there a tree, or a bush, growing within many miles.

From this uncomfortable place, we prepared to hasten away the next morning; but, as we were getting on our mules, comes a huge young fellow demanding money for a goat which he affirmed that Captain Wray's dog had killed; expostulating the matter, and impatient of staying in the cold, we set spurs and endeavoured to ride away, when a multitude of people being by this time gotten together about us (for it being Sunday morning and attending for the priest to say mass), they stopped our mules, beat us off our saddles, and, disarming us of our carbines, drew us into one of the rooms of our lodging, and set a guard upon us. Thus we continued prisoners till mass was ended, and then came half a score grim Swiss, who, taking on them to be magistrates, sate down on the table, and condemned us to pay a pistole for the goat, and ten more for attempting to ride away, threatening that if we did not pay it speedily, they would send us to prison, and keep us to a day of public justice, where, as they perhaps would have exaggerated the crime, for they pretended we had primed our carbines and would have shot some of them (as indeed the Captain was about to do), we might have had our heads cut off, as we were told afterwards, for that amongst these rude people a very small misdemeanour does often meet that sentence. Though the proceedings appeared highly unjust, on consultation among ourselves we thought it safer to rid ourselves out of their hands, and the trouble we were brought into; and therefore we patiently laid down the money, and with fierce countenances had our mules and arms delivered to us, and glad we were to escape as we did. This was cold entertainment, but our journey after was colder, the rest of the way having been (as they told us) covered with snow since the Creation; no man remembered it to be without; and because, by the frequent snowing, the tracts are continually filled up, we passed by several tall masts set up to guide travellers, so as for many miles they stand in ken of one another, like to our beacons. In some places, where there is a cleft between two mountains, the snow fills it up, whilst the bottom, being thawed, leaves as it were a frozen arch of snow, and that so hard as to bear the greatest weight; for as it snows often, so it perpetually freezes, of which I was so sensible that it flawed the very skin of my face.

Beginning now to descend a little, Captain Wray's horse (that was our sumpter and carried all our baggage) plunging through a bank of loose snow, slid down a frightful precipice, which so incensed the choleric cavalier, his master, that he was sending a brace of bullets into the poor beast, lest our guide should recover him, and run away with his burden; but, just as he was lifting up his carbine, we gave such a shout, and so pelted the horse with snow-balls, as with all his might plunging through the snow, he fell from another steep place into another bottom, near a path we were to pass. It was yet a good while ere we got to him, but at last we recovered the place, and, easing him of his charge, hauled him out of the snow, where he had been certainly frozen in, if we had not prevented it, before night. It was as we judged almost two miles that he had slid and fallen, yet without any other harm than the benumbing of his limbs for the present, but, with lusty rubbing and chafing he began to move, and, after a little walking, performed his journey well enough. All this way, affrighted with the disaster of this horse, we trudged on foot, driving our mules before us; sometimes we fell, sometimes we slid, through this ocean of snow, which after October is impassable. Towards night, we came into a larger way, through vast woods of pines, which clothe the middle parts of these rocks. Here, they were burning some to make pitch and rosin, peeling the knotty branches, as we do to make charcoal, reserving what melts from them, which hardens into pitch. We passed several cascades of dissolved snow, that had made channels of formidable depth in the crevices of the mountains, and with such a fearful roaring as we could hear it for seven long miles. It is from these sources that the Rhone and the Rhine, which pass through all France and Germany, derive their originals. Late at night, we got to a town called Briga, at the foot of the Alps, in the Valteline. Almost every door had nailed on the outside and next the street a bear's, wolf's, or fox's head, and divers of them all three; a savage kind of sight, but, as the Alps are full of the beasts, the people often kill them. The next morning, we returned to our guide, and took fresh mules, and another to conduct us to the Lake of Geneva, passing through as pleasant a country as that we had just travelled was melancholy and troublesome. A strange and sudden change it seemed; for the reverberation of the sunbeams from the mountains and rocks that like walls range it on both sides, not above two flight-shots in breadth, for a very great number of miles, renders the passage excessively hot. Through such extremes we continued our journey, that goodly river, the Rhone, gliding by us in a narrow and quiet channel almost in the middle of this Canton, fertilizing the country for grass and corn, which grow here in abundance.

We arrived this night at Sion, a pretty town and city, a bishop's seat, and the head of Valesia. There is a castle, and the bishop who resides in it, has both civil and ecclesiastical jurisdiction. Our host, as the custom of these Cantons is, was one of the chiefest of the town, and had been a Colonel in France; he treated us with extreme civility, and was so displeased at the usage we received at Mount Sampion, that he would needs give us a letter to the Governor of the country, who resided at St. Maurice, which was in our way to Geneva, to revenge the affront. This was a true old blade, and had been a very curious virtuoso, as we found by a handsome collection of books, medals, pictures, shells, and other antiquities. He showed two heads and horns of the true capricorn, which animal he told us was frequently killed among the mountains; one branch of them was as much as I could well lift, and near as high as my head, not much unlike the greater sort of goat's, save that they bent forwards, by help whereof they climb up and hang on inaccessible rocks, from whence the inhabitants now and then shoot them. They speak prodigious things of their leaping from crag to crag, and of their sure footing, notwithstanding their being cloven-footed, unapt (one would think) to take hold and walk so steadily on those horrible ridges as they do. The Colonel would have given me one of these beams, but the want of a convenience to carry it along with me, caused me to refuse his courtesy. He told me that in the castle there were some Roman and Christian antiquities, and he had some inscriptions in his own garden. He invited us to his country-house, where he said he had better pictures, and other rarities; but, our time being short, I could not persuade my companions to stay and visit the places he would have had us see, nor the offer he made to show us the hunting of the bear, wolf, and other wild beasts. The next morning, having presented his daughter, a pretty well-fashioned young woman, with a small ruby ring, we parted somewhat late from our generous host.

Passing through the same pleasant valley between the horrid mountains on either hand, like a gallery many miles in length, we got to Martigni, where also we were well entertained. The houses in this country are all built of fir boards, planed within, low, and seldom above one story. The people very clownish and rusticly clad, after a very odd fashion, for the most part in blue cloth, very whole and warm, with little variety of distinction betwixt the gentleman and common sort, by a law of their country being exceedingly frugal. Add to this their great honesty and fidelity, though exacting enough for what they part with. I saw not one beggar. We paid the value of twenty shillings English, for a day's hire of one horse. Every man goes with a sword by his side, the whole country well-disciplined, and indeed impregnable, which made the Romans have such ill success against them; one lusty Swiss at their narrow passages is sufficient to repel a legion. It is a frequent thing here for a young tradesman, or farmer, to leave his wife and children for twelve or fifteen years, and seek his fortune in the wars in Spain, France, Italy, or Germany, and then return again to work. I look upon this country to be the safest spot of all Europe, neither envied nor envying; nor are any of them rich, nor poor; they live in great simplicity and tranquillity; and, though of the fourteen Cantons half be Roman Catholics, the rest Reformed, yet they mutually agree, and are confederate with Geneva, and are its only security against its potent neighbours, as they themselves are from being attacked by the greater potentates, by the mutual jealousy of their neighbours, as either of them would be overbalanced, should the Swiss, who are wholly mercenary and auxiliaries, be subjected to France or Spain.

We were now arrived at St. Maurice, a large handsome town and residence of the President, where justice is done. To him we presented our letter from Sion, and made known the ill-usage we had received for killing a wretched goat, which so incensed him, as he sware if we would stay he would not only help us to our money again, but most severely punish the whole rabble; but our desire of revenge had by this time subsided, and glad we were to be gotten so near France, which we reckoned as good as home. He courteously invited us to dine with him; but we excused ourselves, and, returning to our inn, whilst we were eating something before we took horse, the Governor had caused two pages to bring us a present of two great vessels of covered plate full of excellent wine, in which we drank his health, and rewarded the youths; they were two vast bowls supported by two Swisses, handsomely wrought after the German manner. This civility and that of our host at Sion, perfectly reconciled us to the highlanders; and so, proceeding on our journey, we passed this afternoon through the gate which divides the Valais from the Duchy of Savoy, into which we were now entering, and so, through Montei, we arrived that evening at Beveretta. Being extremely weary and complaining of my head, and finding little accommodation in the house, I caused one of our hostess's daughters to be removed out of her bed, and went immediately into it whilst it was yet warm, being so heavy with pain and drowsiness that I would not stay to have the sheets changed; but I shortly after paid dearly for my impatience, falling sick of the small-pox so soon as I came to Geneva, for by the smell of frankincense and the tale the good woman told me of her daughter having had an ague, I afterwards concluded she had been newly recovered of the small-pox.

BACCHUS IN GRAUBÜNDEN

FROM *Our Life in the Swiss Highlands*

JOHN ADDINGTON SYMONDS

Scholars know John Addington Symonds for his critical studies in the Renaissance, Elizabethan drama, and Greek poetry. Mountain lovers know him for *Our Life in the Swiss Highlands,* written with his daughter, Margaret.

Symonds lived in Switzerland for a good portion of his life. He had been ordered to Egypt to arrest an incipient tuberculosis. On the way he stopped at Davos to look into the new method of Alpine open-air treatment. He was so taken with Davos that he never left. He built a house in the mountains, became part of the life of the community, devoted the proceeds of his writings to its welfare. In this selection on the wine industry of the Swiss Alps he writes about the people with a warmth generated by familiarity and affection.

LONG RESIDENCE IN THIS CANTON MADE ME FAMILIAR WITH ALL SORTS OF VAL-telline wine: with rough Inferno, generous Forzato, delicate Sassella, harsher Montagner, the raspberry flavour of Grumello, the sharp invigorating twang of Villa. The colour, ranging from garnet to almandine or ruby, told me the age and quality of the vintage; and I had learned many secrets about the proper way of handling it. I furthermore arrived at the conclusion, which is certainly a just one, that good Valtelline can only be tasted at a very considerable height above the sea; for this wine matures slowly in the cold of a mountain climate, and acquires a bouquet here unknown at lower levels. In a word, it amused my leisure to make or think myself a connoisseur. My literary taste was tickled by the praise bestowed in the Augustan age on Rhætic grapes by Virgil—

> Et quo te carmine dicam
> Rhætica? nec cellis ideo contende Falernis.

I piqued myself on thinking that, could the poet but have drunk one bottle of old Grumello at Samaden—where Stilicho, by the way, in his famous recruiting expedition, described so eloquently by the poet Claudian, may perhaps have drunk it—he would have been less chary in his panegyric. For the point of inferiority on which he seems to insist—namely, that Valtelline wine does not ripen well in the cellar—is only proper to this vintage in Italian climate. Here it attains its maximum of excellence after it has been kept a quarter of a century in wood; and certainly no Falernian manufactured at the present day can compete with it.

Such meditations led my fancy on the path of history. Is there truth, then, in the dim tradition that this mountain-land was colonized by Etruscans? Is *Ras* the root of Rhætia? The Etruscans were accomplished winegrowers, we know. It was their Montepulciano which drew the Gauls to Rome, if Livy can be trusted. Perhaps they first planted the vine in Valtelline. Perhaps its superior culture in that district may be due to ancient use surviving in a secluded Alpine valley. One thing is certain, that the peasants of Sondrio and Tirano understand viticulture better than the Italians of Lombardy.

Then my thoughts ran on to the period of modern history, when the Grisons seized the Valtelline in lieu of war-pay from the Dukes of Milan. For some three centuries they held it as a subject province. From the Rathhaus at Davos or Chur they sent their nobles—Von Salis and Buol, Planta and Sprecher von Bernegg—across the hills as governors or podestàs to Poschiavo, Sondrio, Tirano, and Morbegno. In those old days the Valtelline wines came duly every winter over snow-deep passes to fill the cellars of the Signori Grigioni. That quaint traveller, Tom Coryat, in his so-called *Crudities,* notes the custom early in the seventeenth century. And as that custom then obtained, it still subsists with little alteration. The wine-carriers—Weinführer, as they are called—first scaled the Bernina Pass, halting then as now, perhaps, at Poschiavo and Pontresina. Afterwards, in order to reach Davos, the pass of the Scaletta rose before them—a wilderness of untracked snowdrifts. The country-folk still point to narrow, light hand-sledges, on which the casks were charged before the last pitch of the pass. Some wine came, no doubt, on pack-saddles. A meadow in front of the Dischma Thal, where the pass ends, still bears the name of the Ross-Weid, or horse-pasture. It was here that the beasts of burden used for this wine service rested after their long labours. In favourable weather the whole journey from Tirano would have occupied at least four days, with scanty halts at night. . . .

With so much practical and theoretical interest in the produce of the Valtelline to stimulate my curiosity, I determined to visit the district at the season when the wine was leaving it. It was the winter of 1881–82, a winter of unparalleled beauty in the high Alps. Day succeeded day without a cloud. Night followed night with steady stars, gliding across clear mountain ranges and forests of dark pines unstirred by wind. I could not hope for a more prosperous season; and indeed I made such use of it, that between the months of January and March I crossed six passes of the Alps in open sleighs—the Fluela, Bernina, Splügen, Julier, Maloja, and Albula—with less difficulty and discomfort in mid-winter than the traveller may often find on them in June.

At the end of January my friend Christian and I left Davos long before the sun was up, and ascended for four hours through the interminable snow-drifts of the Fluela in a cold grey shadow. The sun's light seemed to elude us. It ran along the ravine through which we toiled; dipped down to touch the topmost pines above our heads; rested in golden calm upon the Schia-horn at our back; capriciously played here and there across the Weisshorn on our left, and made the precipices of the Schwartzhorn glitter on our right. But athwart our path it never fell until we reached the very summit of the pass. Then we passed quietly into the full glory of the winter morn-ing—a tranquil flood of sunbeams pouring through air of crystalline purity, frozen and motionless. White peaks and dark brown rocks soared up, cutting a sky of almost purple blueness. A stillness that might be felt brooded over the whole world; but in that stillness there was nothing sad, no suggestion of suspended vitality. It was the stillness rather of untroubled health, of strength omnipotent but unexerted.

From the Hospiz of the Fluela the track plunges at one bound into the valley of the Inn, following a narrow cornice carved from the smooth bank of snow, and hung, without break or barrier, a thousand feet or more above the torrent. The summer road is lost in snow-drifts. The galleries built as a protection from avalanches, which sweep in rivers from those grim, bare fells above, are blocked with snow. Their useless arches yawn, as we glide over or outside them, by paths which instinct in our horse and driver traces. As a fly may creep along a house-roof, slanting downwards we de-scend. One whisk from the swinged tail of an avalanche would hurl us, like a fly, into the ruin of the gaping gorge. But this season little snow has fallen on the higher hills; and what still lies there is hard frozen. Therefore we have no fear as we whirl fast and faster from the snow-fields into the black forests of gnarled cembras and wind-wearied pines. Then Süss is reached, where the Inn hurries its shallow waters, clogged with ice-floes, through a sleepy hamlet. The stream is pure and green, for the fountains of the glaciers are locked by winter frosts, and only clear rills from perennial sources swell its tide. At Süss we lost the sun, and toiled in garish gloom and silence, nipped by the ever-deepening cold of evening, upwards for four hours to Samaden. . . .

The chief feature of the Bernina—what makes it a dreary pass enough in summer, but infinitely beautiful in winter—is its breadth; illimitable undulations of snow-drifts; immensity of open sky; unbroken lines of white, descending in smooth curves from glittering ice-peaks.

A glacier hangs in air above the frozen lakes, with all its green-blue ice-cliffs glistening in intensest light. Pitz Palü shoots aloft like sculptured marble, delicately veined with soft aerial shadows of translucent blue. At the summit of the pass all Italy seems to burst upon the eyes in those steep serried ranges, with their craggy crests, violet-hued in noonday sunshine, as though a bloom of plum or grape had been shed over them, enamelling their jagged precipices. The top of the Bernina is not always thus in winter. It has a bad reputation for the fury of invading storms, when falling snow hurtles together with snow scooped from the drifts in eddies, and the weltering white sea shifts at the will of whirlwinds. The Hospice then may be tenanted for days together by weather-bound wayfarers; and a line drawn close beneath its roof shows how two years ago the whole building was buried in one snow-shroud. This morning we lounged about the door, while our horses rested and postillions and carters pledged one another in cups of new Veltliner.

The road takes an awful and sudden dive downwards, quite irrespective of the carefully engineered post-track. At this season the path is badly broken into ruts and chasms by the wine traffic. In some places it was indubitably perilous: a narrow ledge of mere ice skirting thinly-clad hard-frozen banks of snow, which fell precipitately sideways for hundreds of sheer feet. We did not slip over this parapet, though we were often within an inch of doing so. Had our horse stumbled, it is not probable that I should have been writing this.

When we came to the galleries which defend the road from avalanches, we saw ahead of us a train of over forty sledges ascending, all charged with Valtelline wine. Our postillions drew up at the inner side of the gallery, between massive columns of the purest ice dependent from the rough-hewn roof and walls of rock. A sort of open *loggia* on the farther side framed vignettes of the Valtelline mountains in their hard cerulean shadows and keen sunlight. Between us and the view defiled the wine-sledges; and as each went by, the men made us drink out of their *trinketti*. These are oblong, hexagonal wooden kegs, holding about fourteen litres, which the carter fills with wine before he leaves the Valtelline, to cheer him on the homeward journey. You raise it in both hands, and when the bung has been removed, allow the liquor to flow stream-wise down your throat. It was a most extraordinary Bacchic procession—a pomp which, though undreamed of on the banks of the Ilissus, proclaimed the deity of Dionysos in authentic fashion. Struggling horses, grappling at the ice-bound floor with sharp-spiked shoes; huge, hoarse drivers, some clad in sheepskins from Italian valleys, some brown as bears in rough Graubünden homespun; casks, dropping their spilth of red wine on the snow; greetings, embracings; patois of Bergamo, Romansch, and German roaring around the low-browed vaults and tingling ice pillars; pourings forth of libations of the new strong Valtelline on breasts and beards;—the whole made up a scene of stalwart jollity and manful labour such as I have nowhere else in such wild circumstances witnessed. Many Davosers were there, the men of Andreas Gredig, Valär, and so forth; and all of these, on greeting Christian, forced us to drain a *Schluck* from their unmanageable cruses. Then on they went, crying, creaking, struggling, straining through the corridor, which echoed deafeningly, the gleaming crystals of those hard Italian mountains in their winter raiment building a background of still beauty to the savage Bacchanalian riot of the team.

How little visitors who drink Valtelline wine at San Moritz or Davos reflect by what strange ways it reaches them. A sledge can scarcely be laden with more than one cask of 300 litres on the ascent; and this cask, according to the state of the road, has many times to be shifted from wheels to runners and back again before the journey is accomplished. One carter will take charge of two horses, and consequently of two sledges and two casks, driving them both by voice and gesture rather than by rein. When they leave the Valtelline, the carters endeavour, as far as possible, to take the pass in gangs, lest bad weather or an accident upon the road should overtake them singly. At night they hardly rest three hours, and rarely think of sleeping, but spend the time in drinking and conversation. The horses are fed and littered; but for them, too, the night-halt is little better than a baiting-time. In fair weather the passage of the mountain is not difficult, though tiring. But woe to men and beasts alike if they encounter storms! Not a few perish in the passes; and it frequently happens that their only chance is to unyoke the horses and leave the sledges in a snow-wreath, seeking for themselves such shelter as may possibly be gained, frost-bitten, after hours of battling with impermeable drifts. The wine is frozen into one solid mass of rosy ice before it reaches Pontresina. This does not hurt the young vintage, but it is highly injurious to wine of some years' standing. The perils of the journey are aggravated by the savage temper of the drivers. Jealousies between the natives of rival districts spring up; and there are men alive who have fought the whole way down from Fluela Hospice to Davos-Platz with knives and stones, hammers and hatchets, wooden staves and splintered cartwheels, staining the snow with blood, and bringing broken pates, bruised limbs, and senseless comrades home to their women to be tended.

"I WUZ BORN AN' RAISED IN THE OZARK HILLS AN' DON'T KNOW NOTHIN' ELSE"

FROM *Pioneers of the Ozarks*

LENNIS L. BROADFOOT

The people of the Ozarks whose stories Lennis Broadfoot records here with so authentic and fresh a flavor are vanishing. Our urban civilization has impinged even on these isolated Missouri hills. Broadfoot is himself a native of the Ozarks, part Cherokee Indian, as his name suggests. His father picked the highest spot in the mountains to build a cabin and from boyhood Broadfoot looked down on the life of the hills below. Before it had gone, he wanted to record this older and simpler way of life. He carried his easel for miles into the canyons and up the peaks to draw the portraits of the old pioneers and to listen to their stories.

Broadfoot has worked all through the western country as ranch hand and artist and he says he would rather "draw a picture of an Ozark grandmother loitering around her cabin home with a pipe in her mouth than all the glamour girls of Hollywood." We can be glad for his preference.

KATHERINE BURK

Timber, Missouri

Mrs. Burk Says:

"I AM ONE HUNDRED AN' ELEVEN YEARS OL', AN' WUZ BORN AN' RAISED IN THE Ozark hills, an' don't know nothin' else.

"I wuz born February 13, 1829. I guess I am about the oldest person in these hills.

"I have smoked an' chawed terbacker ever since I wuz a little girl, an' I don't believe terbacker hurts a body either, if they use it right, but the way young people use it nowdays, I think it hurts 'em. They sit around, suckin' cigarettes an' draw the smoke down in their lungs, an' soon they get to coughin' an' wheezin' in their lungs like a pig that's sick with cholera, an' their health is gone an' they die young.

"My pappy an' mammy smoked an' chawed too, but they smoked a clay pipe like I do, an' we never smoked or chawed nothin' only what we raised ourselves.

"I reckon I'm ol'-fashioned an' foagy, but I believe the ol' way of life is best.

"I believe in moon signs, witches, an' all them things. People used to think I wuz a witch. Lots of people don't know what a witch is.

"If you don't know, I'll tell ye: A witch is an ol' person—usually a womern, with humpback, an' goosenecked with long chin an' nose, with stringy, frizzlie hair, deep wrinkles in her face, an' her eyes as glassy an' glairy as a dyin' calf's eye, an' sets aroun' or snoops aroun' an' says nothin' to nobody, an' has the power to send their spirit away to work around the homes of others an' do things.

"The reason why they won't talk is 'cause their mind an' spirit is allers away somewheres else. An' ye cain't become a witch or have the power of witchcraft till ye air at least seventy years ol'.

"I can recognize every witch as soon as I look at 'em. They can shore do ye a lot of torment. We have had 'em to come to our home in the night an' tie knots in our hosses' an' cows' tails, an' pick all the feathers out of our ol' gray rooster's tail an' sich things as that, an' here's what we done to stop it, or kill the spirit:

"The witch usually has a rabbit to carry her spirit here an' there, doin' devilment, an' we watched our chance to shoot an' kill the rabbit, or if we didn't kill the rabbit, we would keep our minds good an' strong on the person we thought wuz the witch while we stuck a dishrag full of pins an' throw it in the fire an' burn it, or take a ball of yarn an' pierce it with a darnin' needle with our minds concentrated on that certain ol' witch.

"We would get 'em that way."

MILLER BELL

Iron County, Missouri

Mr. Bell Says:

"I am seventy-five years ol' an' was born an' raised in the Iron County hills, an' have worked at this, that, an' t'other all my life, till I am broke down an' hain't no good any more, an' now all I can do is jist plod around with this ol' 'walkin' cane' an' see what others air doin', an' hear 'em talk.

"I usually come to town on Saturday if I can get here, an' after I plod around on the streets fer a while, shakin' hands with ol' timers, an' findin' out if their folks air all well, an' how the crops air, I go into a grocer store an' sit down on a sack ov taters or a sack ov shorts or a goods' box, an' hear 'em talk about how to run the givernment.

"Now I hain't no idea much how to run this givernment, an' don't claim to be so dad-burn smart, but I know there's a screw loose somewhere! I live on a little patch ov land an' have allers been a little one-horse farmer, raisin' a few pigs an' calves down here in the hills, an' have jist worked my hocks off, an' still somebody else got it! An' who wuz it, the packers, or the merchant?

"Why gee whizz! us fellers can raise a hog an' ship it to St. Louis, an' not even get enough out ov it to pay the freight ov the dad-burn thing, an' sometimes haft to send a basket ov eggs along to help pay the freight; an' the packers will take that durned hog, an' butcher it, an' save everything, hoof, hair, an' all, an' even bottle up the squeal an' sell it fer more than we get fer the whole hog!

"Now I think the givernment ort to look into things like that, take the whole works apart an' fix the loose wheels. Course, ye can allers get plenty ov goods' box an' tater sack advice around the little grocer store, ov how to run the givernment, but now actually, fellers, there's shore a magget in the apple somewhere, 'cause us fellers don't get enough money for a three-year-ol' steer when we ship it out to buy enough ov its taller to grease a shot gun barrel after it makes the round an' comes back to our small town butcher!

"Sometimes I think I could set on a sack ov shorts, or sack ov taters, an' run a better givernment than some ov 'em do. These duck-billed, beer-bellied politicians, come around at election time, makin' their soap-box speeches, an' tellin' us ol' humpy farmers how they're goin' to take the whole works apart an' see what makes it tick, an' they're goin' to put in a new cogwheel an' make it free wheelin' fer us fellers, but ever' time one ov these greasy tongued liars puts in a new wheel, it's one that grinds a new kink in our legs, an' a hump on our backs.

"I've been comin' to town fer a long time an' talkin' it over with these fellers an' we hain't never got it fixed yet, an' I can see that if we ever get anywhere, we've got to do somethin' besides set on a sack ov taters an' talk; 'cause things air gettin' in a mess, an' taxes goin' higher'n a giraff's back, an' all ye can hear is, 'Revenue! revenue! revenue!' an' the first thing ye know, ye'll haf to wear a revenue stamp on the seat ov yer pants to have the right to set down.

"I've hearn so much talk an' had so many promises I'm fed up an' disgusted; an' I've worked my life away, an' all I've got to show fer it, is this ol' walkin' cane, an' a hump on my back like a camel. I reckon us ol' farmers air about the only animal on earth that can stand more than one skinnin', an' we git it, ever time we vote, or sell a pig."

ELY HAYES

Gaino, Missouri

Ely Says:

"I am seventy-nine years ol' an' hain't never been married yet, an' don't guess I want a womern now, 'cause I'm gettin' too old, an' don't know what I'd do with one. I've been around a whole lot in my life an' see'd lots ov people, but never see'd any womern that I wanted to marry.

"When I wuz young, I worked with the wreckers' crew on the Iron Mountain Railroad, at DeSoto, Missouri, for a while, then I went to St. Louis an' stayed fer a short spell, an' I jist got so gol-durned lonesome I couldn't live there, an' I don't like ol' noisy city life, an' druther live down here in the hills where I can sleep good, get a good fresh breath, an' drink spring water out ov an ol' gourd.

"I've lived alone in this little shack fer forty years, an' every year I plant gourd seeds around my house an' let 'em vine all over this little ol' hut. I like to see these long-necked gourds hangin' on the vines around my porch an' the corners ov my house. The gourd vine makes a fine shade for the house, an' they're awful purty too, an' the gourds are fine an' healthy to drink out ov.

"When I first moved here, I tried to raise corn, but after I had worked hard an' raised it, the wild turkeys would eat it up. I never see'd the like! Why, I've killed as many as five an' six in a single night! An' the deer wuz jist as bad, 'cause they'd jump in the fields an' eat the corn an' beans before it wuz ripe, an' many a time I've sit around an' killed three or four in a day, cut the hams off an' sell 'em, an' leave the rest lie; but I'd like to see you do that today, 'cause if you'd kill a deer now, you'd get your head cut off.

"Some people wonder how I live down in the hills like this all alone, but I'm gettin' along fine.

"I druther live a bachelor's life down in the hills, drink muddy water out ov a gourd, sleep in a holler log, fry me own fritters, an' eat cracklin's, than to take chances on livin' in war like some ov 'em, an' havin' a sack ov beans threshed out over my head or the cookstove throwed at me, jist 'cause I might happen to say the biscuits wuz a little too hard or the corn bread had a little too much soda in it."

DR. JOHN ROBERT HUFFER
CORN AND WART DOCTOR OF THE OZARKS

Turtle, Missouri

Dr. Huffer Says:

"You hear lots said about the Ozarks an' Ozarkians, but I reckon I know more people in these hills, an' have been in more Ozark counties an' homes than any other man ov my age, 'cause I have a profession that calls me out here an' there at all hours.

"I am seventy-three years ol', an' am known as the 'corn an' wart doctor' ov the Ozarks, an' can cure any case ov headache too by rubbin' my hands together till I git up the electricity, an' my hands become hot, then apply them gently to the patient's head, an' with a few light strokes ov rubbin', the pain leaves, an' the patient goes off to sleep. It is the electricity I have in me that does the work. I am full ov it.

"I cure all my own headaches the same way, an' for years an' years I have been goin' frum house to house, through the hills takin' off warts an' corns, bringin' relief to the sufferin'.

"I hain't made no money out ov it, but sometimes I git a chicken, a few eggs, a gallon ov molasses, or a little terbacker, but, after all, it's a lot ov pleasure to me to know that I am able to step into the ol' cabin homes an' remove frowns frum faces an' make glad hearts by liftin' that painful corn frum the ol' toe, an' that's worth somethin'.

"Ol' sore achin' corns have caused many a fuss between husband an' wife 'cause a man may come in frum his work sometimes, an' say somethin' to his wife that don't sound jist right to her 'cause that ol' corn is givin' her fits, an' they git into a big fuss an' separate, when nothin' in the world caused it but the miserable ol' corn. So I think I have kept peace in many families jist that way.

"If you have a wart on the end ov your nose or some place, I can jist rub my finger over it gently, with a few hocus-pocus remarks, an' the wart magically disappears.

"The Ozarkians know me well an' are glad to see Dr. Huffer comin' when that ol' wart or corn is givin' 'em thunder."

ANDEAN RAILROAD

FROM *Casual Wanderings in Ecuador*

BLAIR NILES

Blair Niles is partial to explorers as husbands. She was married to William Beebe, the naturalist, and traveled with him on his many scientific expeditions to Central and South America. After they separated she married Robert Niles, by avocation an explorer and photographer. Together they have explored many of the wilder areas of the world. She has a reporter's eye for illuminating color and detail and the evocative imagination to project them for the reader. This narrative of a railroad cut through the jungle and across the Andes is from one of her early books, *Casual Wanderings in Ecuador.*

AT SEVEN MINUTES PAST SEVEN THE TRAIN OUT OF DURÁN WAS RUNNING smoothly along over flat fields spread with pale lavender convolvulus fresh in the early morning. A hawk with a neatly white-banded tail was swooping hungrily close to the ground. On the margins of reedy marshes were plovers and charming jacanas, who continually stretched their dainty wings as if to show how lovely a lemon-yellow they were in the early sunlight. Tall cotton-trees bare of leaves were covered with yellow blossoms—the clear yellow of a crocus in spring sunshine. And other trees were hung with the pendant oriole nests of black and gold caciques.

The day was so gaily young, and in the long cane-seated first-class coach where we were packed two to each seat every one seemed in the humor for adventure, glad now to have risen while it was yet dark, and to have come upon a train which ran thus smoothly along through a flowery kingdom of birds. It seemed in that kingdom to be a feast-day, a day of celebration. It was scarcely credible that every morning could be so colorful, so vibrant with flutter and song.

At a quarter to eight we halted before a collection of dilapidated houses with dejected balconies. Along the roofs grim rows of vultures sat and stared at us. Even the palms and orange-trees and long rustling banana leaves did not succeed in mitigating the forlornness.

This was Yaguachi, where fifty years ago the track of the first railroad in Ecuador was laid for a short distance across the fields. Little by little this track was added to until some years later it was extended as far as Chimbo, where it stopped abruptly, near the foot of the stupendous, the forbidding Andes. . . .

At Bucay we exchanged our wood-burning locomotive for an enormous oil-burner. Here, fifty miles from Guayaquil, the Andes rise precipitously eleven thousand feet. For two generations it was the dream of Ecuador to scale this wall of the Andes and to connect the seaport of Guayaquil with the mountain capital, Quito.

As the years passed frequent attempts were made to realize that dream. Under various administrations elaborate surveys were made between Chimbo and the towering plateau, and contract after contract was let for the continuation of the road. But all efforts failed. The Andes frowned down upon the trains which puffed into Chimbo only to return ignominiously to Durán. The vague superstition that these Andes of Ecuador could not be surmounted grew into a settled conviction. The Guayaquil to Quito Railroad was an ambitious and patriotic scheme, but, alas, an impossibility. There stood the Andes to prove it!

Meanwhile traffic between the interior and the coast continued to pass laboriously over century-old trails. It passed on the backs of Indians and mules and llamas, up and down the mountain sides, over primitive swaying bridges suspended above torrential rivers, across desert *páramos,* along the face of precipitous cliffs, through jungle swamps where men and beasts floundered in mire, and along trails often so narrow that the muleteers had to run on ahead shouting to make sure that no caravan approached from the opposite direction.

In this traffic more than seventy thousand mules were employed. How the trail must have echoed with the familiar shouts of *"Mula! . . . Pasa! . . . Lado! . . . Pasa!"*

And then each December would come the rains—the deluge! For six months traffic would cease, only the letter-carriers maintaining a fitful communication between the coast and the capital. No wonder the railroad had been for so long the dream of every administration!

Eloy Alfaro came to the presidency of Ecuador in 1896. His years of political exile in the United States led him to declare that only North Americans could build the Guayaquil to Quito Railroad.

Accordingly two such North Americans were found—Archer and John Harman, Virginians, the sons of a Civil War colonel, and thus born not

only in the shadow of those lost and mistaken battles, but in the light of a
valiant spirit inherited from colonial cavaliers.

They were young and full of faith. What to them was the settled
conviction that a thing could not be done? Their vision did not stop at
Chimbo. As for the manifold difficulties . . . difficulties were, like the Andes, made to be mastered.

Archer Harman raised the funds to finance the proposed road and
helped the new president, Alfaro, to reëstablish the then demoralized credit
of Ecuador. But it was John Harman who was the chief engineer in charge of
the difficult enterprise of actual construction. In person he led his staff
of engineers up and down over that obstructing Andean wall, surveying,
plotting, considering all possible routes. Nothing disheartened him. . . .

I can fancy with what preoccupation Harman lay down at night and
rose up in the morning; how absently he went through the routine of existence; his mind absorbed in one thing, the creation of the Guayaquil to
Quito Railroad; a procession of problems passing always through his brain;
the construction of a mule trail from Bucay to the Pass over which supplies
and equipment might be transported . . . the grading . . . so difficult
. . . heavy . . . running as high as a hundred and seventy-five thousand
yards to the mile . . . very heavy . . . earth . . . loose rock . . . solid
rock . . . earth . . . by wheelbarrows . . . almost entirely by wheelbarrows . . . carts and scrapers not much use . . . mountains too steep . . .
difficult grading . . . with wheelbarrows. . . .

Thus it came about that at Bucay, at the foot of the Western Cordilleras,
we were changing locomotives, taking on the powerful engine which was to
pull us up the Andes.

We began at once to climb. Green bamboo plumes gathered about the
banks of clear stony brooks. The hills were covered with high trees. There
was an elusive difference in the air that came in with the opening and closing of the doors, when the conductor passed through the train. It was crisp
air, and in the streams there was a mountain sparkle, although bananas and
palms still grew along the track clearing.

We crossed the Chan-Chan River. The engine was working hard. We
could feel the throb of its mighty effort. We were now pulling only four
cars, all that the biggest locomotives can drag from Bucay to the Pass.

We began to see cactus in abundance and maguey. There were also
lovely little shrubs with dark-green foliage and pink and white flowers,
silky and fluffy like thistle-down. There were purple flowering vines and
yellow trumpet blossoms. In the high valleys sky-bound mists paused before
drifting on.

We stopped to take on water from a stream gushing out of the mountain-
side. The engine seemed to draw great tired breaths.

And then we went on again. The bamboos along the streams had become smaller. Organ cactus appeared. All other growth was stunted.

Just before noon we reached Huigra. At Huigra the trains wait twenty minutes for lunch; and there, if one is going to Cuenca, the third largest city in the republic, one leaves the train to ride three days on muleback over trails which even in Ecuador have an evil reputation.

The air at Huigra was already sufficiently keen to be mildly exciting, and we remembered that down at Guayaquil, four thousand feet below us, this was the sultry sleepy noon hour, when the vender of iced *chicha* drowsily proclaims his beverage up and down the arcades.

Leaving Huigra the hills were bare and dry, rugged and stern. In air brilliantly clear, under a sky pale blue flecked with clouds of fleece, we negotiated the difficult "Devil's Nose."

The Nose rises up a conical mountain, standing at the end of the valley, barring the way. It is without vegetation, arid and precipitous. It is an arrogant Nose, seeming to stand forth contemptuously, dominating the valley.

Here had been a problem for John Harman. Thus far, following the cañon of the Chan-Chan River, he had encountered no extraordinary engineering difficulties. But at the base of the Nose the valley divided, separating into two ravines, each of which ran straight against the wall of the Andes. There was nothing to do but somehow, by way of that Nose, to reach the apparently inaccessible higher level, from which it would be possible to continue the ascent.

We ran along the left fork of the valley, skirting the base of the Nose. Looking up we could see the lines of track, one above the other; a daring zigzag cut out of so sheer a mountain-side that supporting walls of rock had, here and there, been constructed to reinforce the crumbling surface. But how were we to mount to those lines of track stretched like mere threads high upon the mountain?

We had reached the sudden end of the ravine. It had led us into a *cul-de-sac.* There was no going forward, and the ravine had so narrowed, hemmed in by almost perpendicular hills, that a loop was impossible. We dropped off the brakeman, who waited for us to pass and then threw the switch connecting us with the track which led up along the Nose. Up this track we began now to back. The brakeman swung on board again. Very slowly, the locomotive laboring with ponderous measured chugs, we were pushed up a grade incredibly steep, backing along a single track cut out of a ledge of rock.

Below us was the line over which we had just come. As we mounted, it dropped away from us, growing rapidly smaller.

We climbed with great sobbing breaths, spaced far apart—so far apart that it would not have been surprising had their rhythm come abruptly to an end. We climbed toward the bridge of the Nose . . . slowly . . . heavily . . . and then rounded the bridge to the other side, where there was another switch, and where the line up which we were backing came to a dead end. We felt perilously suspended there, looking out over the valley of the Chan-Chan River, a narrow valley shut in on either side by mountains, with our tiny track many times crossing and recrossing the shining river: all seeming, like the past, ever so far away . . . a thing experienced long ago.

To the east the line of the proposed Cuenca Railroad, of which only about thirty kilometers have been laid, wound up from the valley and wandered off among the tumbled hills. Ahead of us stretched the third arm of the great zigzag which was to complete the ascent of the Devil's Nose.

This time it was the fireman who threw the connecting switch. The engine now went forward, while we, looking dizzily down upon the two lines of track directly beneath us, watched them, too, recede and diminish . . . until at last they could no longer be seen, and we knew that we had passed from the Nose to the mountains behind it!

We had come up into a world where hills were heaped high. Often the valleys were cultivated, and irrigated fields were thrown like vast patchwork quilts upon the mountain sides—quilts made of squares and rectangles and triangles. The dark patches were plowed earth; the tan and gold patches were ripening grain; the vivid blue-green were fields of alfalfa. These patches were separated by the irrigation ditches showing as dark lines, by hedges, and occasionally by straight rows of the slender eucalyptus-trees. Sometimes the fields extended to the very summits, growing smaller as they advanced, until at the apex the patch was composed of only a few stalks of corn, waving there eleven thousand feet above the sea.

And still we climbed. . . . The Alausi loop gained for us with one bold flourish an added elevation of 290 feet.

Alausi itself is a tiny adobe settlement, two miles high in the sun, with cabbages and corn growing about it. The Indian women who gathered to watch the train come in wore round full skirts of native weave—orange, blue, and red. They were long, those skirts, touching the dusty earth. And I saw at Alausi the sweetest little Indian girl, not more than three years old, dressed to match the women in a full, orange skirt down to her small bare toes, and a tiny gray shawl over her head. There were boy muleteers, too, scarcely out of their babyhood, clad in scarlet ponchos and loose white trousers, in exact imitation of their fathers. They had an air of poise, of being masters of their environment, which reminded me of the capable childish hands which had brought our boat to dock on that first day in Guayaquil.

The Indians of Ecuador, though very different in their dress from Tibetans, yet in many ways recalled them. They both have the sturdy, stocky build of mountain people. The shape and cast of their features are astonishingly similar, for the Ecuadorian Indian of the highlands is of a decidedly Mongolian type. The warm red blood glows under their yellowish brown skins just as it does in the faces of the Tibetans who flock about the station at Darjeeling; so that it seemed strange not to see here, too, an old Buddhist priest twirling his prayer-wheel!

Beyond Alausi mountains unroll, fold upon fold, to the horizon, with, ever so far below, the deep gorge of the river.

Still we climbed . . . And when we stopped it seemed entirely to let the great panting locomotive catch its breath. . . .

At an elevation of nearly eleven thousand feet we came over the Palmira Pass. In a distance of forty-seven miles we had risen ten thousand feet. We had at last surmounted the Andes!

The Guayaquil and Quito Railroad had been first a vision; then a plan, a road upon paper; then in all its details operating in a man's brain, in the brain of John Harman; and finally a reality, coming to be known familiarly as the "G. & Q."

CONDOR

THE MOUNTAIN DIALECT

FROM *Our Southern Highlanders*

HORACE KEPHART

Horace Kephart wrote *Our Southern Highlanders* in 1913. It quickly went through a number of editions and even now, forty years later, it ranks high among books on the American mountaineers. Kephart was a university librarian and authority on woodcraft and camping who lived in close intimacy with the people of the Carolina Smokies, the small farmers who lived off the traveled roads and whose lives and work and customs were shaped almost completely by the isolation and inbreeding of their mountain living. The chapter heads in Kephart's book give the flavor of this rapidly disappearing life: "The Blood Feud," "The Revenuer," "Moonshine Land." Among the most interesting chapters is the one on "Mountain Dialect" from which this selection has been taken.

ONE DAY I HANDED A VOLUME OF JOHN FOX'S STORIES TO A NEIGHBOR AND asked him to read it, being curious to learn how those vivid pictures of mountain life would impress one who was born and bred in the same atmosphere. He scanned a few lines of the dialogue, then suddenly stared at me in amazement.

"What's the matter with it?" I asked, wondering what he could have found to startle him at the very beginning of a story.

"Why, that feller *don't know how to spell!*"

Gravely I explained that dialect must be spelled as it is pronounced, so far as possible, or the life and savor of it would be lost. But it was of no use. My friend was outraged. "That tale-teller then is jest makin' fun of the mountain people by misspellin' our talk. You educated folks don't spell your own words the way you say them."

A most palpable hit; and it gave me a new point of view.

To the mountaineers themselves their speech is natural and proper, of course, and when they see it bared to the spotlight, all eyes drawn toward it by an orthography that is as odd to them as it is to us, they are stirred to wrath, just as we would be if our conversation were reported by some Josh Billings or Artemas Ward. . . .

Seldom is a "hill-billy" at a loss for a word. Lacking other means of expression, there will come "spang" from his mouth a coinage of his own. Instantly he will create (always from English roots, of course) new words by combination, or by turning nouns into verbs or otherwise interchanging the parts of speech.

Crudity or deficiency of the verb characterizes the speech of all primitive peoples. In mountain vernacular many words that serve as verbs are only nouns of action, or adjectives, or even adverbs. "That bear'll meat me a month." "They churched Pitt for tale-bearin'." "Granny kept faultin' us all day." "Are ye fixin' to go squirrelin'?" "Sis blouses her waist a-purpose to carry a pistol." "My boy Jesse book-kept for the camp." "I disgust bad liquor." "This poke salat eats good." "I ain't goin' to bed it no longer" (lie abed). "We can muscle this log up." "I wouldn't pleasure them enough to say it." "Josh ain't much on sweet-heartin'." "I don't confidence them dogs much." "The creek away up thar turkey-tails out into numerous leetle forks."

A verb will be coined from an adverb: "We better git some wood, bettern we?" Or from an adjective: "Much that dog and see won't he come along" (pet him, make much of him). "I didn't do nary thing to contrary her." "Baby, that onion'll strong ye!" "Little Jimmy fell down and benastied himself to beat the devil."

Conversely, nouns are created from verbs. "Hit don't make no differ." "I didn't hear no give-out at meetin'" (announcement). "You can git ye one more gittin' o' wood up thar." "That Nantahala is a master shut-in, jest a plumb gorge." Or from an adjective: "Them bugs—the little old hatefuls!" "If anybody wanted a history of this county for fifty years he'd git a lavish of it by reading that mine-suit testimony." Or from an adverb: "Nance tuk the biggest through at meetin'!" (shouting spell). An old lady quoted to me in a plaintive quaver:

> "It matters not, so I've been told,
>   Where the body goes when the heart grows cold;

"But," she added, "a person has a rather about where he'd be put." . . .

Everywhere in the mountains we hear of biscuit-bread, ham-meat, rifle-gun, rock-clift, ridin'-critter, cow-brute, man-person, women-folks, preacher-man, granny-woman and neighbor-people. In this category belong the famous double-barreled pronouns: we-all and you-all in Kentucky, we-uns and you-uns in Carolina and Tennessee. (I have even heard such locution as this: "Let's we-uns all go over to youerunses house.") Such usages are regarded generally as mere barbarisms, and so they are in English, but

Miss Murfree cites correlatives in the Romance languages: French *nous autres,* Italian *noi altri,* Spanish *nosotros.*

The mountaineers have some queer ways of intensifying expression. "I'd *tell* a man," with the stress as here indicated, is simply a strong affirmative. "We had one more *time*" means a rousing good time. "P'int-blank" is a superlative or an epithet: "We jist p'int-blank got it to do." "Well, p'int-blank, if they ever come back again, I'll move!"

A double negative is so common that it may be crowded into a single word: "I did it the unthoughtless of anything I ever done in my life." Triple negatives are easy: "I ain't got nary none." A mountaineer can accomplish the quadruple: "That boy ain't never done nothin' nohow." Yea, even the quintuple: "I ain't never seen no men-folks of no kind do no washin'." . . .

Our highlander oftens speaks in Elizabethan or Chaucerian or even pre-Chaucerian terms. His pronoun hit antedates English itself, being the Anglo-Saxon neuter of he. Ey God, a favorite expletive, is the original of egad, and goes back of Chaucer. Ax for ask and kag for keg were the primitive and legitimate forms, which we trace as far as the time of Laya-mon. When the mountain boy challenges his mate: "I dar ye—I ain't afeared!" his verb and participle are of the same ancient and sterling rank. Afore, atwixt, awar, heap o' folks, peart, up and done it, usen for used, all these everyday expressions of the backwoods were contemporary with the *Canterbury Tales.* . . .

When one dines in a cabin back in the hills he will taste some strange dishes that go by still stranger names. Beans dried in the pod, then boiled "hull and all," are called leather-breeches (this is not slang, but the regular name). Green beans in the pod are called snaps; when shelled they are shuck-beans. The old Germans taught their Scotch and English neighbors the merits of scrapple, but here it is known as poor-do. Lath-open bread is made from biscuit dough, with soda and buttermilk, in the usual way, except that the shortening is worked in last. It is then baked in flat cakes, and has the peculiar property of parting readily into thin flakes when broken edgewise. I suppose that poor-do was originally poor-doin's, and lath-open bread denotes that it opens into lath-like strips. But etymology cannot be pushed recklessly in the mountains, and I offer these clews as a mere surmise.

Your hostess, proffering apple sauce, will ask, "Do you love sass?" I had to kick my chum Andy's shin the first time he faced this question. It is well for a traveler to be forewarned that the word love is commonly used here in the sense of like or relish.

If one is especially fond of a certain dish he declares that he is a fool about it. "I'm a plumb fool about pickle-beans." Conversely, "I ain't much of a fool about liver" is rather more than a hint of distaste. "I et me a bait" literally means a mere snack, but jocosely it may admit a hearty meal. If the provender be scant the hostess may say, "That's right at a smidgen," meaning little more than a mite; but if plenteous, then there are rimptions.

To "grabble 'taters" is to pick from a hill of new potatoes a few of the best, then smooth back the soil without disturbing the immature ones.

If the house be in disorder it is said to be all gormed or gaumed up, or things are just in a mommick.

When a man is tired he likely will call it worried; if in a hurry, he is in a swivvet; if nervous, he has the all-overs; if declining in health, he is on the down-go. If he and his neighbor dislike each other, there is a hardness between them; if they quarrel, it is a ruction, a rippit, a jower, or an up-scuddle—so be it there are no fatalities which would amount to a real fray.

A choleric or fretful persion is tetchious. Survigrous (ser-*vi*-grus) is a superlative of vigorous (here pronounced *vi*-grus, with long *i*): as "a survigrous baby," "a most survigrous cusser." Bodaciously means bodily or entirely: "I'm bodaciously ruint" (seriously injured). "Sim greened him out bodaciously" (to green out or sap is to outwit in trade). To disfurnish or discon*fit* means to incommode: "I hope it has not disconfit you very bad."

To shamp means to shingle or trim one's hair. A bastard is a woods-colt or an outsider. . . .

Evening, in the mountains, begins at noon instead of at sunset. Spell is used in the sense of while ("a good spell atterward") and soon for early ("a soon start in the morning"). The hillsmen say "a year come June," "Thursday 'twas a week ago," and "the year nineteen and eight."

Many common English words are used in peculiar senses by the mountain folk, as call for name or mention or occasion, clever for obliging, mimic or mock for resemble, a power or a sight for much, risin' for exceeding (also for inflammation), ruin for injure, scout for elude, stove for jabbed, surround for go around, word for phrase, take off for help yourself. Tale always means an idle or malicious report.

Some highland usages that sound odd to us are really no more than the original and literal meanings, as budget for bag or parcel, hampered for shackled or jailed. When a mountain swain "carries his gal to meetin' " he is not performing so great an athletic feat as was reported by Benjamin Franklin, who said, "My father carried his wife with three children to New England" (from Pennsylvania).

A mountaineer does not throw a stone; he "flings a rock." He sharpens tools on a grindin'-rock or whet-rock. Tomato, cabbage, molasses and baking powder are always used as plural nouns. "Pass me them molasses." "I'll have a few more of them cabbage." "How many bakin'-powders has you got?" . . .

The speech of the southern highlanders is alive with quaint idioms. "I swapped hosses, and I'll tell you fer why." "Your name ain't much common." "Who got to beat?" "You think me of it in the mornin'." "I 'low to go to town to-morrow." "The woman's aimin' to go to meetin'." "I had in head to plow to-day, but hit's come on to rain." "I've laid off and laid off to fix that fence." "Reckon Pete was knowin' to the sarcumstance?" "I'll name it to Newt, if so be he's thar." "I knowed in reason she'd have the mully-grubs over them doin's." "You cain't handily blame her."

"Air ye plumb bereft?" "How come it was this: he done me dirt." "I ain't carin' which nor whether about it." "Sam went to Andrews or to Murphy, one." "I tuk my fut in my hand and lit out." "He lit a rag fer home." "Don't much believe the wagon 'll come to-day." " 'Tain't powerful long to dinner, I don't reckon." "Phil's Ann give it out to each and every that Walt and Layunie 'd orter wed."

"Howdy, Tom: light and hitch."

"Reckon I'd better git on."

"Come in and set."

"Cain't stop long."

"Oh, set down and eat you some supper!"

"I've been."

"Won't ye stay the night? Looks like to me we'll have a rainin', windin' spell."

"No: I'll haffter go down."

"Well, come agin, and fix to stay a week."

"You-uns come down with me."

"Won't go now, I guess, Tom."

"Giddep! I'll be back by in the mornin'."

"Farwell!"

3

Men Against the Mountains

The ancients feared the high places. The traders of the Mediterranean world, of Northern Europe, later of Western America, searched for passes and circumventing routes. It was not alone the dangerous terrain that deterred them, but the unknown and mysterious heights, peopled by fear and folklore with dragons and giants and obscene, hairy half-men. But there were frontiersmen, then and later, some driven by hunger, some by dreams, some by needs only half understood, who climbed the great barriers and looked over the edge.

Among these records and stories of man against the mountains—against storm and avalanche and shifting rock, against cold and hunger and the hallucinations of high altitudes—are some of the most stirring pieces of writing in any language. Some end in tragedy, others in high comedy, but all are part of the great record of man's reconnaissance of the unknown.

THE STORM
HIS ADVERSARY

FROM *The Magic Mountain*

THOMAS MANN

It was in 1912 that Thomas Mann's wife spent three weeks at a sanitarium in Davos, Switzerland, to cure a catarrh of the lung. Mann spent the time with her and thought of writing a short story on the fascination with death, one which would give "the droll conflict between macabre adventure and bourgeois sense of duty." The story occupied him for twelve years, until 1924, and resulted in *The Magic Mountain,* a great epic of civilization in decay.

Hans Castorp, the major character, is symbolic of a middle-class sense of order and duty. Coming to visit at a Swiss sanitarium, a healthy man surrounded by decay, he discovers that he too is touched with disease. Our civilization, Mann intimates, is one enormous sanitarium. In this extract from the novel, Hans Castorp challenges the storm— symbol of the forces of nature which are utterly indifferent to man's fate.

IT WAS THREE IN THE AFTERNOON. HE HAD SET OUT SOON AFTER LUNCHEON, with the idea of cutting part of the long rest-cure, and tea as well, in order to be back before dark. He had brought some chocolate in his breeches pocket, and a small flask of wine; and told himself exultantly that he had still several hours to revel in all this grandeur.

The position of the sun was hard to recognize, veiled as it was in haze. Behind him, at the mouth of the valley, above that part of the mountains that was shut off from view, the clouds and mist seemed to thicken and move forward. They looked like snow—more snow—as though there were pressing demand for it! Like a good hard storm. Indeed, the little soundless flakes were coming down more quickly as he stood.

Hans Castorp put out his arm and let some of them come to rest on his sleeve; he viewed them with the knowing eye of the nature-lover. They looked mere shapeless morsels; but he had more than once had their like under his good lens, and was aware of the exquisite precision of form displayed by these little jewels, insignia, orders, agraffes—no jeweller, however skilled, could do finer, more minute work. Yes, he thought, there was a difference, after all, between this light, soft, white powder he trod with his skis, that weighed down the trees, and covered the open spaces, a difference between it and the sand on the beaches at home, to which he had likened it. For this powder was not made of tiny grains of stone; but of myriads of tiniest drops of water, which in freezing had darted together in symmetrical variation—parts, then, of the same anorganic substance which was the source of protoplasm, of plant life, of the human body. And among these myriads of enchanting little stars, in their hidden splendour that was too small for man's naked eye to see, there was not one like unto another; an endless inventiveness governed the development and unthinkable differentiation of one and the same basic scheme, the equilateral, equiangled hexagon. Yet each, in itself—this was the uncanny, the anti-organic, the life-denying character of them all—each of them was absolutely symmetrical, icily regular in form. They were too regular, as substance adapted to life never was to this degree—the living principle shuddered at this perfect precision, found it deathly, the very marrow of death—Hans Castorp felt he understood now the reason why the builders of antiquity purposely and secretly introduced minute variation from absolute symmetry in their columnar structures.

He pushed off again, shuffling through the deep snow on his flexible runners, along the edge of the wood, down the slope, up again, at random, to his heart's content, about and into this lifeless land. Its empty, rolling spaces, its dried vegetation of single dwarf firs sticking up through the snow, bore a striking resemblance to a scene on the dunes. Hans Castorp nodded as he stood and fixed the likeness in his mind. Even his burning face, his trembling limbs, the peculiar and half-intoxicated mingled sensations of excitement and fatigue were pleasurable, reminding him as they did of that familiar feeling induced by the sea air, which could sting one like whips, and yet was so laden with sleepy essences. He rejoiced in his freedom of motion, his feet were like wings. He was bound to no path, none lay behind him to take him back whence he had come. At first there had been posts, staves set up as guides through the snow—but he had soon cut free from their tutelage, which recalled the coast-guard with his horn, and seemed inconsistent with the attitude he had taken up toward the wild.

He pressed on, turning right and left among rocky, snow-clad elevations, and came behind them on an incline, then a level spot, then on the mountains themselves—how alluring and accessible seemed their softly covered gorges and defiles! His blood leaped at the strong allurement of the distance and the height, the ever profounder solitude. At risk of a late return he pressed on, deeper into the wild silence, the monstrous and the menacing, despite that gathering darkness was sinking down over the region like a veil, and heightening his inner apprehension until it presently passed into actual fear. It was this fear which first made him conscious that he had deliberately set out to lose his way and the direction in which valley and settlement lay—and had been as successful as heart could wish. Yet he knew that if he were to turn in his tracks and go downhill, he would reach the valley bottom—even if at some distance from the Berghof—and that sooner than he had planned. He would come home too early, not have made full use of his time. On the other hand, if he were overtaken unawares by the storm, he would probably in any case not find his way home. But however genuine his fear of the elements, he refused to take premature flight; his being scarcely the sportsman's attitude, who only meddles with the elements so long as he knows himself their master, takes all precautions, and prudently yields when he must—whereas what went on in Hans Castorp's soul can only be described by the one word challenge. It was perhaps a blame-worthy, presumptuous attitude, even united to such genuine awe. Yet this much is clear, to any human understanding: that when a young man has lived years long in the way this one had, something may gather—may accumulate, as our engineer might put it—in the depths of his soul, until one day it suddenly discharges itself, with a primitive exclamation of disgust, a mental "Oh, go to the devil!" a repudiation of all caution whatsoever, in short with a challenge. So on he went, in his seven-league slippers, glided down this slope too and pressed up the incline beyond, where stood a wooden hut that might be a hayrick or shepherd's shelter, its roof weighted with flat stones. On past this to the nearest mountain ridge, bristling with forest, behind whose back the giant peaks towered upward in the mist. The wall before him, studded with single groups of trees, was steep, but looked as though one might wind to the right and get round it by climbing a little way up the slope. Once on the other side, he could see what lay beyond. Accordingly Hans Castorp set out on this tour of investigation, which began by descending from the meadow with the hut into another and rather deep gully that dropped off from right to left.

He had just begun to mount again when the expected happened, and the storm burst, the storm that had threatened so long. Or may one say "threatened" of the action of blind, non-sentient forces, which have no purpose to destroy us—that would be comforting by comparison—but are merely horribly indifferent to our fate should we become involved with them? "Hullo!" Hans Castorp thought, and stood still, as the first blast whirled through the densely falling snow and caught him. "That's a gentle zephyr—tells you what's coming." And truly this wind was savage. The air was in reality frightfully cold, probably some degrees below zero; but so long as it remained dry and still one almost found it balmy. It was when a wind came up that the cold began to cut into the flesh; and in a wind like the one that blew now, of which that first gust had been a forerunner, the furs were not bought that could protect the limbs from its icy rigours. And Hans Castorp wore no fur, only a woollen waistcoat, which he had found quite enough, or even, with the faintest gleam of sunshine, a burden. But the wind was at his back, a little sidewise; there was small inducement to turn and receive it in the face; so the mad youth, letting that fact reinforce the fundamental challenge of his attitude, pressed on among the single tree-trunks, and tried to outflank the mountain he had attacked.

It was no joke. There was almost nothing to be seen for swimming snow-flakes, that seemed without falling to fill the air to suffocation by their whirling dance. The icy gusts made his ears burn painfully, his limbs felt half paralysed, his hands were so numb he hardly knew if they held the staff. The snow blew inside his collar and melted down his back. It drifted on his shoulders and right side; he thought he should freeze as he stood into a snow-man, with his staff stiff in his hands. And all this under relatively favouring circumstances; for let him turn his face to the storm and his situation would be still worse. Getting home would be no easy task—the harder, the longer he put it off.

At last he stopped, gave an angry shrug, and turned his skis the other way. Then the wind he faced took his breath on the spot, so that he was forced to go through the awkward process of turning round again to get it back, and collect his resolution to advance in the teeth of his ruthless foe. With bent head and cautious breathing he managed to get under way; but even thus forewarned, the slowness of his progress and the difficulty of seeing and breathing dismayed him. Every few minutes he had to stop, first to get his breath in the lee of the wind, and then because he saw next to nothing in the blinding whiteness, and moving as he did with head down, had to take care not to run against trees, or be flung headlong by uneven-nesses in the ground. Hosts of flakes flew into his face, melted there, and he anguished with the cold of them. They flew into his mouth, and died away with a weak, watery taste; flew against his eyelids so that he winked, over-flowed his eyes and made seeing as difficult as it was now almost impossible for other reasons: namely, the dazzling effect of all that whiteness, and the veiling of his field of vision, so that his sense of sight was almost put out of action. It was nothingness, white, whirling nothingness, into which he looked when he forced himself to do so. Only at intervals did ghostly-seeming forms from the world of reality loom up before him: a stunted fir, a group of pines, even the pale silhouette of the hay-hut he had lately passed.

He left it behind, and sought his way back over the slope on which it stood. But there was no path. To keep direction, relatively speaking, into his own valley would be a question far more of luck than management; for while he could see his hand before his face, he could not see the ends of his skis. And even with better visibility, the host of difficulties must have combined to hinder his progress: the snow in his face, his adversary the storm, which hampered his breathing, made him fight both to take a breath and to exhale it, and constantly forced him to turn his head away to gasp. How could anyone—either Hans Castorp or another and much stronger than he— make head? He stopped, he blinked his lashes free of water drops, knocked off the snow that like a coat of mail was sheathing his body in front—and it struck him that progress, under the circumstances, was more than anyone could expect.

And yet Hans Castorp did progress. That is to say, he moved on. But whether in the right direction, whether it might not have been better to stand still, remained to be seen. Theoretically the chances were against it; and in practice he soon began to suspect something was wrong. This was not familiar ground beneath his feet, not the easy slope he had gained on mounting with such difficulty from the ravine, which had of course to be retraversed. The level distance was too short, he was already mounting again. It was plain that the storm, which came from the south-west, from the mouth of the valley, had with its violence driven him from his course. He had been exhausting himself, all this time, with a false start. Blindly, enveloped in white, whirling night, he laboured deeper and deeper into this grim and callous sphere.

"No, you don't," said he, suddenly, between his teeth, and halted. The words were not emotional, yet he felt for a second as though his heart had been clutched by an icy hand; it winced, and then knocked rapidly against his ribs, as it had the time Rhadamanthus found the moist cavity. Pathos in the grand manner was not in place, he knew, in one who had chosen defiance as his rôle, and was indebted to himself alone for all his present plight. "Not bad," he said, and discovered that his facial muscles were not his to command, that he could not express in his face any of his soul's emotions, for that it was stiff with cold. "What next? Down this slope; follow your nose home, I suppose, and keep your face to the wind—though that is a good deal easier said than done," he went on, panting with his efforts, yet actually speaking half aloud, as he tried to move on again: "but something has to happen, I can't sit down and wait, I should simply be buried in six-sided crystalline symmetricality, and Settembrini, when he came with his little horn to find me, would see me squatting here with a snow-cap over one ear." He realized that he was talking to himself, and not too sensibly— for which he took himself to task, and then continued on purpose, though his lips were so stiff he could not shape the labials, and so did without them, as he had on a certain other occasion that came to his mind. "Keep quiet, and get along with you out of here," he admonished himself, adding: "You seem to be wool-gathering, not quite right in your head, and that looks bad for you."

But this he only said with his reason—to some extent detached from the rest of him, though after all nearly concerned. As for his natural part, it felt only too much inclined to yield to the confusion which laid hold upon him with his growing fatigue. He even remarked this tendency and took thought to comment upon it. "Here," said he, "we have the typical reaction of a man who loses himself in the mountains in a snow-storm and never finds his way home." He gasped out other fragments of the same thought as he went, though he avoided giving it more specific expression. "Whoever hears about it afterwards, imagines it as horrible; but he forgets that disease— and the state I am in is, in a way of speaking, disease—so adjusts its man that it and he can come to terms; there are sensory appeasements, short circuits, a merciful narcosis—yes, oh yes, yes. But one must fight against them, after all, for they are two-faced, they are in the highest degree equivocal, every- thing depends upon the point of view. If you are not meant to get home, they are a benefaction, they are merciful; but if you mean to get home, they become sinister. I believe I still do. Certainly I don't intend—in this heart of mine so stormily beating it doesn't appeal to me in the least—to let myself be snowed under by this idiotically symmetrical crystallometry."

In truth, he was already affected, and his struggle against oncoming sen- sory confusion was feverish and abnormal. He should have been more alarmed on discovering that he had already declined from the level course— this time apparently on the other slope. For he had pushed off with the wind coming slantwise at him, which was ill-advised, though more convenient for the moment. "Never mind," he thought, "I'll get my direction again down below." Which he did, or thought he did—or, truth to tell, scarcely even thought so; worst of all, began to be indifferent whether he had done or no. Such was the effect of an insidious double attack, which he but weakly combated. Fatigue and excitement combined were a familiar state to our young man—whose acclimatization, as we know, still consisted in getting used to not getting used; and both fatigue and excitement were now present in such strength as to make impossible any thought of asserting his reason against them. He felt as often after a colloquy with Settembrini and Naphta, only to a far greater degree: dazed and tipsy, giddy, a-tremble with excitement. This was probably why he began to colour his lack of resistance to the stealing narcosis with half-maudlin references to the latest-aired com- plex of theories. Despite his scornful repudiation of the idea that he might lie down and be covered up with hexagonal symmetricality, something with- in him maundered on, sense or no sense: told him that the feeling of duty which bade him fight against insidious sensory appeasements was a purely ethical reaction, representing the sordid bourgeois view of life, irreligion, Philistinism; while the desire, nay, craving, to lie down and rest, whispered him in the guise of a comparison between this storm and a stand-storm on the desert, before which the Arab flings himself down and draws his burnous over his head. Only his lack of a burnous, the unfeasibility of drawing his woollen waistcoat over his head, prevented him from following suit— this although he was no longer a child, and pretty well aware of the conditions under which a man freezes to death.

There had been a rather steep declivity, then level ground, then again an ascent, a stiff one. This was not necessarily wrong; one must of course, on the way to the valley, traverse rising ground at times. The wind had turned capriciously round, for it was now at Hans Castorp's back, and that, taken by itself, was a blessing. Owing, perhaps, to the storm, or the soft whiteness of the incline before him, dim in the whirling air, drawing him toward it, he bent as he walked. Only a little further—supposing one were to give way to the temptation, and his temptation was great; it was so strong that it quite lived up to the many descriptions he had read of the "typical danger-state." It asserted itself, it refused to be classified with the general order of things, it insisted on being an exception, its very exigence challenged comparison—yet at the same time it never disguised its origin or aura, never denied that it was, so to speak, garbed in Spanish black, with snow-white, fluted ruff, and stood for ideas and fundamental conceptions that were characteristically gloomy, strongly Jesuitical and anti-human, for the rack-and-knout discipline which was the particular horror of Herr Settembrini, though he never opposed it without making himself ridiculous, like a hand-organ man for ever grinding out *"ragione"* to the same old tune.

And yet Hans Castorp did hold himself upright and resist his craving to lie down. He could see nothing, but he struggled, he came forward. Whether to the purpose or not, he could not tell; but he did his part, and moved on despite the weight the cold more and more laid upon his limbs. The present slope was too steep to ascend directly, so he slanted a little, and went on thus awhile without much heed whither. Even to lift his stiffened lids to peer before him was so great and so nearly useless an effort as to offer him small incentive. He merely caught glimpses: here clumps of pines that merged together; there a ditch or stream, a black line marked out between overhanging banks of snow. Now, for a change, he was going downhill, with the wind in his face, when, at some distance before him, and seeming to hang in the driving wind and mist, he saw the faint outline of a human habitation.

''A HEAVY SHOWER OF ASHES RAINED UPON US''

FROM *Letters*

PLINY

Pliny the Younger—not to be confused with his uncle who wrote the *Natural History*—was born in Rome circa 62 A.D. The son of a wealthy family, he studied rhetoric under Quintilian, became consul and one of the most noted attorneys of the day. His letters were written with an eye to publication and have the character of graceful, even if artificial, prose compositions. They are frequently more revealing of the writer than the subject he takes to hand—a certain vanity, an occasional humorlessness, a vast concern with the amenities of rhetoric, and a certainty that the Roman was the best of all possible worlds. In these two letters to Cornelius Tacitus, however, he drops most of his poses and writes with the vividness, the immediacy, and the excitement of an eyewitness to a great natural catastrophe.

To Tacitus

YOUR REQUEST THAT I WOULD SEND YOU AN ACCOUNT OF MY UNCLE'S DEATH, in order to transmit a more exact relation of it to posterity, deserves my acknowledgments; for, if this accident shall be celebrated by your pen, the glory of it, I am well assured, will be rendered forever illustrious. And notwithstanding he perished by a misfortune, which, as it involved at the same time a most beautiful country in ruins, and destroyed so many populous cities, seems to promise him an everlasting remembrance; notwithstanding he has himself composed many and lasting works; yet I am persuaded, the mentioning of him in your immortal writings, will greatly contribute to render his name immortal. Happy I esteem those to be to whom by provision of the gods has been granted the ability either to do such actions as are worthy of being related or to relate them in a manner worthy of being read; but peculiarly happy are they who are blessed with both these uncommon talents: in the number of which my uncle, as his own writings and your history will evidently prove, may justly be ranked. It is with extreme willingness, therefore, that I execute your commands; and should indeed have claimed the task if you had not enjoined it. He was at that time with the fleet under his command at Misenum. On the 24th of August, about one in the afternoon, my mother desired him to observe a cloud which appeared of a very unusual size and shape. He had just taken a turn in the sun, and, after bathing himself in cold water, and making a light luncheon, gone back to his books: he immediately arose and went out upon a rising ground from whence he might get a better sight of this very uncommon appearance. A cloud, from which mountain was uncertain, at this distance (but it was found afterwards to come from Mount Vesuvius), was ascending, the appearance of which I cannot give you a more exact description of than by likening it to that of a pine tree, for it shot up to a great height in the form of a very tall trunk, which spread itself out at the top into a sort of branches; occasioned, I imagine, either by a sudden gust of air that impelled it, the force of which decreased as it advanced upwards, or the cloud itself being pressed back again by its own weight, expanded in the manner I have mentioned; it appeared sometimes bright and sometimes dark and spotted, according as it was either more or less impregnated with earth and cinders. This phenomenon seemed to a man of such learning and research as my uncle extraordinary and worth further looking into. He ordered a light vessel to be got ready, and gave me leave, if I liked, to accompany him. I said I had rather go on with my work; and it so happened he had himself given me something to write out. As he was coming out of the house, he received a note from Rectina, the wife of Bassus, who was in the utmost alarm at the imminent danger which threatened her; for her villa lying at the foot of Mount Vesuvius, there was no way of escape but by sea; she earnestly entreated him therefore to come to her assistance. He acccordingly changed his first intention, and what he had begun from a philosophical, he now carries out in a noble and generous spirit. He ordered the galleys to put to sea, and went himself on board with an intention of assisting not only Rectina, but the several other towns which lay thickly strewn along that beautiful coast. Hastening then to the place from whence others fled with the utmost terror, he steered his course direct to the point of danger, and with so much calmness and presence of mind as to be able to make and dictate his observations upon the motion and all the phenomena of that dreadful scene. He was now so close to the mountain that the cinders, which grew thicker and hotter the nearer he approached, fell into the ships, together with pumice stones, and black pieces of burning rock: they were in danger too not only of being a-ground by the sudden retreat of the sea, but also from the vast fragments which rolled down from the mountain, and obstructed all the shore. Here he stopped to consider whether he should turn back again; to which the pilot advising him, "Fortune," said he, "favours the brave; steer to where Pomponianus is." Pomponianus was then at Stabiae, separated by a bay, which the sea, after several insensible windings, forms with the shore. He had already sent his baggage on board; for though he was not at that time in actual danger, yet being within sight of it, and indeed extremely near, if it should in the least increase, he was determined to put to sea as soon as the wind, which was blowing dead in-shore, should go down. It was favourable, however, for carrying my uncle to Pomponianus, whom he found in the greatest consternation: he embraced him tenderly, encouraging and urging him to keep up his spirits, and, the more effectually to soothe his fears by seeming unconcerned himself, ordered a bath to be got ready, and then, after having bathed, sat down to supper with great cheerfulness, or at least (what is just as heroic) with every appearance of it. Meanwhile broad flames shone out in several places from Mount Vesuvius, which the darkness of the night contributed to render still brighter and clearer. But my uncle, in order to soothe the apprehensions of his friend, assured him it was only the burning of the villages, which the country people had abandoned to the flames: after this he retired to rest, and it is most certain he was so little disquieted as to fall into a sound sleep: for his breathing, which, on account of his corpulence, was rather heavy and sonorous, was heard by the attendants outside. The court which led to his apartment being now almost filled with stones and ashes, if he had continued there any time longer, it would have been impossible for him to have made his way out. So he was awoke and got up, and went to Pomponianus and the rest of his company, who were feeling too anxious to think of going to bed. They consulted together whether it would be most prudent to trust to the houses, which now rocked from side to side with frequent and violent concussions as though shaken from their very foundations; or fly to the open fields, where the calcined stones and cinders, though light indeed, yet fell in large showers, and threatened destruction. In this choice of dangers they resolved for the fields: a resolution which, while the rest of the company were hurried into by their fears, my uncle embraced upon cool and deliberate consideration. They went out then, having pillows tied upon their heads with napkins; and this was their whole defence against the storm of stones that fell round them. It was now day everywhere else, but *there* a deeper darkness prevailed than in the thickest night; which however was in some degree alleviated by torches and other lights of various kinds. They thought proper to go farther down upon the shore to see if they might safely put out to sea, but found the waves still running extremely high, and boisterous. There my uncle, laying himself down upon a sail-cloth, which was spread for him, called twice for some cold water, which he drank, when immediately the flames, preceded by a strong whiff of sulphur, dispersed the rest of the party, and obliged him to rise. He raised himself up with the assistance of two of his servants, and instantly fell down dead; suffocated, as I conjecture, by some gross and noxious vapour, having always had a weak throat, which was often inflamed. As soon as it was light again, which was not till the third day after this melancholy accident, his body was found entire, and without any marks of violence upon it, in the dress in which he fell, and looking more like a man asleep than dead. During all this time my mother and I, who were at Misenum—but this has no connection with your history, and you did not desire any particulars besides those of my uncle's death; so I will end here, only adding that I have faithfully related to you what I was either an eye-witness of myself or received immediately after the accident happened, and before there was time to vary the truth. You will pick out of this narrative whatever is most important: for a letter is one thing, a history another; it is one thing writing to friend, another thing writing to the public. Farewell.

To Cornelius Tacitus

The letter which, in compliance with your request, I wrote to you concerning the death of my uncle has raised, it seems, your curiosity to know what terrors and dangers attended me while I continued at Misenum; for there, I think, my account broke off:

> Though my shock'd soul recoils, my tongue shall tell.

My uncle having left us, I spent such time as was left on my studies (it was on their account indeed that I had stopped behind), till it was time for my bath. After which I went to supper, and then fell into a short and uneasy sleep. There had been noticed for many days before a trembling of the earth, which did not alarm us much, as this is quite an ordinary occurrence in Campania; but it was so particularly violent that night that it not only shook but actually overturned, as it would seem, everything about us. My mother rushed into my chamber, where she found me rising, in order to awaken her. We sat down in the open court of the house, which occupied a small space between the buildings and the sea. As I was at that time but eighteen years of age, I know not whether I should call my behaviour, in this dangerous juncture, courage or folly; but I took up Livy, and amused myself with turning over that author, and even making extracts from him, as if I had been perfectly at my leisure. Just then, a friend of my uncle's, who had lately come to him from Spain, joined us, and observing me sitting by my mother with a book in my hand, reproved her for her calmness, and me at the same time for my careless security: nevertheless I went on with my author. Though it was now morning, the light was still exceedingly faint and doubtful; the buildings all around us tottered, and though we stood upon open ground, yet as the place was narrow and confined, there was no remaining without imminent danger: we therefore resolved to quit the town. A panic-stricken crowd followed us, and (as to a mind distracted with terror every suggestion seems more prudent than its own) pressed on us in dense array to drive us forward as we came out. Being at a convenient distance from the houses, we stood still, in the midst of a most dangerous and dreadful scene. The chariots, which we had ordered to be drawn out, were so agitated backwards and forwards, though upon the most level ground, that we could not keep them steady, even by supporting them with large stones. The sea seemed to roll back upon itself, and to be driven from its banks by the convulsive motion of the earth; it is certain at least the shore was considerably enlarged, and several sea animals were left upon it. On the other side, a black and dreadful cloud, broken with rapid, zigzag flashes, revealed behind it variously shaped masses of flame: these last were like sheet-lightning, but much larger. Upon this our Spanish friend, whom I mentioned above, addressing himself to my mother and me with great energy and urgency: "If your brother," he said, "if your uncle be safe, he certainly wishes you may be so too; but if he perished, it was his desire, no doubt, that you might both survive him: why therefore do you delay your escape a moment?" We could never think of our own safety, we said, while we were uncertain of his. Upon this our friend left us, and withdrew from the danger with the utmost precipitation. Soon afterwards, the cloud began to descend, and cover the sea. It had already surrounded and concealed the island of Capreae and the promontory of Misenum. My mother now besought, urged, even commanded me to make my escape at any rate, which, as I was young, I might easily do; as for herself, she said, her age and corpulency rendered all attempts of that sort impossible; however she would willingly meet death if she could have the satisfaction of seeing that she was not the occasion of mine. But I absolutely refused to leave her, and, taking her by the hand, compelled her to go with me. She complied with great reluctance, and not without many reproaches to herself for retarding my flight. The ashes now began to fall upon us, though in no great quantity. I looked back; a dense dark mist seemed to be following us, spreading itself over the country like a cloud. "Let us turn out of the high-road," I said, "while we can still see, for fear that, should we fall in the road, we should be pressed to death in the dark, by the crowds that are following us." We had scarcely sat down when night came upon us, not such as we have when the sky is cloudy, or when there is no moon, but that of a room when it is shut up, and all the lights put out. You might hear the shrieks of women, the screams of children, and the shouts of men; some calling for their children, others for their parents, others for their husbands, and seeking to recognise each other by the voices that replied; one lamenting his own fate, another that of his family; some wishing to die, from the very fear of dying; some lifting their hands to the gods; but the greater part convinced that there were now no gods at all, and that the final endless night of which we have heard had come upon the world. Among these there were some who augmented the real terrors by others imaginary or wilfully invented. I remember some who declared that one part of Misenum had fallen, that another was on fire; it was false, but they found people to believe them. It now grew rather lighter, which we imagined to be rather the forerunner of an approaching burst of flames (as in truth it was) than the return of day: however, the fire fell at a distance from us: then again we were immersed in thick darkness, and a heavy shower of ashes rained upon us, which we were obliged every now and then to stand up to shake off, otherwise we should have been crushed and buried in the heap. I might boast that, during all this scene of horror, not a sigh, or expression of fear, escaped me, had not my support been grounded in that miserable, though mighty, consolation, that all mankind were involved in the same calamity, and that I was perishing with the world itself. At last this dreadful darkness was dissipated by degrees, like a cloud or smoke; the real day returned, and even the sun shone out, though with a lurid light, like when an eclipse is coming on. Every object that presented itself to our eyes (which were extremely weakened) seemed changed, being covered deep with ashes as if with snow. We returned to Misenum, where we refreshed ourselves as well as we could, and passed an anxious night between hope and fear; though, indeed, with a much larger share of the latter: for the earthquake still continued, while many frenzied persons ran up and down heightening their own and their friends' calamities by terrible predictions. However, my mother and I, notwithstanding the danger we had passed, and that which still threatened us, had no thoughts of leaving the place, till we could receive some news of my uncle.

And now, you will read this narrative without any view of inserting it in your history, of which it is not in the least worthy; and indeed you must put it down to your own request if it should appear not worth even the trouble of a letter. Farewell.

CAMP OF DEATH

FROM *The Mothers*

VARDIS FISHER

The most tragic and most horrifying of all the experiences in the overland migration to California was suffered by the Donner party. The wagon train of emigrants set out across the plains in 1846. They took a new cutoff south of the Great Salt Lake and were so delayed that they were blocked by the early snows in the Sierra Nevada. During that winter when the snow piled in drifts two and three times as high as the cabins they had hastily thrown together, half the party starved to death. Rescue parties from California brought out the survivors in the early spring. They had survived by eating their dead.

Vardis Fisher tells the story in *The Mothers*. He knows the country. His childhood memories, he writes of himself, are "of howling wolves, screaming cougars, venison, deer skin for bedding and neighborless loneliness."

IT WAS CHRISTMAS MORNING, AND IT WAS THE WILDEST MORNING THESE PERsons had ever seen. A great wind poured over the mountains and whipped the falling snow into a terrific blizzard. During the night, snow had piled softly on their tent of quilts, but with the coming of dawn the quilts were whipped bare. The quilts would have been blown away if those under them had not sat on their edges. They were chilled through, and if hope still burned in any heart here, there was no record of it in haggard faces. Pat Dolan still muttered in delirium.

Those with clear minds knew that a dead man lay with them under the blankets. Mary drew her sister a little to one side and whispered to her, telling her what their father had said; and then the two girls clung to one another and wept. At one side the Indians lay together and seemed to sleep. Bill Eddy strove to quiet Pat, but at last Pat broke free, hurled the quilt off him, and staggered out into the blizzard, cursing his companions and howling threats against them. He stood and menaced them, a shouting and infuriated skeleton. He said he was going to California. He said he would be there by sundown.

"Bill Eddy," he howled, "he's the only man here! Bill will go with me! Come on, Bill!"

The others covered themselves against the blizzard, but Bill framed his face with a quilt and looked out, watching Pat to see what he would do. Pat staggered away, still crying that he would cross the mountains before sunset. Bill drew his face in and spoke to Mary.

"He's going. I guess I should try and drag him back."

Mary said nothing, but when Bill left the shelter, she framed her face to watch him. She saw Bill overtake Pat and seize him, and then both men struggled and fell. They seemed to be wrestling in the storm. Then Bill came back and crawled under the quilts. He was trembling all over.

"I'm not strong enough," he said.

"He'll be lost," said Mary.

A little later they were astonished when Pat raised the quilt and crawled in.

"We'd better hold him," Bill said; and he grasped Pat and drew him down. He spread the man on his back and laid one arm out and sat on it, and Foster sat on the other arm. Mary and the two Harriets sat on Pat's legs. Thus pinned, he could only curse and slobber and writhe under them. He bit his tongue and his lips, and blood ran into his beard. What he was saying, nobody could understand. After he became quieter, erupting only now and then in low mutterings, Bill tried in the gloom to see how the others fared. Lem lay across the lap of one of his sisters and seemed to be unconscious. Jay Fosdick was talking to himself, but Bill was unable to tell if the man was asleep or awake.

It was sometime in the afternoon when Bill realized that Pat was very quiet. He moved off the arm and lowered an ear to Pat's breast.

"He's dead," Bill said to the women. After a moment he added: "Now we are eleven."

Pat had been their jester. During the nine bitter days of this journey he had tried to cheer them; but he was gone now, and in none of those who lived was there a witticism for this terrible Christmas day.

Bill said: "I guess I'd better roll him outside. It will give us more room." Mary held a quilt up, and he rolled Frank Graves out. Then on the other side of the tent he pushed Pat Dolan out into the storm. Bill thought they would all feel better if the dead did not lie within sight and touch of the living.

As night approached. Lem began to mutter and then to shriek; and they held him as they had held Pat. Some held his legs and arms; his sister Sarah held his tossing head on her lap. In death from starvation, they had learned, wild delirium was a herald of the end. Their number would be ten before morning.

And what would the ten do? Except Bill, who had eaten about three ounces of his bear meat, they had gone four days and nights without food. They had covered hardly more than a third of the distance across the mountains. If this storm lasted as long as those by the lake, it might rage for a week or ten days.

It was probably about midnight when brave little Lem breathed his last. His two sisters kissed his face and then Bill rolled him outside. Bill seemed to like to toll off the grim count.

"Now we are ten," he said.

"Nine and then eight," said Mary. "Then seven, six, five. I guess you'll be the last one."

"No. Ten men started and five women. Five men are gone but the women are all alive."

"I don't want to be last. That would be hardest of all."

"Why do we talk this way? We are going on."

"Yes, we're going on. How, Bill?"

"On grit."

It was morning of the next day when Mary moved over to Bill and told him what her father had said. She spoke in whispers, and nobody else could hear her; but her sister Sarah knew what she was saying. Horrified and speechless, Bill listened to her. His romantic soul did not know that Mary was speaking the bravest words he had ever heard. After a few moments, he rose and left the shelter.

In his mind was the thought that he, and he alone, must save those who still lived. He would gather the wood and build a fire under the quilts—but first he would eat another mouthful of his precious meat. He cut off a thin slice and devoured it, and then gathered some dry twigs and returned to the tent. With his wood he crawled under, and set a long limb upright to serve as a tentpole.

Then, using powder and flint, he tried to start a fire. The first spark exploded the powder with a terrifying bang, and the explosion burned his hands and face, as well as the faces of Mary and Sarah Fosdick who had been assisting him.

"Damn," Bill said. "You hurt?"

"A little," Mary said.

The explosion aroused the Indians, who came bolt upright, ready to flee. Will Foster awoke from stupor.

"What in hell you doing?"

"Trying to make a fire."

"What was that noise?"

"The powder blew up."

There was a smell of burnt powder under the quilts. Bill reached out-side for snow and with it bathed his face and hands. He threw off a quilt to let in light and then looked at the faces of Mary and her sister. There were dark stains on their cheeks; a part of their eyebrows had been burned off.

"Well," Bill said, feeling very silly.

Later he tried again, but he could not find any bark or twigs dry enough to ignite with a flint. Mary remembered that Harriet Pike's blanket was lined with cotton. Bill cut a corner off the blanket. The storm had broken away. He took a handful of cotton and the flint and went to a dry tree; and there, after an hour of desperate effort, he brought to life a tiny flame. He nursed it under his hands and fed small twigs to it and soon he had a healthy fire. Then he set fire to the big dry tree, and a magnificent torch blazed in the desolation.

The sight of the fire aroused the others; but it was only little by little, as if the knowledge came to him through the murk of a nightmare, that Bill realized what they were doing. He saw them dig Pat Dolan out of the snow, but he thought nothing of that. Then the two Indians came over and broke off a flaming fagot and went to another tree to build their own fire. That, too, meant nothing to Bill. Not until Foster came over, with a green stick thrust through a piece of raw meat, did the full shock of it overwhelm Bill's senses. He drew back, horrified.

"Will, what is that?"

"Never mind," said Will quietly. "Some of us intend to reach Califor-nia."

Then the women came over, and all of them were weeping so bitterly that Bill turned sick when he looked at them. He withdrew, as if to search for wood, and peered around a tree at the seven of them by the fire. They were eating, but the women still wept. While hunting for the axe, Bill cut off another slice of meat and ate it. An hour passed before he joined the group. He did not look at them, and when he became aware of their in-quiring gaze he felt impatient with himself. After all, in the only way left to them they were restoring their strength so they could march again. If Bill had not had the bear meat, he might have shared their fellowship now— and their courage; but he had not been driven, like them, to the last des-perate extremity. He had the foolish notion that his few ounces of meat would see him through.

The women had all wept bitterly, but they felt a little stronger now; and they went off together to break green twigs for a mattress on the snow. After piling the twigs they laid blankets on them and lay down, and Will and Jay lay with them. The seven skeletons stretched out on the quilts and drew quilts over them. The two Indians had wrapped blankets round them and were sitting by their fire. And still Bill Eddy stood by the burning tree, thinking stubbornly of what had happened.

He tried not to think of it. Over at the camps, had any of them been driven to cut flesh from the dead? Would any of them be alive there when help came? What were Jim Reed and Mac doing? Trying to cross the mountains, no doubt, and dying in the snow.

"Bill," Mary said.

"Yes?"

"You better lie down."

"Pretty soon."

"Did you find the axe?"

"No."

Bill wondered if he should strike out alone. To test his strength, he went over to the two Indians. He asked Luis if they were off the route. Luis said they were.

"South of it?" Luis nodded. "Are we lost?" Yes, Luis said. Luis did not wish to answer any more questions. Like the philosopher he was, he wanted to sit quietly and hoard his strength.

Bill returned to the burning tree. A twig, or a small branch maned with flame, fell now and then and struck the bed. A hand would come out and brush it away. These seven persons would not have moved if the burning tree had fallen across them. None of them had strength to move, now that they had lain down and were warm. Bill raised a quilt and crawled in by Foster. The women all lay on one side, with Jay Fosdick next to his wife.

Bill's feet had frozen and thawed and frozen so many times that he could feel no life in them. That was true, he reflected, of all their feet. Before long their toes would begin to rot and drop off, and they would be unable to walk, even if they had the strength. He hoped the other nine would be ready to set out in the morning. On this thought he closed his eyes and slept.

But none of them really slept. Those who had eaten meat were filled with cramps and nightmares. Some of them only moaned and fretted, but now and then one would yell and sit up, pawing at the quilts. Neither awake nor asleep, they were drugged by exhaustion and pain and terrifying dreams. Bill was awake most of the night, studying the sensations in his body and wondering if he was approaching the end. He had enough bear meat to allow him two ounces a day for two or three days; but it was still sixty or seventy miles across the mountains. At their former rate of speed, that meant two weeks.

Once during the night, Bill heard Harriet McCutchen talking to her baby, and he realized that she thought the baby was in her arms. She was crooning to it in a way that chilled him. He drew a blanket around his ears to shut out the sound.

When morning came, none of them would go with Bill. None of them was able to, and Bill himself could not have walked five miles to save his life.

"Be sensible," Mary said. "We have to rest up."

She spoke, it seemed to him, like a very old woman. There was no emotion in her voice. Her words were merely words, and that was all.

"There's no sense in going without food. You know that."

Yes, Bill knew that, but his sentimental soul wanted to get away from this camp of death. A braver man than Bill Eddy never set out on a perilous journey; but his prejudices were strong, and his distaste for this spot filled him with nausea. He wanted to go, even if he had to lie down and die at the end of a mile. But there were five clear-headed and determined women here; and now that they had wept the first shock out of them in bitter grief, now that the horrible taboo had been broken, they were resolved to be guided only by intelligence and duty.

Among themselves they agreed that nobody was to touch the body of a relative. With that understanding they set to work, and neither tears nor horror stayed their hands. The meat had to be dried and placed in their packs. Then they could march again. Then, with God's help, they would get through and bring relief to the camps.

If there had been only men in this group, undoubtedly they would all have perished. It took the desperation of mothers in an hour like this. It took their hard and unfaltering courage to roll the bodies out of the snow and kneel by them with a knife. Jay Fosdick did not assist. His wife did, but she was a Graves and the sister of Mary. Will Foster did not assist, but his wife was a mother and a Murphy. The Indians also remained aloof, but with impassive faces they accepted their portions when these were offered. Bill slipped away from time to time to chew on his bear meat and bring wood for the fire.

Another day passed and he wanted to push on, but Mary said they were not ready. Another night passed, and another day, and still the women would not budge. Mixed with physical exhaustion was horror now, and they needed to be stronger before they went. It was not until Wednesday morning, December thirtieth, after five days in a camp of death, that Mary said they were ready to go. On this morning Bill had nothing to eat, nor had he had the day before; and though he did not know it, he had come to the end of his amazing endurance.

They set out in deep new snow, the ten of them, with Bill leading. Mary was next in line. The rawhide laces in their boots were rotting. Their frozen feet cracked open and bled and felt like numbed and aching weights attached to their legs. Sunken-eyed, and hardly more than skin and bones, they staggered on, with Bill turning now and then to exhort those who fell behind. Jay Fosdick was weakest. He reeled like a man who at any moment would fall and never rise again.

They went into the southwest, guided by the haze of the sun. About noon they paused, and nine of them ate a little meat; but when Mary offered some to Bill he said no.

"You're silly," she said. "Eleanor would tell you that."

When they moved off again, Bill Eddy sank. He sank slowly, as if easing himself down. Looking up at Mary, he said he felt queer; he felt saturated with deep and holy peace. The others came up and stood around Bill and looked at him.

Mary said: "You should know what this means. You've seen others feel queer and peaceful. Get up."

"I don't want to."

They argued with him, but Bill sat like a child and said he felt fine. They should go on, he said, and he would overtake them soon.

"That's what Charley Stanton said. Bill, please."

The seven white persons looked at one another, their eyes asking what should be done. Then Mary remembered Bill's deep love for his wife.

"Bill?—are you listening?"

"Yes."

"Do you understand me?"

"Yes."

"Over at the lake, Bill, you have a wife and two babies. You set out to bring help. If you give up now, what will Eleanor think of you?"

"Eleanor. You mean my wife?"

"Your wife, yes. You're giving up. This—this peace, it's what comes just before death. You know that."

"Is it?"

Mary turned to Foster. "Shake him," she said.

Will hadn't enough strength to shake a child but he clutched Bill's long shaggy hair and pulled. "Bill, you cuss, get up."

"Sure," said Bill, and with Foster's help he rose.

Mary now led. She had gone no more than a hundred yards when, on looking back, she saw that Bill had fallen again. She went back, and he told her he felt a marvelous peace all through him. He thought this was what heaven would be like. Without arguing, Mary took off her pack and fetched out a small strip of meat.

"You have to eat this. If you don't I'll poke it down you."

Bill looked at the flesh and shuddered. He turned away.

To Foster, Mary said: "Hold him." Foster grasped Bill's hair and bent over him, thrusting his knees against Bill's neck; and Mary shoved the piece of meat against Bill's lips. He closed his mouth stubbornly and strove to duck his head.

Mary knelt by him. "Bill, you're a coward. Eleanor would despise you if she could see you now."

"You mean my wife?"

"Your wife would say you're being a coward."

As if the words relaxed him, Bill opened his mouth and Mary thrust the meat in. "Chew," she said, and Bill began to chew. His eyes were strange to look at. They seemed to say that he expected to explode at any moment or die in a convulsion. He was such a ridiculous fellow that Mary laughed and gave him more meat. Bill now ate without protest and felt his strength returning.

"Feel better?"

"I feel fine."

He wanted to go on, but Mary thought they had better camp here. There was dry wood close by, and they were in a ravine that sheltered them from the wind. After they had a fire going, Foster and Fosdick and the women opened their packs and each of them gave to Bill a few strips of meat. They all shared generously, and his supply of food was equal to that of the others; but none of them had food for more than two or three days.

During the twilight, while sitting round the fire, they nursed their swollen and bleeding feet, but there was little they could do for them. Their shoes had been soaked and dried so many times that the leather was rotting. Always they had slept with their shoes on. During the nights the leather had dried on their feet, and when they set out in the morning it was stiff and hard and chafed their feet to raw sores. Then as they walked the snow softened the leather and eased the pain.

The next morning they came to a deep canyon, but instead of going down into it they went southwest along a ridge. They climbed the ridge to a summit. Mary, who had been leading, stopped suddenly and cried aloud and then sank as if she had fainted. When the others came up she said "Look!" and pointed into the west. There, far away, was a broad valley, and they all knew it was the valley of the Sacramento. Somewhere at the eastern side of it was Sutter's Fort, and scattered over it were dwellings in which people were warm and had food. The ten of them stood on the summit and stared at the valley, and tears came to the eyes of all except the Indians.

THE GREAT MOGUL
CROSSES THE HIMALAYAS

FROM *Memoirs of Baber, Emperor of India, First of the Great Moguls*

EDITED BY

F . G . T A L B O T

Baber, emperor of Hindustan, begins his memoirs, "In the month of Ramzân, in the year fourteen hundred and twenty-four, in the twelfth year of my age, I became king." He was of the house of Tamerlane, scourge of Asia, and was descended on the maternal side from Ghengiz Khan. He was as proud of his verse-making as of his conquests. Perhaps more so; poets were scarcer than conquerors in those times. In this selection he describes a military expedition in which his army is caught in the mountains in a winter storm—an unusual military report which on no provocation swings into verse.

Baber's *Memoirs*, little known, give a portrait of an uncommon man, let alone an emperor, frank, warm and human, and even through indifferent translation, make very pleasurable reading.

IN THE LATTER END OF THE MONTH OF THE LATTER RABÎA, BY THE BLESSING OF Almighty God, I gained possession of Kâbul and Ghazni, with the country and provinces dependent on them, without battle or contest.

The country of Kâbul is situate in the midst of the inhabited part of the world. It is surrounded on all sides by hills. In winter all the roads are shut for five months save one alone. The Kaffir robbers issue from the mountains and narrow paths and infest this passage. The country of Kâbul is very stony, and difficult of access to foreigners or enemies. Its warm and cold districts are close to each other. You may go in a single day to a place where snow never falls, and in the space of two astronomical hours you may reach a place where snow lies always. To the north-west lie the meadows of Chalak, but in the summer mosquitoes greatly annoy the horses.

Kâbul is not fertile in grain—a return of four or five to one is reckoned favourable. The fruits are grapes, pomegranates, apricots, peaches, pears, apples, quinces, damsons, almonds, and walnuts. I caused the cherry-tree to be brought here and planted. It produced excellent fruit and continues thriving. It was I who planted the sugar-cane.

Drink wine in the citadel of Kâbul, and send round the cup without stop-
    ping;
For it is at once a mountain and a sea, a town and a desert.

. . . The winter was come, and the snow began to fall in the mountains
that separated me from my dominions. I still felt considerable alarm as to
the situation of things in Kâbul. At length, compelled by necessity, and unable to explain my real motives, I left under pretence of going into winter
quarters. From the time we left it snowed incessantly. The farther we advanced, the deeper was the snow. Two or three days later the snow became
excessively deep; it reached up above the stirrups. In many places the horses'
feet did not reach the ground, and the snow still continued to fall. One
Bishâi was our guide. I do not know whether it was from old age, or from
his heart failing him, or from the unusual depth of the snow, but having
once lost the road, he never could find it again, so as to point out the way.
He and his sons, anxious to preserve their reputation, dismounted, and,
after beating down the snow, discovered a road, by which we advanced.
Next day, as there was much snow, and the road was not to be found with
all our exertions, we were brought to a complete stand. Seeing no remedy
left, we returned back to a place where there was abundance of firewood,
and dispatched sixty or seventy chosen men, to return by the road we had
come, and, retracing our footsteps, to find, under the higher grounds, any
Hazâras or other people who might be wintering there, and to bring a
guide who was able to point out the way. We halted at this spot for three
or four days, waiting the return of the men whom we had sent out. They did
indeed come back, but without having been able to find a proper guide.
Placing our reliance on God, therefore, and sending on Bishâi before us, we
again advanced by that very road in which formerly we had been stopped
and forced to return. In the few days that followed, many were the difficulties and hardships that we endured; indeed, such hardships and suffering
as I have scarcely undergone at any other period of my life. It was at this
time that I composed the following verses:

There is no violence or injury of fortune that I have not experienced;
This broken heart has endured them all. Alas! is there one left that I have
    not encountered?

For about a week we continued pressing down the snow, without being
able to advance more than two or three miles. I myself assisted in depressing
the snow. Accompanied by ten or fifteen of my household, and by Kâsim
Beg, his two sons, and two or three of his servants, we all dismounted and
worked in beating down the snow. Every step we sank up to the middle or
the breast, but we still went on trampling it down. As the vigour of the

person who went first was generally expended after he had advanced a few paces, he stood still, while another advanced and took his place. The ten, fifteen, or twenty people who worked in trampling down the snow next succeeded in dragging on a horse without a rider. The first horse sank up to the stirrups and girths, and after advancing ten or fifteen paces, was worn out. Drawing this horse aside, we brought on another, and in this way ten, fifteen, or twenty of us trampled down the snow, and contrived to bring forward the horses of all our number. The rest of the troops, even our best men, and many that bore the title of Beg, without dismounting, advanced along the road that had been beaten for them, hanging down their heads. This was no time for plaguing them or employing authority. Every man who possesses spirit or emulation hastens to such works of himself. Continuing to advance by a track which we had beat in the snow in this manner, we proceeded by a place named Anjukan, and in three or four days reached a cave at the foot of the Zirrîn pass. That day the storm of wind was dreadful. The snow fell in such quantities that we all expected to meet death together. We halted at the mouth of it. The snow was deep, and the path narrow, so that only one person could pass at a time. The horses, too, advanced with difficulty over the road that had been beaten and trampled down, and the days were at the shortest. The first of the troops reached this cave while it was yet daylight. About evening and night prayers the troops ceased coming in, after which every man was obliged to dismount and halt where he happened to be. Many men waited for morning on horseback. The cave seemed to be small. I took a hoe, and having swept away and cleared off the snow, made for myself at the mouth of the cave a resting-place about the size of a prayer-carpet. I dug down in the snow as deep as my breast, and yet did not reach the ground. This hole afforded me some shelter from the wind, and I sat down in it. Some desired me to go into the cavern, but I would not go. I felt that for me to be in a warm dwelling and in comfort while my men were in the midst of snow and drift—for me to be within, enjoying sleep and ease, while my followers were in trouble and distress, would be inconsistent with what I owed them, and a deviation from that society in suffering that was their due. It was right that whatever their sufferings and difficulties were, and whatever they might be obliged to undergo, I should be a sharer with them. There is a Persian proverb, that "Death in the company of friends is a feast." I continued, therefore, to sit in the drift, in the sort of hole which I had cleared and dug out for myself, till bed-time prayers, when the snow fell so fast that, as I had remained all the while sitting crouching down on my feet, I now found that four inches of snow had settled on my head, lips, and ears. That night I caught a cold in my ear. About bed-time prayers a party, after having surveyed the cave, reported that the cave was very extensive, and was sufficiently large to receive all our people. As soon as I learned this, I shook off the snow that was on my head and face, and went into the cave. I sent to call in all such of the people as were at hand. A comfortable place was found within for fifty or sixty persons; such as had any eatables, stewed meat, preserved flesh, or anything else in readiness, produced them; and thus we escaped from the terrible cold, and snow, and drift, into a wonderfully safe, warm, and comfortable place, where we could refresh ourselves.

Next morning the snow and tempest ceased. Moving early, we trampled down the snow in the old way, and made a road. Before we reached the bottom of the pass, the day closed on us. We halted in the defiles of the valley. The cold was dreadful, and we passed that night in great distress and misery. Many lost their hands and feet from the frost. Kepek lost his feet, Sewendûk his hands, and Akhi his feet, from the cold of that night. Early next morning we moved down the glen. Although we knew that this was not the usual road, yet, placing our trust in God, we advanced down the valley, and descended by difficult and precipitous places. It was evening prayer before we extricated ourselves from the mouth of the valley. It was not in the memory of the oldest man, that this pass had ever been descended, when there was so much snow on the ground; nay, it was never known that anybody even conceived the idea of passing it at such a season. Although for some days we endured much from the depth of the snow, yet, in the issue, it was this very circumstance which brought us to our journey's end. For, if the snow had not been so deep, how was it possible to have gone, as we did, where there was no road, marching over precipices and ravines? Had it not been for the extreme depth of the snow, the whole of our horses and camels must have sunk into the first gulph that we met with.

Every good and evil that exists,
If you mark it well, is for a blessing.

It was bed-time prayers when we reached Auleng, and halted. The people of Auleng, who had heard of us as we descended, carried us to their warm houses, brought out fat sheep for us, a superfluity of hay and grain for our horses, with abundance of wood and dried dung to kindle us fires. To pass from the cold and snow, into such a village and its warm houses, on escaping from want and suffering, to find such plenty of good bread and fat sheep as we did, is an enjoyment that can be conceived only by such as have suffered similar hardships, or endured such heavy distress. We staid one day at Auleng to refresh and recruit the spirits and strength of our men; after which we marched on eight miles, and halted. Next morning was the festival of the Ramzân. The Turkomân Hazâras had taken up their winter quarters in the line of my march, with their families and property, and had not the smallest intimation of my approach. Next morning, on our march, we came among their huts, close by their sheep-folds, two or three of which we plundered; whereupon the whole of the Hazâras taking the alarm, abandoned their huts and property, and fled away to the hills with their children. Soon afterwards information was brought from the van, that a body of them, having posted themselves right in our line of march, had stopped our people in a narrow defile, were assailing them with arrows, and effectually prevented their advance. Immediately on learning this I hurried forward. On coming up, I found that there really was properly speaking no strait; but that some Hazâras had posted themselves on a projecting eminence, where they had gathered together their effects, had taken up a position, and were making discharges of arrows on our men.

(*Tûrki verse.*)
They marked the distant blackening of the foe,
And stood panic-struck and confounded;
I came up and hastened to the spot,
And pressing on, exclaiming, Stand! Stand!
My aim was to make my troops alert,
To fall briskly upon the foe.
Having brought on my men, I placed myself behind;
When not a man minded my orders;
I had neither my coat of mail, nor horse-mail, nor arms,
Except only my bow and arrows.
When I stood still, all my men stood still also,
As if the foe had slain them all.
"He who hires a servant, hires him for his need,
That he may one day be useful in time of danger,
Not that he should stand still while his lord advances,
That he should stand at ease while his lord bears the burden of the day.
He who is a servant should serve in due season,
Not loiter in thy service, so as not even to be seasoning to thy food."
At length I spurred on my horse and advanced,
And, driving the foe before me, ascended the hill;
My men, on seeing me advance, advanced also,
Leaving their terror behind.
Pushing forward, we quickly climbed the hill;
We went on without heeding their arrows,
Sometimes dismounting, sometimes on horseback.
First of all came on the boldest warriors:
The enemy showered down arrows from above,
But marking our resolution gave way and fled.
We gained the top of the hill, and drove the Hazâras before us,
We skipped over the heights and hollows like deer;
We cut off the heads of the slain like deer;

We plundered them, we divided their property and sheep;
We slew the Tûrkoman Hazâras,
And made captives of their men and women;
Those who were far off too we followed and made prisoners:
We took their wives and their children.

The purport of these verses is, that when the Hazâras stopped the van, on its route, our men were all rather perplexed, and halted. In this situation I came up singly. Having called out to the men who were fleeing, "Stand! stand!" I attempted to encourage them. Not one of them would listen to me, or advance upon the enemy, but they stood scattered about in different places. Although I had not put on my helmet, my horse's mail, or my armour, and had only my bow and quiver, I called out that servants were kept that they might be serviceable, and, in time of need, prove their loyalty to their master; not for the purpose of looking on while their master marched up against the foe: after which I spurred on my horse. When my men saw me making for the enemy, they followed. On reaching the hill which the Hazâras occupied, our troops instantly climbed it, and, without minding the arrows which poured down on them, made their way up, partly on horseback, partly on foot. As soon as the enemy saw that our men were in real earnest, they did not venture to stand their ground, but took to flight. Our people pursued them up the hills, hunting them like deer or game. Such property or effects as our troops could lay hold of, they brought in with them, and made the families and children of the enemy prisoners. We also gathered in some of their sheep, which we gave in charge to Yârek, while we proceeded forward. We traversed the heights and eminences of the hill-country, driving off the horses and sheep of the Hazâras, and brought them to Lenger, where we encamped. Fourteen or fifteen of the most noted insurgents and robber chiefs of the Hazâras had fallen into our hands. It was my intention to have put them to death with torture at our halting-ground, as an example and terror to all rebels and robbers; but Kâsim Beg happening to meet them, was filled with unseasonable commiseration, and let them go;

To do good to the bad is the same thing
As to do evil to the good:
Salt ground does not produce spikenard;—
Do not throw away good seed on it.

FLIGHT TO THE
SOUTH POLE

FROM *Exploring with Byrd*

RICHARD BYRD

🦌 Richard Byrd was fifteen years old when the Wright brothers flew at Kittyhawk. He took his first air ride at twenty-five and was thirty before he piloted a plane. Since that time he has flown over most of the inhabited and uninhabited areas of the globe, including the North and South Poles. His four most important flights resulted in the discovery of the following: five new mountain ranges, five islands, more than 100,000 square miles of territory, a large peninsula, and 700 miles of previously unknown stretches of Antarctic coast—a big piece of discovery for any man. This selection describes his almost disastrous flight over the South Pole in 1929.

THANKSGIVING DAY, NOVEMBER 25TH, BROUGHT WHAT WE WANTED. AT NOON the Geological Party radioed a final weather report: "Unchanged. Perfect visibility. No clouds anywhere." Harrison finished with his balloon runs, Haines with his weather charts. The sky was still somewhat overcast, and the surface wind from the east southeast. Haines came into the library, his face grave. Together we went out for a walk and a last look at the weather. What he said exactly I have forgotten, but it was in effect: "If you don't go now, you may never have another chance as good as this." And that was that.

The mechanics, Bubier, Roth and Demas, went over the plane for the last time, testing everything with scrupulous care. A line of men passed five-gallon cans of gasoline to several men standing on the wing, who poured them into the wing tanks. Another line fed the stream of gear which flowed into the plane. Black weighed each thing before passing it on to McKinley and June, who were stowing the stuff in the cabin. Hanson went over the radio equipment. With de Ganahl I made a careful check of the sextant and the watches and chronometers, which were among the last things put aboard. For days de Ganahl and I had nursed the chronometers, checking them against the time tick broadcast every night from the United States. We knew their exact loss or gain.

The total weight was approximately 15,000 pounds.

Haines came up with a final report on the weather. "A twenty-mile wind from the south at 2,000 feet." I went into my office and picked up a flag weighted with a stone from Floyd Bennett's grave. It seemed fitting that something connected with the spirit of this noble friend, who stood with me over the North Pole, on May 9th, 1926, should rest as long as stone endures at the bottom of the world.

There were handshakes all around, and at 3:29 o'clock we were off. The skis were in the air after a run of 30 seconds—an excellent take-off. A calm expectation took hold of my mind.

Had you been there to glance over the cabin of this modern machine which has so revolutionized polar travel, I think you would have been impressed most of all—perhaps first of all—with the profusion of gear in the cabin. There was a small sledge, rolled masses of sleeping bags, bulky food sacks, two pressure gasoline stoves, rows of cans of gasoline packed about the main tank forward, funnels for draining gasoline and oil from the engines, bundles of clothing, tents and so on *ad infinitum*. There was scarcely room in which to move.

June had his radio in the after bulkhead on the port side. From time to time he flashed reports on our progress to the base. From the ear phones strapped to his helmet ran long cords so that he might move freely about the cabin without being obliged to take them off. His duties were varied and important. He had to attend to the motion picture camera, the radio and the complicated valves of the six gasoline tanks. Every now and then he relieved Balchen at the wheel, or helped him to follow the elusive trail.

McKinley had his mapping camera ready for action either on port or starboard side. It was for him and the camera he so sedulously served that the flight was made. The mapping of the corridor between Little America and the South Pole was one of the major objectives of the expedition.

Balchen was forward, bulking large in the narrow compartment, his massive hands on the wheel, now appraising the engines with a critical eye, now the dozen flickering fingers on the dials on the instrument board. Balchen was in his element. His calm fine face bespoke his confidence and sureness. He was anticipating the struggle at the "Hump" almost with eagerness.

It was quite warm forward, behind the engines. But a cold wind swept through the cabin, making one thankful for heavy clothes. When the skies cleared, a golden light poured into the cabin. The sound of the engines and propellers filled it. One had to shout to make oneself heard. From the navigation table aft, where my charts were spread out, a trolley ran to the control cabin. Over it I shot to Balchen the necessary messages and courses; he would turn and smile his understanding.

That, briefly, is the picture, and a startling one it makes in contrast with that of Amundsen's party, which had pressed along this same course eighteen years before. A wing, pistons and flashing propellers had taken the place of runner, dogs and legs. Amundsen was delighted to make 25 miles per day. We had to average 90 miles per hour to accomplish our mission. We had the advantages of swiftness and comfort, but we had as well an enlarged fallibility. A flaw in a piece of steel, a bit of dirt in the fuel lines of carburetor jets, a few hours of strong head winds, fog or storm— these things, remotely beyond our control, could destroy our carefully laid plans and nullify our most determined efforts.

Still, it was not these things that entered our minds. Rather it was the thought of the "Hump," and how we should fare with it.

Soon after passing the crevasses we picked up again the vast escarpment to the right. More clearly than before we saw the white-blue streams of many glaciers discharging into the Barrier, and several of the higher snow-clad peaks glistened so brightly in the sun as to seem like volcanoes in eruption.

Now the Queen Maud Range loomed ahead. I searched again for the "appearance of land" to the east. Still the rolling Barrier—nothing else.

At 8:15 o'clock we had the Geological Party in sight—a cluster of beetles about two dark-topped tents. Balchen dropped overboard the photographs of the Queen Maud Range and the other things we had promised to bring. The parachute canopy to which they were attached fluttered open and fell in gentle oscillations, and we saw two or three figures rush out to catch it. We waved to them, and then prepared for a settlement of the issue at the "Hump."

Up to this time, the engines had operated continuously at cruising revolutions. Now Balchen opened them full throttle, and the Ford girded its loins for the long, fighting pull over the "Hump." We rose steadily. We were then about 60 miles north of the western portal of Axel Heiberg, and holding our course steadily on meridian 163° 45' W. with the sun compass.

I watched the altimeters, of which there were two in the navigation department. The fingers marched with little jumps across the face of the dial—3,000 feet, 3,500, 4,000, 4,500. The Ford had her toes in, and was climbing with a vast, heaving effort.

Drawing nearer, we had edged 30° to the west of south, to bring not only Axel Heiberg but also Liv Glacier into view. This was a critical period. I was by no means certain which glacier I should choose for the ascent. I went forward and took a position behind the pilots.

The schemes and hopes of the next few minutes were beset by many uncertainties. Which would it be—Axel Heiberg or Liv Glacier?

There was this significant difference between flying and sledging: we could not pause long for decision or investigation. Minutes stood for gasoline, and gasoline was precious. The waste of so little as half an hour of fuel in a fruitless experiment might well overturn the mathematical balance on which the success of the flight depended. The execution of the plan hung on the proper choice of the route over the "Hump."

Yet, how well, after all, could judgment forecast the ultimate result? There were few facts on which we might base a decision. We knew, for example, from Amundsen's report, that the highest point of the pass of Axel Heiberg Glacier was 10,500 feet. We should know, in a very few minutes, after June had calculated the gasoline consumption, the weight of the plane. From that we could determine, according to the tables we had worked out and which were then before me, the approximate ceiling we should have. We should know, too, whether or not we should be able to complete the flight, other conditions being favorable.

These were the known elements. The unknown were burdened with equally important consequences. The structural nature of the head of the pass was of prime importance. We knew from Amundsen's descriptions and from what we could see with our own eyes, that the pass on both sides was surrounded by towering peaks, much higher than the maximum ceiling of the heavily loaded plane. But whether the pass was wide or narrow; whether it would allow us room to maneuver in case we could not rise above it; whether it would be narrow and running with a torrent of down-pressing wind which would dash a plane, already hovering near its service ceiling, to the glacier floor—these were things, naturally, we could not possibly know until the issue was directly at hand.

I stood beside Balchen, carefully studying the looming fortress, still wondering by what means we should attempt to carry it. With a gesture of the hand Balchen pointed to fog vapor rising from the black rock of the foothills which were Nansen's high priests—caused no doubt by the condensation of warm currents of air radiated from the sun-heated rocks. A thin layer of cloud seemed to cap Axel Heiberg's pass, and extended almost to Liv Glacier. But of this we were not certain. Perhaps it was the surface of the snow. If cloud, then our difficulties were already upon us. Even high clouds would be resting on the floor of the uplifted plateau.

There was, then, a gamble in the decision. Doubtless a flip of the coin would have served as well. In the end, we decided to choose Liv Glacier, the unknown pass to the right which Amundsen had seen far in the distance and named after Dr. Nansen's daughter. It seemed to be broader than Axel Heiberg, and the pass not quite so high.

A few minutes after 9 o'clock we passed near the intermediate base, which, of course, we could not see. Our altitude was then about 9,000 feet. At 9:15 o'clock we had the eastern portal on our left, and were ready to tackle the "Hump." We had discussed the "Hump" so often, had anticipated and maligned it so much, that now that it was in front of us and waiting in the flesh—in rock-ribbed, glacierized reality—it was like meeting an old acquaintance. But we approached it warily and respectfully, climbing steadily all the while with maximum power, to get a better view of its none too friendly visage.

June, wholly unaffected by the immediate perplexities, went about his job of getting the plane in fighting trim. He ripped open the last of the fuel cans, and poured the contents into the main tank. The empty tins he dropped overboard, through the trapdoor. Every tin weighed two pounds; and every pound dropped was to our gain. June examined the gauges of the five wing tanks, then measured with a graduated stick the amount of fuel in the main tank. He jotted the figures on a pad, made a few calculations and handed me the results. Consumption had thus far averaged between 55 and 60 gallons per hour. It had taken us longer to reach the mountains than we had expected, owing to head winds. However, the extra fuel taken aboard just before we left had absorbed this loss and we actually had a credit balance. We had, then, enough gasoline to take us to the Pole and back.

With that doubt disposed of, we went at the "Hump" confidently.

We were still rising, and the engines were pulling wonderfully well. The wind was about abeam, and, according to my calculations, not materially affecting the speed.

The glacier floor rose sharply, in a series of ice falls and terraces, some of which were well above the (then) altitude of the plane. These glacial waterfalls, some of which were from 200 to 400 feet high, seemed more beautiful than any precipitous stream I have ever seen. Beautiful yes, but how rudely and with what finality they would deal with steel and duralumin that crashed into them at 100 miles per hour.

Now the stream of air pouring down the pass roughened perceptibly. The great wing shivered and teetered as it balanced itself against the changing pressures. The wind from the left flowed against Fisher's steep flanks, and the constant, hammering bumps made footing uncertain in the plane. But McKinley steadily trained his 50-pound camera on the mountains to the left. The uncertainties of load and ceiling were not his concern. His only concern was photographs—photographs over which students and geographers might pore in the calm quiet of their studies.

The altimeters showed a height of 9,600 feet, but the figure was not necessarily exact. Nevertheless there were indications we were near the service ceiling of the plane.

The roughness of the air increased and became so violent that we were forced to swing slightly to the left, in search of calmer air. This brought us over a frightfully crevassed slope which ran up and toward Mount Nansen. We thus escaped the turbulent swirl about Fisher, but the down-surging currents here damped our climb. To the left we had the "blind" mountain glacier of Nansen in full view; and when we looked ahead we saw the plateau—a smooth, level plain of snow between Nansen and Fisher. The pass rose up to meet it.

In the center of the pass was a massive outcropping of snow-covered rock, resembling an island, which protruded above and separated the descending stream of ice. Perhaps it was a peak or the highest eminence of a ridge connecting Fisher and Nansen which had managed through the ages to hold its head above the glacial torrent pouring down from the plateau. But its particular structure or relationship was of small moment then. I watched it only with reference to the climb of the plane; and realized, with some disgust and more consternation, that the nose of the plane, in spite of the fact that Balchen had steepened the angle of attack, did not rise materially above the outcropping. We were still climbing, but at a rapidly diminishing rate of speed. In the rarefied air the heavy plane responded to the controls with marked sluggishness. There is a vast difference between the plane of 1928 and the plane of 1937.

It was an awesome thing, creeping (so it seemed) through the narrow pass, with the black walls of Nansen and Fisher on either side, higher than the level of the wings, and watching the nose of the ship bob up and down across the face of that chunk of rock. It would move up, then slide down. Then move up, and fall off again. For perhaps a minute or two we deferred the decision; but there was no escaping it. If we were to risk a passage through the pass, we needed greater maneuverability than we had at that moment. Once we entered the pass, there would be no retreat. It offered no room for turn. If power was lost momentarily or if the air became excessively rough, we could only go ahead, or down. We had to climb, and there was only one way in which we could climb.

June, anticipating the command, already had his hand on the dump valve of the main tank. A pressure of the fingers—that was all that was necessary—and in two minutes 600 gallons of gasoline would gush out. I signaled to wait.

Balchen held to the climb almost to the edge of a stall. But it was clear to both of us that he could not hold it long enough. Balchen began to yell and gesticulate, and it was hard to catch the words in the roar of the engines echoing from the cliffs on either side. But the meaning was manifest. "Overboard—overboard—200 pounds!"

Which would it be—gasoline or food?

If gasoline, I thought, we might as well stop there and turn back. We could never get back to the base from the Pole. If food, the lives of all of us would be jeopardized in the event of a forced landing. Was that fair to McKinley, Balchen and June? It really took only a moment to reach the decision. The Pole, after all, was our objective. I knew the character of the three men. McKinley, in fact, had already hauled one of the food bags to the trapdoor. It weighed 125 pounds.

The brown bag was pushed out and fell, spinning, to the glacier. The improvement in the flying qualities of the plane was noticeable. It took another breath and resumed the climb.

Now the down-currents over Nansen became stronger. The plane trembled and rose and fell, as if struck bodily. We veered a trifle to the right, searching for helpful rising eddies. Balchen was flying shrewdly. He maintained flight at a sufficient distance below the absolute ceiling of the plane to retain at all times enough maneuverability to make him master of the ship. But he was hard pressed by circumstances; and I realized that, unless the plane was further lightened, the final thrust might bring us perilously close to the end of our reserve.

"More," Bernt shouted. "Another bag."

McKinley shoved a second bag through the trapdoor, and this time we saw it hit the glacier, and scatter in a soundless explosion. Two hundred and fifty pounds of food—enough to feed four men for a month—lay strewn on the barren ice.

The sacrifice swung the scales. The plane literally rose with a jump; the engines dug in, and we soon showed a gain in altitude of from 300 to 400 feet. It was what we wanted. We should clear the pass with about 500 feet to spare. Balchen gave a shout of joy. It was just as well. We could dump no more food. There was nothing left to dump except McKinley's camera. I am sure that, had he been asked to put it overboard, he would have done so instantly; and I am equally sure he would have followed the precious instrument with his own body.

The next few minutes dragged. We moved at a speed of 77 nautical miles per hour through the pass, with the black walls of Nansen on our left. The wing gradually lifted above them. The floor of the plateau stretched in a white immensity to the south. We were over the dreaded "Hump" at last. The Pole lay dead ahead over the horizon, less than 300 miles away. It was then about 9:45 o'clock. (I did not note the exact time. There were other things to think about.)

FOURTEEN MONTHS
ON TABLE MOUNTAIN

FROM *The Life and Adventures of Joshua Penny*

JOSHUA PENNY

Joshua Penny was a *cause célèbre* in a small but very vocal area of the Republic during the War of 1812. Besides his harrowing experiences on Table Mountain, described in this selection, his *Life and Adventures,* published by himself, gives an account of his "being taken out of his bed by Commodore Hardy on the night of August 21, 1813, and carried to Halifax, where he suffered nine months imprisonment."

The case of Joshua Penny was the subject of considerable correspondence between Commodore Hardy, later Vice-Admiral of the British Navy, and the citizens of East Hampton, Long Island, who demanded Penny's release on the double ground that he was a resident of their township and a noncombatant.

A squib from the *Long Island Star* gives the flavor of the exchange: "By our attentive correspondent at Sag Harbor, it appears that Commodore Hardy's persecution of Joshua Penny is principally on account of his having piloted a torpedo boat. . . . The Commodore threatens to lay waste the towns and show no mercy to the inhabitants that harbor torpedoes which had given him so much inquietude that it had taken almost all the hair from his head."

The Life and Adventures of Joshua Penny, a native of South-old, Long Island, Suffolk County, New-York: Who was Impressed into the British Service, and in one of his attempts to escape was fourteen months on the Table Mountain, at the Cape of Good Hope, and saw no human being during that time. In another instance he resided some time among the Hottentots. Interspersed with Many Curious Incidents and Hair Breadth Escapes.

NOT LONG AFTER THIS THE 4TH OF JUNE CAME, WHEN THE SEAMEN ARE AL-lowed to get drunk, because this is their king's birth day; and when the 4th of July came, I applied to Lt. Pingally for liberty to get drunk. He said "go along forward, you yankee rascal." The captain then spoke to him, when he, as I suppose, informed him of my request. He called me to him, and asked—What do you mean, sir, by asking permission to do what you know is contrary to the regulations of this ship? I recollect sir, said I, that about a month ago you gave the English liberty to get drunk because it was their king's birth day; and now I want the liberty to rejoice on my nation's birth day. The captain laughing heartily, ordered that two gallons of wine and one of brandy be procured from the shore for me and my *yankee mess* to rejoice. We all liked this captain. The glass passed merrily round in our *yankee mess,* of thirty in number, and they began to sing *Hail Columbia, happy land!* A north countryman, who called himself the bully of the ship, came along for the purpose of fomenting a quarrel, and told us—"get out of the way, you d—d yankee buggers." This was, consequently, taken as an insult. I gave him an unceremonious box on the ear, and asked if that was what he meant. Yes, he answered, it is exactly what I want. A few blows were passed between us, when the officer between decks coming up, ordered *fair play*—he had observed that several others were aiding my antagonist by pelting me. A few more passes were made at each other; at last I struck him with the left hand, and in drawing back found two of the bully's teeth sticking in the joint of one of my fingers. My antagonist, on losing his front teeth, yielded immediately.

I was then put on the surgeon's list as unfit for duty. The finger is stiff to the present time. This appeared to me a good opportunity to improve for my deliverance, so that I resolved to counterfeit inability, if necessary to attain this end. I continued six months under the doctor's care, and he reported me *incurable;* but the captain said "the yankee feigns his sickness, so as to get at liberty—to run away from the hospital." This the surgeon told me; but soon after put me once more on the list of *incurables.* The captain then told the surgeon that I was not so sick as I represented.— The surgeon replied, he understood his own business, and I was immediately ordered into the boat with a sick company going to the hospital, under the care of the surgeon's mate, who was to attend us on shore. The hospital was situated at the foot of Table mountain, half a mile from the shore. I was put into a blanket, slung on an oar and carried by two men.

The doctor's mate, ordered the men to follow him through town in single rank, and I was in the rear of this procession. We had not proceeded far before we came to a wine-house, where I begged the sailors to set me down, as I was very *thirsty.* They very readily complied, knowing they should get some wine.—I called on the landlord, as we entered his house, for a bottle of Constantia wine and three tumblers. I took my glass, and paid the landlord while the sailors were drinking theirs. I proposed going immediately, judging however that they would never budge while any wine remained. As soon as they became engaged, I pretended an occasion of necessity to retire out of the back door, and helped myself by the chairs until fairly out, and it was safe to become as well as ever I was in my life. I went hastily through the back yard into another street, which enabled me to get through the town and reach the thicket of bushes at the skirts of Table mountain, which I had often looked to as a place of refuge. I had this in contemplation long before, because I had been acquainted with the mode of living in similar places, and had taken the precaution to provide myself with a belt to fasten around me, containing a knife, a small brass tinder-box, and eleven dollars.

Here, feeling myself secure from pursuit, I meditated leisurely, and at length determined to spend the residue of my days on this mountain, if the British ships should not leave the Cape. I resolved to become a breakfast for a lion, sooner than be taken to another floating dungeon.

I returned into the town in the dark, and laid in my supply of goods—this was two loaves of bread, a calabash of brandy and a flint. This was as much as I could take, although my money was not all spent, which had been saved out of my rations of grog for this purpose. My dress was composed of one shirt, one Guernsey frock, and one pair of duck trowsers, with a hospital cap.

Thus equipped I marched on my tour up the mountain, without waiting to hear what return the doctor's mate would make to our captain of the sick *Jonas Ingleberg,* for that was my name on board the ship. My destiny seemed providential; for the first news I had of the Sceptre, was that she sunk soon after I left her, in a gale of wind, without weighing her anchors, and every soul on board perished in her.

There are no trees on Table mountain, and I climbed the cragged rocks through the bushes, and ascended, or attempted to ascend, all night; yet frequently returned to the place last left. I was much fatigued, and sometimes found a spring of water, where my calabash was very useful. It was unsafe to make a fire that night on a mountain fronting the ships, yet I was in danger from the wild beasts, who were often near me, and seemed reluctant to get out of my way. I knew the wild beasts were numerous here, and of almost every species. The next morning, I perceived that the ships lay far below, and could not discover me.

This mountain is green in every season, and it seems, from the water, that a cat might be discovered upon it: but I found nothing else than gullies, cragged rocks piled on each other, and scrubby bushes in their crevices. Here I began to think of preparing for subsistence, and, on searching, soon found a hive of bees among the rocks. This wild honey is so plenty, that a man from Cape Town will return home, loaded, the same day he leaves it.

The Hottentots had taught me the process of obtaining this honey, and having a wooden pipe, I proceeded to the cavity of the rock, covered with wax, and introducing the stem of my pipe through the entrance of the bees, blew in the smoke, which caused the bees to retreat into the interior. The second night I could make a fire under the cover of a rock, and regale myself with brandy and honey.

When I had ascended four days from the mountain's foot, I lost sight of the fleet and the bay. My course now was over level rocky spots, of 30 or 40 feet in width, on which I saw innumerable herds of goats, hosts of antelopes, wolves, tygers, and leopards. The three latter are the only animals considered dangerous here, except the venomous snakes. The baboons are here numerous and large. At first, they would apparently take no notice of me; but soon after would be seen on a precipice, 100 feet above, throwing stones at me.

At last I reached the summit, and selected a spot, in view of the Western Ocean, for my residence. I occupied a cavern which secured me from storms, near a spring of good water. My whole stock of provisions being nearly exhausted, I thought it time to recruit. Necessity invents the means in these cases. I sallied out with a stone in my hand, and had not advanced a great distance when I espied an antelope on the brow of a precipice. I threw the stone at the back of his head, and tumbled him to the bottom; where, by a circuitous route, I found my game, whose skin I drew over his head, and cutting the meat into strings, hung it on sticks put into the crevices of my habitation. This meat when dried, I broiled and eat with toad-sorrel for my sauce. Besides this I had honey and good water. It seemed rather hard at first, to live without bread, salt, and articles deemed necessary in former days; but at the end of two or three weeks I lived very contentedly. While among the Hottentots I had learned their method of making a very pleasant beverage resembling metheglin. I was fortunate enough to find an old hollow tree, which I cut off with my knife, and seized a green hide on one end for a bottom. Into this tub honey and water was put to stand twenty-fours hours; then was added some pounded root to make it foment. This root, in use among the frontier Hottentots, does not resemble any of my acquaintance in America, but makes an excellent drink in this preparation. I had ground-nuts and a root with a stem one inch above the ground, with three leaves as small as those of the garden pink. This root, of the size of a junk bottle, is eatable; yet is not as good as the water-melon, which the Dutch call it. It is probable the *kameroo* from the description given me of its size and shape.

My clothes, by creeping through the rocks and bushes, were so tattered that I had become almost naked. In this extremity I made a needle from the bone of a beast; the eye of which being made with my sharp pointed knife, enabled me to sew with the sinews of my antelopes. With the skins I equipped myself completely from head to foot. The skins were dressed by rubbing sand on the flesh side with a stone; and furnished me with moccasins, *shin-fenders,* or leggings to the knee; a short petticoat fastened round my waist, and a hunting frock. The hair was worn inside when cold, and turned outside when warm. It is almost unnecessary to add that I wore a *superb cap.*

Thus accoutred, it is natural to suppose me somewhat elevated, although without a looking-glass. Pride must have a fall—I was soon afflicted with lice. By procuring an entire new suit, and changing my residence, these tenants of the skin abandoned me. It was not troublesome to change my quarters; and by often shifting my abode for a new tenement, I acquired by occupation dwellings enough to make my territory called a city. Thus I lived, unannoyed by wild beasts or press-gangs; until one day I crept out of some cragged rocks, and came inadvertently into a large concourse of wolves, in their season of making love. They soon surrounded me; some within 20 feet. I stood ready with my knife to defend myself; when at last, one turned off, another followed, till they all had sneaked off apparently ashamed of themselves and left me alone. I used to kill *darsies* or mountain rats, which eat grass, and are choice food.

At each full moon I cut a notch in the root, which hung to a silken cord about my neck; and this was the only account I kept of time.

Once I undertook to descend the western side of the mountain to the sea shore, where I could often see vessels in clear weather; but the mountain being very steep on that side, with so many rocks that I frequently let myself down by taking hold of bushes, until I seemed sliding into the sea without power to stop. In two days I returned, and gave up experiments in that direction. My practice was to eat twice in the day; and when cooking in the evening always heard the howling of wild beasts, and often saw the light of their eyes, when attracted about me by the smell of meat.

My residence was not on the summit, but in a convenient place for hunting; near some height, on which I could cramp my game. I often went over to the eastern front to view the ships; and continued to do so until twelve notches were made upon the calender fastened to my neck. I had become perfectly reconciled to my condition—had abundance of meat, sorrel, honey and water; and every night could sing my song with as much pleasure as at any period of my life. In fine, I never enjoyed life better than while I lived among the ferocious animals of Table Mountain; because I had secured myself against the more savage English. I now discovered some vessels at sea, on the western side of the mountain, but was unable to distinguish them as ships or other vessels, the clouds being so far below me.*
However, I suspected the fleet had sailed from the Cape—mustered my pro-

* This mountain is 1350 feet high.

visions, and stowed them in a knapsack, made of a skin drawn over the head, after splitting it on the hind-legs. The skin of each hind leg was tied to that of the fore-leg on the same side, and my arms passed through the loop, the neck hung at the bottom down my back.

I now left my numerous habitations for the last time. During my residence I had never been able to discover the vestige of a human being, except myself, having ever ventured here. I travelled one day and part of a night, without being able to discover any shipping, on account of intervening clouds. I often was compelled to travel five miles on the mountain, without gaining in descent one hundred rods. The second day in my descent, the air being clear, I saw the bay, and one vessel only. I concluded to pursue my course until I could ascertain her character. Continuing on the next day, I perceived that vessel to be a brig; and having no top-gallant-masts, took her for a merchantman.

Determined to push for her immediately, I descended to the foot of the mountain, and rested there till after day break. It was only half a mile to the shore. A British regiment I supposed to be stationed in the town; yet I thought no person would know me after so long an absence; especially in my mountain dress: But to avoid their notice of my uncouth habit, I turned the hair side inwards. I marched through the town unobserved by any one except two or three servants, who continued to gaze obliquely at me as long as I could see them. The boat was coming to the shore as I approached it, with two men and the captain, as I supposed.

I tried my power of speech to prepare myself. The captain landing advanced guardedly towards me, I stepped up to meet him and asked if he wanted to ship a man? He was surprised to hear me speak, and asked "What in the name of God are you! man or beast?" He at last stepped up to me and giving me his hand, said "this is no place to talk—jump into the boat and go on board." The boat was ordered to return for him in half an hour; into it I sprung, and was soon snug on board.

When the captain returned he sent for me in the cabin and ordered me two suits of clothes. I put them on, and took my beard off for the first time in fourteen months. He then heard a short story of myself, and said he supposed me to be a deserter; but that I had nothing to fear if I would go with him.

This brig was under Danish colors, but the captain and property were English, as he told me—and was bound to St. Helena, and thence to London. On learning that I had deserted the Sceptre, he informed me that she had been sunk fourteen months: he pointed to a monument on shore over the bodies of her crew, which had been driven on shore and there interred.

AVALANCHE

FROM *Other Gods*

PEARL BUCK

🦁 Pearl Buck has been associated more intimately with China than any other western writer. Her novel *The Good Earth,* whose theme was the struggle of man against hunger, made literary history when it was published. It won her the Pulitzer prize, the medal of the American Academy of Arts and Letters, and subsequently the Nobel Prize.

Besides her many Chinese novels and translations of Chinese classics, she has written equally compelling novels of western life which are much less familiar to many of her great body of readers. In *Other Gods,* from which this selection is taken, she shifts her locale to the Himalayas and her theme to the struggle of men against the mountains.

UPON THE CLOUD UNDER WHICH THE BASE CAMP SLEPT, BERT LOOKED DOWN AS on a floor. His luck held. Just when he was thinking he had to take his choice of wind with clear sky, or snow every time the wind fell, this floor of white cloud came up around the mountain, shutting off the wind and the warmth which made it. The temperature rose nearly ten degrees that morning in the last camp where he and Brugh had spent the night before, together. It had been a bad night. He knew now why he didn't like Brugh. It wasn't only because he was an Englishman, but because he did not trust him. It occurred to him in the middle of the night that Brugh might pull the same trick on him now that he had pulled on old Fessaday, get up while he was still asleep and make the dash up the last thousand feet alone. The peak was definitely between the two of them now. Blastel and Brewer had given up at the end of the second day. The wind had sent the thermometer down until Brewer had to be slapped to keep him awake. Finally Blastel had said he'd take him back to the camp they had made the night before. And before night of the next day Calloway had begun to see double for some reason or other, and Mayhew complained of snow blindness. He'd told them to stay at the camp yesterday morning and left them most of the oxygen. Mayhew saw more clearly after a little oxygen. But there was no use dragging him on. Fessaday used to say every man had his own height, and you couldn't make him go higher and have him any use.

What his own height was he did not know. Certainly it was higher than Therat. Up there he had felt the air thin enough to make him careful about breathing, but he didn't feel stupid with it. He could still feel that last great lift when he stepped to the topmost rock. It was like nothing on earth. He panted to feel it again. Every step upward brought him nearer to it.

But Brugh was as good at climbing as he was. Brugh showed no sign of being tired. He could bear the cold as no one he had ever seen could bear it; last night before they turned in they went outside their tent for a moment, and Brugh had stood looking at the stars as though he were at home. The air was solid ice. When you breathed it you felt like you were drawing chunks of it into your lungs and it cut. But Brugh stood as though he were made of ice and did not mind breathing it.

"One does not become acquainted with the heavenly bodies," he said, "until one climbs mountains." Brugh could not open his mouth without long words coming out of it. "I used to think I was familiar with the stars," he said. "Now I know I was merely presumptuous."

He did not know what to answer Brugh and so he said nothing. He was always safe if he said nothing.

The stars were hanging there big as pumpkins around them and near enough to pick. Kit would like them. He looked in the direction of the base camp but the edge of a col hid the right saddle of the mountain. He'd like her to know he was all right. But then he had told her he would be. It was swell of her to come along so far. But why shouldn't she when she was his wife? And when he came down tomorrow she could be proud of him all over again.

"Difficult to imagine human beings down there," Brugh was saying. "Difficult to believe in all that little life stirring about as it does, generation after generation, never getting out of its own mud!"

Brugh was putting on airs again, Bert thought. People didn't talk like that unless they were putting on airs.

"Guess I'll turn in," he said. No use standing out in such cold just to hear Brugh talk!

He went inside and then wondered if Brugh had gone crazy. He heard him out there still talking—no, singing, in a big clear voice, loud enough to start an avalanche. The words were some foreign language. He could hear them coming back in echoes.

"Here you!" he shouted. "I don't know about so much noise up here. We don't know the lay of things—might start vibrations or something and peel down an avalanche!"

Brugh shut up instantly. "Right," he said and came into the tent.

They did not speak again. But it had been queer enough to make him feel Brugh was a little off and could do a thing like getting up and going on by himself. It was a bad night anyway, and the wind forced snow into every crack of the tent. Then suddenly it dropped. When Bert woke in the morning the floor of cloud was not five hundred feet below them and there was no wind.

Brugh was still asleep. Bert looked down into that long thin English face and was suddenly burning with temptation. Suppose he just slipped out and went on?

The moment he thought of it he knew he had to do it. Now that he looked at him, it seemed to him he had never liked Brugh. Why should Brugh be the one to get to the top with him?

Brugh did not move. His pale long face looked frozen, but it was not. He was breathing evenly in slow breaths. When he got up, Bert thought scornfully, he would have to have tea to drink before he could start, even though they couldn't get water to boil up here, and tea was nothing but brown tepid water. That one delay was reason enough why he should go on.

It took only a minute to make up his mind and get things together and he knew how to be perfectly quiet when he wanted to be. So now, slipping into his extra garments, picking up his crampons to put on outside, stuffing his pockets with food, he was outside the tent in ten minutes wrapped in his fur parka, with three sweaters underneath and three pairs of trousers, and under his hood two caps, ready to begin the long steady climb which Pangbat spread before him. What he was doing now that he had begun it seemed the only thing he could do, and he remembered, besides, that he and Brugh had already half-decided yesterday that this last day they would climb independently and without a rope to tie them together. He chuckled. He was only being a little more independent. . . .

There had been a light snowfall during the night. That must have been after the wind died. Upon the old ice of now more sharply increasing slopes, the new snow was three inches deep, and right for crampons to stick into and hold. Luck was still following him. By a miracle the wind had not begun again and yet the sky was clear. After noon the sky would cloud, and by midafternoon there might be snow. But he would be at the top by noon, if his luck held. . . .

He could see nothing of Brugh coming after him. For a long time the tent had been visible, a dark inverted cone upon the snow. Then he had lost it behind a bergschrund and going between that and the mountain he saw that the easiest way was not up the face he had been climbing, but around its base and up the irregularities of the side at right angles with it. The smooth face, he now saw was deceptive. It ended in that sharp cornice at the top which might prove impossible for him just when he needed his utmost strength. Or, if the day went on as quietly as it now was under the sun, the weight of the cornice, pressing upon the sheet of snow upon the blue ice beneath, might cause the sheet to peel off the ice into an avalanche. It was better to get to rough ground, even if it meant slower going. It occurred to him that yesterday he and Brugh, planning this last dash for the top, had decided that the smooth north face which he was now climbing was the best way up and that now he had no way to tell Brugh that he had changed his mind. But Brugh was an older climber and he would see for himself the threat of the cornice.

"At least he ought to see it, and it's not my fault if he don't," he told himself.

By mid-morning he was beginning to feel dull with the altitude. He had heard men talk about that dullness, though he had never had it before. But he was already higher than he had ever been in his life. Dull and heavy-footed, his breath difficult to draw, and the weight of his ice ax trebling, he stopped a moment to take in oxygen, and for the first time it occurred to him that Brugh had no oxygen! He had not thought of that when he lifted the tank this morning. He thought about it now for an instant and then was comforted. Brugh wouldn't get near the top, so why would he need oxygen? He felt better and went steadily upward.

He had forgotten Brugh by eleven o'clock. He had forgotten everything except his wonderful luck in the weather and this push within him to go on up and up. Imperceptibly as a poison gas the dullness grew upon him, and oxygen, though it relieved his lungs, did not clear his mind. He could not remember things. He tried to remember Kit's face and could not see her. He entirely forgot Brugh, and he tried for a long time to remember why he was here. And all the time he worried himself over these things, he kept on climbing, step by step. Just before noon he was delayed by a steep face of blue ice from which the snow had slipped into a heap at its bottom. He had to cut steps in the ice, hard as rock with depth and age. His arms seemed anchored to his thighs when he lifted them, and he had to cling to the wall gasping between every step. Still he could think, "That snow—soft to fall on—if I fall—luck!"

But he did not fall. He crawled over the edge of the highest cliff and lay panting for a few moments, remembering always to breathe through his mouth. Then he looked ahead and his heart gave a thick jump. Pangbat had given up. From where he lay the rise to the flattened knob of the crest was as gentle as a sloping meadow. He had only to gather himself together, leave his ice ax, because it was so heavy, leave his camera—the oxygen tank —leave everything, and walk across that hundred feet or so, to the top. He would feel no worse than he felt now. The crest was scarcely higher.

He rose slowly and plodded forward, step by step. Weights were upon his feet and against his knees and his blood had stopped running, though he was not cold, but the engine in him drove him on. He went to the end of the rise, stepped up twice, and Pangbat was beneath him.

He stood, dizzy and panting, and then his head began to clear. She was under his feet, this mountain! He was on her where nobody had ever been. He was doing something nobody had done before—maybe would never do again, because nobody might have just his luck again of sun and no wind. It was not all luck, though. It was partly him, a big part of it him and his push that always made him want to get to the top. He was at the top and Pangbat was his mountain. He felt like a king.

He stood looking around. Then he saw the cornice of snow was in his way. It was like a frozen wave springing up against the top of the mountain and curling away again and it kept him from being able to see everything. It was only a small cornice of snow. If he gave it a push it might crash down and let him see over the edge of the top. He wanted to see the whole world lying beneath him.

He struggled to it and looked down and saw a fissure a foot wide where the cornice clung to the ice crag on which he stood. If he gave the stiffly frozen snow even a touch, it might drop and he could see over. He put out his hand against the wall of snow which was just higher than his eyes. It was safe enough. There was plenty of room where he stood, and from it the sides of Pangbat's crest sloped gently to the supporting cliffs. He pushed, and heard a creak of parting snow surfaces and a slight crash. The top of the cornice had fallen and was beginning to slide downward. He could see over now. The noonday sun was shining upon the vast spreading snowy skirts of Pangbat.

And then, upon that whiteness he saw, a hundred feet, two hundred feet, beneath him a slowly moving speck of black. Brugh! It must be Brugh! He had forgotten Brugh.

"Brugh!" he yelled. "Brugh! Look out there!" The thickness of his head cleared completely. He was as much himself as he would have been at sea level.

"Look out!" he screamed.

For, in an instant so short he could not grasp it, the whole cornice began slowly to peel itself from the rocklike ice beneath it. The thing he had dreaded for himself was about to happen to Brugh. He could not stop it. He saw the harmless edge of the wave pull after it the whole frozen wall, and that weight of snow crashed downward and suddenly it seemed to him the whole side of Pangbat began to move in deep wrinkles and then in waves and then in torrents.

He kept on looking, not able to imagine what it would do when it struck

Brugh. It struck him. He saw the crinkled, slipping edge of the moving mass catch him at the knees. He saw Brugh fling up his hands, and his ice ax flew away and then the roaring grinding mass of snow overwhelmed him in a tide and swept downward, on and on, to be caught and held at last by the bergschrund they had rounded last night. The small valley where their tent had stood filled like a bowl, and snow brimmed to the top and frothed over it in a coomb of white.

He stood motionless and dazed, and, as though that downward rush had released some demon locked in Pangbat, he heard the familiar growl of a rising wind.

RIDING THE AVALANCHE

A JOURNEY TO CAINTUCK

FROM *Diary, 1775*

WILLIAM CALK

🐦 Daniel Boone in 1775 had blazed a trail—the Wilderness Road—from the edge of the settlements in the east, across the mountains to the land of Kentucke. It was the first time that the heart of the American wilderness had been invaded, not by Indians or hunters or traders, but to chop a road for people who wanted land and homes. From the settlements the first parties of men, women, and children, carrying their muscle and brain and courage, their farm tools and stock, set out across Boone's Trace to the western lands. It was the beginning of that vast migration that would in time push America to the Pacific Ocean. Boone's Trace was not an easy road to travel. All around it was the untouched wilderness and fear. But ahead was a promise. And a little of the fear and much of the courage we can read in this original diary of William Calk of Virginia, who started from Prince William County in that colony on March 13th, 1775, and reached Boone's Fort on April 20th.

1775, Mon. 13th—I SET OUT FROM PRINCE WM. TO TRAVEL TO CAINTUCK ON tuesday Night our company all got together at Mr. Priges on rapadon which was Abraham hanks philip Drake Eanock Smith Robert Whitledge and my Self thear Abrams Dogs leg got broke by Drakes Dog.

Wednesday, 15th—We started early from priges made a good Days travel and lodge this night at Mr. Cars on North fork James River.

Thursday, 16th—We started early it rained Chief part of the day Snowed in the Eavening very hard and was very Coald we traveled all day and got to Mr. Blocks at the foot of the Blue Ridge.

Friday 17th—We started early cross the Ridge the wind Blowsz very hard and cold and lodge at James loyls.

Monday 20th—We start early cross the ferry and lodge this night at Wm. Adamses on the head of Catauby.

Wedns 22nd—We start early and git to foart Chissel whear we git some good loaf Bread and good whiskey.

fryday 24th—we start early and turn out of the wagon Road to go across the mountains to go by Danil Smiths we loose Driver Come to a turable mountain that tired us all almost to death to git over it and we lodge this night on the Lawrel fork of holston under a granite mountain and Roast a fine fat turkey for our suppers and Eat it without aney Bread.

Satrd 25th—We start early over Some more very Bad mountains one that is called Clinch mountain and we git this night to Danil Smiths on Clinch and there we staid till thursday morning on tuesday night and wednesday morning it snowed Very hard and was very Coald and we hunted a good deal there while we staid in Rough mountains and kild three deer and one turkey Eanock Abram and I got lost tuesday night and it a snowing and Should a lain in the mountains had not I a had a pocket compas by which I got in a littel in the night and fired guns and they heard them and caim in By the Repoart.

thusd 30th—We set out again and went down to Elk gardin and there suplid our Selves With Seed Corn and irish tators then we went on a littel way I turned my hors to drive before me and he got scard ran away threw Down the Saddel Bags and broke three of our powder goards and Abrams beast Burst open a walet of corn and lost a good Deal and made a turrabel flustration amongst the Reast of the Horses Drakes mair run against a sapling and noct it down we cacht them all again and went on and lodged at John Duncans.

fryd 31st—We suplyed our Selves at Dunkans with a 103 pounds of Bacon and went on again to Brileys mill and suployed our Selves with meal and lodged this night on Clinch By a large cainbraike and cuckt our Supper.

April Saturday 1st—This morning there is ice at our camp half inch thick we start early and travel this Day along a verey Bad hilley way cross one creek whear the horses almost got mired some fell in and all wet their loads we cross Clinch River and travell till late in the Night and camp on Cove Creek having two men with us that wair pilates.

mond 3rd—We start early travel Down the valey cross powels river go some through the woods without aney track cross some Bad hills git in to hendersons Road camp on a creek in powels valey.

Tuesday 4th—Raney we Start about 10 oclock and git down to Capt. martins in the valey where we over take Col. henderson and his Company Bound for Caintuck and there we camp this Night there they were Broiling and Eating Beef without Bread.

Wednesday 5th—Breaks away fair and we go down the valey and camp on indian Creek we had this creek to cross maney times and very bad banks Abrams saddel turned and the load all fell in we got out this Eavening and kill two Deer.

thursd 6th—this morning is a hard frost and we wait at Camp for Col. henderson and company to come up they come up about 12 oclock and we goin with them and camp there still this night waiting for some part of the company that had their horses ran away with their packs.

fryday 7th—this morning is a very bad snowey morning we still continue at Camp being in number about 40 men and some neagros this Eaven. Comes a letter from Capt. Boone at caintuck of the indians doing mischief and some turns back.

Saturday 8th—We all pack up and started crost Cumberland gap about one oclock this Day Met a good many peopel turned back for fear of the indians but our Company goes on Still with good courage we came to a very ugly Creek with steep Banks and have to cross it several times on this Creek we camp this night.

tuesday 11th—this is a very loury morning and like for Rain but we all agree to start Early and we cross Cumberland River and travel Down it about 10 miles through some turrabel cainbrakes as we went down Abrams mair Ran into the River with her load and swam over he followed her and got on her and made her swim back agin it is a very raney Eavening we take up camp near Richland Creek they kill a beef Mr. Drake Bakes Bread without washing his hands we Keep Sentry this Night for fear of the indians.

Wednesday 12th—this is a Raney morning But we pack up and go on we come to Richland Creek it is high we tote our packs over on a tree and swim our horses over and there we meet another Companey going Back they tell such News abram and Drake is afraid to go aney farther there we camp this night.

thursday 13th—this morning the weather seems to brake and Be fair Abram and Drake turn Back we go on and git to loral River we come to a creek Before wheare we are able to unload and to take our packs over on a log this day we meet about 20 more turning Back we are obliged to toat our packs over loral river and swim our horses one hors ran in with his pack and lost it in the river and they got it agin.

sunday 16th—cloudy and warm we start early and go on about 2 miles down the river and then turn up a creek that we crost about 50 times some very bad foards with a great Deal of very good land on it in the Eavening we git over to the waters of Caintuck and go a little down the creek and there we camp keep sentel the fore part of the night it Rains very har all night.

tuesday 18th—fair and cool and we go on about 10 oclock we meet 4 men from Boones camp that caim to conduck us on we camp this night just on the Beginning of the good land near the Blue lick they kill 2 bofelos this Eavening.

thursday 20th—this morning is clear and cool. We start early and git Down to caintuck to Boons foart about 12 o'clock where we stop they come out to meet us and welcome us in with a voley of guns.

fryday 21st—warm this Day they begin laying off lots in the town preparing for people to go to work to make corn.

Sunday 23rd—this morning the peopel meets and draws for chois of lots this is a very warm day.

monday 24th—We all view our lots and some Dont like them about 12 oclock the combses come to town and Next morning they make them a bark canew and set off down the river to meet their Companey.

wednesday 26th—We Begin Building us a house and a plaise of Defense to Keep the indians off this day we begin to live without bread.

Satterday 29th—We git our house kivered with Bark and move our things into it at Night and Begin housekeeping Eanock Smith Robert Whitledge and myself.

THE DESTRUCTION OF THE ISLE OF ST. VINCENT

FROM *Mist's Journal*

DANIEL DEFOE

Daniel Defoe holds an eminent place in literature. His *Journal of the Plague Year* is documentary writing yet to be surpassed. He is acknowledged the father of English journalism and a satirist who frequently approaches the stature of Swift. In other areas, however, his accomplishments were distinctly less admirable. He was a government spy and informer. Both Whigs and Tories used him and both distrusted him. An unsavory but representative episode in his career was his editorship of *Mist's Journal,* a Jacobite paper, in which position his function was to act as provocateur and to report to the government on Jacobite activities.

Defoe's news item on the destruction of the Isle of St. Vincent, happily not political, appeared in *Mist's Journal* for July 5th, 1718. In the issue of August 2nd he published the following curiously phrased retraction: "The Island of St. Vincent not Destroyed. They pretend to tell us a strange Story, viz., that the Island of St. Vincent is found again, and is turn'd into a Volcano, or burning Mountain; but we must acknowledge we do not believe one word of it."

WE HAVE A PIECE OF PUBLIC NEWS THIS TIME OF SUCH CONSEQUENCE, AND SO necessary for all our readers to be fully acquainted with, that our friends who have written several letters to us, which otherwise deserve publishing, must excuse us for this week.

This relates to the entire desolation of the island of St. Vincent, in the West Indies, by the immediate hand of nature, directed by Providence, and in a manner astonishing to all the world, the like of which never happened since the creation, or, at least, since the destruction of the earth by water in the general Deluge.

Our accounts of this come from so many several hands, and several places, that it would be impossible to bring the letters all separately into this journal; and when we had done so, or attempted to do so, would have

the story confused, and the world not perfectly informed. We have therefore thought it better to give the substance of this amazing accident in one
collection, making together as full and as distinct account of the whole as
we believe is possible to come at by any intelligence whatsoever; and at the
close of this account we shall give some probable guesses at the natural cause
of so terrible an operation. The relation is as follows, viz:

An account of the island of St. Vincent, in the West Indies, and of its entire
destruction on the 26th of March last, with some rational suggestions
concerning the causes and manner of it.

The island of St. Vincent is the most populous of any possessed by the Caribbeans; its latitude is sixteen degrees north from the line. Those who have
seen the island Ferro or Fietre, one of the Canaries, affirm that this is much
of the same figure. It may be about eight leagues in length, and six in
breadth. There are in it several high mountains, and very fruitful plains, if
they were cultivated. The Caribbeans have many fair villages, where they
live pleasantly, and without any disturbance; and though they have a jealousy of strangers, yet do they not deny them the bread of the country, which
is cossava, water, fruits, and other provisions growing in their country, if
they want them, taking in exchange wedges, hooks, and other implements
of iron, which they much esteem.

On the 24th March a French sloop arrived at Martinico that passed by
the island of St. Vincent the 22nd, and, as the master reported, he bought
some fish of some of the savages who inhabited there, and who came off to
him in three canoes. He says that all was safe and in very good condition
there, for anything he perceived, only that some of his seamen report, since
the disaster, that one of the Indians told them they had been terribly frighted
with earthquakes for some time, and with flashes of fire like lightning, which
did not come out of the clouds as usual, but out of the earth; and that they
had felt these earthquakes for a month past, to their very great amazement.

On the 27th, in the morning, the air was darkened in a dreadful manner;
which darkness, by all accounts, seems to have extended over all the colonies
and islands which were within 100 miles of the place, but was perceived to
be more or less dark as those islands were farther or nearer from the place.

But that which is most remarkable of all is, that at some of the islands,
and at Martinico in particular, a dreadful flash of lightning, as they called
it, was seen on the 26th about eleven o'clock at night. This flash, which they
called lightning, we shall account for in the following part of this relation.

It is to be observed, in the next place, that as there were several ships,
or other vessels at sea, in several ports among the islands, some of these had
a more terrible sight of this thing than others; particularly they write that
in one sloop, which is come into Martinico, the men are so terrified still, and

were so amazed at what they saw and heard, that they appear perfectly stupe-fied, and gave little or no account. Others are come into other ports so hor-ribly frighted that they scarce retain their senses; other give confused ac-counts, and so, more or less distinct, as they were nearer or farther from the place; the sum of what may be gathered from them all is this:

That they saw in the night that terrible flash of fire, and after that they heard innumerable clashes of thunder—some say it was thunder they heard—others that it was cannon—only that the noise was a thousand times as loud as thunder or cannon, considering that it appeared to be at a great distance from them.

That the next morning, when the day began to break, the air looked dismally, viz., all overhead was a deep, impenetrable darkness; but below, all round the edge of the horizon, it looked as if the heavens were all on fire. As the day came on, still the darkness increased, till it was far darker than it had been in any part of the night before; and, as they thought, the cloud descended upon them. The darkness still increased after this, viz., in the afternoon they were surprised with the falling of something upon them as thick as smoke, but fine as dust, and yet solid as sand; this fell thicker and faster as they were nearer or farther off—some ships had it nine inches, other a foot thick, upon their decks; the island of Martinico is covered with it at about seven to nine inches thick; at Barbadoes it is frightful, even to St. Christopher's it exceeded four inches; it is fallen over the whole extent of the Isle of Hispaniola, and there is no doubt but it has been seen on the continent of New Spain, about the point of Guiana, or the mouth of the Orinoco; all of which will perhaps be accounted for in some measure in the following narrative.

This continued falling for two or three days and nights successively; and it was impossible for any man to find out or so much as guess at the meaning of it, or of any natural cause to produce it, till the whole came to discover itself; but all people stood amazed at the cause, and several letters were sent to England of it, from Barbadoes in particular; as of a strange miraculous shower of sand, of which we gave an account in our journal of the 20th past. The first news that was given of the whole thing was by some vessels that were under sail, in the night of the 26th, belonging to Martinico, by which we had the following particulars: that on the said 26th, about midnight, the whole island of St. Vincent rose up into the air, with a most dreadful erup-tion of fire from underneath the earth and an inconceivable noise in the air at its rising up; that it was not only blown up, but blown out of the very sea, with a dreadful force, as it were torn up by the roots, or blown up from the foundations of the earth.

That the terror was inexpressible, and cannot be represented by words; that the noise of the bursting of the earth at first is not possible to be described; that the force of the blow or blast was such, and the whole body of the island was raised so furiously, that the earth was entirely separated into small particles like dust; and as it rose to an immense height, so it spread itself to an incredible distance, and fell light and gradually, like a small but thick mist. This part, we suppose, must be occasioned by the force of the blow effectually separating the parts, otherwise they would have fallen with a violence of motion, proportioned to the weight of the whole, the particles pressing one another; whereas now every grain was loose and independent in the air, and fell no faster than it was pressed by its own weight, as in a shower of snow or rain.

The more solid parts of this land, which were lifted up by this blast, and supposed to be of stone, slate, or clay, or such solid matter as would not dissipate or separate in the air, like the rest, being lifted to an immense height, and then plunging, by a mighty force, received by their own weight, into the sea, must of necessity make a noise or blow equal to that of the loudest cannon, and perhaps to thunder itself; and these we think to be the several reports or blows which were heard even to St. Christopher's Island (which is a vast distance from that of St. Vincent), and of which the people in these islands, as well as in the ships, heard about a thousand or twelve hundred distinct blows or reports, and supposed it to be the noise of guns.

As soon as it was understood by the inhabitants in other islands what it was, that is to say, that it was an eruption of the earth at the island of St. Vincent or thereabouts, sloops, barks, and other small vessels came from all parts to see how it was, to inquire into the damage suffered, and to get an account of the particulars; but how astonished must these inquirers be when, meeting from all parts upon the same errand, they may be supposed to go cruising about to find the island, some examining their books to cast up the length they had sailed, some blaming their own negligence for not keeping a right reckoning, some their men for mistaking their distance, others taking observations to know the latitude they were in; at last, all concluding, as it really was, to their great confusion, that the said island was *no more;* that there appeared no remains, except three little rocks, no, not any tokens that such an island had been there; but that, on the contrary, in the place of it, the sea was excessive deep, and no bottom to be found at two hundred fathom.

As this is an event so wonderful as no history can give us an account of the like, so it cannot be unpleasant to our readers to consider briefly some natural causes which may be assigned for it.

An earthquake it cannot be—though that is the first thing which offers to our view. Had the island sunk into the water, it had been well enough accounted for in that way; nor are we without examples in history, when earthquakes have raised islands where they had not been seen before, as particularly in the Archipelago, and sunk islands which have been, so that they have been seen no more, as is said of the great island Atlantis, from which some fancy the Atlantic Ocean received its name.

But for an island to be blown up into the air as if it were undermined and blown up by gunpowder, like a bastion in a town besieged, and for the force to be such as to blow up the solid earth into the third region, as we may say—to such a stupendous, prodigious height as to have it go up an island, and come down in sand; to go up in bulk, and come down in atoms; to go up perpendicular, and be spread about to a hundred miles' distance— this is unaccountable but by some force superior to that of ten millions of barrels of gunpowder.

Some, we hear, by casting up the dimensions of the island, to reduce it to cubical inches, are pretending to tell us what weight of earth this blast has raised up, and consequently would tell us what force it was that must raise it; but this is a perfectly needless inquiry, and many ways impracticable also.

But it may not be an unfruitful search if we endeavour to inquire, and offer some probable essay at the manner, how such a wonderful thing as this is in Nature has been, or may be, performed. There seems to be only two several ways for us to conceive of the possibility of such a thing—we mean, by the ordinary course of Nature, and concurrence of causes.

What infinite Power, who made the world, may be supposed to do, we have nothing to say to, nor is it to our purpose in this case to inquire into it.

Infinite Power might as easily blow this whole earth up and dissipate every part of it into the first atoms, from which it may be supposed to have been made, as He could, by the power of His word, form this beautiful figure from the unshaped chaos; but this, we say, is out of the present question.

Our inquiry is into natural and probable causes which might produce such a terrible eruption in Nature as this has been, the like whereof was never heard of before.

First, a concurrence or conjunction of sulphureous and nitrous particles in the subterranean caverns of the earth, of which some might happen to be under this island, of a vast extent, according to the quantity of which particles the force would be; and there's no question but that these particles taking air, by some chasm or vent given to them by some accident of an earthquake or otherwise, might be able to perform this terrible operation.

As to the nature of an earthquake, it is needless to enter into inquiries here of a thing so well known, or to prove that this might open the hollows and vast caverns in the bowels of the earth, at a great depth, perhaps many hundred fathoms under the bottom of the sea; for as an earthquake effects a dislocation of the parts, it is most natural to suppose it might so open those subterranean hollows, so as to bring air to those particles which were before big with that contracted fire, which, when dilated, would blow up all above them.

The second method in Nature by which this may be supposed to be performed, might be subterranean fires, which, having kindled themselves in the body of the earth, do, in several places, extend themselves to a prodigious space, and often discover to us, more or less, as their magnitude or distance from the surface of the earth may be, sometimes by warming the springs of water which flow near them (from whence our hot baths and warm springs of water are produced), other times by volcanoes or burning mountains, as Mount Gibell or Etna, in Sicily; Mount Vesuvius, near Naples; and Strombolo; Mount Hecla, in Iceland, and the like.

Supposing, then, by the shocks of an earthquake near the cavities where these treasures of fire are reserved, the earth may be opened so as that the sea might come pouring into the vast body of fire, which we may imagine to be kindled there, and which may have burned several hundred years—this, having no vent, would not fail to blow up, not such an island as St. Vincent only, but an island forty times as big in proportion to the extent of the fire below, and to the quantity of water which might come in; and this we believe is the only way we can account for the dreadful eruptions which sometimes happen in those burning mountains mentioned above, and of which we have not room to enlarge here.

The experiment of this may be made familiar by the throwing a pail of water hastily into a furnace—suppose such as a brewer's furnace—which will immediately burst out again, with a violence proportioned to the quantity of water; and, if it were possible, at the same time, to shut the door of the furnace, the force of it would blow up all above it. This also may be illustrated, with great exactness to our imagination, by reflecting on a very sad accident which happened not many years ago in London, and which most people have heard of, viz., at the foundry at Windmill Hill, by Moorfields, where the metal for the casting of a great gun, running into a mould ill prepared, and which had received some water, though by the relation of all concerned in it, and that were alive, that water, by the cavity of the mould, could not be equal to a gallon, yet it blew up the whole work, and blew the melted metal up, as light as if it had been the lightest earth, throwing it about the whole place, separated in small parts like drops, so that it overwhelmed, as with a shower of molten brass, those that were near, and almost all who were in the place were either killed or terribly hurt with it.

We have not room to say any more of this affair in this paper: we shall only add, that as by either of these two ways this terrible event of blowing up the island of St. Vincent may be supposed possible in Nature, so we do believe that all the philosophers in the world cannot find a third.

''GOOD GOD!

LOOK AT BROOKS''

FROM *Conquest of Mount McKinley*

BELMORE BROWNE

Mount McKinley is the highest and most inaccessible mountain in North America. Belmore Browne's book, from which this selection is taken, is the story of three expeditions through the Alaskan wilderness to climb the peak.

In the preface to his book, Browne tries to explain to the reader who has never felt "the lure of the wilderness," why he and his companions undertook so hazardous a venture. There was the exciting task of mapping unknown country; there was the absorbing interest in geological and botanical findings; there were other good, material, practical, scientific reasons. But more compelling than any of these was the much less rational, less logical, certainly less material reason—to challenge the unknown.

IT WAS THE EVENING OF JULY 6TH. PROFESSOR PARKER WAS RESTING INSIDE THE big tent. La Voy, Aten, and I had been drying and airing our mountain tent and duffle and doing odd jobs around camp. The sky was a sickly green colour, and the air seemed heavy and lifeless. After finishing our work we rested in the heather and talked of our plans for our coming journey to the Yukon.

The sky reminded me of sinister skies that I had seen on the eastern seacoast before heavy storms, and I turned to Aten and said that were I on a boat I would overhaul the ground tackle and see that everything was snug because it looked like "dirty weather." The words were scarcely out of my mouth before a deep rumbling came from the Alaskan Range. I can only compare the sound to thunder, but it had a deep hollow quality that was unlike thunder, a sinister suggestion of overwhelming power that was terrifying. I remember that as I looked, the Alaskan Range melted into mist and that the mountains were bellowing, and that Aten was yelling something that I could not understand and that the valley above us turned white—and then the earth began to heave and roll, and I forgot everything but the desire to stay upright. In front of me was a boulder weighing about two hundred pounds. We had pulled it there with a sled and dog team to anchor our tent; it had sunk into the moss from its own weight, and as I watched, the boulder turned, broke loose from the earth, and moved several feet.

Then came the crash of our falling caches, followed by another muffled crash as the front of our hill slid into the creek, and a lake near by boiled as if it was hot.

The mossy surfaces of the hills were opening all about us, and as the surface opened the cracks filled with liquid mud, and then suddenly everything was still. We stood up dazed and looked about. The Alaskan Range was still wrapped in the haze of avalanche dust, and the country far and near was scarred, and stripped of vegetation where the earth had slid. Our dogs had fled at the beginning of the quake and we could hear them whimpering and running about through the willows.

Aten, with his pocket full of tobacco, was asking me impatiently for mine—and then we began to laugh. We ran to the tent to see how Professor Parker had fared, and then we howled again, for as we pulled the flaps aside it seemed as if everything that was movable, including the stove, had fallen in a heap. The stove had overturned and a great flat rock which we used as a base for the stove had moved towards the tent door.

While we were restoring order out of chaos, Aten, who was standing by the tent door, exclaimed: "Good God! Look at Brooks!" As we dashed out of the tent an awe-inspiring sight met our eyes. Just east of Mount McKinley stood a magnificent 12,000-foot peak. It was somewhat like the Matterhorn in shape, and formed the culminating pinnacle in a range some six miles in length that formed the eastern wall of the main eastern fork of the Muldrow Glacier. As this mountain was the finest peak east of Mount McKinley we were anxious to give it a worthy name and we decided to name it after Alfred Brooks, who had led the first survey party through this part of Alaska. While we were uncertain as to whether or not Brooks's name had already been attached to some other Alaskan mountain, we always spoke of the great peak as Mount Brooks. Now, as we reached the open and turned our eyes towards the mountain, we saw that the whole extent of the mountain wall that formed its western flank was avalanching. I have never seen a sight of such overpowering grandeur. The avalanche seemed to stretch along the range for a distance of several miles, like a huge wave, and like a huge wave it seemed to poise for an instant before it plunged downward onto the ice-fields thousands of feet below. The mountain was about ten miles away and we waited breathlessly until the terrific thunder of the falling mass began to boom and rumble among the mountains.

Following the inspiring salvos of nature's artillery came the aftermath we had learned to look for. Beyond the range that rimmed our valley a

SHEPHERDING IN THE SCOTTISH HIGHLANDS

HIGHLAND DANCERS

GRAPE HARVEST NEAR BOLZANO, ITALY

CANADIAN LUMBERJACKS AT WORK

right: EMIGRANTS CLIMBING THE PER-
ILOUS CORDUROY ROAD OVER THE
ROCKY MOUNTAINS, 13,000 FEET
ABOVE SEA LEVEL, INTO LEADVILLE,
COLORADO, 1879

below: PEASANTS OF MÜNSTER, A
MOUNTAIN VILLAGE IN THE VALAIS
REGION OF SWITZERLAND, TRANSPORT
LOGS BY SLED

A THICK FROSTING OF SNOW COVERS THE HUTS ON ALP OBER-LAREIN, ALONG THE PARSENN
DOWNHILL RUN TO JENAZ, SWITZERLAND

PINSEC IS A TYPICAL WANDERING SETTLEMENT IN VALAIS, SWITZERLAND. HERE THE HOUSES
ARE INHABITED ACCORDING TO THE SEASONS. THE OWNERS MOVE TO SIMILAR SETTLEMENTS
HIGHER UP THE MOUNTAINS AND IN THE VALLEYS BELOW WHEN WORK MUST BE DONE IN THE
FIELDS ON THOSE LEVELS

SWISS SHEPHERDS CARRYING COWBELLS

CHAMOIS HUNTER

POSITANO, AN ITALIAN TOWN, CLINGS TO THE STEEP SLOPES OF THE MOUNTAINS RISING FROM
THE MEDITERRANEAN

great white cloud began to rise. As it came into view and began to obscure the Brooks range we could almost check off its growth as it billowed upward with startling rapidity, two—three—four thousand feet until it hung like a huge opaque wall against the main range, and then it fell—the range that rimmed our valley was blotted out and the great wave of avalanche débris came rushing down our valley. We were already at work, strengthening our tent in frantic haste.

We knew that the cloud was advancing at a rate close to sixty miles an hour and that we did not have much time to spare. But with boulders to hold the bottom and tautened guy-ropes, we made the tent as solid as possible and got inside before the cloud struck us. The tent held fast, but after the "wullies" passed, the ground was spangled with ice-dust that only a few minutes before had formed the icy covering of a peak ten miles away!

Before we rolled up in our sleeping-bags, we took a last look about us. In every direction the earth and mountains were seamed and scarred and a great dun-coloured cloud of ice- and rock-dust hid the Alaskan Range. The streams, too, were flooding their banks, and ran chocolate-coloured from the earth-slides that had dammed them. As we compared our adventures and sensations, we thought of the band of fifty caribou that we had seen in the head of the valley—what a sight they must have presented when the earthquake struck them! Fifty wild beasts plunging, falling, and wild-eyed with terror—I would give much to have been on a hillside nearby!

The earthquakes continued at regular intervals for about thirty-six hours. None of them could compare in strength with the first shock, but many of them were severe enough to wreck a modern city. Strangely enough most of the shocks were preceded by a deep detonation. The sound resembled the noise made by exploding steam, and it came always from the same place—Mount McKinley. Experts on seismic disturbances have told me that the sound does not precede the disturbance, but in our case the reverse was true. We would be sitting in our tent, when suddenly the deep, explosive noise would reach our ears. One of us would say, "Here comes another," and if the explosion was of sufficient power we would take the precaution of seeing that our teapot was in a safe place. And then, after a few seconds had elapsed, the quake would reach us. After going through such an experience as the big quake, one realises, for the first time, the gigantic power of the forces of nature, and understands with what ease great mountain ranges have been formed.

My strongest impression immediately after the quake was one of surprise at the elasticity of the earth. We speak of being on "solid ground," but while the earthquake was occurring one felt as if the earth's crust was a quivering mass of jelly.

GLORY

FROM *Ascent of F 6*

W . H . A U D E N
AND
C H R I S T O P H E R   I S H E R W O O D

During the early 1930's W. H. Auden and Christopher Isherwood were acknowledged among the most promising of the younger generation of English writers. Auden's place in contemporary poetry was under-scored a few years later when he was awarded the King's Poetry Medal, the second of these medals to be awarded. Isherwood is a novelist and playwright. *I am a Camera,* which enjoyed a long theatrical run in this country, was adapted from his Berlin stories.

Ascent of F 6, from which this selection was taken, is one of a number of plays upon which the two have collaborated. Auden writes the poetry and Isherwood the prose. The theme of the play is that question which will almost certainly never be answered completely: Why do men climb, sometimes to glory, but as frequently to death?

[*The* STAGE-BOX *on the right is illuminated.*
The A.'s *are having breakfast.*]

MRS A. Give me some money before you go
There are a number of bills we owe
And you can go to the bank today
During the lunch-hour.

MR A.   I dare say;
But, as it happens, I'm overdrawn.

MRS A. Overdrawn? What on earth have you done
With all the money? Where's it gone?

MR A. How does money always go?
Papers, lunches, tube-fares, teas,
Tooth-paste, stamps and doctor's fees,
Our trip to Hove cost a bit, you know.

MRS A.   Can we never have fun? Can we never have any
         And not have to count every single penny?
         Why can't you find a way to earn more?
         It's so degrading and dull to be poor.
         Get another job.
MR A.   My job may be small
         But I'm damned lucky to have one at all.
         When I think of those I knew in the War,
         All the fellows about my age:
         How many are earning a decent wage?
         There was O'Shea, the middle-weight champion; slouches from bar
             to bar now in a battered hat, cadging for drinks;
         There was Morgan, famous for his stories; sells ladies' underwear
             from door to door;
         There was Polewhele, with his university education; now Dan the
             Lavatory Man at a third-rate night-club;
         And Holmes in our office, well past fifty, was dismissed last week
             to bring down expenses;
         Next week another: who shall it be?
         It may be anyone. It may be me.
         [*A newspaper is dropped through the door into the back of the
         Box.* MR A. *goes to fetch it.*]
MRS A.   It's all this foreign competition:
         Czechoslovakia, Russia, Japan,
         Ostnia and Westland do all they can
         To ruin our trade with their cheap goods,
         Dumping them on our market in floods.
         It makes my blood boil! You can find
         No British goods of any kind
         In any of the big shops now.
         The Government ought to stop it somehow——
MR A.   Listen to this. [*Reads.*] Our Special Correspondent reports that the
         Ostnian Expedition to F 6, headed by Blavek, has crossed the Tung
         Desert and is about to commence its final assault on the mountain.
         Blavek is confident of success and, in mountaineering circles, it is be-
         lieved that the British climbers will have to make very strenuous efforts
         indeed if they are to beat their formidable opponents. . . .
MRS A.   You see? The foreigner everywhere,
         Competing in trade, competing in sport,
         Competing in science and abstract thought:
         And we just sit down and let them take
         The prizes! There's more than a mountain at stake.

MR A. The travelogue showed us a Babylon buried in sand.

MRS A. And books have spoken of a Spain that was the brilliant centre of an Empire.

MR A. I have found a spider in the opulent board-room.

MRS A. I have dreamed of a threadbare barnstorming actor, and he was **a** national symbol.

MR A. England's honour is covered with rust.

MRS A. Ransom must beat them! He must! He must!

MR A. Or England falls. She has had her hour
And now must decline to a second-class power.
[*Puts on his bowler hat and exit, brandishing his newspaper. The* STAGE-BOX *is darkened.*]

ACT II, SCENE II

[*On F 6. At the foot of the West Buttress. The back of the stage rises slightly, suggesting a precipice beyond. A magnificent panorama of distant mountains. On the right of the stage, the wall of the buttress rises, with an overhang.*]

[*Midday.* RANSOM, SHAWCROSS *and* LAMP *stand roped on the edge of the precipice, assisting the* DOCTOR *and* GUNN, *who are still out of sight, below. The rope is belayed round a rock.*]

RANSOM [*looking down*]. There's a hold to your left, Tom. No, a little higher up. Good. Now you're all right.

GUNN'S VOICE [*from below*]. Look out, Doc.! Don't tread on my face!

RANSOM. Now then. . . .
[*After a moment, the* DOCTOR *hoists himself into view, panting.*]
Now you take it easy, Tom. Fifteen minutes' rest, here.

LAMP. We've made good time, this morning.

RANSOM [*looking down*]. You all right, David?

GUNN'S VOICE [*from below*]. I think so. . . . No! Ooh, er! Gosh, this rock is soft! Here we come! [*He appears.*]

DOCTOR. Well, thank goodness, that couloir's behind us, anyhow. Though how we shall ever get down it again is another matter.

RANSOM. You were splendid, Tom. Never known you in better form.

DOCTOR. I must have lost at least two stone. That's one comfort.

GUNN. While we were in the chimney, I felt his sweat dripping on to me like a shower-bath. . . . I say, isn't there anything more to eat?

RANSOM. I'm afraid we must keep to our rations, David. We're only carrying the minimum, you know.

SHAWCROSS. I should have thought you'd eaten enough to satisfy even *your* appetite—considering you had all my chocolate, as well.

GUNN. Well, you needn't make a grievance out of it. You didn't want it,
  did you?

DOCTOR. Still feeling sick, Ian?

SHAWCROSS [*crossly*]. I'm all right.

DOCTOR. You don't look any too good.

SHAWCROSS. Anyhow, I don't see that it helps much to keep fussing about
  trifles and thinking of one's comfort.

[*A pause.*]

LAMP. Well, if we've got another ten minutes to spare, I think I'll be taking
  a look round. Might spot a clump of Polus Naufrangia. You never know.
  It's about the right altitude, now.

  [*He goes to the back of the stage and looks over, through his
  binoculars.*]

GUNN [*following him*]. See anything? [LAMP *shakes his head.*] Gosh, that's a
  drop! [*He balances on the edge and pretends to wobble.*]
  Ooh, er! Help!

RANSOM. Come away from there, David.

  [GUNN *obeys and begins wandering about the stage.*]

DOCTOR [*pointing upwards*]. How high do you make that buttress?

RANSOM. About seventeen hundred feet. We shall be on it all this afternoon.
  We ought to reach the ridge easily by sunset.

GUNN [*poking about*]. Hullo, what's this? [*Picks up a skull.*] Doctor Living-
  stone, I presume?

  [*The others, except* LAMP, *who continues to peer through his
  binoculars, collect round* GUNN.]

How on earth did he get here?

DOCTOR. Goodness knows. May have fallen from above. See this crack? It's
  hardly likely to have been murder, up here.

SHAWCROSS. Anyhow, he must have been a pretty useful climber to have got
  as far as he did. I suppose there's no doubt it's a native skull?

DOCTOR. Impossible to say. It may have been some mad European who
  thought he'd have a shot at F 6 on his own; but that's scarcely possible.
  Some herdsman, probably. . . . What do you think, M.F.?

[*Hands him the skull.*]

LAMP [*shouting excitedly*]. Come here! Look!

GUNN. What's the matter, Teddy?

LAMP. Polus Naufrangia! Five-leaved! A beauty! Only just spotted it. And
  it was right under my nose!

[*He begins lowering himself over the edge.*]

DOCTOR. Wait a moment, Teddy. Better do that on the rope.

GUNN [*looking over*]. He'll be all right. It's a broad ledge. Only about twenty
  feet down.

DOCTOR [*looking over*]. Careful, Teddy. Careful. Take your time.

LAMP'S VOICE [*from below*]. I'm all right.

> [*The others, except* RANSOM, *stand looking over the edge.*]

RANSOM [*to skull*]. Well, Master; the novices are here. Have your dry bones no rustle of advice to give them? Or are you done with climbing? But that's improbable. Imagination sees the ranges in the Country of the Dead, where those to whom a mountain is a mother find an eternal playground. There Antoine de Ville scales pinnacles with subtle engines; Gesner drinks water, shares his dreams with Saussure, whose passion for Mont Blanc became a kind of illness. Paccard is reconciled with Balmont, and Bourrit, the cathedral precentor, no longer falsifies their story. Marie-Coutett still keeps his nickname of The Weasel; Donkin and Fox are talking of the Caucasus; Whymper goes climbing with his friends again and Hadow, who made the slip of inexperience, has no faults. While, on the strictest buttresses, the younger shadows look for fresher routes: Toni Schmidt is there and the Bavarian cyclists; and that pair also whom Odell saw on the step of Everest before the cloud hid them for ever, in the gigantic shadow of whose achievement we pitch our miserable tent——

> [*The roar of an approaching avalanche is heard.*]

DOCTOR. An avalanche! My God!

> [RANSOM *runs to join the others.*]

Look out, Teddy! Look out!

GUNN. Quick, man!

SHAWCROSS. Stay where you are!

GUNN. Jump for it!

DOCTOR. Oh, God! He's done for!

> [*The roar of the avalanche drowns their voices; then gradually dies away.*]

SHAWCROSS. He was just stooping to pick the flower, when the first stone got him.

DOCTOR. It was all over in a moment. He was probably knocked right out.

SHAWCROSS. As he went over the edge, you could see the flower in his hand.

GUNN. Gosh, I feel beastly! [*Sits down on a rock.*]

SHAWCROSS. He was a damn good man!

DOCTOR. I'm glad he found the Naufrangia, anyway. We must tell them that in London. Perhaps the five-leaved kind will be named after him. He'd like that, I think.

SHAWCROSS. I just can't believe it. Five minutes ago, he was standing here.

DOCTOR [*looking at* LAMP'S *rucksack, which is lying on a rock*]. What do you think we ought to do with this? His people might like to have it.

SHAWCROSS. We can't very well take it with us now. I think we'd better bury it here. We can pick it up on our way down.

DOCTOR. Right you are. I'll help you. [*Begins collecting stones.*]

[SHAWCROSS *picks up the rucksack.*]

GUNN. Poor old Teddy! [*To* SHAWCROSS.] Half a minute! [*Feels in the pocket of the rucksack.*] Oh, good!

[*Pulls out a piece of chocolate and begins eating it.*]

SHAWCROSS [*horrified*]. My God! Haven't you any decency left in you at all?

GUNN [*with his mouth full*]. Why, what's the matter now?

SHAWCROSS. Of all the filthy callousness!

GUNN. But, honestly, I don't see anything wrong. He doesn't want it now, does he?

SHAWCROSS. If that's the line you take, I suppose there's no more to be said. . . Get some stones!

[*While the others are burying the rucksack,* RANSOM *stoops and picks up* LAMP'S *snow-glasses, which he has left lying on the rocks at the back of the stage.*]

RANSOM. The first victim to my pride. If I had never asked him, he would not have come. The Abbot was perfectly right. My minor place in history is with the aberrant group of Caesars: the dullard murderers who hale the gentle from their beds of love and, with a quacking drum, escort them to the drowning ditch and the death in the desert. . . . [*To the others.*] You have forgotten these. [*Gives glasses.*] Hurry up. We must be getting on. Ian, will you change places with David?

[*Music. They rope up in silence.* RANSOM *begins the traverse round the buttress, as the* CURTAIN *slowly falls.*]

[*Both* STAGE-BOXES *are illuminated. In the left-hand box,* STAGMANTLE *is at the microphone. In the right-hand box, the* A.'s *sit, listening.* MR A. *is playing Patience.* MRS A. *is darning socks.*]

STAGMANTLE. It is with the deepest regret that we have to announce the death of Mr Edward Lamp, a member of the F 6 Expedition. He was climbing along a ridge on the north face after a rare botanical specimen when he was caught by an avalanche and killed. He was twenty-four years of age.

In Edward Lamp, Science has lost one of her most brilliant recruits. At Cambridge he carried everything before him; and his career, so tragically cut short, promised to be of the highest distinction. He died as he had lived: in the service of his austere mistress. This is as he would have wished; and no man can do more. Nor could one design him a more fitting grave than among the alpine flowers he loved so passionately and with such understanding. . . . [*Exit.*]

MRS A. [*moved*].

> Death like his is right and splendid;
> That is how life should be ended!
> He cannot calculate nor dread
> The mortifying in the bed,
> Powers wasting day by day
> While the courage ebbs away.
> Ever-charming, he will miss
> The insulting paralysis,
> Ruined intellect's confusion,
> Ulcer's patient persecution,
> Sciatica's intolerance
> And the cancer's sly advance;
> Never hear, among the dead,
> The rival's brilliant paper read,
> Colleague's deprecating cough
> And the praises falling off;
> Never know how in the best
> Passion loses interest;
> Beauty sliding from the bone
> Leaves the rigid skeleton.

MR A.

> If you had seen a dead man, you would not
> Think it so beautiful to lie and rot;
> I've watched men writhing on the dug-out floor
> Cursing the land for which they went to war;
> The joker cut off halfway through his story,
> The coward blown involuntary to glory,
> The steel butt smashing at the eyes that beg,
> The stupid clutching at the shattered leg,
> The twitching scarecrows on the rusty wire;
> I've smelt Adonis stinking in the mire,
> The puddle stolid round his golden curls,
> Far from his precious mater and the girls;
> I've heard the gas-case gargle, green as grass,
> And, in the guns, Death's lasting animus.
> Do you think it would comfort Lamp to know
> The British Public mourns him so?
> I tell you, he'd give his rarest flower
> Merely to breathe for one more hour!
> What is this expedition? He has died
> To satisfy our smug suburban pride. . . .

[*The* STAGE-BOXES *are darkened.*]

THE IMMEDIATE
PRESENCE OF DEATH

FROM *The Path to Rome*

HILAIRE BELLOC

An epic theme has sometimes the force of shaping a style so that it measures up to the size of the subject. Hilaire Belloc proves the reverse of that proposition true also—at least for Hilaire Belloc. He is one of those greatly gifted essayists who can take a theme of very small dimension—a trivial contact, a casual landscape, a homely incident—and so surround it with ideas and dress it in wit that it becomes a richly embroidered commentary. All of his writing in history, travel, even his delightful books for children, are colored by his humor, his deeply religious feeling, and his sense for the past. In this selection, Belloc, on a pilgrimage to Rome, attempts a crossing of an Alpine pass during a *tourmente*, the mountain people's fitting name for a wild storm.

AND THIS IS A PECULIAR THING I HAVE NOTICED IN ALL MOUNTAINS, AND HAVE never been able to understand—namely, that if you draw a plan or section to scale, your mountain does not seem a very important thing. One should not, in theory, be able to dominate from its height, nor to feel the world small below one, nor to hold a whole countryside in one's hand—yet one does. The mountains from their heights reveal to us two truths. They suddenly make us feel our insignificance, and at the same time they free the immortal Mind, and let it feel its greatness, and they release it from the earth. But I say again, in theory, when one considers the exact relation of their height to the distances one views from them, they ought to claim no such effect, and that they can produce that effect is related to another thing—the way in which they exaggerate their own steepness. . . .

Well, so it was here from the Grimsel when I overlooked the springs of the Rhone. . . . Where there was no mist, the air was so surprisingly clear that I could see everything clean and sharp wherever I turned my eyes. The mountains forbade any very far horizons to the view, and all that I could see was as neat and vivid as those coloured photographs they sell with bright green grass and bright white snow, and blue glaciers like precious stones.

I scrambled down the mountain, for here, on the south side of the pass, there was no snow or ice, and it was quite easy to leave the road and take the old path cutting off the zig-zags. As the air got heavier, I became hungry, and at the very end of my descent, two hundred feet or so above the young Rhone, I saw a great hotel. I went round to their front door and asked them whether I could eat, and at what price. "Four francs," they said.

"What!" said I, "four francs for a meal! Come, let me eat in the kitchen, and charge me one." But they became rude and obstinate, being used only to deal with rich people, so I cursed them, and went down the road. But I was very hungry.

The road falls quite steeply, and the Rhone, which it accompanies in that valley, leaps in little falls. On a bridge I passed a sad Englishman reading a book, and a little lower down, two American women in a carriage, and after that a priest (it was lucky I did not see him first. Anyhow, I touched iron at once, to wit, a key in my pocket), and after that a child minding a goat. Altogether, I felt myself in the world again, and as I was on a good road, all down hill, I thought myself capable of pushing on to the next village. But my hunger was really excessive, my right boot almost gone, and my left boot nothing to exhibit or boast of, when I came to a point where at last one looked down the Rhone valley for miles. It is like a straight trench, and at intervals there are little villages, built of most filthy châlets, the said châlets raised on great stones. There are pine-trees up, up on either slope, into the clouds, and beyond the clouds I could not see. I left on my left a village called "Between the Waters." I passed through another called "Ehringen," but it has no inn. At last, two miles farther, faint from lack of food, I got into Ulrichen, a village a little larger than the rest, and the place where I believed one should start to go either over the Gries or Nufenen Pass. In Ulrichen was a warm, wooden, deep-eaved, frousty, comfortable, ramshackle, dark, anyhow kind of a little inn called "The Bear." And entering, I saw one of the women whom God loves.

She was of middle age, very honest and simple in the face, kindly and good. She was messing about with cooking and stuff, and she came up to me stooping a little, her eyes wide and innocent, and a great spoon in her hand. Her face was extremely broad and flat, and I had never seen eyes set so far apart. Her whole gait, manner, and accent proved her to be extremely good, and on the straight road to heaven. I saluted her in the French tongue. She answered me in the same, but very broken and rustic, for her natural speech was a kind of mountain German. She spoke very slowly, and had a nice soft voice, and she did what only good people do, I mean, looked you in the eyes as she spoke to you. . . .

She put food before me and wine. The wine was good, but in the food was some fearful herb or other I had never tasted before—a pure spice or scent, and a nasty one. One could taste nothing else, and it was revolting; but I ate it for her sake.

Then, very much refreshed, I rose, seized my great staff, shook myself and said, "Now it is about noon, and I am off for the frontier."

At this she made a most fearful clamour, saying that it was madness, and imploring me not to think of it, and running out fetched from the stable a tall, sad, pale-eyed man who saluted me profoundly and told me that he knew more of the mountains than any one for miles. And this by asking many afterwards I found out to be true. He said that he had crossed the Nufenen and the Gries whenever they could be crossed since he was a child, and that if I attempted it that day I should sleep that night in Paradise. The clouds on the mountain, the soft snow recently fallen, the rain that now occupied the valleys, the glacier on the Gries, and the pathless snow in the mist on the Nufenen would make it sheer suicide for him, an experienced guide, and for me a worse madness. Also he spoke of my boots and wondered at my poor cotton coat and trousers, and threatened me with intolerable cold.

It seems that the books I had read at home, when they said that the Nufenen had no snow on it, spoke of a later season of the year; it was all snow now, and soft snow, and hidden by a full mist in such a day from the first third of the ascent. As for the Gries, there was a glacier on the top which needed some kind of clearness in the weather. Hearing all this I said I would remain—but it was with a heavy heart. Already I felt a shadow of defeat over me. The loss of time was a thorn. I was already short of cash, and my next money was at Milan. My return to England was fixed for a certain date, and stronger than either of these motives against delay was a burning restlessness that always takes men when they are on the way to great adventures.

I made him promise to wake me next morning at three o'clock, and, short of a tempest, to try and get me across the Gries. As for the Nufenen and Crystalline passes which I had desired to attempt, and which were (as I have said) the straight line to Rome, he said (and he was right), that let alone the impassability of the Nufenen just then, to climb the Crystal Mountain in that season would be as easy as flying to the moon. Now, to cross the Nufenen alone, would simply land me in the upper valley of the Ticino, and take me a great bend out of my way by Bellinzona. Hence my bargain that at least he should show me over the Gries Pass, and this he said, if man could do it, he would do the next day; and I, sending my boots to be cobbled (and thereby breaking another vow), crept up to bed, and all afternoon read the school-books of the children. They were in French, from lower down the valley, and very Genevese and heretical for so devout a household. But the Genevese civilisation is the standard for these people, and they combat the

Calvinism of it with missions, and have statues in their rooms, not to speak of holy water stoups.

The rain beat on my window, the clouds came lower still down the mountain. Then (as is finely written in the Song of Roland), "the day passed and the night came, and I slept." But with the coming of the small hours, and with my waking, prepare yourselves for the most extraordinary and terrible adventure that befel me out of all the marvels and perils of this pilgrimage, the most momentous and the most worthy of perpetual record, I think, of all that has ever happened since the beginning of the world.

At three o'clock the guide knocked at my door, and I rose and came out to him. We drank coffee and ate bread. We put into our sacks ham and bread, and he white wine and I brandy. Then we set out. The rain had dropped to a drizzle, and there was no wind. The sky was obscured for the most part, but here and there was a star. The hills hung awfully above us in the night as we crossed the spongy valley. A little wooden bridge took us over the young Rhone, here only a stream, and we followed a path up into the tributary ravine which leads to the Nufenen and the Gries. In a mile or two it was a little lighter, and this was as well, for some weeks before a great avalanche had fallen, and we had to cross it gingerly. Beneath the wide cap of frozen snow ran a torrent roaring. I remembered Colorado, and how I had crossed the Arkansaw on such a bridge as a boy. We went on in the uneasy dawn. The woods began to show, and there was a cross where a man had slipped from above that very April and been killed. Then, most ominous and disturbing, the drizzle changed to a rain, and the guide shook his head and said it would be snowing higher up. We went on, and it grew lighter. Before it was really day (or else the weather confused and darkened the sky), we crossed a good bridge, built long ago, and we halted at a shed where the cattle lie in the late summer when the snow is melted. There we rested a moment.

But on leaving its shelter we noticed many disquieting things. The place was a hollow, the end of the ravine—a bowl, as it were; one way out of which is the Nufenen, and the other the Gries. . . . First, all that bowl or cup below the passes was a carpet of snow, save where patches of black water showed, and all the passes and mountains, from top to bottom, were covered with very thick snow; the deep surface of it soft and fresh fallen. Secondly, the rain had turned into snow. It was falling thickly all around. Nowhere have I more perceived the immediate presence of great Death. Thirdly, it was far colder, and we felt the beginning of a wind. Fourthly, the clouds had come quite low down.

The guide said it could not be done, but I said we must attempt it. I was eager, and had not yet felt the awful grip of the cold. We left the

Nufenen on our left, a hopeless steep of new snow buried in fog, and we attacked the Gries. For half-an-hour we plunged on through snow above our knees, and my thin cotton clothes were soaked. So far the guide knew we were more or less on the path, and he went on and I panted after him. Neither of us spoke, but occasionally he looked back to make sure I had not dropped out.

The snow began to fall more thickly, and the wind had risen somewhat. I was afraid of another protest from the guide, but he stuck to it well, and I after him, continually plunging through soft snow and making yard after yard upwards. The snow fell more thickly and the wind still rose.

We came to a place which is, in the warm season, an alp; that is, a slope of grass, very steep but not terrifying; having here and there sharp little precipices of rock breaking it into steps, but by no means (in summer) a matter to make one draw back. Now, however, when everything was still Arctic it was a very different matter. A sheer steep of snow whose downward plunge ran into the driving storm and was lost, whose head was lost in the same mass of thick cloud above, a slope somewhat hollowed and bent inwards, had to be crossed if we were to go any farther; and I was terrified, for I knew nothing of climbing. The guide said there was little danger, only if one slipped one might slide down to safety, or one might (much less probably) get over rocks and be killed. I was chattering a little with cold; but as he did not propose a return, I followed him. The surface was alternately slabs of frozen snow and patches of soft new snow. In the first he cut steps, in the second we plunged, and once I went right in and a mass of snow broke off beneath me and went careering down the slope. He showed me how to hold my staff backwards as he did his alpenstock, and use it as a kind of brake in case I slipped.

We had been about twenty minutes crawling over that wall of snow and ice; and it was more and more apparent that we were in for danger. Before we had quite reached the far side, the wind was blowing a very full gale and roared past our ears. The surface snow was whirring furiously like dust before it: past our faces and against them drove the snow-flakes, cutting the air: not falling, but making straight darts and streaks. They seemed like the form of the whistling wind; they blinded us. The rocks on the far side of the slope, rocks which had been our goal when we set out to cross it, had long ago disappeared in the increasing rush of the blizzard. Suddenly as we were still painfully moving on, stooping against the mad wind, these rocks loomed up over as large as houses, and we saw them through the swarming snow-flakes as great hulls are seen through a fog at sea. The guide crouched under the lee of the nearest; I came up close to him and he put his hands to my ear and shouted to me that nothing further could be done—he had so to shout because in among the rocks the hurricane made a roaring sound, swamping the voice.

I asked how far we were from the summit. He said he did not know where we were exactly, but that we could not be more than 800 feet from it. I was but that from Italy and I would not admit defeat. I offered him all I had in money to go on, but it was folly in me, because if I had had enough to tempt him and if he had yielded we should both have died. Luckily it was but a little sum. He shook his head. He would not go on, he broke out, for all the money there was in the world. He shouted me to eat and drink, and so we both did.

Then I understood his wisdom, for in a little while the cold began to seize me in my thin clothes. My hands were numb, my face already gave me intolerable pain, and my legs suffered and felt heavy. I learnt another thing (which had I been used to mountains I should have known), that it was not a simple thing to return. The guide was hesitating whether to stay in this rough shelter, or to face the chances of the descent. This terror had not crossed my mind, and I thought as little of it as I could, needing my courage, and being near to breaking down from the intensity of the cold.

It seems that in a *tourmente* (for by that excellent name do the mountain people call such a storm) it is always a matter of doubt whether to halt or to go back. If you go back through it and lose your way, you are done for. If you halt in some shelter, it may go on for two or three days, and then there is an end of you.

After a little he decided for a return, but he told me honestly what the chances were, and my suffering from cold mercifully mitigated my fear. But even in that moment, I felt in a confused but very conscious way that I was defeated. I had crossed so many great hills and rivers, and pressed so well on my undeviating arrow-line to Rome, and I had charged this one great barrier manfully where the straight path of my pilgrimage crossed the Alps—and I had failed! Even in that fearful cold I felt it, and it ran through my doubt of return like another and deeper current of pain. Italy was there, just above, right to my hand. A lifting of a cloud, a little respite, and every downward step would have been towards the sunlight. As it was, I was being driven back northward, in retreat and ashamed. The Alps had conquered me.

Let us always after this combat their immensity and their will, and always hate the inhuman guards that hold the gates of Italy, and the powers that lie in wait for men on those high places. But now I know that Italy will always stand apart. She is cut off by no ordinary wall, and Death has all his army on her frontiers.

Well, we returned. Twice the guide rubbed my hands with brandy, and once I had to halt and recover for a moment, failing and losing my hold.

Believe it or not, the deep footsteps of our ascent were already quite lost and covered by the new snow since our halt, and even had they been visible, the guide would not have retraced them. He did what I did not at first understand, but what I soon saw to be wise. He took a steep slant down-ward over the face of the snow-slope, and though such a pitch of descent a little unnerved me, it was well in the end. For when we had gone down perhaps 900 feet, or a thousand, in perpendicular distance, even I, half numb and fainting, could feel that the storm was less violent. Another two hun-dred, and the flakes could be seen not driving in flashes past, but separately falling. Then in some few minutes we could see the slope for a very long way downwards quite clearly; then, soon after, we saw far below us the place where the mountain-side merged easily into the plain of that cup or basin whence we had started.

When we saw this, the guide said to me, "Hold your stick thus, if you are strong enough, and let yourself slide." I could just hold it, in spite of the cold. Life was returning to me with intolerable pain. We shot down the slope almost as quickly as falling, but it was evidently safe to do so, as the end was clearly visible, and had no break or rock in it.

So we reached the plain below, and entered the little shed, and thence looking up, we saw the storm above us; but no one could have told it for what it was. Here, below, was silence, and the terror and raging above seemed only a great trembling cloud occupying the mountain. Then we set our faces down the ravine by which we had come up, and so came down to where the snow changed to rain. When we got right down into the valley of the Rhone, we found it all roofed with cloud, and the higher trees were white with snow, making a line like a tide mark on the slopes of the hills.

I re-entered "The Bear," silent and angered, and not accepting the humiliation of that failure. Then, having eaten, I determined in equal silence to take the road like any other fool; to cross the Furka by a fine highroad, like any tourist, and to cross the St. Gothard by another fine high-road, as millions had done before me, and not to look heaven in the face again till I was back after my long detour, on the straight road again for Rome.

But to think of it! I who had all that planned out, and had so nearly done it! I who had cut a path across Europe like a shaft, and seen so many strange places!—now to have to recite all the litany of the vulgar; Bellinzona, Lugano, and this and that, which any railway travelling fellow can tell you. Not till Como should I feel a man again. . . .

Indeed it is a bitter thing to have to give up one's sword.

HUNGER

FROM *The Track of the Cat*

WALTER VAN TILBURG CLARK

When Walter Van Tilburg Clark's first novel, *The Oxbow Incident*, was published, critics talked of it in superlatives. The writer, they said, had taken the western horse opera and had given it astonishing literary depth; he had combined the thriller with the psychological novel and had produced a book both new and perfect.

For many readers his second novel, *The Track of the Cat*, from which this extract is taken, is as perfect in its own way—a subtle psychological study with great dramatic force, of the warping effect of isolation upon a mountain family.

BUT NOW THERE CAME MOMENTS WHEN A SINGLE, ACTIVE, QUICKLY MOVING fear ran out through him, escaped from the small, dark core in his middle. The monitor set it off each time, by suggesting that perhaps none of his calculations had been even close to right, that perhaps the lapses into inattention had been much longer than he believed, and that first eagerness and then fear had made him travel much faster than he thought he was traveling.

Maybe, the monitor would keep suggesting, you're way to hell and gone west and south, in mountains you've never even seen before.

Maybe, it would say, you might just as well be looking across the winter roof of Asia, for all the good it's ever going to do you.

These spells of fear were short and well separated, though. Most of the time he was hopeful. When he had the food packet again, and was out the other end of the pass, and going north on the east slope, he kept telling himself, he'd know where he was.

You'll be able to see then, insisted the monitor's optimistic antagonist.

You'll see something you know for sure from there, it said again, almost gaily.

Even if it gets dark on you now, it added, a couple of minutes later, there'll be stars out. They can't get you tangled with stars out; you can keep right on going all night, if you have to.

He continued to plow rapidly north, slowing to rest now and then, but always resuming the hurried shuffle again as soon as his knees and his lungs would permit, and always peering ahead, or across at the gleaming sea of mountains in the west, through the little, protective clouds of his lashes. Gradually the monitor began to speak up, if at all, only to suggest his confidence was approaching insolence again. He was getting so warm that, in spite of the light, he pushed the hood back to let the wind work on his head.

He had to pull the hood forward a few minutes later, though, and across his face from the left as much as he could and still see. He had come around a sharply drifted buttress of the mountain, and the wind was suddenly much stronger against him, and much colder, and full of a twisting, glittering scud of ground-snow. It blinded him, for the moment he was pulling the hood up, and he stopped until it slacked off and he could see again. Then his growing confidence received its first serious setback. The wide, crooked wake of the bear-paws, which he'd been trusting all this time to the point of not even giving it a thought, was barely visible, and not as a distinct, broken track at all, but only as a narrow, shallow depression, as smooth as the slope on both sides of it.

"Goddam," he muttered violently. "Everything, even the goddam wind."

The spur of time struck into him deeply again. He hurried forward faster than ever along the faint depression, keeping up the bent-kneed running without a break, until he was breathing all the time in gasps through his mouth and the champagne dizziness was constant and produced no elation whatever. Yet he didn't go fast enough. Before he was off that buttress of the range, the trace had vanished completely. There was only the smooth, trackless snow, with the glittering serpents of scud slithering up and across it at him. He let his pace slack off a little. There was no use hurrying that much any longer.

What the hell, he challenged the fear. It can't be far to the pass now. I've come back most of the way, that's a cinch. And nobody could miss a pass like that.

Actually he was not at all sure that nobody, himself in particular, could miss a pass like that. He was watching the slope and the skyline above him anxiously, peering ahead along them again and again, and they were no more familiar anywhere than the shining sea of mountains in the west. At the first break in the skyline, a wide but shallow dip, with a shallow, drifted draw going up to it, he paused and studied it uncertainly.

"Not deep enough," he declared finally. "It's no real pass. It ain't it."

He really wasn't that sure, though. The snow was deep and light, and it drifted fast in a wind like this. Also, he discovered that he wasn't at all sure what the mouth of the pass had looked like in the falling snow, let alone what it would look like now. He went on after a minute, watching constantly ahead again, scanning the ridge as far north as he could see it, each time the clouds of windy crystals broke or subsided. It began to seem possible to him that he had already gone by the mouth of the pass.

Twice more great dents in the snow wall halted him. He didn't believe he'd ever seen them before, but he knew now that he hadn't really seen anything around him that morning, only the snow. He believed, trying to think back, that he hadn't even turned around, when he came out of the pass, to take a good look at the mouth of it. It worried him that he had been capable of such incredible carelessness.

The fourth of these troublesome depressions of the ridge particularly disturbed him. It could quite justly be called a pass. It was very high and not very deep but it went all the way through, there wasn't a doubt of that. He finally decided against it, though. The mouth of the pass he'd come through couldn't be that high above him, even allowing for a lot of heavy drifting, and maybe for his being a little farther down now. The white domes of the timberline trees had been more numerous in the mouth of it, too.

Nevertheless, he began to be troubled, as he went on, by all four breaks he had passed. They pulled back upon something within him, as if he were a spider simultaneously reeling out four lines behind him. The farther he went, the more strongly the four threads tugged at him, until at last he was forced to stop and turn around and look back as far as he could. He couldn't make out, for sure, any of the notches he'd passed.

What he did make out, beyond any question, however, was the fact that the sun had already gone far past the height of its arc. He felt that it had taken a great, curving leap while his back was turned, and that made it seem likely that he'd gone by the pass long since, maybe even before he'd started to watch for it. If so, however, there was nothing to do but give it up, and the food packet with it. He was profoundly alarmed by that leaping sun. He turned north again, and began to hurry on, the four threads dragging at him as heavily as cables now. He even began to debate, as his belief grew stronger and stronger that the pass was behind him, whether he hadn't better go up over the ridge any time now. . . .

He worked his way swiftly out around one more great bastion of the range, and at the first look beyond it, the four cables let go. There, not far ahead, was the mouth of the real pass, the unquestionable pass. Now that he saw it, he was amazed that he'd ever been troubled by those four shallow fakes. The end of the ridge he was on sloped down northward toward the pass, and then broke off steeply into it. The north wing of the V shone blindingly in the sun, but its height and its slant were unmistakable.

He hailed it joyfully. "That's you, you son-of-a-bitch."

The joy, however, died quickly, squeezed out under the terrible burden of the time that had already passed. The shadows of the evergreen spires below him were now clearly pointing uphill as well as north, and each of them pointed toward coming darkness. He hurried on along the side of the ridge and up into the mouth of the pass. The wind, blowing fiercely now, along the spine of the range, was repeatedly hurling the snow in great clouds off the edge of the north wall and out over the hollow. It sank in long shimmering curtains into the cut and around him. A little way into the pass, he salvaged another moment of certainty. There was the wake of his webs, going right up the middle ahead of him. He followed it as fast as he could among the watching trees, and through the shining, soundless rain of crystals from above.

The pass seemed much longer to him now than it had in the morning. Twice he stopped and looked attentively along the dark rock cliffs of the north side, thinking he must have gone as far as the cave, even though he could see the half-erased track meandering on ahead of him. And once he even stopped to study the south wall, being assailed by a brief doubt as to which he had stayed in after all. In this matter, as in the case of the pass, however, there was no mistaking the right cave when he saw it. The break he'd made coming out and the buttress of hand-packed snow, and the little section of uncovered wall in the upper, far corner, tiny as they were in the base of the great wall, like the work of some improbable survivor of cliff dwellers, did not for a moment appear to be an accident of nature. . . .

When he came right under it, he stared up at it and said softly, "God, a blind cat with no nose could of picked it out. And knocked it in, too," he added, "knocked it in like nothing."

He went straight up toward it as far as he could, and then climbed sideways in what was left of the steps he had made that morning. When he reached the top of the talus slope he went across at once to the corner of the wall that had no snow on it. There was no time to waste mooning over the strange hold the cave had on him. He would knock in a few slabs of the shale and reach out the oilskin packet without taking off the webs, and get going again as fast as he could.

At the thought of having the packet, of opening it and finding the buttered bread and the salt jerky, his mouth filled with saliva so that he had to spit. He would eat it all, and go the rest of the way tonight, wherever he was when it got dark. That's the way he would do it; no more dallying, no more silly notions.

He pushed, and the loose shale fell, clattering with short, thick echoes inside, and let in enough light so he could see the ledges he wanted to see. There was no sign of the yellow oilskin of the packet. He reached in as far as he could, and felt to the back of one ledge after another, but couldn't find it. Everything else—time, distance, darkness, the now only half-believable cat—vanished from his mind. Nothing mattered except to get hold of that packet. His watering mouth and the growling hollow of his stomach demanded it fiercely.

He leaned the carbine against the cliff, and tore away the rest of the wall, throwing it down the slope behind him, shale and snow together. When the opening was large enough, he crawled up into the cave and searched in the crevices, at first carefully, but then, before he would be convinced, with his mittens off and frantically. There was nothing in any crevice.

After a moment of kneeling there, blank with despair, he unlaced the webs and let them fall outside, by the carbine, and then crawled along over the stones he'd pushed in, and searched the other end. He found the sheath of the knife, and slipped the knife into it, and dropped it back into his pocket, but the oilskin wasn't there either, on the floor or in any of the crevices. He thought wildly, for an instant, that he must have taken it with him after all, and lost it somewhere along the side of the mountain in the snow. He corrected the notion savagely. "No, by God," he declared, "I left it here. I didn't eat this morning. I never touched it this morning. It's gotta be here."

There was only one chance left. He began to hurl the slabs of shale from the floor out the opening onto the slope. He had thrown out only four or five of them when he saw the yellow patch between two stones on the bottom, and exulted. Furiously he tossed away the last slabs that kept it from him, and then, suddenly, with his hands out in the air, ready to grasp another slab, he knelt there motionless, staring down at it. The oilskin itself had been clumsily unrolled and then ripped, in places practically shredded, and there was not a single visible crumb of bread or scrap of jerky in it.

At first it seemed to him that the mountain itself must have developed a malignant spirit, an evil, trivial, crumb-eating thing that delighted in tormenting him. Then it crossed his mind that the cougar might have entered the cave after he was gone. A moment more, however, during which his disappointment and revived despair brought tears to his eyes, and he knew that it must have been the work of some of the little rock mice or chipmunks of the heights. They must live in there under those back ledges, farther than he had been able to see or feel. This guess did nothing but embody the malice he had imputed in general to the mountain. He continued to kneel there for some time, staring blindly down at the empty, shredded oilskin.

At last, slowly, almost as dazed as when he had left that morning, he crawled out onto the edge again, and laced on the bear-paws and drew on his mittens. He lifted the carbine into the crook of his right arm, where it felt now like part of himself restored, and stepped slowly, both feet upon each step, down the slope of snow into the bottom of the pass again.

"Even the mice now," he muttered. "Even the durned, stinking, little tiny bits of mice now. Everything. Every goddam thing in the world."

THE HORROR HORN

FROM *Visible and Invisible*

E . F . BENSON

It was inevitable that the Abominable Snowman should become a character in a story. Here E. F. Benson takes the legend, mixes with it small parts of fact and large parts of terror to make a chilling potion.

E. F. Benson was an incredibly fertile writer. At the time of his death he had published eighty volumes of fiction and biography, many of them graced with the ease and urbanity which characterize this story. We can ascribe at least a part of his facility as storyteller to the fact that he and his brothers were each required by their father, later Archbishop of Canterbury, to contribute a weekly quota of four pages of prose or one page of poetry to the family magazine.

I HAD COME OUT HERE WITH MY COUSIN, PROFESSOR INGRAM, THE CELEBRATED physiologist and Alpine climber. During the serenity of the last fortnight he had made a couple of notable winter ascents, but this morning his weather-wisdom had mistrusted the signs of the heavens, and instead of attempting the ascent of the Piz Passug he had waited to see whether his misgivings justified themselves. So there he sat now in the hall of the admirable hotel with his feet on the hot-water pipes and the latest delivery of the English post in his hands. This contained a pamphlet concerning the result of the Mount Everest expedition of which he had just finished the perusal when I entered.

"A very interesting report," he said, passing it to me, "and they certainly deserve to succeed next year. But who can tell what that final six thousand feet may entail? Six thousand feet more when you have already accomplished twenty-three thousand does not seem much, but at present no one knows whether the human frame can stand exertion at such a height. It may affect not the lungs and heart only, but possibly the brain. Delirious hallucinations may occur. In fact, if I did not know better, I should have said that one such hallucination had occurred to the climbers already."

"And what was that?" I asked.

"You will find that they thought they came across the tracks of some naked human foot at a great altitude. That looks at first sight like an hallucination. What more natural than that a brain excited and exhilarated by the extreme height should have interpreted certain marks in the snow as the footprints of a human being? Every bodily organ at these altitudes is exerting itself to the utmost to do its work, and the brain seizes on those marks in the snow and says, 'Yes, I'm all right, I'm doing my job, and I perceive marks in the snow which I affirm are human footprints.' You know, even at this altitude, how restless and eager the brain is, how vividly, as you told me, you dream at night. Multiply that stimulus and that consequent eagerness and restlessness by three, and how natural that the brain should harbour illusions! What after all is the delirium which often accompanies high fever but the effort of the brain to do its work under the pressure of feverish conditions? It is so eager to continue perceiving that it perceives things which have no existence!"

"And yet you don't think that these naked human footprints were illusions," said I. "You told me you would have thought so, if you had not known better."

He shifted in his chair and looked out of the window a moment. The air was thick now with the density of the big snowflakes that were driven along by the squealing northwest gale.

"Quite so," he said. "In all probability the human footprints were real human footprints. I expect that they were the footprints, anyhow, of a being more nearly a man than anything else. My reason for saying so is that I know such beings exist. I have even seen quite near at hand—and I assure you I did not wish to be nearer in spite of my intense curiosity—the creature, shall we say, which would make such footprints. And if the snow was not so dense, I could show you the place where I saw him."

He pointed straight out of the window, where across the valley lies the huge tower of the Ungeheuerhorn with the carved pinnacle of rock at the top like some gigantic rhinoceros-horn. On one side only, as I knew, was the mountain practicable, and that for none but the finest climbers; on the other three a succession of ledges and precipices rendered it unscalable. Two thousand feet of sheer rock form the tower; below are five hundred feet of fallen boulders, up to the edge of which grow dense woods of larch and pine.

"Upon the Ungeheuerhorn?" I asked.

"Yes. Up till twenty years ago it had never been ascended, and I, like several others, spent a lot of time in trying to find a route up it. My guide and I sometimes spent three nights together at the hut beside the Blumen glacier, prowling round it, and it was by luck really that we found the route, for the mountain looks even more impracticable from the far side than it does from this. But one day we found a long, transverse fissure in the side which led to a negotiable ledge; then there came a slanting ice couloir which you could not see till you got to the foot of it. However, I need not go into that."

The big room where we sat was filling up with cheerful groups driven indoors by this sudden gale and snowfall, and the cackle of merry tongues grew loud. The band, too, that invariable appanage of tea-time at Swiss resorts, had begun to tune up for the usual potpourri from the works of Puccini. Next moment the sugary, sentimental melodies began.

"Strange contrast!" said Ingram. "Here are we sitting warm and cozy, our ears pleasantly tickled with these little baby tunes and outside is the great storm growing more violent every moment, and swirling round the austere cliffs of the Ungeheuerhorn: the Horror-horn, as indeed it was to me."

"I want to hear all about it," I said. "Every detail: make a short story long, if it's short. I want to know why it's *your* Horror-horn?"

"Well, Chanton and I (he was my guide) used to spend days prowling about the cliffs, making a little progress on one side and then being stopped, and gaining perhaps five hundred feet on another side and then being confronted by some insuperable obstacle, till the day when by luck we found the route. Chanton never liked the job, for some reason that I could not fathom. It was not because of the difficulty or danger of the climbing, for he was the most fearless man I have ever met when dealing with rocks and ice, but he was always insistent that we should get off the mountain and back to the Blumen hut before sunset. He was scarcely easy even when we had got back to shelter and locked and barred the door, and I well remember one night when, as we ate our supper, we heard some animal, a wolf probably, howling somewhere out in the night. A positive panic seized him, and I don't think he closed his eyes till morning. It struck me then that there might be some grisly legend about the mountain, connected possibly with its name, and next day I asked him why the peak was called the Horror-horn. He put the question off at first, and said that, like the Schreckhorn, its name was due to its precipices and falling stones; but when I pressed him further he acknowledged that there was a legend about it, which his father had told him. There were creatures, so it was supposed, that lived in its caves, things human in shape, and covered, except for the face and hands, with long black hair. They were dwarfs in size, four feet high or thereabouts, but of prodigious strength and agility, remnants of some wild primeval race. It seemed that they were still in an upward stage of evolution, or so I guessed, for the story ran that sometimes girls had been carried off by them, not as prey, and not for any such fate as for those captured by cannibals, but to be bred from. Young men also had been raped by them, to be mated with the females of their tribe. All this looked as if the creatures, as I said, were tending towards humanity. But naturally I did not believe a word of it, as applied to the conditions of the present day. Centuries ago, conceivably, there may have been such beings, and, with the extraordinary tenacity of tradition, the news of this had been handed down and was still current round the hearths of the peasants. As for their numbers, Chanton told me that three had been once seen together by a man who owing to his swiftness on skis had escaped to tell the tale. This man, he averred, was no other than his grandfather, who had been benighted one winter evening as he passed through the dense woods below the Ungeheuerhorn, and Chanton supposed that they had been driven down to these lower altitudes in search of food during severe winter weather, for otherwise the recorded sights of them had always taken place among the rocks of the peak itself. They had pursued his grandfather, then a young man, at an extraordinarily swift canter, running sometimes upright as men run, sometimes on all-fours in the manner of beasts, and their howls were just such as that we had heard that night in the Blumen hut. Such at any rate was the story Chanton told me, and, like you, I regarded it as the very moonshine of superstition. But the very next day I had reason to reconsider my judgment about it.

"It was on that day that after a week of exploration we hit on the only route at present known to the top of our peak. We started as soon as there was light enough to climb by, for, as you may guess, on very difficult rocks it is impossible to climb by lantern or moonlight. We hit on the long fissure I have spoken of, we explored the ledge which from below seemed to end in nothingness, and with an hour's step-cutting ascended the couloir which led upwards from it. From there onwards it was a rock-climb, certainly of considerable difficulty, but with no heart-breaking discoveries ahead, and it was about nine in the morning that we stood on the top. We did not wait there long, for that side of the mountain is raked by falling stones loosened, when the sun grows hot, from the ice that holds them, and we made haste to pass the ledge where the falls are most frequent. After that there was the long fissure to descend, a matter of no great difficulty, and we were at the end of our work by midday, both of us, as you may imagine, in the state of the highest elation.

"A long and tiresome scramble among the huge boulders at the foot of the cliff then lay before us. Here the hillside is very porous and great caves extend far into the mountain. We had unroped at the base of the fissure, and were picking our way as seemed good to either of us among these fallen rocks, many of them bigger than an ordinary house, when, on coming round the corner of one of these, I saw that which made it clear that the stories Chanton had told me were no figment of traditional superstition.

"Not twenty yards in front of me lay one of the beings of which he had spoken. There it sprawled naked and basking on its back with face turned up to the sun, which its narrow eyes regarded unwinking. In form it was completely human, but the growth of hair that covered limbs and trunk alike almost completely hid the sun-tanned skin beneath. But its face, save for the down on its cheeks and chin, was hairless, and I looked on a countenance the sensual and malevolent bestiality of which froze me with horror. Had the creature been an animal, one would have felt scarcely a shudder at the gross animalism of it; the horror lay in the fact that it was a man. There lay by it a couple of gnawed bones, and, its meal finished, it was lazily licking its protuberant lips, from which came a purring murmur of content. With one hand it scratched the thick hair on its belly, in the other it held one of these bones, which presently split in half beneath the pressure of its finger and thumb. But my horror was not based on the information of what happened to those men whom these creatures caught, it was due only to my proximity to a thing so human and so infernal. The peak, of which the ascent had a moment ago filled us with such elated satisfaction, became to me an Ungeheuerhorn indeed, for it was the home of beings more awful than the delirium of nightmare could ever have conceived.

"Chanton was a dozen paces behind me, and with a backward wave of my hand I caused him to halt. Then withdrawing myself with infinite precaution, so as not to attract the gaze of that basking creature, I slipped back round the rock, whispered to him what I had seen, and with blanched faces we made a long detour, peering round every corner, and crouching low, not knowing but that at any step we might come upon another of these beings, or that from the mouth of one of these caves in the mountain-side there might not appear another of those hairless and dreadful faces, with perhaps this time the breasts and insignia of womanhood. That would have been the worst of all.

"Luck favoured us, for we made our way among the boulders and shifting stones, the rattle of which might at any moment have betrayed us, without a repetition of my experience, and once among the trees we ran as if the Furies themselves were in pursuit. Well now did I understand, though I dare say I cannot convey, the qualms of Chanton's mind when he spoke to me of these creatures. Their very humanity was what made them so terrible, the fact that they were of the same race as ourselves, but of a type so abysmally degraded that the most brutal and inhuman of men would have seemed angelic in comparison."

The music of the small band was over before he had finished the narrative, and the chattering groups round the tea-table had dispersed. He paused a moment.

"There was a horror of the spirit," he said, "which I experienced then, from which, I verily believe, I have never entirely recovered. I saw then how terrible a living thing could be, and how terrible, in consequence, was life itself. In us all I suppose lurks some inherited germ of that ineffable bestiality, and who knows whether, sterile as it has apparently become in the course of centuries, it might not fructify again. When I saw that creature sun itself, I looked into the abyss out of which we have crawled. And these creatures are trying to crawl out of it now, if they exist any longer. Certainly for the last twenty years there has been no record of their being seen, until we come to this story of the footprint seen by the climbers on Everest. If that is authentic, if the party did not mistake the footprint of some bear, or what not, for a human tread, it seems as if still this bestranded remnant of mankind is in existence."

Now, Ingram had told his story well; but sitting in this warm and civilised room, the horror which he had clearly felt had not communicated itself to me in any very vivid manner. Intellectually, I agreed, I could appreciate his horror, but certainly my spirit felt no shudder of interior comprehension.

"But it is odd," I said, "that your keen interest in physiology did not disperse your qualms. You were looking, so I take it, at some form of man more remote probably than the earliest human remains. Did not something inside you say, 'This is of absorbing significance'?"

He shook his head.

"No: I only wanted to get away," said he. "It was not, as I have told you, the terror of what, according to Chanton's story, might await us if we were captured; it was sheer horror at the creature itself. I quaked at it."

The snowstorm and the gale increased in violence that night, and I slept uneasily, plucked again and again from slumber by the fierce battling of the wind that shook my windows as if with an imperious demand for admittance. It came in billowy gusts, with strange noises intermingled with it as for a moment it abated, with flutings and moanings that rose to shrieks as the fury of it returned. These noises, no doubt, mingled themselves with my drowsed and sleepy consciousness, and once I tore myself out of a nightmare, imagining that the creatures of the Horror-horn had gained footing on my balcony and were rattling at the window-bolts. But before morning the gale had died away, and I awoke to see the snow falling dense and fast in a windless air. For three days it continued, without intermission, and with its cessation there came a frost such as I have never felt before. Fifty degrees were registered one night, and more the next, and what the cold must have been on the cliffs of the Ungeheuerhorn I cannot imagine. Sufficient, so I thought, to have made an end altogether of its secret inhabitants: my cousin, on that day twenty years ago, had missed an opportunity for study which would probably never fall again either to him or another.

I received one morning a letter from a friend saying that he had arrived at the neighbouring winter resort of St. Luigi, and proposing that I should come over for a morning's skating and lunch afterwards. The place was not more than a couple of miles off, if one took the path over the low, pine-clad foothills above which lay the steep woods below the first rocky slopes of the Ungeheuerhorn; and accordingly, with a knapsack containing skates on my back, I went on skis over the wooded slopes and down by an easy descent again on to St. Luigi. The day was overcast, clouds entirely obscured the higher peaks though the sun was visible, pale and unluminous, through the mists. But as the morning went on, it gained the upper hand, and I slid down into St. Luigi beneath a sparkling firmament. We skated and lunched, and then, since it looked as if thick weather was coming up again, I set out early, about three o'clock, for my return journey.

Hardly had I got into the woods when the clouds gathered thick above, and streamers and skeins of them began to descend among the pines through which my path threaded its way. In ten minutes more their opacity had so increased that I could hardly see a couple of yards in front of me. Very soon I became aware that I must have got off the path, for snow-cowled shrubs lay directly in my way, and, casting back to find it again, I got altogether confused as to direction. But, though progress was difficult, I knew I had only to keep on the ascent, and presently I should come to the brow of these low foothills, and descend into the open valley where Alhubel stood. So on I went, stumbling and sliding over obstacles, and unable, owing to the thickness of the snow, to take off my skis, for I should have sunk over the knees at each step. Still the ascent continued, and looking at my watch I saw that I had already been near an hour on my way from St. Luigi, a period more than sufficient to complete my whole journey. But still I stuck to my idea that though I had certainly strayed far from my proper route a few minutes more must surely see me over the top of the upward way, and I should find the ground declining into the next valley. About now, too, I noticed that the mists were growing suffused with rose-colour, and, though the inference was that it must be close on sunset, there was consolation in the fact that they were there and might lift at any moment and disclose to me my whereabouts. But the fact that night would soon be on me made it needful to bar my mind against that despair of loneliness which so eats out the heart of a man who is lost in woods or on mountain-side, that, though still there is plenty of vigour in his limbs, his nervous force is sapped, and he can do no more than lie down and abandon himself to whatever fate may await him. . . . And then I heard that which made the thought of loneliness seem bliss indeed, for there was a worse fate than loneliness. What I heard resembled the howl of a wolf, and it came from not far in front of me where the ridge— was it a ridge?—rose still higher in a vestment of pines.

From behind me came a sudden puff of wind, which shook the frozen snow from the drooping pine-branches, and swept away the mists as a broom sweeps the dust from the floor. Radiant above me were the unclouded skies, already charged with the red of the sunset, and in front I saw that I had come to the very edge of the wood through which I had wandered so long. But it was no valley into which I had penetrated, for there right ahead of me rose the steep slope of boulders and rocks soaring upwards to the foot of the Ungeheuerhorn. What, then, was that cry of a wolf which had made my heart stand still? I saw.

Not twenty yards from me was a fallen tree, and leaning against the trunk of it was one of the denizens of the Horror-horn, and it was a woman. She was enveloped in a thick growth of hair grey and tufted, and from her head it streamed down over her shoulders and her bosom, from which hung withered and pendulous breasts. And looking on her face I comprehended not with my mind alone, but with a shudder of my spirit, what Ingram had felt. Never had nightmare fashioned so terrible a countenance; the beauty of sun and stars and of the beasts of the field and the kindly race of men could not atone for so hellish an incarnation of the spirit of life. A fathomless bestiality modelled the slavering mouth and the narrow eyes; I looked into the abyss itself and knew that out of that abyss on the edge of which I leaned the generations of men had climbed. What if that ledge crumbled in front of me and pitched me headlong into its nethermost depths? . . .

In one hand she held by the horns a chamois that kicked and struggled. A blow from its hindleg caught her withered thigh, and with a grunt of anger she seized the leg in her other hand, and, as a man may pull from its sheath a stem of meadow grass, she plucked it off the body, leaving the torn skin hanging round the gaping wound. Then putting the red, bleeding member to her mouth she sucked at it as a child sucks a stick of sweetmeat. Through flesh and gristle her short, brown teeth penetrated, and she licked her lips with a sound of purring. Then dropping the leg by her side, she looked again at the body of the prey now quivering in its death convulsion, and with finger and thumb gouged out one of its eyes. She snapped her teeth on it, and it cracked like a soft-shelled nut.

It must have been but a few seconds that I stood watching her, in some indescribable catalepsy of terror, while through my brain there pealed the panic-command of my mind to my stricken limbs, "Begone, begone, while there is time." Then, recovering the power of my joints and muscles, I tried to slip behind a tree and hide myself from this apparition, but the woman —shall I say?—must have caught my stir of movement, for she raised her eyes from her living feast and saw me. She craned forward her neck, she dropped her prey, and half rising began to move towards me. As she did this, she opened her mouth and gave forth a howl such as I had heard a moment before. It was answered by another, but faintly and distantly.

Sliding and slipping, with the toes of my skis tripping in the obstacles below the snow, I plunged forward down the hill between the pine-trunks.

The low sun already sinking behind some rampart of mountain in the west reddened the snow and the pines with its ultimate rays. My knapsack with the skates in it swung to and fro on my back, one ski-stick had already been twitched out of my hand by a fallen branch of pine, but not a second's pause could I allow myself to recover it. I gave no glance behind, and I knew not at what pace my pursuer was on my track, or indeed whether any pursued at all, for my whole mind and energy, now working at full power again under the stress of my panic, were devoted to getting away down the hill and out of the wood as swiftly as my limbs could bear me. For a little while I heard nothing but the hissing snow of my headlong passage, and the rustle of the covered undergrowth beneath my feet, and then, from close at hand behind me, once more the wolf-howl sounded and I heard the plunging of footsteps other than my own.

The strap of my knapsack had shifted, and as my skates swung to and fro on my back it chafed and pressed on my throat, hindering free passage of air, of which, God knew, my labouring lungs were in dire need, and without pausing I slipped it free from my neck, and held it in the hand from which my ski-stick had been jerked. I seemed to go a little more easily for this adjustment, and now, not so far distant I could see below me the path from which I had strayed. If only I could reach that, the smoother going would surely enable me to out-distance my pursuer, who even on the rougher ground was but slowly overhauling me, and at the sight of that riband stretching unimpeded downhill, a ray of hope pierced the black panic of my soul. With that came the desire, keen and insistent, to see who or what it was that was on my tracks, and I spared a backward glance. It was she, the hag whom I had seen at her gruesome meal; her long grey hair flew out behind her, her mouth chattered and gibbered, her fingers made grabbing movements, as if already they closed on me.

But the path was now at hand, and the nearness of it I suppose made me incautious. A hump of snow-covered bush lay in my path, and, thinking I could jump over it, I tripped and fell, smothering myself in snow. I heard a maniac noise, half scream, half laugh, from close behind, and before I could recover myself the grabbing fingers were at my neck, as if a steel vise had closed there. But my right hand in which I held my knapsack of skates was free, and with a blind back-handed movement I whirled it behind me at full length of its strap, and knew that my desperate blow had found its billet somewhere. Even before I could look round I felt the grip on my neck relax, and something subsided into the very bush which had entangled me. I recovered my feet and turned. There she lay, twitching and quivering. The heel of one of my skates piercing the thin alpaca of the knapsack had hit her full on the temple, from which the blood was pouring, but a hundred yards away I could see another such figure coming downwards on my tracks, leaping and bounding. At that panic arose again within me, and I sped off down the white smooth path that led to the lights of the village already beckoning. Never once did I pause in my headlong going: there was no safety until I was back among the haunts of men. I flung myself against the door of the hotel, and screamed for admittance, though I had but to turn the handle and enter; and once more as when Ingram had told his tale, there was the sound of the band, and the chatter of voices, and there, too, was he himself, who looked up and then rose swiftly to his feet as I made my clattering entrance.

"I have seen them too," I cried. "Look at my knapsack. Is there not blood on it? It is the blood of one of them, a woman, a hag, who tore off the leg of a chamois as I looked, and pursued me through the accursed wood. I—"

Whether it was I who spun round, or the room which seemed to spin round me, I knew not, but I heard myself falling, collapsed on the floor, and the next time that I was conscious at all I was in bed. There was Ingram there, who told me that I was quite safe, and another man, a stranger, who pricked my arm with the nozzle of a syringe, and reassured me. . . .

A day or two later I gave a coherent account of my adventure, and three or four men, armed with guns, went over my traces. They found the bush in which I had stumbled, with a pool of blood which had soaked into the snow, and, still following my ski-tracks, they came on the body of a chamois, from which had been torn one of its hindlegs and one eye-socket was empty. That is all the corroboration of my story that I can give the reader, and for myself I imagine that the creature which pursued me was either not killed by my blow or that her fellows removed her body. . . .

Anyhow, it is open to the incredulous to prowl about the caves of the Ungeheuerhorn, and see if anything occurs that may convince them.

CHAMOIS

4

Men Study the Mountains

People accept almost as a truism the notion that there are no new places left to explore. That, of course, depends upon where you set boundaries. If you set none, then the world becomes infinite. There are worlds we have only begun to explore, the incalculably populated submicroscopic world, the world of the ocean floor, the interstellar spaces. Even the tiny surface of our planet has enormous areas that civilized man has never seen and of whose existence he has only recently become aware. Much of the global map ought still to be shown with a question mark—mountain ranges unseen and unexplored in China, Siberia, New Guinea, the Antarctic continent; ranges, it is suspected, higher than any now known.

There is a gigantic wall of rock discovered not too long ago in the interior of Brazil towering 9,000 feet into the sky, surfaced with a pre-Cambrian sandstone a half billion years old—a piece of a world that existed long before man. There is another in British Guiana, a flat mass of rock 7,860 feet high, where scientists found species of birds and plants unknown anywhere else in the world.

These scientists are our new adventurers, the explorers of new worlds. High among them rank the mountaineering geologists and naturalists who have chipped rock from the biggest mountains in the world, who have ventured into volcanoes, and have reached into impossible crevices for a new species of mountain flower. With brain and courage and the patience of the scientist, they have stretched the elastic boundaries of knowledge. From the writings of these mountaineer scientists we have chosen their best, those that communicate the excitement and wonder of their explorations into the unknown.

WHEN MT. PELÉE, A 4,000-FOOT VOLCANO ON THE ISLAND OF MARTINIQUE, ERUPTED IN A FLASH OF FIRE ON MAY 8, 1902, IT BLOTTED OUT ST. PIERRE, A SEAPORT SEVERAL MILES AWAY, AND KILLED 30,000 PEOPLE INSTANTLY. THIS PHOTOGRAPH, TAKEN A SHORT TIME AFTER THE ERUPTION, SHOWS A TOWER OF BLACK, GLASSLIKE ROCK, THEN CALLED PELÉE'S SPINE, WHICH WAS PUSHED UPWARD OUT OF THE CRATER TO A HEIGHT OF NEARLY 1,000 FEET. IT IS NOW BELIEVED TO HAVE BEEN THE PLUG THAT BLOCKED THE CRATER'S THROAT FOR HUNDREDS OF YEARS. IT DISAPPEARED FROM SIGHT AFTER A YEAR

Wide World

AN AERIAL VIEW OF THE MOUTH OF BOQUERON VOLCANO, OFF THE WEST COAST OF MEXICO

IN 1883, KRAKATOA, A VOLCANIC ISLAND NEAR JAVA, EXPLODED IN ONE ENORMOUS BLAST, AND COLLAPSED INTO THE SEA. THIS IS ALL THAT IS LEFT: A RING OF LOW ISLANDS, AND AN OCCASIONAL PUFF OF STEAM. 35,000 PEOPLE WERE KILLED BY THE TIDAL WAVES

Bettmann Archive

left: AN ETCHING OF THE DONNER PARTY, A GROUP OF EMIGRANTS WHO WERE TRAPPED IN THE HEAVY SNOWS OF THE SIERRA NEVADAS IN 1846–1847 AND SURVIVED ONLY THROUGH RECOURSE TO CANNIBALISM

below: IRONICALLY, THIS BEAUTY SPOT IN THE UINTA MOUNTAINS OF NORTHEASTERN UTAH BECAME A DEATH TRAP FOR A LUXURY AIR LINER THAT FAILED TO CLEAR THE TOP OF THE PEAK AND CARRIED 19 PERSONS TO THEIR DEATHS IN 1937. THIS PICTURE WAS MADE AS A RESCUE PARTY APPROACHED THE WRECKAGE OF THE FALLEN SHIP

United Press Photo

TOURISTS OF 1885, REPLETE WITH WALKING STICKS AND PARASOLS, PICK THEIR WAY NEATLY
OVER THE MER DE GLACE IN CHAMONIX, SWITZERLAND

CLIMBING THE CREST OF KLEINGLOCKNER IN THE DOLOMITES, AUSTRIAN ALPS

Georgia Engelhard: Monkmey

THE EARTH IS ALIVE!

FROM *Conversation with the Earth*

HANS CLOOS

🐉 It is the rare scientist who can establish so close a communion with his study as to give the layman not only knowledge but a sensory perception of the physical laws by which our universe operates. For that he needs to be both scientist and poet. Hans Cloos was one of the prominent geologists of this century, but he was, in addition, an artist who could paint with both brush and word. His scientific work took him throughout the world, to the mountains of Africa, the polar regions, Europe, America. He spent months in the Sierra Nevadas, inquiring into the structural characteristics of the American Cordilleras. Before his death in 1951, he published his *Conversation with the Earth,* from which these extracts have been taken. It is a conversation we are privileged to listen to.

Naples

WHEN I ARRIVED AT NAPLES, IT WAS A WARM TURMOIL OF NOISE AND LIGHTS under a starless sky. From the hotel window I heard nothing but the soft lapping of the sea on the mole.

The next morning, however, I experienced the great moment which made me a real geologist. As I threw the shutters open, the whole splendor of the famous picture before me was unveiled like a vast triptych. From right to left; the sparkling bay hemmed in by mountainous shores; then, close by, the gloomy little fort on the beach; and finally, the colorful city rising landward in a thousand steps.

Upward the vision was cut off by a low cloud. Somewhat disappointed, I was about to turn back into the room when I saw a bright sheen above the clouds.

There the clear-cut triangular silhouette of the summit of Vesuvius seemed to be floating in the air, gleaming white with the new winter's snow, and from its sunken crater a little cloud of smoke idly detached itself. . . .

So it was really true!

Year after year I had read and learned little else but this: that our old earth had changed in countless ways during its endless history, and that the whole variegated mass of strata and rocks of the primeval world and of the present mountain ranges was but the result or relic of such changes; that the earth is still active today, living and working on its old material, adding new matter and energy to its old stores; that it is but an optical illusion to assume that the earth has reached a stability that provides an unshakeable foundation for human planning, and that recent changes are only superficial.

These teachings I had heard and believed. I had defended them against the incredulous and recited them before stern judges in searching examinations. But now I had to realize in an unguarded moment that in reality I had learned nothing at all because that concept of the physical world had not yet become a true possession of my own—not till this unique and unforgettable moment when I became a geologist forever by seeing with my own eyes: THE EARTH IS ALIVE!

Up there in those noble isolated heights above seas and crowds the monstrous happens: the earth, this permanent and time-honored stage of our growing, being, and dying, of our digging and building, thunders and bursts and blows acrid fumes from dark caverns into the pure air we breathe. It spits red fire and flings up hot rocks to let them crash to the ground and smash to bits. There, too, glowing waves rise and flow, burning all life on their way, and freeze into black, crusty rock which adds to the height of the mountain and builds land, thereby adding another day to the geological past.

So it is that the earth itself growing, grows and renews itself.

And as we look, the bright cloud fades into the blue sky and a second one gushes up from the peak. It swells and rises, parting easily, like a soap bubble, from the stony crater rim, which remains bound by terrestrial gravity.

A third cloud follows. Hundreds more; some larger, and more powerful, wrecking the peak; and others, more gentle ones, quietly covering the mountain with dust and ashes, building it step by step to new heights.

Countless eruptions have preceded them, building and destroying, piling up and shattering again. In such fashion, this mountain, softly and smoothly contoured, this cone within a cone, has become for people all over the world the symbol of another, hotter, and more active realm under the cooler one we know, an ever-growing product of a cosmic process of construction patiently carried on through the ages.

The student of the earth thus sees for the very first time the significant relationship between the shape, structure, and history of the terrestrial formation. Deeply moved, he senses the inseparable bonds of matter and space with time and history. And he learns that mountain- and land-forms are the handwriting of the earth, and that he who wanders attentively over the earth's surface can follow the traces of their history. . . .

Africa

To the south, too, Africa looks out from a precipitous escarpment. Before it another vast space spreads out, almost empty, furnished only with the indispensable inventory of the desert. This is the Karroo. But then, still farther to the south, there is not simply a row of hills such as the Lebombos, but a complete range of fold-mountains, as extensive and half as high as the Alps. Like the Alps, these ranges show thrusts and overturned folds leaning asymmetrically to the north, with a small central crystalline zone.

However, everything looks quite different here, at least at first sight—both landscape and geology.

Cape Town, Port Elizabeth, George—these are large, medium, and small cities for white people. These towns have villas and gardens and are surrounded by vineyards and orchards, planted fields, and wooded places where some forest culture is practiced. Here are springs, rivers, aqueducts, and firm bridges. How European would Africa be if it reached farther to the south? Like North and South America, Greenland and India, Africa is a wedge pointing southward. But its point is dull. Thus it terminates along an oblique coastline of about 600 miles just where it begins to become a pleasant abode for spoiled white settlers.

Unlike the southeast coast of Africa, this southern coast is rimmed by two or three rows of folds. The folded mountains of the Cape are found in every school atlas. The blunt point has been long in the making, and is firmly secured by a pair of ramparts.

This is no great trick for the earth. It draws the upper layers into a few folds, like a tablecloth on a table. A few thousand yards are shale and dirty sandstones (graywacke), and, as re-enforcement, a thick plate of quartzite hard as glass. The folds rise toward the north, bend over and dip, then flatten out; beyond, the pattern is repeated. Now there are two folds (anticlines), with a depression (syncline) between them. On these large folds rise several hundred smaller ones, for each good layer likes to have its private tectonics. This is all there is to the Cape mountains; its mechanics are easily understood, and the folding process can be made clear in experiments.

But in nature! What an effort for the short-legged geologist to assemble a picture of even one single larger fold out of some thousands of observations and measurements, or to recognize it as a fold, not to speak of making out the details of its origin and construction. Petroleum geologists, for whom the fold is both the source bed and the container of their liquid fuel, who perforce have to study its shape and structure with extreme care, can tell you some interesting stories about folds.

In dry or in high mountains the study of folds is easier because the large form can be seen from afar. But how arduous it is to crawl about these tectonic giants! An ant, crawling over the trunk of a tree with its prey, need conquer the obstacle only physically. The geologist must conquer it intellectually as well, and must bring it back with him, transformed accurately into black and white drawings. . . .

The Indies

I was looking at the volcano Gunong Tengger. Risen to great heights above the common earth, veiled in clouds, there the dark gates of the underworld yawned, breathing their deadly glow into the cool, pure air.

Or was it a hemisphere that I saw? Did not the round mountainous mass, almost two miles high, with its flattened top, look like a hemisphere of the earth reduced to one two-thousandth part of its terrestrial counterpart? Was I not really planning an abbreviated trip around the world, a scaling of the earth? Out of the moist and hot equatorial zone which girdled the mountain base like a ring of Saturn, through jungle and steppe, through temperate, cloud-bound reaches into polar heights, where, before my eyes, the hollow axis of the earth could appear.

Metaphors, fancies which I spin while impatiently waiting. My gaze goes back and forth between the high peaks, over the palms and the flimsy conveyance now being hitched up in front of the little railroad station for the exciting trip.

Two hours of imperceptible ascent to the foot of the mountain. The sun burned down fiercely on the lowland. Rice and sugar cane fields drank in the warm moisture led to their roots from the mountain; they almost drowned in the superabundance of water.

But as we started up the mountain proper the steppe began. The blessed moisture was abruptly cut off. For it is not feasible to irrigate at this level, and rains fall during only half the year. Blocks of lava were strewn about on the yellow clay soil like meteorites.

We exchanged our wagon for saddle-horses and continued up a steeper grade into a tropical rain forest. At 2,000 feet altitude we entered into a new climate and a third landscape: columnar white trunks held up a portico of green into which lianas climbed, and ferns and orchids built pulpits and nests in the vaulted branches, and sent down roots and shoots like bell-ropes. Seen from the dark ground below, the decorative, feathery crowns of tree ferns rose up like branched candelabra.

After an hour of hard climbing we were released from the forest and came out into a bright land of cultivated fields, gardens, and villages. In the lower Nongkodjadjar eternal spring reigns; higher up at an elevation of about 6,000 feet, there is a misty autumnal region shot through with sunlight. Here the white man comes to life and pokes fun at the shivering Malayans. Here are stone houses and hotels that look like castles. In Tosari we found windows, blankets, fireplaces, and tourist traffic. We were surrounded there by a ring of clouds. Fog drifted over the roofs, and glided through the gorges. Visibility was very poor. Somewhere far below were the hot lowlands. For us island-dwellers they were like deep sea bottoms.

But in the first hour the newcomer feels that up there is something more than alpine air and recuperation, something unseen, yet clearly sensed. There he is in an ominous neighborhood; he has a premonition of great events.

Everybody talks about it: the mountain system, which continues to rise steeply toward invisible peaks; the lulling regularity of its thousands of ravines and ridges which lead upward like the ribs of an opened umbrella; the layers of ashes and slag which slope outward in the form of the underlying mountain. Each layer is but a few inches thick, but each represents the hail of an eruption. How many thousands of explosions, catastrophes, hotly oppressive downpouring of ashes were needed to build up, by such laborious addition, a mountain which reaches from the tropics into the realm of cool clouds and 6,000 feet beyond? One looks, uneasily apprehensive, at volcanic bombs weighing tons embedded in fine volcanic ash. Is it not possible that today, or perhaps day after tomorrow, the mountain may discharge more of these missiles, annihilating the feeble life that has nested on its flanks for a spell?

The hotel guests discuss it; those who had been on top talk differently from the newcomers, and each one has his individual reaction. Among the guests are mothers with their offspring who want only to cool off here and are content to spend the day worrying about their clothes and children. For them Tosari is only less hot than Soerabaja, and for most of them really too cold for comfort.

I too rejoiced a few days in the change to cool mountain air and clouds. Then I took the road into the sacred land. I climbed another 3,000 feet and the tough ponies hardly noticed the even climb. Above the cultivated zone a new forest received me. It consisted exclusively of casuarina trees. Their foliage is feathery, thin, and light, like that of conifers, and provides shadow enough against the sun as it filters through the fog. In a few hours I approached the rim of the crater and met returning visitors. I thought that they would be all smiles and wonder, renewed by the sight of a miracle. This was not the case. They littered the ground with film-wrappings and fruit peels and argued about which road to take, and about the price of rubber.

Meanwhile the casuarina wood became low and wild, the sky showed through, and then, very suddenly and unexpectedly, I stood in a pass-like notch in the high rim. To one side there was a shelter with a bench. Before me the abyss. . . .

I cannot define my feelings on this November in 1911 when I looked down from the Mungal Notch to the gigantic floor of the crater of Tengger. I could not do it then, and can hardly do so now. There, inside the crater, were four volcanic cones, each a sizable mountain, one of them an open crater, smoking. Far beyond this group I could see the steep cone of Seme-roe, one of the highest volcanoes in Asia, which at that moment shot a gnarled vapor cloud into the pure air. My feelings were indescribable.

Among an educated man's strongest experiences are: a view of a broad, interesting landscape; participation in the unfolding of powerful forces and movements of a natural event; and sympathetic pleasure in the simple, rhythmic organization of a work of art. That hour included some of all three. Most volcanoes possess a beautifully simple basic contour, corresponding to their development about a center. In Mount Tengger, however, this geom-etry is compounded and multiplied gigantically in such fashion that it suggests a place of reverence beyond ordinary human concepts. At Mungal Pass I stood on a high ring-like wall which slopes gently on the outside, but drops perpendicularly into the crater. It rises above a plain, almost treeless, as if swept bare, a veritable lake of sand. Within the ring are three open cones; among them the smallest and only active one is Bromo. A fourth, a high, closed cone nearby, looks down on these three.

The cones look as if they had been turned out on a lathe. They remind one of circles with various diameters drawn playfully, one large circle on the outside, and four smaller ones, some touching each other, some inter-secting.

This mathematical fancy bespeaks a deeper meaning. Each later circle is a bit smaller than the preceding one. The constructive forces were sim-ple, and subject to rule both in space and time. In the course of its develop-ment this huge volcano has lived actively five different times, and each life was shorter and weaker than the one before. Its youngest rebirth is Bromo: through its torn crater the soul of the mountain escaped before my eyes, thick white steam in the morning and evening coolness, and during the heat of the day transparent blue clouds of sulphurous gas. Slow, very slow is the mountain's geological death. But from millennium to millennium it becomes quieter, its periods of quiescence longer. The time will come when Bromo, like its predecessors, will be extinct. Then this dark abode of Vul-can, or of the Hindu Brahma, will cover itself with forest and fall into ruins, assuming the pleasing colors of other mountains on the earth.

WIND-STORM
IN THE FOREST

FROM *The Mountains of California*

JOHN MUIR

John Muir, whose exploration of a canyon we include elsewhere in this volume, here writes of the mountain forests of the West. Muir was the most eloquent and the most persistent advocate for the preservation of our American forests by turning them into national parks.

The Yosemite in particular might, with gratitude, have been named for him. But perhaps the Mountain Pine, the Juniper, the Silver Fir, the Hemlock Spruce, are the memorials that he himself would have preferred.

THE MOUNTAIN WINDS, LIKE THE DEW AND RAIN, SUNSHINE AND SNOW, ARE measured and bestowed with love on the forests to develop their strength and beauty. However restricted the scope of other forest influences, that of the winds is universal. The snow bends and trims the upper forests every winter, the lightning strikes a single tree here and there, while avalanches mow down thousands at a swoop as a gardener trims out a bed of flowers. But the winds go to every tree, fingering every leaf and branch and furrowed bole; not one is forgotten; the Mountain Pine towering with outstretched arms on the rugged buttresses of the icy peaks, the lowliest and most retiring tenant of the dells; they seek and find them all, caressing them tenderly, bending them in lusty exercise, stimulating their growth, plucking off a leaf or limb as required, or removing an entire tree or grove, now whispering and cooing through the branches like a sleepy child, now roaring like the ocean; the winds blessing the forests, the forests the winds, with ineffable beauty and harmony as the sure result.

After one has seen Pines six feet in diameter bending like grasses before a mountain gale, and ever and anon some giant falling with a crash that shakes the hills, it seems astonishing that any, save the lowest thickset trees, could ever have found a period sufficiently stormless to establish themselves; or, once established, that they should not, sooner or later, have been blown down. But when the storm is over, and we behold the same forests tranquil

again, towering fresh and unscathed in erect majesty, and consider what
centuries of storms have fallen upon them since they were first planted—hail,
to break the tender seedlings; lightning, to scorch and shatter; snow, winds,
and avalanches, to crush and overwhelm—while the manifest result of all this
wild storm-culture is the glorious perfection we behold; then faith in
Nature's forestry is established, and we cease to deplore the violence of her
most destructive gales, or of any other storm-implement whatsoever.

There are two trees in the Sierra forests that are never blown down,
so long as they continue in sound health. These are the Juniper and the
Dwarf Pine of the summit-peaks. Their stiff, crooked roots grip the storm-
beaten ledges like eagles' claws, while their lithe, cord-like branches bend
round compliantly, offering but slight holds for winds, however violent.
The other alpine conifers—the Needle Pine, Mountain Pine, Two-leaved
Pine, and Hemlock Spruce—are never thinned out by this agent to any
destructive extent, on account of their admirable toughness and the close-
ness of their growth. In general the same is true of the giants of the lower
zones. The kingly Sugar Pine, towering aloft to a height of more than 200
feet, offers a fine mark to storm-winds; but it is not densely foliaged, and its
long, horizontal arms swing round compliantly in the blast, like tresses of
green, fluent algæ in a brook; while the Silver Firs in most places keep their
ranks well together in united strength. The Yellow or Silver Pine is more
frequently overturned than any other tree on the Sierra, because its leaves
and branches form a larger mass in proportion to its height, while in many
places it is planted sparsely, leaving open lanes through which storms may
enter with full force. Furthermore, because it is distributed along the lower
portion of the range, which was the first to be left bare on the breaking
up of the ice-sheet at the close of the glacial winter, the soil it is growing
upon has been longer exposed to post-glacial weathering, and consequently
is in a more crumbling, decayed condition than the fresher soils farther up
the range, and therefore offers a less secure anchorage for the roots.

While exploring the forest zones of Mount Shasta, I discovered the path
of a hurricane strewn with thousands of Pines of this species. Great and
small had been uprooted or wrenched off by sheer force, making a clean
gap, like that made by a snow avalanche. But hurricanes capable of doing
this class of work are rare in the Sierra, and when we have explored the
forests from one extremity of the range to the other, we are compelled to
believe that they are the most beautiful on the face of the earth, however
we may regard the agents that have made them so.

There is always something deeply exciting, not only in the sounds of
winds in the woods, which exert more or less influence over every mind, but
in their varied water-like flow as manifested by the movements of the trees,
especially those of the conifers. By no other trees are they rendered so

extensively and impressively visible, not even by the lordly tropic Palms or tree-ferns responsive to the gentlest breeze. The waving of a forest of the giant Sequoias is indescribably impressive and sublime, but the Pines seem to me the best interpreters of winds. They are mighty waving goldenrods, ever in tune, singing and writing wind-music all their long century lives. Little, however, of this noble tree-waving and tree-music will you see or hear in the strictly alpine portion of the forests. The burly Juniper, whose girth sometimes more than equals its height, is about as rigid as the rocks on which it grows. The slender lash-like sprays of the Dwarf Pine stream out in wavering ripples, but the tallest and slenderest are far too unyielding to wave even in the heaviest gales. They only shake in quick, short vibrations. The Hemlock Spruce, however, and the Mountain Pine, and some of the tallest thickets of the Two-leaved species bow in storms with considerable scope and gracefulness. But it is only in the lower and middle zones that the meeting of winds and woods is to be seen in all its grandeur.

One of the most beautiful and exhilarating storms I ever enjoyed in the Sierra occurred in December, 1874, when I happened to be exploring one of the tributary valleys of the Yuba River. The sky and the ground and the trees had been thoroughly rain-washed and were dry again. The day was intensely pure, one of those incomparable bits of California winter, warm and balmy and full of white sparkling sunshine, redolent of all the purest influences of the spring, and at the same time enlivened with one of the most bracing wind-storms conceivable. Instead of camping out, as I usually do, I then chanced to be stopping at the house of a friend. But when the storm began to sound, I lost no time in pushing out into the woods to enjoy it. For on such occasions Nature has always something rare to show us, and the danger to life and limb is hardly greater than one would experience crouching deprecatingly beneath a roof.

It was still early morning when I found myself fairly adrift. Delicious sunshine came pouring over the hills, lighting the tops of the Pines, and setting free a steam of summery fragrance that contrasted strangely with the wild tones of the storm. The air was mottled with pine-tassels and bright green plumes, that went flashing past in the sunlight like birds pursued. But there was not the slightest dustiness, nothing less pure than leaves, and ripe pollen, and flecks of withered bracken and moss. I heard trees falling for hours at the rate of one every two or three minutes; some uprooted, partly on account of the loose, water-soaked condition of the ground; others broken straight across, where some weakness caused by fire had determined the spot. The gestures of the various trees made a delightful study. Young Sugar Pines, light and feathery as squirrel-tails, were bowing almost to the ground; while the grand old patriarchs, whose massive boles had been tried in a hundred storms, waved solemnly above them, their long, arching branches streaming fluently on the gale, and every needle thrilling and ringing and shedding off keen lances of light like a diamond. The Douglas Spruces, with long sprays drawn out in level tresses, and needles massed in a gray, shimmering glow, presented a most striking appearance as they stood in bold relief along the hilltops. The Madroños in the dells, with their red bark and large glossy leaves tilted every way, reflected the sunshine in throbbing spangles like those one so often sees on the rippled surface of a glacier lake. But the Silver Pines were now the most impressively beautiful of all. Colossal spires 200 feet in height waved like supple goldenrods chanting and bowing low as if in worship, while the whole mass of their long, tremulous foliage was kindled into one continuous blaze of white sun-fire. The force of the gale was such that the most steadfast monarch of them all rocked down to its roots with a motion plainly perceptible when one leaned against it. Nature was holding high festival, and every fiber of the most rigid giants thrilled with glad excitement.

I drifted on through the midst of this passionate music and motion, across many a glen, from ridge to ridge; often halting in the lee of a rock for shelter, or to gaze and listen. Even when the grand anthem had swelled to its highest pitch, I could distinctly hear the varying tones of individual trees —Spruce, and Fir, and Pine, and leafless Oak—and even the infinitely gentle rustle of the withered grasses at my feet. Each was expressing itself in its own way—singing its own song, and making its own peculiar gestures— manifesting a richness of variety to be found in no other forest I have yet seen. The coniferous woods of Canada, and the Carolinas, and Florida, are made up of trees that resemble one another about as nearly as blades of grass, and grow close together in much the same way. Coniferous trees, in general, seldom possess individual character, such as is manifest among Oaks and Elms. But the California forests are made up of a greater number of distinct species than any other in the world. And in them we find, not only a marked differentiation into special groups, but also a marked individuality in almost every tree, giving rise to storm effects indescribably glorious.

Toward midday, after a long, tingling scramble through copses of hazel and ceanothus, I gained the summit of the highest ridge in the neighborhood; and then it occurred to me that it would be a fine thing to climb one of the trees to obtain a wider outlook and get my ear close to the Æolian music of its topmost needles. But under the circumstances the choice of a tree was a serious matter. One whose instep was not very strong seemed in danger of being blown down, or of being struck by others in case they should fall; another was branchless to a considerable height above the ground, and at the same time too large to be grasped with arms and legs in climbing; while others were not favorably situated for clear views. After cautiously casting about, I made a choice of the tallest of a group of Douglas

Spruces that were growing close together like a tuft of grass, no one of which seemed likely to fall unless all the rest fell with it. Though comparatively young, they were about 100 feet high, and their lithe, brushy tops were rocking and swirling in wild ecstasy. Being accustomed to climb trees in making botanical studies, I experienced no difficulty in reaching the top of this one, and never before did I enjoy so noble an exhilaration of motion. The slender tops fairly flapped and swished in the passionate torrent, bending and swirling backward and forward, round and round, tracing indescribable combinations of vertical and horizontal curves, while I clung with muscles firm braced, like a bobolink on a reed.

In its widest sweeps my tree-top described an arc of from twenty to thirty degrees, but I felt sure of its elastic temper, having seen others of the same species still more severely tried—bent almost to the ground indeed, in heavy snows—without breaking a fiber. I was therefore safe, and free to take the wind into my pulses and enjoy the excited forest from my superb outlook. The view from here must be extremely beautiful in any weather. Now my eye roved over the piny hills and dales as over fields of waving grain, and felt the light running in ripples and broad swelling undulations across the valleys from ridge to ridge, as the shining foliage was stirred by corresponding waves of air. Oftentimes these waves of reflected light would break up suddenly into a kind of beaten foam, and again, after chasing one another in regular order, they would seem to bend forward in concentric curves, and disappear on some hillside, like sea-waves on a shelving shore. The quantity of light reflected from the bent needles was so great as to make whole groves appear as if covered with snow, while the black shadows beneath the trees greatly enhanced the effect of the silvery splendor.

Excepting only the shadows there was nothing somber in all this wild sea of Pines. On the contrary, notwithstanding this was the winter season, the colors were remarkably beautiful. The shafts of the Pine and Libocedrus were brown and purple, and most of the foliage was well tinged with yellow; the laurel groves, with the pale undersides of their leaves turned upward, made masses of gray; and then there was many a dash of chocolate color from clumps of Manzanita, and jet of vivid crimson from the bark of the Madroños, while the ground on the hillsides, appearing here and there through openings between the groves, displayed masses of pale purple and brown.

The sounds of the storm corresponded gloriously with this wild exuberance of light and motion. The profound bass of the naked branches and boles booming like waterfalls; the quick, tense vibrations of the pine-needles, now rising to a shrill, whistling hiss, now falling to a silky murmur; the rustling of laurel groves in the dells, and the keen metallic click of leaf on leaf—all this was heard in easy analysis when the attention was calmly bent.

The varied gestures of the multitude were seen to fine advantage, so that one could recognize the different species at a distance of several miles by this means alone, as well as by their forms and colors, and the way they reflected the light. All seemed strong and comfortable, as if really enjoying the storm, while responding to its most enthusiastic greetings. We hear much nowadays concerning the universal struggle for existence, but no struggle in the common meaning of the word was manifest here; no recognition of danger by any tree; no deprecation; but rather an invincible gladness as remote from exultation as from fear.

I kept my lofty perch for hours, frequently closing my eyes to enjoy the music by itself, or to feast quietly on the delicious fragrance that was streaming past. The fragrance of the woods was less marked than that produced during warm rain, when so many balsamic buds and leaves are steeped like tea; but, from the chafing of resiny branches against each other, and the incessant attrition of myriads of needles, the gale was spiced to a very tonic degree. And besides the fragrance from these local sources there were traces of scents brought from afar. For this wind came first from the sea, rubbing against its fresh, briny waves, then distilled through the Redwoods, threading rich ferny gulches, and spreading itself in broad undulating currents over many a flower-enameled ridge of the coast mountains, then across the golden plains, up the purple foot-hills, and into these piny woods with the varied incense gathered by the way.

VIEW OF MOUNT WASHINGTON

THE TRUE STATE
OF ICELAND

FROM Hakluyt's *English Voyages*

ARNGRIMUS JONAS

Richard Hakluyt spent a lifetime gathering an invaluable store of original reports of travels and explorations which he published under the title *Principal Navigations, Traffiques, and Discoveries (The English Voyages)*. He evaluated this enormous project modestly when he said that it had "brought to light many rare and worthy monuments which long have lien miserably scattered in mustie corners . . . and were very like for the greatest part to have been buried in perpetuall oblivion." He lived during the golden age of Elizabethan discovery on ecclesiastical stipends granted him by the Queen for his writings.

This selection from his *Navigations* is a polemical work written in Latin by Arngrimus Jonas, or Arngrimur Jonnsson, sometime after 1600. Jonas, or Jonnsson, was a geographer who, incensed at the slanders regarding Iceland and its mountains, spread by fellow geographers Munster, Frisius, Ziegler and others, set out to refute their findings. We will wager that the reader has never read so original a scientific paper.

A BRIEFE COMMENTARIE OF ICELAND: *wherein the errors of such as have written concerning this Iceland, are detected, and the slanders, and reproaches of certaine strangers, which they have used over-boldly against the people of Iceland are confuted by Arngrimus Jonas, of Iceland.*

There be in this Iland mountaines lift up to the skies, whose tops being white with perpetuall snowe, their roots boile with everlasting fire. The first is towards the West, called Hecla: the other the mountaine of the crosse: and the third Helga. Item: Zieglerus. The rocke or promontorie of Hecla boileth with continuall fire. Item: Saxo. There is in this Iland also a mountaine, which resembling the starrie firmament, with perpetuall flashings of fire, continueth alwayes burning, by uncessant belching out of flames.

MUNSTER AND FRISIUS BEING ABOUT TO REPORT THE WOONDERS OF ISLAND DOE
presently stumble, as it were, upon the thresholde, to the great inconvenience
of them both. For that which they heere affirme of mount Hecla, although
it hath some shew of trueth: notwithstanding concerning the other two
mountaines, that they should burne with perpetuall fire, it is a manifest
errour. For there are no such mountaines to be found in Island, nor yet any
thing els (so farre foorth as wee can imagine) which might minister occasion
of so great an errour unto writers. Howbeit there was seene (yet very lately)
in the yeere 1581 out of a certaine mountaine of South Island lying neere the
Sea, and covered over with continuall snow and frost, a marveilous eruption
of smoake and fire, casting up abundance of stones and ashes. But this mountaine is farre from the other three, which the sayd authours doe mention.
Howbeit, suppose that these things be true which they report of firie mountaines: is it possible therefore that they should seeme strange, or monstrous,
whenas they proceed from naturall causes? What? Doe they any whit pre-
vaile to establish that opinion concerning the hell of Island, which followeth
next after in Munster, Ziegler, and Frisius? For my part, I thinke it no way
tollerable, that men should abuse these, and the like miracles of nature, to
avouch absurdities, or, that they should with a kinde of impietie woonder
at them, as at matters impossible. As though in these kindes of inflamma-
tions, there did not concurre causes of sufficient force for the same purpose.
There is in the rootes of these mountaines a matter most apt to be set on fire,
comming so neere as it doeth to the nature of brimstone and pitch. There
is ayer also, which insinuating it selfe by passages, and holes, into the very
bowels of the earth, doeth puffe up the nourishment of so huge a fire, together with Salt-peter, by which puffing (as it were with certeine bellowes)
a most ardent flame is kindled. For, all these thus concurring, fire hath those
three things, which necessarily make it burne, that is to say, matter, motion,
and force of making passage: matter which is fattie and moyst, and therefore
nourisheth lasting flames: motion which the ayer doeth performe, being
admitted into the caves of the earth: force of making passage, and that the
invincible might of fire it selfe (which can not be without inspiration of ayre,
and can not but breake foorth with an incredible strength) doeth bring to
passe: and so (even as in undermining trenches, and engines or great warre-
like ordinance, huge yron bullets are cast foorth with monstrous roaring,
and cracking, by the force of kindled Brimstone, and Salt-peeter, whereof
Gunne-powder is compounded) chingle and great stones being skorched in
that fiery gulfe, as it were in a furnace, together with abundance of sande
and ashes, are vomitted up and discharged, and that for the most part not
without an earthquake: which, if it commeth from the depth of the earth
(being called by Possidonius, Succussio), it must either be an opening or a

quaking. Opening causeth the earth in some places to gape, and fall a sunder. By quaking the earth is heaved up and swelleth, and sometimes (as Plinie saith) casteth out huge heaps: such an earth-quake was the same which I even now mentioned, which in the yere 1581 did so sore trouble the South shore of Island. And this kinde of earth-quake is most clearkely described by Pontanus in these verses:

> The stirring breath runnes on with stealing steppes, urged now up, and now enforced downe:
> For freedome eke tries all, it skips, it leaps, to ridde it selfe from uncouth dungeon.
> Then quakes the earth as it would burst anon,
> The earth yquakes, and walled cities quiver,
> Strong quarries cracke, and stones from hilles doe shiver.

I thought good to adde these things, not that I suppose any man to be ignorant thereof: but least other men should thinke that we are ignorant, and therefore that we will runne after their fables, which they do from hence establish. But yet there is somewhat more in these three fained mountaines of Island, which causeth the sayd writers not a little to woonder, namely whereas they say that their foundations are alwayes burning, and yet for all that, their toppes be never destitute of snowe. Howbeit, it beseemeth not the authority and learning of such great clearks to marveile at this, who can not but well know the flames of Mount Aetna, which (according to Plinie) being full of snowe all Winter, notwithstanding (as the same man witnesseth) it doth alwayes burne. Wherefore, if we will give credit unto them, even this mountaine also, sithens it is covered with snowe, and yet burneth, must be a prison of uncleane soules: which thing they have not doubted to ascribe unto Hecla, in regard of the frozen top, and the firie bottome. And it is no marveile that fire lurking so deepe in the roots of a mountaine, and never breaking forth except it be very seldome, should not be able continually to melt the snowe covering the toppe of the sayd mountaine. For in Caira (or Capira) also, the highest toppes of the mountaine are sayd continually to be white with snowe: and those in Veragua likewise, which are five miles high, and never without snowe, being distant notwithstanding but onely 10 degrees from the equinoctiall. We have heard that either of the forsayd Provinces standeth neere unto Paria. What, if in Teneriffa (which is one of the Canarie or fortunate Ilands) the Pike so called, arising into the ayre, according to Munster, eight or nine Germaine miles in height, and continually flaming like Aetna: yet (as Benzo an Italian, and Historiographer of the West Indies witnesseth) is it not able to melt the girdle of snowe embracing the middest thereof. Which thing, what reason have we more to admire in the mountaine of Hecla? And thus much briefly concerning firie mountaines.

Now that also is to be amended, whereas they write that these mountaines are lifted up even unto the skies. For they have no extraordinarie height beyond the other mountaines of Island, but especially that third mountaine, called by Munster Helga, and by us Helgafel, that is the holy mount, standing just by a monastery of the same name, being covered with snowe, upon no part thereof in Summer time, neither deserveth it the name of an high mountaine, but rather of an humble hillocke, never yet (as I sayd in the beginning of this section) so much as once suspected of burning. Neither yet ought perpetuall snowe to be ascribed to Hecla onely, or to a few others; for Island hath very many such snowy mountaines, all which the Cosmographer (who hath so extolled and admired these three) should not easily finde out, and reckon up in a whole yere. And that also is not to be omitted, that mount Hecla standeth not towards the West, as Munster and Ziegler have noted, but betweene the South and the East: neither is it an headland, but rather a mid-land hill.

Continueth alwayes burning &c. whosoever they be that have ascribed unto Hecla perpetuall belching out of flames, they are farre besides the marke: insomuch that as often as it hath bene enflamed, our countreymen have recorded it in their yerely Chronicles for a rare accident: namely in the yeeres of Christ 1104, 1157, 1222, 1300, 1341, 1362, and 1389: For from that yeere we never heard of the burning of this mountaine untill the yeere 1558, which was the last breaking foorth of fire in that mountaine. In the meane time I say not that is impossible, but that the bottome of the hill may inwardly breed and nourish flames, which at certaine seasons (as hath bene heretofore observed) have burst out, and perhaps may do the like hereafter.

Neare unto the mountaines (the 3. fornamed Hecla &c.) there be three vaste holes, the depth whereof, especially at mount Hecla, cannot be discerned by any man, be he never so sharpe sighted: but there appeare to the beholders thereof certaine men at that instant plunged in, & as yet drawing their breath, who answere their friends (exhorting them with deepe sighs to returne home) that they must depart to mount Hecla: and with that, they suddenly vanish away.

TO CONFIRME THE FORMER LIE, OF AN EARTHLY & VISIBLE HELL (ALBEIT I WILL easily grant that Frisius in writing these things did not entend to reproch any, but only to blaze abroad new & incredible matters) certaine idle companions knowing neither hell nor heaven have invented this fable, no lesse reprochfull then false, and more vaine & detestable then Sicilian scoffes.

Which fellowes these writers (being otherwise men of excellent parts, and to whom learning is much indebted) have followed with an over hastie judgement.

But it were to be wished, that none would write Histories with so great a desire of setting foorth novelties & strange things, that they feare not, in that regard to broch any fabulous & old-wives toyes, & so to defile pure gold with filthy mire. But I pray you, how might those drowned men be swimming in the infernal lake, & yet for al that, parleing with their acquaintance & friends? What? Will you conjure, & raise up unto us from death to life old Orpheus conferring with his wife Euridice (drawen backe againe down to the Stigian flood) & in these parts of the world, as it were by the bankes of snowey Tanais, & Hebrus descanting upon his harpe? But in very deed although others will not acknowledge the falshood, & vanity of these trifles, yet Cardane being a diligent considerer of all things in his 18. booke de subtilitate, doth acknowledge & find them out. Whose words be these. There is Hecla a mountaine in Island, which burneth like unto Ætna at certain seasons, & hereupon the common people have conceived an opinion this long time, that soules are there purged: some, least they should seeme liars, heape up more vanities to this fable, that it may appeare to be probable, & agreeable to reason. But what be those vanities? namely, they feine certaine ghosts answering them, that they are going to mount Hecla: as the same Cardane saith. And further he addeth. Neither in Island only, but every where (albeit seldome) such things come to passe. And then he tels this storie following of a man-killing spright. There was (saith he) solemnized this last yeare the funerall of a common citizen, in the gate neare unto the great Church, by that marketplace, which in regard of the abundance of herbs, in our toong hath the name of the herbmarket. There meets with me one of mine acquaintance: I (according to the custome of Phisitians) presently aske of what disease the man died? he giveth me answere that this man used to come home from his labour 3. houres within night: one night among the rest he espied an hobgoblin pursuing him: which to avoid, he ran away with al speed: but being caught by the spright, he was throwne down upon the ground. He would faine have made a shout, & was not able. At length (when the spright & he had struggled together upon the ground a good while) he was found by certain passengers, & carried home halfe dead. And when he was come to himselfe againe, being asked what was the matter, he up and tolde this strange relation. Hereupon (being utterly daunted, & discouraged, when neither by his friends, nor by Phisitians, nor by Priests, he could be perswaded, that these things were but his owne conceits, & that there was no such matter) 8. daies after he died. I heard also afterward of others which were his neighbors, that no man could more constantly affirme himselfe to be wounded of his enemy, then this man did, that he was cast upon the ground by a ghost. And when some demanded what he did, after he was tumbled on the earth? The dead man (quoth he) laying his hands to my throat, went about to strangle me: neither was there any remedy, but by defending my selfe with mine own hands. When others doubted least he might suffer these things of a living man, they asked him how he could discerne a dead man from a living? To this, he rendered a very probable reason, saying that he seemed in handling to be like Cottum, & that he had no weight, but held him down by maine force. And presently after he addeth. In like manner as in Island, so in the desert sands of Ægypt, Æthiopia, and India, where the sunne is hoat, the very same apparitions, the same sprights are wont to delude wayfaring men. Thus much Cardane. Yet from hence (I trow) no man will conclude as our writers of Island do, that in the places of Ægypt, Æthiopia, and India, there is a prison of damned soules.

I thought good to write these things out of Cardane, that I may bring even the testimony of strangers on our sides, against such monstrous fables. This place of Cardane implieth these two things, namely y^t apparitions of sprights are not proper to Island alone (which thing al men know, if they do not maliciously feigne themselves to be ignorant). And secondly that that conference of the dead with the living in ye gulfe of Hecla is not grounded upon any certainty, but only upon fables coined by some idle persons, being more vaine then any bubble, which the brutish common sort have used, to confirme their opinion of the tormenting of soules. And is there any man so fantasticall, that wilbe induced to beleeve these gulfes, mentioned by writers, to be any where extant, although they be never so ful of dead mens miracles? yea doubtlesse. For from hence also they say, y^t reproches are justly used against our nation: namely, y^t there is nothing in all the world more base, & worthlesse then it, which conteineth hell within the bounds therof. This verely is the good that we have gotten by those historiographers, who have bin so greedy to publish novelties. But this opinion, bred by the sottishnes of the common people hath hitherto (as I hope) bene sufficiently overthrown as a thing foolish & vaine, and as being devised for the upbrayding of our nation. Wherefore, proceede (friendly Reader) and be farther instructed in this philosophy of infernall secrets.

MOUNTAIN FOXES
AND FLOWERS

FROM *Swiss Essays*

L L E W E L Y N P O W Y S

It may be distorting a parallel to venture a judgment that the writings of Llewelyn Powys and John Addington Symonds have a quality in common by virtue of the fact that both were prone to tuberculosis and spent long periods in the Swiss Alps. One seems to find a self-centeredness in their writing that might well have resulted from a closer intimacy with death than most of us have; and perhaps thereby, greater intensity of feeling and delicacy of perception for a living flower, a moving animal, a falling snow—for all the small details of living that well people always assume they will have time to notice later.

Whether the analogy is valid or not, these qualities are accented in Powys' writing. His books, whatever their surface subject, are all highly subjective reflections of himself, his *Swiss Essays,* from which these selections are taken, particularly so. They offer glimpses of that poetic vision which Powys thought "the best clue to life."

IN THE MOUNTAINS OF SWITZERLAND DURING THE MONTHS OF FEBRUARY AND March the hillsides begin to ring with a reiterated tinkling as though the larch-tree tops, already brushed to a faint yellow by the first upflowing of the sap, were each one hung with little icicle bells. The gay notes come from the throats of innumerable little tits who, aware of the increased warmth of the sun upon their tiny backs, realize that the snows will soon be melting and that the days of love-making are very near, days of short dancing flights across sloping lawns covered with flowers virginal and fresh. The calling of the tits is accompanied by sounds of running water continually audible under the deep snow.

In the dead of winter, except for the hoarse croaking of solitary crows, nature is strangely silent, held, as it were, under a spell of an ubiquitous contraction sharp and bright as the rarefied air. Only at night, when the glitter of the stars is blinding, there may be heard from the freezing snow-slopes of the forests the husky barking of the hunting fox. It is a deeper and more resonant sound than the ghost-yapping we listen to from the foot-paths of our island meadows. The humour of the Alpine foxes, with their whitish moonlight buttocks, is incomparably fiercer than that of the little harried red creature with which we are acquainted. It is true that a good dog is able to master an Alpine fox in single fight, but should a second fox come to the help of the first then the dog will be most surely killed and eaten. It is no uncommon thing for a forester to come upon the remains of a deer that has fallen a prey to these truculent animals. If the snow is too soft to support the roe-deer's narrow hoofs, and yet has a surface hard enough to leave unhampered the movements of her tormentor, she will soon sink exhausted from the savage bites given to her neck as she flounders about helpless. These mountain foxes are not only physically formidable, but the extreme privations endured by them through the long winters have sharp-ened their wits to a sinister degree.

In Dorset I have disturbed cliff foxes searching the rock-pools under White Nose for shell-fish, and the foxes of Switzerland will haunt the banks of a mountain stream in the same way with the prospect of snatching a trout out of a shallow pool or picking up a fresh-water crab. In the winter they sustain life for the most part on hares, birds, and mice, but it is no uncom-mon thing to find a little pad of half-digested moss in their bellies. In the summer they fare better, feasting themselves as often as they can with the flesh of a plump marmot. They will eat hedgehogs also. They have devised a most knavish trick for persuading these quaint creatures to uncurl them-selves. They will stand over them with lifted hindleg until the obstinate urchin no longer being able to tolerate such an ignominy, will unroll itself sufficiently to allow of its intestines being bitten into. Small wonder that a creature capable of inventing so discreditable a monkey-trick should have won a reputation in the folklore of every country for being "wise in coun-cil."

In medieval times the skin of a fox was called its "case." Shakespeare uses the expression when the Duke reproaches Viola for her deceits:

> O thou dissembling cub! What wilt thou be
> When Time hath sow'd a grizzle on thy case?

These mountain foxes are so lazy that if they can help it they will never dig out their own earths. Just as wart-hogs in Africa leave heavy excavating to the ant bears, so do these rangers abandon such dull labour to their sober and courteous neighbour the badger. And so good-natured is that great weasel that it will share lodgings, no doubt reluctantly, with the lithe rogue whose habits are constitutionally and notoriously unfastidious and insani-tary. I know of just such a double tenement in the forests here. The smell that comes from the entrance of this hole is not of amber, and testifies to the presence of Dan Russel. Such mountain earths are often so large that it is possible for a peasant hunter to crawl down them, and I am told that the badger is never to be feared, for, friendly and magnanimous as always, he merely displays his displeasure at so unexpected an intrusion by a series of pats with his forepaws; whereas the fox will rush up to the man, give him one shrewd bite, and scuttle back to the further recesses of the burrow.

Yet though he lacks the simple dignity of the badger there is something appealing about the feckless nonchalance of the fox, who, like our own race, has ever depended more upon his brain than upon his brawn. Chaucer puts into the mouth of his farmyard cock an admirable description of this marauder who everywhere survives against odds. The philosophic chanticleer tells his wife Pertelote of the dread monster he has seen in his nightmare:

> His colour was bitwixe yelow and reed
> And tipped was his tail, and bothe his eeres
> With blak, unlik the remnaunt of his heres.
> His snowt was smal, with glowynge eyen tweye;
> Yet of his look for fear almost I deye;
> This caused me my gronyng doubteles.

On my coming down from Cambridge in the year nineteen hundred and seven I got work as a schoolmaster at Bromsgrove. It was not a happy period of my life and if anything redeems it in retrospect it is the interest that I learned to take in wild flowers. I discovered that the finding of these seely weeds, and the learning of their names, offered me a sure escape from my spiritual imprisonments. Issuing one afternoon from "the Steps"—a fine old eighteenth-century house where I dwelt in dolorous unease with my colleagues—I happened to notice in a damp ditch a little yellow flower that was obviously neither a hawkweed nor a dandelion. I enclosed it in my Sunday letter to my mother and soon received an answer: "Your dear father says that the flower you have found is a very common one and that its name is coltsfoot." The ancients used to call coltsfoot *Filius ante Patrem* and in after years a chance sight of this flower never failed to bring back the discomfiture I experienced over my father's casual comment.

It so happened that for five years I lived in the centre of a garden preserve of these very flowers. This was when we rented one of the coastguard cottages on the top of White Nose in Dorset. Here in a neglected glistening sea-salt parterre—square as a barrack plot—they grew in great profusion as early as February, lifting up their narrow faces of good cheer, and in the late spring covering the ground with their broad sheltering leaves, under the cool shadows of which I have known more than one meadow-pippet to rear its brood in safety. It is the appearance of this same gallant flower that encourages the Swiss to believe, when all is still crisp and hard, that the snows of the long winter will presently really and truly take their departure. Indeed the flower is sometimes called *Lauene,* on account of its being seen on the edges of the earth-avalanches that are so often laved and loosened in the universal thaw. The plant takes its name, of course, from the shape of its leaf rather than from that of the flower, the leaf being supposed to resemble a hoof, the hoof of a donkey or filly—*fulli fuess.* Swiss children are fond of making toy sunshades and looking-glasses out of these singular leaves. The looking-glasses are contrived by removing the furry white gossamer-like veil that is spread over the leaf's underside, a procedure that exposes to the view, beyond all expectation, a miraculous surface of shining satin-like green, a ready enough mirror to a child's fancy for the reflection of the pert, privy face of a darling doll.

The coltsfoot is quickly followed by the spring crocus, which before the dung has even been spread, populates the meadows in unnumbered hosts, offering to goat and sheep a dainty diet, but one villainously ungrateful to man and cattle. Then follow the gentian and the spring anemone, the latter featly furnished with mantles of fur to clout it from the cold. Dr. Martha Egli, in an excellent little book, tells of an old play that children have with gentians, with this matchless mountain flower that borrows its hue from the sea, from the sapphire, from the sky, *Herrgottsblumen,* God's flower, as it is called. Holding the gentian between finger and thumb the little girls boldly chant the words, "Dead, dead, come out," and at the same time squeeze and twist at the flower until its pistil—a little pale corpse—is propelled from the bell. By this ritual they actually think to surprise and exorcise death himself, curiously couched for the nonce in the orifice of these triumphant trumpets.

The gentians are in their glory when the goat-boys first begin to bring down from the high mountains bunches of Alpine roses, still only in bud. The fragrance of these tough immature nosegays is as dear to a true Swiss as is the first sight of an edelweiss. The odour that these wild rough bunches emit is feral beyond all conception. They smell of mountain winds, of mountain rains, of moss, of bark, of lichens cold to the touch, of the fells of chamois, and of the breath of eagles. This wild rhododendron gives a glow to the high slopes, a glow like the dawn, the colour of its flower strikingly contrasting with the dark green of its lancet-shaped leaves. Another name for this low bushy plant is mountain-hen-flower, *Hühnerbluest,* a reference to the impenetrable shelter it offers to these shy game birds.

The Alpine roses are still in full blossom when the dandelions begin to gladden the valleys on every side with their fairy gold. Not a footpath way, not a lane, not a grey fence or swart stable but is fringed with the gaudy discs of these life-affirming flowers. I have often met children carrying them home by the basket-full, the little girls, as much as the flowers at their elbows, savouring of the first hot sunshine of the year; bland and blameless and sun-saturated as window-sill kittens. These same children are fond of using the milk-filled stems of this gypsy salad for the making of shepherd's pipes so that they may play to toads and snails and dutiful lady-birds the plaintive nursery ditties of long ago.

> O evil day! if I were sullen
> While Earth herself is adorning
> This sweet May-morning,
> And the children are culling
> On every side
> In a thousand valleys far and wide,
> Fresh flowers; while the sun shines warm
> And the babe leaps up on his mother's arm.

When the dandelion clocks are all "telling the time," and the Alpine roses are past their blossoming, the valley meadows lie ready for the first swath to be cut. Often it happens that the butterflies and faltering moths which, hour after hour, wander and waver above the clustering flower-heads, hold their frivolous surveillance over fields of separate colour-patches, certain flowers dominating certain acres, or creating in wide patterns monochrome carpets of gold, of pink, of violet, of Chinese white, according to the wealth of the ranunculi, of the pink campions, of the hearts'-ease, of the Queen Anne's-Lace, that occupies this or that portion of the sloping grounds. I once visited the tents of two little sisters, Marteli and Anneli, tents pitched at the edge of the wide green seas of these quilted plots; honey-plots that would have outdone in their light loveliness even the floors of Botticelli's imagination. And when I looked at these broad prospects of jostling flowers, I could not but believe that life in itself is its own justification, and that however transitory its passage, and however charged it may be with execrable savagery, it can indeed be rightly carried upon wings of trust without despair.

It would serve us little to make an over-scrupulous list of the flowers that decorate the hay-fields of the valley, those valleys where "azure pillars of the hearth arise" from the houses of the peasants. Rampions, snake-weeds, wild pink, and man's troth are perhaps the most conspicuous. Man's troth, or *Nigritella,* is a heavily scented dark-headed little orchis that has gathered about it in the passing of the centuries much romantic lore. The peasants regard it with suspicion, not only because it flourishes best on poor soil and is rumoured to give a bluish colour to the milk of the cows that eat it, but also on account of other less ponderable properties. Women, it is rumoured, know how to brew love-potions out of it. It is likely enough the very plant that the wife of Lucretius put to such ill use, for a single one of its flowers slipped beneath the pillow of a too light-hearted boy will make him utterly besotted, just as a mountain girl, before free as the wind, can be made complaisant by the lodging of the head of one of these worts in the pocket of her apron.

The second mowing sees the valley sadly scanted of its flowers. The grass is luxuriant enough, but the scythes are sharpened before ungarnished slopes. As at the earlier time, the implements glitter and glance like swords at the hour before dawn, but the honour of the fields has departed. It is an emerald aftermath. This is not yet the case on the mountain tops, with the hay made upon those heights that brush against the ceilings of the sky:

> Mountains on whose barren breast
> The labouring clouds do often rest.

On the very crest of the Jacob's Horn above Clavadel there grows a pasture patch of the yellow flower called Villous hawkweed (*Pervière Villeuse*). It is a favourite food of the chamois, a golden food that dances and nods against those lofty spaces.

> In the house of the moon where I was born
> They fed a silver unicorn
> On golden flowers of the sun.

Gone now and forgotten in the dales is the soldanella with its fringed edges, gone the water-avens, gone the grass of Parnassus, the white dryas, and the heaven-keys (*Primula auricula*). A few white clovers only remain— God's flesh, or heaven's bread, as they are called. Then follows the idle season of Martinmas when every hour the rowan tree berries ripen and redden, and the days grow shorter and the nights grow longer, and the spirits of men and women are troubled by vague misgivings. It is a time of recollections; and there is suddenly to be seen everywhere the last lonely flower of the year. This flower is the autumn crocus, the saffron crocus. In all directions they open their frail petals with solicitude, decorating the lifeless faded fields before the winter whiteness envelops all. This colchicum autumnale, or *Herbstzeitlose,* as the Germans have named it, is a flower wistful as a solitary street-cry heard at Michaelmas by a weeping child.

Its appearance is a sure sign of the nearness of the dark solstice. In the old days it was the custom of women to pick the first autumn crocus that they saw and to cover their hands with its juice, hoping that some occult virtue in it would preserve the suppleness of their fingers through the long "spinning evenings."

To a poet's eye the smockless nakedness of these flowers is a delight, and yet the mere look of them has provoked cruelty. If a girl's chastity is suspected it is an ancient usage to strew the path that leads from her father's house to the family washing-well with handfuls of these flowers. A happier association may be found in the name *Chilte-blumen*, meaning the flower that shows itself at that time of the year when young men, after the evening milking is over, are drawn to the houses of their sweethearts; the windows, because of the thickening autumn twilight, being already lamplit.

Then at the end of November, or at the beginning of December, the snow falls in real earnest, and all the bulbs and seeds and tiny twisting roots of the fugitive summer flowers hide and huddle for months together under massy snows, not under snow that easily melts away as in England, but under weighty loads that day after day press down ever more ponderously upon the wintry grass.

In the high mountains the only living thing that thrives is the lichen known as Icelandic moss. Legend declares that this moss was at one time a succulent grass-green herb, a herb that provided the cows with so much milk that the men of the mountains grew careless and made, out of their plenary surplus, cheese-balls for their children to sport with, and, worse still, washed their women in the white fluid.

> Up he has taken his fair lady,
> Gar'd was her wi' the milk!

The legend relates that one day, out from a grove of arven-trees, Jesus appeared in the form of a beggar. He accosted those luxurious dairy-men, and on being refused the alms he craved of them, the gentle God who had always prized highly the grass of the fields, punished these come-day-go-day rogues by changing their valuable milk-producing weed, nish as water-cress, into Icelandic moss, into "the misery that grows under the snow." He made it a sapless dead dry lichen that never again would have anything to do with the spring-time meadow-valleys, where fieldmice, blunt of nose and as large as water-rats, frolic at the breaking of their hibernating fast; and where "the myriads of rivulets hurrying thro' the lawn" mingle their tinkling with the tinkling of cattle-bells and with the haunting sounds of children's voices intermittently heard shouting through the happy hollow air of an April afternoon.

ON THE STRUCTURE AND ACTION OF VOLCANOS

FROM *Views of Nature*

ALEXANDER VON HUMBOLDT

When Alexander von Humboldt died in 1859 at the age of ninety, the world went into mourning for "the greatest man since Aristotle." Time and history tend to diminish these sweeping verdicts. There is no denying, however, Humboldt's enormous intellectual stature. He made original contributions to botany, geography, meteorology, oceanography, zoology, anthropology; currents, bays, and mountain peaks were named for him; he corresponded with the most famous men of his day and kings were proud to talk with him.

Humboldt compared his own style to a "Warsaw dressing gown with forty pockets of parentheses." That his Warsaw dressing gown with its many pockets was both functional and decorative we can see from this extract from his *Views of Nature*.

LANGUAGE, WHICH SO FREQUENTLY IMPARTS PERMANENCE AND AUTHORITY TO first, and often also erroneous views, but which points, as it were, instinctively to the truth, has applied the term *volcanic* to all eruptions of subterranean fire and molten matter; to columns of smoke and vapour which ascend sporadically from rocks, as at Colares, after the great earthquake of Lisbon; to Salses, or argillaceous cones emitting moist mud, asphalt, and hydrogen, as at Girgenti in Sicily, and at Turbaco in South America; to hot Geyser springs, which rise under the pressure of elastic vapours; and, in general, to all operations of impetuous natural forces which have their seat deep in the interior of our planet. In Central America (Guatimala) and in the Philippine Islands, the natives even formally distinguish between *Volcanes de agua y de fuego,* volcanos emitting water, and those emitting fire; designating by the former appellation, mountains from which subterranean waters burst forth from time to time, accompanied by a dull hollow sound and violent earthquakes.

Without denying the connection, which undoubtedly exists among the phenomena just referred to, it would seem advisable to apply more definite terms to the physical as well as to the mineralogical portion of the science of geology, and not at one time to designate by the word *volcano* a mountain terminating in a permanent fire-emitting mouth, and at another to apply it to any subterranean cause, be it what it may, of volcanic action. . . .

Volcanos which communicate with the atmosphere by means of fire-emitting mouths, such as conical basaltic hills, and dome-like craterless trachytic mountains (the latter being sometimes low, like the Sarcouy, and sometimes high, like the Chimborazo), form various groups. Comparative geography draws our attention, at one time, to small Archipelagos or independent mountain-systems, with craters and lava streams, like those in the Canary Isles and the Azores, and without craters or true lava streams, as in the Euganean hills, and the Siebengebirge near Bonn; at another time, it makes us acquainted with volcanos arranged in single or double chains, and extending for many hundred miles in length, either running parallel with the main direction of the range, as in Guatimala, Peru, and Java, or intersecting its axis at right angles, as in tropical Mexico. In this land of the Aztecs fire-emitting trachytic mountains alone attain the high snow limit: they are ranged in the direction of a parallel of latitude, and have probably been upheaved from a chasm extending over upwards of 420 miles, intersecting the whole continent from the Pacific to the Atlantic.

This crowding together of volcanos, either in rounded groups or double lines, affords the most convincing proof that their action does not depend on slight causes located near the surface, but that they are great and deep-seated phenomena. The whole of the eastern portion of the American continent, which is poor in metals, has in its present condition no fire-emitting openings, no trachytic masses, and perhaps no basalt containing olivine. All the volcanos of America are united in the portion of the continent opposite to Asia, along the chain of the Andes, which runs nearly due north and south over a distance of more than 7200 miles.

The whole elevated table-land of Quito, which is surmounted by the high mountains of Pichincha, Cotopaxi, and Tunguragua, constitutes one sole volcanic hearth. The subterranean fire bursts sometimes from one and sometimes from another of these openings, which have generally been regarded as independent volcanos. The progressive movement of the fire has, for three centuries, inclined from north to south. Even the earthquakes, which so fearfully devastate this portion of the globe, afford striking evidence of the existence of subterranean communications, not only between countries where there are no volcanos—as has long been known—but likewise between volcanic apertures situated at a distance from each other. Thus the volcano of Pasto, east of the river Guaytara, continued during three months of the year 1797, to emit, uninterruptedly, a lofty column of smoke, until it suddenly ceased at the moment of the great earthquake of Riobamba (at a distance of 240 miles), and the mud eruption of the "Moya," in which from thirty to forty thousand Indians perished.

The sudden appearance, on the 30th of January, 1811, of the island of Sabrina, in the group of the Azores, was the precursor of the dreadful earthquakes which, further westward, shook, from May, 1811, to June, 1813, almost uninterruptedly, first the Antilles, then the plains of the Ohio and Mississippi, and lastly, the opposite coasts of Venezuela or Caracas. Thirty days after the total destruction of the beautiful capital of the province, there was an eruption of the long inactive volcano of St. Vincent, in the neighbouring islands of the Antilles. A remarkable phenomenon accompanied this eruption: at the moment of this explosion, which occurred on the 30th of April, 1811, a terrible subterranean noise was heard in South America, over a district of more than 35,000 square miles. The inhabitants of the banks of the Apure, at the confluence of the Rio Nula, and those living on the remote sea-coast of Venezuela, agreed in comparing this sound to the noise of heavy artillery. The distance from the confluence of the Rio Nula with the Apure (by which I entered the Orinoco) to the volcano of St. Vincent, measured in a straight line, is no less than 628 miles. This noise was certainly not propagated through the air, and must have arisen from some deep-seated subterranean cause; its intensity was, moreover, hardly greater on the shores of the Caribbean sea, near the seat of the raging volcano, than in the interior of the country in the basin of the Apure and the Orinoco.

It would be useless to multiply examples of this nature, by adducing others which I have collected: I will therefore only refer to one further instance, namely, the memorable earthquake of Lisbon, an important phenomenon in the annals of Europe. Simultaneously with this event, which took place on the 1st of November, 1755, not only were the Lakes of Switzerland and the sea off the Swedish coasts violently agitated, but in the eastern portion of the Antilles, near the islands of Martinique, Antigua, and Barbadoes, the tide, which never exceeds thirty inches, suddenly rose upwards of twenty feet. All these phenomena prove, that subterranean forces are manifested either dynamically, expansively, and attended by commotion, in earthquakes; or possess the property of producing, or of chemically modifying substances in volcanos; and they further show, that these forces are not seated near the surface in the thin crust of the earth, but deep in the interior of our planet, whence through fissures and unfilled veins they act simultaneously at widely distant points of the earth's surface. . . .

If, in the newspaper reports of great eruptions, we often find assertions made of an entire change of form in Mount Vesuvius, and if these assertions appear to be confirmed by the picturesque views of the volcano made at Naples, the cause of the error arises from the outlines of the margins of the crater having been confounded with those of the cones of eruption accidentally formed in its centre, the bottom of which has been raised by the force of vapours. A cone of eruption of this kind, formed by the accumulation of masses of rapilli and scoriæ, gradually came to view, above the south-eastern margin of the crater, between the years 1816 and 1818. The eruption in the month of February, 1822, increased this cone to such an elevation, that it projected from 107 to 117 feet above the north-western margin of the crater (the Rocca del Palo). This remarkable cone, which was at length regarded at Naples as the actual summit of Vesuvius, fell in with a fearful crash at the last eruption, on the night of the 22nd of October; in consequence of which, the bottom of the crater, which had continued uninterruptedly accessible from the year 1811, is now nearly 800 feet below the northern and 213 feet below the southern margin of the volcano. The varying form and relative position of the cones of eruption, the apertures of which must not, as they sometimes are, be confounded with the crater of the volcano, give to Vesuvius at different epochs a peculiar physiognomy; so much so, that the historiographer of this volcano, by a mere inspection of Hackert's landscapes in the Palace of Portici, might guess the exact year in which the artist had made his sketch, by the outline of the summit of the mountain, according as the northern or southern side is represented in respect to height.

Twenty-four hours after the fall of the cone of scoriæ, which was 426 feet high, and when the small but numerous streams of lava had flowed off, on the night between the 23rd and 24th of October, there began a fiery eruption of ashes and rapilli, which continued uninterruptedly for twelve days, but was most violent during the first four days. During this period the explosions in the interior of the volcano were so loud that the mere vibrations of the air caused the ceilings to crack in the Palace of Portici, although no shocks of an earthquake were then or had previously been experienced. A remarkable phenomenon was observed in the neighbouring villages of Resina, Torre del Greco, Torre del' Annunziata, and Bosche Tre Case. Here the atmosphere was so completely saturated with ashes that the whole region was enveloped in complete darkness during many hours in the middle of the day. The inhabitants were obliged to carry lanterns with them through the streets, as is often done in Quito during the eruptions of Pichincha. Never had the flight of the inhabitants been more general, for lava streams are less dreaded even than an eruption of ashes, a phenomenon unknown here in any degree of intensity, and one which fills the imaginations of men with images of terror from the vague tradition of the manner in which Herculaneum, Pompeii, and Stabiæ were destroyed.

The hot aqueous vapour which issued from the crater during the eruption, and diffused itself through the atmosphere, formed, on cooling, a dense cloud, which enveloped the column of ashes and fire, that rose to an elevation of between 9000 and 10,000 feet above the level of the sea. So sudden a condensation of vapour, and, as Gay Lussac has shown, the formation of the cloud itself, tended to increase electric tension. Flashes of forked lightning darted in all directions from the column of ashes, while the rolling thunder might be clearly distinguished from the deep rumbling sounds within the volcano. In no other eruption had the play of the electric forces been so powerfully manifested as on this occasion.

On the morning of the 26th of October the strange report was circulated that a stream of boiling water was gushing from the crater, and pouring down the cone of cinders. Monticelli, the zealous and learned observer of the volcano, soon perceived that this erroneous report originated in an optical illusion, and that the supposed stream of water was a great quantity of dry ashes which issued like drift sand from a crevice in the highest margin of the crater. The long drought, which had parched and desolated the fields before this eruption of Vesuvius, was succeeded, towards the termination of the phenomenon, by a continued and violent rain, occasioned by the *volcanic storm* which we have just described. A similar phenomenon characterizes the termination of an eruption in all zones of the earth. As the cone of cinders is usually wrapped in clouds at this period, and as the rain is poured forth with most violence near this portion of the volcano, streams of mud are generally observed to descend from the sides in all directions. The terrified peasant looks upon them as streams of water that rise from the interior of the volcano and overflow the crater, while the deceived geologist believes that he can recognise in them either sea-water or muddy products of the volcano, the so-called *eruptions boueuses,* or, in the language of the old French systematisers, products of an igneo-aqueous liquefaction.

Where, as is generally the case in the chain of the Andes, the summit of the volcano penetrates beyond the snow-line, attaining sometimes an elevation twice as great as that of Mount Etna, the inundations we have described are rendered very frequent and destructive, owing to the melting and permeating snow.

These are phenomena which have a meteorological connection with the eruptions of volcanos, and are variously modified by the heights of the mountains, the circumference of the summits which are perpetually covered with snow, and the degree to which the walls of cinder cones become heated; but they cannot be regarded in the light of true volcanic phenomena. Subterranean lakes, communicating by various channels with the mountain streams, are frequently formed in deep and vast cavities, either on the declivity or at the base of volcanos. When the whole mass of the volcano is powerfully shaken by those earthquakes which precede all eruptions of fire in the Andes, the subterranean vaults open, and pour forth streams of water, fishes, and tuffaceous mud. This singular phenomenon brings to mind the *Pimelodes Cyclopum,* or the Silures of the Cyclops, which the inhabitants of the plateau of Quito call Preñadilla, and of which I gave a circumstantial account soon after my return to Europe. When, on the night between the 19th and 20th of June, 1698, the summit of Mount Carguairazo, situated to the north of Chimborazo, and having an elevation of more than 19,000 feet, fell in, all the country for nearly 32 square miles was covered with mud and fishes. A similar eruption of fish from the volcano of Imbaburu was supposed to have caused the putrid fever, which, seven years before this period, raged in the town of Ibarra.

I refer to these facts because they throw some light on the difference between the eruption of dry ashes and mud-like inundations of tuff and trass, investing fragments of wood, charcoal, and shells. The quantity of ashes recently erupted from Mount Vesuvius, like every phenomenon connected with volcanos and other great and fearful natural phenomena, has been greatly exaggerated in the public papers; and two Neapolitan chemists, Vicenzo Pepe and Guiseppe di Nobili, even asserted that the cinders were mixed with given proportions of gold and silver, notwithstanding the counter-statements of Monticelli and Covelli. According to my researches the stratum of ashes which fell during the twelve days was only three feet in thickness in the direction of Bosche Tre Case, on the declivity of the cone, where they were mixed with rapilli, while in the plains its greatest thickness did not exceed from 16 to 19 inches. Measurements of this kind must not be made at spots where the ashes have been drifted by the wind, like snow or sand, or where they have been accumulated in pulp-like heaps by means of water. The times are passed in which, after the manner of the ancients, nothing was regarded in volcanic phenomena save the marvellous, and when men would believe, like Ctesias, that the ashes from Etna were borne as far as the Indian peninsula. A portion of the Mexican gold and silver veins is certainly found in trachytic porphyry, but in the ashes of Vesuvius which I myself collected, and which were, at my request, examined by that distinguished chemist Heinrich Rose, no trace of either gold or silver was to be discovered.

NURSLINGS OF THE SKY

FROM *The Land of Little Rain*

MARY AUSTIN

There is an excitement one has on first coming to Mary Austin, as though one had made a personal and intimate discovery. And with it a need to share the experience. For Mary Austin was a writer with greatness, not alone for the rhythm of her prose, but for the richness and humanity of her visions. "She had a standard by which to measure the world," Carl Van Doren says of her, "the desert and the mountains." She wrote of landscape and climate, of storm and trees and water, but always of people. In this essay from *Land of Little Rain,* her earliest book, Mary Austin carries us with her to the high Sierras on a rare and glowing journey.

CHOOSE A HILL COUNTRY FOR STORMS. THERE ALL THE BUSINESS OF THE WEATHER is carried on above your horizon and loses its terror in familiarity. When you come to think about it, the disastrous storms are on the levels, sea or sand or plains. There you get only a hint of what is about to happen, the fume of the gods rising from their meeting place under the rim of the world; and when it breaks upon you there is no stay nor shelter. The terrible mewings and mouthings of a Kansas wind have the added terror of viewlessness. You are lapped in them like uprooted grass; suspect them of a personal grudge. But the storms of hill countries have other business. They scoop watercourses, manure the pines, twist them to a finer fibre, fit the firs to be masts and spars, and, if you keep reasonably out of the track of their affairs, do you no harm.

They have habits to be learned, appointed paths, seasons, and warnings, and they leave you in no doubt about their performances. One who builds his house on a water scar or the rubble of a steep slope must take chances. So they did in Overtown who built in the wash of Argus water, and at Kearsarge at the foot of a steep, treeless swale. After twenty years Argus water rose in the wash against the frail houses, and the piled snows of Kearsarge slid down at a thunder peal over the cabins and the camp, but you could conceive that it was the fault of neither the water nor the snow.

The first effect of cloud study is a sense of presence and intention in storm processes. Weather does not happen. It is the visible manifestation of the Spirit moving itself in the void. It gathers itself together under the heavens; rains, snows, yearns mightily in wind, smiles; and the Weather Bureau, situated advantageously for that very business, taps the record on his instruments and going out on the streets denies his God, not having gathered the sense of what he has seen. Hardly anybody takes account of the fact that John Muir, who knows more of mountain storms than any other, is a devout man.

Of the high Sierras choose the neighborhood of the splintered peaks about the Kern and King's river divide for storm study, or the short, wide-mouthed cañons opening eastward on high valleys. Days when the hollows are steeped in a warm, winey flood the clouds come walking on the floor of heaven, flat and pearly gray beneath, rounded and pearly white above. They gather flock-wise, moving on the level currents that roll about the peaks, lock hands and settle with the cooler air, drawing a veil about those places where they do their work. If their meeting or parting takes place at sunrise or sunset, as it often does, one gets the splendor of the apocalypse. There will be cloud pillars miles high, snow-capped, glorified, and preserving an orderly perspective before the unbarred door of the sun, or perhaps mere ghosts of clouds that dance to some pied piper of an unfelt wind. But be it day or night, once they have settled to their work, one sees from the valley only the blank wall of their tents stretched along the ranges. To get the real effect of a mountain storm you must be inside.

One who goes often into a hill country learns not to say: What if it should rain? It always does rain somewhere among the peaks: the unusual thing is that one should escape it. You might suppose that if you took any account of plant contrivances to save their pollen powder against showers. Note how many there are deep-throated and bell-flowered like the pentstemons, how many have nodding pedicels as the columbine, how many grow in copse shelters and grow there only. There is keen delight in the quick showers of summer cañons, with the added comfort, born of experience, of knowing that no harm comes of a wetting at high altitudes. The day is warm; a white cloud spies over the cañon wall, slips up behind the ridge to cross it by some windy pass, obscures your sun. Next you hear the rain drum on the broad-leaved hellebore, and beat down the mimulus beside the brook. You shelter on the lee of some strong pine with shut-winged butterflies and merry, fiddling creatures of the wood. Runnels of rain water from the glacier-slips swirl through the pine needles into rivulets; the streams froth and rise in their banks. The sky is white with cloud; the sky is gray with rain; the sky is clear. The summer showers leave no wake.

Such as these follow each other day by day for weeks in August weather.

Sometimes they chill suddenly into wet snow that packs about the lake gardens clear to the blossom frills, and melts away harmlessly. Sometimes one has the good fortune from a heather-grown headland to watch a rain-cloud forming in mid-air. Out over meadow or lake region begins a little darkling of the sky—no cloud, no wind, just a smokiness such as spirits materialize from in witch stories.

It rays out and draws to it some floating films from secret cañons. Rain begins, "slow dropping veil of thinnest lawn"; a wind comes up and drives the formless thing across a meadow, or a dull lake pitted by the glancing drops, dissolving as it drives. Such rains relieve like tears.

The same season brings the rains that have work to do, ploughing storms that alter the face of things. These come with thunder and the play of live fire along the rocks. They come with great winds that try the pines for their work upon the seas and strike out the unfit. They shake down avalanches of splinters from sky-line pinnacles and raise up sudden floods like battle fronts in the cañons against towns, trees, and boulders. They would be kind if they could, but have more important matters. Such storms, called cloud-bursts by the country folk, are not rain, rather the spillings of Thor's cup, jarred by the Thunderer. After such a one the water that comes up in the village hydrants miles away is white with forced bubbles from the wind-tormented streams.

All that storms do to the face of the earth you may read in the geographies, but not what they do to our contemporaries. I remember one night of thunderous rain made unendurably mournful by the houseless cry of a cougar whose lair, and perhaps his family, had been buried under a slide of broken boulders on the slope of Kearsarge. We had heard the heavy detonation of the slide about the hour of the alpenglow, a pale rosy interval in a darkling air, and judged he must have come from hunting to the ruined cliff and paced the night out before it, crying a very human woe. I remember, too, in that same season of storms, a lake made milky white for days, and crowded out of its bed by clay washed into it by a fury of rain, with the trout floating in it belly up, stunned by the shock of the sudden flood. But there were trout enough for what was left of the lake next year and the beginning of a meadow about its upper rim. What taxed me most in the wreck of one of my favorite cañons by cloud-burst was to see a bobcat mother mouthing her drowned kittens in the ruined lair built in the wash, far above the limit of accustomed waters, but not far enough for the unexpected. After a time you get the point of view of gods about these things to save you from being too pitiful.

The great snows that come at the beginning of winter, before there is yet any snow except the perpetual high banks, are best worth while to watch. These come often before the late bloomers are gone and while the migratory birds are still in the piney woods. Down in the valley you see little but the flocking of blackbirds in the streets, or the low flight of mallards over the tulares, and the gathering of clouds behind Williamson. First there is a waiting stillness in the wood; the pine-trees creak although there is no wind, the sky glowers, the firs rock by the water borders. The noise of the creek rises insistently and falls off a full note like a child abashed by sudden silence in the room. This changing of the stream-tone following tardily the changes of the sun on melting snows is most meaningful of wood notes. After it runs a little trumpeter wind to cry the wild creatures to their holes. Sometimes the warning hangs in the air for days with increasing stillness. Only Clark's crow and the strident jays make light of it; only they can afford to. The cattle get down to the foothills and ground inhabiting creatures make fast their doors. It grows chill, blind clouds fumble in the cañons; there will be a roll of thunder, perhaps, or a flurry of rain, but mostly the snow is born in the air with quietness and the sense of strong white pinions softly stirred. It increases, is wet and clogging, and makes a white night of midday.

There is seldom any wind with first snows, more often rain, but later, when there is already a smooth foot or two over all the slopes, the drifts begin. The late snows are fine and dry, mere ice granules at the wind's will. Keen mornings after a storm they are blown out in wreaths and banners from the high ridges sifting into the cañons.

Once in a year or so we have a "big snow." The cloud tents are widened out to shut in the valley and an outlying range or two and are drawn tight against the sun. Such a storm begins warm, with a dry white mist that fills and fills between the ridges, and the air is thick with formless groaning. Now for days you get no hint of the neighboring ranges until the snows begin to lighten and some shouldering peak lifts through a rent. Mornings after the heavy snows are steely blue, two-edged with cold, divinely fresh and still, and these are times to go up to the pine borders. There you may find floundering in the unstable drifts "tainted wethers" of the wild sheep, faint from age and hunger; easy prey. Even the deer make slow going in the thick fresh snow, and once we found a wolverine going blind and feebly in the white glare.

No tree takes the snow stress with such ease as the silver fir. The star-whorled, fan-spread branches droop under the soft wreaths—droop and press flatly to the trunk; presently the point of overloading is reached, there is a soft sough and muffled dropping, the boughs recover, and the weighting goes on until the drifts have reached the midmost whorls and covered up the branches. When the snows are particularly wet and heavy they spread over the young firs in green-ribbed tents wherein harbor winter-loving birds.

All storms of desert hills, except wind storms, are impotent. East and east of the Sierras they rise in nearly parallel ranges, desertward, and no rain breaks over them, except from some far-strayed cloud or roving wind from the California Gulf, and these only in winter. In summer the sky travails with thunderings and the flare of sheet lightnings to win a few blistering big drops, and once in a lifetime the chance of a torrent. But you have not known what force resides in the mindless things until you have known a desert wind. One expects it at the turn of the two seasons, wet and dry, with electrified tense nerves. Along the edge of the mesa where it drops off to the valley, dust devils begin to rise white and steady, fanning out at the top like the genii out of the Fisherman's bottle. One supposes the Indians might have learned the use of smoke signals from these dust pillars as they learn most things direct from the tutelage of the earth. The air begins to move fluently, blowing hot and cold between the ranges. Far south rises a murk of sand against the sky; it grows, the wind shakes itself, and has a smell of earth. The cloud of small dust takes on the color of gold and shuts out the neighborhood, the push of the wind is unsparing. Only man of all folk is foolish enough to stir abroad in it. But being in a house is really much worse; no relief from the dust, and a great fear of the creaking timbers. There is no looking ahead in such a wind, and the bite of the small sharp sand on exposed skin is keener than any insect sting. One might sleep, for the lapping of the wind wears one to the point of exhaustion very soon, but there is dread, in open sand stretches sometimes justified, of being over blown by the drift. It is hot, dry, fretful work, but by going along the ground with the wind behind, one may come upon strange things in its tumultuous privacy. I like these truces of wind and heat that the desert makes, otherwise I do not know how I should come by so many acquaintances with furtive folk. I like to see hawks sitting daunted in shallow holes, not daring to spread a feather, and doves in a row by the prickle bushes, and shut-eyed cattle, turned tail to the wind in a patient doze. I like the smother of sand among the dunes, and finding small coiled snakes in open places, but I never like to come in a wind upon the silly sheep. The wind robs them of what wit they had, and they seem never to have learned the self-induced hypnotic stupor with which most wild things endure weather stress. I have never heard that the desert winds brought harm to any other than the wandering shepherds and their flocks. Once below Pastaria Little Pete showed me bones sticking out of the sand where a flock of two hundred had been smothered in a bygone wind. In many places the four-foot posts of a cattle fence had been buried by the wind-blown dunes.

It is enough occupation, when no storm is brewing, to watch the cloud currents and the chambers of the sky. From Kearsarge, say, you look over Inyo and find pink soft cloud masses asleep on the level desert air; south of you hurries a white troop late to some gathering of their kind at the back of Oppapago; nosing the foot of Waban, a woolly mist creeps south. In the clean, smooth paths of the middle sky and highest up in air, drift, unshepherded, small flocks ranging contrarily. You will find the proper names of these things in the reports of the Weather Bureau—cirrus, cumulus, and the like—and charts that will teach by study when to sow and take up crops. It is astonishing the trouble men will be at to find out when to plant potatoes, and gloze over the eternal meaning of the skies. You have to beat out for yourself many mornings on the windly headlands the sense of the fact that you get the same rainbow in the cloud drift over Waban and the spray of your garden hose. And not necessarily then do you live up to it.

Bettman Archive

BALD EAGLE

ON THE BEHAVIOUR
OF A CHAMOIS:
AND INCIDENTALLY
OF SOME OTHER MATTERS

FROM *Essay*

JULIAN HUXLEY

🦅 Whether by virtue of Weissman's theory of genetics or Lamarck's theory of the inheritance of acquired characteristics, it would be a startling exception to either theory if a Huxley were not a writer, and a good one. Julian Huxley, whose charming and intimate essay on the chamois of the Swiss Alps and various related and unrelated matters follows, is a grandson of Thomas Huxley, a grand-nephew of Matthew Arnold, a nephew of Mrs. Humphrey Ward, and elder brother to Aldous Huxley. He looks much like Thomas Huxley, whose writing appears elsewhere in this book, and has never denied the remark his famous grandfather was said to have made about him when Julian was very young indeed, "I like that chap. I like the way he looks you straight in the face and disobeys you." Julian Huxley is a zoologist by profession and a mountain climber by avocation.

THOSE WHO KNOW ROSENLAUI WILL ALSO KNOW THAT FINELY POINTED LITTLE peak, an outlying spur of the Wetterhorn, that looks straight down into the front windows of the hotel—the Dossenhorn. That was my first climb. I confess that it was nothing very thrilling, though I enjoyed it thoroughly. We had a guide—an aged, aged man, whose downhill, bent-knee walk was if anything slower than his very slow but quite automatic and invariable upward pacing. We had a rope, which appeared to me perfectly unnecessary, and was a great nuisance to the airily independent spirit and body of the novice. Two ice-axes lent to our party (of five) an air of considerable distinction. Very little of the day's happenings have remained to me. I still remember how very easy the rocks of the last arête were; how fine the Wetterhorn looked across the snow plateau; how I wondered why my uncle, a considerable climber in his day, wore trousers instead of knickerbockers; how I ran down most of the way home after unroping; and how, in my innocence, I plunged my face, scarlet from its exposure all unvaselined to the snow-fields, into a basin of cold water—with what results those know who have tried it. Among all this intolerable deal of bread, however, we had a half-penny worth of something more intoxicating. There is a long snow slope to be crossed slantingly before the col and the hut are reached. It is not at all steep, sloping up to the lower border of the rock pile that forms the pyramidal top of the mountain; but the old guide had ordered the rope, and so there we were plodding diagonally upwards in single file.

All of a sudden there was a rattle, and then a stone leapt off the rocks above to bound down the snow slope some four hundred yards ahead of us. The old guide looked around, and said: "Chamois."

This set us all agog—two or three had never seen the chamois on his native heath. However, the brown coat of the chamois is a good piece of cryptic colouring; he—or they—remained absolutely invisible against the brown rocks. But we had startled him, and he went on moving—for some reason towards us, as we soon discovered when a second stone came down. The third alarmed us a little, for it crossed our path not fifty yards ahead of the leader; so we resolved to halt and keep our eyes open for the next. This was not long in coming; it came with a bound off the rocks, and seemed to be heading for the gap between the last two on the rope. It must have been going at a great pace, for it devoured that snow slope in great hungry leaps, clearing eighty or a hundred feet at a bound, though never rising a yard above the snow; it hummed as it came, with a deep buzzing sound. Altogether it was extremely alarming (I was one of the two hinder-most), and it was a considerable relief to see, after it was half-way to us, that it had a slight curl on it, and an outward curl, which caused it to hum past five or six yards behind the tail of our procession. The chamois passed, still invisible, on his way, and we on ours, discussing what would have been the best thing to do supposing his aim had been straighter.

It was that scene that came into my head years later. I had been trying to master some of the rudiments of geology, of which science I was lamentably ignorant, and had at least begun to get into my head the idea of denudation —how the shapes of mountains as we see them are as much due to cutting away as to heaving up—and was grasping the strength of the denuding forces that would go on thus cutting and cutting until nothing was left but one flat plain, did they not thus once more liberate the forces of upheaval. In my textbook there were examples given of the many and various activities working together this work of destruction—wind and sun, rain and frost, sand, rivers, little plants—"and chamois!" came suddenly into my mind.

A little nail will serve to hang a large picture; and so the whole idea of denudation was fixed in my brain by that one Bernese chamois.

It perhaps, more than any other single thing, taught me to see the transience of the hills. For here, as so often elsewhere, the judgments of the natural man must be unlearnt. "The hills stand about Jerusalem," says the natural man,—"The Eternal Hills!" They are not eternal; they are as transitory, as much slaves of Time, as anything with life. The title is but one more witness to the arrogance, the unimaginativeness of man, who thinks that everything is of the same order of magnitude as he himself; and if he does not notice the hour hand move while he trips along some fraction of the circumference of the seconds dial—why, then, it must be motionless!

But man possesses also a brain, and therein an intelligence, a logical faculty, by means of which he discovers presently that things are not always what they seem; and one of these apparent contradictions is that the mountains must be changing, rising up and wearing down, even though he cannot perceive it directly; and yet even though he can prove that it must be so, it is still very difficult for him to realise it happening.

Our intelligence, indeed, although it thus transcends the senses' immediate judgments, has to go back to them and ask their aid if it is to attain to fullest knowledge. It is a very imperfect instrument, so built up on the foundations of the five senses that if we cannot feel, bear, taste, smell or, more particularly, see what there is to be dealt with, but only reason about it, we may *know* quite well that reasoning has led to the only right conclusion, but yet do not *feel* fully and unquestioningly the rightness of it. We all believe the moon to be a globe; but I must confess that on my first sight of her through a telescope, I experienced a veritable shock of surprise and pleasure to realise, as I saw the craters passing from full face in the centre to profile at the edge, how globular she really was. With the mountains no such ocular demonstration is possible to us. I say to us, for to our descendants it may be. You have but to take a series of photographs of some peak from exactly the same spot at intervals of fifty years or so; then, putting these together in their order, run them through a cinematograph, and you would see your everlasting citadel crumble, shrinking before your eyes like a pricked balloon. Such a condensation of events has already been practised to render such slow processes as the growth of twigs or the complex unfolding of the egg more patent and striking; and there is no reason why it should not be applied to matters of centuries instead of days.

To-day we cannot have the change rendered thus visible to us. We have only indirect methods to help us, methods which demand reflection and imagination. Imagination and reflection, however, are processes demanding more mental energy than the average man is willing to expend, for the average man is mentally of extreme laziness. So the mountains remain eternal, to the average man.

But there is no harm in trying to exercise powers of reflection and of imagination, if I may persuade you to it. Stand on the bridges at Geneva and look at the Rhone slipping down from the lake, clear and blue with a wonderful and almost unreal blue. Then walk down to the junction of the Rhone and the Arve, and see that other river, turbid, greyish-white, a regular glacier stream; identity and name may be taken from it in the union, but it still has strength to rob the robber of his own especial beauty. That discolouring flood—what is it? As you walk back again, the top of Mont Blanc comes gradually from behind the Grande Salève into sight. If you reflect, you will know that those white waves were white from carrying away what only yesterday had been a part of those famous mountains; to-day it is dust, and nameless; to-morrow it will be laid down upon the ocean floor, there to be hardened, kneaded, and baked into the bricks that shall build other, as yet unchristened, hills. If you imagine, you will see in the mind's eye those same summits, thus continually attacked, gradually shrinking; preserving their beauty to the last, no doubt, like our lovely lake mountains, which though in respect of their former height they be but as roots when the trunk is fallen, yet in themselves show not a trace of decay, and lift their heads as strong and fresh as ever. Yet they dwindle, and will in the end be mountains no more; they will no more have form and shape, no more be named and almost live, endowed with that strong appearance of vivid and obvious personality; mere undulations, they will no more exercise the mountain power upon the mind of man.

What else will help you to see the transience of the hills? Go and stand by a mountain stream where it runs in quick swishing rapids; as I have done by the Drance de Bagnes, and heard sounds as of groaning and muffled giant hammering—great boulders grinding each other in the press of the current, and moving always downwards. Go and look at the enormous moraines that wind down into Italy—each would be a range of hills in England. Had not the Alps another aspect before these were heaped up? And yet, say the geologists, great cenotaphs of the ice were raised in but a fraction of the time since the Alps were born. Try to tackle a rock-and-ice gully with strong sun on it, or (preferably) stay on one side and watch the stones come down: down they come like that every sunny day.

Look at the Matterhorn, and be told how like it is to Strasburg Cathedral; but rock spires are not built upwards like ones of stone and mortar; they are monoliths, cut out of the solid rock. The stony layers of the rock, once lying flat and soft upon the sea-bottom, then hardened, then gripped and crumpled by the ageing earth like so many sheets of wet paper, now are cut through, and show their free edges on the steep flanks of the mountain

Fixed long ago in waves and curves, now they are immobile, but they treasure within themselves the forms which the ice and the sun are to reveal. As if the sculptor were to have but half the shaping of his work, and the block of marble almost of itself disclose its hidden Oenus, or turn a Hercules planned into a Hylas accomplished, so the rock masses contain within themselves no infinite possibility of forms—there is, to start with, a quality of mountain concealed in the rock, so that the aerial sculptors may work as they please, and never find a Dent du Midi in the Mont Blanc range, or fashion a Weisshorn from the Dolomites. But that is another story. Even though the rocks thus decree that the instruments of their destruction shall be as well instruments to reveal their hidden beauties, yet destruction none the less it is. How gigantic a destruction those cut, upcurving layers of rock can testify.

But in the same way as our mind can know and yet not feel the mutability of the mountains, so it may know and yet not grasp their size and its extent. Here again the new lesson is hard to be learnt by brain alone: "Everest 29,002, Mont Blanc 15,786, Scawfell Pike 3210"—the figures convey but a part. The hills must take the mind by assault through the breaches of sense. . . .

I shall never forget the impression of colossal grandeur that showed itself at a turn of the road opposite the gate of the Glacier de la Neuvaz. Nothing was lacking in the chain. In the foreground, below a grassy bank, flowed the Drance de Ferret—only a smallish stream, but big enough and swift enough unbridged to stop such a small animal as man from gaining its other side. Across it lay a fallen pine; and from this, better than from the standing trees, you realised to what a height the pine-trunks grow. Of these there was a thick wood filling up the level bottom left by the receding glacier; the green sea extended back and back until the tops of the separate trees were not to be made out, and the whole wood tapered away in perspective like a band of clouds towards the setting sun. In the end it turned a corner to the right—a thin green line beyond the grey terminal moraine. This corner filled a little indentation in the hill behind. The eye travelled up naturally from the green line of trees to the green slope, and saw that slope as part of a great rounded hill, rather like a bit of the Downs in general appearance; but had it been hollow you could have gone on pouring your Chanctonburies and Sinoduns and Beachy Heads and Hogs backs into it, and they would have rattled about like small-shot inside. The stream of trees let you see how big it was, as hills on the horizon show the greatness of the setting moon. I think the hill was nameless. Beyond it, in another plane of distance, rose another peak—this one brown, of bare rock, and rather jagged; the vegetation had ended on the part concealed behind the green hill. Up and up the eye travelled, and was amazed to find that if the green had been but a spur of the brown, so the brown was but a spur of the white. Mont Dolent arose from behind it like the pursuing peak in the *Prelude*. All its rocky middle and its snowline were in their turn hidden by the brown spur before them; only the white slanting chisel edge of the summit soared up to sight. Stream—tree—wood—mountains: one, two, and three . . . each formed a stepping-stone to the one beyond, making it possible for the whole grandeur of the peak to slip down, as it were, and find place within the narrow limits of the brain waiting at the other end.

There it was able to take up its station beside that other thought which entered there, not charioted by Bacchus and his pards, but by the swift chamois and the mountain torrents. The two, holding mutual colloquy, together tell what Wordsworth learnt in another fashion, that the mountains are

> Huge and mighty forms, that do not live
> Like living men.

But live they do, in their own way—not only in their form and individuality, but in the constant cycle of their changeableness. They approach to being closed systems, independent in some degree of the rest of the world; partial individuals, they have a share in determining their future selves. Once raised to mountains, they contain within themselves the germs of their own destiny; and if not possessing such power as true life possesses of blossoming into a predetermined form, scarcely to be altered by all the efforts of the outside world, yet at least marking down beforehand the limits beyond which the outer influences cannot mould them, preordaining the main succession of their future history, and the essential quality of the forms they are to take. And again, though they have not the true vital property of reproducing their kind by means of a mere particle of their own substance, that grows, and in its growth takes up the atoms of outer matter and moulds them to its will, they have a kind of reproduction scarcely less strange, where like generates not like, but unlike. In their decay they are laying new foundations. Grain torn from grain of solid rock, boulder from boulder is swept away; layer after layer of grains or boulder is laid—"well and truly laid"; rock system piled upon rock system; till the time comes, and all this is upheaved into a chain of peaks which, though their every particle were taken from the substance of that older chain, will be like it in being a mountain range, but in that alone. So they have their being, in a different and vaster cycle than man's, their life only another fragment of that change which is the single fixed reality.

And what is the moral of all this? You may well ask; for I do not know that I know myself. Proceed to the fact that our mountains are but crinkles on the rind of a small satellite of one star among the millions, and we deduce the littleness of man: which has been done before. Point out how, in spite of all their size and their terrors, they fall one by one to the climber, and we with equal facility prove his greatness: which also others have successfully attempted. Insist on their mutability, and it merely takes us back to Heraclitus and his πάντα ῥεῖ. Perhaps one moral is that feeling as well as reasoning, reasoning as well as feeling, is necessary to true knowledge; a conclusion which would appeal to followers of Mr. Bergson, but hardly falls within the scope of this book.

The chief moral is, I expect, that the mountains can give the climber more than climbing, and will do so if he but keep his eyes open. From them there will come to him flashes of beauty and of grandeur, light in dark places, sudden glimpses of the age, the glory, and the greatness of the earth.

HERD OF CHAMOIS

A DELUGE AND THE REPRESENTATION OF IT IN PAINTING

FROM *Notebooks*

LEONARDO DA VINCI

🐦 Genius, someone said, is the capacity for seeing what is not there. History tells of no man gifted in the same degree as Leonardo da Vinci for seeing what had previously been hidden from sight. Nor could the life of any man have been long enough to complete a small fraction of the projects he attempted: in mechanics, hydraulics, architecture, military and civil engineering, painting, music, sculpture, anatomy, chemistry, geology—experimentation in almost every branch of knowledge.

As painter he is yet to be surpassed. The theory of art by which he worked was that the artist who did not look beneath the surface of things to search for the hidden reality beneath was reproducing nothing more than surface illusions. His method of study and observation is evidenced in this selection from his *Notebooks,* "Of a Deluge and the Representation of it in Painting."

FIRST OF ALL LET THERE BE REPRESENTED THE SUMMIT OF A RUGGED MOUNTAIN with certain of the valleys that surround its base, and on its sides let the surface of the soil be seen slipping down together with the tiny roots of the small shrubs, and leaving bare a great part of the surrounding rocks. Sweeping down in devastation from these precipices, let it pursue its headlong course, striking and laying bare the twisted and gnarled roots of the great trees and overturning them in ruin. And the mountains becoming bare should reveal the deep fissures made in them by the ancient earthquakes; and let the bases of the mountains be in great part covered over and clad with the débris of the shrubs which have fallen headlong from the sides of the lofty peaks of the said mountains, and let these be mingled together with mud, roots, branches of trees, with various kinds of leaves thrust in among the mud and earth and stones. And let the fragments of some of the mountains have fallen down into the depth of one of the valleys, and there form a barrier to the swollen waters of its river, which having already burst the barrier rushes on with immense waves, the greatest of which are striking and laying in ruin the walls of the cities and farms of the valley. . . . The waves of the sea that beats against the shelving base of the mountains which confine it, rush foaming in speed up to the ridge of these same hills, and in turning back meet the onset of the succeeding wave, and after loud roaring return in a mighty flood to the sea from whence they came. A great number of the inhabitants, men and different animals, may be seen driven by the rising of the deluge up towards the summits of the hills which border on the said waters.

WILD GOAT

MOUNTAIN ROOTS

FROM *Biography of the Earth*

GEORGE GAMOW

George Gamow is in the tradition of Thomas Huxley, a ranking scientist who has the gift for translating the complex findings of science into imaginative English. He is professor at George Washington University and has made important contributions in theoretical physics, particularly in the application of nuclear reactions to the evolution of the stars. He has won a large audience of lay readers with his witty, simply written, but at the same time authoritative popularizations of physics, mathematics, and geology. His book *Biography of the Earth,* from which this selection is taken, is a most readable account of what is known and surmised about the earth.

WHEN WE LOOK AT A HIGH MOUNTAIN RANGE RISING THOUSANDS OF FEET ABOVE the surrounding plain, we are inclined to consider it merely a gigantic excrescence of rock piled on the surface of the Earth, much as an artificial hill constructed by engineers. Such a primitive point of view, which regards mountains as wholly a surface feature, was quite common in scientific geology a century ago; only comparatively recently was it recognized that *the bulk of any mountain is situated under the surface of the Earth.*

The discovery of these "mountain roots," going very deep under the surface, resulted from the study of the gravitational action of a mountain upon two pendulums suspended on opposite sides of it. One would expect that, in accordance with the general law of gravity, the great mass of the mountain would deflect the pendulums from the vertical to an extent proportional to the size of the mountain. Of course, in this instance the word "vertical" is defined, not as a plumb line, but in respect to a fixed direction in space as given by observation of the stars. To the great surprise of the scientists who carried out such measurements for the first time, the observed deviations of the pendulums caused by the proximity of a mountain turned out to be much smaller than was expected on the basis of the mountain's size.

In the case of Mount Everest, for example, the observed deviation is about three times smaller than should be expected from its giant mass, while the Pyrenees even seem to repel the pendulum instead of attracting it! The absence of the expected gravitational attraction clearly indicated that a certain amount of mass was lacking, inside or under the mountain, which led to the hypothesis that mountains were hollow: something like a broken eggshell placed on a table.

It must be clear to a reader who has carefully followed our argument up to this point that this "eggshell" hypothesis can hardly stand up under criticism based on our present knowledge of the properties of the Earth's crust, and that the true explanation of the apparently missing mass under the mountain must lie in deformations of the crust by the weight of the material piled on it. According to present views, the mountains on the surface of the Earth represent formations similar to the ice hills produced on the polar ice fields by the compression of ice. Every arctic explorer knows that when blocks of ice, broken by compression, are piled on top of one another, most of the ice sinks below the water in order to keep the rest afloat. Thus, while a polar bear will see a high hill rising above the surface of the ice field, a seal swimming under it will notice an even larger bulge protruding into the water. Similarly, *to each mountain rising above the surface of the Earth there corresponds, so to speak, a "negative mountain" formed by the granite masses protruding into the underlying plastic layer of basalt.*

According to Archimedes' law, the mass of a floating body must be equal to the mass of the displaced material underneath, so that the *presence of an elevation that is in isostatic equilibrium does not signify any actual increase of mass in this region.*

Thus, instead of asking the question: "Why does the mountain not affect the plumb line as much as would correspond to its apparent mass?" we must rather ask: "Why is there any deflection at all?" To answer this last question we must bear in mind that, although the solid crust of the Earth is not strong enough to support the whole mountain, it still possesses sufficient elasticity to prevent the mountain from sinking as deep as it would in the case of a completely plastic substratum. Hence the mountain will be elevated a little higher above the surface than corresponds to complete isostatic equilibrium, and the pendulum suspended alongside it will show a slight deviation from the vertical line. It must also be borne in mind that under the weight of smaller mountains and hills (as well as under "manmade mountains" such as the Egyptian pyramids or the New York skyscrapers) the crust will not bend at all, and the deviation of the plumb line in this case will exactly correspond to the excess of mass above the surface.

The elasticity of the crust also prevents the "negative mountain" from being something like a mirror image of the corresponding elevation above the surface; an imaginary mountain climber making his way through the masses of plastic basalt deep under the Alps will look in vain for anything resembling the upside-down Jungfrau or Matterhorn. Probably all that he will find there is an extensive smooth bulge of granite protruding several kilometres downward into the basaltic layer.

We have mentioned more than once that those parts of the continental massifs above sea level, especially the high mountains raised by the crumpling of the crust, are subject to the continuous destructive action of water, which pours down on them from the sky during rainy periods and carries large quantities of dissolved and mechanically eroded material into the surrounding seas. We have also said that the amount of salt alone carried to the ocean as the result of the past erosion of continental blocks totals about 20,000,000 cubic kilometres. *If we were able to extract all this salt from the sea and distribute it uniformly over the land surface* of the Earth, it would form a layer 135 metres (about 450 feet) thick. But salt represents only a very small portion of the granite rocks (about 5 per cent), so that *in order to wash out the amount of salt now dissolved in the ocean, rain water has had to erode a granite layer more than 2 kilometres thick!* Whereas the salt extracted from the rocks remains in solution, the other products of erosion, such as sand and gravel, are deposited on the ocean bottom bordering the shore line or on the bottoms of intracontinental seas, forming the steadily growing layer of sedimentary rocks.

The idea that rain water can wash away thousands of feet of continental surface and level the highest mountain ranges will not seem so strange if we bear in mind the enormous periods of time during which this destructive process has been steadily going on.

Direct measurements of the amount of mud carried away by rivers indicate that the surface of the United States alone loses about 800,000,000 tons of its rocky material annually. *Denudation by rain water reduces the average height of the continents by 0.02 millimetre per year.* Since Columbus first stepped on the shore of the New World, an outer layer of about 4 inches thick has been carried away into the oceans and seas.

Erosion by rain water is responsible for such peculiar features of the Earth's surface as the Bad Lands of South Dakota, or the deep canyons cut into the solid rock by comparatively unimportant rivers and creeks. Since the surface of the Earth consists of various kinds of rocks with varying resistance to the destructive action of water, the landscape of denuded areas often assumes strange and fantastic shapes. One example is the peculiar structure known as the Devil's Tower, familiar to travellers who have driven through South Dakota along U. S. Highway 9. Once upon a time this spot was occupied by a magnificent volcano, an outlet for the masses of molten magma from below. Later, the volcanic activity in this region ceased, and the solidified lava filling the volcanic crater formed a long vertical column of basalt. Rain water worked on the dead volcano for centuries upon centuries, and it took hundreds of thousands of years until it finally succeeded in washing away the outer part of the cone formed by the volcanic ashes of numerous eruptions. The remaining tower is merely the original column of solidified lava, and since basalt withstands erosion much better than the softer material of the cone, it will probably take many more hundreds of thousands of years for the rain to obliterate completely this last remainder of the ancient volcano.

Since the destruction of mountains by the rapid streams rushing down their steep slopes proceeds considerably faster than the erosion of flatlands, we must expect that *the general effect of the action of rain water will be to obliterate all the characteristic features produced by the crumpling of the crust and transform the continental surfaces into extensive low plains.* It must be noted, however, that to wash away a mountain, rain water must do considerably more work than would seem necessary at first sight. In fact, the process of isostatic adjustment described above operates so that, while the material of the mountain is being carried away by rushing streams, new rocks slowly rise up from below, giving the water additional work to do. *To remove the mountain completely from the surface of the Earth it is necessary, not only to take away its visible protruding part, but also to remove its "roots," which penetrate deep into the crust.* If some ambitious railway company, constructing a new line through a mountainous region, should decide to remove the whole mountain instead of digging a tunnel through it, the advantage obtained by this gigantic construction job would be only temporary, since in a few hundred thousand years a new mountain, of only slightly smaller size, would again rise on the same spot!

Parallel with the permanent upward movement of the mountain regions there goes the slow sinking of those parts of the Earth's surface on which the streams and rivers deposit their loads of eroded material. Since the mountains are raised mainly along the continental shore lines, and since the rain water falling on a mountain runs down both its sides, these sinking regions of the crust must evidently correspond to the oceanic bottoms bordering the continents and to the bottoms of the comparatively shallow seas that are often formed in the lower central portions of the continental massifs. . . . As we have said, the deformation of the Earth's crust resulting from processes of this kind may cause some additional wrinkling of the surface and the formation of local mountain chains.

From the observed rate of denudation it is estimated that *the time necessary for rain waters to obliterate the mountains raised during a revolutionary epoch of mountain formation is several times shorter than the period between two such revolutions.* Hence we must conclude that *the surface of the Earth was quite featureless and flat during most of its history, with many areas completely covered by shallow seas,* and that it is our special privilege to live during one of the comparatively short epochs when the mountains raised by the last revolution are still standing proudly.

CLOUDS THAT STAND STILL

FROM *Song of the Sky*

GUY MURCHIE

The things we understand we label; those we do not understand we call Nature or "mystery" or religion. It is only recently, as science measures time, that the "mystery" of the new dimension, air, has begun to be labeled—the clouds, winds, the atmosphere.

In his book *Song of the Sky*, Guy Murchie has taken those things we are beginning to know about meteorology and aerodynamics, and has woven them together with a fine prose.

Murchie is, among other things, a flyer. He was instructor in navigation for the Air Transport Command. In this selection he gives us an understanding of the clouds that are born on the mountain tops.

MOST ORDINARY CLOUDS, AS YOU'VE NOTICED IF YOU HAVE EVER LAIN ON YOUR back in the grass, drift slowly along on the wind, eventually disappearing below the horizon. But they have some strange cousins that behave very differently, defying the winds as if literally tied to the earth. You see these generally near mountain peaks and they are in fact tied to the earth by invisible thongs of humid air that spring from solid ground, that may reach up from any orographic configuration bold enough to deflect moist currents up into the cold. The island lighthouse cloud . . . is sometimes in this category though usually created more by heat than a hill.

The best known of fixed clouds is probably the banner cloud which streams like a flag from a high peak—continuously gaining new substance as valley air, riding up a mountainside on the wind's back, condenses near the crest—continuously evaporating old substance at its tattered flagtail end perhaps a mile to leeward as the air mixes with drier air or subsides to a warmer level. Thus the wind blows right through the banner cloud instead of carrying it along—just as if it were a flag of cloth.

Another stand-still cloud familiar to mountaineers is the crest or cap cloud, a kind of tablecloth of fog that drapes itself snugly upon summits. Like the banner cloud it lets the wind blow through it, eating condensation on the one side, voiding evaporation on the other. It is also called the helm cloud or foehn wall through which the foehn winds blow.

The third stay-put cloud is the strangest and loveliest of all, the lenticular or lens cloud. It is usually shaped like an almond or a surreal convex lens with tapering pointed edges and, like a lens, often shows iridescent colors around its circumference. It looks as if it might have been painted by Dali. As with the last two clouds, it remains stationary in the windy sky, balancing condensation with evaporation, often miles from a hill so that its air leash from earth is hard to trace. Yet it is anchored securely by a standing wave of air that billows up from some irregularity of ground to windward. It may be high enough to mark the beginning of the stratosphere or it may float close to the low stratus level. Wherever it is found it is a living graph of the wind's true path, the fixed white cap of a standing billow of air—as real as a stopped clock, as graceful as the flying tresses of Aura—cool, beautiful, unearthly.

A special form of the lenticular in mountain skies is the moazagotl cloud or "foe's beard," so called because of its reputation as an omen of trouble. This dangerous cloud, part of the complex condensation in standing air waves to leeward of high mountain ranges, was recently explored with its associated violent winds in a special "Mountain Wave Project" of the Geophysics Research Directorate of the United States Air Force. The objective was to discover the full pattern of the wave and the causes of its most violent disturbances which have so often led pilots to disaster, particularly in sudden turbulent downdrafts that dropped them from apparently safe altitudes to the crags below.

Flying sail planes that are too slow to be seriously buffeted by rough air, the research men gradually accumulated facts. They found that the many waves of wind in the lee of the Sierras near Bishop, California, flow up and down in almost regular rhythm between two layers of rotating, eddying air, the upper moving invisibly in the stratosphere, the lower outlined by a long succession of revolving moazagotl clouds, now better known to meteorologists as rotor clouds because of their roller-bearing action under the leaping wind. At the base of each of a long series of multiple lenticular clouds arranged like stacks of airplane wings in a factory, the rotor clouds are the focal points of the wild lower turbulence that extends to the ground and includes treacherous jetlike downdrafts in the lee of each roller.

More mysterious but of a similar ilk are the shy nacreous or mother-of-pearl clouds that stand still at an altitude of from fourteen to twenty miles: three times the height of cirrus. These rare clouds that are seldom seen except in polar regions when a foehn wind is blowing at ground level are now known to be lenticular in nature and normally composed of ice crystals which by refraction create the pearly iridescence observed. They are perhaps best known to Norwegian weather men in Oslo who see them in the clear evening skies as the dry west wind descends from the mountains in the wake of a storm. They show up at night almost as plainly as by day, sometimes remaining luminous three hours after sunset. Might they be more than the remote spoondrift of a mountain wave stirred by the passing jet stream? What significance that "an exceptionally lovely development of mother-of-pearl clouds was seen on May 19, 1910, the day when the earth passed through the tail of Halley's comet"?

I know of only one kind of earth cloud loftier and rarer than the nacreous, and that is the very aloof one called noctilucent. Measured at more than fifty miles above the ground and illumined by the sun virtually all night, it is believed to be composed of very fine, dry volcanic dust, or perhaps the faint, powdery ash of meteors. It is seen in the north only from the latitude of Canada and northern Europe, mysteriously lingering close to the horizon, seldom observed as high as 10°. Few noctilucent clouds have been reported since World War I, although they were frequently seen on summer nights for a few years after the 1883 explosion of Krakatoa, the Siberian meteor of 1908, and the lesser blowup of Katmai in 1912. They are silvery white at the top, yellowish gold nearer the bottom, rarely faintly bluish but never iridescent. And sometimes among them at the same low angle lurk darker clouds which, curiously enough, are not lucent at all.

FLOWER CLIMB

FROM *Among the Hills*

REGINALD FARRER

🦌 Few people think of plant collecting as either an arduous or a dangerous occupation. It would seem offhand that there could be nothing easier or more pleasant than picking flowers. This selection from Reginald Farrer's *Among the Hills* will serve quickly enough to disabuse the reader.

Plant collecting is far from a simple business. The serious plant expedition is usually subsidized by a syndicate at home and must get results. An expedition will climb to a high mountain meadow many times to catch the seasonal seeding and flowering periods.

Farrer, naturalist and collector, climbed the European and Asian mountains for his specimens and had the hazards of both hostile mountains and people to overcome.

IT IS IN THE GREEN CHILLS OF DAWN THAT ONE SETS OUT FROM CASTELLAR FOR Rocca Longa. The air is cold and solemn, to fit the solemnity of the occasion; for you are sallying forth now on a good solid climb of six hours or so, to pay your respects to a plant which is among the rarest and most beautiful in the world. Not only that, but the most impregnably seated; more than that, the most remote and difficult to see. "Non cuivis homini contingit adire Rupestrim." For a few hundred yards one follows the level road running south from Castellar, then a track diverges, and begins steadily climbing the enormous mountain on your left. All the rock of the district is calcareous: and here there are screes that might be lying under Robin Proctor or the Long Scar, so exact is their resemblance to the screes of the mountain-limestone. . . .

In the gloom of stormy daybreak the path mounts rapidly. Dense darkness covered the hills across the valley of the Ronca; all that we ever saw that day of the alpine sunrise was a livid bronze that ultimately tinged their masses of cold blue. The worst of weather threatened; vast snowfields up in the north gleamed lurid for a while amid the shifting volumes of storm, and then were finally shrouded from view as the clouds settled lower and lower. However, there was no help for it but to continue. One does not come all the way to Castellar, to be beaten back from the Rocca by rain or hail. Besides, the weather is generally open to a bluff; the worst of clouds, if firmly confronted, very often turns, like the devil, and flees from you. And there is always the chance here, that the tempests will pass away to the greater ranges in the north. This in the end proved to be the reward of our pertinacity; for, as we mounted, the lowering darkness grew lighter and lighter; the banks of gloom began to shift clearly northward; and at last the day was fully on us, open and grey, but without imminence of wet.

All that hill lies in shadow through the morning; this is the reason why one chooses this side, by which to ascend to the Rocca, so as to come down again in the afternoon, through the glen of the Val Riario into the Valbonne, which will then be in the shade, while this slope would be in full sun by that time. The ascent is extraordinarily long and high; yet seems achieved with extraordinary rapidity. The fact is that I have made it before—ask me not the story of that first ascent—"Infandum, regina, jubes renovare dolorem." In that former attempt on the Daphne, I was ignominiously baffled by cloud within a hundred yards of it, on the very topmost ridge itself. Let us say no more, but hastily turn our attention to the rocks of limestone beneath which the track is now ascending.

For not only are there here beginning Primulas of different and interesting sorts, but also there is abundance of *Phyteuma comosum*. Now this is a rare treasure, not to be collected but with hammer and chisel; for it inhabits only the smallest crevices of the hardest mountain limestone. To the limestone it is firmly faithful, and is a species restricted to the southern ranges. In the Dolomites it is especially notable: on a cliff behind Cortina you will see it in rock more hard than iron, making wide masses. The plant forms a huge, fat and waxy yellow rootstock, which pours and moulds itself deep into soil-less crannies, drawing nourishment from the lime; from the cliff-face, no crevice being visible at all, hang the tufts of foliage. This is of a very dark, livid leaden green, almost black in general effect; the basal leaves are stalked, broad, irregular, roughly ivy-shaped, pointed and jagged. Sometimes they are almost grey with a fine down, but normally are quite smooth and glossy. The flowers come up in dense heads, on stems of two or three inches. They are wonderful and weird, a bunch of long dark blue tubes, like elongated, twisted Chianti-bottles, from each of which protrudes a stigma like an immense fine feeler whisking about this way and that. Contrary to reasonable expectation, *Phyteuma comosum* is not only very good-natured about growing on and striking fresh root from a mutilated stump, but it is also very easy-going with regard to ordinary conditions of culture in the rock-garden—easy-going, that is, for a plant which has every right, by all appearances, to be so difficult and exacting. A good chink or crevice, with deep good soil, will suit it well. The one drawback, as I have said before, is that slugs adore it with so notorious a passion. So notoriously, indeed, that when, right up on the Ciriegia, close to eternal snow, my companion found a big fat black slug perambulating the cliff, he had much reason on his side in announcing that this must be a sign that *Phyteuma comosum* was near.

Having collected a few convenient plants of this by smashing away the rock, we continued on our way. The track was loose and stony, most awkward to walk on; but all around there were so many plants that one hardly noticed the climb. Indeed, it is well that the Rocca should be so remote and hard to get at; for the whole range is prodigiously rich in rare plants. As we went, there shone orange lilies, and *Genista radiata* spidery amid the scrub; but now we were getting almost too high for the noble leaves of the Christmas Rose which abounds in every bush and in all the stony grass at the very roadsides round Castellar, and must be a snowy glory in winter and early spring. Soon after this one emerges above the first range of cliffs which had looked so stupendous from the village, and comes out of the copse upon a smooth shoulder of mown grass where there are châlets. On the other side of this the track goes mounting stiffly again, through more copse, towards yet another hitherto unsuspected wall of precipice, over which, be sure, will be found to loom another and yet another after that; so that you never seem to get to any definite top at all. This is the disheartening part of these Alps, their lack of finality. You are always finding one more wall of cliff above the one you have just laboriously surmounted in the fond hope that it was really the last. So we go zigzagging up now, under more rock, until the path through the thick brushwood gives a little holiday by meandering along a shoulder, where there are a few limestone bluffs to be profitably explored.

. . . On these rocks there was a happening. For, as my companion was plucking trunks of Primula from their nook, a little dormouse walked straight out of them, and sat on his hand, and blinked at him with expressionless eyes like beads. We were overjoyed, and received the visitor with sweet words. To none of these did it pay any attention. Ultimately my companion put it in his pocket for future reference. I entered cautions against this step, being afraid that the mouse might get squeezed against a rock in the excitement and difficulty of climbing after *Daphne rupestris*. However, mouse's finder seemed properly impressed with the peril, and a sense of responsibility. He walked forward as carefully as if he had been carrying roc's eggs for the Sultan of Babylon. Mouse, however, behind his silence, concealed wisdom and much strength of mind and will. For, when at last we sat down to administer milk and air to the captive, it was discovered that without saying a word, he had inconspicuously vanished into his native wilds again.

Now the path was really drawing near, through thinning woodland, to the shoulder of the huge mountain range which had blocked out the sky from Castellar. In the silt of the track-side there were a few pieces of *Saxifraga mutata,* and, just where the path turns over the actual shoulder, a mass of weathered boulders, on which were growing *Primula Auricula* and *Saxifraga aeizoon.* From the shoulder itself, which was a down of short grass, with a few pine trees, and here and there a rosy flower of *Cephalanthera rubra* unexpectedly appearing, we had a clear prospect right over the Varronca, where the Ronca river swells again and again into little bright blue lakes that lay motionless like patches of sky that morning, deep down between the tumbled pale-green ranges of the hills. On the other side, away into the northern distance, rolled other high ranges. Beyond these, and higher still in the north, all the snowfields lay buried in violet storm. From this prospect we turned away sharp to the left, up over the ridge. Here we entered on a pass of meadow-grass, diversified with big rocks, and bushy with dwarf beech. Among these were tufts of the larger Hellebore, and on the rocks little hovering flowers. It was so perfect a fairy-glade that one expected every moment to see its occupants come forth and dance. And this was the summit of that first pass.

And then suddenly, for the first time, we set eyes on Rocca Longa. And Rocca Longa struck us with terror as we gazed; for it seemed twenty miles away at the least, an enormous, enormously distant range of limestone, misty-blue against the risen sun, jagging up in ridge after ridge, to the highest summit, which also happened to be the most remote. Yet ours had been, perhaps, quite the nearest way to the Rocca. Thus securely defended is the Daphne, on a range that rises right from the very centre of a mountain pedestal, wholly devoid of roads or any means of access; besides being well cut off from any known corner of the earth. However, we justly attributed our momentary depression to lack of food, and advanced to where there is a dairy-farm on the Col, and innumerable cows, there to purchase milk, and drink it to the accompaniment of our own eggs and bread and chocolate. It was a lovely halting-spot—when you got away from the trampled muck of the cows and pigs.

For we were up now, in the cleared air of morning, fresh and sparkling with cool breezes, yet warm with the first virgin rays of the sun. Away before us, over an amphitheatre of meadow and valley, ranged the long mass of the Rocca, and now we could see that its extreme remoteness had been the result of atmospheric effect. For, standing against the sun, its whole bulk was in flat soft tones, devoid of relief or salient detail. Far and high though it undoubtedly was, it was neither quite so high nor nearly so far as it had looked at first sight. Up behind us as we sat there rose also a wonderful hill, precipitous and peaked, with rose-pink pinnacles sticking out all over it; and pine-scrub in the gullies. It bristled with points like a hedgehog, and was even more densely spiky than those puddings which are adorned with almonds stuck in on end; a fashion adopted from the style of rock-gardening favoured in the fifties.

Reluctantly we stirred from our rest, and renewed our journey towards the remote Rocca. But now, as the sun rose, relief and shadows were being quickly mapped out upon its slopes, and the distances diminished. The way led round, under the rampart of soil that upholds this high valley. There were curious bare pans of black silt to cross; otherwise grass and scattered coppice, composed of charming little isolated beech trees, dwarfed and Japanesed by wind and weather, which one longed to carry off bodily, but that one felt certain they would revert and grow big as soon as they had surroundings more sympathetic. A final pull up among Rhododendrons, and we were fairly embarked on the last climb. And by now the day was wholly fair and fine. It was with dancing spirits that we strode along the track, rising gradually at every step, towards the goal. At length it reached the foot of the ridge, and then began briskly to mount, though at an easy slant, round each successive buttress of the towering calcareous wall which is Rocca Longa.

The going was over a certain amount of loose white limestone, with limestone cliffs becoming bigger and more imposing as one drew towards the upper bulwarks of the ridge. . . .

But now we are dropping into a wide grassy hollow, immediately under the culminating point of Rocca Longa. Here there is a little cowshed called the Casa della Rocca, or the Refuge d'Arlet, according as you choose to use the language of one frontier or another. And the mortal moment is very near. To fortify ourselves we eat our lunch, and force our trembling fingers to collect Primulas, which our souls, meanwhile, are too deeply excited to care about, or our eyes to see. Fortunately, then, it is simply a matter of kicking sods and tussocks out of the hillside that is matted with them, and then absentmindedly cleaning the individual roots, as one separates the clumps into their component plants. Straight behind us rises a stark rosy cliff of limestone, above a rippling slope of Primula; and, just beyond this (which is the southern face of the actual summit), there looms another, which is the actual seat of *Daphne rupestris*. For, on one cliff, and on that one cliff only, will that exclusive plant take up its residence. Neither to the right nor to the left of its chosen precipice will you see a sign of it, though the others may have exactly the same rock, and exactly the same exposure.

However, this wisdom is proleptic; at the moment I had no inclination to wisdom of any sort; my brain felt dissolved into an icy liquid somewhere in the pit of my stomach. The little warm hollow was filled with a silence so complete that it seemed as if the Earth-mother herself was sharing in the solemnity of the moment. A second failure could not be borne or thought of; and already the clouds were driving noiselessly up at us over the lower rim of the bowl where we sat; and though they were still so thin that the sun made them into a veil of gold as they drifted, I could bear the suspense at last no longer, bolted my remaining fragment of egg, and began scrambling at a slant across the slope that led to the further cliff. Up I scrambled, and up, until its crannies, and the growths in them, grew clear to view. And there, over the whole of that face, was *Daphne rupestris*.

Where should we naturally look for *Daphne rupestris,* you and I? Where, but in places like those favoured by the rest of the family: that is to say, on ridges and slopes of hard peaty turf? As for its name, it might easily be called the Rock-Daphne from haunting such open banks up among the rocks. And now look at that naked precipice, and give me news. For the specific name is not a blind guide as it so often is. *Daphne rupestris* is the most absolutely saxatile of all rock-plants; it is more saxatile than anything I know except *Androsace imbricata.* Even *Saxifraga florulenta* and *Phyteuma* occasionally seed into unlikely places, such as silt-beds and moraines; but the Rock Daphne will practically never be seen at all, and certainly never be seen in full health, except in the cracks of a sheer limestone cliff facing due south. Indeed, it precisely matches the habit of the *Androsace,* except that it is as passionately attached to the limestone as the *Androsace* to the granite.

Here, in microscopic crannies, it roots back into chinks where no soil can be, but perhaps, a little humus at first, and then only moisture and lime. Here it forms bushes that lie tight and hard against the cliff, hugging the rock as closely as any willow or cotoneaster. Each thick little wooden twig, gnarled and pressed against the stone, is crowned with a tuft of dark green, tiny, narrow-oval leaves, solid and lucent, roughly resembling those of the common alpine *globularia,* as, indeed, does the whole look of the plant at first sight. And on these mats, in heads of two or three, are scattered the great rosy trumpets, flat and firm on the firm flat mass. They did not appear to seed, though seed one supposes they must: but one big sheet would send out a sucker, here and there, to emerge from some apparently unconnected crevice half a yard away, and there, in time, splay out into another sheet of flower and leaf, plastered close on the blank wall of the rock.

It is a marvellous sight, that little Daphne, up and up the cliff, from base to summit. It was still in flower in the highest chinks, so that I had the joy of craning up from below when I had climbed as high as I dared, to see its waxy-pink loveliness in display. The plant, of course, is very rare indeed. It is almost entirely confined to one or two small districts; in these districts has not many stations, and is, even in those stations, narrowly restricted. For, although abundant where it does occur, it ceases, abruptly (as here), to right and left of just the one precipice that has happened to take its fancy. All along the south side of the Rocca, for instance, there are cliffs that seem made for it; yet the Daphne won't even trouble to try them. It will have exactly what it likes, and only what it likes, this domineering small shrub. It *must* have limestone, and it *must* have a cliff both sheer and sound, and it *must* have an exposure facing full due south, it appears; but a cliff may take pains to fulfil faithfully all these requirements, without ever succeeding in winning the favour of the Daphne.

Also, *Daphne rupestris* is quite the most difficult plant I have ever had to collect. Collecting *Saxifraga florulenta* and *Phyteuma comosum* is, by comparison, like plucking bushes of groundsel out of my moraines. The precipice is hard as iron, and solid as the British intelligence; impossible to find a cleavage anywhere; as you smite at it with futile hammer the rock rings derisively at you again, like adamant, chips a little, and does no more. The cracks, too, are of the tiniest; the Daphne wedges itself into them with a fanatical tightness. Its roots go far, far in, and it is also dangerously, curiously, breakable just at the neck. All along the lines of the cliff one has to clamber here and there, questing for a chink that may not prove so inexorable as the others—and a Daphne more amenable to suasion. Below you long banks of grass and lesser buttresses of limestone slope abruptly into infinity. There are cows under one's feet, near a path; they look like fleas, or grains of pepper. And down below these again, below all the green mountains that descend and descend in successive laps—there, through swirling grey-and-golden glimpses of the cloud, one snatches a rare glimpse of Savinanza Water, lying like a sapphire pavement, among ranges that seem, from here, to be mere mole-hummocks on a lawn.

Up and up above one's head towers the wall of the cliff: and all of it, from top to bottom, is lined and seamed with flat masses of the Daphne, from the cracks at eye-level to those far up on the bare face, where no depredator can get them. Not, as you will judge, that the Daphne is inclined to be tender to the depredator, anyhow, or to give him a chance; the Daphne has its own methods of dealing with the depredator. Unfortunately, in the vile soul of man this resistance has been held to justify reprisals; and the depredator has, accordingly, developed a foul habit of tearing out the Daphne, in rage and desperation, by rootless masses from its chinks, thus certainly killing alike what he takes and what he leaves. He is maddened by its obduracy, as men are maddened who murder their obdurate mistresses. I have suffered under this insanity of his myself (hardly less indeed, than the Daphne), receiving moribund or lifeless twigs and rootless chunks, when I had paid good money in the hope of good plants.

After which, do I need to justify my own action? Many were the plants, indeed, that I collected with pious care that day; and many were the pieces into which they were subsequently divided. But not a piece did I attempt that was not amenable to the persuasions of hammer and chisels; not a piece

I took but had roots; not a piece I took but has lived and thrived and surmounted the shock of removal. And the cliffs of the Rocca certainly show
no less rich than before. This is not to say that *Daphne rupestris* is exactly
an easy plant in cultivation, as you will have gathered from all this; it is apt
to damp off in the wetness of open ground in the garden; it really wants its
sunny crevice, in limy humus and vegetable soil, with perfect drainage, and
rather excess of drought than of humidity. Altogether, what with its remoteness, the altitudes and inconveniences of the Rocca, and its wild neighbourhood, the dense hardness of the rock, and the difficulty, for experienced and
inexperienced alike, of getting out sound plants and starting them again
when got, I am not afraid that *Daphne rupestris* will suffer from the wandering tourist. As for the professional depredator, I throw the plant upon
his mercy and sense of decency; let him take, indeed, if he needs, and if he
can, and if he must, but let him take with care and courtesy and consideration; and realise the ugly, futile cruelty of spoiling what he cannot safely
get, merely in order that some fragments of the wreckage he makes may
ultimately die miserably in English gardens, instead of in their sacked home
on the Rocca, when their tale of years is full.

MOUNTAIN FRINGE

SNOW AND ICE

FROM *Physiography: An Introduction to the Study of Nature*

THOMAS HENRY HUXLEY

Thomas Henry Huxley labeled himself agnostic, "without faith in any truth save that reached by the patient application of scientific methods." To the Victorian fundamentalists that was heresy and damnation and they fought him with no holds barred. In defense of Darwin's theory of evolution he battled with Gladstone and Bishop Wilberforce and stood firm through two decades of abuse and calumny from lesser men. His London lectures for workingmen on "A Piece of Chalk" and "A Grain of Sand" opened for them a new world of scientific causes and relations, and gathered audiences of hundreds. These talks, published, are among the best of his writings, models of popular scientific presentation. In this extract from his *Physiography* we have the same blend of precise thinking and lucid writing.

WHEN SNOW FALLS UPON A MOUNTAIN IN WINTER, IT MAY LIE THERE UNMELTED until the warmth of summer returns to thaw it. But, if the mountain be very high, the summer-heat may never be strong enough to melt all the ice on its top, and the top will therefore be enveloped in perpetual snow. A line drawn at the level above which the snow never melts is called the *snow-line*. On the north side of the Himálaya Mountains this line is 16,600 feet high; that is to say, all the snow which falls below this height is melted in summer, but all above remains unmelted. In the Andes of Peru the limit of perpetual snow is about 15,500 feet; but in passing northwards or southwards from these hot regions, we expect to find the snow-line descending; in the Swiss Alps, for example, it comes down to about 8,500 feet above the sea. Still farther north it reaches yet lower, and, in the Arctic regions, descends to the very sea-level; the winter's accumulation of snow is never completely melted by the summer-sun, and the snow consequently lies on the ground all the year round. . . .

When a snow-storm occurs in this country, the snow does little or nothing in the way of denudation, beyond what it may effect indirectly, by giving rise to floods when a rapid thaw takes place. In fact, the snow, as snow, protects rather than destroys. But the result is different in a mountainous country, such as that of the Swiss Alps. The greater part of the snow which falls there above the snow-line, lies all the year round unmelted; and, therefore, every fall must needs add to the thickness of the heap piled upon the mountain-top. It is true that the snow evaporates, but the evaporation is extremely slow, and is far from equal to the additions constantly received; and, though the heat of the sun during the day, may melt the surface layer, the water thus formed sinks in and becomes frozen in the interior of the mass. Occasionally, the accumulation is relieved by a great mass of snow sliding down the mountain slope, as an *avalanche*. Usually, however, the pressure of the heaped-up snow gets rid of the surplus by gently squeezing it into the valleys below, where it moves down with extreme slowness. Yet it does not come down as a mass of white opaque snow. It has been shown in an earlier part of this work that snow is white and opaque in consequence of the air entangled among its crystals. In squeezing a handful of snow into a snowball, some of this air is forced out, and the loose crystals begin to adhere to one another; while, by compressing snow very tightly in a hydraulic press, it may be rendered almost homogeneous and thus brought nearly to the condition of ice. In this way, the great pressure exerted by the piles of snow in the Alpine snow-fields compresses the lower layers, and converts them more or less completely into ice. The imperfectly consolidated substance, partly snow and partly ice, is known in Switzerland as *Névé* or *Firn*. Moreover, the water produced by temporary thaw, during sunshine, becomes frozen into ice; and, in these and other ways, the water, which fell on the mountain-top as loose white snow, is ultimately sent down into the valleys in the form of solid ice. The river of ice which thus drains the high snow-fields is termed a *glacier*.

Although we have just spoken of a "river of ice," it is not easy, at first, to believe that a substance so solid and rigid can really move in any way like a mobile liquid. Yet the fact that the glacier does so move can easily be demonstrated. Drive a row of stakes firmly into the ice across a glacier and opposite to some well-marked point, so that you may know exactly their position. If you examine these stakes a week or two afterwards, you will find that they are no longer at A, but at some point lower down the glacier, say opposite to B. The ice has therefore moved during this time from A to B, carrying the stakes with it.

From this experiment it is seen that the ice really moves. But the experiment teaches something more than this; for it will be observed that the stakes have not only moved down, but have changed their relative positions. Instead of forming a straight line across the ice, as at A, they now form a curve at B; the stakes in the middle of the row have got farther from A than those at the sides, and it is therefore clear that they must have moved faster. But the movement of the stakes is due simply to the movement of the ice, so that if the middle stakes move faster than the side ones, it shows that the middle of the glacier moves faster than its sides. Exactly the same thing may be observed in a river: light bodies floated on a stream move like the stakes carried down by the glacier. Nor is it difficult to see why a river should flow more rapidly in the middle than at its sides. The particles of water at the sides rub against the banks, and consequently are not so free to move as the particles in the middle of the stream. In like manner, friction against the rocky walls on the flanks of a glacier causes the ice at the sides to move more sluggishly than the ice in the middle. Again, it is known that, in a river, the particles at the bottom drag along the bed and move less rapidly than those at the surface. The ice of a glacier behaves in precisely the same way. It is concluded, therefore, that the motion of a glacier is like the motion of a river. If the glacier enters a gorge, it becomes contracted and the flow is rapid: while, if its bed widens, it spreads out and the movement becomes slower. In truth, in all points, the motion of a glacier resembles that of a river; the movement is essentially the same in kind but different in degree, the rate of movement of the glacier being perhaps only a few inches or, at most, a yard or two, daily.

This sluggish motion of a glacier, and the way in which it accommodates itself to all the inequalities of the surface over which it travels, long ago gave rise to the supposition that ice is a plastic or viscous substance, something like dough or even treacle, so that it can sink into a depression, or ride over a ridge, without losing its continuity. Yet, as a matter of fact, ice is so brittle that if you pull, or try to bend, it, it will snap, without stretching to any appreciable extent. How, then, can the apparent plasticity be reconciled with the undoubted brittleness? Prof. Tyndall has shown the way out of this difficulty.

When a schoolboy makes a snowball, he squeezes a handful or two of light snow into a hard compact lump; and it is worth noting that, if the snow be just on the point of thawing, he will be able to weld it into a firmer mass than if he employed perfectly hard and dry snow. Snow, as we have seen, is nothing but a confused mass of ice-crystals; and the snowball becomes hard, partly, because it contains less air, and, partly, because the little pieces of ice of which it is composed, instead of remaining loose, stick firmly to one another. But why do they thus become welded together? Experiment shows that when two pieces of damp ice are pressed together, they immediately freeze into one solid mass. Faraday observed this curious fact five-and-twenty years ago, and the phenomenon has been termed *regelation*. Hence, when snow is strongly squeezed, the icy particles freeze together into a compact substance; and, hence, the snow from which a glacier takes its birth, is

H. Armstrong Roberts

THE LANDWASSER VIADUCT OF THE RHAETIAN RAILWAY NEAR FILISUR IN THE GRISONS, SWITZERLAND, IS A TRIUMPH OF ENGINEERING SKILL

THE DEVIL'S BRIDGE BETWEEN BALTCHENEN AND AUDER-
INALL, SWITZERLAND

PLAN FOR A RAILROAD TO ASCEND A MOUNTAINSIDE WITH THE HELP OF BALLOONS.
PROPOSED BY FRIEDRICH ALBRECHT, 1859

A TRAIN OF THE AIGLE-SÉPEY-DIABLERETS RAILWAY IN THE VAUDOIS ALPS, SWITZERLAND, TAKES
WINTER SPORTS LOVERS TO THE SNOW FIELDS

Bradford Washburn

EXTRAORDINARY TWISTING AND BANDING OF THE ICE IN THE GREAT BERING GLACIER WHERE IT
FLOWS THROUGH A GAP IN THE ST. ELIAS RANGE, ALASKA

THIS HUGE ALPINE "MUSHROOM" WAS FORMED WHEN THE INTENSE SWISS SUNSHINE MELTED
ALL BUT A THIN SHAFT OF ICE BENEATH A ROCK CARRIED DOWN THE GLACIER TABLE

Bachmann Getshertisch
Swiss National Travel Office

Bradford Washburn

THE 190-FOOT ICE CLIFF WHERE THE SOUTH CRILLON GLACIER PLUNGES INTO THE FRIGID
WATERS OF CRILLON LAKE IN ALASKA. THS GLACIER MOVES AT THE RATE OF MORE THAN TWO
FEET A DAY

EXTRAORDINARY MEDIAL MORAINES ON BARNARD GLACIER, ALASKA, SHOWING HOW A MAIN-
TRUNK GLACIER IS FORMED FROM A LARGE NUMBER OF SMALL TRIBUTARIES

Bradford Washburn

STEPS LEADING TO AN ANCIENT INCA OBSERVATORY IN PERU

THE RUINS OF PETRA, IN JORDAN, WHOSE TEMPLES, TOMBS, AND DWELLINGS WERE CARVED IN COLORED LIMESTONE, WERE DISCOVERED IN 1812

LINES OF HOLES IN SOUTHERN PERU. THEIR PURPOSE IS NOT KNOWN, ALTHOUGH IT MAY HAVE BEEN FOR DEFENSE

AERIAL VIEW OF VOLCANIC CONES IN PERU

pressed by the weight above into a hard mass, more or less like true ice. A number of pieces of ice, powerfully squeezed together in a hydraulic press, are readily united into a solid lump, or a single mass may be crushed, and the fragments built up into a differently shaped body. In a similar manner, when a glacier is forced over an obstacle, the ice, being brittle, cracks and snaps, but the enormous pressure of the sliding mass behind, squeezes it together again, and regelation immediately heals the fractures. The glacier therefore accommodates itself to irregularities in its bed, not by virtue of any real plasticity, but by being successively fractured and frozen. In fact, by suitable means, ice may be artificially moulded at will, as though it possessed true plasticity; and a similar operation is doubtless carried on in nature.

As it creeps down the valley, the glacier transports, from higher to lower levels, any detrital matter that may happen to fall upon its surface. From the neighbouring rocks, fragments are constantly being loosened by atmospheric agents, and these, sooner or later, tumble down upon the glacier. In this way, a line of débris fringes each side of the glacier, some of the stones being perhaps several tons in weight. Such accumulations of detritus are known as *moraines;* and, as those which are now being described, occur on the two sides of the ice-river they are distinguished as *lateral moraines.* As the glacier moves along, the moraine-matter is carried forwards, until, at length, it reaches the end of the glacier; and thus fragments of rock may be transported down the valley, far from the heights above. The water which issues from the melting ice, at the end of the glacier, is unable to carry off this burden of stones which the ice has deposited; and, hence, we generally find, across the end of the glacier, a confused heap of rubbish, known as a *terminal moraine. . . .*

A glacier resembles a river, not only in its power of thus transporting detritus from a higher to a lower level, but also in acting as a direct agent of denudation. Just as a river wears away its banks and its bed, so the ice acts on the sides and bottom of the valley along which it travels. If the ice has to turn a sharp corner, or make an abrupt descent, it is forced to split, and in this way yawning chasms, perhaps hundreds of feet in depth, are produced in the glacier. Such rents are termed *crevasses.* Stones, sometimes of great size, fall with a crash down these clefts, and reaching the bottom of the glacier get frozen into its base. As the glacier moves, these stones, pressed by the weight of ice above, scratch and score the rocky bed in the direction of the ice-flow; while the stones themselves, jammed in between the ice and its floor, get bruised in turn, so that by the time they are discharged at the terminal moraine they may be covered with parallel scratches.

At the same time, the smaller fragments worn off the rocks by the passage of a glacier get ground down into fine gravel, sand, and mud, which may be carried in suspension by the stream of water which flows over the bed of the glacier. For it should be noted that the bottom layer of ice, pressed by the weight above, and grinding along the floor, is generally in a state of thaw; and, moreover, water finds it way from the surface to the bottom through crevasses. Hence, a little liquid stream separates the bottom ice from the rocky bed; and at the end, or snout, of the glacier this water issues forth, not indeed as a clear bright spring, but as a thick stream laden with detritus. The Rhine, the Rhone, the Po, the Ganges, and many other large rivers, may be traced back to muddy streams springing from glaciers. The fine detrital matter which the water thus carries along polishes the surface of the rock over which it flows. The action of a glacier is consequently twofold: the fine sandy matter polishes the surface, while the large stones scratch furrows. It is, in fact, as though some giant hand had rubbed the surface of the rock with fine emery powder, and at the same time rasped it with a huge file.

All rough points of rock in the path of a glacier are thus rubbed down, and projecting masses are smoothed to the form of rounded bosses. The flat-domed hummocks of rock produced in this way are termed *sheep-backs* or *roches moutonnées,* since, if seen in the distance, they bear some resemblance to a flock of sheep. Hence, the passage of a glacier across a country gives rise to peculiar features not produced by any other agent of denudation; and, by these peculiarities, we may tell, with certainty, that ice has been at work in a district where there is, perhaps, not a vestige of ice at the present day. Thus, in many of the valleys of Switzerland, not now occupied by glaciers, the rocks are rounded, polished, and scratched, showing that the Swiss glaciers must formerly have been of gigantic proportions and that they extended far beyond the limits retained by their present successors.

On travelling northwards, the snow-line is found to descend until, in the Arctic Regions, it comes down to the very sea-level. Hence, in such regions, the entire surface of land may be enveloped in a mantle of ice. This ice-sheet creeps down towards the shore, until its foot at length advances into the sea. Huge masses of ice then become detached, and are sent drifting away as icebergs. These mountains of ice often assume most fantastic shapes; and their vast mass produces so great a depression of temperature in the neighbouring air that, when they are carried into the Atlantic, they are usually obscured by a shroud of mist. The icebergs, like glaciers, are laden with fragments of rock worn from the land over which the ice-sheet travelled; and when, on reaching warmer waters, they melt, they discharge this freight of stones and earth, which may thus get carried far from their original home. When blocks of rock are borne along by running water, they become rounded by the friction to which they are subjected; but, when a fragment of rock is transported on an iceberg, it may retain much of its angularity and be dropped upon the sea-bed in an almost unworn state. The finer detritus which the berg carries will be diffused through the water in which the ice melts; and currents may transport it far away into southern latitudes. If a glacier descends to the edge of a lake, exactly the same thing occurs as in the formation of an iceberg. A tongue of ice is pushed into the water, and bergs break off and float away, carrying their burden of moraine matter to be strewn over the bottom of the lake on the melting of the floating ice. If the bottom of the lake, or of the sea, should at any time be upheaved, the glacial mud and gravel, with angular blocks and ice-scratched boulders, may be exposed to view; and may thus furnish evidence of glacial denudation in countries which are now free from anything like glaciers or icebergs.

Other evidence of ice-action is afforded by the peculiar position of large angular blocks of stone, poised perhaps upon the very edge of a precipice, or balanced upon a mere point. Such stones, known as *perched blocks* or *blocs perchés,* could hardly have been brought into their strange position by mere rolling, or by the action of running water; but it is easy to see that they might have been dropped by an iceberg, or left stranded by the gradual melting of a glacier on which they were originally seated.

5

Men Fight on the Mountains

It is a particular kind of war that is fought on the mountains, not one of massed armies and regular formations, but one where individual skill, daring, ingenuity are the decisive factors. It is the terrain of the guerrilla fighter, of the small detachment, where speed and mobility decide defeat or victory.

For armies, war in the mountains is a war of speed and surprise, of great risks and great daring. Hannibal lost 36,000 of his army of 55,000 crossing the Pyrenees and the Alps, but he defeated the Roman army. Napoleon had to push his heavy artillery over the St. Bernard pass in hollow logs, but he held Europe. The special character of mountain war that makes its literature so powerful is that the fighting is always against two enemies—against other men and against the mountains themselves.

HANNIBAL CROSSING THE ALPS

HANNIBAL CROSSES
THE ALPS

FROM *Book XXI*

L I V Y

One of the most spectacular episodes related by Livy in his history of Rome is Hannibal's Alpine crossing in 218 B.C. What caught the wonder of the ancient world was not that Hannibal had made the treacherous crossing—that had been done before by the Latins—but that the Carthaginian had in five months moved an army with its batteries of weapons, including a great herd of elephants, from Spain, across the Pyrenees, over the Rhone, across the Alps and into the Italian peninsula, had slipped behind a Roman army, had rested, refitted and then attacked to catch the Romans unaware and unprepared.

Scholars have questioned Livy's accuracy as historian. That he had either the historical insight or the critical judgment of such historians as Thucydides is debatable, but there is no disagreement as regards his enthusiasm and his sense for the dramatic.

HANNIBAL, LEAVING THE DRUENTIA, AND ADVANCING FOR THE MOST PART through a champaign country, reached the Alps without being molested by the Gauls who inhabited those regions. Then, though report, which is wont to exaggerate uncertain dangers, had already taught them what to expect, still, the near view of the lofty mountains, with their snows almost merging in the sky; the shapeless hovels perched on crags; the frost-bitten flocks and beasts of burden; the shaggy, unkempt men; animals and inanimate objects alike stiff with cold, and all more dreadful to look upon than words can tell, renewed their consternation. As their column began to mount the first slopes, mountaineers were discovered posted on the heights above, who, had they lain concealed in hidden valleys, might have sprung out suddenly and attacked them with great rout and slaughter. Hannibal gave the command to halt, and sent forward some Gauls to reconnoitre. When informed by them that there was no getting by that way, he encamped in the most extensive valley to be found in a wilderness of rocks and precipices. He then employed these same Gauls, whose speech and customs did not differ greatly from those of the mountaineers, to mingle in their councils, and in this way learned that his enemies guarded the pass only by day, and at night dispersed, every man to his own home. As soon as it was light, he advanced up the hills, as though he hoped to rush the defile by an open attack in the daytime. Then having spent the day in feigning a purpose other than his real one, he entrenched a camp on the spot where he had halted. But no sooner did he perceive that the mountaineers had dispersed from the heights and relaxed their vigilance, than, leaving for show more fires than the numbers of those who remained in camp demanded; leaving, too, the baggage and the cavalry and a great part of the infantry, he put himself at the head of some light-armed soldiers—all his bravest men—and, marching swiftly to the head of the defile, occupied those very heights which the enemy had held.

With the ensuing dawn the Carthaginians broke camp and the remainder of their army began to move. The natives, on a signal being given, were already coming in from their fastnesses to occupy their customary post, when they suddenly perceived that some of their enemies were in possession of the heights and threatened them from above, and that others were marching through the pass. Both facts presenting themselves at the same time to their eyes and minds kept them for a moment rooted to the spot. Then, when they saw the helter-skelter in the pass and the column becoming embarrassed by its own confusion, the horses especially being frightened and unmanageable, they thought that whatever they could add themselves to the consternation of the troops would be sufficient to destroy them, and rushed down from the cliffs on either side, over trails and trackless ground alike, with all the ease of habit. Then indeed the Phoenicians had to contend at one and the same time against their foes and the difficulties of the ground, and the struggle amongst themselves, as each endeavoured to outstrip the rest in escaping from the danger, was greater than the struggle with the enemy. The horses occasioned the greatest peril to the column. Terrified by the discordant yells, which the woods and ravines redoubled with their echoes, they quaked with fear; and if they happened to be hit or wounded, were so maddened that they made enormous havoc not only of men but of every sort of baggage. Indeed the crowding in the pass, which was steep and precipitous on both sides, caused many—some of them armed men—to be flung down to a great depth; but when beasts of burden with their packs went hurtling down, it was just like the crash of falling walls. Dreadful as these sights were, still Hannibal halted for a little while and held back his men, so as not to augment the terror and confusion. Then, when he saw that the column was being broken in two, and there was danger lest he might have got his army over to no avail, if it were stripped of its baggage, he charged down from the higher ground and routed the enemy by the very impetus of the attack, though he added to the disorder amongst his own troops. But the flurry thus occasioned quickly subsided, as soon as the roads were cleared by the flight of the mountaineers; and the whole army was presently brought over the pass, not only without molestation but almost in silence. Hannibal then seized a stronghold which was the chief place in that region, together with the outlying hamlets, and with the captured food and flocks supported his troops for three days. And in those three days, being hindered neither by the natives, who had been utterly cowed at the outset, nor very greatly by the nature of the country, he covered a good deal of ground.

They came next to another canton, thickly settled for a mountain district. There, not by open fighting, but by his own devices, trickery and deception, Hannibal was all but circumvented. The elder headmen of the strongholds waited on him, as a deputation, and said that, taught by other men's misfortunes—a useful warning—they preferred to experience the friendship of the Phoenicians rather than their might; they were ready, therefore, to carry out his orders, and they requested him to accept provisions and guides and also hostages as a guarantee of good faith. Hannibal, neither blindly trusting nor yet repulsing them, lest, being spurned, they might become openly hostile, returned a friendly answer, accepted the proffered hostages, and used the supplies, which they had brought down, themselves, to the road. But he drew up his column, before following their guides, by no means as though for a march through a friendly country. The van was made up of elephants and cavalry; he himself, with the main strength of the infantry, came next, looking warily about him and watching everything. When they had got to a narrow place, which was overhung on one side by a ridge, the tribesmen rose up on every quarter from their ambush and assailed them, front and rear, fighting hand to hand and at long range, and rolling down huge boulders on the marching troops. The rear-guard bore the brunt of the attack, and as the infantry faced about to meet it, it was very evident that if the column had not been strengthened at that point, it must have suffered a great disaster in this pass. Even so, they were in the utmost peril and came near destruction. For while Hannibal was hesitating to send his division down into the defile, since he had no troops left to secure the rear of the infantry, as he himself secured that of the horse, the mountaineers rushed in on his flank, and breaking through the column, established themselves in the road, so that Hannibal spent one night without cavalry or baggage.

On the following day, since by now the barbarians were attacking with less vigour, his forces were re-united and surmounted the pass; and though they suffered some casualties, still they lost more baggage animals than men. From this point on the mountaineers appeared in smaller numbers, and, more in the manner of brigandage than warfare, attacked sometimes the van, sometimes the rear, whenever the ground afforded an advantage, or the invaders, pushing on too far ahead or lagging behind, gave opportunity. The elephants could be induced to move but very slowly along the steep and narrow trails; but wherever they went they made the column safe from its enemies, who were unaccustomed to the beasts and afraid of venturing too near them.

On the ninth day they arrived at the summit of the Alps, having come for the most part over trackless wastes and by roundabout routes, owing either to the dishonesty of their guides, or—when they would not trust the guides—to their blindly entering some valley, guessing at the way. For two days they lay encamped on the summit. The soldiers, worn with toil and fighting, were permitted to rest; and a number of baggage animals which had fallen among the rocks made their way to the camp by following the tracks of the army. Exhausted and discouraged as the soldiers were by many hardships, a snow-storm—for the constellation of the Pleiades was now setting—threw them into a great fear. The ground was everywhere covered deep with snow when at dawn they began to march, and as the column moved slowly on, dejection and despair were to be read in every countenance. Then Hannibal, who had gone on before the standards, made the army halt on a certain promontory which commanded an extensive prospect, and pointing out Italy to them, and just under the Alps the plains about the Po, he told them that they were now scaling the ramparts not only of Italy, but of Rome itself; the rest of the way would be level or downhill; and after one, or, at the most, two battles, they would have in their hands and in their power the citadel and capital of Italy.

The column now began to make some progress, and even the enemy had ceased to annoy them, except to make a stealthy raid, as occasion offered. But the way was much more difficult than the ascent had been, as indeed the slope of the Alps on the Italian side is in general more precipitous in proportion as it is shorter. For practically every road was steep, narrow, and treacherous, so that neither could they keep from slipping, nor could those who had been thrown a little off their balance retain their footing, but came down, one on top of the other, and the beasts on top of the men.

They then came to a much narrower cliff, and with rocks so perpendicular that it was difficult for an unencumbered soldier to manage the descent, though he felt his way and clung with his hands to the bushes and roots that projected here and there. The place had been precipitous before, and a recent landslip had carried it away to the depth of a good thousand feet. There the cavalry came to a halt, as though they had reached the end of the road, and as Hannibal was wondering what it could be that held the column back, word was brought to him that the cliff was impassable. Going then to inspect the place himself, he thought that there was nothing for it but to lead the army round, over trackless and untrodden steeps, however circuitous the detour might be. But that way proved to be insuperable; for above the old, untouched snow lay a fresh deposit of moderate depth, through which, as it was soft and not very deep, the men in front found it easy to advance; but when it had been trampled down by the feet of so many men and beasts, the rest had to make their way over the bare ice beneath and the slush of the melting snow. Then came a terrible struggle on the slippery surface, for it afforded them no foothold, while the downward slope made their feet the more quickly slide from under them; so that whether they tried to pull themselves up with their hands, or used their knees, these supports themselves would slip, and down they would come again! Neither were there any stems or roots about, by which a man could pull himself up with foot or hand—only smooth ice and thawing snow, on which they were continually rolling. But the baggage animals, as they went over the snow, would sometimes even cut into the lowest crust, and pitching forward and striking out with their hoofs, as they struggled to rise, would break clean through it, so that numbers of them were caught fast, as if entrapped, in the hard, deep-frozen snow.

At last, when men and beasts had been worn out to no avail, they encamped upon the ridge, after having, with the utmost difficulty, cleared enough ground even for this purpose, so much snow were they obliged to dig out and remove. The soldiers were then set to work to construct a road across the cliff—their only possible way. Since they had to cut through the rock, they felled some huge trees that grew near at hand, and lopping off their branches, made an enormous pile of logs. This they set on fire, as soon as the wind blew fresh enough to make it burn, and pouring vinegar over the glowing rocks, caused them to crumble. After thus heating the crag with fire, they opened a way in it with iron tools, and relieved the steepness of the slope with zigzags of an easy gradient, so that not only the baggage animals but even the elephants could be led down. Four days were consumed at the cliff, and the animals nearly perished of starvation; for the mountain tops are all practically bare, and such grass as does grow is buried under snow. Lower down one comes to valleys and sunny slopes and rivulets, and near them woods, and places that begin to be fitter for man's habitation. There the beasts were turned out to graze, and the men, exhausted with toiling at the road, were allowed to rest. Thence they descended in three days' time into the plain, through a region now that was less forbidding, as was the character of its inhabitants.

Such were the chief features of the march to Italy, which they accomplished five months after leaving New Carthage—as certain authorities state—having crossed the Alps in fifteen days.

THREE TONS OF BRONZE CANNON

FROM *The Gun*

C. S. FORESTER

Captain Horatio Hornblower is a very familiar character to English and American readers. He won for himself a place in the galaxy of romantic heroes and for his creator a stellar position among historical novelists.

The Gun, from which this extract is taken, is a less familiar book of Forester's. It is a novel of the Peninsular Wars, not a narrative of grand strategy, but of war as it comes to people in the mountain villages of an occupied country, told with that quietness and understatement that make Forester such exciting reading. William McFee, a considerable writer himself, says of Forester that he "writes as if nobody had ever told a tale before." Long before the reader finishes the selection, he will have found himself in thorough agreement with this evaluation.

A DEFEATED ARMY WAS FALLING BACK THROUGH THE MOUNTAINS FROM ESPI-nosa. Such was its condition that an ignorant observer would find it easier to guess that it had been defeated than that it had been an army. The twenty thousand men of whom it was composed were strung out along twenty miles of road; its sick and its dead littered the edges of the road for a hundred miles to the rear. At the head came such of the cavalry as were fortunate enough still to have horses to ride; they felt safer there than in their proper place, covering the retreat. Next came the infantry, in groups, in herds, or in ones and twos. Their white Bourbon uniforms were now in strips and tatters, and their skin, blue with disease and cold, showed through the rents. Perhaps half of them still retained their muskets, and of these perhaps a quarter had bayonets as well. Here and there little groups still displayed some soldierly bearing, and marched steadily beneath the cased regimental colours, but these groups were few, for most of the colours had been lost at Espinosa.

The long column of misery tended continually to grow longer, as the more robust struggled forward to get as far as possible from the pursuing French, and as the weaker fell farther and farther behind. There were enough weaklings, in all conscience; even in summer the men had been badly clothed, and even in victory insufficiently fed, and now it was winter, and Espinosa had been fought and lost, and the route of the retreat lay away from the fertile plains and up into the inhospitable mountains. The rain had fallen upon them in deluges for days, and now, as they climbed higher, it was turning into sleet, and a bitter cold wind blew. Ahead of them they could see the snow lying thick on the mountain passes through which they would have to climb, without food or fuel or rest, and with the terror of the French to urge them on. Disease had come, inevitably, to complete the work so well begun by hunger, exposure, and the sword. The typhus—the Black Death—was in among them, along with dysentery and rheumatism and pneumonia. Men dropped dying in the very middle of the road, to be trodden and spurned by comrades too sick and weary to step out of the way, and whose shoeless feet left blood at every step.

If such were the state of affairs at the head of the column, the condition of the rear can hardly be imagined. Here were the men whose legs had given way beneath them, and who still tried to struggle along on hands and knees. Here were the women and the children, left ever farther and farther behind, gazing back apprehensively down the road to see when the dreaded helmets of the French dragoons would appear over the rise. Here were the last few relics of the impedimenta of the army, all that had survived the disaster of Espinosa and the hundred miles of the retreat. The horses were all dead, and the few guns and wagons were being dragged along by dying mules, goaded by the drivers who limped along at their sides. It was bad luck on the sick who fell in the highway incapable of moving, for the gun teams were quite incapable of hauling the guns out of the deep central ruts; they could only go straight on, regardless.

If any part of the wretched Spanish Bourbon Army could boast *esprit de corps* and devotion to duty, it was the artillery. The gunners of the few guns which had escaped from Espinosa had no real motive in imperilling their lives in dragging their guns on in this fashion. They knew that if they were to cut the traces and leave their pieces behind no one would ever have the energy to make inquiries into the matter. But either their own natural obstinacy or that ingrained by discipline had caused them to drag the things thus far.

The very last unit in the Spanish column—if we except the dying—was a bigger, heavier, and more imposing gun than the iron six-pounders which led the artillery column. Thirteen feet long, it was, and two feet in diameter at the breech, and a foot in diameter at the muzzle. It was an eighteen-pounder bronze gun, of that handsome dark alloy which is still known as

"gunmetal." Around the vent and forward along the barrel it was orna-
mented with blazonry and heraldic traceries, beautifully designed, and cast
as part of the gun itself; it was evidently a gun which had had a mould made
expressly for itself at the time of casting, and had clearly been intended as
an ornament for some wealthy noble's castle. Round the muzzle, in boldly
raised lettering, was a Latin inscription, a fragment of the liturgy of Noc-
turne—"And our mouths shall show forth Thy praise." The gun must have
been one of a pair; its brother must have borne the inscription "Oh, Lord,
open Thou our lips," and the two must have stood on each side of the entrance ramp of a castle in the South. When the Spaniards rose against the
French invaders, and the nation flew to arms after a French army had been
engulfed at Baylen, these two guns must have been taken from their ornamental duties to help eke out the woefully inadequate equipment of the
Spanish artillery. The other gun had fallen into French hands at some one
or other of the disasters which had befallen Spain when Napoleon in his
wrath led the Grand Army across the Pyrenees—at Gamonal, perhaps, or Rio
Seco, or Tudela, and was probably relegated again by now to ornamental
duties at the Tuileries or at Compiègne, to grace Imperial splendour.

It seemed likely enough that the same fate would overtake its fellow,
trailing along at the rear of Blake's defeated army. The dozen mules which
were dragging its three tons of weight along the rocky road were in the last
stages of exhaustion. To force them to take every single step the drivers had
to stick their goads into their raw and bleeding sides; the big lumbering gun
surged forward only a yard at a time, and every yard with pain and difficulty,
crashing and bumping over the rocks which surfaced the road. They reached
a point where all the gradients which they had already climbed up into the
mountains were inconsiderable, compared with the one which now faced
them. It seemed to rise before them like the sides of a house; ahead they
could see it at intervals winding on interminably, looping back and forth
up the mountain side, as far as the eye could see through the driving sleet.
At every hairpin bend the pull of the long string of mules was necessarily
at an angle to the length of the gun, with much consequent wastage of
power. The drivers shouted, and stuck their goads into the mules' sides until
the blood ran in streams; the gunners toiled at the spokes of the wheels
with what feeble strength was left them. The wind shrieked round them,
dazing them with its force and with the sleet which it hurled along with it.
Then the inevitable occurred. One last spasmodic effort carried one wheel
up to the top of the rock which had been impeding it; the mules lunged
forward under the goads, and the whole thing tottered and fell over on its
side in the midst of the road, dragging the limber over with it, and the
wheelers in their traces, and they the pair in front, and so on, until half the

team was down, while the gun lay, huge and ungainly, on its side with one wheel still slowly rotating.

In this fashion the question was settled for the gunners. It would take hours to put that three tons of bronze on to its wheels again. And the mules were past further effort. Those which had fallen lay quietly on the rocky road, their only movement being the distressed heaving of their flanks. With most of them no amount of goading or kicking or cursing could get them on their feet again. When a dying mule finds himself lying down, he nearly always decides to lie and die quietly, and no stimulus whatever will get him on his feet again to expend his last few breaths in the service of mankind. The wretched animals who were still on their feet huddled together and tried, as well as their traces would allow, to turn their tails to the sleet-laden wind. At any moment the dragoons might appear in pursuit; the gunners had seen them in among the rear-guard once or twice already during the retreat, slashing about with their swords like a schoolboy among thistles. The wind and the cold and fatigue and hunger had left the gunners too dazed for intelligent effort with levers and ramps. They had just sense enough to open the limber and allow its small content of ammunition to cascade into the road, and then, detaching the limber from the gun, they were able to right the former and hitch the last few mules to it. With this light load, they were able to struggle forward again up the interminable mountain road, into the fast falling winter night, while the gun still lay grotesquely with one wheel in the air and the dying mules around it, like some fantastic god surrounded by sacrificed animals—a simile which is not so far from the truth.

The Spanish Army went on its way, leaving the gun behind it. Thirty thousand men had fought at Espinosa, and twenty thousand had escaped from that disaster. The march through the mountains, and a winter among their desolate slopes, left some eight thousand fever-ridden phantoms alive next spring to appear again in another corner of Spain and to be sacrificed in some further foolish battle. For the French left their retreat unharried from the morning of the day when the gun was abandoned. Not even a French army could penetrate farther into that desolate tangle of mountains, with no more motive than the destruction of a beaten enemy; they wheeled aside and marched down into the plains to Madrid.

The men of the mountain valleys, the charcoal burners and the miners, found the gun still lying in the road when next they descended it. They eyed it with curiosity; for familiar though they were with small arms, a cannon was a rare sight among those precipices. So far, in this lost corner of the

Peninsula, the war had barely touched them. Indeed, they had suffered more up to now from the depredation of the starving Spaniards than from the French. The sight of the long desolate road, littered with dead men and dead animals and all the pitiful paraphernalia abandoned in a retreat, was their first introduction to the horrors which were to overwhelm Spain during the next four years. They were men of the mountains, not of the towns. The news that the French Emperor had kidnapped their king and had determined on setting his own brother in his place had been slow in reaching them, and these Galician peasantry did not feel the same intense national pride as did the Castilians and the townsfolk. It was the sight of the dead men along the road, and the tales told by the few living stragglers, and the shameful news of Espinosa, which roused them at last to take their part in the national uprising.

In every mountain village the parish priest mounted his mule and rode off to the nearest town for news, and came back with stories of the formation of provincial governments, of decrees of universal military service, of the organization of new armies to take the place of the old. So that when Father Ciro Prieto came riding up the road in reply to a hurried message, and saw the group of peasants round the gun, he reined in and dismounted with a thrill of pleasure. Artillery was rare among the mountains.

"Good morning, children," said Father Ciro Prieto, shaking his cassock out of the disorder consequent upon riding astride.

"Good morning, Father," said they respectfully, and waited for him to take charge of operations. He was a little man with sharp grey eyes, and a great snuff taker, and much respected all round about as a fount of wisdom. Those sharp eyes of his took in the whole story; the wheel marks in the road, the position of the gun, turned over at a bend, and the dead mules, made it all obvious to him.

"The French are no farther off than Camino Real," he said. "The sooner we get this gun into a place of safety, the better."

"Yes, Father, certainly," said Vigil the woodcutter. "But how?"

The priest spread his hands.

"I leave that to you, my sons," he said. "Use any means you think will serve."

Father Prieto's worldly wisdom stopped short at the problem of righting three-ton guns, but he was not going to admit it. He sat at the edge of the road holding the reins of his mule and taking snuff, while his parishioners bustled about the task.

At first their efforts were feeble and ill advised. It was hard for them to realize the enormous weight with which they were dealing. Their early pullings and pryings availed them not at all. It was the copper miners among them who initiated the correct method; they were more used to such difficulties. Two woodcutters were despatched to get a couple of big tree branches as levers. When these were brought back, there was at last a real promise of progress. A little hole was dug beneath the barrel of the gun, just in front of the swell of the breach, and the end of a lever thrust into it. Then, when ten men flung all their weight upon the other end, behold, the gun moved! It stirred a little in the rut in which it had buried itself. Every one else promptly flung himself upon the lever. It sank under the combined weight, the gun lifted itself a full foot, and then, the lever slipping from under it, it fell again with a shattering crash upon the road.

"Gently, children, gently," said Father Prieto from the roadside. His life's experience among these wild mountain people had taught him that they needed far more to be restrained from headlong excess of zeal than to be urged on.

"Gently, you fools," said Comas the miner. "That is not the way. Listen —oh, Mother of God!"

Already the wild enthusiasts had pushed the lever under the gun again and were swinging on to it.

"Listen to Andres," said Father Prieto sharply, and his flock ceased their heavings while Comas gave a hurried lecture on the use of alternating levers. This time, when the gun was heaved up out of its bed, Comas was ready. He pushed the second lever under the gun, and a rock beneath it as a fulcrum, and in response to his shouts, half the party now flung themselves upon the second lever. The gun rose farther still—Andres' wild exhortations, backed up by Father Prieto, just sufficed to stop them overdoing it again. While the gun hung precariously on the tip of the lever, Comas built yet a higher fulcrum, rested the first lever upon it, thrust the lever under the gun, and called to the others to heave again. In this fashion the gun rose steadily, turning over with its carriage to an upright position. There was a tense moment when the rim of the lower wheel took the ground and the gun began to rise upon it. Comas imperilled his life by rushing beneath the swaying mass to pile rocks against the wheel rim when it threatened to slip. As the fulcrums grew higher and higher, the effort of turning the gun grew greater and greater; to the very end success hovered in the balance. Just before the gun was ready to fall into the upright position, it seemed as if they would never be able to lift it the last necessary six inches. Every one piled upon the lever, their feet seeking out some grip which might increase their weight; they tugged and they strained, their joints cracking and the sweat running in streams in the cold mountain air. At last Father Prieto left his mule by the roadside and ran to the lever. He found a foot of it unoccupied, grasped it, and lifted his feet from the ground, his legs kicking absurdly within his cassock. His little additional weight turned the scale. The gun swung over, falling with a crash upon its other wheel, tottered, and kept its position, on its two wheels again, pointing with defiance down the road towards the French, while the lever, slipping from beneath it, deposited the whole mass of mountaineers in an ungraceful heap on the road.

Everybody rose, panting and full of pride. They swarmed about the gun, examining it with curiosity. They plied Father Prieto with questions about it, most of which the poor man was quite unable to answer. The minute education of a Spanish parish priest did not extend to a knowledge of siege artillery. He could tell them nothing about the employment of the elevating screw and wedge beneath the breech, but he could at least read out the legend round the muzzle—they heard the Latin words with a respectful intake of breath—and translate it for them—"And our mouths shall show forth Thy praise"—and he found the touchhole for them (the gun did not boast the elaborate firing arrangements with lock and lanyard which modern artillery possesses) and was able to explain how to load and fire. His flock could understand that; it was just the same simple method that they used with their own muskets, and Father Prieto's economic use of the little knowledge he possessed quite concealed from them his complete ignorance of anything like laying and elevating an eighteen-pounder. They were quite enthralled by his little lecture. Diego Cabrera picked up one of the half-dozen rusty cannon balls which the gunners had spilt from the limber, and weighted it in his hands. Every one looked longingly at every one else. The thought was in the minds of all, big children that they were, that it would be fine to load the gun and fire it off, just once. But they looked at the width of the bore and at the cavernous depths of the barrel. A single charge for the monster would consume as much powder as the whole community possessed. Diego let the cannon ball fall reluctantly from his hands.

"Now, into a place of safety with it, children," said Father Prieto.

That started a new discussion. Any one could guess that an enormous team would be necessary to drag the gun up the mountain side. Although these peasantry were ready enough to risk their lives, they were all of them peculiarly unwilling to risk their cattle. Horses and mules and draught oxen had been hurried away, along with the flocks and herds, into safe recesses of the upper valleys even before there was fear of the French coming—the unpaid Spanish armies were just as careless about the rights of property. But no one could disclaim the possession of draught animals to neighbours who knew every detail of his affairs, whatever tales he was willing to tell to commissaries and tax gatherers. Each in turn was gradually provoked into offering the use of a mule or a yoke of oxen, and at last there was a general dispersion to assemble a team, while the few unpropertied men remained behind with the gun, fingering the relief work along its barrel, peeping into the muzzle to see the tiny bit of light which crept in through the touchhole, passing wise comment on the solidity of the carriage work, while all the time the gun, huge and impassive, stood glaring defiantly down the mountain side. It was well that the French made no move.

Then, when the team was got together, in the late afternoon, and harness had been devised, a new difficulty arose. They began by attaching the traces to the iron loop at the tip of the trail of the gun, and found that thus it was impossible to pull the thing along. The trail was devised for limiting recoil and simply dug itself into the ground when they applied any pull. Clearly the trail must be lifted, and the muzzle depressed, and the gun drawn along in that position. But no cattle on earth were strong enough to maintain sufficient tension on the traces to hold the ponderous weight of the trail in the air. Even Clemente Cagorno's renowned yoke of draught oxen, weighing a ton and a half between them, were dragged backwards as though they had been no more than a pair of nanny-goats, while the trail sank back to the ground.

A stray memory came into Father Prieto's mind at last, illuminating it like day. It was a memory ten years old, of an occasion when he had ridden into Burgos, an enormous journey, to consult with the Bishop's secretary. In Burgos he had seen an army on the march, on its way to the Pyrenees to fight the French, who were then Red revolutionaries instead of Imperial king makers. There had been guns with that army, clattering through Burgos, and by an excruciating effort Father Prieto remembered how they had been pulled along. The trails of the guns had been swung from limbers —stout two-wheeled carts, to which the horses were harnessed.

With dignity Father Prieto intervened in his parishioners' despairing discussion and explained how the thing should be done, and every one instantly saw the soundness of the advice. And at the same time every one— save one—instantly decided who should supply the cart which would take the place of the limber. Isidoro Botto had been the least helpful of any of the group. He had not done much in the matter of righting the gun, and his contribution to the team had been only one unhappy ass, which every one knew to be sixteen years old if a day. Yet he was the wealthiest of them all, and they knew he owned just the right cart for the business. Each solid pair of wheels was of one piece with the six-inch axles, and they were attached to the wooden cheek pieces with iron staples of best Galician smiths' work, and every bit of wood was of solid Spanish oak. A clamour arose for Botto to offer his cart. He demurred; it was unsuitable for the job in hand; it was out of repair; he had lent it last week to a man from the Asturias; he could not afford to be without it. But he swallowed his objections when Diego Cabrera drew his knife and was imitated by half a dozen others. He went sullenly off with them to his farm to fetch the cart.

It was nearly nightfall when they returned, and humorists declared they could still hear Granny Botto's imprecations, which she had hurled at them when she saw that beloved cart being commandeered, and was presumably still continuing to hurl, some four miles away.

And now the trail of the gun was swung up and fastened to the back axle of the cart, and the motley team was harnessed up. Those who had whips cracked them joyfully; those who had goads plied them with a will, and those with neither ran up and down, shouting encouragement. Cart and gun lurched, heaved, and then unmistakably got under way. The difficult corner was rounded, and they set themselves to the climb. Lanterns made their appearance from here and from there, and by their light each successive hairpin bend was negotiated, and the rising of the moon found them over the shoulder of the mountain. Then every one decided he had done enough for that day.

The further progress of the gun into the heart of the mountains can hardly be followed in so much detail. Certainly it was the very next day that the would-be gunners discovered a truth which the artillery teamster learns speedily enough—that going downhill is more difficult even than going uphill. Three tons of solid metal on a steep slope constitute a Juggernaut which exacts a cruel toll of lives and broken limbs. The first runaway was only terminated by a crash into the ditch at a bend, with half the team disabled, and incredible labour necessitated in the way of building of ramps and working with levers to get the thing on the road again. If the wheels were locked for a descent, they ploughed so deep into the road that it was necessary to dig them out again. And if the strain on the ropes which locked the wheels rose above breaking point, so that one wheel was suddenly released, that meant another capsizing and more heartbreaking toil to right the gun. Diego Cabrera and Clemente Cagorno and the others came to hate the huge thing which had taken possession of their lives. Isidoro Botto watched with dismay the gradual disintegration of his beloved cart under the shocks and strains to which it was subjected.

But there was some compensation in the fact that the passage of the gun through the mountain villages excited enormous attention. Men who were still hesitating to take up arms were carried away by the spectacle and attached themselves to the party, which increased in snowball fashion. To those unsophisticated mountaineers a force of a thousand peasants with an eighteen-pounder appeared an irresistible army. Father Prieto, rather to his dismay, found himself at the head of one of the most considerable forces of the province, and in consequence a man of weight in the councils of the Junta, when the point of concentration was at last reached.

BLIZZARD IN THE PYRENEES

FROM *The Horned Pigeon*

GEORGE MILLAR

George Millar's *Horned Pigeon* is one of the highly praised personal narratives of the last war. Millar served as correspondent for a London newspaper on the western front. Impatient with his auxiliary role, he joined the 8th Army as lieutenant, fought in Africa, and was captured in the desert. He was interrogated by Rommel himself, then turned over to the Italians and interned in a punishment camp in Italy after an unsuccessful try at escape. When Italy surrendered he was transferred to Germany and en route escaped by jumping from a train window. He crossed Germany in a sealed freight car and escaped through France into Spain. The strains and apprehensions of the climb across the border Pyrenees are vividly described in this selection.

WE BEGAN CLIMBING WHEN WE CAME TO THE OLIVE-GROVES. IT WAS HARD WORK on the terraced ground. Then we left the olives and climbed up woodland paths. At one of our short halts I took off Pedro's oiled silk coat, which I had carried in a roll over one shoulder. I took it off to make a seat on the damp ground. And when we went on I forgot it. That forgetfulness might have cost me my life.

At 5 A.M. we cleared the woods, and the bare mountains were above us. The guide told us to sleep in some bushes while he and his assistant went to a cottage farther up the hill. We had been walking for nine hours. All of us went to sleep among the sparse bushes and were awakened by strange noises like the barking of a small lap-dog. They were made by the guide.

"More climbing now," he said. "Fill your water-bottles passing the cottage. I apologise for leaving you outside. But there are often German patrols here. If they found us they would take us for visiting shepherds. If they found you they would kill everybody, burn the cottage, rape my friend's wife, and eat his sheep."

At the back door of the cottage a thin woman wearing a jacket of sheepskin and trousers of some soft leather filled our bottles with earthy-tasting water. Then we went on climbing up a narrow path over and through big rocks. Often tough thorn-bushes closed behind the man in front, lashing those who followed with tearing branches. It was bitterly cold, although we could see a strong-looking sun beginning to rise over the sea horizon. We were tired, but would have liked to go on climbing to keep warm. At eight o'clock, however, the guide said that it was getting dangerously light.

He shepherded us into the thorn-scrub below the mountain path.

"You will enjoy several hours of sunshine here to-day," he said. "Tell your friends that if they get a good sleep and eat solidly in the evening, they should be in Spain to-morrow morning. Warn them not to drink too much water, because that is bad for crossing the mountains, and this crossing is never easy in winter. My friend and I are going back to sleep the day away in the cottage below. Au revoir, and don't move about. That big house down there is the headquarters of the German frontier guards. They occasionally send patrols over the hills during the daytime, and some of them have dogs."

I faithfully transmitted his instructions to the Americans. They had borne up bravely all through the night. Now they seemed to have an enormous thirst. Before the end of the morning all our water had been drunk. I attributed their thirst to their unfit condition. The one we had called Clark Gable looked quite ill. He lay near me, heavily asleep, his face a greenish-grey against his mossy pillow.

The air at that height was cold and crisp, even when the sun was on our hill-face. A heavy coastal battery of German guns had firing practice during the afternoon. The shells fell a long way out to sea. The guns themselves were sited nearly a mile inland.

From our high resting-place we could see all our little mile-stones of the past three weeks stretched out below us in a huge relief map. We could see Perpignan, the first river, the Tech, and the subsequent rivers. There were the two roads making a wish-bone forking towards us from Perpignan. And down below us, where the hills ran into the sea, lay Port Vendres, such a dramatic little port in the Spanish Civil War. Pale wisps of wood smoke rose from its distant chimneys against the pale winter blue of the Mediterranean.

Although I could not sleep, I ate all that I carried and lay as relaxed as possible on the slope. At the beginning of this attempt I had not had enough money to buy provisions. I had left Perpignan with two tins of French Army meat, two small loaves and one of the cakes that Serge and I had bought for the second attempt. The Americans wondered to see me finish my provisions, but I told them that it was better to have a full stomach before we set off on the worst part of the journey than to save up for a meal when we were across.

Within myself I felt an immense exultation, for I was convinced that in twenty-four hours I should be safe from the Germans.

The guides arrived promptly at five, but we had to wait until six before the old man considered it dark enough for us to begin climbing. The early going was good on a bare, rocky path.

We stopped at a spring to fill all our water-bottles. While we were there, three of the Americans got down on their knees and lapped at the water like dogs. When he saw this the guide stood on a rock above them and jabbered at them in his high voice.

"Bad, bad, bad. Water is bad on the hills. Much better drink wine." He offered his wine-skin, but nobody felt like drinking wine.

The guide now wore a kind of fluffy woollen helmet, which covered all but his sharp nose and his restless eyes. He led us up small paths made perhaps by goats, perhaps by men. Sometimes he left the paths to slither across steep hill-faces. He explained that he did this to avoid German posts which were often placed on the high ground.

A bitter north wind cut into our backs. I deeply regretted the loss of Pedro's coat, for even with the climbing I could not keep warm.

"This wind is the *tramontane*," said the guide. "It will get much worse and it will bring snow."

"To-night?"

"When else?"

We had been walking and climbing for two hours and a half when we stopped to rest in a small dark pine-wood. All of the Americans were extremely tired and were feeling their feet.

"Of what do they speak?" asked the guide.

"They speak of the possibilities of victory next year," I lied.

"I know that they are talking about their tired limbs. That is because they have drunk too much water. Tell them they drink no more water. Let them ask for wine. Eh, *amigo,* pass your skin."

His companion passed the wine with some grumbling, and this time we all drank, including the guide himself.

"Tell your comrades to have courage, for with courage man conquers all," he continued with a chuckle. "Tell them I lost my brother here one year ago."

My translation of his morbid injunction was met by hollow groans from the Americans, for their extreme fatigue could not yet prevent them from laughing at everything, including themselves.

After this rest we slithered down a hill so steep that it just failed to be a precipice. At the bottom was a raging torrent which had to be crossed by leaping from boulder to boulder. Two of the Americans, the Chauve Souris and Gable, fell heavily but followed on. The Chauve Souris had been lagging for some time.

We had not, it appeared, traversed the main block of the mountains, and we turned west, paralleling what the guide said was the last ridge before the Spanish frontier. This paralleling was the most arduous work of all, for there were continual high ridges running across our path so that we were like some infinitely small animals climbing in and out of the squares of a giant honeycomb. Now too, we were walking in snow, although it was not deep enough to present much of a handicap.

I explained to the Americans that we were working along the high ridge on our left, keeping well below the summit because there were German frontier posts and patrols there, and that the guide would turn up it at a place where he knew it would be safe to cross. But an exhausted man finds it difficult to reason and easy to complain. Our line grew more and more strung out. The guide frequently had to halt to allow the Chauve Souris, Charlie and Gable to catch up. I would have liked to push on much faster, for it was the cold, not fatigue, that worried me. My back was freezing in the *tramontane*.

Charlie told me at one point that he had seen cows and I thought he must be going mad.

"Can't you tell a cow from a goat?"

But a little later I saw them myself, a large half-wild herd of small cows. And I suddenly remembered Laurence talking with Alpine scorn of the Pyrenees as *"Montagnes des vaches."*

The blizzard became so bad and so heavy with wet snow that the guide led us into a small cave in the hill-side. Here there was just room for all of us to rest, squeezed together and dripping water from our soaking clothes. The others smoked. Some shepherd had left a crude oil-lamp there. The guide lit it and I was able to look at my companions.

My heart would have bled for them had I been less intent on surmounting this final obstacle. Except for Fritz, who seemed to thrive on the work, they were plainly in the last stages of exhaustion.

Gable, the biggest and toughest-looking of us all, told me that he could not go much farther.

"Why not?"

"My legs are passing out on me."

The Chauve Souris and Charlie seemed to be equally miserable. The Trapper was little better, although he complained less since he came from tougher, less citified stock.

They begged me to ask the guide if we could either stop there for the night or if he could take us by a quick, direct route to the frontier.

"If we wait here we shall die from the cold," he answered. "I must take you by the proper route. Tell them it is only one hour from here to the frontier if this blizzard dies down, as I think it will very soon."

The going was more difficult when we started out again, and the Americans, excepting Fritz, were slower than ever. At one short halt, when the guide left us for a moment to look at the crest of the ridge, Gable lay down on a patch of snow and shouted: "I can't go on, I can't go on."

Fritz and I went back to him.

"My legs have given out," he said. "Ask the old man if he can give us five minutes' rest."

"Certainly not," said the guide indignantly. "Tell him to be a man."

He now noticed that some of them were stuffing lumps of snow into their mouths. For although it was deathly cold and eerie and wet on the mountain-top, we were parched with thirst. "If you drink like that you will die," shrieked the guide.

So we moved on slowly to what he said was the last slope. It was very steep, and the snow was deeper and softer. The four weak Americans were all in grave difficulties. Fritz and I had to divide all that they carried between us. They struggled bravely at the slope. But there were times when they all lay down in the bitter cold, and we despaired of ever getting them over.

The guide and his assistant did nothing to help. They only got angry, screaming at us and jabbering in fast, incomprehensible Catalan. I have never given so many encouraging discourses in such a short time. They sounded false to me, up there in the whistling wind, and they had little effect on Gable who, poor soul, was now almost unconscious with pain from his powerful legs. The others somehow, little by little, managed to drag themselves up. The Trapper and Charlie hung together and kept going inch by inch with a rest every few yards. The Chauve Souris, brave spirit, negotiated the whole slope on hands and knees. This left the two of us to deal with Gable.

At first he lay on the snow saying: "I can't, I tell you."

Fritz gave him a "You're doing fine, boy," piece of nonsense.

He responded by walking with our help for twenty yards, then he sank down again. While he lay there Fritz talked to him and the Chauve Souris passed us, crawling. I was reminded of the hare and the tortoise and burst out laughing. The old guide chose this moment to come back and scream that this was the most dangerous part of the whole trip.

"Kick him into activity. Does he want to kill us all?"

"Ask him to let me rest here for a half-hour, just a half-hour," moaned Gable, his voice trailing away slowly into a sleepy drawl.

"Rest?" yelled the guide (I had not dared to translate the "half-hour" request). "Rest, I'll give him rest, the pig."

He danced down the slope and slapped Gable sharply several times on the face. This roused the poor man, and, supported by Fritz and me, he did another fifty yards.

Then he collapsed finally. Fritz and I tried everything we could think of, praise, vilification, encouragement, massage, wine from the Spaniard's skin, alcohol from Fritz's little bottle. The big man would not move. Tears oozed from his eyes.

"Leave me here to die, you fellows. I can't go on."

The Chauve Souris passed us again, going bravely on hands and knees. I pointed him out to Gable.

The only comment this drew was: "Just give me a half-hour and I think I'll be O.K."

Charlie and the Trapper were nearly over the ridge. The guide and his assistant were ahead of them. The Chauve Souris was nearing the top.

Fritz and I managed to raise big Gable. He sagged. We each got a shoulder under him, twining his heavy thick arms like dead pythons round our straining necks. We gathered ourselves together and managed to stagger up to the top and over the ridge. He kept saying maddening things like: "Let me be, fellows. Just let me rest."

The summit of the ridge was narrow and smooth; below it lay a few yards of scrub, then stunted pine-trees. The three of us fell in a heap. I lay there with the blood pounding in my ears.

When I picked myself up Gable again was asking for "a half-hour's rest."

Fritz and I worked on him. We ran the full gamut of first-aid, we talked to him lovingly, angrily. Nothing happened. The other three lay around us in the scrub, offering advice. The two Spaniards stood sourly under a tree, watching us. Occasionally the guide hurled piping invective at us. At last he came over to look at the prostrate giant.

"The Spanish frontier is thirty minutes' easy walking from here," he said. "We go down to the burn below us, over it, up on the other side, and then across that plateau. At the far edge of the plateau is the frontier, and you can see the lights of the Spanish town of Figueras from there."

"Why don't you leave me then?" said Gable. "I'll make it when my legs get some strength back in them."

"We won't leave you. You must come with us now. It's too cold to lie here."

"I'll cover myself with leaves. See," he began to scrabble leaves over his legs. "After an hour or two I'll go on down to Spain. Now I got to get some rest. . . ."

"Enough of this foolery," screamed the guide. "I have been taking men across all this winter and I never saw such women. This is the worst part.

Sooner or later Germans will pass here. Are you all going to throw your chance away for one weakling?"

He suddenly darted on Gable.

"I will *make* you go on," he shouted. Before we could stop him he seized two handfuls of Gable's black hair and began to bash his big head against a tree-trunk. Gable only moaned gently.

"I don't care what you do to me. I can't go on."

When I had translated the guide's remarks about German patrols to him he only replied: "What do I care about Germans? My legs hurt so badly. Please go on without me. I'll be O.K. I see the way. You none of you'll make it if you take me along. It's the only hope, to leave me. When I've rested I'll go on down into Spain. . . ."

After all the ground that had been covered I could practically see the Spanish frontier. After the help of Wally Binns, the French prisoners, the Strasbourg café plotters, Ramon and Alban, Greta, Scherb, Dolores, Pascal, La Pepette, Xavier, Elizabeth, Clément, Laurence, Serge, Estève, Cartelet— after all that, I was stuck here, almost within jumping distance of the frontier. Stuck, stuck, stuck! Because one American had been too lazy to do three deep knee bends each day that he was hidden up in Paris. Was my duty to this man, or to all that lay behind me and all that lay ahead?

I could not decide. I asked Fritz.

"I reckon we should leave him as he asks. He may make it in the morning. If we stop here it may mean all of us get lost."

I asked the Trapper, Charlie, and the Chauve Souris. They were all of the same opinion as Fritz. By this time the guide, who did not understand what this talk was about, was screaming: "To perdition with you all, you bunch of women! I am going on. I will not throw myself away for you. . . ."

We covered Gable's body with leaves and left him what food and wine remained. We showed him the road to the frontier again.

The others moved off. He had relaxed, and looked much better now that he knew he was to be allowed to rest. When I was hurrying after the others, I bumped into a man in the darkness.

"Who is it?"

"It's me," said the Chauve Souris. "Listen, lieutenant. I was in the same house with him for six months in Paris. I'm going to stay with him. Furthermore, my legs are just about all in too, and I would be a drag on the rest of the party. I could never make the frontier to-night. We'll go on down together in the daylight. See you in Spain. . . ."

"Keep each other awake," I told him. "It's too cold, dangerously cold, to go to sleep. If you go to sleep you may never wake. Drink all the wine and eat the food. Rub each other's legs and get on down as soon as you feel you can move. I'm glad you're staying with him. It's a good thing to do.

A decent thing. . . ." But already we had separated in the wood, and I was running down towards the burn, after the others.

The Trapper and Charlie were both in a bad way, and the effort of carrying Gable had taken a lot out of Fritz and me. We worked our way slowly up the wooded slope beyond the burn. There seemed to be a numbness in my legs. The guide was nervous and ill at ease. He repeatedly hissed at us to be silent or to hurry.

At last we came out on the plateau. It looked unnatural, like the face of the moon. The bitter wind swept across it, bludgeoning us forward, stabbing us forward. The guide nudged me and pointed to a kind of hillock at the far edge of the plateau.

"Keep that on your left hand," he said. "It marks the Spanish frontier. But you must make them run across here. We are in full view. It's not far. Look. Only 300 metres."

He and the other Spaniard began to run away in front of us.

"Run," I shouted. "That's the frontier. Run. Run."

The Trapper and Fritz ran on. Charlie was too tired. He stumbled after them. A wild exaltation gripped me, filled me, maddened me.

"Just 300 yards now, Charlie boy," I shouted at him. "Run with me."

"I can't."

"Run. Run. Run."

I took him by the hand and pulled him as you might an unwilling child. The pair of us broke into a shambling trot. I pulled and the wind pushed. Charlie responded nobly. Our speed increased. We crossed the plateau; and suddenly we were running away with ourselves as we dropped over the edge of the plateau—into Spain.

"A PARTICULAR MANNER OF FORTIFYING PLACES SITUATED ON EMINENCES"

FROM *The Field of Mars, being an Alphabetical Digestion of the Principal Naval and Military Engagements of Great Britain and her Allies from the Ninth Century to the Peace of 1801*

ANONYMOUS

We can give neither credit nor biography for the nameless author of this curiously phrased but instructive essay on how one goes about fortifying mountains. Writers of encyclopedia articles in 1801 had apparently not yet won the distinction of a signature. The editor's preface, however, is reassuring. The articles, he indicates, were "selected from the best historians and journalists and adjusted from the greatest authority." He appeals to the patriotic fervor of every British book buyer. "Such a publication cannot but be acceptable . . . at a time when every British subject glows with emulation in defence of his Native Country and the support of its dignity. . . . The perusal of a well executed work on this Plan, cannot but excite a desire to pursue the well-trod paths of our Ancestors, in an exertion to prove ourselves worthy of enjoying the fruits of their labours."

THE CITIES WHICH ARE SITUATED ON EMINENCES, AS MONS AND STRASBURG, are much exposed, because neither the houses nor the streets can be covered by the fortifications; though without this inconveniency, such places are very proper to be fortified; but the fortifications on a mountain ought to be made very high at the bottom: it is best to make them by degrees, covering them with parapets and traverses.

None but small forts and citadels are built on high rocks, because of the narrowness of the space. The best method is to adapt, as much as possible, the lines of the fortification to the sides and figure of the mountain. The ramparts must be made low; and as the ditches are commonly dry, the best defence must be at the bottom. The road to the fortress must have, from distance to distance, retrenchments very well defended. The engineer must also take care to make all sorts of works, whence the foot of the mountain can be beaten most: they ought to be disposed in such a manner, that those who defend them may retreat from them in safety, and annoy without interruption the enemy, when he has rendered himself master of them.

Against the eminences which are near a fortress, there should be erected not only good ravelins on the ramparts, but those eminences themselves should also be fortified by works capable to resist the enemy. At the highest place of the mountain is drawn a line of the height and thickness of a parapet, so that it may be enfiladed by the cannon of the fortress. Farther towards the fortress, where the mountain grows lower, are erected redoubts of stone, which are open on the side of the fortress, and distant from one another a musket-shot, and contrived so low, that they should raze the mountain. Taking care besides, lest the enemy should cut off the retreat into the fortress to the soldiers who are lodged on those redoubts, or annoy them with his cannon.

A LONELY WAR

FROM *War Below Zero*

BERNT BALCHEN,
COREY FORD,
AND
OLIVER LA FARGE

🐎 We are sharply reminded of the global nature of modern war in this
account by Bernt Balchen of war in the Arctic. It was a war of
weather, of silence, of desolate icy wastes. Balchen is a veteran of
the ice, both in peace and war. He was chief pilot of Byrd's Antarctic
Expedition in 1926. His first flight experience was in the Arctic and he
has to his credit more logged hours over ice and snow than any other
airman in the world. In 1943 he was assigned by the United States Army
Air Corps to command a secret expedition to Greenland to establish
the northernmost American air base in the world. His book, written
together with Corey Ford and Oliver La Farge, is the story of that military expedition.

WAR IN THE ARCTIC IS A LONELY WAR. IT IS NOT A BIG SHOW LIKE RUSSIA OR
Italy; there are no vast armies, no major campaigns, no epic battles or a million men. It is a war of long distances and longer silences: a war of waiting.
Events are far apart and small. A trawler halts in a hidden cove. A group of
men in green German army tunics set up their equipment on the barren
beach. A passing dog-sled driver is ambushed and shot. And between these
events is nothing but the waiting and the silence. . . .

Evidently the driver of the sled never heard the command to halt. The
wind off Greenland's Ice Cap was sharp, the flying snow crystals stung his
face as the team of huskies trotted ahead of him; he pulled his parka hood
tighter over his head against the cold. With two other members of the Greenland Sledge Patrol he was hurrying back to Eskimonaes after an uneventful
two weeks' reconnaissance to the north; there had been no sign of enemy
installations along the coast. Nothing aroused his suspicions as he led the
way over the shore ice toward the deserted trapper's cabin at Sandodden,
where they planned to spend the night.

The first shot, fired from the door of the cabin, struck his lead dog; the animal dropped in its traces, kicking once or twice convulsively. Before the driver realized what had happened, his second dog leaped into the air and doubled over, biting at a spreading red stain on its white fur. Instinctively he stooped to grab his rifle from the bottom of the sled; a bullet drilled him through the temple, and he fell face forward onto the snow.

That shot, by a Nazi trooper, marked our first fatal conflict with the enemy in Greenland: it was the initial contact with an armed German invasion force anywhere in the Western Hemisphere. You did not know—the facts could not be revealed until now—that the Nazis had actually established a foothold on this side of the Atlantic. You did not know, all last year, that their planes were flying within bombing distance of the shores of North America. Their U-boats, refueling in Greenland's silent fjords, were striking at will at our convoys to England and Murmansk. Their well-equipped weather station, on the island's undefended east coast, was in daily radio communication direct with Berlin.

Perhaps you did not even know there was a war in Greenland. It was a secret war, waged in semi-darkness north of the Arctic Circle, on a remote battlefield perpetually locked under ten thousand feet of solid ice. The weapons were not tommy-guns and tanks; the real heroes of this war were nameless enlisted men working in Air Force ground crews at fifty below zero, or standing guard on Coast Guard cutters fighting through the pack-ice, or living all winter long in isolated weather stations along the Ice Cap, buried under eighteen feet of snow. Once each day they would tunnel to the surface to take their wind and temperature readings; the rest of the time there was nothing to do but wait.

But in Greenland we were not fighting to defeat a division or capture a ridge. It was not a war for territory. It was a war for weather. . . .

When you fight the Arctic, you fight on the Arctic's terms. On the trail you fight sudden thaws, and treacherous snow-bridges that give way under your weight, and crevasses into which a driver and team of dogs may plunge and never be seen again. If you are flying, you fight icing conditions that overload your wings with tons of ice; you fight eccentric whirlwinds over the Ice Cap that rack a ship and drop it several thousand feet in a second; you fight the fog. Most of the time you win, but sometimes you lose, and the Arctic shows no mercy to a loser. . . .

The fog had been building for several days, born of the ice-pack that moves down slowly from the polar basin in June, drifts around the southern tip of Greenland, and strikes the warmer current of the Gulf Stream off Labrador. It had been stirred to life by turbulent winds blowing off the high plateau of ice in the interior, and now it eddied and sucked around the jagged coast, flooding the narrow fjords, obliterating all landmarks and navigational guides in a limitless white ocean. Here and there an uncharted mountain-peak protruded like a vicious reef; and the pilots of the four B–17's, proceeding from a field in Labrador toward our base in Greenland, fought their way higher and higher in a desperate attempt to get above the stuff. Their gas was getting low, radio contact was poor, their S.O.S.'s came through to us faintly all night as we tried in vain to bring them in.

At two in the morning, one Fortress found our field and managed a successful landing. A second Fort was forced down in the water near a base in southern Greenland; all of the crew were saved. The third pilot crashed his ship behind a small Eskimo colony north of us; the plane was completely wrecked, but miraculously no one was hurt. We learned of their landing through the Danish radio, evacuated them safely in two PBY's, and dispatched a crew of our own mechanics to dismantle the plane and salvage as much as possible.

The fourth Fortress, with Lieutenant Stinson as pilot, made a wheels-up landing on the Ice Cap itself, about one hundred and twenty-five miles south of our base. His crew showed the greatest presence of mind and ingenuity: no sooner had the ship skidded on its belly to a full stop than they set to work with hacksaws, cut off the twisted propellers from one engine, dug out a space beneath it in the snow. Thus they obtained a power source by which they could run the generators and recharge their batteries in order to maintain constant radio communication. In addition, they cleaned out the hydraulic and heating system and installed a stove inside the plane, using engine oil for fuel. We got radio bearings on them, located them the following afternoon, and dropped standard emergency supplies: sleeping bags, C rations, coffee, a complete new set of polar clothing for each man. The next job was to get them out.

They had come down in a heavily crevassed area of the Greenland Ice Cap, inaccessible except on foot. A rescue by boat would have involved at least two weeks of travel over this rough terrain in order to bring them to the coast. Our best bet was to fly in to them. On previous flights across the Cap, I had noticed that shallow lakes of melting snow and slush formed occasionally in large sinks on the Ice Cap itself. A hasty survey disclosed a lake three miles long, not more than a dozen air-miles from the spot where the plane was wrecked. In a Navy PBY, with Lieutenant Parunak, we flew low over this lake a couple of times, and decided that it was large enough for a Catalina to land and, more important, take off again. That same evening the PBY dropped me off at the lake with two experienced sled-drivers, Sergeant Dolleman and Sergeant Healey, who had both been with Byrd in the Antarctic. We paddled our rubber boat ashore through the watery snow and landed on a weird beach of sloping blue ice, as bare and smooth as the side of a porcelain bathtub. There we bedded down in sleeping bags for the night.

We woke next morning, the Fourth of July, to a drizzling cold rain that turned into sleet and then snow. We made ourselves as comfortable as we could, and waited out the weather. By noon it had stopped raining, with only light squalls of sleet and snow, so Healey and I decided to make a stab at it. We left Sergeant Dolleman at the camp, with orders to send up smoke signals from time to time so we could find our way back, and we set out on skis, each with our own pack-sack, a couple of days' rations, and ropes for crossing the crevasses.

You think of the Greenland Ice Cap as a solid substance, but actually this is not the case. Ice in the Arctic is fluid, constantly moving and shifting as it works toward the sea; and near the coast, where the glaciers break off into the ocean, the bending produces deep vertical cracks in the surface of the Cap. Some of these crevasses are virtually bottomless: you can drop an object into one of them and listen in vain for it to land. Most of the fissures are covered by thin roofs of snow, called snow-bridges, which vary in width and thickness. Sometimes the ice will shift, and one side of a bridge will break loose, forming a natural booby trap in the trail: the only safe procedure is to test ahead of you with your ski-pole every step of the way. In good light conditions, you can tell when you are over a crevasse because the snow-bridge sags a little in the middle; but in fog these warning hollows are imperceptible, and you must go roped constantly. A moment of carelessness may prove fatal.

The fog was growing worse and worse as we proceeded through the heavily crevassed area along the coast. The surface was so broken that sometimes, with only a hundred feet of rope, there would be as many as three deep fissures between Healey and myself. We could hear water running constantly beneath the ice, eating it away underfoot. Several times, as we felt our way blindly forward, the rear end of our skis would drop sickeningly into an unseen opening. At last we gave up, back-tracked ourselves into camp, put on dry clothing, and waited to make another try that evening.

For our second attempt we avoided the hazardous coastal area, and made for the better ice in the interior. Swollen glacial rivers were running down over the Cap, and we had to wade them knee-deep, linking our arms together and fighting to keep our balance on the slippery-smooth bottom. Occasionally a river would be so large that we would have to detour many miles upstream before we could find a place to cross. Altogether we covered over fifty miles that night, crawling and sliding, and now and then plunging clean over our heads into hidden potholes filled with slush. From my previous aerial reconnaissance, I knew that we were traveling in the general direction of the plane; and at last, toward morning, we made out the low throb of a motor running. We reached the plane about nine o'clock, thoroughly soaked and exhausted, after twenty hours of steady traveling; but there was no time to sleep. A PBY, flying over the wrecked ship with additional snow-shoes and provisions, had dropped a warning. Another storm was on its way.

We made hasty preparations all that day for our trek back to the lake. Our plan was to travel by night; the surface then is drier and more firm, due to the lowered temperature when the sun is low in the north, and the glacial streams are apt to be less formidable. The thirteen men in the Fortress crew put on the new polar clothing they had been issued, adjusted their snow-shoes, and packed their sleeping bags for the long march. I warned them that they could take only a day's rations, and everything else would have to be left behind; but the men had no idea of the ordeal that they were about to face and smuggled into their bags various personal belongings they wanted to salvage.

Our caravan started out single file across the ice; I led the way, and Healey, like a loyal sheep-dog, brought up the rear to herd any stragglers along. For the first couple of miles the men were enthusiastic; but after they had waded waist-deep through a couple of rivers of ice-water, and hauled themselves by ropes over an endless series of fissures, their ardor began to cool. One by one they discarded the items they had tried to bring back, and presently our trail was marked by an increasing succession of cameras, electric razors, fountain pens, wallets, uniform caps, a pair of officer's dress-shoes, a girl's picture in a leather frame. By midnight most of them wanted to drop their sleeping bags as well; but this was a risk we could not afford to take. The wind was building fast, the storm warnings were increasingly apparent. I tried to urge them along a little faster: "See that hill over there, the lake's just behind it," but they could only shuffle at a dead walk, faces set, eyes half-closed in utter weariness.

By six o'clock that morning we made out the lake in the distance; an hour later we reached camp, where Sergeant Dolleman had a steaming pot of pemmican waiting for us. The men were too tired to eat. They flopped down where they were and did not move until the PBY landed to take them back to the base.

Our rescue had been none too soon. Two days later I happened to fly over the same area. In vain I looked for the lake on which we had landed. A large fissure had opened in the ice directly under it; all the water had poured down through, the entire lake had disappeared overnight. . . .

It was a constant miracle, as the flow of traffic increased over this new and shortest air route to Europe, that the number of accidents remained so low. As the weather cleared, a mounting stream of bombers roared overhead across the top of the world, bound for the fighting fronts. Mediums and fighters, en route to our Eighth Air Force in Britain, now were break-ing their ocean hop halfway in order to avoid burning out their motors. Greenland was becoming a vital link in our chain of victory.

Our six-months' old base on Greenland's west coast was growing fast. Construction crews labored tirelessly to enlarge our landing field and in-crease our housing facilities, in order to accommodate the growing air traf-fic over the North Atlantic. Ground-crew mechanics of the Air Force worked day and night, often at forty or fifty below zero, to service the transient air-craft and send them on their way. Meteorologists in isolated stations at the heads of lonely fjords, or along the rim of the Ice Cap itself, sent out daily weather observations that cut down to a minimum the danger of forced landings on the ice.

Every now and then the feasibility of emergency airfields on the surface of the Cap itself has been discussed; but it is my own conclusion, after several years of operations in Greenland, that they would not be practicable for the type of aircraft we operate today. When you fly over the Ice Cap in winter, the low sun throws long shadows which etch the innumerable rolls and ridges beneath you; then you see clearly that the surface is not really flat, but undulates like a restless ocean, deep green and blue and purple. Flying low, you are aware of the hard ridges of broken crust, called "sastrugi," which corduroy much of the ice and make landings hazardous. The snow itself shifts like desert sands after each severe blow, drifting deep over any runway; it is never firm enough to land an airplane on wheels, and operations would have to be restricted to aircraft with skis or floats tough enough to stand the gaff. Furthermore, storms over the Ice Cap are un-predictable and violent; gales have been measured up to one hundred and seventy-four miles an hour, and they shift with incredible speed. I have seen an eighty-knot wind move around a complete 360° circle in a minute and a half.

All that summer the possibility of enemy attack was never out of our minds. Since the outbreak of the war, long-range Nazi planes—Focke-Wulfs, JU-88's and Blohm und Voss 135's—had been patrolling Greenland's east coast; more than once they had flown directly over our base. So far no enemy installations had been discovered in Greenland; but we knew that on several previous occasions enemy operators, hiding on small sealing vessels, had been picked up offshore by cutters of the United States Coast Guard's valiant and little-known Greenland Patrol. As long ago as the spring of 1941, Lieutenant Commander McCluskey, of the Coast Guard cutter *Northland,* on routine anti-submarine patrol, had halted a dubious-looking Danish ice-breaking vessel named the *Buskoe,* and learned from the crew that a group of alleged hunters—with guns and radio equipment—had been set ashore at a cabin several hundred miles to the south. Proceeding to the suspected site, Commander McCluskey and a dozen heavily armed Coast Guard Commandos had landed in a midnight blizzard, raided the shack, and captured some twenty Nazi troopers in army uniforms who were asleep in their bunks: the men are interned in England today. In July we were given further reason to suspect that the Germans had actually established themselves somewhere on Greenland's undefended east coast.

On the fifteenth of July a group of two B–17's and four P–38's were being ferried across Greenland en route to England. It was their second try in a week; an earlier attempt had nearly ended in disaster when they had run into bad weather over the Ice Cap, and for several hours had wandered lost in the fog, the smaller peashooters hugging the wings of the bigger bombers like a flock of frightened chicks as they dove and climbed again in search of a break in the stuff. The clouds dripped freezing moisture, the P–38's loaded with ice, the pilots bent back the throttles and sought to maintain formation; if they ever became separated in this fog, they knew it would mean curtains. With their gas down to the last teacupful, they managed to land at my base, where they waited a week for the weather to clear.

Bad luck seemed to dog them, however; on their next attempt to fly the Cap they ran into a solid front between Greenland and Iceland, their heaters and Pitot tubes froze as they climbed to get above the clouds. At last they asked, in secret code, for a weather report on an auxiliary field in southern Greenland. The reply came—also in secret code—that this field was locked in solid, with visibility zero, but that another field to the north was open to receive them. As they headed north, the bad weather increased rather than diminished; again they asked for a weather report, and again the reply in secret code ordered them on. They throttled back and reduced engine r.p.m. to conserve fuel, dropped their auxiliary tanks, held on grimly as long as they could; at last Lieutenant McManus in a P–38 called that he would have to set down. He dragged the Cap for several miles, decided that the surface was smooth enough to try a wheels-down landing, dropped both flaps and prepared to come in under power. For a moment all went well; then the nose wheel buckled, the ship over-ended at fifty miles an hour, there was an ominous puff of black smoke, and silence. Without hesitation the rest of his comrades in the flight set down their ships one by one, sliding on their bellies to safe stops, and floundered knee-deep across the soft white snow toward Mac's ship. The last peashooter made a pass over the wreckage, then pulled straight up from a 350-mile per hour dive and executed a triumphant slow-roll: the signal to the rest that Mac was alive and only slightly hurt. You can't lick a peashooter pilot.

The six ships—twenty-five men in all—had come down in perhaps the largest successful crash landing in history: save for the bitter sight of their broken planes, which they knew would never fly again, they were okay. Hurriedly they set to work making camp, divided their rations to last for fifteen days, detailed the gunners to melt snow for drinking-water, sat down to their first meal in twenty hours. The radiomen meantime set up aerials suspended from box-kites and ran the engines to recharge the batteries; by evening they got through a report to the auxiliary field giving their positions which the navigators had checked accurately by sun shots.

That night the storm closed in and they knew the rescue planes might be delayed for days. With great ingenuity they made themselves comfortable and settled down to wait. They devised a cooking-stove for each B–17, using a large oxygen bottle and an engine exhaust stack, with supercharger oil for fuel and a parachute strap for a wick. Walls of snow hung with tarpaulins made a cozy kitchen. For recreation they practiced target-shooting with their forty-fives, destroying the bomb-sights and other secret paraphernalia on the wrecked planes. They even set up a battery-operated radio-beam receiving-set and got music from Reykjavik in Iceland; they all staged an old-fashioned square dance on the wing of the B–17. The pilot of the first rescue plane, circling overhead as the storm broke three days later, remarked enviously that he was tempted to land himself and join the happy party.

With the end of bad weather, the rescue ships made up for lost time, swarming above the wreck in an aerial circus: two transports, two Army B–24's, a Navy Catalina. They dropped food, medical supplies, even a quart of Scotch whiskey wrapped in a sleeping bag, to ward off colds. Unfortunately, the cork came out of the bottle on the way down; there was a mad scramble to see who would be the one to use the bag that night. The Catalina sent added word that Navy Lieutenant Crockett, who had been with Byrd at the South Pole, was starting toward them with a dog team. Eight days after their crash landing, the entire party was successfully evacuated to a near-by base and returned to the States.

Later we checked our own weather records with the orders the pilots had received in secret code. The reports concerning the two auxiliary fields had been deliberately reversed. The flight had been lured on to disaster by false information, sent either from an enemy submarine or from a secret German radio station located somewhere on Greenland's eastern coast. . . .

War in the Arctic is a silent war; and in the silence and the vast distances an enemy moves undetected. A man is only a dot in all that whiteness; huts and radio-towers are invisible from the air amid the boulders and uneven patches of snow; the drifts cover an intruder's tracks as fast as they are made. Only the scouts of the Sledge Patrol, traveling by dog sled up and down the barren shore, may stumble on a secret hiding-place.

Formerly the members of this unique Patrol were Danish and Norwegian trappers, as well as a few Eskimos, who made their living running traplines during the winter along Greenland's east coast. Their tiny cabins were scattered at intervals along the trail, they owned equipment and teams of dogs, their knowledge of the country could not be duplicated. In the fall of 1941, Rear Admiral E. H. Smith, U.S.C.G., Commander of the Greenland Naval Patrol, organized these civilians, and they were hired by the United States Army to form a regular military patrol of the east coast of Greenland as far north as 77°, working out of various stations along the coast, visiting the unoccupied huts along the trails, and reporting any signs of enemy occupation.

On March 13, 1943, as three members of the Patrol were approaching Sabine Island in northwestern Greenland, they observed a couple of tiny figures moving along the ridge of Tafelberg Mountain. Realizing that no human beings were supposed to be in that area, they made for a near-by trapper's cabin at Cape Wan, on the south side of Clavring Strait, planning to investigate further in the morning. In the hut they found two strange sleeping bags and a green uniform tunic with a swastika on the sleeve. As they were searching for further evidence, their alert ears detected someone approaching; they had no time to harness up their dogs, but set out on skis for the nearest Patrol station at Eskimonaes, some ninety-five miles south.

Their precipitate flight had given the enemy two good dog teams. On the twenty-fourth of March, a small party of Germans commanded by Lieutenant Ritter arrived at Eskimonaes in the sledges abandoned by the Danes. They attacked the base with rifles, automatics, and hand-grenades, firing a machine gun into the air to give the semblance of being in force. The occupants, equipped only with hunting rifles, evacuated hurriedly. Fortunately they had a portable radio transmitter; less than twenty-four hours after the station was silenced, they were able to report what had happened. The Germans seized three additional dog teams and sledges, confiscated a number of soft-nosed cartridges which the trappers used for hunting game, and placed all personal effects of the Danes in one hut, together with the Danish flag and about a hundred fox-skins; everything else they destroyed. Beside the flag they left a characteristic note:

March 24: The U.S.A. protects its defense interests here in Greenland. We do the same also. We are not at war with Denmark. But the administration on Greenland gave orders to capture or shoot us, and besides that you gave weather reports to the enemy. You are making Greenland into a place of war. We have stayed quietly at our posts without attacking you. Now you want war, so you shall have war. But remember that if you shoot with illegal weapons (dumdum bullets) which you have at hand here in the loft of the radio station, then you must take full responsibility for the consequences, because you are placing yourselves outside the rules of war. Note we have put all personal effects of the hunters and all pelts in this hut, while we have destroyed the radio apparatus operating for the U.S.A. (Signed) *Commandant of the German Wehrmacht Detail in Eskimonaes.*

Our war in Greenland was not a big war, as wars go. There were no major battles, no epic encounters of planes or tanks, no headlines in the home-town papers. Loneliness doesn't rate a citation; they don't give medals for waiting. The casualties were not very glamorous: frozen lungs, a couple of missing fingers or toes, an amputated leg. There are no fields of crosses today to mark its battlefield: only a broken fuselage drifted deep in snow, a pair of crossed skis beside the trail, a forgotten dog sled lying forever at the bottom of a black crevasse.

But it was an important war, for the knowledge of the Arctic that we gained, at the cost of these men who gave their lives on the Ice Cap, will insure the safety of tomorrow's aerial travel in the North. The bases and weather stations they fought to maintain, amid the darkness and silence and cold, will be future stops along the new air route to Europe. Some day our whole conception of geography will be changed; the earth itself will be rolled over on its side, and the spindle of the globe will run, not from Pole to Pole, but from one side of the Equator to the other. Then the Arctic will be the very center of our new world; and across Greenland and northern Canada and Alaska will run the commercial airways from New York to London, from San Francisco to Moscow to India. Today's highway of war will be tomorrow's avenue of peace.

ON THE GENIUS OF WAR
IN THE MOUNTAINS

FROM *Memoirs*

NAPOLEON

An interesting light is thrown on the character of Napoleon by an essay he wrote a few years after he had been graduated from the military school in Paris. The question "What truth and sentiments is it most important to inculcate in men for their happiness?" brought the answer from Napoleon that men must admit the claims of reason and sentiment. The essay contended vigorously against the follies and crimes of ambitious men. The judges, prophetic men, placed his essay fifteenth in merit among the sixteen submitted in the contest.

It was Napoleon's reason and sentiment which freed Europe; it was his ambition which re-enslaved it. But in the years during which he held a continent by the throat, there was manifest a military brilliance which the world had not seen before. His *Memoirs*, from which this selection "On the Genius of War in the Mountains" is taken, will long remain required reading for students of military strategy and tactics.

I SPENT PART OF MARCH IN VISITING THE POSITIONS OCCUPIED BY THE ARMY, and collecting information respecting the various actions which had taken place in 1792. I remained several days at the camp of Brouis occupied by General Macquart, and convinced myself of the strength of the enemy's positions, and the imprudence of the attacks of the 8th and 12th of June, which had proved disastrous to the army. Amongst mountains there are many positions to be found of great natural strength, which we must take care not to attack. The genius of this kind of warfare consists in occupying camps, either on the flanks or in the rear of those of the enemy, which leave him only the alternative of evacuating his positions without fighting, or of coming out of them to attack you. In mountain-war, he who attacks is always under a disadvantage; even in offensive war, the art consists in engaging only in defensive actions, and in obliging the enemy to attack. The enemy's positions were well connected; the right was supported in a solid manner, but the left not so well; the country was much more practicable on that side. I, therefore, conceived a plan of operations, which, without engaging the army in difficult affairs, was adapted to put it in possession of the upper chain of the Alps, and to oblige the enemy to abandon of his own accord the formidable camps of Raus and Fourches. There was no reason to fear that the enemy would avail themselves of the detachment which would be made by the French army on its right, in order to act on the offensive; such a movement in a hilly country would only be formidable in proportion to the time that might be lost in striking the decisive blow; for if the troops have gained a few marches on the enemy, they have arrived on his flanks, and then it is too late for him to take the offensive part. In mountain warfare, to oblige the enemy to leave his positions to attack yours, is, as we have already said, the spirit and true method of conducting this kind of war.

This plan was laid before a council, at which were present the two popular representatives, commissioners to the army, General Dumerbion, the general of the artillery (myself), General Massena, General Vial of the engineers, and Brigadier-General Rusca, a light-infantry officer, born in these mountains, and particularly acquainted with them. The reputation of the author saved him all long discussions. My predictions concerning Toulon were remembered, and my plan was adopted. . . .

On 6 April a division of 14,000 men, forming five brigades, passed the Roya, and took possession of the castle of Vintimiglia; one brigade, commanded by Massena, marched on Mount Tanardo, and took up a position there; a second, after having passed the Taggia, took up a position at Monte-Grande; the three others, under my immediate command, advanced on Oneglia and overthrew an Austrian division posted on the heights of Sainte-Agatha. The French Brigadier-General Brulé was killed in this affair. The next day the army entered Oneglia, where twelve pieces of cannon were found. The whole population of the town and valley had fled.

The loss of the army was slight. The fall of Saorgia and of all those grand positions for which so many plans had been formed, and so much blood shed, increased my reputation in the army; and public opinion already called me to the chief command.

The Piedmontese Army, encamped in the plains and hills at the foot of the Alps, enjoyed the greatest abundance; it was recovering from its fatigues and repairing its losses; and was daily reinforced by the arrival of fresh Austrian battalions: whilst the French armies, encamped on the ridges of the upper chain of the Alps, on a semi-circumference of sixty leagues in extent, between Mont Blanc and the sources of the Tanaro, were perishing through want and sickness. All communication was attended with great difficulty, provisions were scarce and very expensive, the horses suffered, and all the material of the army was damaged. The hard waters of those elevated regions caused much sickness. The losses which the army suffered every three months in hospital might have supplied the casualties of a great battle; these defensive operations were more burthensome to our finances, and more perilous to the men, than an offensive campaign.

Defensive operations in the Alps, in addition to these disadvantages, are attended with others which arise from the topography of the country. The different corps encamped on these summits cannot assist each other; they are insulated; twenty days are necessary for proceeding from right to left, whilst the army defending Piedmont is in a fine plain, occupies the diameter, and can, in a few days, assemble in force at the point which it is intended to attack. The Committee of Public Safety was desirous that the army should assume the offensive. I had conferences on this subject at Colmar, with officers from the Army of the Alps: but a difference of opinion prevailed; it was necessary, in the first place, that these two armies should be under one commander-in-chief.

I spent the rest of the autumn in fortifying the promontories from Vado to the Var with good coast-batteries, in order to protect the passage from Genoa to Nice. In January I passed one night on the Col di Tende, whence, at sunrise, I surveyed those fine plains which were already the subject of my meditations. *Italiam! Italiam!*

THE TYPOGRAPHICAL
HOWITZER

FROM *Comstock Bonanza*

SAM DAVIS

Silver in Nevada was the cry, mountains of silver, ledges ten thousand feet deep, solid masses of silver. And the wild and crazy race began to Virginia City, to Carson City, to Washoe—a brawling race to the end of the Comstock rainbow. Sam Davis was the chronicler of that fantastic period in American life. He was editor of the *Morning Appeal* at Carson City and his sketches were subsequently collected in a book of short stories now long out of print.

Of the characters in this story, a little-known classic of American humor, Mark Twain needs no introduction except the note that he was a reporter for the *Territorial Enterprise* at that time and earned himself the name "the Wild Washoe Humorist." Dan de Quille, who fights the Indians with him, worked on the same paper from 1862 to 1893, a period which spanned the Comstock boom and its decline.

IT WAS NEARLY TWENTY YEARS AGO WHEN DAN DE QUILLE AND MARK TWAIN attempted to start a paper in Mendocino County. They took the type and material of their recently defunct newspaper establishment in San Francisco, and, loading the stuff on a big wagon, struck out into the country to retrieve their fortune. They packed their type just as it stood in the forms, tied up the articles with stout cords by a process well known to printers, and, packing them closely in boxes, vowed to establish a newspaper somewhere which would be the leading exponent of politics and history for the Pacific Coast. Had not an unfortunate circumstance taken place, it is evident that the newspaper which they contemplated founding would have been alive today. Their journey over the mountains was utterly uneventful until they reached Simpson's Station, a spot well known to old travelers on that route. Here they met a party of emigrants making for Lower California, and the latter had with them a small mountain howitzer which they had brought with them across the plains.

Twain took a great fancy to this gun, and offered fifty dollars for it, with two kegs of powder. The emigrants were glad enough to part with it, as they concluded the time for its use had passed. Dan thought the purchase of the artillery and military supplies was a reckless piece of extravagance, and said as much, but Mark replied:

"When we start our paper we must fire a salute. A newspaper office with artillery has a big bulge on the business. No well-regulated office in California should be without a howitzer. If a man comes in for a retraction, we can blow him into the next county. The howitzer goes."

This silenced the argument, and the next day the two journalists took to the road with their printing outfit and artillery.

The next night they camped in a mountain ravine, fifteen miles from Simpson's, and after building the usual campfire, fell asleep. About eleven o'clock the horses wakened them by prancing about, and the two journalists were led to the conclusion that a party of Indians was making arrangements for a night attack. In the clear moonlight, human forms could be distinguished about half a mile away at the foot of the ravine. The idea of encountering Indians had never entered the heads of the two fortune-seekers, and they had no arms. Suddenly Twain brightened up, remarking:

"The howitzer?"

"We've got nothing but powder," said Dan.

"Well, powder'll scare 'em; and we'll load her up."

The piece was immediately loaded with a good big charge, and the two men felt quite certain that the Indians, hearing the roar of the gun, would beat an unconditional retreat. The piece was hardly loaded and placed in position when about forty of the Redskins came charging up the ravine.

Twain seized a brand from the campfire and was about to lay it on the touch-hole when Dan yelled "Hold on!" as he rammed something into the mouth of the piece and remarked:

"Turn 'er loose."

The roar of the howitzer echoed through the lonely forest, and the savages, with frantic cries of pain, reeled down the ravine in wild confusion.

"What in hell did you put in?" asked Mark.

"A column of solid nonpareil and a couple of sticks of your spring poetry."

"The poetry did the business, Dan. Get one of your geological articles ready for the next charge, and I guess it'll let the red devils out for the present campaign."

The savages again advanced. Mark attended to the powder, and Dan assorted the shot, so to speak.

"Jeems Pipe's Song, 'My Mountain Home.'"

"Good for three Indians—sock 'er in."

"An acrostic by John B. Ridge, in long primer."

"It'll paralyze 'em."

"Frank Pixley on the Constitution—half a column of leader brevier."

"If it hits 'em, the day is won."

"Your leader on 'Law and Order.' "

"Save it as a last resort."

Dan pulled the type out of the boxes and stuffed column after column in the howitzer's mouth as the savages came charging on. Another round from the gun, and the Redskins rolled over and over each other like boulders swept away by a mountain cloudburst. Mark, in an ecstasy of delight, pulled an American flag out of his effects, nailed it to the tail-board of the wagon, and was about to make a speech, when the dusky figures of the foe were once more seen moving to the attack.

The piece was again loaded, and this time with a double charge. Mark's leader on "Law and Order"; the puff of an auction house, by Fred Mc-Crellish, "as a sickener," Dan said; Frank Gross's verses on "The Rebel Yell"; an agricultural article by Sam Seabaugh, showing the chemical properties of corn-juice as an educational lever; a maiden poetical effort by Olive Harper, and some verses by Colonel Cremony and Frank Soule completed the load.

"That poetry reaching 'em first will throw 'em into confusion, and my editorial coming up on the heels of the rest will result in a lasting demoralization. It will be like the last cavalry charge of the French troopers at the battle of Austerlitz."

For the third and last time the faithful howitzer belched its typographical compliments to the advancing foe. The havoc was terrible. There was a wild yell from a score of savage throats, and then the low groans of the dying floated up the ravine on the gentle wind. The two men walked over the field of slaughter and counted fifty-six aboriginals lying in heaps. The bodies were horribly mutilated with nonpareil, bourgeois, "caps," misery dashes, and unassorted pi.

"My leader cooked that man's goose," said Mark, pointing to a savage hanging over the limb of a cedar.

"My geological article did the business for him," rejoined Dan, nodding carelessly at an Indian whose head was lying twenty yards away.

"The pen is mightier than the sword."

"You bet. Hurrah for Faust [sic] and Gutenberg [sic]!"

"Is there any type left?"

"Not a pound."

Ten days later the two journalistic tramps reached Virginia City, weary, discouraged, and foot-sore, and secured places on the *Enterprise*.

A few days ago Dan received the following from his former partner:

Hartford, Connecticut
January 1, 1880

Dear Dan:

I send you the congratulations of the New Year. Do you recollect the time we exterminated the tribe of unlettered (?) savages in Mendocino County? If you can spare the time I wish you would make a pilgrimage to that historic spot, gather the ghostly relics together, and plant a tablet (not too expensive, and at your own expense) to the memory of the departed. Having a shooting-stick lying across a long bow, with our monogram and coat-of-arms entwined, and some appropriate epitaph carved on the stone; an extract from Carl Schurz's views on the "Peace Policy" might do. Enclosed is a dollar and a half for your incidental expenses.

Yours,
Mark Twain

P.S.—Send a thigh bone of the fallen chief by next express.

M.T.

Dan will attend to the matter in the spring. The old howitzer used on the occasion is still in his possession.

ON THE TRAIL

MUSSOLINI'S ESCAPE FROM GRAN SASSO

FROM *Commando Extraordinary*

CHARLES FOLEY

One of the most theatrical exploits of the last war was Otto Skorzeny's kidnaping of Mussolini. Italy had already signed an armistice. Mussolini was held prisoner in the high mountains of the Apennines for delivery to the Allies. The Germans, their armies disintegrating, needed a dramatic propaganda coup for the crumbling home front. Skorzeny, in charge of Hitler's Commando forces, proposed a daring and suicidal plan to kidnap Mussolini. In the face of impossible odds, he delivered Mussolini to Hitler.

Charles Foley, author of *Commando Extraordinary,* tracked the evasive Skorzeny through half the countries of Europe and South America to get the story.

ALREADY AN ARMISTICE HAD SECRETLY BEEN SIGNED IN SICILY AND NOW BADOglio had to spin out the time until the Allies landed in Italy.

The suspense was hard on the Italians, who held the capital. But the Germans, too, were playing with a caution worthy of the stakes: Mussolini, Rome, perhaps all Italy. Their troops were disposed on the hills outside the city. Who would move first?

Keeping doggedly to his search for Mussolini, Skorzeny was rewarded with a series of false trails and assignations, in this villa and that café, each requiring minute investigation. He longed for Friedenthal as the days went on. Suddenly he was galvanised by an intercepted code message to the Italian Ministry of Interior. It said: "Security measures around Gran Sasso completed." That was all, but it was signed "Cueli"—and Skorzeny's spies had told him that a General Cueli was the Ministry's official responsible for Mussolini's safety.

The Gran Sasso, if Mussolini were really there, would present a problem. It was the loftiest peak in the Apennines, and in this area, a hundred miles from Rome as the crow flies, the mountain groups and ranges towered up to ten thousand feet.

Where in this cloudland could you house a prisoner of state with a regiment to guard him? According to their pre-war maps, nowhere; but a winter-sports centre called the Hotel Campo Imperatore had recently been built on a crag six thousand feet up. A gaudy tourist leaflet was produced. While maddeningly vague about the site and building it did say that the hotel could be reached only by funicular—and such a mountain railway was an easily broken link with the outer world: ideal for achieving quick isolation.

Agents soon found that roads to the Gran Sasso through the pine forests were blocked. Nobody knew what was happening in a wide area all around. Skorzeny decided that he and Radl would have to fly over and find out.

In a plane fitted with an automatic camera, they took off on September 8. Nothing went right; as they flew over the Gran Sasso they found the camera had jammed. So Skorzeny had to struggle with a hand camera, hanging head-first out of the rear gunner's turret in the freezing air while Radl, laughing uproariously, held his legs. In a second run over the spot Skorzeny insisted on reversing the rôles; he pulled Radl back into the plane with the laughter frozen on his lips.

They got their pictures: the hotel, square and massive as a blockhouse set on a spur, and beside it, a triangle of ground and the little upper station of the funicular.

More trouble on the way back; they had to skim the ground to avoid a swarm of American bombers and fighters which were dropping an avalanche of explosives on the German headquarters and barracks at Frascati. As luck would have it they landed just in time to dash over to their own quarters, which were in flames, and salvage a few things, but the photographic studio which would have made stereoscopic enlargements of the Gran Sasso pictures had been blown to bits.

Rome was in uproar; the air-raid was in celebration of an Allied radio announcement that Italy had surrendered. That night the Allies landed at Salerno. The game of make-believe was over. Italy had changed sides—officially. Scattered fighting between Germans and Italians had already begun. Now that pretences were at an end, Mussolini could hardly be rescued without a battle; but at least, as Radl pointed out, the threat of Himmler's padded cell was removed. The show-down had come, and any brusque action against the Italians would not be fraught with diplomatic perils. They could go ahead.

Skorzeny had seen the Campo Imperatore from the air; independent checking now seemed to clinch the issue of Mussolini's presence there. A day or two earlier, Skorzeny had suggested to a German army doctor that if he wanted to requisition an Alpine hotel for a convalescent home he knew just the place—it was on the Gran Sasso mountain. The doctor had set off right away; now he returned dejected. The Armistice, he supposed, had put paid to the idea anyway, but Skorzeny might as well know that he had sent him on a fool's errand. He had not been able to get within miles of the hotel; the whole area was sealed up. He must have run into at least a battalion of carabinieri, and another two hundred and fifty were said to be billeted in the hotel itself. He had telephoned from a village and asked for the manager: a short-tempered Italian officer had sent him to the devil.

This looked really hopeful; and then Skorzeny got a report that trade unionists were complaining about the injustice of expelling the hotel's civilian staff at a moment's notice, "simply to accommodate that Fascist Mussolini." That was it, then: the Gran Sasso was the place.

Looking at it all from the Italians' point of view, Skorzeny conceded they could be proud of themselves. Even if Mussolini's whereabouts became known his prison was obviously impregnable. Merely to surround the mountain and ensure that Mussolini was not moved out would need a full German division; huge losses would have to be taken among those jagged peaks: long before the Germans reached the prisoner—if they ever did—he could be hidden in some rocky cave or killed.

The Italians could sit back; their defences were impassable. They had overlooked nothing; nothing, that is, except an individual's determination to get through.

Skorzeny had his facts, such as they were, and his photographs, such as *they* were—holiday snaps four inches square—on which to base a plan of attack. If an orthodox land assault were ruled out, there was only the sky left, and the altitude had even ruled that out: paratroops plummeting through the thin air would be dashed to pieces; planes had nowhere to land; gliders—

He looked again at his pictures, at that triangular patch by the hotel. If it were really flat and smooth, a few gliders might land there. In that event shock troops might just reach Mussolini before his guards put a bullet in him; they could rush him to the funicular—the lower end having been seized by paratroops at exactly the same moment—and away. Skorzeny calculated that with everything going perfectly they should reach Mussolini within three minutes of the shock attack. Time to get away? That must be left to luck.

Student raised a scarred eyebrow when Skorzeny put the scheme to him; both men were weary after three almost sleepless nights of crisis and the general was in no mood for hair-brained escapades. He sent for two technical officers of the Airborne staff, and Skorzeny had to expound the scheme again in detail as plausibly as he could.

The staff officers were not to be beguiled; experts never are. A glance at his snapshots told them that the proposed landing space was ridiculously small; nor had gliders ever come down in such rarefied air. They estimated that of a hundred men who made the trip twenty might survive—twenty men to storm a fortress defended by two hundred and fifty!

Skorzeny argued; the experts would not budge. At last he offered to drop the plan if they could put forward a better one. Student looked anxious; unless they were to abandon the mission given them by Hitler, there was no alternative in sight—and no time to look for one. Finally he yielded: but it would need three days, he said, to get the gliders from the south of France. Ninety of the men must be drawn from his trained airborne battalion; the rest Skorzeny could supply. D-day would be on September 12, with a seven-A.M. take-off.

That night Skorzeny called his men together and told them that he was going to lead a group of them on a dangerous and difficult operation ordered personally by Hitler.

"Candidly," he said, "the experts don't give much for our chances. They expect us to lose most of our strength even before the fighting starts. I hope it won't be as bad as all that, but losses are bound to be high. No one is ordered to take part. Anybody who wants to think twice about coming, or who has a family to worry about, can drop out now. He will have nothing to fear. His refusal will not be known outside our ranks nor put into any record, and we shall respect him no less."

Skorzeny might have spared his pains. Every man stepped forward and he had trouble persuading them that only eighteen could be picked. The remaining hours before D-day hurried by as they tried to catch up with a thousand details: direction of approach, position of gliders *en route* and in landing, distances, altitudes, timing.

Skorzeny and Radl spent the last evening together with their soldiers. They drank a bottle of champagne to their chances and agreed on the principle that life was diverting and it was a shame to leave it.

Skorzeny summed up. "There are some things you can't work out with a slide-rule. That's just where our experts may be wrong; and the Italians too. The safer the enemy feel, the better our chances of catching them unawares. Well, we'll soon know."

Just after the paratroops left that night for the drop into the valley, Allied radio put out an announcement: Mussolini had been handed over by the Italians; an Italian battleship had brought him to North Africa.

For a moment Skorzeny could not get his breath. Then he remembered where the Italian capital ships had been stationed; it could not have been done in time. The broadcast must be a hoax to throw the Germans off Mussolini's trail. Italian brains were still at work.

It was bright and windless, that September morning which the knot of men waiting at the airfield knew must be the last for quite a few of them. Great banks of white cloud lying athwart their north-easterly course might help to get them on their way unhindered; and the still, transparent morning would have softened the trials of their landing—if only they could have taken off as planned.

The start had been set for dawn—when they might hope to float down unperceived by a sleepy enemy—but the gliders were held up on their journey from the Riviera; they could not arrive before eleven A.M. at the earliest.

That meant, by Student's reckoning, twenty-four hours' delay—but there were not twenty-four hours to spare. They would simply have to accept the further risk of approaching in daylight and, moreover, at an hour when they would be the sport of warm air currents which might whisk the gliders from their path like so many paper darts.

Certainly, Skorzeny thought, since nobody in his senses would expect a glider operation at high noon, an added measure of surprise, if they lived to exploit it, might be achieved. So he went cheerfully among his men, distributing boxes of fresh fruit that he had bought to lend a picnic touch to the expedition. They were to take off at exactly one P.M., which would give them a landing time of about two o'clock.

The delay allowed Radl to follow a fancy of his own; he hurried into Rome, where uneasy truce still reigned, and returned with an otherwise unimportant Italian, General Soletti, who had shown much favour to the Germans. Soletti was told his help was needed in "an important enterprise," it being Radl's hope that the sight of an Italian among the attackers might help to upset the garrison on the Gran Sasso.

The expedition, twelve gliders with their towing planes, was to be led to the dropping zone by the pilot who had taken Skorzeny and Radl on their numbing reconnaissance flight. Ten men in the first two gliders would cover the landing of the third with Skorzeny and Warger aboard; Radl was to follow in a fourth.

By half-past twelve the aircraft were drawn up, ready for the men to board them—and at that instant the sirens wailed. By the time they were all in shelter, Allied bombs were bursting all over the place—one of those jests of Providence as cruel as the rainstorm which wrecks the family outing. Yet when the all-clear sounded, Skorzeny found his gliders were untouched; the damage, as far as their interest went, was confined to craters on the runway.

Skorzeny followed his men into his glider and pulled Soletti after him into the front seat. With this extra passenger between his knees he signalled: the armada began to leave.

They took off dead on time. Skorzeny did not know till later that two machines behind him ran into bomb-holes and never left the ground. What he did see, once they had emerged from the bank of white cloud and had risen to twelve thousand feet, was that his two leading gliders had vanished.

They had lost their guide, and also the covering party. So much the worse; since they would soon be approaching the Gran Sasso area Skorzeny would have to tax his memory of the photographic trip to lead the way in. But wedged in his seat he could not see where he was going.

He pulled out a knife and began to hack at the canvas deck and bulk-heads. As they gave way, he blessed the flimsy fabric. Cool air rushed into the overheated shell, crammed as it was with men and weapons, and, peer-ing through the rents, he could see the granite mountains below.

The Gran Sasso came into view. Soon they were a-top of it: there was the hotel again, and on that dizzy perch alongside, the triangular ledge on which they would alight.

"Let go!" he told the pilot. The tow-rope parted and they were swoop-ing freely, with no sound but the gush of the wind on their wings. Then the pilot was jabbing with his finger at the triangle below while he turned his goggled face towards Skorzeny. By no flight of hyperbole could the space be called a landing-field: it was a sloping shelf, for all the world like a ski-jump; and as they lost more height they saw it to be studded with outcrop rock.

General Student had provided against such a contingency. At a final briefing he had categorically laid down that unless they could make a smooth landing they must abandon the attack and glide to safety in the valley. Those were his unquestioned orders; in a spasm of defiance Skorzeny elected to disobey. He shouted to the pilot: "Dive—crash-land! As near the hotel as you can."

They hurtled towards the mountain, the parachute brake whipping from their tail. In another instant the glider was jolting and pitching over the boulders like a dinghy flung upon a reef. A shuddering crash, then it was still.

He was alive, was Skorzeny's first thought; his second: *three minutes.*

He burst out of the wrecked glider; before him, like a cliff-face twenty yards ahead, was the wall of the hotel. An Italian carabinier was standing there, rooted to the spot; he was stupefied by this apparition which had fallen almost at his feet out of the silent sky.

Skorzeny plunged past him to the first doorway: inside was a signalman tapping at a transmitter. A kick sent the chair from under him; Skorzeny's gun smashed the radio. But the room led nowhere.

Out again and full-tilt round a corner; he heard his men pounding be-hind him. A ten-foot terrace—they hoisted him up to it. From there, at an upper window, he spotted an unmistakeable shorn head. "Get back!" he yelled to Mussolini. "Get back from the window." And dashed off round the terrace.

At last: the main entrance, flanked by two sentry posts. The guards wore a look of wild amazement; before they could get their breath, Skorzeny's men had booted their machine-guns off the supports and scrambled through the door. A voice far behind was shouting in Italian; Soletti was adding to the confusion.

Skorzeny butted his way through a press of soldiers in the lobby; they were at too-close quarters to shoot, even had they known what had come on them. He took a flight of stairs, turned a corner and flung open a door. The first thing he saw—Mussolini, with two Italian officers.

One of Skorzeny's brawniest subalterns, Lieut. Schwerdt, panted into the room after him. And just then two shining faces bobbed through the window: a couple of his men had swarmed up the lightning conductor to be with him. They overcame the Italian officers and dragged them from the room. Schwerdt took over as Mussolini's bodyguard.

From the window Skorzeny saw how other friends were faring. Radl was in sight, bounding towards the hotel; his glider had made a tolerable landing. Skorzeny hailed him with a shout: "We've got him here. All well so far. You look after the ground floor for me."

Three more gliders crash-landed, and men poured out. A fourth, landing some distance away, was smashed to pieces—no one moved from the wreckage. He could not hope for much more strength, so he turned back across the room, threw open the door and shouted in his bad Italian: "I want the commander. He must come at once." Some bewildered shouting— an Italian colonel appeared.

"I ask your immediate surrender," Skorzeny said in French. "Mussolini is already in our hands. We hold the building. If you want to avert senseless bloodshed you have sixty seconds to go and reflect."

Before the anxious minute was up the colonel came back. This time he carried a goblet brimming with red wine. "To a gallant victor," he bowed. Skorzeny thanked him and drained the beaker—he was thirsty. Cheers arose from the Germans below as a white sheet was flung from the window.

And now Skorzeny could spare time for Mussolini, who had been put into a corner of the room and there shielded by the bulk of Lieut. Schwerdt. He came forward: a stocky man looking older than his portraits showed him, in a blue suit that was too large. He wore a stubble of beard; his pate sprouted grey bristle. But his eyes were black, ardent and excited.

It was a moment for history—the thought crossed Skorzeny's mind. He spoke in German: "Duce, I have been sent by the Leader to set you free." And Mussolini, who always considered his public, replied for posterity: "I knew my friend Adolf Hitler would not abandon me. I embrace my liberator."

Skorzeny went to see to the disarming of the Italian garrison and discovered he had captured an important personage from Rome—none other than the General Cueli who was responsible for keeping Mussolini sealed up and shut away. Having, through his intercepted code message, unwittingly put Skorzeny on the scent leading to the Gran Sasso, he was further unfortunate in choosing this day for a visit to his charge. Skorzeny was delighted to see him.

But now for a more urgent matter: the get-away. Both ends of the funicular were in German hands; a telephone call from the valley station said the paratroops had carried out their part. Since Mussolini could never hope to reach Rome by road once the alarm was given, it had been arranged that paratroopers should capture the nearby airfield at Aquila and hold it briefly while Mussolini was taken off by three Heinkel planes. But now Skorzeny's luckless radio operator could not get through to signal the rescue planes to set out from Rome. The alternative plan worked out in advance called for a single light aircraft to land in the valley: this had been done, but in coming down its landing gear was damaged. There remained a third, desperate choice: Captain Gerlach, Student's personal pilot, might try to land a tiny Stork spotter plane alongside the hotel itself and pick up Mussolini from the mountain ledge—an operation so hair-raising that Skorzeny and Radl had put it to General Student as the most theoretical of possibilities.

Now it was their only hope.

Skorzeny glanced heavenwards, and there, sure enough, the Stork was circling. Well, there was nothing for it. It had been said that Gerlach could do miracles in the air—let him perform one now.

Skorzeny got his troops, helped by some prisoners, to move the biggest boulders from a strip of the landing ledge and at a signal Gerlach came delicately down on it. Gerlach was ready for anything until he heard what was actually wanted. Then he recoiled. To weigh down his frail craft with the united loads, each in its own right substantial, of Mussolini and Skorzeny! It was mad: he refused point-blank to consider it.

Skorzeny took him aside. He told how Hitler had personally commanded him, Skorzeny, to deliver Mussolini: now Gerlach had in his hands the only means through which that mission could be fulfilled; if he should stand aloof he would be defying Hitler's wishes. And what would there be left to them to do if they failed the Leader? Blow their brains out; that was all.

At last Gerlach gave in: "Have it your own way. If it's neck or nothing anyway we had better be on the move."

Squads hurriedly set to work again on the strip; even Mussolini lent a hand in rolling one or two boulders.

They squashed into the plane; Mussolini behind the pilot, Skorzeny behind Mussolini. With the engine turning, twelve men clung to the Stork, digging their heels in for a tug-of-war. Gerlach held a hand aloft until the engine's pitch rose in a crescendo; as he dropped his hand the men let go and the plane catapulted across the scree.

Skorzeny grasped the steel spars on either side of him, throwing his weight from side to side against the swaying motion as one wheel or the other was lifted by a rock. Suddenly a crevasse yawned before them; the plane shot over it and continued its career beyond, with the port wheel buckled. Then it went hurtling over the edge of the ravine.

In the group of Germans standing on the Gran Sasso, there was suddenly a gap. Radl had collapsed; he had fainted.

Gerlach brought off his miracle. With consummate skill he lifted the Stork gently from its nose-dive to flatten out a few hundred feet above the valley floor.

The rest seemed smooth sailing; even the glissade at Rome on starboard and rear wheels. And there, immaculate on the dusty airfield, forewarned by that instinct for an Occasion that animates aides-de-camp and diplomatic vice-marshals, there waited General Student's A.D.C., standing stiffly at the salute while the three crumpled figures stepped on to friendly soil.

PLATOON LEADER

FROM *The Naked and the Dead*

NORMAN MAILER

As happens not infrequently, many of the values of Norman Mailer's novel of the Second World War, *The Naked and the Dead,* were forgotten in the peripheral discussion of the dialogue of his characters, an almost literal transcription of G.I. talk. The book was rejected by at least one publisher because Mailer refused to eliminate certain frank, if familiar enough, words.

On publication, critics talked of the book as "brutal" but as "an incredibly finished performance," and G.I.'s who had fought in the Pacific gave it the rare praise of "That's the way it was."

Mailer was a rifleman in a division which fought its way across the Philippines. In this selection from his book, a platoon crosses a mountain to attack a Japanese detachment.

THE PLATOON PASSED AN UNEASY NIGHT IN THE HOLLOW. THE MEN WERE TOO tired to sleep well, and shivered in their blankets. When it came each man's turn for guard, he would stumble up to the crest of the hill and stare over the grass into the valley below. Everything was cold and silver in the moonlight, and the hills had become gaunt. The sleeping men in the hollow beneath him were removed and distant. Each man on guard felt alone, terribly alone, as though looking out on the valleys and craters of the moon. Nothing moved, and yet nothing was still. The wind was wistful and reflective; the grass rustled, advanced and retreated in shimmering rustling waves. The night was intensely silent and pendant.

In the dawn they folded their blankets, made their packs, and ate a K ration, chewing slowly, and without relish, the cold tinned ham and eggs and the square graham crackers. Their muscles were stiff from the previous day's march, and their clothing was damp with yesterday's perspiration. The older men were wishing that the sun was higher; there seemed no warmth left in their bodies. Red's kidneys were aching again, Roth's right shoulder was rheumatic, and Wilson had a spasm of diarrhea after he ate. They all felt dull, without volition; they scarcely thought of the march ahead.

Croft and Hearn had gone to the top of the hill again, and were discussing the morning's march. In the early morning, the valley was still hazy with mist and the mountain and pass were obscured. They squinted into the north, looking at the Watamai Range. It extended as far as they could see like a cloud bank in the haze, rising precipitously to its peak at Mount Anaka, and dropping abruptly, shudderingly, into the pass at its left, before mounting again.

"Damn sure seems like the Japs would be watching that pass," Croft commented.

Hearn shrugged. "They probably have enough to do without that, it's pretty far behind their lines."

The haze was dissolving, and Croft squinted through the field glasses into the distance. "I wouldn't say, Lootenant. That pass is narrow enough for a platoon to hold it till hell freezes over." He spat. "Course we got to find that out." The sun was beginning to outline the contours of the hills. The shadows in the hollows and draws were considerably lighter.

"There's not a damn thing else we can do," Hearn murmured. Already he could sense the antipathy between Croft and himself. "With any luck we'll be able to bivouac behind the Jap lines tonight, and then tomorrow we can scout the Jap rear."

Croft was doubtful. His instincts, his experience, told him that the pass would be dangerous, probably futile, and yet there was no alternative. They could climb Mount Anaka, but Hearn would never hear of that. He spat again. "Ain't nothin' else to do, I suppose." But he felt disturbed. The more he looked at the mountain . . .

"Let's start," Hearn said.

They went down again to the men in the hollow, put on their packs, and began to march. Hearn alternated with Brown and Croft in leading the platoon, while Martinez acted as point and scouted ahead, almost always thirty or forty yards in front of them. The grass was slick from the night's dew, and the men slipped frequently as they moved downhill, panted hoarsely as they toiled up an ascending slope. Hearn, however, was feeling good. His body had reacted from the preceding day's march, and was stronger now, the waste burned out of him. He had awakened with stiff muscles and a sore shoulder, but rested and cheerful. This morning his legs were firm, and he sensed greater reserves of endurance. As they crossed the first ridge-line, he hefted his pack higher on his broad shoulders, and turned up his face to the sun for an instant. Everything smelled fine, and the grass had the sweet fresh odor of early morning. "Okay, men, let's hit it," he called to them cheerfully as they passed by. He had dropped back from the point, and he moved from man to man, slowing his stride or increasing it in order to keep pace with them. . . .

There was a resistance they had toward him. They were cautious, perhaps distrustful. He was an officer, and instinctively they would be wary. But there was more to it, he felt. Croft had been with them so long, had controlled the platoon so completely, that probably they could not believe Croft was no longer the platoon leader. They were afraid to respond to him, afraid Croft would remember whenever he resumed his command. The thing was to make them understand that he would be with the platoon permanently. But that would take time. If only he had had a week with them in bivouac, a few minor patrols before this. Hearn shrugged again, wiped some sweat from his forehead. The sun was fierce once more.

And the hills were always rising. All morning the platoon plodded through the tall grass, climbing slowly, trudging through valleys, laboring awkwardly around the slopes of the hills. Their fatigue started again, their breath grew short, and their faces burned from the sun and the exertion. Now, no one was talking, and they progressed sullenly in file.

The sun clouded over, and it began to rain. This was pleasant at first, for the rain was cool and stirred a breeze along the top of the grass, but soon the ground turned soft and their shoes fouled with mud. By degrees they became completely wet again. Their heads drooping, their rifle muzzles pointed toward the ground to avoid the rain, the file of men looked like a row of wilted flowers. Everything about them sagged.

The terrain had altered, become rockier. The hills were steeper now, and some of them were covered with a waist-high brush of low thickets and flat-leafed plants. For the first time since they had left the jungle they passed a grove of trees. The rain halted, and the sun began to burn again, directly overhead. It was noon. The platoon halted in a tiny grove, and the men stripped their packs, and ate another ration. Wilson fingered his crackers distastefully, mouthed down a square of cheese. "Ah heard this binds a man up," he said to Red.

"Hell, it must be good for something."

Wilson laughed, but he was confused. All morning his diarrhea had plagued him, his back and groin had ached. He could not understand why his body had deserted him so. He had always prided himself on being able to do as much as any other man, and now he had to drag along at the tail of the column, pulling himself over even the smallest hills by tugging at the kunai grass. He had been doubled up with cramps, had sweated terribly, his pack abusing his shoulders like a block of concrete. . . .

In a few minutes Hearn gave the order to move again, and the platoon filed out of the grove, and trudged forward in the sun. Although the rain had halted, the hills were mucky, and steam arose from them. The men marched with drooping bodies, the line of hills extending endlessly before them. Slowly, strung out in a file almost a hundred yards long, they weaved through the grass, absorbed in the varied aches and sores of their bodies. Their feet were burning, and their thighs quivered with fatigue. About them the hills shimmered in the noon heat, and a boundless nodding silence had settled over everything. The whirring of the insects was steady and not unpleasant. . . .

The sunlight, the heat, was everywhere, dazzling.

For an hour they marched uphill almost constantly, and then halted at a stream to fill their canteens. They rested for fifteen minutes and went on again. Their clothing had been wet at least a dozen times, from the ocean spray, from the river, their sweat, from sleeping on the ground, and each time it dried it left its stains. Their shirts were streaked with white lines of salt, and under their armpits, beneath their belts, the cloth was beginning to rot. They were chafed and blistered and sunburned; already some of them were limping on sore feet, but all these discomforts were minor, almost unnoticed in the leaden stupor of marching, the fever they suffered from the sun. Their fatigue had racked them, exploited all the fragile vaults of their bodies, the leaden apathy of their muscles. They had tasted so many times the sour acrid bile of labor, had strained their overworked legs over so many hills, that at last they were feeling the anesthesia of exhaustion. They kept moving without any thought of where they went, dully, stupidly, waving and floundering from side to side. The weight of their packs was crushing, but they considered them as a part of their bodies, a boulder lodged in their backs.

The bushes and thickets grew higher, reached almost to their chests. The brambles kept catching in their rifles, and hooking onto their clothing. They thrashed forward, plunging through the brush until halted by the barbs clinging to their clothing, and then stopped, picked the barbs loose, and swooped forward again. The men thought of nothing but the hundred feet of ground in front of them; they almost never looked upward to the crest of the hill they were climbing,

In the early afternoon, they took a long break in the shadow of some rocks. The time passed sluggishly in the chirping of the crickets, the languid flights of the insects. The men, wretchedly tired, began to sleep. Hearn had no desire to move, but the break was too prolonged. He stood up slowly, hitched on his pack, and called out, "Come on, men. On your feet." There was no response, which furnished him with a sharp irritation. They would have obeyed Croft quickly. "Come on, let's get going, men. We can't sit around on our butts all day." His voice was taut and impersonal, and the soldiers rose out of the grass slowly and sullenly. He could hear them muttering, was aware of a glum crabbed resistance.

His nerves were more keyed than he had realized. "Quit the bitching and let's go," he heard himself piping. He was damn tired of them, he realized suddenly.

"That sonofabitch," one of them muttered.

It shocked him, and generated resentment. He repressed it, however. What they were doing was understandable enough. In the fatigue of the march, they had to have someone to blame, and no matter what he did they would hate him sooner or later. His approach would end by confusing and annoying them. Croft they would obey, for Croft satisfied their desire for hatred, encouraged it, was superior to it, and in turn exacted obedience. The realization depressed him. "We've still got a long way to go," he told them more quietly.

They continued to plod on. They were much closer to Mount Anaka now. Every time they crossed a ridge-line they could see the towering cliff walls bordering the pass, could distinguish even the individual trees in the forests on its middle slopes. The country, even the air, had changed. It was cooler here, but the air was perceptibly thinner, and burned faintly in their lungs.

They reached the approach to the pass by three o'clock. Croft climbed the crest of the last hill, crouched behind a bush, and examined the land before them. Beneath the hill, a valley extended for perhaps a quarter of a mile, an island of tall grass surrounded by the mountain range in front, and by hills to the left and right. Beyond the valley the pass wound through the range in a twisting rocky gorge between sheer walls of stone. The floor of the defile was hidden in foliage, and might conceal any number of men.

He stared at the few knolls set in the opening of the pass, searching the jungle that circled about its foot. He had a quiet satisfaction that he had come so far. A damn lot of land we crossed, he told himself. Through the silence which hung over the hills, he could hear the muffled rumble of artillery on the other side of the mountains, the sporadic grumble of a battle.

Martinez had come up beside him. "All right, Japbait," he whispered, "let's keep to the hills around the edge of this valley. If they's anyone sitting at the entrance to the pass, they'll see us if we go through the field." Martinez nodded, crouched over the top of the hill, and turned to the right to circle the valley. Croft waved his arm to the rest of the platoon to follow, and started down the hill.

They moved very slowly, keeping close to the tall grass. Martinez would advance only thirty yards at a time, and then halt, before moving forward again. Something of his caution was transferred to the men. Without anything being said, they all were wary. They roused themselves from their fatigue, alerted their dulled senses, even restored to some extent a necessary delicate control of their limbs. They were careful where they placed their feet, and they lifted their legs at each step, and set them down firmly, trying to make no noise. They were all acutely conscious of the silence in the valley, and started at unexpected rustles, halted every time an insect began its chirping. Their tension increased. They expected something to happen, and their mouths became dry, their heartbeats pounded high in their chests.

It was only a few hundred yards from the place where Croft had studied the valley to the approaches of the pass, but the route Martinez took was more than half a mile. It took them a long time to circle around, perhaps half an hour, and their alertness diminished. The men in the rear of the column had to wait minutes at a time, and then jog forward on the half-run to keep up with the rest of the platoon. It was trying, it was exhausting, and it grated on them. Their fatigue became alive again, and throbbed in their backs, in the exhausted hamstrings of their thighs. They would stand in a partial crouch, waiting for the signal to move ahead, their packs resting cruelly on their shoulders. The sweat would run into their eyes, and their eyes would tear. They lost the fine edge of their tension, became surly. A few of them began to grumble, and in one of the longer halts Wilson stopped to relieve himself. They began to move while he was still occupied and the column was confused. The men in the rear whispered up the file to halt the leaders, and for a minute or so men were moving back and forth and whispering to each other. When Wilson was ready, they advanced again, but discipline was broken. Although none of the men talked aloud, the sum of their whispers, their decreased caution in walking, added up to a detectable murmur of sound. Occasionally Croft would give a hand signal to be silent, but it did not have enough effect.

They reached the cliffs at the base of Mount Anaka, and bore to the left again, darting toward the pass from rock to rock. They reached a place where there was no defilade; an open field, a cove of the larger valley extended for a hundred yards to the first saddle in the pass. There was nothing to do but walk across it. Hearn and Croft squatted behind a ledge and discussed their strategy.

"We got to divvy up into the two squads, Lootenant, and have one of them go across the field while the other covers."

"I guess that's it," Hearn nodded. It was oddly, incongruously pleasant, to be sitting on the rock ledge, absorbing the warmth of the sun on his body. He took a deep breath. "That's what we'll do. When the first squad reaches the pass, the other one can come on up."

"Yeah." Croft massaged his chin, examining the Lieutenant's face. "I'll take the squad, huh, Lootenant?"

No! This was where he had to step in. "I'm going to take it, Sergeant. You cover me."

"Well . . . all right, Lootenant." He paused a moment. "You better take Martinez's squad. Most of the older men are in it."

Hearn nodded. He thought he had detected a trace of surprise and disappointment in Croft's expression and it pleased him. But immediately afterward he was annoyed with himself. He was getting childish.

He motioned to Martinez and held up one finger to indicate he wanted the first squad. After a minute or two, the men formed about him. Hearn could feel some tension in his throat, and when he spoke his voice was hoarse, a whisper. "We're going to move into that grove, and the second squad will cover us. I don't have to tell you to keep your eyes open." He fingered his throat, feeling as though he had forgotten something. "Keep at least five yards apart." Some of the men nodded in agreement.

Hearn stood up, climbed over the ledge, and began to walk across the open field toward the foliage that covered the entrance to the pass. Behind him and to his left and right, he could hear the footsteps of the squad. Automatically he held his rifle at his side, both hands gripping the stock. The field was a hundred yards long, and perhaps thirty yards wide, bordered by the cliffs on one side and the valley of tall grass on the other. It sloped downward slightly over a run of scattered small rocks. The sun beat on it fiercely, refracting brightly from the stones and the barrels of their rifles. The silence was intense again, laving itself in layers of somnolence.

Hearn could feel the impact of each step on the sore bruised ball of his foot, but it seemed to exist at a great distance from his body; he knew remotely that his hands were slippery on the gun. The tension banked itself in his chest only to flare forth at any unexpected sound, anyone kicking a stone or scuffling his feet. He swallowed, looked behind him for a moment at the squad of men. His senses were exceptionally alert. Behind everything, he had a suppressed joy and excitement.

Some of the foliage in the grove seemed to move. He halted abruptly, and stared across the fifty yards which separated them. Seeing nothing, he waved his hand forward again, and they continued to advance.

BEE-YOWWWWW!

The shot ricocheted off a rock and went singing into the distance. Suddenly, terrifyingly, the grove crackled with gunfire, and the men in the field withered before it like a wheat prairie in a squall. Hearn dropped to the ground behind a rock, looked behind him to see the rest of the men crawling for cover, squirming and cursing and shouting at each other. The rifle fire continued, steady and vicious, mounting in crescendo with the parched snapping sound of wood in a forest fire. The bullets chirruped by in the soft buzzing sound of insects on the wing, or glanced off a rock and went screaming through the air with the tortured howl of metal ripping apart. BEE-YOWWWWWW! BEEE-YOWWWWWWW! TEE-YOOOOOOOOONG!

The men in the field flopped behind their rocks, quivered, helpless, afraid to raise their heads. Behind them, back of the rock ledge, after a pause, Croft and his squad had begun to fire into the grove at the other end of the field. The walls of the cliff refracted the sound, bounced it back into the valley, where it rushed about in disorder, the echoes overlapping like conflicting ripples in a brook. A wash of sound beat over the men, almost deafening them.

Hearn lay prone behind a rock, his limbs twitching, sweat running into his eyes. He stared for long seconds at the granite veins and tissues of the rock before him, looking with numb absorption, without volition. Everything in him had come undone. The impulse to cover his head and wait passively for the fight to terminate was very powerful. He heard a sound trickle out of his lips, was dumbly surprised to know he had made it. With everything, with the surprising and unmanning fear was a passionate disgust with himself. He couldn't quite believe it. He had never been in combat before, but to act like this . . .

BEE-YOWWWWWW! Rock fragments and powder settled on his neck, itched slightly. The gunfire was spiteful, malevolent. It seemed directed at him, and he winced unconsciously every time a bullet passed. All the water in his body had rushed to the surface. Perspiration dripped steadily, automatically, from his chin, the tip of his nose, from his brow into his eyes. The skirmish was only fifteen or twenty seconds old, and he was completely wet. A steel band wrenched at his clavicle, choked his throat. His heart pounded like a fist beating against a wall. For ten seconds he concentrated only on knitting his sphincter, roused to a pitch of revulsion by the thought of soiling himself. "NO! NO!" The bullets whirred past with an ineffable delicate sound.

He had to get them out of here! But his arms cushioned his head, and he flinched each time a bullet ricocheted off a rock. Back of him he heard the men bawling to each other, shouting words back and forth incoherently. Why this fear? He had to shake it. What had happened to him? This was unbelievable. . . . He felt as though he could hear everything, the scattered men breathing hoarsely behind their rocks, the Japanese in the grove calling to each other, even the rustling of the grass and the tense humming sounds of the crickets in the valley. Behind him, Croft's squad was still firing. He ducked behind the rock, scrounging his body as a volley of Japanese fire ricocheted off it. The stone and dust stung the back of his neck.

Why didn't Croft do something? And abruptly he realized that he had been waiting here for Croft to take over, waiting for the sharp voice of command that would lead him out of this. It roused a vivid rage. He slid his carbine around the side of the rock, started to squeeze the trigger.

But the gun wouldn't fire; the safety catch was still on. This mistake in-

EDELWEISS, A PLANT NATIVE TO THE ALPS OF CENTRAL EUROPE. IT IS A SMALL HERB REACHING ABOUT SIX INCHES HIGH, WITH NARROW WHITE WOOLLY LEAVES AND FLOWER HEADS ENVELOPED IN WOOLLY BRACTS. ITS COVERING ENABLES IT TO THRIVE IN EXPOSED SITUATIONS

Fosco Maraini: Monkmeyer

MONSOON-MISTS IN THE HIMALAYAN VALLEYS SEEM TO DISSOLVE TRUNKS, FERNS, AND TREES

John Sumner: Monkmeyer

A JEFFREY PINE, NORMALLY A SYMMETRICAL TREE, ON THE SUMMIT OF SENTINEL DOME IN YOSEMITE PARK. THE GRIMNESS OF ITS STRUGGLE FOR SURVIVAL IS READILY APPARENT

A MOUNTAIN CARNATION IN BLOOM IN THE SWISS ALPS

Black Star

GOLDEN EAGLES DEVOURING THE CARCASS OF A DEER

MOUNTAIN GOATS BECAUSE OF THEIR AGILITY AND INCREDIBLE SURE-FOOTEDNESS ARE ABLE TO MAKE THEIR HOME AMONG THE HIGH ROCKS AND CRAGS OF MOUNTAINS

Fritz Henle: Monkmeyer

A VIEW OF THE GREAT WALL OF CHINA, SNAKING ITS WAY OVER THE MOUNTAINS

AMERICAN INFANTRYMEN ON A RIDGE IN KOREA

Official Department of Defense Photo: Acme

A SWISS MOUNTAINEER PATROL DURING A DOWNHILL SKI RUN IN THE BERNE HIGHLANDS

SWISS ARMY RESERVISTS TRAINING IN WINTER WARFARE IN THE BERNE HIGHLANDS

furiated him. Not quite conscious of what he was doing, he stood up, pressed
the safety and fired a volley of three or four shots into the grove.

"GET BACK, GET BACK," he roared. "COME ON, GET UP, GET
UP! . . . BACK!" Numbly he heard himself shouting, his voice shrill and
furious. "COME ON, GET UP AND RUN!" There were bullets whipping
past him, but standing on his feet they seemed insignificant. "GET BACK
TO THE OTHER SQUAD!" he roared again, running from rock to rock,
his voice bellowing like something apart from himself. He turned and fired
again, five shots as quickly as he could squeeze them off, and waited dumb,
motionless. "GET UP AND FIRE. GIVE THEM A VOLLEY!"

A few of the men in the squad stood up and fired. Awed, confused, the
grove was silent for a few seconds. "COME ON, RUN!"

The men straggled to their feet, looked mutely at him, and began to race
toward the ledge from which they had started. They faced the grove, fired a
few shots, and ran back for twenty yards, stopped to fire again, retreating
pell-mell, sobbing like animals in anger and fear. The Japanese in the grove
were firing once more, but they paid no attention. All of them were frantic.
In motion, they wanted only one thing—to reach the safety of the ledge.

One by one, gasping, panting angrily, they climbed the last shelf of rock
and dropped behind its bank, their bodies pungent with sweat. Hearn was
one of the last.

THE GREEKS BATTLE
THE BARBARIANS

FROM *Anabasis*

XENOPHON

Xenophon was an Athenian born sometime about 430 B.C. He knew Socrates and wrote about him. He was something of a jack-of-all-trades—in politics, writing, military strategy. Classical scholars observe that his writings show him "a lover of country, pious to the gods, a lucid and agreeable writer, sensible but not profound"—a carefully measured judgment. In 401 he joined a military expedition as commander of the Ten Thousand Greeks allied with Cyrus. One of the battles at a mountain pass during which he maneuvered the Greeks out of a dangerously untenable position is described in this extract from his *Anabasis*.

AS SOON AS THEY REACHED A HALTING PLACE, XENOPHON WENT STRAIGHT TO Cheirisophus, just as he was, and proceeded to reproach him for not waiting, but compelling them to flee and fight at the same time; "and now," he went on, "two fine, brave fellows have lost their lives, and we were not able to pick up their bodies or bury them." Cheirisophus' reply was, "Take a look," said he, "at the mountains, and observe how impassable all of them are. The only road is the one there, which you see, a steep one, too, and on that you can see the great crowd of people who have taken possession of it and are guarding our way out. That's the reason why I was hurrying and why I would not wait for you, for I hoped to reach the pass and occupy it before they did. The guides that we have say there is no other road." And Xenophon answered, "Well, I also have two men. For at the time when the enemy were giving us trouble, we set an ambush. It allowed us, for one thing, to catch our breath; but, besides, we killed a number of them, and we took especial pains to get some prisoners for this very purpose, of being able to employ as guides men who know the country."

They brought up the two men at once and questioned them separately as to whether they knew any other road besides the one that was in plain sight. The first man said he did not, despite all the numerous threats that

were made to him; and since he would give no information, he was slaugh-
tered before the eyes of the second one. The latter now said that the reason
why this first man had maintained that he did not know any other road, was
because he chanced to have a daughter living in that neighborhood with a
husband to whom he had given her; but as for himself, he said that he
would lead the Greeks by a road that could be traversed even by baggage
animals. Upon being asked whether there was any point on it which was
difficult to pass, he replied that there was a height which they could not possibly pass unless they should seize it beforehand.

Thereupon it was decided to call together the captains, both of peltasts
and hoplites, to set forth to them the existing situation, and to ask if there
was any one among them who would like to prove himself a brave man and
to undertake this expedition as a volunteer. Volunteers came forward, from
the hoplites Aristonymus of Methydrium and Agasias of Stymphalus, while
in rivalry with them Callimachus of Parrhasia said that he was ready to
make the expedition and take with him volunteers from the entire army;
"for I know," he continued, "that many of the young men will follow if I
am in the lead." Then they asked whether any one among the captains of
light troops wanted to join in the march. The volunteer was Aristeas of
Chios, who on many occasions proved himself valuable to the army for
such services.

It was now late afternoon, and they ordered the volunteers to take a
snatch of food and set out. They also bound the guide and turned him over
to the volunteers, and made an agreement with them that in case they
should capture the height, they were to guard it through the night and
give a signal at daybreak with the trumpet; then those on the height were
to proceed against the Carduchians who were holding the visible way out,
while the main army was to come to their support, pushing forward as fast
as it could. This agreement concluded, the volunteers, about two thousand
in number, set out on their march; and there was a heavy downpour of
rain; at the same time Xenophon with the rearguard began advancing toward the visible way out, in order that the enemy might be giving their
attention to that road and that the party taking the roundabout route
might, so far as possible, escape observation. But as soon as the troops of
the rearguard were at a gorge which they had to cross before marching up
the steep hill, at that moment the barbarians began to roll down round
stones large enough for a wagon-load, with larger and smaller ones also;
they came down with a crash upon the rocks below and the fragments of
them flew in all directions, so that it was quite impossible even to approach
the ascending road. Then some of the captains, unable to proceed by this
route, would try another, and they kept this up until darkness came on. It
was not until they imagined that their withdrawal would be unobserved

that they went back to dinner—and it chanced that they had had no breakfast either. The enemy, however, never stopped rolling down their stones
all through the night, as one could judge from the noise.

Meanwhile the party with the guide, proceeding by a roundabout route,
found the guards sitting around a fire, and after killing some of them and
chasing away the others they remained at the post themselves, supposing
that they held the height. In fact, they were not holding it, for it was a
round hill above them and past it ran this narrow road upon which the
guards had been sitting. Nevertheless, from the place they did hold there
was a way of approach to the spot, upon the visible road, where the main
body of the enemy were stationed. At this place, then, they passed the night,
and when day was beginning to break, they took up their march silently in
battle array against the enemy; for there was a mist, and consequently they
got close up to them without being observed. When they did catch sight of
one another, the trumpet sounded and the Greeks raised the battle cry
and rushed upon the enemy. And the Carduchians did not meet their
attack, but abandoned the road and took to flight; only a few of them,
however, were killed, for they were agile fellows. Meanwhile Cheirisophus
and his command, hearing the trumpet, charged immediately up the visible
road; and some of the other generals made their way without following any
road from the points where they severally chanced to be and, clambering up
as best they could, pulled one another up with their spears; and it was they
who were first to join the troops that had already gained possession of the
place.

But Xenophon with half the rearguard set out by the same route which
the party with the guide had followed, because this was the easiest route for
the baggage animals; and behind the baggage animals he posted the other
half of the rearguard. As they proceeded they came upon a hill above the
road which had been seized by the enemy, and found themselves compelled
either to dislodge them or be completely separated from the rest of the
Greeks; and while, so far as the troops themselves were concerned, they
might have taken the same route that the rest followed, the baggage animals
could not get through by any other road than this one by which Xenophon
was proceeding. Then and there, accordingly, with words of cheer to one
another, they charged upon the hill with their companies in column, not
surrounding it, but leaving the enemy a way of retreat in case they chose
to use it. For a while, as the Greeks were climbing up by whatever way they
severally could, the barbarians discharged arrows and other missiles upon
them; they did not let them get near, however, but took to flight and abandoned the place. No sooner had the Greeks passed by this hill, than they
saw a second one ahead similarly occupied by the enemy, and decided to
proceed against this one in its turn. Xenophon, however, becoming appre-

hensive lest, if he should leave unoccupied the hill he had just captured, the enemy might take possession of it again and attack the baggage train as it passed (and the train stretched out a long way because of the narrowness of the road it was following), left three captains upon the hill, Cephisodorus, son of Cephisophon, an Athenian, Amphicrates, son of Amphidemus, also an Athenian, and Archagoras, an Argive exile; while he himself with the rest of the troops proceeded against the second hill, which they captured in the same fashion as the first.

There still remained a third round hill, far the steepest of them all, the one that rose above the guard post, by the fire, which had been captured during the night by the volunteers. But when the Greeks got near this hill, the barbarians abandoned it without striking a blow, so that everybody was filled with surprise and imagined that they had quit the place out of fear that they might be surrounded and blockaded. As it proved, however, they had seen, looking down from their height, what was going on farther back, and were all setting out to attack the Greek rearguard. Meanwhile Xenophon proceeded to climb the abandoned height with his youngest troops, ordering the rest to move on slowly in order that the hindmost companies might catch up; then they were to advance along the road and halt under arms on the plateau at the top of the pass.

At this time Archagoras the Argive came up in flight and reported that the Greeks had been dislodged from the first hill, that Cephisodorus and Amphicrates had been killed, and likewise all the rest except such as had leaped down the rocks and reached the rearguard. After accomplishing this achievement the barbarians came to a hill opposite the round hill, and Xenophon, through an interpreter, held a colloquy with them in regard to a truce and asked them to give back the bodies of the Greek dead. They replied that they would give them back on condition that the Greeks should not burn their houses. To this Xenophon agreed. But while the rest of the army was passing by and they were engaged in this conference, all the enemy from that neighbourhood had streamed together to the spot; and as soon as Xenophon and his men began to descend from the round hill, in order to join the rest of the Greeks at the place where they were halted under arms, the enemy took this opportunity to rush upon them in great force and with a great deal of uproar. When they had reached the crest of the hill from which Xenophon was descending, they proceeded to roll down stones. They broke one man's leg, and Xenophon found himself deserted by the servant who was carrying his shield; but Eurylochus of Lusi, a hoplite, ran up to him and, keeping his shield held out in front of them both, fell back with him; and the rest also made good their retreat to the main array.

S T R E T C H E R   C A S E S

FROM *Man's Hope*

A N D R É   M A L R A U X

🦎 André Malraux has lived his two major novels. He abandoned his studies in archaeology to join the Young Annam League in the Indo-Chinese fight for independence. As his political interests widened, he played a leading part in the early Kuomintang movement and in *Man's Fate* dramatized the Chinese revolution of 1924. During the Civil War in Spain he organized an air corps for the Loyalists, flew sixty-five flights, and wrote *Man's Hope*. It was hailed as a magnificent imaginative work and won him the Goncourt Prize and stature as one of France's great contemporary writers. This selection from *Man's Hope* describes the grim aftermath of a guerrilla battle in the Pyrenees.

AT LAST LINARES ANSWERED. NO, THE AIRMEN WERE NOT THERE. THEY HAD come down near a little hamlet called Valdelinares. Higher up, in the snow.

What village would he have to call now? "Higher up, in the snow!" But the friendly tone in which the answers were given made Magnin feel more than ever that this was the real Spain which surrounded him, as though in each hospital, in each committee, in each post office a peasant were waiting with comradely greetings. At last there was a ring. The postmaster lifted the receiver; Valdelinares was answering. He listened, then turned round.

"One of the airmen can walk. He has gone to fetch him."

The little boy no longer dared to move. A cat's shadow flitted across the window.

The postmaster handed Magnin the antiquated receiver, from which came a muffled voice.

"Hullo! Who is that?"

"Magnin speaking. That's Pujol, isn't it?"

"Yes."

"Who has been killed?"

"Saïdi."

"And the wounded?"

"Gardet, badly: eyes in danger. Taillefer, left leg broken in three places, Mireaux, four bullets in the arm. Scali, an explosive bullet in the foot. Langlois and I will be all right."

"Can anyone walk?"

"All the way down?"

"Yes."

"No, nobody."

"Or ride down on mules?"

"Langlois and I. Perhaps Scali, with help; but I'm not sure."

"How are you being looked after?"

"The sooner we get down, the better. They're doing all they can, but . . ."

"Are there any stretchers?"

"Not here. Wait, the doctor's saying something."

He could hear the doctor's voice.

"Hullo!" Magnin said. "Can all the wounded be moved?"

"Yes—if you have stretchers."

Magnin questioned the postmaster. He didn't know. Perhaps there were stretchers at the hospital. But certainly not six. Magnin picked up the receiver again.

"Can you fix up litters with branches, straps and mattresses?"

"Well . . . I think so."

"I'm bringing what I can in the way of stretchers. Get them on to making the litters right away, and start down. I am waiting here for an ambulance. It will come up as far as it can."

"What about the body?"

"Bring everything down. Hallo! Hallo! And you might tell the men that sixteen enemy planes were destroyed. Don't forget."

The journey through the streets began again; past the brightly coloured houses, the square and its fountains, the steeply pitched bridges and the sharp cobbles, still shining after the showers which had fallen that morning from the low clouds. There were two stretchers in all and they were tied on to the roof of the car.

"Won't that be too high to go through the gate?"

At last, Magnin left for Linares.

From now on, he was in contact with the very soul of Spain. Passing through a village of houses with open balustrade-fronted lofts, the car came to a gorge where the spreading horns of a fighting bull showed dimly outlined on the grey sky. A dark, primitive hostility seemed rising from the soil, on which these un-European villages had left their scars; a hostility intensified for Magnin by the way the rocks continually reminded him, in between glances at his watch, of their pitilessness towards the wounded airmen. Nowhere to land; nothing but rocks, trees and fields terraced like steps. Every time the car ran down a slope Magnin imagined the plane sinking down towards that merciless ground.

Linares has a wall round it. Children were sitting on the ramparts, on either side of the gate. At the inn, where the ground floor was jammed full of carts with their shafts sticking up in the air, there were mules waiting. At the Committee there was one doctor, who had come up from the valley, and fifteen or twenty young men. They stared curiously at the tall stranger with the drooping moustache who wore the uniform of the Spanish air force.

"We don't need all those bearers," said Magnin.

"They all insist on coming," said the delegate.

"Right. What about the ambulance?"

The delegate phoned Mora; it hadn't arrived yet. Their carts drawn up in a semicircle around them, the mule-drivers were sitting in the courtyard eating from the communal pot, in this case an enormous inverted bell. It was full of bubbling olive oil, and covered with soot, which hid the inscription on it. Above the doorway was engraved: 1614.

At last the caravan got under way.

"How long will it take to get up there?"

"Four hours. You'll meet them coming down."

Magnin was walking two hundred yards ahead, his burly silhouette— uniform cap and leather coat—clear-cut against the mountainside. There was hardly any mud, only stones to impede progress. Behind him came the doctor on a mule; farther behind, the stretcher-bearers wearing jerseys and Basque berets (the local costumes were kept for fête-days and old age); in the distance, mules and stretchers.

Soon there were no more bulls or fields; nothing but rocks, the rocks of Spain, that sparkle red and yellow in the sun, but now were pale beneath the overcast sky, with shadows lurking in the huge clefts. They fell away in two or three precipitous tiers from the snow on the skyline right down to the bottom of the valley. Pebbles fell over the edge of the path as they walked, clattering down from rock to rock until the silence of the gorge engulfed them. It seemed to be engulfing the noise of a mountain-stream they were leaving behind them. After more than an hour the valley down which Linares could still be seen came to an end. The moment they rounded the spur of the mountain which separated them from it, Magnin could no longer hear the noise of the water. The track went behind a sheer wall of rock which overhung it in places. At the point where it changed direction was an apple-tree, outlined against the sky; in the centre of a minute field, recalling a Japanese landscape. Its apples had not been picked. Strewn on the ground, they formed a thick ring round it, which merged gradually into grass again. This apple-tree was the only living thing among the rocks, living with the mute ageless indifference of endlessly reincarnated plant-life.

Magnin could feel the fatigue growing steadily in his shoulders and leg-muscles as he climbed. Gradually the feeling of effort invaded his whole body, driving everything else from his mind. By now the litters would be making their way down these same precipitous paths, with their load of shattered arms and broken legs. His eyes wandered from the short stretch of path visible in front to the snow-clad peaks fretting the white clouds, and each new effort brought home to him with vivid intensity the comradeship that bound him to his leader.

The Linares peasants, who had not seen any of the wounded yet, followed him in silence, keeping him stern and dignified company. He was thinking about the lorries from the villages.

He had been climbing for at least two hours when the path which they had been following round the face of a spur of the mountain came to an end. The track now led through snow, up a new gorge, towards the higher and much less rugged part of the mountains that the aeroplanes had seen rising beside the other when they left for Teruel. From here on, the mountain-streams were frozen. Where the path changed direction again a Saracen warrior was waiting, like the apple-tree lower down, black against the background of sky, and foreshortened like a statue on a high pedestal seen from below. The horse was a mule, and the Saracen was Pujol, complete with flying-helmet. He turned round, his profile thrown into relief like a carving, and shattered the intense silence with a shout. "There's Magnin!" . . .

The mules in front were vanishing round another corner, following the original direction again. The new line of descent led straight to Linares: Magnin recognized the apple-tree.

What forest was that on which the rain was beating down, on the far side of the rock, where the path turned? Magnin coaxed his mule to a trot, went past all the others, and arrived at the turning. No rain; it was the sound of the streams which the cliff wall had screened from him, as a rock wall hides a landscape, and which could not be heard from the other slope. The sound was rising from Linares, as though the ambulances and the new lease of life which lay before them were sending up this insistent rustling, as of a high wind on leaves, from the far depths of the valley. Night had not fallen yet, but the light was failing. Like an equestrian statue, Magnin was sitting askew on his saddleless mule, gazing at the little apple-tree standing surrounded by its dead fruit. Langlois' bristling crest of bloodstained hair came into view in front of the branches. In the silence suddenly grown murmurous with the sound of rippling water, the ring of decaying fruit seemed to typify the passage from life to death that not only was the doom of men but was an immutable law of the universe. Magnin's eyes wandered from the tree to the ageless ravines. One after another, the stretchers were going past. The branches reached forward on either side over the swaying stretchers, as above Langlois' head; above the corpselike smile of Taillefer, the childlike face of Mireaux, Gardet's flat bandage and Scali's lacerated lips; above each bloodstained body gently borne along by comrades' hands. The coffin went by, with its machine-gun twisted like the branch of a tree. Magnin moved on again.

Without his quite knowing why, the deep gorges into which they now were plunging, as if into the bowels of earth, seemed imbued with the same agelessness as the trees. He thought of the quarries in which prisoners were left to die in former days. But that shattered leg which the muscles barely held together, that sagging arm, that obliterated face, that machine-gun on a coffin, all these were the results of risks voluntarily accepted, sought after. The solemn, primitive march of that line of stretchers had something as compelling about it as the pale rocks that merged into the lowering sky, something as fundamental as the apples scattered on the ground. Birds of prey were crying again, close beneath the clouds. How many years had he to live? Twenty?

"What made the Arab airman join in?"

One of the women was approaching him again, accompanied by two others.

Up above the birds were wheeling through the air with rigid wings, like so many aeroplanes.

"Can they really give people new noses now?"

The path widened steadily as the valley approached Linares; the peasants were walking beside the stretchers now. The black-clothed women, scarves on their heads and baskets on their arms, were still bustling around the wounded, moving from one to another. The men were keeping pace with the stretchers, without ever getting in front of them, walking abreast of each other, holding themselves with the stiff erectness of those who have been carrying a weight on their shoulders. At each change-over, the new bearers abandoned their stiff walk as they took up the shafts with affectionate care, moving off again to the accompaniment of the grunts which tell of physical effort, as if anxious to mask the betrayal of their emotions which their solicitude denoted. Their attention concentrated on the stones which obstructed the path, thinking only of the necessity not to jolt the stretchers, they moved steadily forward, slowing up a little on the steeper inclines. And the steady rhythm of their tread over the long, pain-burdened journey seemed to fill the vast ravine, down which the last cries still came floating from the birds above, with a solemn beat like a funeral drum. But it was not death which haunted the mountains at that moment; it was triumphant human will.

They were beginning to be able to make out Linares at the bottom of the valley, and the stretchers were drawing closer together; the coffin was level with Scali. The machine-gun had been tied on where a wreath would normally have been laid; the whole procession recalled a funeral as precisely as that twisted machine-gun recalled the wreaths which it replaced. Near the Saragossa road down below, around the fascist planes, the fires of black wood were still burning in the fading light. They would never reach Guadalajara. And all that long line of black-clothed peasants, the women with their hair hidden beneath the scarves which they had worn from time immemorial, seemed to have more of the character of an austere triumphal progress than a relief party bringing home wounded men.

The gradient was easy now. Leaving the path, the stretchers spread out across the grass, and the hill men scattered out fanwise. Children were running up from Linares; a hundred yards from the stretchers they moved aside, let them pass, and followed on behind. The road followed the fortifications up to the gate; its cobbles, set edgewise, were more slippery than the mountain-path.

The whole town was massed behind the battlements. Night had not yet fallen, but there was little daylight left. Though there had been no rain, the cobbles were moist and shining and the bearers picked their way carefully. In the houses which projected above the battlements lamps were glimmering.

The bomber still headed the line. The women on the battlements looked at him gravely, but without surprise; only the face of the wounded man appeared above the blanket, and it showed no sign of injury. Scali and Mireaux likewise, Langlois gave them a shock; with a bleeding bandage round his head, and toes sticking into the air (he had removed the shoe from his sprained foot), he looked like Don Quixote. Was this how war in the air ended, war in its most romantic form? The atmosphere grew tenser when Pujol went past; there was still light enough for observant eyes to see the large bloodstains on his leather coat. When Gardet arrived a hush so profound fell upon the crowd that the noise of the distant mountain-torrents suddenly became audible.

All the other wounded could see; and all, even the bomber, had made an effort to smile when they saw the crowd. Gardet did not look at them; he was alive, but that was all. From the battlements the crowd could make out the thick coffin behind him. Covered with a blanket up to his chin, and with the bandage under his flying-helmet lying so flat that it was impossible that there could be any nose beneath it, this stretcher was the visible incarnation of the peasants' immemorial conception of war. And nobody had forced him to fight. For a moment they hesitated; not knowing what to do, but determined to make some gesture. Then, as at Valdelinares, they silently raised their clenched fists.

It had begun to drizzle. The last stretchers, the peasants from the mountains, and the last mules were advancing between the vast background of rocky landscape over which dark rainclouds were massing, and the hundreds of peasants standing motionless with raised fists. The women were weeping quietly, and the procession seemed to be fleeing from the eerie silence of the mountains, its noise of clattering hoofs and clogs linking the everlasting clamour of the vultures with the muffled sound of sobbing.

AT MISSIONARY RIDGE

FROM *No Bugles Tonight*

BRUCE LANCASTER

In this selection from Bruce Lancaster's Civil War novel, we see death brought not by the enemy, but by military stupidity, incompetence, misjudgment—it goes by many names, but is death all the same—even more horrifying because it is more futile.

This is a detail from the larger canvas of the battle of Missionary Ridge. The episode concerns an artillery battery in Sherman's Army. Whip is platoon leader and Kinyard battery commander.

Bruce Lancaster is no stranger to field guns. He served for two years with the Field Artillery in France during the First World War and writes like a man who has seen a big gun from both ends.

FOUR HUNDRED MILES AND MORE, KINNYARD'S BATTERY HAD ROLLED AND TUGGED its way with the rest of Sherman's artillery and wagon trains from Memphis on the Mississippi to Bridgeport on the Tennessee. Now, in late November, the four Napoleons with their attendant caissons and wagons moved across the swaying bridge at Kelly's Ferry and plunged into the high-walled pass that led across the great tongue of land formed where the river bent sharply north, then west and then south again. The paint of gun, limber, and caisson showed deep nicks and scars; the horses were worn and bony; officers and men pressed on in stained uniforms made up of a weird medley of government issue, civilian clothes, and hastily converted gray from the captured Vicksburg stores; some of the elements of the battery were drawn by six-horse hitches although most of the sections were reduced to four. But the horses were well-groomed, the marching cannoneers kept steadily on. Not an axle shrieked from lack of grease and the harness was supple and uncracked.

Just inside the pass Whip pulled up the slope a little and watched his platoon bend to the rough road. Satisfied with what he saw, he paced along the column. There was nothing to be seen for the first mile or so, save the slant of the hills, the road choked with men and guns and horses and, far ahead of the first section, the bayonets of Miller's 6th Iowa, Corse's brigade, Ewing's division, as they led the battery on to Brown's Ferry and its bridge.

All at once the ridge on the right of the road fell away and Whip unconsciously checked his mount. There, not much more than a mile to his right front, the Tennessee swung in its dart to the north and, towering hard above the bend, Lookout Mountain caught the late sun. Far beyond it he saw the roofs and spires of Chattanooga and, more distant, the harsh shoulder of Missionary Ridge. . . .

The battery lurched on along the rough road, the drivers leading their teams. Whip walked with them, his roan following docilely. The woods were cleared, the column turned right toward the river, and Whip stared in astonishment. Off across the flats, where there had been empty river the night before, a broad pontoon bridge rocked gently in the current. Across it rolled a battery, guidon bright at its head, while other batteries were already massed on the south shore. As he watched, another line of guns and caissons swung onto the planks and he recognized it for James Williams's 1st Iowa, which had been camped not far beyond Kinnyard's.

The shore came closer and closer, the planks rang to the pound of hoof and wheel. He craned his neck. The drizzle still held. He could see that the southern fields were thick with infantry and artillery, all moving inland. But the broad nose of Missionary Ridge was mist-wrapped almost to ground level.

On the south shore he swung into the saddle, motioned the drivers to mount and gave the signal to trot as the other sections slanted off toward the west, heading for the right flank of a heavy mass of infantry that was forming. As he rode, he saw other bodies, full divisions he estimated, grouping center and left.

He cantered across abandoned field works, then saw, beyond the waiting infantry, fresher dirt. The infantry that had ferried itself over in pontoons during the night must have started digging at once, for they had created a well-protected bridgehead. Kinnyard signaled to him and he joined the head of the battery. "How'd you like riding across that beautiful target?" grinned Tom.

"I'd have gone under that bridge if a kid had snapped a popgun behind me." He looked at Kinnyard. "What are orders?"

Kinnyard nodded toward the troops just ahead. "Ewing's 4th Division," he said. "We're supporting it along with three Illinois batteries and one Missouri. Sherman's moving right up the nose of the ridge in echelon. Morgan Smith's division's on the far left, then John E. Smith's center, and then Ewing. We'll roll along Ewing's right flank. We can expect to hit anything at any time. Be sure your sections can go into action without the slightest delay. I'm going to halt the column by that apple tree over there. When the whole shebang starts, we go into line, first piece on the left. That'll make you the extreme right. When we go into action, Nick and Escholtz will run the limbers to cover, no matter how far they have to go. I'm not going to have my horses picked off by Reb sharpshooters. Nick knows about it."

The battery halted by the apple tree that Kinnyard had pointed out. Whip stared ahead of the waiting infantry, who, in the manner of seasoned veterans, were saving their legs by stretching out on the wet grass. Beyond them the ground rose in a steady, gentle slope that melted away in the mist. Scattered pale patches began to wink up in the clouds and bullets whined high in the air. There was a hidden, deep-toned thud and a shell screeched away to burst with a flat smack in the soggy ground close by the river. Whip saw the cannoneers of his platoon cocking their ears toward the unseen heights.

Beyond the head of Ewing's massed division, Sherman was reining in beside his brother-in-law, his head moving in animated jerks and his arm stabbing the air. Then he wheeled his mount and raced off toward the advanced left division, Morgan Smith's.

Bugles suddenly blared and drums rolled. The three divisions, in staggered formation, moved at a slow, steady gait up the slope, their heads vanishing into the mists. Whip stood in his stirrups and watched Kinnyard. When he saw his arm go up, he nodded to his chiefs of section and sent his platoon off at a sharp trot, then wheeled it left front so that it formed the right end of the battery line, some fifty yards behind the rearmost of Ewing's elements.

The horses fought their bits, threw their shoulders into their collars. Whip crooked his arm across his forehead in signal to decrease the gait. He called, "Steady! What are you trying to do? Run over Ewing's boys?" The pace slowed to a walk and he felt a quick glow of pride as he looked along the line that was dressed so smoothly and maintained such precise intervals. He hoped that the Illinois gunners, over by Ewing's center, could see them.

The lead driver of the fourth piece swerved his pair suddenly, swung the section far to the right. Whip shouted at him, then saw that he had swerved to avoid the end of a trench where a few blue and gray bodies were scattered. The first outworks! Carried in a single rush! Whip shouted and waved his arm. Kinnyard's little bugler galloped up beside him, saluted. "Sir, Cap'n says don't try to keep formation. Ground's all broke ahead and there's trenches. He says try to keep roughly in line and use your own judgment."

Whip nodded in acknowledgment and the bugler raced off. The ground was growing steeper and the mist seemed to be thinning. There was sharp firing all along the line. Here and there he could make out groups of Ewing's men halting, dropping to the ground to fire, creeping on cautiously.

Another fifty yards and he made out a great shoulder rising to his right front. It bristled with men who ducked their heads, drove forward out of sight, reappeared to throw themselves to the ground in the shelter of the summit. He looked left across the trampled ground. More blue figures and gray scattered about. The first platoon was moving on steadily, the drivers seeming to try to weave their way on without touching the bodies. A man with a bloody face raised himself to his knees, hands high and pleading. The lead team of the second piece swung to avoid him. Hands still high, he tottered to his feet, staggered and pitched headlong under the gun wheels. Whip heard the cannoneers cry out in horror. The piece jolted sickeningly, rolled on.

The firing was heavier than ever as he drew closer to the ridge. Past a burning hut a dismounted officer ran madly, saw the sections and threw up both hands. "Who's in command? Who's in command?"

"I am," said Whip, trotting over to him.

The officer, a major, took off his hat and a quick spurt of blood ran down his cheek. He pointed to the right with a trembling hand. "Give us some fire there. Right away. You can take a whole line of Rebs in enfilade. Get 'em up there! Quick!"

Whip looked at the steep slope, rough and rock-strewn. He nodded to the major. "Right away, sir." He held up one hand, shouting, "Action right! Pieces, by hand to the front!"

The major waved his arms and his voice broke to a screech. "No, no! God damn it, no! It'll take too long. You drivers—hit straight ahead."

"Hold it," shouted Whip. "We can't take that slope, not with horses. We'll use ropes and cannoneers on the wheels."

"You'll use your horses. God damn it, a whole battalion's getting wiped out there. You'll take orders from me or get a court-martial." He ran over to the lead pairs. "Get going now! Straight ahead. Unhook your guns at the crest. I'll show you where. Come on."

The drivers and the chiefs of section looked inquiringly at Whip, who threw out his hands, helpless. The drivers shrugged, leaned forward in their saddles and started their teams up the slope, their boots drumming against their horses' ribs.

Whip circled his mount behind the caissons, watching with a growing sense of sick defeat. The major was walking backwards up the slope, urging the drivers on. The third piece, taking advantage of a fairly smooth stretch, got into the lead by a carriage length. Then the slope pitched steeper. He could hear the pound of hoofs, the snorting of the horses, and the tense voices of the drivers urging them on. The drivers leaned farther and farther forward, eyes straining. Little by little the horses slowed down, wove from side to side. The great muscles of their haunches cracked with the effort and their heads swayed in slow arcs. Ahead of them the major yelled and waved.

Whip rode up beside the third piece. Even the great black wheelers, the best pullers in the battery, were advancing a step at a time, their powerful legs trembling and their collars cutting into their shoulders. Suddenly they stopped, checked at last by the frightful slope. Whip cut across to the major. "Sir, I tell you, no team in the army can make this. They—"

He whirled his horse about as the wheel driver yelled.

The hoofs of the two wheelers began to slip. Slowly the spokes of the limber and piece turned backward. The wheelers reared, lashed out with their forefeet. The swing and lead pair gave ground. The wheels turned faster and faster. Whip flung himself to the ground yelling, "Unlimber! For God's sake unlimber." He saw the chief of section, George Beal, dismount and jump for the pintle catch. Then, in a horrible cascade of men, metal, and horseflesh, the third piece surrendered itself to the slope. The horses reared and bucked. Men shouted. One horse went down, dragging another with it. A trace snapped. There were screams, ugly, dull snappings, a sudden high-pitched wail, a terrific crash. The piece was abruptly checked by a high stump jutting out of the hillside, the limber canting sharply to the right. Beyond the limber was a writhing, lashing, kicking tangle of men and horses and harness that reddened horribly.

Whip yelled, "Cut 'em clear. Get the drivers free!" He dodged a heavy hoof that struck with spasmodic viciousness at him and tugged at the shoulders of the lead driver who screamed, "My leg! My leg!"

Two cannoneers jumped beside Whip, wedged fence rails under the horse, trying to lever it up enough to pull the driver clear. Two more joined them and Whip moved on to the swing pair. The driver was lying, white-faced but cool, pinned by his mount. "I'm all right. Just get Polly off me. I'll—" Something whizzed past Whip, knocked up his kepi. There was a horrible thud and the swing driver's white face turned to crimson pulp. Whip jumped back before the hoof swung again and pulled out his Colt. "Shoot the horses if you have to. Shoot anyway if their legs are broken. Beal! George Beal. Plug that off lead!"

A sudden crash from the crest jerked his head up and his mind away from the hideous wreckage. The fourth piece teams stood farther down the slope. On the crest, the fourth-section gun crew had fired a round and now were swarming about the barrel, ready for the second shot. Whip braced himself. This was a mere incident, militarily speaking. The third piece must be brought up beside the fourth, must go into action. He yelled, "John Hummel! Take charge here. Cannoneers—by hand to the front. Get 'em going, Beal!"

He raced to the limber and stumbled over a body, two bodies. The nearer must have been George Beal by the stripes on his sleeve. In trying to unlimber at the first alarm, he must have slipped and the wheel had gone over his head. The other was Doughty, a cannoneer, whose chest was scored by a deep, bloody rut, wide as the iron tire of the piece. Whip waved on the survivors as he pulled up the pintle catch. "On the wheels, now. Twenty yards right of the fourth piece." He threw his full strength against the spokes and the Napoleon began its slow ascent.

Someone yelled in his ear and he looked up, crimson with effort, at the bloody-faced major of infantry. The major whacked at his shoulder. "It'll mean a court-martial. One of your men struck me and then disobeyed my orders by unlimbering."

Straining against the dead weight of the piece, Whip snapped, "Get the hell out of here and don't annoy me! And if you're thinking about courts-martial, take a look down the slope at what your orders did to this section. Keep out of my sight. I'll take this right to General Sherman. For God's sake, boys, *heave!*"

Suddenly there was level ground under his feet, the piece moved smoothly. Whip jumped aside as the cannoneers slewed the trail about, dropped it to the ground. Then he looked across the fourth section. The crew was calmly swabbing out the bore. He shouted, "What's the target?"

The gun crew turned sweat-streaked, panting faces toward him. Roy Abbot, the sergeant, threw down his kepi in disgust. "Target? Ten Rebs back of a pile of rocks! They lit out before we'd rammed home a charge. Wish to hell Honker Bell had planked that Goddamn fool major another one." Then he looked down the slope and his face went white. "Holy God, what happened?"

"Trouble," said Whip tersely as a mixed squad of drivers and cannoneers manhandled the caisson up the slope. John Hummel, the caisson corporal, his jaw set like a trap, reported to Whip in a cold, expressionless voice. They had been able to drag out Moulton, the wheel driver, with nothing more than severe bruises, but Williams, the swing, was dead from the effects of the kick in the head and Pomictor, the lead, had a leg broken so badly that the bone jutted through the flesh. He probably would not survive an operation. Five of the six horses had had to be shot and the sixth, the offwheeler, had a severe gash on the shoulder that would take weeks to heal. The caisson team was intact, the drivers having been able to swing the hitch at right angles to the slope. Of the cannoneers, Beal and Doughty were dead.

"I know about them," said Whip shortly. "Hitch a pair from the caisson to the piece limber and borrow another team from the fourth section. Take charge of both sections and stay where you are at the foot of the slope. How about Pomictor?"

"Surgeon from the 26th Illinois looking after him," said Hummel.

"All right. Get back and start shuffling your teams," said Whip, turning to the sections.

The crews were cursing in a dull, sullen rage and went about their duties with dragging slackness. Whip snapped, "Get your tails up! God damn it, we're in action."

He looked ahead through the mist but could see little. Thin lines of infantry to the left and right moved ahead ghostlike, carrying their rifles at port and stepping high as though they were wading through the heavy air. At fifty yards they were lost to sight. Off to the far left, small arms and artillery slammed and crashed, but he could make out no details. The air above him hummed to the passage of scattered shots and occasional shells arched high on their way to the river, obviously fired at random. To the right front, Chattanooga Valley and Lookout Mountain beyond it were completely veiled. There was little sound from Thomas in the valley, but beyond the great ridge a steady thrumming told of Hooker on the move.

Off to the left someone hailed and Whip saw Kinnyard walking calmly toward him, a riding crop flicking at his boots. The captain's face was powder-stained but his frogged jacket and red-striped breeches could have passed on parade. Whip took renewed strength from Kinnyard's unruffled grave calm. "Look here, sir, a Goddamned infantry major—"

Kinnyard held up a gloved hand. "I heard about it, Whip. There was nothing else you could have done. We'll go over it all when the action's finished. We haven't got time now." He pointed to the left. "See that tree with its branches sticking up through the mist? The first platoon's there. Run your guns over by hand. I'll send Nick along to pick up your teams."

"Right," said Whip. "What's been happening?"

"We got the high ground and Ewing's consolidating it. We'll be on the west slope, pretty much to the extreme right. Heath's 100th Indiana's covering us."

"Going to push on?"

Kinnyard shook his head. "Just one of those things that happen. The maps show this crest as the beginning of the Ridge. It isn't. There's a deep dip, a railroad tunnel that the Rebs hold, and another, higher peak beyond it. That's where their main force is. Now get your sections moving. The Rebs don't like seeing us where we are and they'll come a-booming at us."

Whip turned to the sections. "All right. Hook on your prolonges. Cannoneers on the wheels! By the left flank!"

Whip led the way to the tree that Kinnyard had indicated, and carefully sited his two pieces. Tom came over to join him, shaking his head. "Tough luck, Whip."

Whip set his chin. "If I think about the damn thing, I'll vomit."

MOUNTAINEERS DARK
AND FIERCE

FROM *A Pilgrimage to Meccah and Medinah*

RICHARD BURTON

Sir Richard Burton is in the great tradition of adventurers. It was said that he had crowded into his one lifetime more adventure, study, hardship than would have sufficed for six ordinary men. The well-nigh perfect translation of the *Arabian Nights* for which he is best known was only a by-product of his skills as archaeologist, explorer, and linguist. It was his unorthodox way of traveling that gave him the insights into peoples and customs which make his books so fascinating. The raw material for *A Pilgrimage to Meccah and Medinah* was collected in 1853 when he joined a caravan at Cairo disguised as a Pathan hadji and climbed across the mountains of the Sahara to visit the sacred Mohammedan shrines.

AS WE WERE NOW NEAR THE HOLY CITY, ALL THE MECCANS WERE BUSY CANvassing for lodgers and offering their services to pilgrims. Quarrels, too, were of hourly occurrence. In our party was an Arnaut, a white-bearded old man, so decrepit that he could scarcely stand, and yet so violent that no one could manage him but his African slave, a brazen-faced little wretch about fourteen years of age. Words were bandied between this angry senior and Shaykh Masud, when the latter insinuated sarcastically, that if the former had teeth he would be more intelligible. The Arnaut in his rage seized a pole, raised it, and delivered a blow which missed the camel-man, but brought the striker headlong to the ground. Masud exclaimed, with shrieks of rage, "Have we come to this, that every old woman Turk smites us?" Our party had the greatest trouble to quiet the quarrellers. The Arab listened to us when we threatened him with the Pasha. But the Arnaut, whose rage was "like red-hot steel," would hear nothing but our repeated declarations, that unless he behaved more like a pilgrim, we should be compelled to leave him and his slave behind.

At four P.M. we left El-Birkat, and travelled eastwards over rolling ground thickly wooded. There was a network of footpaths through the thickets, and clouds obscured the moon; the consequence was inevitable loss of way. About two A.M. we began ascending hills in a south-westerly direction, and presently we fell into the bed of a large rock-girt Fiumara, which runs from east to west. At six A.M. (9th Sept.) we left the Fiumara, and, turning to the west, we arrived about an hour afterwards at the station. El-Zaribah, "the valley," is an undulating plain amongst high granite hills. In many parts it was faintly green; water was close to the surface, and rain stood upon the ground. During the night we had travelled about twenty-three miles, and our present station was south-east 56° from our last.

Having pitched the tent and eaten and slept, we prepared to perform the ceremony of *El-Ihram* (assuming the pilgrim-garb), as El-Zaribah is the Mikat, or the appointed place. Between the noonday and the afternoon prayers a barber attended to shave our heads, cut our nails, and trim our mustachios. Then, having bathed and perfumed ourselves—the latter is a questionable point—we donned the attire, which is nothing but two new cotton cloths, each six feet long by three and a half broad, white, with narrow red stripes and fringes: in fact, the costume called *El-Eddeh* in the baths at Cairo. One of these sheets, technically termed the *Rida,* is thrown over the back, and, exposing the arm and shoulder, is knotted at the right side in the style *Wishah*. The *Izar* is wrapped round the loins from waist to knee, and, knotted or tucked in at the middle, supports itself. Our heads were bare, and nothing was allowed upon the instep. It is said that some clans of Arabs still preserve this religious but most uncomfortable costume; it is doubtless of ancient date, and to this day, in the regions lying west of the Red Sea, it continues to be the common dress of the people.

After the toilette, we were placed with our faces in the direction of Meccah, and ordered to say aloud, "I vow this Ihram of Hajj (the pilgrimage) and the Umrah (the little pilgrimage) to Allah Almighty!" Having thus performed a two-bow prayer, we repeated, without rising from the sitting position, these words, "O Allah! verily I purpose the Hajj and the Umrah, then enable me to accomplish the two, and accept them both of me, and make both blessed to me!" Followed the *Talbiyat,* or exclaiming—

"Here I am! O Allah! here am I—
No Partner hast Thou, here am I:
Verily the Praise and the Beneficence are Thine, and the Kingdom—
No Partner hast Thou, here am I!"

And we were warned to repeat these words as often as possible until the conclusion of the ceremonies.

Then Shaykh Abdullah, who acted as director of our consciences, bade us be good pilgrims, avoiding quarrels, immorality, bad language, and light conversation. We must so reverence life that we should avoid killing game, causing an animal to fly, and even pointing it out for destruction; nor should we scratch ourselves, save with the open palm, lest vermin be destroyed, or a hair uprooted by the nail. We were to respect the sanctuary by sparing the trees, and not to pluck a single blade of grass. As regards personal consider-ations, we were to abstain from all oils, perfumes, and unguents; from washing the head with mallow or lote leaves; from dyeing, shaving, cutting, or vellicating a single pile or hair; and though we might take advantage of shade, and even form it with upraised hands, we must by no means cover our sconces. For each infraction of these ordinances we must sacrifice a sheep; and it is commonly said by Moslems that none but the Prophet could be perfect in the intricacies of pilgrimage. Old Ali began with an irregular-ity: he declared that age prevented his assuming the garb, but that, arrived at Meccah, he would clear himself by an offering.

The wife and daughters of a Turkish pilgrim of our party assumed the Ihram at the same time as ourselves. They appeared dressed in white gar-ments; and they had exchanged the Lisam, that coquettish fold of muslin which veils without concealing the lower part of the face, for a hideous mask, made of split, dried, and plaited palm-leaves, with two "bulls'-eyes" for light. I could not help laughing when these strange figures met my sight, and, to judge from the shaking of their shoulders, they were not less suscep-tible to the merriment which they had caused.

At three P.M. we left El-Zaribah, travelling towards the south-west, and a wondrously picturesque scene met the eye. Crowds hurried along, habited in the pilgrim-garb, whose whiteness contrasted strangely with their black skins; their newly shaven heads glistening in the sun, and their long black hair streaming in the wind. The rocks rang with shouts of *Labbayk! Lab-bayk!* At a pass we fell in with the Wahhabis, accompanying the Baghdad Caravan, screaming "Here am I"; and, guided by a large loud kettle-drum, they followed in double file the camel of a standard-bearer, whose green flag bore in huge white letters the formula of the Moslem creed. They were wild-looking mountaineers, dark and fierce, with hair twisted into thin Dalik or plaits: each was armed with a long spear, a match-lock, or a dagger. They were seated upon coarse wooden saddles, without cushions or stirrups, a fine saddle-cloth alone denoting a chief. The women emulated the men; they either guided their own dromedaries, or, sitting in pillion, they clung to their husbands; veils they disdained, and their countenances certainly belong not to a "soft sex." These Wahhabis were by no means pleasant companions. Most of them were followed by spare dromedaries, either un-laden or carrying water skins, fodder, fuel, and other necessaries for the march. The beasts delighted in dashing furiously through our file, which being lashed together, head and tail, was thrown each time into the greatest confusion. And whenever we were observed smoking, we were cursed aloud for Infidels and Idolaters.

Looking back at El-Zaribah, soon after our departure, I saw a heavy nimbus settle upon the hill-tops, a sheet of rain being stretched between it and the plain. The low grumbling of thunder sounded joyfully in our ears. We hoped for a shower, but were disappointed by a dust-storm, which ended with a few heavy drops. There arose a report that the Bedawin had attacked a party of Meccans with stones, and the news caused men to look exceeding grave.

At five P.M. we entered the wide bed of the Fiumara, down which we were to travel all night. Here the country falls rapidly towards the sea, as the increasing heat of the air, the direction of the watercourses, and signs of violence in the torrent-bed show. The Fiumara varies in breadth from a hundred and fifty feet to three quarters of a mile; its course, I was told, is towards the south-west, and it enters the sea near Jeddah. The channel is a coarse sand, with here and there masses of sheet rock and patches of thin vegetation.

At about half-past five P.M. we entered a suspicious-looking place. On the right was a stony buttress, along whose base the stream, when there is one, swings; and to this depression was our road limited by the rocks and thorn-trees which filled the other half of the channel. The left side was a precipice, grim and barren, but not so abrupt as its brother. Opposite us the way seemed barred by piles of hills, crest rising above crest into the far blue distance. Day still smiled upon the upper peaks, but the lower slopes and the Fiumara bed were already curtained with grey sombre shade.

A damp seemed to fall upon our spirits as we approached this Valley Perilous. I remarked that the voices of the women and children sank into silence, and the loud Labbayk of the pilgrims were gradually stilled. Whilst still speculating upon the cause of this phenomenon, it became apparent. A small curl of the smoke, like a lady's ringlet, on the summit of the right-hand precipice, caught my eye; and, simultaneous with the echoing crack of the matchlock, a high-trotting dromedary in front of me rolled over upon the sands—a bullet had split its heart—throwing the rider a goodly somersault of five or six yards.

Ensued terrible confusion; women screamed, children cried, and men vociferated, each one striving with might and main to urge his animal out of the place of death. But the road being narrow, they only managed to jam the vehicles in a solid immovable mass. At every matchlock shot, a shudder ran through the huge body, as when the surgeon's scalpel touches some more sensitive nerve. The irregular horsemen, perfectly useless, galloped up and down over the stones, shouting to and ordering one another. The Pasha of the army had his carpet spread at the foot of the left-hand precipice, and debated over his pipe with the officers what ought to be done. No good genius whispered "Crown the heights."

Then it was that the conduct of the Wahhabis found favour in my eyes. They came up, galloping their camels, with their elf-locks tossing in the wind, and their flaring matches casting a strange lurid light over their features. Taking up a position, one body began to fire upon the Utaybah robbers, whilst two or three hundred, dismounting, swarmed up the hill under the guidance of the Sherif Zayd. I had remarked this nobleman at El-Medinah as a model specimen of the pure Arab. Like all Sherifs, he is celebrated for bravery, and has killed many with his own hand. When urged at El-Zaribah to ride into Meccah, he swore that he would not leave the caravan till in sight of the walls; and, fortunately for the pilgrims, he kept his word.

Presently the firing was heard far in our rear, the robbers having fled. The head of the column advanced, and the dense body of pilgrims opened out. Our forced halt was now exchanged for a flight. It required much management to steer our desert-craft clear of danger; but Shaykh Masud was equal to the occasion. That many were lost was evident by the boxes and baggage that strewed the shingles. I had no means of ascertaining the number of men killed and wounded: reports were contradictory, and exaggeration unanimous. The robbers were said to be a hundred and fifty in number; their object was plunder, and they would eat the shot camels. But their principal ambition was the boast, "We, the Utaybah, on such and such a night, stopped the Sultan's Mahmal one whole hour in the Pass."

At the beginning of the skirmish I had primed my pistols, and sat with them ready for use. But soon seeing that there was nothing to be done, and wishing to make an impression—nowhere does Bobadil now "go down" so well as in the East—I called aloud for my supper. Shaykh Nur, exanimate with fear, could not move. The boy Mohammed ejaculated only an "Oh, sir!" and the people around exclaimed in disgust, "By Allah, he eats!" Shaykh Abdullah, the Meccan, being a man of spirit, was amused by the spectacle. "Are these Afghan manners, Effendim?" he inquired from the Shugduf behind me. "Yes," I replied aloud, "in my country we always dine before an attack of robbers, because that gentry is in the habit of sending men to bed supperless." The Shaykh laughed aloud, but those around him looked offended. I thought the bravado this time *mal placé;* but a little event which took place on my way to Jeddah proved that it was not quite a failure.

As we advanced, our escort took care to fire every large dry Asclepias, to disperse the shades which buried us. Again the scene became wondrous wild. On either side were ribbed precipices, dark, angry, and towering above, till their summits mingled with the glooms of night; and between them formidable looked the chasm, down which our host hurried with shouts and dis-

charges of matchlocks. The torch-smoke and the night-fires of flaming
Asclepias formed a canopy, sable above and livid red below; it hung over
our heads like a sheet, and divided the cliffs into two equal parts. Here the
fire flashed fiercely from a tall thorn, that crackled and shot up showers of
sparks into the air; there it died away in lurid gleams, which lit up a truly
Stygian scene.

As usual, however, the picturesque had its inconveniences. There was
no path. Rocks, stone-banks, and trees obstructed our passage. The camels,
now blind in darkness, then dazzled by a flood of light, stumbled frequently;
in some places slipping down a steep descent, in others sliding over a sheet
of mud. There were furious quarrels and fierce language between camel-men
and their hirers, and threats to fellow-travellers; in fact, we were united
in discord. I passed that night crying, "Hai-Hai!" switching the camel, and
fruitlessly endeavoring to fustigate Masud's nephew, who resolutely slept
upon the water-bags. During the hours of darkness we made four or five
halts, when we boiled coffee and smoked pipes; but man and beasts were
beginning to suffer from a deadly fatigue.

Dawn (Saturday, September 10) found us still travelling down the
Fiumara, which here is about a hundred yards broad. The granite hills on
both sides were less precipitous; and the borders of the torrent-bed became
natural quays of stiff clay, which showed a water-mark of from twelve to
fifteen feet in height. In many parts the bed was muddy; and the moist
places, as usual, caused accidents. I happened to be looking back at Shaykh
Abdullah, who was then riding in old Ali bin Ya Sin's fine Shugduf; suddenly the camel's four legs disappeared from under him, his right side
flattening the ground, and the two riders were pitched severally out of
the smashed vehicle. Abdullah started up furious, and with great zest abused
the Bedawin, who were absent. "Feed these Arabs," he exclaimed, quoting
a Turkish proverb, "and they will fire at Heaven!" But I observed that,
when Shaykh Masud came up, the citizen was only gruff.

We then turned northward, and sighted El-Mazik, more generally known
as Wady Laymun, the Valley of Limes. On the right bank of the Fiumara
stood the Meccan Sherif's state pavilion, green and gold: it was surrounded
by his attendants, and he had prepared to receive the Pasha of the Caravan.
We advanced half a mile, and encamped temporarily in a hill-girt bulge of
the Fiumara bed. At eight A.M. we had travelled about twenty-four miles
from El-Zaribah, and the direction of our present station was south-west 50°.

Shaykh Masud allowed us only four hours' halt; he wished to precede
the main body. After breaking our fast joyously upon limes, pomegranates,
and fresh dates, we sallied forth to admire the beauties of the place. We
are once more on classic ground—the ground of the ancient Arab poets, and
this Wady, celebrated for the purity of its air, has from remote ages been

a favorite resort of the Meccans. Nothing can be more soothing to the brain than the dark-green foliage of the limes and pomegranates; and from the base of the southern hill bursts a bubbling stream, whose flow through the gardens, filling them with the most delicious of melodies, the gladdest sound which Nature in these regions knows.

Exactly at noon Masud seized the halter of the foremost camel, and we started down the Fiumara. Troops of Bedawi girls looked over the orchard walls laughingly, and children came out to offer us fresh fruit and sweet water. At two P.M., travelling south-west, we arrived at a point where the torrent-bed turns to the right; and, quitting it, we climbed with difficulty over a steep ridge of granite. Before three o'clock we entered a hill-girt plain, which my companions called "Sola." In some places were clumps of trees, and scattered villages warned us that we were approaching a city. Far to the left rose the blue peaks of Taif, and the mountain road, a white thread upon the nearer heights, was pointed out to me.

Here I first saw the tree, or rather shrub, which bears the balm of Gilead, erst so celebrated for its tonic and stomachic properties. I told Shaykh Masud to break off a twig, which he did heedlessly. The act was witnessed by our party with a roar of laughter; and the astounded Shaykh was warned that he had become subject to an atoning sacrifice. Of course he denounced me as the instigator, and I could not fairly refuse assistance. The tree has of late years been carefully described by many botanists; I will only say that the bark resembled in color a cherry-stick pipe, the inside was a light yellow, and the juice made my fingers stick together.

At four P.M. we came to a steep and rocky Pass, up which we toiled with difficulty. The face of the country was rising once more, and again presented the aspect of numerous small basins divided and surrounded by hills. As we jogged on we were passed by the cavalcade of no less a personage than the Sherif of Meccah. Abd el-Muttalib bin Ghalib is a dark, beardless old man with African features derived from his mother. He was plainly dressed in white garments and a white muslin turban, which made him look jet black; he rode an ambling mule, and the only emblem of his dignity was the large green satin umbrella borne by an attendant on foot. Scattered around him were about forty matchlock men, mostly slaves. At long intervals, after their father, came his four sons, Riza Bey, Abdullah, Ali, and Ahmed, the latter still a child. The three elder brothers rode splendid dromedaries at speed; they were young men of light complexion, with the true Meccan cast of features, showily dressed in bright-colored silks, and armed, to denote their rank, with sword and gold-hilted dagger.

We halted as evening approached, and strained our eyes, but all in vain, to catch sight of Meccah, which lies in a winding valley. By Shaykh Abdullah's direction I recited, after the usual devotions, the following prayer.

The reader is forewarned that it is difficult to preserve the flowers of Oriental rhetoric in a European tongue.

"O Allah! verily this is Thy Safeguard *(Amn)* and Thy Sanctuary *(Haram)!* Into it whoso entereth becometh safe *(Amin)*. So deny *(Harrim)* my Flesh and Blood, my Bones and Skin, to Hell-fire. O Allah! save me from Thy Wrath on the Day when Thy Servants shall be raised from the Dead. I conjure Thee by this that Thou art Allah, besides whom is none (Thou only), the Merciful, the Compassionate. And have Mercy upon our Lord Mohammed, and upon the Progeny of our Lord Mohammed, and upon his Followers, One and All!" This was concluded with the "Talbiyat," and with an especial prayer for myself.

We again mounted, and night completed our disappointment. About one A.M. I was aroused by general excitement. "Meccah! Meccah!" cried some voices; "The Sanctuary! O the Sanctuary!" exclaimed others; and all burst into loud "Labbayk," not unfrequently broken by sobs.

MOUNT SINAI AND MOUNT HOREB

6

Men Wonder at the Mystery of the Mountains

From the placatory songs of aboriginal man to his gods on the mountain to Shelley's sonnet on Mont Blanc is a remove, not in time, but in language, a way of phrasing man's awe and fear and wonder at the mountains. Both the first man who stood on the hill above his native valley and the men who climbed the Matterhorn, or Everest, or Annapurna looked at the infinity of space before and below them and held their breath. They stood in a place where only the gods and the demons had stood before them. For the old attitudes are slow-changing, and are still part of our language and consciousness. And such words as awe and taboo, beauty and superstition, mystery and veneration, have many connotations in common.

From Olympus, Zeus threw his thunderbolts; Prometheus, the Titan, was chained to Mt. Caucasus for daring to snatch fire from heaven. The witches, it is said, still hold their Walpurgisnacht on the highest peak of the Harz Mountains, and Mexican peons will tell you that the crater of Popocatepetl is the entrance to hell.

But whatever the attitude—whether veneration, fear, awe—man's effort to explain his wonder of the mountains has produced some of the most moving and most impassioned writing we have.

D E D I C A T I O N   T O   A
M O U N T A I N

FROM *Pierre: or, The Ambiguities*

H E R M A N   M E L V I L L E

🐾 Herman Melville is so much identified with *Moby Dick* that it needs an effort to remember that he wrote *Typee* and *Omoo,* among the freshest and most interesting narratives of the South Pacific. His books are by no means all dark allegories of the struggle against evil.

Pierre: or, The Ambiguities is one of his less successful books. It has the unique distinction, however, of being the only book ever dedicated to a mountain. We give here the dedication:

TO GREYLOCK'S MOST EXCELLENT MAJESTY

IN OLD TIMES AUTHORS WERE PROUD OF THE PRIVILEGE OF DEDICATING THEIR works to Majesty. A right noble custom, which we of Berkshire must revive. For whether we will or no, Majesty is all around us here in Berkshire, sitting as in a grand Congress of Vienna of majestical hill-tops, and eternally challenging our homage.

But since the majestic mountain, Greylock—my own more immediate sovereign lord and king—hath now, for innumerable ages, been the one grand dedicatee of the earliest rays of all the Berkshire mornings, I know not how his Imperial Purple Majesty (royal born: Porphyrogenitus) will receive the dedication of my own poor solitary ray.

Nevertheless, forasmuch as I, dwelling with my loyal neighbours, the Maples and the Beeches, in the amphitheatre over which his central majesty presides, have received his most bounteous and unstinted fertilisations, it is but meet, that I here devoutly kneel, and render up my gratitude, whether, thereto, The Most Excellent Purple Majesty of Greylock benignantly incline his hoary crown or no.

Pittsfield, Mass.

AS THE HILLMEN DESIRE THEIR HILLS

FROM *Kim*

RUDYARD KIPLING

Rudyard Kipling made himself the apologist in story and verse for British imperial policy. The Colonial Office could not itself have evolved a more perfect combination of background, zeal, and talent for that onerous task. It is doubtful whether the total body of his work, much of it puerile and obscurantist, would have won him the Nobel Prize today. But whatever his diminished stature, there is no critic who does not grant him an exceedingly high place as storyteller.

Kim, from which this extract is taken, is in spirit, if not altogether in fact, autobiographical. Kipling was born in India and learned Hindustani concurrently with English. There are few literary craftsmen who have been able to paint so skillful and understanding a picture of a life and culture not their own.

"WHO GOES TO THE HILLS GOES TO HIS MOTHER."

They had crossed the Sewaliks and the half-tropical Doon, left Mussoorie behind them, and headed north along the narrow hill-roads. Day after day they struck deeper into the huddled mountains, and day after day Kim watched the lama return to a man's strength. Among the terraces of the Doon he had leaned on the boy's shoulder, ready to profit by wayside halts. Under the great ramp to Mussoorie he drew himself together as an old hunter faces a well-remembered bank, and where he should have dropped exhausted swung his long draperies about him, drew a deep double lungful of the diamond air, and walked as only a hillman can. Kim, plains-bred and plains-fed, sweated and panted astonished. "This is *my* country," said the lama. "Beside Suchzen, this is flatter than a rice-field"; and with steady, driving strokes from the loins he strode upwards. But it was on the steep downhill marches, three thousand feet in three hours, that he went utterly away from Kim, whose back ached with holding back, and whose big toe was nigh cut off by his grass sandal-string. Through the speckled shadow of the great deodar forests; through oak feathered and plumed with ferns, birch, ilex, rhododendron, and pine, out on to the bare hillsides' slippery sunburnt grass, and back into the woodlands' coolth again, till oak gave way to bamboo and palm of the valley, he swung untiring.

Glancing back in the twilight at the huge ridges behind him and the faint, thin line of the road whereby they had come, he would lay out, with a hillman's generous breadth of vision, fresh marches for the morrow; or, halting in the neck of some uplifted pass that gave on Spite and Kulu, would stretch out his hands yearningly towards the high snows of the horizon. In the dawns they flamed windy red above stark blue, as Kedarnath and Badjunath—kings of that wilderness—took the first sunlight. All day long they lay like molten silver under the sun, and at evening put on their jewels again. At first they breathed temperately upon the travellers, winds good to meet when one crawled over some gigantic hogback; but in a few days, at a height of nine or ten thousand feet, those breezes bit; and Kim kindly allowed a village of hillmen to acquire merit by giving him a rough blanket coat. The lama was mildly surprised that any one could object to the knife-edged breezes that had cut the years off his shoulders.

"These are but the lower hills, *chela*. There is no cold till we come to the true mountains."

"Air and water are good, and the people are devout enough, but the food is very bad," Kim growled; "and we walk as though we were mad—or English. It freezes at night, too."

"A little, maybe; but only enough to make old bones rejoice in the sun. We must not always delight in the soft beds and rich food."

"We might at the least keep to the road."

Kim had all a plains-man's affection for the well-trodden track, not six feet wide, that snaked among the mountains; but the lama, being Tibetan, could not, for the life of him, refrain from short-cuts over spurs and the rims of gravel-strewn slopes. As he explained to his doubting disciple, a man bred among mountains can prophesy the course of a mountain-road, and though low-lying clouds might be a hindrance to a short-cutting stranger, they made no earthly difference to a thoughtful man. Thus, after long hours of what would be reckoned very fair mountaineering in civilised countries, they would drop over a saddle-back, sidle past a few landslips, and drop through forest at an angle of forty-five onto the road again. Along their tracks lay the villages of the hill-folk—mud and earth huts, timbers now and then rudely carved with an axe—clinging like swallows' nests against the steeps; huddled on tiny flats half-way down a three-thousand-foot glissade; jammed into a corner between cliffs that funnelled and focused every wandering blast; or, for the sake of summer pasture, cowering down on a neck that in winter would be ten feet deep in snow. And the people—the sallow, greasy, duffle-clad people, with short bare legs and faces almost Esquimaux—would flock out and adore. The Plains—kindly and gentle—had treated the lama as a holy man among holy men. But the Hills worshipped him as one in the confidence of all the devils. Theirs was an almost obliterated Buddhism, overlaid with a nature-worship fantastic as their own landscapes, elaborate as the terracing of their tiny fields; but they recognised the big hat, the clicking rosary, and the rare Chinese texts for great authority, and they respected the man under the hat.

"We saw thee come down over the black breasts of Eua," said a Betah who gave them cheese, sour milk, and stone-hard bread one evening. "We do not use that often—except when calving cows stray in summer. There is a sudden wind among those stones that casts men down on the stillest day. But what should such folk care for the Devil of Eua!"

Then did Kim, aching in every fibre, dizzy with looking down, footsore with cramping desperate toes into inadequate crannies, take joy in the day's march—such joy as a boy of St. Xavier's who had won the quarter-mile in the flat might take in the praises of his friends. The hills sweated the *ghi* and sugar suet off his bones; the dry air, taken sobbingly at the head of cruel passes, firmed and built out his upper ribs; and the tilted levels put new hard muscles into calf and thigh.

They meditated often on the Wheel of Life—the more so since, as the lama said, they were freed from its visible temptations. Except the gray eagle and an occasional far-seen bear grubbing and rooting on the hillside, the vision of a furious painted leopard seen at dawn in a still valley devouring a goat, and now and again a bright-coloured bird, they were alone with the winds and the grass singing under the wind. The women of the smoky huts over whose roofs the two walked as they descended the mountains were unlovely and unclean wives of many husbands, and afflicted with goitre. The men were wood-cutters when they were not farmers—meek, and of an incredible simplicity. But that suitable discourse might not fail, Fate sent them, overtaking and overtaken upon the road, the courteous Dacca physician, who paid for his food in ointments good for goitre and counsels that restore peace between men and women. He seemed to know these hills as well as he knew the hill dialects, and gave the lama the lie of the land towards Ladakh and Tibet. He said they could return to the plains at any moment. Meantime, for such as loved mountains, yonder road might amuse. This was not all revealed in a breath, but at evening encounters on the stone threshing-floors, when, patients disposed of, the doctor would smoke and the lama snuff, while Kim watched the wee cows grazing on the house-tops, or threw his soul after his eye across the deep blue gulfs between range and range. And there were talks apart in the deep woods, when the doctor would seek herbs, and Kim, as budding physician, must accompany him. . . .

They crossed a snowy pass by cold moonlight, and the lama, mildly chaffing Kim, went through up to his knees, like a Bactrian camel—the snow-bred, shag-haired sort that come into the Kashmir Serai. They dipped across beds of light snow and snow-powdered shale, where they took refuge from a gale in a camp of Tibetans hurrying down tiny sheep, each laden with a bag of borax. They came out upon grassy shoulders still snow-speckled, and through forest, to pass anew. For all their marchings, Kedarnath and Badrinath were not impressed; and it was only after days of travel that Kim, uplifted upon some insignificant ten-thousand-foot hummock, could see that a shoulder-knot or horn of the two great lords had—ever so slightly—changed outline.

At last they came into a world within a world—a valley of leagues where the high hills were fashioned of the rubble and refuse from off the knees of the mountains. Here one day's march carried them no farther, it seemed, than a dreamer's clogged pace bears him in a nightmare. They skirted a shoulder painfully for hours, and, behold, it was but an outlying boss in an outlying buttress of the main pile! A rounded meadow revealed itself, when they had reached it, as a vast tableland running far into the valley. Three days later, it was but a fold in the earth to southward.

"Surely the Gods live here," said Kim, beaten down by the silence and the appalling sweep and dispersal of the cloud-shadows after rain. "This is no place for men."

"Long and long ago," said the lama, as to himself, "it was asked of the Lord whether the world were everlasting. To this the Excellent One returned no answer. . . . When I was in Ceylon, a wise Seeker confirmed that from the gospel which is written in Pali. Certainly, since we know the way to Freedom, the question was unprofitable, but—look, and know illusion, *chela!* These are the true hills! They are like the hills by Suchzen. Never were such hills!"

Above them, still enormously above them, earth towered away towards the snow-line, where from east to west across hundreds of miles, ruled as with a ruler, the last of the bold birches stopped. Above that, in scarps and blocks upheaved, the rocks strove to fight their heads above the white smother. Above these again, changeless since the world's beginning, but changing to every mood of sun and cloud, lay out the eternal snow. They could see blots and blurs on its face where storm and wandering *wulli-wa* got up to dance. Below them, as they stood, the forest slid away in a sheet of blue green for mile upon mile; below the forest was a village in its sprinkle of terraced fields and steep grazing-grounds; below the village they knew, though a thunderstorm worried and growled there for the moment, a pitch of twelve or fifteen hundred feet gave to the moist valley where the streams gather that are the mothers of young Sutlej.

A STRANGE DREAM

FROM *The Celebrated Jumping Frog of Calaveras County, and Other Sketches*

SAMUEL CLEMENS

It was to be expected that when Mark Twain visited Hawaii in 1866, one of the by-products would be some of his inimitable foolery. His "Dreamed at the Volcano House" is a search under the guidance of spirits for the bones of King Kamehameha in the bowels of the crater. Twain was clearly partial to the Hawaiian volcanoes. He spent several hours at the lookout house, a half mile away, watching the stupendous fireworks, and wrote later, "I have seen Vesuvius since, but it is a mere toy, a child's volcano, a soup kettle compared with this."

Dreamed at the Volcano House, crater of "Kilauea," Sandwich Islands, April 1, 1866.

ALL DAY LONG I HAVE SAT APART AND PONDERED OVER THE MYSTERIOUS OCCURrences of last night. . . . There is no link lacking in the chain of incidents—my memory presents each in its proper order with perfect distinctness, but still——

However, never mind these reflections—I will drop them and proceed to make a simple statement of the facts.

Toward eleven o'clock, it was suggested that the character of the night was peculiarly suited to viewing the mightiest active volcano on the earth's surface in its most impressive sublimity. There was no light of moon or star in the inky heavens to mar the effect of the crater's gorgeous pyrotechnics.

In due time I stood, with my companion, on the wall of the vast cauldron which the natives, ages ago, named *Hale mau mau*—the abyss wherein they were wont to throw the remains of their chiefs, to the end that vulgar feet might never tread above them. We stood there, at dead of night, a mile above the level of the sea, and looked down a thousand feet upon a boiling, surging, roaring ocean of fire!—shaded our eyes from the blinding glare, and gazed far away over the crimson waves with a vague notion that a supernatural fleet, manned by demons and freighted with the damned, might presently sail up out of the remote distance; started when tremendous thunder-bursts shook the earth, and followed with fascinated eyes the grand jets of molten lava that sprang high up toward the zenith and exploded in a world of fiery spray that lit up the sombre heavens with an infernal splendor.

"What is your little bonfire of Vesuvius to this?"

My ejaculation roused my companion from his reverie, and we fell into a conversation appropriate to the occasion and the surroundings. We came at last to speak of the ancient custom of casting the bodies of dead chieftains into this fearful caldron; and my comrade, who is of the blood royal, mentioned that the founder of his race, old King Kamehameha the First—that invincible old pagan Alexander—had found other sepulture than the burning depths of the *Hale mau mau.* I grew interested at once; I knew that the mystery of what became of the corpse of the warrior king had never been fathomed; I was aware that there was a legend connected with this matter; and I felt as if there could be no more fitting time to listen to it than the present. The descendant of the Kamehamehas said:

"The dead king was brought in royal state down the long, winding road that descends from the rim of the crater to the scorched and chasm-riven plain that lies between the *Hale mau mau* and those beetling walls yonder in the distance. The guards were set and the troops of mourners began the weird wail for the departed. In the middle of the night came a sound of innumerable voices in the air, and the rush of invisible wings; the funeral torches wavered, burned blue, and went out. The mourners and watchers fell to the ground paralyzed by fright, and many minutes elapsed before any one dared to move or speak; for they believed that the phantom messengers of the dread Goddess of Fire had been in their midst. When at last a torch was lighted, the bier was vacant—the dead monarch had been spirited away! Consternation seized upon all, and they fled out of the crater. When day dawned, the multitude returned and began the search for the corpse. But not a footprint, not a sign was ever found. Day after day the search was continued, and every cave in the great walls, and every chasm in the plain, for miles around, was examined, but all to no purpose; and from that day to this the resting-place of the lion king's bones is an unsolved mystery. But years afterward, when the grim prophetess Wiahowakawak lay on her deathbed, the Goddess *Pele* appeared to her in a vision, and told her that eventually the secret would be revealed, and in a remarkable manner, but not until the great *Kauhuhu,* the Shark God, should desert the sacred cavern *Aua Puhi,* in the Island of Molokai, and the waters of the sea should no more visit it, and its floors should become dry. Ever since that time the simple, confiding natives have watched for the sign. And now, after many and many a summer has come and gone, and they who were in the flower of youth then have waxed old and died, the day is at hand! The great Shark God has deserted the *Aua Puhi:* a month ago, for the first time within the records of the ancient legends, the waters of the sea ceased to flow into the cavern, and its stony pavement is become dry! As you may easily believe, the news of this event spread like wildfire through the islands, and now the natives are looking every hour for the miracle which is to unveil the mystery and reveal the secret grave of the dead hero."

After I had gone to bed I got to thinking of the volcanic magnificence we had witnessed, and could not go to sleep. I hunted up a book and concluded to pass the time in reading. The first chapter I came upon related several instances of remarkable revelations, made to men through the agency of dreams—of roads and houses, trees, fences, and all manner of landmarks, shown in visions and recognized afterward in waking hours, and which served to point the way to some dark mystery or other.

At length I fell asleep, and dreamed that I was abroad in the great plain that skirts the *Hale mau mau.* I stood in a sort of twilight which softened the outlines of surrounding objects, but still left them tolerably distinct. A gaunt, muffled figure stepped out from the shadow of a rude column of lava, and moved away with a slow and measured step, beckoning me to follow. I did so. I marched down, down, down, hundreds of feet, upon a narrow trail which wound its tortuous course through piles and pyramids of seamed and blackened lava, and under overhanging masses of sulphur formed by the artist hand of nature into an infinitude of fanciful shapes. The thought crossed my mind that possibly my phantom guide might lead me down among the bowels of the crater, and then disappear and leave me to grope my way through its mazes, and work out my deliverance as best I might; and so, with an eye to such a contingency, I picked up a stone, and "blazed" my course by breaking off a projecting corner, occasionally, from lava walls and festoons of sulphur. Finally we turned into a cleft in the crater's side, and pursued our way through its intricate windings for many a fathom down toward the home of the subterranean fires, our course lighted all the while by a ruddy glow which filtered up through innumerable cracks and crevices, and which afforded me occasional glimpses of the flood of molten fire boiling and hissing in the profound depths beneath us. The heat was intense, and the sulphurous atmosphere suffocating; but I toiled on in the footsteps of my stately guide, and uttered no complaint. At last we came to a sort of rugged chamber whose sombre and blistered walls spake with mute eloquence of some fiery tempest that had spent its fury here in a bygone age. The spectre pointed to a great boulder at the farther extremity— stood and pointed, silent and motionless, for a few fleeting moments, and then disappeared! "The grave of the last Kamehameha!" The words swept mournfully by, from unknown source, and died away in the distant corridors

of my prison-house, and I was alone in the bowels of the earth, in the home
of desolation, in the presence of death!

My first frightened impulse was to fly, but a stronger impulse arrested
me and impelled me to approach the massive boulder the spectre had
pointed at. With hesitating step I went forward and stood beside it—nothing there. I grew bolder, and walked around and about it, peering shrewdly
into the shadowy half-light that surrounded it—still nothing. I paused to
consider what to do next. While I stood irresolute, I chanced to brush the
ponderous stone with my elbow, and lo! it vibrated to my touch! I would
as soon have thought of starting a kiln of bricks with my feeble hand. My
curiosity was excited. I bore against the boulder, and it still yielded; I gave
a sudden push with my whole strength, and it toppled from its foundation
with a crash that sent the echoes thundering down the avenues and passages
of the dismal cavern! And there, in a shallow excavation over which it had
rested, lay the crumbling skeleton of King Kamehameha the Great, thus
sepulchred in long years, by supernatural hands! The bones could be none
other; for with them lay the rare and priceless crown of *pulamalama* coral,
sacred to royalty, and *tabu* to all else beside. A hollow human groan issued
out of the—

I woke up. How glad I was to know it was all a dream! "This comes of
listening to the legend of the noble lord—of reading of those lying dream
revelations—of allowing myself to be carried away by the wild beauty of
old *Kileana* at midnight—of gorging too much pork and beans for supper!"
And so I turned over and fell asleep again. And dreamed the same dream
precisely as before; followed the phantom—"blazed" my course—arrived at
the grim chamber—heard the sad spirit voice—overturned the massy stone—
beheld the regal crown and the decaying bones of the great king!

I woke up, and reflected long upon the curious and singularly vivid
dream, and finally muttered to myself, "This—this is becoming serious!"

I fell asleep again, and again I dreamed the same dream, without a single
variation! I slept no more, but tossed restlessly in bed and longed for daylight. And when it came, I wandered forth, and descended to the wide plain
in the crater. I said to myself, "I am not superstitious; but if there is any
thing in that dying woman's prophecy, I am the instrument appointed to
uncurtain this ancient mystery." As I walked along, I even half expected to
see my solemn guide step out from some nook in the lofty wall, and beckon
me to come on. At last when I reached the place where I had first seen him
in my dream, I recognized every surrounding object, and there, winding
down among the blocks and fragments of lava, saw the very trail I had
traversed in my vision! I resolved to traverse it again, come what might.
I wondered if, in my unreal journey, I had "blazed" my way, so that it
would stand the test of stern reality; and thus wondering, a chill went to my

heart when I came to the first stony projection I had broken off in my dream, and saw the fresh new fracture, and the dismembered fragment lying on the ground! My curiosity rose up and banished all fear, and I hurried along as fast as the rugged road would allow me. I looked for my other "blazes," and found them; found the cleft in the wall; recognized all its turnings; walked in the light that ascended from the glowing furnaces visible far below; sweated in the close, hot atmosphere, and breathed the sulphurous smoke—and at last I stood hundreds of feet beneath the peaks of *Kileana* in the ruined chamber, and in the presence of the mysterious boulder!

"This is no dream," I said; "this is a revelation from the realm of the supernatural; and it becomes not me to longer reason, conjecture, suspect, but blindly to obey the impulses given me by the unseen power that guides me."

I moved with a slow and reverent step toward the stone and bore against it. It yielded perceptibly to the pressure. I brought my full weight and strength to bear, and surged against it. It yielded again; but I was so enfeebled by my toilsome journey that I could not overthrow it. I rested a little, and then raised an edge of the boulder by a strong, steady push, and placed a small stone under it, to keep it from sinking back to its place. I rested again, and then repeated the process. Before long, I had added a third prop, and had got the edge of the boulder considerably elevated. The labor and the close atmosphere together were so exhausting, however, that I was obliged to lie down then, and recuperate my strength by a longer season of rest. And so, hour after hour I labored, growing more and more weary, but still upheld by a fascination which I felt was infused into me by the invisible powers whose will I was working. At last I concentrated my strength in a final effort, and the stone rolled from its position.

I can never forget the overpowering sense of awe that sank down like a great darkness upon my spirit at that moment. After a solemn pause to prepare myself, with bowed form and uncovered head, I slowly turned my gaze till it rested upon the spot where the great stone had lain.

There wasn't any bones there!

I just said to myself, "Well, if this an't the blastedest, infernalest swindle that ever I've come across yet, I wish I may never!"

And then I scratched out of there, and marched up here to the Volcano House, and got out my old raw-boned fool of a horse, "Oahu," and "lammed" him till he couldn't stand up without leaning against something.

You can not bet any thing on dreams.

KTAADN

FROM *The Maine Woods*

HENRY DAVID THOREAU

Thoreau is one of America's famous prisoners. He was jailed—for one night—for refusing to pay a tax, his protest against slavery. But there is this little-stressed incident which perhaps gives a larger clue to an understanding of the author of *Walden:* He taught school in Concord after his graduation from Harvard in 1837 and was forced to resign because he would not whip his students. He wrote later that the man who loved nature loved man. This proposition, turned end for end, was no less true for him. On his nature walks he wore a suit in brown and green weave so as to blend with the woods. Once a mink came within twenty feet of him, he notes delightedly. He liked to think of himself not as a walker or hiker but as a "saunterer," and he sauntered up Mount Monadnock, Greylock, the Catskills, Mount Washington, Katahdin with a book under one arm to press flowers in, a telescope under the other, and a loaf of bread and a diary in his pocket.

HAVING SLUMPED, SCRAMBLED, ROLLED, BOUNCED, AND WALKED, BY TURNS, OVER this scraggy country, I arrived upon a side-hill, or rather side-mountain, where rocks, gray, silent rocks, were the flocks and herds that pastured, chewing a rocky cud at sunset. They looked at me with hard gray eyes, without a bleat or a low. This brought me to the skirt of a cloud, and bounded my walk that night. But I had already seen that Maine country when I turned about, waving, flowing, rippling, down below.

When I returned to my companions, they had selected a camping-ground on the torrent's edge, and were resting on the ground; one was on the sick list, rolled in a blanket, on a damp shelf of rock. It was a savage and dreary scenery enough; so wildly rough, that they looked long to find a level and open space for the tent. We could not well camp higher, for want of fuel; and the trees here seemed so evergreen and sappy, that we almost doubted if they would acknowledge the influence of fire; but fire prevailed at last, and blazed here, too, like a good citizen of the world. Even at this height we met with frequent traces of moose, as well as of bears. As here was no cedar, we made our bed of coarser feathered spruce; but at any rate the feathers were plucked from the live tree. It was, perhaps, even a more grand and desolate place for a night's lodging than the summit would have been, being in the neighborhood of those wild trees, and of the torrent. Some more aerial and finer-spirited winds rushed and roared through the ravine all night, from time to time arousing our fire, and dispersing the embers about. It was as if we lay in the very nest of a young whirlwind. At midnight, one of my bed-fellows, being startled in his dreams by the sudden blazing up to its top of a fir-tree, whose green boughs were dried by the heat, sprang up, with a cry, from his bed, thinking the world on fire, and drew the whole camp after him.

In the morning, after whetting our appetite on some raw pork, a wafer of hard bread, and a dipper of condensed cloud or waterspout, we all together began to make our way up the falls, which I have described; this time choosing the right hand, or highest peak, which was not the one I had approached before. But soon my companions were lost to my sight behind the mountain ridge in my rear, which still seemed ever retreating before me, and I climbed alone over huge rocks, loosely poised, a mile or more, still edging toward the clouds; for though the day was clear elsewhere, the summit was concealed by mist. The mountain seemed a vast aggregation of loose rocks, as if some time it had rained rocks, and they lay as they fell on the mountain sides, nowhere fairly at rest, but leaning on each other, all rocking-stones, with cavities between, but scarcely any soil or smoother shelf. They were the raw materials of a planet dropped from an unseen quarry, which the vast chemistry of nature would anon work up, or work down, into the smiling and verdant plains and valleys of earth. This was an undone extremity of the globe; as in lignite, we see coal in the process of formation.

At length I entered within the skirts of the cloud which seemed forever drifting over the summit, and yet would never be gone, but was generated out of that pure air as fast as it flowed away; and when, a quarter of a mile farther, I reached the summit of the ridge, which those who have seen in clearer weather say is about five miles long, and contains a thousand acres of table-land, I was deep within the hostile ranks of clouds, and all objects were obscured by them. Now the wind would blow me out a yard of clear sunlight, wherein I stood; then a gray, dawning light was all it could accomplish, the cloud-line ever rising and falling with the wind's intensity. Sometimes it seemed as if the summit would be cleared in a few moments, and smile in sunshine; but what was gained on one side was lost on another. It was like sitting in a chimney and waiting for the smoke to blow away. It was, in fact, a cloud factory—these were the cloud-works, and the wind turned them off done from the cool, bare rocks. Occasionally, when the windy col-

umns broke in to me, I caught sight of a dark, damp crag to the right or
left; the mist driving ceaselessly between it and me. It reminded me of the
creations of the old epic and dramatic poets, of Atlas, Vulcan, the Cyclops,
and Prometheus. Such was Caucasus and the rock where Prometheus was
bound. Æschylus had no doubt visited such scenery as this. It was vast, Titanic, and such as man never inhabits. Some part of the beholder, even some
vital part, seems to escape through the loose grating of his ribs as he ascends.
He is more lone than you can imagine. There is less of substantial thought
and fair understanding in him than in the plains where men inhabit. His
reason is dispersed and shadowy, more thin and subtile, like the air. Vast,
Titanic, inhuman Nature has got him at disadvantage, caught him alone,
and pilfers him of some of his divine faculty. She does not smile on him as in
the plains. She seems to say sternly, Why came ye here before your time.
This ground is not prepared for you. Is it not enough that I smile in the
valleys? I have never made this soil for thy feet, this air for thy breathing,
these rocks for thy neighbors. I cannot pity nor fondle thee here, but forever
relentlessly drive thee hence to where I *am* kind. Why seek me where I have
not called thee, and then complain because you find me but a stepmother?
Shouldst thou freeze or starve, or shudder thy life away, here is no shrine,
nor altar, nor any access to my ear.

> Chaos and ancient Night, I come no spy
> With purpose to explore or to disturb
> The secrets of your realm, but . . .
> .   .   .   .   .   as my way
> Lies through your spacious empire up to light.

The tops of mountains are among the unfinished parts of the globe,
whither it is a slight insult to the gods to climb and pry into their secrets,
and try their effect on our humanity. Only daring and insolent men, perchance, go there. Simple races, as savages, do not climb mountains—their
tops are sacred and mysterious tracts never visited by them. Pomola is always
angry with those who climb to the summit of Ktaadn.

GIGANTIC MUSICAL
STATUES

FROM *Erewhon*

SAMUEL BUTLER

Samuel Butler was one of the sharpest and most unconventional minds of the nineteenth century. His *Way of all Flesh,* largely autobiographical, and thoroughly distasteful to his own period because it exposed so brutally the counterfeit of Victorian piety, has a place as one of the great English novels. Although he thought of painting as his major endeavor, he also wrote music with Handel as his model and did original thinking in the study of heredity. He was much impressed with Darwin's work in evolution. His best-known work, *Erewhon; or, Over the Range,* grew out of a paper he wrote called "Darwin Among the Machines." Erewhon he pictured as an incredible country where sickness and poverty are crimes and where theft is treated as a disease. In this extract the narrator, crossing the mountain range behind which Erewhon lies, comes on enormous statues with hollowed heads.

I ROSE WITH EARLY DAWN, AND IN AN HOUR I WAS ON MY WAY, FEELING strange, not to say weak, from the burden of solitude, but full of hope when I considered how many dangers I had overcome, and that this day should see me at the summit of the dividing range.

After a slow but steady climb of between three and four hours, during which I met with no serious hindrance, I found myself upon a tableland, and close to a glacier which I recognized as marking the summit of the pass. Above it towered a succession of rugged precipices and snowy mountain sides. The solitude was greater than I could bear; the mountain upon my master's sheep-run was a crowded thoroughfare in comparison with this somber sullen place. The air, moreover, was dark and heavy, which made the loneliness even more oppressive. There was an inky gloom over all that was not covered with snow and ice. Grass there was none.

Each moment I felt increasing upon me that dreadful doubt as to my own identity—as to the continuity of my past and present existence—which is the first sign of that distraction which comes on those who have lost them-

selves in the bush. I had fought against this feeling hitherto, and had conquered it; but the intense silence and gloom of this rocky wilderness were too
much for me, and I felt that my power of collecting myself was beginning
to be impaired.

I rested for a little while, and then advanced over very rough ground,
until I reached the lower end of the glacier. Then I saw another glacier,
descending from the eastern side into a small lake. I passed along the western
side of the lake, where the ground was easier, and when I had got about
half way I expected that I should see the plains which I had already seen
from the opposite mountains; but it was not to be so, for the clouds rolled
up to the very summit of the pass, though they did not overlip it on to the
side from which I had come. I therefore soon found myself enshrouded by
a cold thin vapor, which prevented my seeing more than a very few yards in
front of me. Then I came upon a large patch of old snow, in which I could
distinctly trace the half-melted tracks of goats—and in one place, as it seemed
to me, there had been a dog following them. Had I lighted upon a land
of shepherds? The ground, where not covered with snow, was so poor and
stony, and there was so little herbage, that I could see no sign of a path
or regular sheep-track. But I could not help feeling rather uneasy as I
wondered what sort of a reception I might meet with if I were to come
suddenly upon inhabitants. I was thinking of this, and proceeding cautiously
through the mist, when I began to fancy that I saw some objects darker
than the cloud looming in front of me. A few steps brought me nearer, and
a shudder of unutterable horror ran through me when I saw a circle of
gigantic forms, many times higher than myself, upstanding grim and gray
through the veil of cloud before me.

I suppose I must have fainted, for I found myself some time afterwards
sitting upon the ground, sick and deadly cold. There were the figures, quite
still and silent, seen vaguely through the thick gloom, but in human shape
indisputably.

A sudden thought occurred to me, which would have doubtless struck
me at once had I not been prepossessed with forebodings at the time that I
first saw the figures, and had not the cloud concealed them from me—I mean
that they were not living beings, but statues. I determined that I would count
fifty slowly, and was sure that the objects were not alive if during that time
I could detect no sign of motion.

How thankful was I when I came to the end of my fifty and there had
been no movement!

I counted a second time—but again all was still.

I then advanced timidly forward, and in another moment I saw that my
surmise was correct. I had come upon a sort of Stonehenge of rude and barbaric figures, seated as Chowbok had sat when I questioned him in the wool-

shed, and with the same superhumanly malevolent expression upon their faces. They had been all seated, but two had fallen. They were barbarous—neither Egyptian, nor Assyrian, nor Japanese—different from any of these, and yet akin to all. They were six or seven times larger than life, of great antiquity, worn and lichen grown. They were ten in number. There was snow upon their heads and wherever snow could lodge. Each statue had been built of four or five enormous blocks, but how these had been raised and put together is known to those alone who raised them. Each was terrible after a different kind. One was raging furiously, as in pain and great despair; another was lean and cadaverous with famine; another cruel and idiotic, but with the silliest simper that can be conceived—this one had fallen, and looked exquisitely ludicrous in his fall—the mouths of all were more or less open, and as I looked at them from behind, I saw that their heads had been hollowed.

I was sick and shivering with cold. Solitude had unmanned me already, and I was utterly unfit to have come upon such an assembly of fiends in such a dreadful wilderness and without preparation. I would have given everything I had in the world to have been back at my master's station; but that was not to be thought of: my head was failing, and I felt sure that I could never get back alive.

Then came a gust of howling wind, accompanied with a moan from one of the statues above me. I clasped my hands in fear. I felt like a rat caught in a trap, as though I would have turned and bitten at whatever thing was nearest me. The wildness of the wind increased, the moans grew shriller, coming from several statues, and swelling into a chorus. I almost immediately knew what it was, but the sound was so unearthly that this was but little consolation. The inhuman beings into whose hearts the Evil One had put it to conceive these statues, had made their heads into a sort of organ-pipe, so that their mouths should catch the wind and sound with its blowing. It was horrible. However brave a man might be, he could never stand such a concert, from such lips, and in such a place. I heaped every invective upon them that my tongue could utter as I rushed away from them into the mist, and even after I had lost sight of them, and turning my head round could see nothing but the storm-wraiths driving behind me, I heard their ghostly chanting, and felt as though one of them would rush after me and grip me in his hand and throttle me.

WHY MEN CLIMB

FROM *Speaking of Books, The New York Times Book Review*

ISAAC ROSENFELD

In this selection Isaac Rosenfeld, novelist, critic, and teacher of the humanities, argues with moving logic that mountain climbing is not a sport but a branch of theology. He rests his case on the Bible, the sacred Hindu writings, and the mythology of the mountain peoples, and calls as supporting witnesses John Muir of the high Sierras and George Mallory of Everest.

And why not? If the essence of religion is the responsibility of every man for his brother which Buddha and Moses and Christ and Mohammed taught, then what more compelling parable have we today than, let us say, the Annapurna climb, when Maurice Herzog, blinded and crippled, was carried down the man-killing slopes of the mountain on the backs of his companions.

THE MORE I READ THE LITERATURE OF MOUNTAIN CLIMBING, THE MORE CONvinced I am that mountain climbing is not a sport. Surely Maurice Herzog's "Annapurna," with its extreme suffering and misfortune, and Sir John Hunt's "Conquest of Everest"—that masterpiece of logistics—should suggest a revision of the conventional view. For how can one call sport an activity which draws hundreds of men away from home, to shoulder heavy packs and carry them, panting in thin air, up walls of rock, snow and ice, in constant peril of their lives? As an American I have taken my image of sport from baseball: I think of DiMaggio in center, loping off at the crack of the bat, to shag a fly with careless ease. Even the more reckless sports, such as motorcycle or auto-racing, are conducted according to fixed rules, on flat ground, which stays put; a man knows what to expect. At its wildest, sport is safe—in the sense of the known, the natural.

Grace, skill, teamwork, competition and excitement to the contrary, mountain climbing is no sport, but a branch of theology. I base my conclusion on the frequently quoted words of one of the greatest climbers of all time, George Mallory, who lost his life on Mount Everest during the expedition of 1924. When asked why he wanted to climb Everest, Mallory simply replied, "Because it is there."

Now this is hardly a reason. Reasons lead us beyond the thing done, to consideration of intentions and consequences, practical ends. Yet one must not say that Mallory's reply expressed no reason at all, for it was a compelling reason, as anything must be which leads men, presumably sane, to risk and lose their lives. The reason for an activity which is neither practical nor gratuitous can only be intrinsic; it is done for its own sake. But then wouldn't Mallory's famous statement apply to any object of sport, such as swimming the English Channel? That, too, is "there."

The distinguishing characteristic of Mallory's words is that they are primarily religious in nature: their exact equivalent in meaning is to be found in the sacred writings of the Hindus, in our own Holy Bible, and no doubt in similar texts. In the Sanskrit it is written, *Tat vam asi,* which means, "That Thou art"; and the Lord says to Moses, "I am that I am." All three statements are alike in being ontological—they make the assertion of existence, that it is. Moreover all three statements are identical in meaning, and differ only in the person. In the first person, the statement is, "I am . . . ," in the second, "Thou art . . ." and in the third, "It is . . ." Mallory was speaking the language of theology.

My case does not rest on linguistic analysis alone. The connection between mountain and godhead has long been recognized, however vaguely, in mythology and religion. There is Mount Olympus (to say no more of Mount Everest, or Chomolungma, "the home of the gods"), there is Mount Sinai, there is the Sermon on the Mount; and even the tourist taking color shots feels himself in the Presence. An analogy, somewhat nearer the point, would liken the ascent of a mountain to man's striving toward God. Herzog and other climbers have reported the sensations of lightheadedness and extreme impersonality, the double vision and hallucinations induced by lack of oxygen as one nears the top; the analogy to the mystic union should be obvious.

As for the temptations that beset the way, John Muir, the naturalist, recounts many proud impulses toward daring and inevitable self-destruction on the way up, during a climb, if I recall, in the Tetons; these are surely temptations of a demon. That it is a difficult (well nigh impossible) ascent is certainly no news to a Christian, and neither is the fact that the ascent, the symbol of redemption, implies the symbol, and sometimes, alas, the actuality, of the fall. (It is worth noting in this context that the descent from a mountain is the hardest part of the climb. The mystery of Grace is fully symbolized.)

Enough analogies. Whatever man's passion for conquering the highest peaks may mean symbolically (motivations running the range from sex to nationalism have been assigned to it), it has a plain and simple, literal meaning: the impulse, informing all our culture, which has driven the Western world toward the limits of human experience. To stand at the highest point is to occupy such a limit. Here ends the human world, farther one cannot go; at the limit of our experience one encounters that other world, of which one can only say the word *that*—bare being, mere structure, the "thatness" of the universe and of God. Mountain climbing is the literal metaphor of this encounter.

I am not dismayed by the fact that Sir Edmund Hillary, on returning from Mount Everest, spoke of having admired the "grand view." Standing at the topmost point, he had earned the right to look down.

MOSES IS SHOWN THE PROMISED LAND

WHERE THE PRAYER
WHEELS TURN

FROM *Throne of the Gods*

ARNOLD HEIM
AND
AUGUST GANSSER

Arnold Heim is an eminent geologist who headed the first Swiss expedition to the Himalayas. August Gansser is a young colleague who accompanied him. Heim had previously spent twenty years in geological research in the European Alps. The expedition through the Himalayan ranges was to make a comparative study. In addition to their more formidable scientific reports, the two geologists wrote this personal and interesting study of the Himalayan people and the ancient religious rites which are woven so closely into their daily lives. The title of the book, *Throne of the Gods,* the authors explain, was chosen because Indians and Tibetans, both Hindu and Buddhist, believe the gods reign from the Himalayan and trans-Himalayan peaks.

ITS REMARKABLE STRUCTURE, AND THE PECULIAR HARMONY OF ITS SHAPE, JUStify my speaking of Kailas as the most sacred mountain in the world. Here is a meeting-place of the greatest religions of the East, and the difficult journey round the temple of the gods purifies the soul from earthly sins. The remarkable position of this mountain that towers out of the Transhimalayan plateau already indicates that it must present extremely interesting geological problems for solution. Strangely enough, it consists of horizontally stratified conglomerate masses with erratic admixture. In the course of geological aeons, these strata have been elevated many thousands of feet without any change in their horizontal lay-out. Next day, when for the first time the mighty Kailas is displayed to us in its full magnificence, Paldin, my companion, kneels and touches the ground with his forehead. Then he looks round at me questioningly, somewhat anxiously. "No, Paldin," I answer the unspoken enquiry, "this mountain is just as sacred to me as it is to you, for

I too am a pilgrim, just as those two lamas who passed a moment ago are pilgrims. Like you, like them, I am in search of the beautiful, the sacred in this wonderful mountain." I wrestle with my broken Hindustani, interspersed with broken English. But Paldin understands me.

For nearly three-quarters of a mile, our road is bordered by high walls of conglomerate. This is a genuine road, and is marked out in addition on either side by rows of small cairns. There are more of these cairns on the right, for you must always pass to the left of a shrine, and the pilgrimage round Kailas, like that round other holy places in the East, must be made clockwise. Only the Boen-Po, adherents of the pre-Buddhist, originally animist, religion of Tibet, make their pilgrimage counter-clockwise as a protest against the interloping and more orthodox Buddhism.

The very stones of this region are sacred, and to collect specimens is sacrilege. Consequently, though the prospects for geological research are rosy, peculiar methods of work are needed. A gradual adaptation to my surroundings has been produced by exposure to the weather and to the smoke of yak-dung fires. But beneath the veil of dirt and my lama's outer garments, I feel as unreligious as possible, for the geological sketch-books, hammer, compass, small field-glasses, a fair number of geological specimens, a bottle of hydrochloric acid, and a conveniently portable camera, are stored about my person, and give me a paunchy appearance. But in this matter I was outdone by a Tibetan I encountered who, after a deal in which he disposed of four sheep, packed away within his caftan the sugar he received in exchange, thus creating a preposterous bulk above the girdle. Of these hidden impedimenta, the one I use most often is my Bézard compass to help me in making sketch-maps. Fortunately most of the Tibetans wear an amulet round the neck, and the compass is not a bad imitation of one, so I can hang it on a string and have it readily available without attracting too much attention. I have got quite used to the monotonous repetition of "Om mani padme oom," this having been my lullaby when the old Tibetan who camped with us a while ago murmured his refrain far on into the night with the assiduity of a perpetual-motion machine.

The pilgrims' way leads into a lateral valley by which we can reach the northern side of Kailas. Crossing the torrent once more, I enter an area which is highly interesting for a geologist, being the granite pediment of the huge conglomerate mass of Kailas. A little to the side of the track we rested. For a time I was able to divest myself of my lama envelope and climb the opposite slope, from which, while studying the geological structure, I was able to take an excellent photo of Mount Kailas and neighbourhood. There were marmots everywhere, uttering their peculiar cries monotonously. The sound made by these Tibetan beasts was very different from the whistle-like call of the marmots of the Alps, being a "ft, ft, ft," like the noise produced by a wheezy, worn-out lorry; and these marmots are of a foxy-red colour.

Having washed my socks in a snow-water rivulet, I laid them on a hot stone to dry in the sun and sat down to make a sketch, but was soon interrupted by one of those rapid changes in the weather common in the high mountains. Even before the gloomy storm-clouds had gathered, the thunder was rumbling and echoing in the wild upland valley. Our immediate objective to-day was a gompa or lamasery at an altitude of over 16,000 feet on the northern slopes of Kailas. A few leagues short of this we were overtaken by a storm more violent than any I have seen in the Alps. The rain was quickly followed by snow. Lightning flashed amid the snowflakes, illuminating the rugged granite rocks against the background of a dark-grey sky. We have not been bothered by thunderstorms during our sojourn in the Himalayas, but here in Transhimalaya they are an almost daily occurrence. The dense monsoon-clouds which surmount the Himalayas with a huge wall like that produced in the Alps by the föhn, are not seen here in Transhimalaya. All the same, we are not free from the influence of the monsoon, but the chief movement of the rain-clouds is from the west towards the east. The discharges take place mainly in the form of thunderstorms rather than in that of continuous rainfall. Of course I can speak only of the regions I visited, where the local conditions in the Sutlej Valley doubtless have something to do with the matter.

The lightnings flashed from crag to crag, an echoing clap of thunder following each. Night was falling as, amid mighty scattered rocks of granite, we reached the lonely gompa. The walls, picked out with red at the top, were covered with new-fallen snow. As a weary pilgrim, feeling somewhat uneasy, I made my way through the low entry to find myself in a dark, soot-begrimed granite cave, where I could hope that the lamas, however inquisitive, would not notice anything amiss with my aspect. Of course, it was common form for Kailas pilgrims to seek shelter in this monastery, but it was important that my identity as a European should not be pierced. I did not care to let myself dwell on what might happen if it was. The place was lighted by one little candle, which scarcely did more than make darkness visible.

Every pilgrim who considers himself of importance must request the pleasure of an interview with the head-lama. I myself was posing as a lama of importance from a distant region, and must therefore seem eager for an interview. With mixed feelings I stood before the little door leading to the head-lama's quarters. Paldin and one of the Bhotias accompanied me. My other travelling companions had stayed behind at Darchen, for a trade in sheep and goats—always a long business in the East. Paldin, who was familiar with the ways of lamaseries, had given me an hour's private tuition upon the best way of conducting myself in these unfamiliar circumstances. Barefooted, with folded hands and lowered head, I entered the dark chamber which was lighted only by a few small butter-lamps. Behind a long altar, which looked like the table of a medieval alchemist, squatted the high priest, tailor-fashion. Slowly and reverently I approached His Holiness. He had sharply cut features and an intelligent expression, very different from that of most lamas, who look like self-satisfied materialists. Paldin announced me as an extremely holy man from far, far away, and fortunately sanctity connotes the idea of a discreet silence. My head still devoutly lowered, I handed him two small coloured goblets of marbled vulcanite, a somewhat risky gift here, but we have found them effective and comparatively easy to transport. An attendant rummaged in a small chest, and then, with a solemn gesture, His Eminence handed me a strip of red ribbon, which, according to custom, was immediately hung round my neck. I was also given a little bag of tiny pills which would preserve me from every possible mischance. In the dim light, the head-lama evidently had no suspicion that he was receiving a European in audience. Soon we were back in our dark, soot-begrimed cave. Although I was not best pleased to learn that a number of sadhus had arrived during the audience, I soon fell asleep, while from the roof flakes of soot fell upon my face. Every time I awoke from my uneasy slumbers, I heard a peculiar noise as if large stones were being rubbed together. Was this a prayer-wheel in permanent operation, or was tsamba being ground throughout the night? From a furtive enquiry I learned that the latter was the true interpretation.

A glorious morning followed. I was up at peep of day, and, armed with my leica (portable camera), I went out to take what views I could of this remote and inaccessible spot. Hidden behind a big rock, I secured the photo. Slowly I made my way back to the lamasery. In the rays of the rising sun the head-lama was standing on the flat roof, with folded hands, contemplating Kailas, and bowing before the sublime view. Every morning throughout the year, summer and winter alike, he greets the sacred mountain, praying to his god, and praying also to demons. In a granite cave beneath the monastery the gilded emblems of the gods are kept. They grinned at me unmeaningly, for their symbolism was beyond my power of interpretation. We entered this sanctum through a low doorway, after traversing a little library. Everyone who came in had to give the big prayer-drum a turn, and it seemed to me that the head-lama would do well to have the axle greased. If that were done, it would go on turning for a while after being set in motion, and the number of prayers would thereby be greatly increased. Now I stood before the holiest of all the images, that of Kailas. We prostrated ourselves in front of this divinity, who was draped in tulle. Each pilgrim must offer up a little butter-lamp. All around were the strangest figures of demons, whose goggle eyes stared at us from every corner. As was proper to the holiness of the place, on leaving I gave the great prayer-drum an especially vigorous thrust. Drawing a deep breath of relief, I found myself once more in the sunshine. White prayer-flags were fluttering, and Kailas shone down upon us.

Now we are on pilgrimage to Dolma-La, a pass over 18,000 feet high, the highest in the circuit of Kailas. A forest of cairns indicates the holiness of the place. Great piles of human hair are encircled by little walls. A rock is covered with teeth that have been extracted—religious sacrifices made by fanatical pilgrims. Huge and savage granite crags border the pass, which is covered with new-fallen snow. My companions kneel at the tomb of a saint. Hard by is a rock showing what are said to be the holy man's footprints. As usual, in such cases, he must have needed an outsize shoe. Often we have to kowtow and knock the ground with our foreheads, as we get a fresh view of the sacred mountain. A small dust-avalanche rushes down from the peak. The great god up there has smiled.

Beside Dolma-La is an enormous crag surmounted by a flag-staff from which small multi-coloured streamers flutter. The abundance of cairns give the place its peculiar stamp. Almost everyone who goes by erects his own cairn, for which purpose, since stones are scarce, he often has to rob previous structures. A white stone usually crowns the little edifice. Although the summit of Kailas is not visible from this spot, it is of peculiar importance. When we recall that many of the pilgrims are persons who never before have left the plains of India, we cannot but suppose that a number of them fail to get home again, perishing here from the hardships of the journey. The more fanatical of the pilgrims make the circuit of the mountain crawling on their bellies, thus achieving the highest degree of spiritual purification.

Here is a description of the actual process. With hands crossed, the pilgrim prostrates himself. Then, wearing gloves armoured with metal plates, he makes a scratch as far ahead as he can reach. Rising erect at the point where his feet are, he strides to the scratch-mark—the length of the body with arms outstretched—prostrates himself once more, and repeats the process. Thus performed, the circuit of the mountain takes about three weeks.

Several times we overtook such fanatics, once just below the pass. Among them were two Tibetan women, who would occasionally drop from sheer fatigue, lying half-dead for a while, and then resume their laborious pilgrimage. In one place a roaring brook poured across the granite blocks, but even here the pious routine was not in the least interrupted. I was amazed.

Concealed within his garments, our old Tibetan has a reserve of coloured prayer-flags. Again and again I have watched him produce one or more of these on the top of one of the many passes, to weight them with large stones or the branch of a tree; nevertheless, his supply seems inexhaustible. With astounding tenacity, he climbs a huge boulder, shouting "Chaloo, sho, sho, sho, chaloo, sho, sho, sho" alternately with "Om mani padme oom" and then a new streamer is fixed. He stands with clasped and uplifted hands, and then kowtows, knocking the ground with his forehead. So great is the power of this mighty religion.

A little below Dolma-La there is a small sacred lake where the pilgrims make their ablutions—as a rule. But this time the lake, being at an altitude of over 18,000 feet, is frozen and thickly covered with snow. Near the shore we see masses of rock which the pilgrims have flung on to the ice in the vain hope of breaking it. It seems to be an unfavourable year for pilgrimages.

The eastern side of the pass leads steeply into a new and long valley, ending far to the north in a lofty pass which is an important route over the chains of the Transhimalaya. But we turn southward, leaving the savage granitic landscape to find ourselves once again amid imposing walls of conglomerate. Soon we are to reach a new monastery, the Tsumtulphu Gompa. For the moment, however, I am wholly taken up by my geological investigations. The strata of conglomerate, which have hitherto been horizontal, are here somewhat inclined, as if by pressure from the south. As we negotiate a curve in the valley, this impression is confirmed, and suddenly I come across a most interesting geological phenomenon. At a well-marked transitional line, the conglomerate strata have been covered by a number of convoluted strata sharply contrasting with the flat Transhimalayan sedimentary rocks and the granites. Compared with the Transhimalayan rocks, this superposed series must have undergone a recent and intensive convolution. These observations show that we have to do with the northernmost vestiges of the Himalayan chain proper, which has been superimposed upon the Transhimalaya from the south—backwards, that is to say.

"Look out, the sadhus are coming!" This shout of warning from Paldin comes as a sudden interruption to my geological studies. Paldin and I secrete ourselves in a small lateral valley, while my other companions wander ahead with apparent unconcern. They must make for Darchen, while Paldin and I lag behind. It is just as well that they should not know too much about my geological activities, which are peculiarly important here.

On the Pilgrims' Way are advancing four lean figures, wrapped in grey blankets. These four sadhus have fine-looking heads, and wear long, black beards, while their heads are thickly covered with black hair. One of them, in due time, will become our special friend, but for the moment I wish to steer clear of devotees.

As soon as they had passed, I continued my geological work, while Paldin pressed some new botanical specimens, for this branch, too, must not be neglected. Although I have nothing but some old pasteboard biscuit boxes in which to store my herbarium, the specimens have kept very well. Of course, could I have foreseen that most of them were to be lost in a difficult river-crossing amid the southern Himalayas, I should have spared myself a great deal of valuable time.

Night was close at hand when I finished my geological sketches and dark storm-clouds had gathered. We entered Tsumtulphu Gompa as pilgrims, to find it a place lacking interest. Comparative disorder prevailed, for the head-lama had gone to Lhasa, so the inmates were a little out of hand. Still, I found it worth while to visit a number of caves excavated in the cliffs, the habitations of famous ascetics in former days, now vacated. The valley widened here, and we had a good view of the broad plain that lies on the southern side of the Transhimalaya. We are only about six miles from Darchen, whence we started upon the circuit of Kailas. The sanctified sheep await us there. On the way thither, next day, we passed huge heaps of inscribed "mani stones," on which "Om mani padme oom" had been chiselled. When I moved to pick one up Kali cried: "No, no, Sahib, don't touch it; the gods will be angry."

Still, Paldin sympathises with my collector's fever, and would like me to have one of these stones. A storm is threatening, and it grows darker. I look cautiously round, and then secrete a particularly well-carved mani stone beneath my caftan. There comes a loud clap of thunder, followed by a cloudburst, as if the Last Judgment was at hand. "Put down the stone, Sahib, put down the stone!" Paldin is pale from anxiety. Certainly the elemental hubbub is enough to make the poor fellow anxious, and convince him that the gods are angered by my sacrilege. Still, the stone remains in my pouch, where I feel it will prove a mascot. A pitch-dark night has fallen. It is still raining heavily, with lightning-flashes and peals of thunder. Paldin is carrying some of my geological specimens. The space within my caftan is somewhat restricted, and the drenched sheepskin is as heavy as lead. After an arduous tramp, we reach Darchen, stumbling in one place over a lama who lies in the pouring rain, having fallen asleep exhausted after a long day of belly-crawling.

CONCERNING THE RATS
ON STACY MOUNTAIN

FROM *Charms and Powers*

GEORGE WASHINGTON BROWN
AS TOLD TO
JESSIE M. WHITEHEAD

The story goes that the Pied Piper was never seen again after he had piped away the mice and children of Hamelin. That is inaccurate because he appeared again in the Berkshires under an assumed name. The confusion arose from the fact that in America he did not play his flute, for what reason we do not know. But he lived on Stacy Mountain and when there was trouble with the rats eating up the corn, his neighbors called on him to use his powers.

Jessie M. Whitehead has a camp at the foot of Mt. Chocorua, New Hampshire, where the narrator, George Washington Brown, was her nearest neighbor. Brown was part Penobscot Indian. He grew up on his grandmother's farm on Stacy Mountain. When he was sixteen she died, and he returned to his father's people at Old Town, marrying into the tribe and working in logging camps. Then he settled down on a farm of his own at Tamsworth. His grandmother left him some of her "powers" and her lore of herbs and charms. He sometimes "calls her up" when he needs a special charm. He told Miss Whitehead that "it takes a lot out of a man but it's wuth it."

MY GRANDMOTHER MEHITABLE WARD AND DAN'L WARD WAS FARMING ON THE old Stacy Mountain farm here east of Silver Lake and they had one hundred sixty acres all cleaned up, and it was clear all the way for a mile or more to Goe Hill, where John Grover farmed two hundred acres. Those was the two first farms taken up in the north country when Columbus discovered these mountains; and they pastured white-headed cattle there and raised corn, for there warn't no flour to be had, and they took the corn down to Portland to be ground for meal, two bushels of corn before them on a horse. It took them two days to go and two to come, and all for one bushel of meal. They had no stoves in those days, but open fires, and they made their spoons and forks of rock maple. Ross Graves down in South Tamworth has a lot of those; he found a barrel of them in his father's house, when he was laid away. But people don't use them now—that was in the old days.

One evening John Grover come down to the Stacy Mountain farm and Dan'l was crying, and John spoke up and says, "I never seen you cry before, Dan'l. My God! What ails you?" Dan'l says the rats was eating all his corn; he might have six hundred bushels, but there might be three thousand rats and they was eating it all.

John Grover spoke up and says, "I don't care how many rats there be, I'll speak to them and take them home with me."

Mehitable Ward was a Christian woman and never spoke no lie; if she said a thing it was so. (She and Dan'l used to pray every Saturday night, and many is the time I've heard her:

How pleasant is Saturday night,
When we tried all the week to be good,
Not spoken a word that is bad,
And obliged everyone that we could!)

Mehitable spoke up and says, "How are you going to take the rats, Mr. Grover?"

And he spoke and he says, "You watch when I go, and watch the rats foller me up over the pasture in the moonlight through the rocks and foller me home. And you'll never have no more rats on earth bother you so long as you live, and I'll put it so low as a mouse."

And my grandmother lived forty years after and Dan'l died before she did and he was ninety-three, and she was a year of a hundred, but they never again saw no rat on the place, not even a mouse.

Mehitable told her husband to go over to John Grover's place next day and ask how he done it; but he said no, he got it as a gift from his mother and he couldn't give it away without he lost it. But he come down the next night and says to her, "Did you see the rats foller me as I told ye?" and she says, "Yes, John, I did, just as a dog or a cat or a pet, and they was so thick I couldn't see through them for a hundred yards each way, I think there was three thousand."

And my grandmother was a Christian woman, and wouldn't lie, she lived till I was sixteen and I folded her hands and laid the quilt over her before the herb woman come, for the others was afraid to handle the dead, but I never was.

Now, that night she was on her last bed she says, "Georgie, hold me up to look through and see the pastures where I saw John Grover lead the rats." And I held her up and when I laid her down she was dead, and we put her away in Eaton Centre with Dan'l Ward that had died before.

No one knows that charm now, but in those days there was several who could do it. Jim Chancey, who lived in Eaton Centre or Snowville, knew it, but he died before he could give it away.

So did Duke Johnson, who lived down Shawtown Brook, south of Blazo Mountain; he had six hundred acres and perhaps two hundred head of cattle.

Duke Johnson had all kinds of power; he lived to be one hundred nine years old and his wife (I forget her name, but she was Mrs. Johnson) lived to be one hundred twelve years old. When she was eighty she took out all her teeth with her fingers, and no blood started nor nothing and they was all sound and white, and she put them in a box and give them to her husband to bury in that place where she was to be laid away, and Duke told her, he says to her, "I'll try and put you a set of ivory teeth in your head good as ever you had, because I think I've got power enough to do it."

And in one year he grew a set of teeth into her mouth, white ivory just as good as you ever seen in your life, and she was laid aside with them.

When Duke Johnson was ninety-three years old, Peohlia, my brother (he was named for my uncle; my father's great grandmother was a fullblood Indian woman, and my father was born near Old Town, Maine), was mowing in the hayfield and he run in crying, and Duke Johnson come and spoke to him and asked him, "What's the matter, dear boy?" and Peohlia says, "The hornets' stinging me 'most to death." And he says, "Hold on, Peohlia, and I'll take my jackknife and cut them all off out of the field and there sha'n't another hornet hurt you as long as you live." So he cut off all the nests and poured the hornets over his own head and took them out of the field; and Peohlia, who is living in Concord, is four years older than I, and has never been hurt by a hornet again, and he's a truthful boy and man.

That's how it was in the north, that's the power they had in them days; they don't have it now, but that is because they don't have the words and those have to be given as a gift.

A charm can be said any time when the sun goes down, mostly they are a verse from the Bible read backwards, but some is different. Then the power comes to you and lasts about a week and grows greater the more you use it. You can't take money with it till you're sixty years old, then you can feed yourself with it and you don't have to repeat anything to have it come to you; the power is always with you and you can't part with it until you can find a woman to give it to, or a man if you are a woman.

It is hard to say why so many of these powers have been lost; the old ones, they had power, but the young ones, they don't.

PLACES SO LONELY AND
FULL OF SOUNDS

FROM *Ms. Journal of Tour in Lake District, 1802*

SAMUEL TAYLOR COLERIDGE

🐉 The "Rime of the Ancient Mariner" and "Kubla Khan" are familiar to most people as part of their childhood. Coleridge the critic and philosopher is less well known. There are few men whose collected scribblings on book margins become important critical works.

In this selection from his *Journal of Tour in Lake District* we get a happier picture of the man than appears in his biographies. It does not resemble Coleridge the opium eater, the man whose genius was so much greater than his will, the man who wrote the most devastating piece of self-criticism in the English language. Knowing Coleridge, one can perhaps read these things even in this letter, but they are muted by the mountain places, "lonely and savage and full of sounds."

Wed, Afternoon 1/2 past 3, Aug *4* *th* *1802—*
WASTDALE, A MILE AND A HALF BELOW THE FOOT OF THE LAKE, AT AN ALE-house without a Sign, 20 strides from the Door, under the Shade of a huge Sycamore Tree, without my coat—but that I will now put on, in prudence—yes here I am and have been for something more than an hour, and have *enjoyed* a good Dish of Tea. I carried my Tea and sugar with me, under this delightful Tree. In the House there are only an old feeble Woman, and a "*Tallyeur*" Lad upon the Table—all the rest of the Wastdale World is a haymaking, rejoicing and thanking God for this first downright summer Day that we have had since the beginning of May. On Sunday Aug*t*. 1*st* 1/2 after 12, I had a Shirt, cravat, 2 pair of Stockings, a little paper and half a dozen Pens, a German Book (Voss's Poems) and a little Tea and Sugar, with my Night Cap, packed up in my natty green oil-skin, neatly squared, and put into my *net* knap-sack, and the knap-sack on my back and the Besom stick in my hand (which for want of a better, and in spite of M*rs* C. and Mary, who both raised their voices against it, especially as I left the Besom scattered on the Kitchen Floor) off I sallied—over the Bridge, thro' the hop-Field, thro' the Prospect Bridge at Portinscale, so on by the tall Birch that grows

out of the center of the huge Oak, along into Newlands. Newlands is indeed a lovely Place—the houses, each in it's little Shelter of Ashes and Sycamores, just under the Road, so that in some places you might leap down on the Roof, seemingly at least—the exceeding greeness and pastoral beauty of the Vale itself, with the savage wildness of the Mountains, their coves, and long arm-shaped and elbow-shaped Ridges—yet this wildness softened down into a congruity with the Vale by the semicircular Lines of the Crags, and of the bason-like Concavities. The Cataract between Newlands and Kescadale had but little water in it, of course, was of no particular Interest. I passed on thro' the green steep smooth bare Kescadale, a sort of unfurnished Passage or antechamber between Newlands and Buttermere, came out on Buttermere and drank Tea at the little Inn, and read the greater part of the Revelations—the only part of the New Testament, which the Scotch Cobbler read—because why? *Because it was the only part that he understood.* O 'twas a wise Cobbler!

Conceive an enormous round Bason mountain-high of solid Stone, cracked in half and one half gone; exactly in the remaining half of this enormous Bason, does Buttermere lie, in this beautiful and stern Embracement of Rock. I left it, passed by Scale Force, the white downfall of which glimmered thro' the Trees that hang before it like bushy Hair over a Madman's Eyes, and climbed 'till I gained the first Level. Here it was "every man his own path-maker," and I went directly cross it—upon soft mossy Ground, with many a hop, skip, and jump, and many an occasion for observing the truth of the old saying, "where Rushes grow, A Man may go." Red Pike, a dolphin-shaped Peak of a deep red, looked in upon me from over the Fell on my Left; on my right I had, first Melbreak (the Mountain on the right of Crummock, as you ascend the Lake) then a Vale running down with a pretty Stream in it, to Loweswater, then Heck Comb, a Fell of the same height and running in the same direction with Melbreak, a Vale on the other side too, and at the bottom of both these Vales the Loweswater Fells running abreast. Again I reached an ascent, climbed up, and came to a ruined Sheep-fold—a wild green view all around me, bleating of Sheep and noise of Waters. I sate there near 20 minutes, the Sun setting on the Hill behind with a soft watery gleam; and in front of me the upper Halves of huge deep-furrowed Grasmere (the mountain on the other side of Crummock) and the huge Newland and Buttermere Mountains, and peeping in from behind, the Top of Saddleback. Two Fields were visible, the highest cultivated Ground on the Newland side of Buttermere, and the Trees in those Fields were the only Trees visible in the whole prospect.

I left the Sheepfold with regret—for of all things a ruined Sheepfold in a desolate place is the dearest to me, and fills me most with Dreams and Visions and tender thoughts of those I love best. . . .

Thursday Morning, Augt 5th—went down the Vale almost to the Water Head, and ascended the low Reach between Sca' Fell and the Screes, and soon after I had gained it's height came in sight Burnmoor Water, a large Tairn ⬭ nearly of that shape, it's Tail towards Sca' Fell, at its head a gap forming an inverted arch with Black Coomb and a peep of the Sea seen thro' it. It lies directly at the Back of the Screes, and the stream that flows from it down thro' the gap, is called the Mite, and runs thro' a Vale of it's own called Miterdale, parallel with the lower part of Wastdale, and divided from it by the high Ridge called Irton Fells. I ascended Sca' Fell by the side of a torrent, and climbed and rested, rested and climbed, 'till I gained the very summit of Sca' Fell—believed by the Shepherds here to be higher than either Helvellyn or Skiddaw. Even to Black Coomb, before me all the Mountains die away running down westward to the Sea, apparently in eleven ridges and three parallel Vales with their three Rivers, seen from their very Sources to their falling into the Sea, where they form (excepting their Screwlike flexures) the *Trident* of the Irish Channel at Ravenglass. O my God! what enormous Mountains these are close by me, and yet below the Hill I stand on, Great Gavel, Kirk Fell, Green Crag, and behind, the Pillar, then the Steeple, then the Hay Cock, on the other side and behind me, Great End, Esk Carse, Bow-fell and close to my back two huge Pyramids, nearly as high as Sca' Fell itself, and indeed parts and parts of Sca' Fell known far and near by these names, the hither one of Broad Crag, and the next to it (but divided from it by a low Ridge) Doe Crag, which is indeed of itself a great Mountain of stones from a pound to 20 Ton weight embedded in woolly Moss. And here I am *lounded*—so fully lounded—that tho' the wind is strong, and the Clouds are hasting hither from the Sea—and the whole air Seaward has a lurid Look—and we shall certainly have Thunder—yet here (but that I am hunger'd and provisionless) *here* I could lie warm, and wait methinks for tomorrow's Sun, and on a nice Stone Table am I now at this moment writing to you—between 2 and 3 o'Clock as I guess—surely the first Letter ever written from the Top of Sca' Fell! But O! what a look down just under my Feet! The frightfullest Cove that might ever be seen, huge perpendicular Precipices, and one Sheep upon it's only Ledge, that surely must be crag! Tyson told me of this place, and called it Hollow Stones. Just by it and joining together, rise two huge Pillars of bare lead-colored Stone. I am no measurer, but their height and depth is terrible. I know how unfair is to judge of these Things by a comparison of past Impressions with present— but I have no shadow of hesitation in saying that the Coves and Precipices of Helvellin are nothing to these! From this sweet lounding Place I see directly thro' Borrowdale, the Castle Crag, the whole of Derwent Water, and but for the haziness of the Air I could see my own House. I see clear enough where it stands—

Here I will fold up this Letter. I have Wafers in my Inkhorn, and you shall call this Letter when it passes before you the Sca' Fell Letter. I must now drop down how I may into Eskdale—that lies under to my right, the upper part of it the wildest and savagest surely of all the Vales that were ever seen from the Top of an English Mountain and the lower part the loveliest.

Eskdale, Friday, Augt. 6th at an Estate House called Toes
There is one sort of Gambling, to which I am much addicted; and that not of the least criminal kind for a Man who has Children and a Concern. It is this. When I find it convenient to descend from a Mountain, I am too confident and too indolent to look round about and wind about 'till I find a track or other symptom of safety; but I wander on, and where it is first *possible* to descend, there I go, relying upon fortune for how far down this possibility will continue. So it was yesterday afternoon. I passed down from Broad Crag, skirted the Precipices, and found myself cut off from a most sublime Crag-summit, that seemed to rival Sca' Fell Man in height, and to outdo it in fierceness. A Ridge of Hill lay low down, and divided this Crag (called Doe-Crag) and Broad-crag—even as the hyphen divides the words broad and crag. I determined to go thither; the first place I came to, that was not direct Rock, I slipped down, and went on for a while with tolerable ease—but now I came (it was midway down) to a smooth perpendicular Rock about 7 feet high—this was nothing—I put my hands on the Ledge, and dropped down. In a few yards came just such another. I *dropped* that too. And yet another, seemed not higher—I would not stand for a trifle, so I dropped that too—but the stretching of the muscle of my hands and arms, and the jolt of the Fall on my Feet, put my whole Limbs in a *Tremble,* and I paused, and looking down, saw that I had little else to encounter but a succession of these little Precipices—it was in truth a Path that in a very hard Rain is, no doubt, the channel of a most splendid Waterfall. So I began to suspect that I ought not to go on; but then unfortunately tho' I could with ease drop down a smooth Rock of 7 feet high, I could not *climb* it, so go on I must; and on I went. The next 3 drops were not half a Foot, at least not a foot, more than my own height, but every Drop increased the Palsy of my Limbs. I shook all over, Heaven knows without the least influence of Fear. And now I had only two more to drop down—to return was impossible—but of these two the first was tremendous, it was twice my own height, and the Ledge at the bottom was exceedingly narrow, that if I drop down upon it I must of necessity have fallen backwards and of course killed myself. My limbs were all in a tremble. I lay upon my Back to rest

myself, and was beginning according to my Custom to laugh at myself for a Madman, when the sight of the Crags above me on each side, and the impetuous Clouds just over them, posting so luridly and so rapidly to northward, overawed me. I lay in a state of almost prophetic Trance and Delight and blessed God aloud for the powers of Reason and the Will, which remaining no Danger can overpower us! O God, I exclaimed aloud, how calm, how blessed am I now. I know not how to proceed, how to return, but I am calm and fearless and confident. If this Reality were a Dream, if I were asleep, what agonies had I suffered! what screams! When the Reason and the Will are away, what remain to us but Darkness and Dimness and a bewildering Shame, and Pain that is utterly Lord over us, or fantastic Pleasure that draws the Soul along swimming through the air in many shapes, even as a Flight of Starlings in a Wind.—I arose, and looking down saw at the bottom a heap of Stones which had fallen abroad and rendered the narrow Ledge on which they had been piled doubly dangerous. At the bottom of the third Rock that I dropt from, I met a dead Sheep quite rotten. This heap of stones, I guessed, and have since found that I guessed aright, had been piled up by the Shepherd to enable him to climb up and free the poor Creature whom he had observed to be crag-fast, but seeing nothing but rock over rock, he had desisted and gone for help and in the mean time the poor Creature had fallen down and killed itself. As I was looking at these I glanced my eye to my left, and observed that the Rock was rent from top to bottom. I measured the breadth of the Rent, and found that there was no danger of my being *wedged* in, so I put my knap-sack round to my side, and slipped down as between two walls, without any danger or difficulty. The next Drop brought me down on the Ridge called the How. I hunted out my Besom Stick, which I had flung before me when I first came to the Rocks, and wisely gave over all thought of ascending Doe-Crag, for now the Clouds were again coming in most tumultuously. So I began to descend, when I felt an odd sensation across my whole Breast—not pain nor itching— and putting my hand on it I found it all bumpy—and on looking saw the whole of my Breast from my Neck—to my Navel, exactly all that my Kamell-hair Breast-shield covers, filled with great red heat-bumps, so thick that no hair could lie between them. They still remain but are evidently less and I have no doubt will wholly disappear in a few Days. It was however a startling proof to me of the violent exertions which I had made. I descended this low Hill which was all hollow beneath me—and was like the rough green Quilt of a Bed of waters. At length two streams burst out and took their way down, one on [one] side a high Ground upon this Ridge, the other on the other. I took that to my right (having on my left this high ground, and the other Stream, and beyond that Doe-crag, on the other side of which is Esk Halse, where the head-spring of the Esk rises, and running down the

mper: Monkmeyer

NOAH'S ARK LANDING ON THE TOP OF THE MOUNTAIN

CLOUD REFLECTIONS IN MONO LAKE, IN THE MOUNTAINS OF CALIFORNIA

Albert Steiner: Black Star

A MOUNTAIN CABIN HIGH ABOVE THE ST. MORITZSEE, SWITZERLAND

YOSEMITE FALLS, 2,600 FEET, YOSEMITE NATIONAL PARK, CALIFORNIA

Bradford Washburn

MASSIVE ICE BLOCKS AT AN ALTITUDE OF 10,000 FEET ON THE APPROACHES TO SILVERTHRONE PASS. NOTE ANNUAL ICE LAYERS

STORM, ON THE EAST SIDE OF THE SIERRA, TAKEN FROM NEAR BIGPINE, CALIFORNIA

right: MUSTAGH TOWER, ONE OF THE WORLD'S MIGHTIEST PEAKS, STILL UNCONQUERED IN THE KARAKORAM HIMALAYAS

Hill and in upon the Vale looks and actually deceived me, as a great Turnpike Road—in which, as in many other respects the Head of Eskdale much resembles Langdale) and soon the Channel sank all at once, at least 40 yards, and formed a magnificent Waterfall—and close under this a succession of Waterfalls 7 in number, the third of which is nearly as high as the first. When I had almost reached the bottom of the Hill, I stood so as to command the whole 8 Waterfalls, with the great triangle-crag looking in above them, and on the one side of them the enormous and more than perpendicular Precipices and *Bull's-Brows,* of Sca' Fell! And now the Thunder-Storm was coming on, again and again! Just at the bottom of the Hill I saw on before me in the Vale, lying just above the River on the side of a Hill, one, two, three, four Objects; I could not distinguish whether Peat-hovels, or hovel-shaped Stones. I thought in my mind, that 3 of them would turn out to be stones—but that the fourth was certainly a Hovel. I went on toward them, crossing and recrossing the Becks and the River and found that they were all huge Stones—the one nearest the Beck which I had determined to be really a Hovel, retained its likeness when I was close beside. In size it is nearly equal to the famous Bowder Stone, but in every other respect greatly superior to it—it has a complete Roof, and that perfectly *thatched* with weeds, and Heath, and Mountain-Ash Bushes. I now was obliged to ascend again, as the River ran greatly to the Left, and the Vale was nothing more than the Channel of the River, all the rest of the interspace between the Mountains was a tossing up and down of Hills of all sizes—and the place at which I am now writing is called—*Te-as,* and spelt, *Toes*—as the Toes of Sca' Fell. It is not possible that any name can be more descriptive of the Head of Eskdale. I ascended close under Sca' Fell, and came to a little Village of Sheep-folds—there were 5 together—and the redding Stuff, and the Shears, and an old Pot, was in the passage of the first of them. Here I found an imperfect Shelter from a Thunder-shower accompanied with such Echoes! O God! what thoughts were mine! O how I wished for Health and Strength that I might wander about for a Month together, in the stormiest month of the year, among these Places, so lonely and savage and full of sounds!

THE ABOMINABLE
SNOWMAN

FROM *The Valley of Flowers*

FRANK S. SMYTHE

The Snowman legend is as much an honored institution among mountaineers as is the Flying Saucer among the air-minded, and as provocative a topic for an evening around the fireplace. There is as much evidence for as against, which means a good deal or none, depending upon what you admit as evidence. Strange tracks have been seen by many climbers far above the permanent snow line of the Himalayas—there is no dispute on that score. The insistent question which remains is, tracks of what?

Frank Smythe, botanist-author of *The Valley of Flowers,* thought he had finally settled the matter. On a holiday in the Himalayas, he had found evidence that the Abominable Snowman was the great white bear. And on his return to England he so reported. But all he accomplished, he complains, was to "rouse a hornet's nest about my ears." The British public was too fond of the Abominable Snowman to let itself be so easily persuaded by logic.

SINCE I HAD FIRST SEEN THAT GRAND MOUNTAIN, 21,264 FEET, NAMED NILGIRI Parbat by Lieutenant R. A. Gardiner of the Survey of India, I had on several occasions turned over in my mind the possibility of an ascent. I had examined the mountain from the west, south, and east, and from these directions there did not seem the least hope of an attempt proving successful. The sole remaining possibility was a route from the north or northwest. There were two possible lines of approach one via the Bhyundar Pass and the Banke Glacier and the other via the snow pass, which I had already visited, and the glacier-filled valley which runs in its uppermost portion roughly parallel with the Bhyundar Valley. I decided on the last-named approach, as it at least involved the exploration of a valley the upper portion of which, as far as I knew, had not been visited by Europeans. . . .

On approaching the pass, I was surprised to notice some tracks in the snow, which I first took to be those of a man, though we had seen no traces of shepherds. But when I came up to the tracks I saw the imprint of a huge naked foot, apparently of a biped, and in stride closely resembling my own tracks. What was it? I was very interested, and at once proceeded to take some photographs. I was engaged in this work when the porters joined me. It was at once evident when they saw the tracks that they were frightened. Wangdi was the first to speak.

"Bad Manshi!" he said, and then "Mirka!" And in case I still did not understand, "Kang Admi (Snowman)."

I had already anticipated such a reply and to reassure him and the other two, for I had no wish for my expedition to end prematurely, I said it must be a bear or snow leopard. But Wangdi would have none of this and explained at length how the tracks could not possibly be those of a bear, snow leopard, wolf or any other animal. Had he not seen many such tracks in the past? It was the Snowman, and he looked uneasily about him.

I am not superstitious. The number thirteen even in conjunction with a Friday means nothing to me. I do not hesitate to walk under a ladder unless there is the danger of a paintpot falling on my head. Crossed knives, spilled salt, sailors drowning when glasses are made to ring, black cats, new moons seen through glass, chimney sweeps and suchlike manifestations leave me unmoved. But there was something queer, and I must admit that Wangdi's argument and fear were not without their effect. The matter must be investigated. So I got out of my rucksack a copy of the *Spectator* and with a pencil proceeded to mark the size and stride of the track, while the men huddled together, a prey to that curious sullenness which in the Tibetan means fear.

About four inches of snow had fallen recently, and it was obvious that the tracks had been made the previous evening after the sun had lost its power and had frozen during the night, for they were perfect impressions distinct in every detail. On the level the footmarks were as much as 13 inches in length and 6 inches in breadth, but uphill they averaged only 8 inches in length, though the breadth was the same. The stride was from 18 inches to 2 feet on the level, but considerably less uphill, and the footmarks were turned outward at about the same angle as a man's. There were the well-defined imprints of five toes, 1½ inches to 1¾ inches long and ¾ inch broad, which, unlike human toes, were arranged symmetrically. Lastly there was at first sight what appeared to be the impression of a heel, with two curious toelike impressions on either side.

Presently the men plucked up courage and assisted me. They were unanimous that the Snowman walked with his toes behind him and that the impressions at the heel were in reality the front toes. I was soon able to disprove this to my own satisfaction by discovering a place where the beast had jumped down from some rocks, making deep impressions where he had landed, and slithering a little in the snow. Superstition, however, knows no logic, and my explanation produced no effect whatever on Wangdi. At length, having taken all the photographs I wanted on the pass, I asked the men to accompany me and follow up the tracks. They were very averse to this at first, but eventually agreed, as they said, following their own "logic," that the Snowman had come from, not gone, in that direction. From the pass the tracks followed a broad, slightly ascending snow ridge and, except for one divergence, took an almost straight line. After some 300 yards they turned off the ridge and descended a steep rock face fully 1,000 feet high seamed with snow gullies. Through my monocular glass I was able to follow them down to a small but considerably crevassed glacier, descending toward the Bhyundar Valley, and down this to the lowermost limit of the new snow. I was much impressed by the difficulties overcome and the intelligence displayed in overcoming them. In order to descend the face, the beast had made a series of intricate traverses and had zigzagged down a series of ridges and gullies. His track down the glacier was masterly, and from our perch I could see every detail and how cunningly he had avoided concealed snow-covered crevasses. An expert mountaineer could not have made a better route and to have accomplished it without an ice axe would have been both difficult and dangerous, while the unroped descent of a crevassed snow-covered glacier must be accounted as unjustifiable. Obviously the Snowman was well qualified for membership in the Himalayan Club.

My examination in this direction completed, we returned to the pass, and I decided to follow the track in the reverse direction. The men, however, said that this was the direction in which the Snowman was going, and if we overtook him, and even so much as set eyes upon him, we should all drop dead in our tracks, or come to an otherwise bad end. They were so scared at the prospect that I felt it was unfair to force them to accompany me, though I believe that Wangdi, at least, would have done so had I asked him.

The tracks, to begin with, traversed along the side of a rough rock ridge below the minor point we had ascended when we first visited the pass. I followed them for a short distance along the snow to one side of the rocks, then they turned upward into the mouth of a small cave under some slabs. I was puzzled to account for the fact that, whereas tracks appeared to come out of the cave, there were none going into it. I had already proved to my own satisfaction the absurdity of the porters' contention that the Snowman walked with his toes behind him; still, I was now alone and cut off from sight of the porters by a mist that had suddenly formed, and I could not altogether repress a ridiculous feeling that perhaps they were right after all; such is the power of superstition high up in the lonely Himalayas. I am ashamed to admit that I stood at a distance from the cave and threw a lump of rock into it before venturing further. Nothing happened, so I went up to the mouth of the cave and looked inside; naturally there was nothing there. I then saw that the single track was explained by the beast having climbed down a steep rock and jumped into the snow at the mouth of the cave. I lost the track among the rocks, so climbed up to the little summit we had previously visited. The mist was now dense and I waited fully a quarter of an hour for it to clear. It was a curious experience seated there with no other human being within sight, and some queer thoughts passed through my mind. Was there really a Snowman? If so, would I encounter him? If I did an ice axe would be a poor substitute for a rifle, but Wangdi had said that even to see a Snowman was to die. Evidently he killed you by some miraculous hypnotism; then presumably gobbled you up. It was a fairy tale come to life.

Then, at last, the mists blew aside. At first I could see no tracks coming off the rock island on which I was seated, and this was not only puzzling but disturbing, as it implied that the beast might be lurking in the rear vicinity. Then I saw that the tracks traversed a narrow and almost concealed ridge to another rock point, and beyond this descended a glacier to the east of our ascending route to the pass. Whatever it was, it lived in the Bhyundar Valley; but why had it left this pleasant valley for these inhospitable altitudes, which involved difficult and dangerous climbing, and an ascent of many thousands of feet?

Meditating on this strange affair, I returned to the porters, who were unfeignedly glad to see me, for they had assumed that I was walking to my death. I must now refer to the subsequent history of this business.

On returning to the base camp some days later, the porters made a statement. It was witnessed by Oliver and runs as follows:

"We, Wangdi Nurbu, Nurbu Bhotia and Pasang Urgen, porters employed by Mr. F. S. Smythe, were accompanying Mr. Smythe on July 17th over a glacier pass north of the Bhyundar Valley when we saw on the pass tracks which we knew to be those of a Mirka or Jungli Admi (wild man). We have often seen bear, snow leopard and other animal tracks, but we swear that these tracks were none of these, but were the tracks of a Mirka.

"We told Mr. Smythe that these were the tracks of a Mirka and we saw him take photographs and make measurements. We have never seen a Mirka because anyone who sees one dies or is killed, but there are pictures of the tracks, which are the same as we have seen, in Tibetan monasteries."

My photographs were developed by Kodak Ltd. of Bombay under conditions that precluded any subsequent accusation of faking and, together with my measurements and observations, were sent to my literary agent, Mr. Leonard P. Moore, who was instrumental in having them examined by Professor Julian Huxley, Secretary of the Zoological Society, Mr. Martin A. C. Hinton, Keeper of Zoology at the Natural History Museum, and Mr. R. I. Pocock. The conclusion reached by these experts was that the tracks were made by a bear. At first, due to a misunderstanding as to the exact locality in which the tracks had been seen, the bear was said to be *Ursus Arctos Pruinosus,* but subsequently it was decided that it was *Ursus Arctos Isabellinus,* which is distributed throughout the western and central Himalayas. The tracks agreed in size and character with that animal and there is no reason to suppose that they could have been made by anything else. This bear sometimes grows as large, or larger, than a grizzly, and there is a well-grown specimen in the Natural History Museum. It also varies in color from brown to silver-gray.

That the tracks appeared to have been made by a biped comes from the fact that this bear, like all bears, puts its rear foot at the rear end of the impression left by its front foot. Only the side toes would show, and this explains the Tibetans' belief that the curious indentations, in reality superimposed by the rear foot, are the front toes of a Snowman who walks with his toes behind him. This also explains the size of the spoor, which when melted out by the sun would appear enormous. Mr. Eric Shipton describes some tracks he saw near the peak of Nanda Ghunti in Garhwal as resembling those of a young elephant. So also would the tracks I saw when the sun had melted them away at the edges.

How did the legend originate? It is known over a considerable portion of Tibet, in Sikkim and parts of Nepal, including the Sola Khombu Valley, the home of the Sherpas on the south side of the Himalayas. The reason for this probably lies in the comparative ease of communication on the Tibetan plateau, as compared with that in the more mountainous regions south of the Himalayan watershed, where it is known only to peoples of Buddhist faith, such as the Sherpas of Nepal and the Lepchas of Sikkim. The Snowman is reputed to be large, fierce, and carnivorous; the large ones eat yaks and the small ones men. He is sometimes white, and sometimes black or brown. About the female, the most definite account I have heard is that she is only less fierce than the male, but is hampered in her movements by exceptionally large pendulous breasts, which she must perforce sling over her shoulders when walking or running.

Of recent years considerable force has been lent to the legend by Europeans having seen strange tracks in the snow, sometimes far above the permanent snowline, apparently of a biped. Such tracks had in all cases been spoiled or partially spoiled by the sun, but if such tracks were made by bears, then it is obvious that bears very seldom wander on to the upper snows, otherwise fresh tracks unmelted by the sun would have been observed by travelers. The movements of animals are incalculable, and there seems no logical explanation as to why a bear should venture far from its haunts of woodland and pasture. There is one point in connection with this which may have an important bearing on the tracks we saw, which I have omitted previously in order to bring it in at this juncture. On the way up the Bhyundar Valley from the base camp, I saw a bear about 200 yards distant on the northern slopes of the valley. It bolted immediately, and so quickly that I did not catch more than a glimpse of it, and disappeared into a small cave under an overhanging crag. When the men, who were behind, came up with me, I suggested that we should try to coax it into the open, in order that I could photograph it, so the men threw stones into the cave while I stood by with my camera. But the bear was not to be scared out so easily, and as I had no rifle it was not advisable to approach too near to the cave. Is it possible that we so scared this bear that the same evening it made up the hillside some 4,000 feet to the pass? There are two objections to this theory: firstly, that it appeared to be the ordinary small black bear, and too small to make tracks of the size we saw and, secondly, that the tracks ascended the glacier fully a mile to the east of the point where we saw the bear. We may, however, have unwittingly disturbed another and larger bear during our ascent to our camp. At all events, it is logical to assume that an animal would not venture so far from its native haunts without some strong motive to impel it. One last and very interesting point—The Sikh surveyor whom I had met in the Bhyundar Valley was reported by the Postmaster of Joshimath as having seen a huge white bear in the neighborhood of the Bhyundar Valley.

It seems possible that the Snowman legend originated through certain traders who saw bears when crossing the passes over the Himalayas and carried their stories into Tibet, where they became magnified and distorted by the people of that superstitious country which, though Buddhist in theory, has never emancipated itself from ancient nature and devil worship. Whether or not bears exist on the Tibetan side of the Himalayas I cannot say. It is probable that they do in comparatively low and densely forested valleys such as the Kharta and Kharma Valleys east of Mount Everest, and it may be that they are distributed more widely than is at present known.

After my return to England I wrote an article, which was published by *The Times,* in which I narrated my experiences and put forward my conclusions, which were based, of course, on the identifications of the zoological experts.

I must confess that this article was provocative, not to say dogmatic, but until it was published I had no idea that the Abominable Snowman, as he is popularly known, is as much beloved by the great British public as the sea serpent and the Loch Ness Monster. Indeed, in debunking what had become an institution, I roused a hornet's nest about my ears. It was even proposed by one gentleman in a letter to *The Times* that the Royal Geographical Society and the Alpine Club should send a joint expedition to the Himalayas in an attempt to prove or disprove my observations and conclusions. It was obvious that the writer hoped that this expedition, if it took place, would not only disprove them, but would prove the existence of the Abominable Snowman. I can only say in extenuation of my crime that I hope there is an Abominable Snowman. The tracks I saw were undoubtedly made by a bear, but what if other tracks seen by other people were made by Abominable Snowmen? I hope they were. In this murky age of materialism, human beings have to struggle hard to find the romantic, and what could be more romantic than an Abominable Snowman, together with an Abominable Snow-woman, and, not least of all, an Abominable Snow-baby?

OF MOUNTAINS AND MICE

FROM *Philosophical Dictionary*

VOLTAIRE

When François Marie Arouet de Voltaire was born in 1694, Louis XIV was absolute ruler of France; eleven years after he died the French Revolution destroyed forever the royal fable of divine right to tyranny. If the responsibility for that epochal shift can be laid to any one man, it would be Voltaire. His caustic wit won him exile, imprisonment, and an unchallenged position as the intellectual leader of Europe. He wrote plays, histories, philosophical pamphlets under his own and assumed names, whose repeated themes were freedom and tolerance.

In his *Philosophical Dictionary,* an alphabetical collection of opinions ranging from "Appearance," to "Climate," to "Luxury," to "War," we have this adroit interpretation of the fable of the mountain which gave birth to a mouse.

IT IS A VERY OLD, VERY UNIVERSAL FABLE THAT TELLS OF THE MOUNTAIN WHICH, having frightened all the countryside by its outcry that it was in labour, was hissed by all present when it brought into the world a mere mouse. The people in the pit were not philosophers. Those who hissed should have admired. It was as fine for the mountain to give birth to a mouse, as for the mouse to give birth to a mountain. A rock which produces a rat is a very prodigious thing; and never has the world seen anything approaching this miracle. All the globes of the universe could not call a fly into existence. Where the vulgar laugh, the philosopher admires; and he laughs where the vulgar open their big, stupid eyes in astonishment.

WOLF SONG

FROM *Driftwood Valley*

THEODORA C. STANWELL-FLETCHER

The writer and J., her artist husband, lived for two years in northern British Columbia, still so far off the beaten path that enormous stretches have not been penetrated—a virgin land of forest and mountain peaks, many still unnamed and unmapped, of animals and birds undisturbed except by natural forces and the rare Indian traveler. They lived on the country, camped and traveled in the same way as the Indians did. They were young and in love and bewitched by the stillness and the solitude, and their book *Driftwood Valley* gives the reader the lyric quality of their feeling about themselves and their wilderness.

LAST NIGHT WE HEARD THE LOVE SONG OF THE WOLF! THERE HAD BEEN FRESH snow followed by clear sky and a full brilliant moon. Our thermometer stood at 24 below. I proposed a snowshoe hike to Wolf Hill on the chance that we might be able to observe wolves down on the lake. J. scouted the notion of actually seeing them, but the night was so beautiful that he couldn't resist the idea any more than I could.

We stepped out in a dazzling world. At least a foot of new powdery snow covered the firm six-foot snow level and made ideal snowshoeing. We traveled swiftly and silently through silver glens and black shadows. Our snowshoes kicked up feathery clouds that twinkled like quicksilver. Our breath froze over jackets and caps and hair so that we were dressed from head to toe in white crystals.

When we reached the top of Wolf Hill, all below us spread the Driftwood Valley, clear as noontime, lit by the moon for a hundred miles, still and primeval as in the days before the few men who know it now had ever seen it. Belts of dark forest were interspersed by willow swamps which, deeply buried, lay like open fields brushed with gold. To the south the mountains of Takla were faint blue in the distance. The jagged, tumbled Frypans jutted like silver spearheads into the deep amethyst, star-studded sky. The Driftwoods, our own mountains, lay serene and golden, so close that we could almost reach out and touch them. The glacial-covered range far behind to the west showed distinctly, and the Bear Lake Mountains stood sharp and shining all around the northern horizon. Finally we moved across to the east side where a rock precipice falls down to Wolf Lake, crisscrossed with fresh black tracks, and looked on the miles of forested hills that rise gradually to the rolling Ominecas.

Utter silence, a deathlike hush over the land, and then, from somewhere below, came a sound that made our hearts stand still. Like a breath of wind, rising slowly, softly, clearly to a high, lovely note of sadness and longing; dying down on two distinct notes so low that our human ears could scarcely catch them. It rose and died, again and again. A wolf singing the beauty of the night, singing it as no human voice had ever done, calling on a mate to share the beauty of it with him, to come to him, to love him. Over and over it sang, so tenderly and exquisitely that it seemed as if the voice were calling to me and I could hardly keep from crying. The whole wilderness was musical with it. After an interval—I have no idea whether it was short or long—from far away across the eastern hills came a soft, distinct, answering call. Three times more the wolf below us sang and was answered. Gradually the other voice grew nearer and nearer, until we thought that the two must have come together, for the sudden quiet was not broken again.

Then I knew that I was shivering like a leaf and my arm, which J. had been grasping, was almost paralyzed.

J. was cussing to himself and saying: "Gad, what luck! What marvelous luck! I've heard wolves howling in India and the Arctic, but I never heard the like of that! Let's go home—if we're not too cold to move."

On the west, Wolf Hill slopes steeply, almost perpendicularly, for several hundred feet, and is clear of trees. Spurred to recklessness by the height of our emotions, we did something that we've never dreamed of daring to do before. We sat on the crossed heels of our snowshoes and tobogganed down the icy slope at terrific speed. Powdered snow flew up in clouds and turned to rainbows where the moon shone through it. That we arrived, unscathed, in a drift below, instead of being smashed to bits against trees, was just a part of the magic of the night.

We reached the warm cabin after midnight, stoked up a roaring fire, and drank hot scalding cocoa. I hardly remember getting into bed and to sleep, but all night in my dreams I thought I could hear a wolf calling and singing and sobbing in a voice of exquisite tenderness.

DREAM OF DEATH ON A MOUNTAIN

FROM *Modern Man in Search of a Soul*

C . G . J U N G

When Freud in the last century developed his theory of the unconscious to explain the workings of the mind, and attempted to apply scientific criteria to dreams and their interpretations, he was following a track which reaches back into prehistory. Dream study has its myths in all cultures.

Freud's method analyzes a patient's dreams and phantasies in terms of his past life to explain a situation in the present. Jungian psychology uses dreams not only to interpret a present situation but to anticipate a future pattern of behavior. Jung was a Swiss psychologist who contributed the association test to modern psychology. In this extract from his writings we have the Jungian method applied to interpreting a dream of a mountain.

DREAMS CONTAIN MORE THAN PRACTICAL HELPS FOR THE DOCTOR, DREAM-analysis deserves very special consideration. Sometimes, indeed, it is a matter of life and death.

Among many cases of this sort, I have been especially impressed with one that concerned a colleague of mine in Zürich. He was a man somewhat older than myself whom I saw from time to time, and who always teased me on these occasions about my interest in dream-interpretation. I met him one day in the street, and he called out to me: "How are things going? Are you still interpreting dreams? By the way, I've had another idiotic dream. Does it mean something too?" He had dreamed as follows: "I am climbing a high mountain over steep, snow-covered slopes. I mount higher and higher—it is marvellous weather. The higher I climb, the better I feel. I think: 'If only I could go on climbing like this for ever!' When I reach the summit, my happiness and elation are so strong that I feel I could mount right up into space. And I discover that I actually can do this. I go on climbing on empty air. I awake in a real ecstasy." When he had told me his dream, I said: "My dear man, I know you can't give up mountaineering, but let me implore you not to go alone from now on. When you go, take two guides, and you must promise on your word of honour to follow their directions." "Incorrigible!" he replied laughing, and said good-bye. I never saw him again. Two months later came the first blow. When out alone, he was buried by an avalanche, but was dug out in the nick of time by a military patrol which happened to come along. Three months after this the end came. He went on a climb accompanied by a younger friend, but without guides. An alpinist standing below saw him literally step out into the air as he was letting himself down a rock wall. He fell on to the head of his friend, who was waiting beneath him, and both were dashed to pieces far below. That was *ecstasis* in the full meaning of the word.

No amount of scepticism and critical reserve has ever enabled me to regard dreams as negligible occurrences. Often enough they appear senseless, but it is obviously we who lack the sense and the ingenuity to read the enigmatical message from the nocturnal realm of the psyche.

TROLLS

FROM *Kristin Lavransdatter*

SIGRID UNDSET

Sigrid Undset is that strange figure, a writer of indisputable greatness who is not at home in her own world. There is a massive gloominess of spirit which broods over all her work, deriving, it is probable, from her conviction that the good life must be built on faith and authority rather than knowledge and experience, and that man's destiny is determined in the last instance by forces he can never hope to understand. It is perhaps this belief, so out of tune with modern thinking, that makes her novels of thirteenth and fourteenth century Norway so superior to her novels of contemporary life.

Kristin Lavransdatter, from which this selection is taken, is her major work, a magnificent novel which, in resurrecting the people of a little-known period, brings them to life with the insights of modern psychology.

KRISTIN HAD EVER THOUGHT THAT COULD SHE BUT WIN OVER THE TOP OF THE home-fells she would look down upon another parish like their own, with tilled farms and dwellings, and 'twas great wonder to her now to see how far it was betwixt the places where folks dwelt. She saw the small yellow and green flecks down below in the dale-bottom, and the tiny clearings with their grey dots of houses amid the hill forests; she began to take tale of them, but when she had reckoned three times twelve, she could keep count of them no longer. Yet the human dwelling-places were as nothing in that waste.

She knew that in the wild woods wolves and bears lorded it, and that under every stone there dwelt trolls and goblins and elfinfolk, and she was afraid, for no one knew the number of them, but there must be many times more of them than of Christian men and women. Then she called aloud on her father, but he could not hear, for the blowing of the wind— he and his men were busy rolling heavy stones up the bare mountain top to pile round the timbers of the beacon.

But Isrid came to the children and showed Kristin where the fell west of

Vaage lay. And Arne pointed out the Grayfell, where folk from the parish took reindeer in pits, and where the King's falcon-catchers lay in stone huts. That was a trade Arne thought to take to some day—but if he did he would learn as well to train the birds for the chase—and he held his arms aloft as though to cast a hawk.

Isrid shook her head.

"'Tis a hard and evil life, that, Arne Gyrdsön—'twould be a heavy sorrow for your mother, boy, should you ever come to be a falcon-catcher. None may earn his bread in those wild hills except he join in fellowship with the worst of men—aye, and with them that are worse still."

Lavrans had come toward them and had heard this last word: "Aye," says he, "there's more than one hide of land in there that pays neither tax nor tithe—"

"Yes, many a thing must you have seen," said Isrid coaxingly, "you who fare so far afield—"

"Aye, aye," said Lavrans slowly. "Maybe—but methinks 'tis well not to speak of such things overmuch. One should not, I say, grudge folks who have lost their peace in the parish, whatever peace they can find among the fells. Yet have I seen yellow fields and brave meadows where few folk know that such things be, and herds have I seen of cattle and small stock, but of these I know not whether they belonged to mankind or to other folk—"

"Oh! aye," says Isrid. "Bears and wolves get the blame for the beasts that are missed from the sæters here, but there are worse thieves among the fells than they."

"Do you call them worse?" asked Lavrans thoughtfully, stroking his daughter's cap. "In the hills to the south under the Boar Fells I once saw three little lads, and the greatest was even as Kristin here—yellow hair they had, and coats of skin. They gnashed their teeth at me like wolf-cubs before they ran to hide. 'Twere little wonder if the poor man who owned them were fain to lift a cow or two—"

"Oh! both wolves and bears have young," says Isrid testily. "And you spare not them, Lavrans, neither them nor their young. Yet they have no lore of law nor of Christendom, as have these evil-doers you wish so well to—"

"Think you I wish them too well, because I wish them a little better than the worst?" said Lavrans, smiling a little. "But come now, let us see what cheer Ragnfrid has sent with us to-day." He took Kristin by the hand and led her with him. And as they went he bent and said softly: "I thought of your three small brothers, little Kristin."

They peeped into the watch-house, but it was close in there and smelt of mould. Kristin took a look around, but there were only some earthen benches about the walls, a hearth-stone in the middle of the floor, and some barrels of tar and faggots of pine-roots and birch-bark. Lavrans thought 'twould be best they should eat without doors, and a little way down among the birches they found a fine piece of green-sward.

The pack horse was unloaded, and they stretched themselves upon the grass. In the wallets Ragnfrid had given them was plenty food of the best— soft bread and bannocks, butter and cheese, pork and wind-dried reindeer meat, lard, boiled brisket of beef, two kegs with German beer, and of mead a little jar. The carving of the meat and portioning it round went quickly, while Halvdan, the oldest of the men, struck fire and made a blaze—it was safer to have a good fire out here in the woods.

Isrid and Arne gathered heather and dwarf-birch and cast it on the blaze. It crackled as the fire tore the fresh green from the twigs, and small white flakes flew high upon the wisps of red flame; the smoke whirled thick and black toward the clear sky. Kristin sat and watched; it seemed to her the fire was glad that it was out there, and free, and could play and frisk.'Twas other-wise than when, at home, it sat upon the hearth and must work at cooking food and giving light to the folks in the room.

She sat nestled by her father with one arm upon his knee; he gave her all she would have of the best, and bade her drink her fill of the beer and taste well of the mead.

"She will be so tipsy she'll never get down to the sæter on her feet," said Halvdan, laughing, but Lavrans stroked her round cheeks:

"Then here are folk enough who can bear her—it will do her good— drink you too, Arne—God's gifts do good, not harm, to you that are yet grow-ing—make sweet, red blood, and give deep sleep, and rouse not madness and folly—"

The men too drank often and deep; neither was Isrid backward. And soon their voices and the roar and crackle of the fire were but a far off hub-bub in Kristin's ears, and she began to grow heavy of head. She was still aware how they questioned Lavrans and would have him tell of the strange things he had met with when out a-hunting. But much he would not say; and this seemed to her so good and so safe—and then she had eaten so well.

Her father had a slice of soft barley-bread in his hands; he pinched small bits of it between his fingers into shapes of horses, and cutting shreds of meat, he set these astride the steeds and made them ride over his thigh and into Kristin's mouth. But soon she was so weary she could neither open her mouth nor chew—and so she sank back upon the ground and slept.

When she came to herself again, she was lying in a warm darkness within her father's arm—he had wrapped his cloak about them both. Kristin sat up, wiped the moisture from her face, and unloosed her cap that the air might dry her damp locks.

The day was surely far spent, for the sunlight was golden, and the shadows had lengthened and fell now toward the southeast. No breath of wind was stirring, and gnats and flies buzzed and swarmed about the group of sleeping men. Kristin sat stock still, scratched her gnat-bitten hands and gazed about her—the mountain-top above them shone white with moss and golden with lichen in the sunshine, and the pile of weather-beaten timber stood against the sky like the skeleton of some wondrous beast.

She grew ill at ease—it was so strange to see them all sleeping there in the naked daylight. At home if by hap she woke at night, she lay snug in the dark with her mother on the one side and on the other the tapestry stretched upon the wall. And then she knew that the chamber with its smoke-vent was shut and barred against the night and the weather without, and sounds of slumber came from the folk who lay soft and safe on the pillows twixt the skins. But all these bodies, lying twisted and bent on the hillside, about the little heap of black and white ashes, might well be dead—some lay upon their faces, some upon their backs with knees updrawn, and the noises that came from them scared her. Her father snored deeply, but when Halvdan drew a breath, it piped and whistled in his nose. And Arne lay upon his side, his face hidden on his arm, and his glossy, light-brown hair spread out amongst the heather; he lay so still Kristin grew afraid lest he be dead. She had to bend forward and touch him—and on this he turned a little in his sleep.

Kristin suddenly bethought her, maybe they had slept through the night and this was the next day—and this frightened her so that she shook her father; but he only grunted and slept on. Kristin herself was still heavy of head, but she dared not lie down to sleep again. And so she crept forward to the fire and raked in it with a stick—there were still some embers aglow beneath. She threw upon it heather and small twigs which she broke off round about her—she dared not pass the ring of sleepers to find bigger branches.

There came a rattling and crashing in the woods near by, and Kristin's heart sank and she went cold with fear. But then she spied a red shape amidst the trees, and Guldsveinen broke out of the thicket. He stood there and gazed upon her with his clear, bright eyes. She was so glad to see him, she leapt to her feet and ran to the stallion. And there, too, was the brown horse Arne had ridden, and the pack-horse as well. Now she felt safe and happy again; she went and patted them all three upon their flanks, but Guldsveinen bent his head so that she could reach up to fondle his cheeks, and pull his yellow-white forelock, while he nosed round her hands with his soft muzzle.

The horses wandered, feeding, down the birch-grown slope, and Kristin went with them—she felt there was naught to fear so long as she kept close to Guldsveinen—he had driven off a bear before now, she knew. And the bilberries grew so thick in here, and the child was thirsty now, with a bad taste in her mouth; the beer was not to her liking any more, but the sweet, juicy berries were good as wine. Away, on a scree, she saw raspberries growing too —so she grasped Guldsveinen by the mane, and sweetly bade him go there with her, and the stallion followed willingly with the little maid. Thus, as she wandered further and further down the hillside, he followed her when she called, and the other two horses followed Guldsveinen.

Somewhere near at hand she heard the gurgling and trickling of a beck; she followed the sound till she found it, and then lay out upon a great slab and washed her hot, gnat-bitten face and hands. Below the slab the water stood, a still, black pool, for over against it there rose a wall of rock behind some small birches and willows—it made the finest of mirrors, and Kristin leaned over and looked at herself in the water, for she wished to see whether 'twas true, as Isrid said, that she bore a likeness to her father.

She smiled and nodded and bent forward till her hair met the bright hair about the round, great-eyed child-face she saw in the beck.

Round about grew a great plenty of those gay, pink flower-clusters they name valerian—redder far and finer here by the fell-beck than at home by the river. Of these Kristin plucked and bound them about with grass, till she had woven herself the finest, thickest wreath of rose-pink. The child pressed it down on her head and ran to the pool to see how she looked now she was decked out like a grown maid who goes a dancing.

She stooped over the water and saw her own dark image rise from the bottom and grow clearer as it came to meet her—and then in the mirror of the pool she saw another figure standing among the birches opposite and bending toward her. In haste she got upon her knees and gazed across. At first she thought it was but the rock and the bushes clinging round its foot. But all at once she was aware of a face amid the leaves—there stood a lady, pale, with waving, flaxen hair—the great, light-grey eyes and wide, pink nostrils were like Guldsveinen's. She was clad in something light, leaf-green, and branches and twigs hid her up to the broad breasts which were covered over with brooches and sparkling chains.

The little girl gazed upon the figure; and as she gazed the lady raised a hand and showed her a wreath of golden flowers;—she beckoned with it.

Behind her Kristin heard Guldsveinen neigh loud in fear—she turned her head—the stallion reared, screaming till the echoes rang, then flung around and fled up the hill with a thunder of hoofs. The other horses followed—straight up the scree, while stones came rumbling down and boughs and roots broke and rattled.

Then Kristin screamed aloud. "Father," she shrieked, "father!" She gained her feet, tore after the horses and dared not look behind. She clambered up the scree, trod on the hem of her dress and slipped back downwards; climbed again, catching at the stones with bleeding hands, creeping on sore bruised knees, and crying now to Guldsveinen, now to her father—sweat started from every pore of her body and ran like water into her eyes, and her heart beat as though 'twould break against her ribs; while sobs of terror choked her throat:

"Oh father, oh father!"

Then his voice sounded somewhere above: she saw him come with great bounds down the scree—the bright, sunlit scree; birch and aspen stood along it and blinked from their small silvered leaves—the hillside was so quiet, so bright, while her father came leaping, calling her by name; and Kristin sank down and knew that now she was saved.

"Sancta Maria!" Lavrans knelt and clasped his daughter—he was pale and strange about the mouth, so that Kristin grew yet more afraid; 'twas as though only now in his face she read how great had been her peril.

"Child, child—" he lifted her bleeding hands, looked at them, saw the wreath upon her bare head, and touched it. "What is it—how came you hither, my little Kristin—?"

"I went with Guldsveinen," she sobbed upon his breast. "I got so afraid seeing you all asleep, but then Guldsveinen came—and then there was someone by the beck down yonder that beckoned me—"

"Who beckoned—was it a man?"

"No, 'twas a lady—she beckoned with a wreath of gold—I think 'twas the dwarf-maiden, father—"

"Jesus-Kristus," said Lavrans softly, and crossed himself and the child.

He helped her up the scree till they came to a grassy slope; then he lifted and bore her. She clung about his neck and sobbed—could not stop for all his soothing.

Soon they met the men and Isrid. The woman smote her hands together, when she heard what had befallen:

"Aye, 'twas the Elf-maiden sure enough—she would have lured the fair child into the mountain, trust you me."

"Hold your peace," bade Lavrans sternly. "Never should we have talked of such things here in the woods as we did—one knows not what may lie beneath the rocks and hearken to each word."

He drew the golden chain from out his shirt and hung it and the relic-holding cross about Kristin's neck and thrust them in upon her bare body.

HIGH COUNTRY

FROM *The Colorado*

FRANK WATERS

High Country is the Colorado basin where everything is bigger, deeper, lower than anywhere else in America—the peaks are higher, the canyons deeper, the deserts lower. It is the backbone of the continent, which we call the Rockies.

When the Frenchmen and Spaniards first saw the Rockies—from a distance—they called them the Shining Mountains. They got the name from the Cree Indians. The first Americans who saw the mountains called them the Stonies—they had to climb them.

Frank Waters writes of the Rockies he knew as a boy. Waters might be called an anthropologist, but of a peculiarly unacademic variety. His concern, as in this selection from his book *The Colorado*, is with the inner drama that lies beneath the surface of scientific observation.

NEXT TIME, BY HOOK OR CROOK, MAKE SURE YOU'RE BORN WITH A MOUNTAIN in the front yard. It comes in mighty handy all the way around.

When you're no bigger than *that* you can hang on to the grimy window curtains and watch it hour after hour. Then you know it best with all its moods and mutations, its sternness, dignity and immeasurable depth. It is like the face of an old medicine man, which only a child can understand. Other times it's just a grand spectacle of a thing—a whole show in itself. In the evening when the sun snags on the rimrock and the hollows fill up with red and lilac, damson blue and purple; when the summer storms explode against its shoulder like soap bubbles filled with father's pipe smoke, and the deer-horn lightning sprouts from the crags; or even in winter when its slopes turn slick and green as Blue Ribbon bottle glass.

But from the day you start to school it begins to be useful. The mountain has drawn back out of your yard, receded across the railroad tracks, even a mite farther. But like you it's got bigger too; you can see it even from behind the schoolhouse privy, so there's no need to worry about losing your way home. Just keep it on the right, on the side where you carry your back-pocket handkerchief. That's the rule to follow when you start camping out in the lower cañons; climb a tree if you can't see it. But besides being a compass the peak is a timekeeper and weather prophet too. A peek out the kitchen window to see what kind of clouds hang over the summit is the way folks always start the day. Later on, when you fancy yourself getting along a bit better than your neighbors, it's something to measure your success by; the peak is pretty chesty itself. Toward the last, of course, it's the best of all. When everything else seems gone and you're just another old fellow sitting alone on the stoop with your pipe, its big cone helps to fill up the heart's emptiness and you know it's one thing that won't pass.

A mountain peak, all in all, is about the handiest thing to have around and strike up friends with. Our mountain was a whopper, a beaut of a peak. We got along fine.

It poured gold into our laps, tons of it. In fact it built the town, both Millionaires' Row and the shanties of Poverty Row across the railroad tracks. It lent a dignity to all our lives, brought into them an enduring sense of mystery, and whetted our appetites with the sharp winds blowing down the Pass—which was no blessing to be sneezed at either, considering the hundreds of poor, sick, half-starved rich people who came to it for just that purpose.

Another thing, you didn't have to travel with the mountain so close. It was the whole world heaped up in layers.

There was the sandy, flat mesa, the first stairstep from the plains, with its garden of queerly eroded red rocks and its dust storms. Halfway up the peak at almost eleven thousand feet was timberline, drawn straight across it as if by a ruler. It separated two more distinct worlds.

Below it to the mesa was a dark and blue world: the forest world of leaf and needle with its silent shadows and singing streams, its chattering squirrels and gossiping magpies, its timid deer and shy brown bear. But like obedient citizens of that still lower world below tide level, none of them ventured upward. No stout exploring fir or spruce, not a single wind-stunted pine, scarcely a blade of grass. Only a mountain sheep sometimes stood poised on a crag, but for no longer than a seal rests on a rock before plunging back down into the green.

Above was a barren world of pink-gray stone—and man, that unbelievable creature to whom no domain is forbidden, even that of the spirit. This was the upper half of the peak that gave life and color to our town.

To reach it one rode the little Short Line that crawled a mile up and eighteen miles around the south slope of the peak. You knew you were getting close when a tourist's nose started bleeding and the ladies drew back dizzy from the windows. Suddenly there it was, unbelievable world: a half dozen little sprawling camps, small clumps of shacks and cabins that seemed to have been dropped out of the sky into the gulches, and everywhere, crowding the streets and littering the hillsides between them, the vast gray dumps and stark gallows frames of the mines. All hanging to an immense slope of rock seamed with great gulches.

Nothing could have been livelier, more entrancing and more pregnant with anticipation. Hills and gulches swarmed with men, burros and machinery. The birth of a monstrous mystery seemed imminent at every moment. Yet one famous and hasty visitor reported it a scene of appalling desolation, adding casually that no cat could live so high.

It was a challenging indictment. Timberline became Catline overnight, and every indignant miner's wife made haste to disprove it. Henceforth our lives were overrun with cats. By dozens they were sent up on the daily train. They roamed the streets and dumps like burros, made the nights hideous with noise, and finally went wild in the lower gulches. Unfortunately the visitor who had instigated the deluge had tarried only long enough to interview a certain Madam on the busiest street. To get even with him, the Town Council promptly renamed this, our local lane of prostitution, in his honor: "Julian Street."

It is a pity that Mr. Street did not remain longer. For the high country above timberline is like no other, and this was its boundary. In the absence of trees and foliage he would have seen here for the first time how everything stood out lucid and stark naked in new perspective. Like the weathered houses, the peeling log cabins, people's lives were stripped of decoration and verbiage by wind and weather. He would have noticed how everything tended to reduce down to stone. The faces of the men coming off shift were gray and colorless. The precious baubles in the parlor were heavy lead-gray samples, not needing roasting to bring out their hidden colors to the appreciative eye. Even the graves were blasted out of the hard granite with dynamite, that man could return not to dust but to stone.

A world, a life which even then seemed in the process of petrification. But still containing inside a hidden warmth. So watching on a winter's dawn the long queue of men plodding up the trail to the portal of a mine, a hasty stranger would be impressed only by the dominant drabness. He will not wait to see, a few minutes later, the window geraniums in their tin cans glowing like tiny fires lighted by the sun. He will not smell the yeasty buckwheat batter in the buckets set out after breakfast on every back stoop down the row of shanties. Nor see inside of an evening the walls livid pink in lamplight with the front sheets of the Denver Post papering the walls against cold. The tall peak itself is the core of an extinct volcano, and the running fire congealed in its veins still reflected the heat of desire which drew men here.

Everything, it seemed then, came from these high wastes of barren stone.

I remember being taken by Jake to an impressive evening's entertainment. We sat next to the plank runway built down the center aisle from the stage, so that Jake in high humor and with boastful familiarity could snap the garters of the beautiful dancing ladies who tripped past. One garter I remember well—and also my unfulfilled ambition to grow big and bold and rich enough to snap it myself. It was a flower that came from no mere vegetable garden, a constellation that had never shone in any midnight sky. It was a beribboned rosette as big as Jake's fist and full of rhinestones and rubies and sapphires and diamonds. It was the most beautiful and vulgar, the most exquisite bad taste, the—"But, Jake, where did it come from? I never seen—"

The huge black-stockinged leg raised and pivoted over our heads, graceful as the steel arm of a crane. There was the close flash of light, color, ribbon and lace, the lusty wink of a dimpled knee, a raucous laugh. Jake made an ineffectual grab, and sank surlily back; it was a man behind him who was allowed to be successful. Girl and garter swept past.

"From the fourth level of the *Sylvanite!* Where the hell do you think it came from?" But Jake's habitual good temper was curiously out of whack; he might have spoken wildly. For certainly neither the fifth nor the sixth level of our mine ever produced anything to compare with it.

But all this, camp and people, still straddled timberline. It was still linked to the lower forested cañons, to the town below.

Our family folly lay even higher. Grandfather called it a mine though he had developed too many good ones to thus misname it. You could see it from the high saddle above the camp, a mere black speck far up the gulch. A bird could wing there in ten minutes. It took a boy on a burro an hour and a half. But if he waited at the station and rode up in the wagon with the supplies it was three hours up.

The speck had grown by the time he got there. There was the great gallows frame bestriding the shaft, a stout log cabin, and a small lean-to and corral of weathered aspen poles. And every great squared timber, every seasoned log and green pole, every stick of firewood, every nail—to say nothing of winch, steel cable and tools for the mine—had been snaked up here by mule and burro. One felt, upon looking downward upon camp and the dark slopes dropping from it, like a swallow resting on the side of a cliff.

Looking upward was worse. You were confronted with a steep terrain of bare frost-shattered granite that rose upward over two thousand feet. Nothing could convince the boy that this was the majestic, familiar peak he had seen from below since childhood. It lacked shape, outline and character. He simply felt imprisoned between sky and earth in a waste of stone. The feeling grew more oppressive daily.

There was no sound of rushing water, nor the sough of wind through pines. There was no smell of living green. No color relieved the surrounding monotone of rock. Only occasionally from deep underground rose a muffled roar, and at night there were new samples to assay. Here in this solitary little world of Grandfather, Abe and Jake, one lived a life of stone.

One blasted it, worked it, dug its dust out of ears and eyes. One cursed it, blessed it, prayed for it. It crawled into the blankets and into the dreams of night. It was at once the bane of your life and a resplendent future that at any crosscut might come to pass. For all that it was merely dead stone.

Then suddenly it happened, the boy did not know how. All this dead stone became intensely, vibrantly alive. Playing on the dump one morning after he had washed the breakfast dishes, he happened to pick up a pinch. In the bright sunlight he saw with microscopic clarity the infinitesimal shapes and colors, the monstrous and miraculous complexity of that single thimbleful of sand. In that instant the world about him took on a new, great and terrifying meaning. Every stone, every enormous boulder fitted into a close-knit unity similar to the one in his sweaty palm. For the first time he saw their own queer and individual shapes, their subtle colors, knew their textures, felt their weight, their strain and stress. It was as if in one instant the whole mountain had become alive and known.

No longer did the nightly assays seem meaningless chores carried out by a perpetually disappointed, white-haired old man and two gaunt, patient helpers. They took on the mystery of rituals that constantly attempted to evoke some deep hidden life within the stone. Each sample brought up from below, the boy eagerly rushed to examine. How did it differ from those on top—these cold, wet pieces wrenched from deep in the bowels of the peak?

"By cracky, the boy's got the makin' of a hard-rock miner!" grinned Jake.

"Dom fool!" snorted Grandfather. "What's he expect—nuggets as big as marbles?"

Late at night, tossing sleeplessly in his bunk, the boy kept wondering. The mountain was not one great big solid rock as it appeared from below. It was a million, trillion pieces all held together without cement: some hard, some soft, in all shapes and patterns, burned brown on the outside and gray inside, some with a purplish streak, but all with a preponderant delicate pink tinge against the snow. But it had lost its benign personality. It reflected a monstrous, impersonal force that pressed him from all sides. He was suddenly, mightily afraid.

"What keeps the Peak from fallin' down on us?" he blurted out in darkness. "I mean—"

From Abe's bunk came the usual silence. Jake let out another snore. But suddenly from across the room came two testy words in answer. "Isostatic equilibrium!" And then a moment later, "God Almighty, this time of night!"

Isostatic equilibrium: it haunted him for years, both the phrase and its ultimate meaning. And not until long afterward did he realize that each of us has his own vocabulary for even Him who made the Word.

Thus he came to know that high realm of rock, the peak itself. Week after week the snowcap steadily receded. By day the drifts melted and trickled down into the cracks and crevices. By night the water froze and wedged the rocks apart. One heard, if only in his imagination, an eternity of sharp reports and booming explosions when the boulders finally split asunder. But to all this expansion and contraction, the rhythmic pulse of constant change, the peak remained immutable, bigger than the sum of its parts.

There came the day when the boy stood on its summit. For only a few moments the foothills, mesas, and the vast flat plains spread out 7,000 feet below to orient him to faraway Kansas and the Universe. Then mists swept up to cloak the forested cañons on all sides; it began to rain. He was standing—isostatic equilibrium to the contrary—on an island of rock floating in the sky. Far off toward Utah was another, and still another like a stepping-stone into Wyoming. It was as it might have been at the Emergence. Or perhaps as it will be at the end of another paragraph in their geological biography when they will be the last to disappear. The feeling was indefinable. He did not know it, but it expressed at best the timelessness which is the core of that we know as time.

ROCKY MOUNTAIN GOAT

HOME FROM THE
MOUNTAIN

FROM *The Web and the Rock*

THOMAS WOLFE

In the flood of words which erupted from Thomas Wolfe during the short span of his life and his writing, one can find some of the noblest prose that ever came out of America. He taught at New York University during the day and wrote all night, living on coffee, canned beans, and cigarettes. In his three novels Wolfe wrote a massive biography of the lonely man. It was his own biography only by indirection. "Loneliness is stamped on the American face," he said. And in this selection from his *The Web and the Rock* we have the theme which dominated and obsessed him. His mountain was an escape from the terrible solitude of people grouped together who have never learned how to reach out to each other to communicate.

THE MOUNTAINS IN THE WINTERTIME HAD A STERN AND DEMONIC QUALITY OF savage joy that was, in its own way, as strangely, wildly haunting as all of the magic and the gold of April. In Spring, or in the time-enchanted spell and drowse of full, deep Summer, there was always something far and lonely, haunting with ecstasy and sorrow, desolation and the intolerable, numb exultancy of some huge, impending happiness. It was a cow bell, drowsy, far and broken in a gust of wind, as it came to him faintly from the far depth and distance of a mountain valley; the receding whistle-wail of a departing train, as it rushed eastward, seaward, towards the city, through some green mountain valley of the South; or a cloud shadow passing on the massed green of the wilderness, and the animate stillness, the thousand sudden, thrumming, drumming, stitching, unseen little voices in the lyric mystery of tangled undergrowth about him.

His uncle and he would go toiling up the mountain side, sometimes striding over rutted, clay-caked, and frost-hardened roads, sometimes beating their way downhill, with as bold and wild a joy as wilderness explorers ever knew, smashing their way through the dry and brittle undergrowth of barren Winter, hearing the dry report of bough and twig beneath their feet, the masty spring and crackle of brown ancient leaves, and brown pine needles, the elastic, bedded compost of a hundred buried and forgotten Winters.

Meanwhile, all about them, the great trees of the mountain side, at once ruggedly familiar and strangely, hauntingly austere, rose grim and barren, as stern and wild and lonely as the savage winds that warred forever, with a remote, demented howling, in their stormy, tossed, and leafless branches.

And above them the stormy wintry skies—sometimes a savage sky of wild, torn grey that came so low its scudding fringes whipped like rags of smoke around the mountain tops; sometimes an implacable, fierce sky of wintry grey; sometimes a sky of rags and tatters of wild, wintry light, westering into slashed stripes of rugged red and incredible wild gold at the gateways of the sun—bent over them forever with that same savage and unutterable pain and sorrow, that ecstasy of wild desire, that grief of desolation, that spirit of exultant joy, that was as gleeful, mad, fierce, lonely, and enchanted with its stormy and unbodied promises of flight, its mad swoopings through the dark over the whole vast sleeping wintriness of earth, as that stormy and maniacal wind, which seemed, in fact, to be the very spirit of the joy, the sorrow, and the wild desire he felt.

That wind would rush upon them suddenly as they toiled up rocky trails, or smashed through wintry growth, or strode along the hardened, rutted roads, or came out on the lonely, treeless bareness of a mountain top. And that wind would rush upon him with its own wild life and fill him with its spirit. As he gulped it down into his aching lungs, his whole life seemed to soar, to swoop, to yell with the demonic power, flight, and invincible caprice of the wind's huge well until he no longer was nothing but a boy of fifteen, the nephew of a hardware merchant in a little town, one of the nameless little atoms of this huge, swarming earth whose most modest dream would have seemed ridiculous to older people had he dared to speak of it.

No. Under the immense intoxication of that great, demented wind, he would become instantly triumphant to all this damning and overwhelming evidence of fact, age, prospect, and position. He was a child of fifteen no longer. He was the overlord of this great earth, and he looked down from the mountain top upon his native town, a conqueror. Not from the limits of a little, wintry town, lost in remote and lonely hills from the great heart, the time-enchanted drone and distant murmur of the shining city of this earth, but from the very peak and center of this world he looked forth on his domains with the joy of certitude and victory, and he knew that everything on earth that he desired was his.

Saddled in power upon the wild back of that maniacal force, not less wild, willful, and all-conquering than the steed that carried him, he would hold the kingdoms of the earth in fee, inhabit the world at his caprice, swoop in the darkness over mountains, rivers, plains, and cities, look under roofs, past walls and doors, into a million rooms, and know all things at once, and lie in darkness in some lonely and forgotten place with a woman, lavish, wild, and secret as the earth. The whole earth, its fairest fame of praise, its dearest treasure of a great success, its joy of travel, all its magic of strange lands, the relish of unknown, tempting foods, its highest happiness of adventure and love—would all be his: flight, storm, wandering, the great sea and all its traffic of proud ships, and the great plantation of the earth, together with the certitude and comfort of return—fence, door, wall, and roof, the single face and dwelling-place of love. . . .

But now, as the boy and his uncle stood there on the mountain top looking into the lonely vistas of the westering sun, watching its savage stripes of gold and red as it went down in the smoky loneliness and receding vistas of the great ranges of the west, the wind would fill the boy's heart with unwalled homelessness, a desire for houses, streets, and the familiar words again, a mighty longing for return.

For now black night, wild night, oncoming, secret, and mysterious night, with all its lonely wilderness of storm, demented cries, and unhoused wandering was striding towards them like an enemy. And around them on the lonely mountain top they heard the whistling of the wind in coarse, sere grasses, and from the darkening mountain side below them they could hear the remote howlings of the wind as it waged its stern, incessant warfare in the stormy branches of the bare and lonely trees.

And instantly he would see the town below, now coiling in a thousand fumes of homely smoke, now winking into a thousand points of friendly light its glorious small design, its aching, passionate assurances of walls, warmth, comfort, food, and love. It spoke to him of something deathless and invincible in the souls of men, like a small light in a most enormous dark that would not die. Then hope, hunger, longing, joy, a powerful desire to go down to the town again would fill his heart. For in the wild and stormy darkness of oncoming night there was no door, and the thought of staying there in darkness on the mountain top was not to be endured.

Then his uncle and he would go down the mountain side, taking the shortest, steepest way they knew, rushing back down to the known limits of the town, the streets, the houses, and the lights, with a sense of furious haste, hairbreadth escape, as if the great beast of the dark was prowling on their very heels.

THE DELECTABLE MOUNTAINS

FROM *Pilgrim's Progress*

JOHN BUNYAN

The mountain has always been the high place, symbol of the high reaches of the spirit toward which man climbs. John Bunyan's Pilgrim makes the slow and tortured ascent, as does every man in search for the meaning of his life.

Bunyan was born in 1628. He was a soldier in Cromwell's army, tinker, dissenting preacher. It was during his twelve years in prison for being a "common upholder of several unlawful meetings and conventicles, to the great disturbance and destruction of the good subjects of this Kingdom," that he wrote *Pilgrim's Progress*. For a century it was only the common people of England, for whom he preached, who read his work. Since then *Pilgrim's Progress* has been translated into every language and dialect; only the Bible has had a larger circulation. Perhaps it is because, as one critic puts it, "the pilgrimage is our own and we have met the people whom Bunyan saw in his dream, and are ourselves whom he describes" that the writing of this inspired Puritan tinker has so much meaning for our own time.

THEY WENT THEN TILL THEY CAME TO THE DELECTABLE MOUNTAINS, WHICH mountains belong to the Lord of that Hill of which we have spoken before; so they went up to the mountains, to behold the gardens and orchards, the vineyards and fountains of water; where also they drank, and washed themselves, and did freely eat of the vineyards. Now there were on the tops of these mountains shepherds feeding their flocks, and they stood by the highway side. The pilgrims therefore went to them, and leaning upon their staves (as is common with weary pilgrims, when they stand to talk with any by the way) they asked, Whose delectable mountains are these? And whose be the sheep that feed upon them?

Shepherds—These mountains are "Immanuel's Land," and they are within sight of his city; and the sheep also are his, and he laid down his life for them.

Christian—Is this the way to the Celestial City?

Shepherds—You are just in your way.

Christian—How far is it thither?

Shepherds—Too far for any but those that shall get thither indeed.

Christian—Is the way safe or dangerous?

Shepherds—Safe for those for whom it is to be safe, "but transgressors shall fall therein."

Christian—Is there in this place any relief for pilgrims that are weary and faint in the way?

Shepherds—The lord of these mountains hath given us a charge "not to be forgetful to entertain strangers"; therefore the good of the place is before you.

I saw also in my dream, that when the shepherds perceived that they were wayfaring men, they also put questions to them (to which they made answer as in other places), as, Whence came you? and, How got you into the way? and, By what means have you so persevered therein? For but few of them that begin to come hither do show their face on these mountains. But when the shepherds heard their answers, being pleased therewith, they looked very lovingly upon them, and said, Welcome to the Delectable Mountains.

The shepherds, I say, whose names were Knowledge, Experience, Watchful, and Sincere, took them by the hand, and had them to their tents, and made them partake of that which was ready at present. They said moreover, We would that ye should stay here a while, to be acquainted with us; and yet more to solace yourselves with the good of these delectable mountains. They then told them that they were content to stay; and so they went to their rest that night, because it was very late.

Then I saw in my dream, that in the morning the shepherds called up Christian and Hopeful to walk with them upon the mountains; so they went forth with them, and walked a while, having a pleasant prospect on every side. Then said the shepherds one to another, Shall we show these pilgrims some wonders? So when they had concluded to do it, they had them first to the top of a hill called Error, which was very steep on the furthest side, and bid them look down to the bottom. So Christian and Hopeful looked down, and saw at the bottom several men dashed all to pieces by a fall that they had from the top. Then said Christian, What meaneth this? The shepherds answered, Have you not heard of them that were made to err, by hearkening to Hymeneus and Philetus, as concerning the faith of the resurrection of the body? They answered, Yes. Then said the shepherds, Those that you see lie dashed in pieces at the bottom of this mountain are they; and they have continued to this day unburied (as you see) for an example to others to take heed how they clamber too high, or how they come too near the brink of this mountain.

Then I saw that they had them to the top of another mountain, and the name of that is Caution, and bid them look afar off; which when they did, they perceived, as they thought, several men walking up and down among the tombs that were there; and they perceived that the men were blind, because they stumbled sometimes upon the tombs, and because they could not get out from among them. Then said Christian, What means this?

The shepherds then answered, Did you not see a little below these mountains a stile, that led into a meadow, on the left hand of this way? They answered, Yes. Then said the shepherds, From that stile there goes a path that leads directly to Doubting Castle, which is kept by Giant Despair; and these men (pointing to them among the tombs) came once on pilgrimages as you do now, even till they came to that same stile; and because the right way was rough in that place, and they chose to go out of it into that meadow, and there were taken by Giant Despair and cast into Doubting Castle; where, after they had been awhile kept in the dungeon, he at last did put out their eyes, and led them among those tombs, where he has left them to wander to this very day, that the saying of the wise man might be fulfilled, "He that wandereth out of the way of understanding shall remain in the congregation of the dead." Then Christian and Hopeful looked upon one another, with tears gushing out, but yet said nothing to the shepherds.

Then I saw in my dream that the shepherds had them to another place, in a bottom, where was a door in the side of a hill, and they opened the door, and bid them look in. They looked in therefore, and saw that within it was very dark and smoky; they also thought that they heard there a rumbling noise as of fire, and a cry as of some tormented, and that they smelt the scent of brimstone. Then said Christian, What means this?

The shepherds told them, This is a by-way to hell, a way that hypocrites go in at; namely, such as sell their birth-right, with Esau; such as sell their Master, as Judas; such as blaspheme the Gospel, with Alexander; and that lie and dissemble, with Ananias and Sapphira his wife. Then said Hopeful to the shepherds, I perceive that these had on them, even every one, a show of pilgrimage, as we have now: had they not?

Shepherds—Yes, and held it a long time too.

Hopeful—How far might they go on in pilgrimage in their day, since they notwithstanding were thus miserably cast away?

Shepherds—Some further, and some not so far as these mountains.

Then said the pilgrims one to another, We had need to cry to the Strong for strength.

Shepherds—Ay, and you will have need to use it when you have it too.

By this time the pilgrims had a desire to go forwards, and the shepherds a desire they should; so they walked together towards the end of the mountains. Then said the shepherds one to another, Let us here show to the pilgrims the gates of the Celestial City, if they have skill to look through our perspective-glass. The pilgrims then lovingly accepted the motion; so they had them to the top of a high hill, called Clear, and gave them their glass to look.

Then they essayed to look, but the remembrance of that last thing that the shepherds had showed them made their hands shake, by means of which impediment they could not look steadily through the glass; yet they thought they saw something like the gate, and also some of the glory of the place.